Crime, Justice, and Society

Fourth Edition

CRIME,

JUSTICE &

SOCIETY

An Introduction to Criminology

Ronald J. Berger
Marvin D. Free, Jr.
Melissa Deller
Patrick K. O'Brien

LYNNE
RIENNER
PUBLISHERS

BOULDER
LONDON

Published in the United States of America in 2015 by
Lynne Rienner Publishers, Inc.
1800 30th Street, Boulder, Colorado 80301
www.rienner.com

and in the United Kingdom by
Lynne Rienner Publishers, Inc.
3 Henrietta Street, Covent Garden, London WC2E 8LU

Library of Congress Cataloging-in-Publication Data
Berger, Ronald J.
Crime, justice, and society : an introduction to criminology / Ronald J. Berger,
Marvin D. Free, Jr., Melissa Deller, and Patrick K. O'Brien. — 4th Edition.
    pages cm
Revised edition of Crime, justice, and society 2009.
    Includes bibliographical references and index.
    ISBN 978-1-62637-225-2 (pb : alk. paper)
    1. Crime—United States—Sociological aspects. 2. Criminal behavior—United States.
3. Criminal justice, Administration of—United States. I. Free, Marvin D. II. Title.
    HV6789.B465 2015
    364.973—dc23

                                                            2014048177

British Cataloguing in Publication Data
A Cataloguing in Publication record for this book
is available from the British Library.

Printed and bound in the United States of America

The paper used in this publication meets the requirements
of the American National Standard for Permanence of
Paper for Printed Library Materials Z39.48-1992.

5   4   3   2   1

We are all witnesses to the life of our times. . . .
We are witnesses to suffering, to violence in its many forms,
to hatred and greed, to inequality and injustice, and to
the possibilities of peace and social justice.

—Richard Quinney,
Bearing Witness to Crime and Social Justice

Contents

Tables and Figures

Tables

Figures

Preface

As the fourth edition of *Crime, Justice, and Society* goes to press, the United States and the world at large continue to experience a deep economic and political malaise. Economic inequality is increasing, the problems of the inner city linger, and the threat of terrorism remains. In its own small way, *Crime, Justice, and Society* bears witness to this state of affairs and sheds light on how we got where we are and where we might go from here. In the book, we explore current events and policy developments and present updated crime data and criminological research in our ongoing effort to provide a timely introduction to the study of crime and criminal justice in the new millennium.

At its core, *Crime, Justice, and Society* is an innovative criminology text written from an explicitly sociological perspective. We place questions of social inequality and power—and particularly class, race/ethnicity, and gender inequality—at the center of criminological inquiry. At the same time, we hope that our approach will advance what C. Wright Mills (1959) famously called the "sociological imagination," in order to help students understand the ways in which *personal or private troubles* are related to *public issues* and how individual lives are influenced by broader historical and social forces. When students embrace their sociological imagination, they become better equipped to appreciate the struggles and sorrows of human life that underlie crime statistics, the war on drugs, the rapacity of unchecked corporate profiteering, and the corruption of political officials. Written in an accessible and compelling manner, *Crime, Justice, and Society* encourages students to think critically about the problems of crime and criminal justice.

* * *

As always, we would like to thank Lynne Rienner and Andrew Berzanskis for their support and valuable suggestions. We also thank Shena Redmond, Jason Cook, and the rest of the staff at Lynne Rienner Publishers for their fine work in bringing the book to publication. We also want to express our gratitude to Patricia Searles for her contribution to earlier editions of this book. And last, we are grateful to Richard Quinney, from whom we have learned much about the intellectual project of sociological criminology and the importance of bearing witness "to the human sufferings of our times" (2000:ix).

Part 1

Introducing Sociological Criminology

1

The Social Problem of Crime

President Franklin Roosevelt famously said that "the only thing we have to fear is fear itself." When it comes to the problem of crime, however, this observation is both true and untrue. It is true that Americans have considerable fear of crime, but this fear does not always comport with reality. For example, studies indicate that a large portion of the public believes that crime rates in their communities or the country at large have been rising, even when they have actually been on the decline (Kappeler & Potter 2005; Roberts & Stalans 2000). Moreover, this fear of crime is often about the wrong things. Take the case of economic inequality, which has increased markedly in the United States over the past few decades (Domhoff 2013; Johnston 2014). Although societies marked by high levels of inequality also experience more social ills, including education and health disparities, as well as crime, the paradox is that we continue to do little to remedy (and in fact we often exacerbate) the very economic conditions that give rise to the social problems we abhor (Glassner 1999).

Criminologist John Hagan (2010) also notes a related change in US crime policy that occurred during the presidential administration of Ronald Reagan in the 1980s, when a more punitive approach to street crime was undertaken, fueled in large part by a "war on drugs," at the same time that a more lenient approach to corporate misconduct was initiated through a policy of business deregulation. The former had a disproportionate impact on racial minorities and the poor, an impact that may be viewed as discriminatory (in result if not intent), insofar as blacks do not use more illegal drugs than whites (Alexander 2010; Tonry 1995). And at the same time that people in the lower economic stratum of society were being incarcerated in increasingly large numbers, fueling a historically unprecedented "incarceration boom" (see Chapter 12), the deregulation of the economy that continued under subsequent presidential administrations resulted in a series of corporate scandals—from the collapse of the savings and loan industry in the late 1980s to the corrupt investment and banking practices that gave rise

3

to the worst financial crisis since the Great Depression in the late 2000s (Madrick 2011).

In his aptly titled book *The Rich Get Richer and the Poor Get Prison,* Jeffrey Reiman (2007) illuminates this paradox by noting that more people are physically harmed, even killed, by exposure to workplace hazards and environmental pollution—some of which is legal, and some of which is illegal—than are harmed by all the assaults and homicides associated with the conventional street crimes that are the priority of the criminal justice system; and more money is stolen through "white-collar" crimes like corporate fraud and illegal price-fixing than from crimes of theft like burglary and robbery. Stephen Rosoff and colleagues observe, for instance, that the cost of the taxpayer bailout of even one corrupt, federally insured savings and loan in the late 1980s "surpassed the total losses of *all* the bank robberies" in the entire history of the United States (2007:xi, emphasis added).

In this book we aim to introduce students to the exciting field of criminology, and in particular sociological criminology, in the hopes of encouraging readers to step outside of conventional understandings of crime. **Criminology*** is a multidisciplinary field of inquiry that involves theoretical explanation and empirical research regarding the process of lawmaking and lawbreaking, and the societal reaction to lawbreaking (Sutherland 1947). The discipline of sociology has occupied a special place among the disciplinary components of criminology, which include biology, psychology, and economics, among others (Guarino-Ghezzi & Treviño 2005), and we agree with Ronald Akers in thinking that **sociological criminology** still constitutes the field's "intellectual center of gravity" (1992:4). For much of the twentieth century, criminology in the United States was most often taught in departments of sociology, and its most widely used textbooks were written by sociologists. Hence the study of criminology was defined as an attempt to understand crime as a *social* rather than an *individual* phenomenon—that is, as a consequence of social relationships and the organization of society.

In the late 1960s, however, sociology began to lose its hold on the field. The federal government provided funds that enabled law enforcement agencies to upgrade their educational requirements and encourage their personnel to obtain postsecondary education degrees. This resulted in an expansion of college and university **criminal justice** programs outside of sociology departments, which became readily apparent by the 1980s. By 1990 there were more than a thousand such programs in the United States offering undergraduate degrees, and nearly a hundred offering graduate degrees (Akers 1992; Sorensen et al. 1994).

---

*Key terms are indicated in **boldface** the first time they appear in the book.

The terms *criminology* and *criminal justice* suggest different orientations. Criminology tends to focus on the phenomena of crime and criminals, while criminal justice tends to focus on the agencies that respond to criminal law violation: the police, courts, and correctional systems. Criminology tends to be more theoretical and research-oriented, while criminal justice is more practical or applied. But in many respects the division between criminology and criminal justice is artificial, and the two are so closely interwoven that a convergence has been under way for some time. As Jonathan Sorensen and colleagues noted, "criminal justice programs often include criminology in the curriculum . . . [and] criminologists often teach in criminal justice programs . . . and conduct research on the criminal justice system. . . . As criminal justice develops further as a discipline, the methodology employed in criminal justice research will become comparable to that used in criminology" (1994:152–153).

In this first chapter of *Crime, Justice, and Society,* we begin our examination by considering the role of the media and politics in shaping public attitudes and opinions about crime and crime policy. We then provide further introduction to a sociological perspective that places issues of inequality at the center of criminological inquiry.

The Media

Our view of reality is drawn not just from personal experience, but also from representations of events that we do not directly experience ourselves. Research indicates that the mass media, politicians, and law enforcement officials are major sources of our opinions about crime. They play a definitive role in generating, shaping, and reinforcing viewpoints and mobilizing support for particular policies. They provide us with a taken-for-granted conceptual framework that helps us identify particular issues as crime-related, interpret the causes of criminal behavior, and apply ready-made solutions to the problem at hand (Beckett 1994; Kappeler & Potter 2005; Surette 2011).

Let us first consider the **mass media**, which may be defined as an institutionalized system of communication that conveys information and symbolic messages to audiences through print and technology. The formative influence of the mass media is pervasive, and there is arguably no single subject matter that provides more content for media communication than crime. As an example, a study called "Dying to Entertain," sponsored by the Parents Television Council, found that violent content (including sexual violence) in prime time was prevalent in about half of all prime-time television programs (Schulenburg 2007). Moreover, most people report relying on the news media to learn about crime and criminals, and readers of newspapers are more likely to read crime items than any other subject matter (Pollak & Kubrin 2007; Surette 2011).

In the late 1980s, a new genre of television crime programming emerged: the tabloid-style **infotainment** shows such as *Cops, America's Most Wanted, Unsolved Mysteries,* and many similar programs. These shows represent "true crime" stories (sometimes in documentary style or as dramatized reenactments) that blur the traditional distinction between news and entertainment. They promote a "shared disgust for anyone alleged to be a criminal" and serve to heighten our fear by suggesting that crime is all-pervasive (Bond-Maupin 1998:33; Fox et al. 2007).

Today, in all sources of news reporting, the distinction between news and entertainment is blurred. Television news emphasizes the sordid details of individual crimes, often packaged in 30- to 60-second time spots, and rarely discusses crime as a social issue. There is heavy reliance on law enforcement officials as convenient sources of information, and deadlines leave little time for independent investigation or follow-up. The novelty or sensational quality of the crime increases its news value—if it bleeds it leads—although through repetition the extraordinary becomes ordinary. In television news, as well as entertainment media, the crimes portrayed are the ones less likely to occur in real life: violent crimes are overrepresented, while property crimes and white-collar crimes are underrepresented (Fox et al. 2007; Pollak & Kubrin 2007; Surette 2011).

The heroes in crime entertainment—in literature, television, and film—are the crime fighters who work both within and, when necessary, outside the formal rules and institutional authority of the legal system. Take the genre of the private eye or private detective, for instance, originally popularized in nineteenth-century print media. Here the "good guy" oddly resembles the criminal he is pursuing: a highly individualistic loner who may be on the side of justice, but who is not bound by the conventional rules of society. The heroics of fictional "super" crime fighters—like Batman, Superman, and Spider-Man—also underscore the need to work outside the official legal order (Newman 1993; Surette 2011).

Dirty Harry, the classic film of the 1970s that spawned several sequels, best illustrates the popular media image of the crime fighter, an image that continues to be relevant to this very day. Harry, played by Clint Eastwood, is a maverick police officer who feels little obligation to abide by "due process" formalities. He is a man of action who has no patience for the Bill of Rights, the constitutionally protected liberties that he holds responsible for allowing scores of dangerous criminals to go free. In the *Dirty Harry* films, the qualities that made Eastwood a film star—"the quiet one with the painfully bottled-up capacity for violence"—break loose, as Harry challenges criminals to resist and "make my day" (Ebert 1986:193).

Another iconic figure of Hollywood film lore is Paul Kersey, played by Charles Bronson in the series of *Death Wish* films, also released in the 1970s. Kersey is an average, law-abiding citizen whose wife and daughter are brutally raped by criminal evildoers; his wife is killed and his daughter is left in a catatonic state. The police tell Kersey that the prospect of catching the assailants is slim. But Kersey also witnesses other violent crimes and, frustrated with the ineffectiveness of the police, decides to take matters into his own hands and become a vigilante killer. The message we are left with is that law-abiding citizens need to arm themselves to protect themselves and their families against bloodthirsty criminals.

Crime Waves and Moral Panics

Another way in which the media influence our perceptions of crime is through the construction of crime waves and moral panics. The concept of a **crime wave** is used by criminologists to refer to a sudden rise (and eventual fall) of a particular type of crime. Crime waves may or may not be related to actual fluctuations in criminal behavior. Typically, media-reported crime

---

FURTHER EXPLORATION
Stand Your Ground: George Zimmerman vs. Trayvon Martin

On February 26, 2012, Trayvon Martin, a 17-year-old black male, was fatally shot by George Zimmerman, a 28-year-old male of white and Hispanic descent, as Martin was walking home from a convenience store while visiting his father in Sanford, Florida. Zimmerman was the coordinator of the neighborhood-watch program in the gated community in which the shooting took place, and just prior to the shooting he called the police to report a "real suspicious" individual after observing a teenager wearing a black hoodie who was "just walking around looking about." The dispatcher told him not to pursue Martin, but Zimmerman did so anyway, telling the dispatcher, "These assholes . . . always get away" (Law Center to Prevent Gun Violence 2013).

Zimmerman had been issued a license to carry a gun, even though he had previously been arrested for assaulting a police officer and was the subject of a restraining order related to a domestic violence dispute. Following the shooting, he was taken into custody and questioned for several hours but subsequently released. Although Martin was unarmed at the time of his death—he was found carrying only a bag of Skittles and a bottle of ice tea—and was not engaged in any illegal activity, the police said they had no evidence to disprove Zimmerman's claim of self-defense under Florida's **stand-your-ground** law, which relieves an individual who feels threatened by another of the obligation to retreat in order to avoid harm (Law Center to Prevent Gun Violence 2013).

Martin's death resulted in intense media coverage and much public outcry, in which Zimmerman was portrayed as a "police wannabe" of sorts or even a *Death Wish*–type vigilante figure. Forty-five days passed before Zimmerman was finally charged for Martin's murder and a criminal trial ensued. The jury was presented with evidence that Zimmerman had incurred

continues

continued

a bloody nose and cuts on his head, but Martin was not alive to dispute Zimmerman's claim that it was Martin, not Zimmerman, who had instigated the altercation. If Zimmerman had never approached Martin, as the police dispatcher advised, Martin would be alive today. Nevertheless, Zimmerman was acquitted of all charges under the terms of Florida's stand-your-ground statute.

The racial overtones of the Martin shooting did not go unnoticed, especially in the wake of other incidents in which white shooters have used stand-your-ground statutes, which have been enacted in more than 20 states, to justify their actions (Cheng & Hoekstra 2013; Yancy & Jones 2013). In another Florida case in 2012, for example, Michael Dunn, a 47-year-old white man, fired multiple shots into a car parked at a convenience store occupied by four black teenagers, killing 17-year-old Jordan Davis. Dunn had apparently asked the youths to turn down their "thug music," as he later described it, and when they refused, an argument ensued. The teenagers were unarmed, but Dunn fired multiple shots into the vehicle, even after the youths were driving away. Unlike Zimmerman, Dunn was convicted of first-degree murder and three counts of attempted murder (Younge 2014).

Gary Younge (2014), commenting on the Zimmerman, Dunn, and similar cases, wonders whether the very presence of "free Black men" remains a threat to gun-carrying white men in certain times and places. As such, Younge would not be surprised by a study conducted by the *Tampa Bay Times*, which found that defendants using stand-your-ground defenses in Florida have been more likely to be acquitted for killing black defendants than white defendants (Hundley et al. 2012). Additionally, a nationwide study of the impact of stand-your-ground laws found that these laws have led to a net increase in the number of homicides (Cheng & Hoekstra 2013).

waves are not. In a classic study that was instrumental in developing the crime wave concept, Mark Fishman (1978) examined a seven-week media-reported crime wave in New York City in the mid-1970s involving an alleged surge in what was labeled "crimes against the elderly." Police statistics, however, did not indicate any particular singling out of the elderly. Crimes increased for people of *all ages* during this period; for some crimes the increases were greater for the elderly and for some they were not. While the media began their coverage of crimes against the elderly with reports of several gruesome murders, and 28 percent of the news stories were about homicides, homicides actually made up less than 1 percent of crimes against the elderly. This theme of "crimes against the elderly" conveniently allowed journalists to cast a particular incident as an instance of something threatening and pervasive, something with greater news value.

Fishman also found that the New York City Police Department (NYPD) was receptive to the media's claims about crimes against the elderly. In fact, the NYPD used the purported crime wave to justify expansion of its Senior Citizens Robbery Unit (SCRU), and images of SCRU officers dressed as elderly people arresting muggers provided attractive subjects for news-camera crews. One newspaper reporter, whose feature articles broke the "crimes against the elderly" story, acknowledged that SCRU officers contacted him with information about muggings or murders of elderly persons and repeatedly complained that the SCRU unit was unappreciated, understaffed, and in need of more resources.

Importantly, the New York City crime wave had a nationwide impact on the public's perception of the crime problem, as the story was disseminated through the wire services and nationally read newspapers like the *New York Times* and *Washington Post*. The Harris polling organization also began to include a new category—crimes against the elderly—in its survey questionnaire, and the majority of polled respondents in a national sample indicated that they believed that such crimes had been increasing in their communities when, in fact, they had not.

Marjorie Zatz's study (1987) of the "gang problem" in the city of Phoenix, Arizona, yielded results that paralleled Fishman's research. In the late 1970s and early 1980s, newspaper accounts relying primarily on information provided by the Phoenix Police Department suggested that the city had experienced a dramatic rise in Chicano (Mexican-American) youth gang activity. The claims of the police that the problem might escalate even further were coupled with well-publicized requests for additional local and federal funding for specialized gang-related law enforcement. The reality was, in fact, more complicated.

The term *gang* evokes a threatening social imagery that has the symbolic power to transform occasional or sporadic acts of delinquency into more purposeful activity. In Phoenix, the police department provided its officers with the *Latin Gang Member Recognition Guide,* which included cartoon caricatures of youths in gang attire, a glossary of relevant Spanish words and expressions, and other criteria that could be used to identify gang members. Increased police surveillance of the Chicano community then yielded an identifiable population of offenders who provided the raw material for media reporting on the gang problem. Zatz found, however, that the claims of the police and the media were disputed by knowledgeable social service workers and counselors who worked with Chicano youths, as well as by representatives of the Chicano community. As one juvenile probation officer noted: "It's fair to say there is some violence and destruction going on. But maybe there is also a bit of an injustice when kids in cowboy hats and pickups, drinking beer and cruising . . . aren't thought of as a gang. But when you have Chicano kids driving lowriders, wearing bandannas, and smoking marijuana, they are singled out as being gangs" (p. 136).

In addition, Zatz analyzed juvenile court records and found that while youths who were officially labeled as gang members were *more likely* than nongang youths to have been arrested in larger groups and for fighting offenses, they were *less likely* than nongang youths to have had prior court referrals and to have been referred for drug offenses. Zatz concluded that gang members "typically engaged in relatively minor squabbles, and not in . . . serious violent crimes that would be dangerous to . . . anyone outside of the gang world" (pp. 140, 143).

Zatz characterized claims about the Phoenix gang problem as a **moral panic**—that is, a discrepancy or disjuncture between a perceived threat and an actual threat that, when reported in the media, generates public support for doing something dramatic about a particular problem (McCorkle & Miethe 2002). In Phoenix, Zatz observed, the more ordinary inclinations of adolescents to congregate in public spaces took on a more ominous appearance and fueled unwarranted fears about Chicano youths as an inherently lawless population. Zatz did not deny that youth gangs existed or that they could pose a serious problem for communities. Nor did she claim that the media always portrayed law enforcement in a positive light. Rather, she cautioned against uncritically accepting police and media accounts of social problems.

However, Fishman (1978) found that there are times in which public officials downplay media stories about crime, being concerned that media reporting causes the public to panic unnecessarily or to believe that the police are ineffective. Thus, for instance, officials from the New York City Transit Authority (NYTA) stopped an emergent theme involving "crimes on the subways" from becoming a media-reported crime wave. In this case, the NYTA police chief told one reporter that there was no such crime wave, and three senior NYTA officials called a news conference to assure the public that "the subways were safer than the city streets" (Fishman 1978:541).

But more often than not, media and law enforcement interests converge in finding mutual benefit from portrayals of escalating crime. Philip Jenkins's study (1994) of the serial murder problem is a case in point. The media, as noted earlier, are attracted to the unusual. During the 1980s, media accounts began to describe serial murder as reaching epidemic proportions. The **serial murderer**—typically described as a psychotically compulsive offender capable of extreme violence who selects multiple victims at random, often while traveling from state to state—was featured in a front-page *New York Times* article in 1984 that suggested serial murders accounted for about 20 percent (about 4,000) of all the homicides committed in the United States each year. Over the next two years, this estimate was repeated in numerous other news reports. The data in these reports were based on Federal Bureau of Investigation (FBI) statistics on "motiveless" and "unsolved" murders and on interviews with law enforcement officials.

In his research, Jenkins was interested in ascertaining whether these numerical estimates were accurate and whether serial murders had, in fact, been on the rise. Jenkins compiled a list of cases that were reported between 1940 and 1990 in three well-indexed and highly regarded newspapers (the *New York Times, Los Angeles Times,* and *Chicago Tribune*), and he supplemented this data with other sources. Jenkins concluded that there had been a significant increase in this type of offense since the late 1960s, but that serial murders still accounted for no more than 2 to 3 percent of all homicides.

Jenkins observed that officials in the US Justice Department and in particular the FBI's Behavioral Sciences Unit (BSU) were the primary sources of information for the exaggerated media claims about the serial murder problem. He also noted that in 1983 concerns about serial murder became a central justification for the development of a new program, the Violent Criminal Apprehension Program (ViCAP), at the FBI Academy in Quantico, Virginia, and for an expanded federal role in law enforcement regarding repeat killers as well as rapists, child molesters, arsonists, and bombers. According to BSU agent Robert Ressler:

> There was somewhat of a media feeding frenzy, if not a panic, over [the serial murder] issue in the mid-1980s, and we at the FBI and other people involved in urging the formation of ViCAP did add to the general impression that there was a big problem and that something needed to be done about it. We didn't exactly go out seeking publicity, but when a reporter called, and we had a choice whether or not to cooperate on a story about violent crime, we gave the reporter good copy. In feeding the frenzy, we were using an old tactic in Washington, playing up the problem as a way of getting Congress and the higher-ups in the executive branch to pay attention to it. (quoted in Ressler & Schachtman 1992:203)

Drug Scares

Craig Reinarman and Harry Levine (1989) identify **drug scares** as a perennial type of crime wave and moral panic that in the United States goes back at least to the early part of the twentieth century. Drug scares typically involve an association between an allegedly "dangerous drug" and a "dangerous class" of individuals: working-class immigrants, racial or ethnic minorities, youths, or some combination thereof. Historically this has been true for the Chinese and opium, African Americans and cocaine, and Mexicans and marijuana (see Chapter 7). During drug scares, antidrug crusaders often receive extended media coverage, which helps mobilize public opinion in support of new drug laws and increased law enforcement against drug offenders. In the 1930s, for example, Harry Anslinger, commissioner of the federal Department of the Treasury's Bureau of Narcotics, led a national campaign against the sale and use of marijuana (Gray 1998). Under Anslinger's leadership the bureau prepared a number of "educational" articles for distribution to magazines and newspapers. These articles included a number of outrageous atrocity stories such as the following incident reported in *American Magazine* in 1937:

> An entire family was murdered by a youthful [marijuana] addict in Florida. When officers arrived at the home they found the youth staggering about in a human slaughterhouse. With an ax he had killed his father, mother, two brothers, and a sister. He seemed to be in a daze. . . . He had no recollection of having committed the multiple crimes. The officers knew him ordinarily as a sane, rather quiet young man; now he was pitifully crazed. They sought the reason. The boy said he had been in the habit of smoking something which youthful friends called "muggles," a childish name for marijuana. (cited in Becker 1963:142)

In the 1980s, crack cocaine emerged in the media as the preeminent dangerous drug (Reeves & Campbell 1994). Crack is a smokable form of cocaine that can be easily manufactured by boiling powdered cocaine (cocaine hydrochloride) with additives like Novocaine and baking soda and placing the boiled mixture in ice water until it hardens. In his book *The Rise and Fall of a Violent Crime Wave: Crack Cocaine and the Social Construction of a Crime Problem,* Henry Brownstein (1996) attributes the rise of crack cocaine to the overproduction of coca leaves (the source of powder cocaine) in the three countries that are the greatest source of cocaine imported into the United States (Bolivia, Colombia, and Peru) and to the consequent opportunity for drug traffickers to expand the cocaine market. Whereas powder cocaine is consumed primarily by middle-class and affluent individuals, crack can be sold in small, inexpensive quantities to low-income people (four ounces of powdered cocaine can serve a thousand).

Media stories about crack cocaine first appeared in a November 1984 *Los Angeles Times* article and in the *New York Times* a year later. At that time crack had only appeared in the impoverished neighborhoods of a few large cities. But by the spring of 1986, drug coverage reached a virtual feeding frenzy in the national media, which claimed that crack cocaine and a "coke plague" had spread to the suburbs and America's heartland and now constituted a "national crisis." Existing crime data, however, suggested that this simply was not true. Even the federal Drug Enforcement Administration (DEA) announced in 1986 that "crack was not a major problem in most areas of the country" (cited in Brownstein 1996:41).

In his research, Brownstein (1996) was especially concerned with media claims, echoed by politicians and law enforcement officials, that crack cocaine was linked to an epidemic of violent criminal behavior.

According to Brownstein, when crack was first introduced, the market was in fact "dominated by young . . . well-armed . . . entrepreneurs who operated independently of established drug trafficking organizations . . . [and who] turned to violence over such things as market share and product quality." But over time this disorganized and rather violent market evolved into "confederations of independent dealers . . . [and] a more highly structured and less violent business-like industry" (p. 40). Moreover, research indicated that while almost all crack users had previously used other illegal drugs, their involvement with crack was for the most part unrelated to increased nondrug or violent criminality (Johnson et al. 1995). Nevertheless, the media constructed a moral panic that suggested that crack-related violence could affect anyone, anywhere. According to *Time* magazine, "A growing sense of vulnerability has been deepened by the belief that deadly violence, once mostly confined to crime-ridden ghetto neighborhoods that the police once wrote off as free-fire zones, is now lashing out randomly at anyone, even in areas once considered relatively safe" (Attinger 1989:38).

Reinarman and Levine (1989) acknowledge that crack is a very dangerous drug. They believe, however, that exaggerated drug scares are an ineffective way to solve the drug problem and may even increase interest in drug use.

The Politics of Crime Control

In many ways the 1960s defined the terms of the contemporary political debate over what to do about crime (Miller 1973). **Liberals** of that era claimed, as they do today, that crime could be prevented through social policies aimed at ameliorating the underlying "root causes" associated with economic inequality and poverty, especially with regard to racial and ethnic minorities, for whom discrimination is a persistent problem. Government-supported social programs that promote economic and educational opportunities and provide needed social services are the prescribed cure. For those already caught up in the cycle of crime, rehabilitation rather than punishment per se is the preferred objective, with those accused and convicted of crimes being guaranteed rights of due process while under the control of the criminal justice system.

Conservatives, on the other hand, emphasized the role of personal responsibility in refraining from criminal behavior. Unfavorable life conditions are no excuse. Criminal behavior is a choice, and those who choose to commit crime must be held accountable. We must resign ourselves to the fact that "wicked people exist" and we have no recourse but to set them apart from the rest of us (Wilson 1975:235). To the extent that there are root causes of crime, these reside in the decay of moral values, not in the absence of opportunities. The government can do little to solve these problems and should get out of people's lives. We need to liberate our criminal justice system from undue restraint so that punishment can be more certain, swift, and severe.

In 1965, President Lyndon Johnson, a Democrat, established the President's Commission on Law Enforcement and Administration of Justice. Johnson asked the commission to "deepen our understanding of the causes of crime and of how society should respond to the challenge" of reducing crime. The commission acknowledged the liberal agenda when it wrote in 1967: "Crime flourishes where the conditions of life are the worst. . . . Reducing poverty, discrimination, ignorance, disease and urban blight, and the anger, cynicism or despair those conditions can inspire, is . . . essential to crime prevention" (p. 279). This apparent statement of liberal principles was a mere footnote, however, to the more conservative-oriented criminal justice strategies that dominated the commission's 17-volume report—that is, strategies that involved "policemen, prosecutors, judges [and] correctional authorities." Even so, in the 1968 presidential campaign, Republican candidate Richard Nixon and right-wing American Independent candidate George Wallace accused the Democrats of being "soft on crime" (Hagan 2010).

The Reagan-Bush Years

In 1974, less than two years after President Nixon was reelected, he was forced to resign for his involvement in a cover-up of a burglary that had been committed on behalf of his reelection campaign at the Democratic National Committee headquarters in the Watergate hotel/office complex (see Chapter 10). The Watergate affair focused public attention on the problem of political corruption and encouraged the pursuit of white-collar crime as an investigative priority of the US Justice Department during the administration of President Jimmy Carter, a Democrat, in the late 1970s (Katz 1980).

In the 1980s, however, President Ronald Reagan, a Republican, shifted federal law enforcement priorities by moving the drug problem to center stage in the political debate about crime. Reagan declared a **war on drugs**, a war that would require not just a redoubling of conventional law enforcement efforts but also an unprecedented involvement of the military in international drug interdiction (Gordon 1994a). Domestically, the slogan **zero tolerance** emphasized "the culpability of casual users" and the belief that "the present problem is [due] to past tolerance . . . [for which] nothing short of wiping out all illicit drug use will do" (p. 33). The war on drugs, in Reagan's words, was "our national crusade" (p. 34). To accomplish this goal, the Reagan administration diverted millions of federal dollars from drug education, treatment, and research to law enforcement. To be sure, the Reagan administration's antidrug agenda was a bipartisan effort, as

Democrats in Congress also favored passage of punitive drug laws in order to curry votes and ward off being perceived by the public as soft on crime (Hagan 2010).

At the same time, the Reagan administration was embroiled in political scandals of its own. On the domestic front, one scandal involved Anne Gorsuch, an antiregulatory state legislator from Colorado who was Reagan's first choice to head the Environmental Protection Agency (EPA). Gorsuch's appointment was sponsored by Joseph Coors, the archconservative Coors brewery mogul who had founded the Mountain States Legal Foundation, a group dedicated to the evisceration of environmental regulations. During Gorsuch's brief term in office, she increasingly staffed the EPA with people who had previously worked for the very corporations the agency was supposed to be regulating. In 1982 the so-called **Sewergate scandal** erupted, which revealed Gorsuch's assurances to polluting corporations that the EPA would not enforce environmental regulations against them. These assurances included arrangements that allowed polluting companies to avoid full payment of environmental cleanup costs, as well as delays in waste-site cleanup timetables. The scandal forced Gorsuch to resign, and Rita Lavelle, who had been appointed to head the EPA's Superfund environmental cleanup program, was convicted on criminal charges of perjury for lying under oath about her antiregulatory activities (Kennedy 2004; Szasz 1986).

On the foreign policy front, the Reagan administration was also embroiled in a foreign policy controversy—dubbed the Iran-Contra scandal—that was related to its covert actions in the Middle East and Central America, which we will consider later in this book (see Chapter 10). But despite its tainted record, the administration managed to gloss over the apparent hypocrisy that might have undermined its claim to be a champion of "law and order" (Hagan 2010). As such, then–vice president George H. W. Bush was not deterred from using the soft-on-crime argument against Massachusetts governor Michael Dukakis, the Democratic candidate, in the 1988 presidential campaign, infamous in the annals of campaign history for the Willie Horton television commercials aired by Bush supporters.

Horton, an African American, had been sentenced to life in prison for his involvement in an armed robbery that resulted in the death of a teenage gas station attendant in Massachusetts. After serving 10 years in prison, he was released for the first of three furloughs (temporary home leaves or community releases). Furlough programs are used by more than half the prison systems in the United States as part of a risk-management policy aimed at the gradual reintegration of convicted felons back into the community. To be sure, furloughs are not without risk. But research on furlough programs in the 1970s and 1980s indicated that on the whole these programs actually reduced criminal recidivism (Skolnick 1996). Horton, however, was not a good candidate for a fourth release. Although prison officials had received complaints about his behavior during his previous fur-loughs, they released him once again. This time he escaped and remained free for almost a year until he burglarized the home of a white suburban couple, Angela Miller and Clifford Barnes, and brutally assaulted them. While Horton was raping Miller, Barnes managed to escape and get help. If he had not, they likely would have been killed (Anderson 1995).

The Horton incident was a tragedy. But Bush supporters used it to por-tray Governor Dukakis as responsible for the release of convicted violent felons. Because Dukakis also opposed the death penalty, Bush was able to portray him as soft on crime. The Democrats, in turn, accused the Bush campaign of exploiting racial stereotypes in an unconscionable way. Never-theless, the ad was extremely effective.

As president, Bush continued his predecessor's focus on drugs. During his first year in office, he addressed the nation in a 1989 televised Labor Day speech that illustrates how politicians exploit the crime issue for polit-ical advantage. In a dramatic gesture, Bush held up a bag of crack cocaine that had been purchased by DEA agents at a park across the street from the White House. We learned later that the arrest had actually been arranged to help dramatize the speech! The Bush administration had asked the DEA to make an illegal drug-buy at the park, but since agents could not find anyone who was selling crack at that location, they lured a dealer to the park in order to make the arrest (Glassner 1999).

The Clinton Years

During the 1992 presidential campaign between the incumbent Bush and Arkansas governor Bill Clinton, it was difficult for Bush to characterize Clinton as a soft-on-crime Democrat. As governor, Clinton had demon-strated his support for the death penalty by signing four execution orders, including the order to execute a mentally impaired African-American felon (Kramer & Michalowski 1995). Clinton also favored the expansion of the nation's police forces, a cornerstone of his crime control policy. On the other hand, Clinton differed from Bush in his support of federal gun control legislation, particularly the Brady Handgun Violence Prevention Act, known simply as the Brady Bill, which required a five-day waiting period for the purchase of a handgun. The Brady Bill was named for James Brady, the press secretary for President Reagan, who had been shot and seriously disabled in 1981 during John Hinckley's attempted assassination of the president (see Chapter 3).

Politically, gun control has received more support from liberals than from conservatives. Many conservatives feel strongly that the Second Amendment to the US Constitution—"A well regulated militia being nec-essary to the security of a free state, the right of the people to keep and bear arms, shall not be infringed"—preserves their right to own any gun of their choice without government interference. Liberals, on the other hand, interpret these words more narrowly, and in their original historical context, viewing the Second Amendment not as providing a constitutionally protected *individual* right to own a firearm, but as preventing the new national government from interfering with the *collective* right of the citizenry to participate in state-regulated militias (Sunstein 2007). As president, Reagan had opposed the Brady Bill, only to endorse it after he left office, perhaps because he no longer needed to worry about incurring the wrath of the National Rifle Association (NRA), a well-funded and influential organization that supports conservative pro-gun political candidates. Unlike Reagan, Bush continued to oppose the bill. But since it was difficult to characterize Clinton's advocacy of gun control as soft on crime, Bush was unable to use the crime issue to his advantage. After Clinton became president, he signed the Brady Bill into law in December 1993.

The Brady Bill expired in 1998 and was replaced by a national computerized system of background checks operated by the FBI. A decade later, in *District of Columbia v. Heller* (2008), the US Supreme Court ruled that the District of Columbia's ban on handguns was in violation of the Second Amendment, thus upholding an individual's right to "keep and bear" a handgun in one's home for the purpose of self-defense. At the same time, this decision did not preclude gun control measures that stopped short of a ban on home handgun ownership.

During the 1992 campaign and the first year of his presidency, Clinton gave indications that he might also be more liberal than his predecessors on other crime issues. He appointed Lee Brown, a former New York City police commissioner, as director of the Office of National Drug Control Policy. Brown, an advocate of prevention and rehabilitation approaches to drug abuse, defined drug abuse "as a public health problem" that should be addressed through "efforts to grow the economy, to empower communities, to curb youth violence, to preserve families, and to reform health care" (quoted in Gordon 1994a:35). However, when Republicans accused Clinton of "slipping into the old permissiveness," he downplayed this view and Brown eventually resigned in frustration (p. 35). Brown was replaced by Barry McCaffrey, a retired four-star general. Similarly, when Attorney General Janet Reno questioned the existing federal policy of lengthy mandatory sentences for even minor drug offenders (which might necessitate shorter sentences for violent offenders to reduce prison overcrowding), she was removed from the White House policymaking loop. And when Jocelyn Elders, Clinton's surgeon general, expressed interest in examining the experiences of other countries that had decriminalized drugs (and made other controversial statements as well), she was forced to resign (Poveda 1994).

The most significant piece of crime legislation passed during the Clinton administration was the Violent Crime Control and Law Enforcement Act of 1994, also called the Federal Crime Bill. The provisions of the bill indicated that the conservative position on crime had prevailed, insofar as law enforcement and punitive strategies far outweighed crime prevention and rehabilitation measures. The bill authorized the spending of more than $30 billion and allocated 45 percent of this amount to the hiring of more police officers and 33 percent to the building of new prisons. The bill also included a "three strikes and you're out" provision (life in prison for violent and drug felons if the third conviction is in federal court), and expanded the death penalty to more than 50 federal crimes (*Milwaukee Journal* 1994b).

The bill was passed in August 1994, while the Democrats were still in control of Congress, and included three provisions that were generally opposed by Republicans. The policing provisions favored by the Clinton administration earmarked federal monies to local police departments willing to implement community policing—law enforcement strategies aimed at putting police in closer touch with the community, including foot patrols, community meetings with residents, and an emphasis on solving community problems rather than just making arrests (see Chapter 11). Republicans would have liked to allow police departments to define their own priorities—for instance, to use the money to buy more equipment, such as squad cars and high-powered weapons, or to expand other law enforcement activities, such as specialized crime units.

Republicans also opposed a provision of the bill that banned the manufacture of 19 specific types of "military-style" assault weapons and other firearms having similar characteristics (this ban expired in 2004 and has not been reauthorized since). In addition, Republicans opposed the portion of the bill that earmarked money (17 percent of the spending) for social programs aimed at crime prevention, such as youth clubs in housing projects, midnight sports leagues, and drug treatment programs. One Republican congressman characterized the bill as "riddled with social welfare spending that is pork and a cops-on-the-streets program that is a sham" (quoted in *Milwaukee Journal* 1994a:A3).

Although the Clinton administration was more favorable to environmental regulation than its Republican predecessors had been, its record of **antitrust law** enforcement was more ambiguous. Antitrust law in the United States has its roots in the Sherman Antitrust Act of 1890, which prohibits business combinations that result in a *restraint of trade* (including noncompetitive agreements to fix prices) or the *monopolization* of an industry. Technically speaking, a monopoly refers to one company, whereas the concentration of corporate power in the US economy is best characterized as an **oligopoly**, whereby a few firms dominate basic industries in society. Nevertheless, the Clinton administration approved corporate mega-mergers that would have been unthinkable a few years earlier and favored the deregulation of the financial industry as well (Berger 2011).

At the same time, the administration did pursue some high-profile antitrust cases. Most notable was the case against Bill Gates's Microsoft Corporation, which was accused of abusing the virtual monopoly it had acquired from its Windows operating system to gain an unfair competitive advantage on sales of other software products. The most egregious action involved Microsoft's pressuring of retailers who sold Windows to also sell its Internet Explorer browser rather than the Netscape Navigator browser, which controlled a larger share of the market at the time. In 1999, a federal judge ruled against Microsoft and suggested that severe sanctions might be in order, including breaking Microsoft into two or more companies and increasing government monitoring of its future acquisitions and its contracts with retailers. Microsoft appealed the ruling, and when the administration of George W. Bush took office, a more modest settlement was reached (Rosoff et al. 2007).

Clinton, like the presidents before him, was embroiled in scandals of his own. But among the many allegations of impropriety that surrounded him, the only one that stuck was the allegation that he had lied under oath about a sexual affair with Monica Lewinsky. Although he was impeached by the US House, he was acquitted by the Senate. And although his transgressions may have been morally discreditable, reasonable people would agree that they pale in comparison to the transgressions that both preceded and followed his administration (see Chapter 10).

The George W. Bush Years
Republican George W. Bush, son of the former president, assumed his presidency amid controversy in the 2000 election over disputed ballots in the state of Florida. In a highly controversial decision, the US Supreme Court stopped a recount vote in Florida, giving Bush a narrow victory in the Electoral College, despite the fact that Vice President Al Gore had won the popular vote nationwide (see Chapter 10).

During the first year of his administration, President Bush and Vice President Dick Cheney's financial and political connections to Enron, a multibillion-dollar energy corporation that went bankrupt due to fraudulent financial practices, were starting to draw attention in the media (Corn 2003; see Chapter 9). But what seemed to be emerging as an ongoing story was moved off the front pages following the September 11, 2001, terrorist attacks on the World Trade Center and the Pentagon, which cost the lives of more than 3,000 people and spurred the subsequent antiterrorism campaign against Al-Qaida ("The Base") and its leader, Osama bin Laden, as well as the US military invasion of Afghanistan and Iraq, the latter justified on the basis of misleading and partly fraudulent evidence (see Chapter 10). Six weeks later, the president signed the USA Patriot Act into law amid complaints by civil libertarians that the law went too far in undermining constitutional liberties (*Patriot* is an acronym for "Providing Appropriate Tools Required to Intercept and Obstruct Terrorism").

The most controversial elements of the Patriot Act included provisions that allowed for warrantless residential searches of individuals deemed a risk to national security, searches of computer files and tracing of Internet communications and library transactions, and detainment of noncitizens without charge for up to six months prior to deportation (Masci & Marshall 2003). Controversial as well was the fact that the law did not contain any "new provisions for the monitoring or control of firearms" (Bergman & Reynolds 2002:21). In fact, Attorney General John Ashcroft did not even allow federal law enforcement investigators to use the national background check system to track potential terrorists. Prior to his appointment as attorney general, as a senator from Missouri, Ashcroft had received thousands of dollars of political campaign contributions from the NRA; and one of his main objectives as attorney general was to eliminate delays in the federal system of background checks for gun buyers. The following year, in 2002, the Department of Homeland Security Act was also passed, creating a massive, cabinet-level department to oversee homeland security (Martin 2003; Shenon 2008).

Proponents of these measures claim they have been successful in preventing another 9/11-type attack, while opponents raise concerns about the massive expansion of a government surveillance apparatus that has been monitoring millions of phone calls and e-mails an hour, both international and domestic, including the monitoring of confidential personal and business matters unrelated to national security (Bamford 2008). The full ramifications of this surveillance system, which continued into the administration of Barack Obama, were not made known to the American public until Edward Snowden released previously undisclosed "top secret" documents in 2013. Snowden, a former Central Intelligence Agency (CIA) employee, was at the time of the leaks working for a private company that had been contracted by the National Security Administration (NSA), an agency in the Department of Defense. *Time* magazine described Snowden's leaks as a revelation about a "massive secret US national security state—$52.6 billion a year, with more than 30,000 employees at the NSA alone" (Scherer 2013:84).

At the time these measures were enacted, the Bush administration claimed that those who opposed them were playing into the hands of terrorists. As Attorney General Ashcroft opined: "To those who scare peace-loving people with phantoms of lost liberty; my message is this: Your tactics only aid terrorists—for they erode our national unity and diminish our resolve. They give ammunition to America's enemies, and pause to America's friends" (quoted in Kappeler & Potter 2005:364). Additionally, Ashcroft linked the "war on terror" to the war on drugs, as if even common drug users were responsible for the spread of terrorism:

The lawlessness that breeds terrorism is also a fertile ground for the drug trafficking that supports terrorism. And the mutually reinforcing relationships between terrorism and drug trafficking should serve as a wake-up call for all Americans. When a dollar is spent on drugs in America, a dollar is made by America's enemies. The Department of Justice is committed to victory over drug abuse and terrorism, and the protection of the freedom and human dignity that both drug abuse and terrorism seek to destroy. (quoted in Kappeler & Potter 2005:354)

Ironically, despite Ashcroft's indignation against those who opposed his post-9/11 policies, before 9/11 he had ignored FBI warnings about the threat of terrorism. As former acting FBI director Thomas Pickard reported, prior to 9/11 Ashcroft told him, "I don't want to hear about al-Qaida anymore. . . . There's nothing I can do about that" (quoted in Shenon 2008:247).

As for the problem of corporate crime, the policies of the George W. Bush administration most resembled those of the Reagan administration. In a cabinet appointment that harkened back to the Sewergate scandal, Gale Norton was selected to head the Department of Interior. Previously, Norton had been a member of an antiregulatory group deceptively called Wise Use, whose founder, Ron Arnold, once said: "Our goal is to . . . eradicate the environmental movement. We want . . . to be able to exploit the environment for private gain" (quoted in Kennedy 2004:27). J. Steven Griles, a lobbyist for the mining industry, was appointed to head the Bureau of Mines. Government scientists and inspectors responsible for evaluating risks and enforcing law violations reported being thwarted in their efforts to protect the public from corporate practices that savaged and polluted the environment. As a result, deaths from mining accidents increased during the Bush years (Frank 2007).

The Obama Years

When Barack Obama, a Democrat, was inaugurated as president in 2009, he inherited a financial crisis that was not of his own making. In order to shore up the economy, he supported a taxpayer bailout of the financial industry. At the same time, he also sought regulatory reforms that would help avoid a repeat of this crisis, signing into law the Wall Street Reform and Consumer Protection Act, also known as the Dodd-Frank Act, in 2010. The law created broad federal guidelines to regulate banks, financial speculation, and credit card companies, but it required the writing and implementation of rules that were opposed by Obama's Republican opposition, who called it "an incomprehensively complex piece of legislation that is harmful to our floundering economy and in dire need of repeal" (quoted in Kuhnhenn 2013:A9).

Also on the domestic front, the issue of gun control reemerged due to several high-profile mass shootings. The first of these incidents involved a shooting by Jared Loughner at a campaign event of Democratic congress-woman Gabrielle Giffords in Tucson, Arizona, in January 2011; Lougher killed six people and seriously injured Giffords and more than a dozen others. The second incident involved a shooting by James Holmes in a movie theater in Aurora, Colorado, in July 2012; Holmes killed 12 people. And the third involved a shooting by Adam Lanza at Sandy Hook Elementary School in Newtown, Connecticut; Lanza killed 20 children and 6 adults. These shootings, especially the Newtown incident, brought forth calls for gun control legislation, especially for a renewal of the assault weapons ban that had expired in 2004, limits on high-capacity magazines, and background checks for gun purchases from unlicensed sellers (not just from licensed dealers). Although the Obama administration and a majority of the public supported these measures, the political clout of the NRA in the US Congress was too strong and no legislation was forthcoming (Fuller 2014). Since Sandy Hook, there have been dozens of other shootings on school grounds, although the calls for gun control reform continue to go unheeded (Frantz et al. 2014).

As for the war on drugs, during the Obama years a movement for retreating from the punitive policies of the past gained momentum. In 2010, the Fair Sentencing Act reduced the disparity between federal criminal penalties for crack cocaine and powder cocaine that had been in place since the mid-1980s (Cratty 2011). Prior to the Fair Sentencing Act, the penalties for possession of crack cocaine, a less expensive form of cocaine consumed primarily by low-income offenders, were a hundred times greater than penalties for possession of comparable amounts of powder cocaine. Also in 2014, Colorado and Washington state led the way by implementing legislation to legalize the recreational use of marijuana. And US attorney general Eric Holder announced his support for lighter sentences for lower-level drug offenders and an end to mandatory minimum sentences that prevented judges from exercising judicial discretion. Expressing a more liberal approach to the problem of crime, Holder said he hoped to break the "vicious cycle of poverty, criminality, and incarceration that traps too many Americans" (quoted in Schworm 2013).

The Sociology of Crime

Earlier we noted our interest in helping students step outside of conventional understandings by acquiring a view of crime as a social rather than an individual phenomenon. At the same time, we do not wish to suggest that we have no interest in individual behavior. Indeed, as sociologist C. Wright Mills (1959) would remind us, the essence of a **sociological imagination** is to understand the ways in which *personal or private troubles* are related to *public issues*. In other words, we want to understand how individ-

FURTHER EXPLORATION
Right-to-Carry Laws

While opposing expanded gun control measures, the NRA and its supporters have advocated the expansion of concealed carry laws, also known as **right-to-carry** (RTC). Recently, more states have adopted "shall issue" laws, which require states to issue right-to-carry permits to citizens who meet certain minimum eligibility requirements, such as passage of a certified gun-safety course, as opposed to "may issue" laws, which give states broader authority to deny permits unless the applicant can show "good cause" for needing a gun.

There is some controversy in the criminological research literature as to whether lenient right-to-carry laws reduce crime, increase crime, or have no effect on crime. The expectation that these laws would reduce crime is based on the assumption that the more law-abiding citizens are able to defend themselves, the more criminals will be deterred (Lott 1998). The expectation that right-to-carry laws would increase crime is based on the expectation that the more guns there are in circulation in the public sphere, the more they will be used in unwarranted situations by irresponsible permit holders, including criminals themselves (Diaz 1999).

In a widely publicized study about right-to-carry laws, economist John Lott (1998) analyzed data from more than 3,000 counties in the United States and found a statistically significant association between right-to-carry laws and lower crime rates. On the other hand, several follow-up studies that critiqued Lott's research methodology failed to confirm his findings, with some even showing that crime rates rose rather than fell as a result of easing restrictions on concealed weapons carrying (Ayres & Donahue 2003; Black & Nagin 1998; Fagan 2003).

Overall, the best that can be said about the effect of right-to-carry laws is that the evidence is mixed, with a review of studies by the National Research Council of the Academies concluding there is no reliable evidence that these laws have a causal impact on crime rates one way or the other (Wellford et al. 2004). Additionally, Anthony Braga and Glenn Pierce (2005) note that legal gun ownership itself is an important source of firearms used by criminals. This occurs not only through theft from legal owners, but also from sales from licensed dealers and private parties at gun shows and flea markets, including "straw purchasers" who buy guns for other people. And even after September 11, the United States has remained "a global shopping center" for gun purchases by "terrorists, mercenaries, and international criminals of all stripes" (Bergman & Reynolds 2002:19). Nevertheless, William Vizzard (2000) is arguably correct in his observation that political ideology, not empirical research, will likely remain the ultimate adjudicator of the debate about guns and gun control.

ual lives are influenced by social forces that define and constrain people's choices and opportunities, their sense of the possible, their very sense of themselves. A sociological imagination helps us understand how individual biographies and the biographies of others intersect with broader social conditions and the relationships people have with each other.

Victimization from crime, for example, is an unfortunate and often traumatic private experience. But when victimization falls disproportionately on a certain group or groups, such as the poor or economically disadvantaged, there is a nonrandom patterning to this problem that requires sociological explanation. Or when large numbers of women experience some form of sexual violence or abuse, mostly from people they know, this cannot be understood without sociological insight.

This perspective is also well illustrated in the following accounts of the lives of African-American gang members. In his book *A Nation of Lords: The Autobiography of the Vice Lords,* David Dawley (1992) gives voice to the experiences of Chicago youths growing up in the late 1950s and 1960s:

> When we got here, *the pattern was already laid out for us.* We weren't aware of what was going on and what we thought, but we were living in the years when you couldn't walk the streets without somebody telling you they were gonna down you. Much of what we did was bad, but we didn't know why, and there just wasn't anybody who could help us. Now we know something about what made us kill each other, but in 1958 we were crammed so close together that the least little thing could touch something off. (p. 3, emphasis added)

Similarly, in *Monster: The Autobiography of an L.A. Gang Member,* Sanyika Shakur (1993), also known as Monster Kody Scott, writes about his life as a member of the Crips in South Central Los Angeles in the 1970s:

> My mind-set was narrowed by *the conditions and circumstances prevailing around me.* Certainly I had little respect for life when practically all my life I had seen people assaulted, maimed, and blown away at very young ages, and no one seemed to care. I recognized early that where I lived, we grew and died in dog years. . . . Where I lived, stepping on someone's toe was a capital offense punishable by death. . . . I did not start this cycle, nor did I conspire to create conditions so that this type of self-murder could take place. . . . To be in a gang in South Central when I joined—and it is still the case today—is the equivalent of growing up in Grosse Pointe, Michigan, and going to college: everyone does it. (pp. 102, 138, emphasis added)

When Dawley and Shakur speak of "the pattern . . . already laid out" or the prevailing "conditions and circumstances" that they "did not start," they are referring to the influence of **social structure** on their lives. Social structure is a concept used by sociologists to refer to the patterns of social interaction and institutional relationships that endure over time and that enable or constrain people's choices and opportunities. Social structures are, in a sense, external to individuals insofar as they are not of their own making and exist prior to their engagement with the world. At the same time, social structures do not exist independently of **social action**. Rather, they are ongoing accomplishments reproduced by individuals acting in particular ways in specific situations (Giddens 1984; Messerschmidt 1997). The members of the Vice Lords and the Crips did not create the social structures that they confronted in their lives, but through their actions they recreated or reproduced the conditions that were already there.

A sociological imagination does not imply a view of individuals as mere dupes or passive recipients of social structures. Individuals are thinking, self-reflexive beings who are capable of assessing their circumstances and choosing among alternative courses of action (Sandstrom et al. 2006). Sociologists refer to this phenomenon as a capacity for **personal agency**—that is, individuals' ability to exercise a degree of control over their lives and at times even manage to transform or reconfigure the social relationships in which they are enmeshed (Berger 2008; Emirbayer & Mische 1998). Social psychologists describe this as a matter of **self-efficacy**—the ability to experience oneself as a causal agent capable of *acting upon* rather than *merely reacting to* the external environment (Bandura 1997; Gecas 1989). To illustrate this point, we need only recall the actions of Rosa Parks, an African-American seamstress who on a December day in 1955 refused to relinquish her seat to a white man on a bus in Montgomery, Alabama, as she was *required by law to do*. Parks had already been actively challenging bus segregation laws, and this "incident sparked a year-long citywide boycott of the public transit system and galvanized the entire civil rights movement of the 1950s and 1960s," dramatically changing the nature of race relations in the United States (Newman 2000:21).

At the same time, many individuals are faced with so many structural deficits that they find it difficult to exercise agency to overcome their social disadvantage. Such circumstances are aptly illustrated by sociologist William Brown's account of his experience with Jimmy, a 15-year-old African-American youth from Detroit. Jimmy was living with his sister, for his mother was in prison and he had never met his father. Brown recalls the day he and his wife took Jimmy out for a birthday celebration:

> Where does a white, middle-class couple take a black soon-to-be-15 gang member for his birthday? . . . [W]e decided that the Detroit Zoo, followed by a movie, and perhaps dinner, would be both appropriate and appreciated. . . . It had never occurred to [us that Jimmy] . . . had never visited a city zoo. The day was absolutely perfect. . . . Jimmy was "hanging" outside his apartment . . . [in] "the projects." Although attempting to maintain the . . . attitude of a streetwise kid, there was a hint of excitement in Jimmy's voice as we exchanged greetings. . . .

I knew that Jimmy had been involved in illegal drug sales . . . [but] he was, as usual, broke. . . . I gave [him] $20 so that he could have some sense of independence. . . . We walked around the zoo for nearly six hours. It was interesting . . . to watch Jimmy eat cotton candy, ice cream bars, [and] popcorn . . . like a normal kid on an outing. I had seen him navigate around a crack house and . . . he had been taking care of himself on the streets of Detroit for several years now! . . .

Following the zoo . . . we went to a movie. . . . Jimmy ate two more boxes of popcorn and one ice cream sandwich and drank an extra-large drink. . . . After the movie we went to a preselected restaurant. At the restaurant we encountered many stares and subtle examples of disapproval from many of the [white] occupants. There were instances during our visit to this restaurant when I wanted to respond to some of the rude onlookers, but this was Jimmy's Day. . . .

My wife and I will never forget Jimmy's 15th birthday. It was a day filled with good intentions . . . [but it] was also filled with cruelty. We removed Jimmy, for a day, from "the projects." . . . We gave him a glimpse of life outside his . . . environment of poverty. . . . The probability of escape for Jimmy, and for the thousands of "Jimmys" like him, is very low—despite all the political rhetoric of "American opportunity." (Shelden et al. 2004:294–297)

Challenges to the Legalistic Definition of Crime

In addition to understanding the relationship between individuals and their society, developing a sociological imagination also requires reconsidering the **legalistic definition** of crime. Paul Tappan was a prominent proponent of the legalistic definition: "Crime is an intentional action in violation of criminal law . . . committed without defense or justification, and sanctioned by the state as a felony or misdemeanor" (1947:100). Tappan believed that criminologists should narrowly confine their subject matter to behaviors that meet this definition. It is inappropriate, he maintained, for criminologists to assert their own values by defining what should or should not be included in the criminal law as "crime."

Edwin Sutherland, one of the most important criminologists of the twentieth century, rejected this approach when he introduced the term **white-collar crime** at his presidential address to the American Sociological Association in 1939. Sutherland (1949), who defined white-collar crime as crime committed by persons of respectability and high social status in the course of their occupations, was especially interested in documenting the extent of law violation among the largest corporations in the United States. He did not wish his study to be constrained by the criminal code, and it was his contention that noncriminal *civil* and *regulatory* law violations should also be considered.

All three systems of law—criminal, civil, and regulatory—are concerned with the social control of actions that are deemed harmful or injurious by a governmental body. These systems of law all involve procedures set up to adjudicate competing claims and to ascertain responsibility regarding such conduct. Technically speaking, **criminal law** defines harmful conduct as a public matter and mandates the intervention of traditional law enforcement authorities such as the police and prosecutors. **Civil law** defines harm as a private matter to be settled by individuals (and their attorneys) as private parties in the courts, although the government may also invoke civil law to litigate actions that affect the government or its employees, and local municipalities may use civil law to enact and enforce ordinances regarding public safety and behavior. **Regulatory law** is concerned with the imposition of rules and standards for business-related activity, and at the federal level involves agencies like the Environmental Protection Agency, the Occupational Safety and Health Administration, and the Securities and Exchange Commission. While the lines of demarcation between these three systems are not always clear, only criminal law allows for the imposition of jail or prison sanctions instead of or in addition to financial penalties, although failure to comply with civil or regulatory rulings may lead to such punishments. Violation of criminal law also carries the greatest moral condemnation, because of the stigma associated with crime.

In his research, Sutherland (1949) uncovered extensive law violations on the part of corporations in areas such as antitrust, misrepresentation in advertising, copyright infringement, and unfair labor practices, although only 16 percent of these violations were prosecuted under criminal law. Nevertheless, Sutherland felt justified in calling these violations crimes. In his view, corporations that engaged in harmful conduct were able to avoid the application of criminal law and the consequent stigma associated with such application because of their economic and political power. Sutherland was unwilling to also allow corporations to exert such influence on criminological research.

The legalistic view expressed by Tappan is often associated with a **consensus perspective** on crime. The consensus approach takes the existing criminal law for granted and assumes there is general agreement in society regarding what is right and what is wrong, regarding those behaviors that should be criminalized and those that should not. In contrast, many of Sutherland's followers prefer a **conflict perspective** on crime, viewing definitions of crime as matters of disagreement, the assertion of economic and political power, and the struggles of competing groups to use the law to their advantage (Chambliss & Seidman 1971; Quinney 1970).

Labeling theory. Thinking about crime from a sociological perspective requires us to move beyond the legalistic-consensus view. **Labeling theory**, for example, encourages us to think about crime as "a label that is attached to behavior and events by those who create and administer the criminal law" (Barlow 1996:10). According to this perspective, legislators establish legal definitions that label some actions as crimes, and criminal justice officials apply these definitions to particular individuals.

The labeling approach assumes that many (if not most) of us have violated the law at one time or another. If we were never caught, however, we were never officially identified or stigmatized as a criminal. What matters most then is the societal reaction to our behavior. Recall the comment of the probation officer whom Zatz cited in her study of the moral panic over Chicano gang violence: "Kids in cowboy hats and pickups, drinking beer and cruising . . . aren't thought of as a gang. But . . . Chicano kids driving lowriders, wearing bandannas, and smoking marijuana . . . are" (1987:136). This type of bias was also documented by William Chambliss (1973) in his classic study "The Saints and the Roughnecks." Chambliss found that the delinquent acts of the lower-class Roughnecks brought forth legal sanctions and community condemnation, while the (quite extensive) delinquencies of the upper-middle-class Saints were treated lightly or ignored. From the perspective of labeling theory, being a criminal is an accorded social status that is relatively independent of actual involvement in lawbreaking (Becker 1963).

Critical criminology. Sociological thinking about crime encourages us to consider the ways in which social advantage and influence affect the process of **criminalization**—that is, the process by which criminal law is selectively applied, making some people and groups more or less vulnerable to or immune from legal control (Hartjen 1974). **Critical criminologists** have been the most radical in their critique of the legal system's bias in the criminalization process, and they have searched for an alternative to the legal definition of crime to broaden the subject matter of criminology. Herman Schwendinger and Julia Schwendinger (1970), for example, advanced a definition of crime as the violation of **human rights**. According to the Schwendingers, egalitarian principles of social justice mandate that all individuals be entitled to certain inalienable rights that are "the fundamental prerequisites for well-being, including food, shelter, clothing, medical services, challenging work and recreational experiences," as well as security from predatory individuals, corporate transgressions, and governmental repression (p. 145). From this perspective, economic or political systems of injustice that deny these rights or that promote racism, sexism, economic exploitation, or environmental degradation, for instance, are proper topics of criminological inquiry.

This human rights definition of crime has been characterized as so broad as to entail the abandonment of criminology as a distinct field of study. Hence Raymond Michalowski (1985) proposed an alternative concept, that of **analogous social injury**, as a way to broaden our understanding of crime. Michalowski defined analogous social injuries as "legally permissible acts or sets of conditions whose consequences are similar to those of illegal acts" (p. 317).

Inequality and Crime

Sociological analysis of social structure and challenges to the legalistic definition of crime merge in efforts to place questions of social inequality at the center of criminological inquiry. Inequality refers to the unequal distribution of valued social resources such as economic, educational, and cultural opportunities; and among the diverse elements of social structure that affect people's lives, criminologists have increasingly emphasized the pivotal role of **class**, **race/ethnicity**, and **gender**.

Class. Most people understand class as a hierarchical relationship that designates individuals on a continuum of lower to middle to upper class based on financial indicators such as wealth (total assets) or annual income. Viewed in this way, the class structure in the United States is marked by considerable inequality. By the end of the first decade of the twenty-first century, for example, the top 1 percent of the country controlled 35 percent of the nation's combined net worth (assets minus debt). The richest 400 families alone had a net worth equal to the combined worth of half of all Americans, some 155 million people. The average annual salary of a chief executive officer of a US corporation was 344 times more than the pay of an average factory worker, up from 42 times more in 1960. In a survey of 134 countries, Sweden ranked first as having the most income *equality,* whereas the United States ranked ninety-third, with more *inequality* than even China, Russia, and Iran. **Intergenerational mobility**, the ability of young people to move up the class hierarchy, to do better than their parents, is also lower in the United States than in countries with less inequality (Domhoff 2013; Frank 2013; Howell 2013).

Most Americans accept the fact that some degree of inequality is necessary in order to reward individual initiative and merit, but they do not favor the extreme inequality that marks the country today. A study by Michael Norton and Dan Ariely (2011) found that most Americans have no idea of the wide distribution of wealth, and when asked about their views on the distributive ideal, they favor a far more equitable distribution than is the case today.

The implications of all this are profound, but it suffices to say here that an individual's class background affects not only their financial status, but also the very nature of their existence. As Michael Lynch observes:

> [Class] affects where you grow up, how you grow up, and the quality of the schools you attend. . . . It affects your occupational choices, your

career path, whom you marry, and . . . even when you have children. It affects your ability to enter politics, and . . . to influence politics. . . . It affects your everyday, mundane decisions, from where you shop, to where you eat, and sometimes, whether you eat at all. (1996:16)

As such, class also affects your incentives and disincentives to engage in criminal behavior, as well as the resources you have at your disposal for committing certain types of crimes (and not others) and for avoiding (or not avoiding) official sanctions for your actions. Crime among the affluent, for example, is facilitated by access to the organizational resources of businesses or governments that are for them "what the gun or knife is for the common criminal—a tool to obtain money from victims," enabling them to perpetrate larger-scale crimes than individuals who act alone (Hagan 1992:9; see also Wheeler & Rothman 1982).

Race and ethnicity. It is arguably true that much progress has been made in the area of race relations in the United States. After all, the country has elected and reelected an African-American president. But the legacy of racial and ethnic discrimination that has marked the history of this country since the days of European colonization—slavery, forcible seizure of land from indigenous peoples, legalized segregation, political disenfranchisement, and lack of economic and educational opportunities—has by no means disappeared, and inequality based on race and ethnicity remains an enduring feature of American life.

Biological typologies of race most often divide humans into three major groups—Caucasoid, Mongoloid, and Negroid—characterized by various physical traits transmitted through heredity. But distinct racial groups hardly exist today due to interracial mixing resulting from migration, exploration, invasions, and involuntary servitude. Speaking of whites and blacks in the United States, Coramae Richey Mann observes that "Euro-Americans are a blend of many ethnic and tribal groups that originated in Africa and Europe . . . [and] many millions of Africans were absorbed into the populations of Mediterranean countries such as Spain, Portugal, Italy, and Greece" (1993:5). Additionally, the rape of black female slaves by their white overseers, as well as consensual interracial mixing, have resulted in millions of mixed-race offspring, making the notion of unitary racial categories somewhat obsolete.

The concept of ethnicity further complicates the subject. Ethnicity refers to distinctions among groups according to cultural characteristics such as language, religion, customs, and family patterns. Often we speak of groups according to their country of origin, such as Irish Americans, Italian Americans, or Mexican Americans. Additionally, people of Hispanic origin may be classified in racial terms as either white or black, and in the United

States the large majority of Hispanics are classified as white. According to census data, about 81 percent of the US population is white, although nearly a fifth of this group is Hispanic. Hispanics overall, including whites and nonwhites, compose about 16 percent of the population. Blacks or African Americans compose about 13 percent. Asians compose about 5 percent. And American Indians, Alaskan Natives, and Pacific Islanders combined compose about 1 percent (US Census Bureau 2012).

Sociologists often use the term **minority** to refer to those racial/ethnic groups who are typically a numerical minority and also distinguished by their disadvantaged social status. In the United States, at the end of the first decade of the twenty-first century, the median net worth of black households was just 5 percent that of white households, and the median net worth of Hispanic households was just 1.3 percent that of white households (Domhoff 2013). Moreover, as suggested earlier, some elements of the US criminal justice system, especially the war on drugs, have had a disproportionate impact on African Americans. Nowadays about one-third of black men can expect to spend some time in prison; among black men with less than a high school education, the figure is nearly 70 percent (Lyons & Pettit 2011; Pettit & Western 2004). Michelle Alexander (2010) dubs this policy the "new Jim Crow," whereby mass incarceration functions as a contemporary legal system of racial control, while Diana Gordon (1994b) believes it reflects a fear of racial minorities and a smokescreen for our inability or unwillingness to address the problems of the inner city.

Gender. In addition to class and race/ethnicity, gender is an element of social structure that is of interest to sociological criminologists. Gender refers to the social statuses and expectations for behavior that are assigned to people who are deemed biologically male and biologically female. The social construction of gender begins at birth (or even before birth) when a child is identified as male or female on the basis of its genitalia. The child is named and dressed in such a way as to make this designation evident to observers, who respond to these gender markers by treating those labeled "boys" differently from those labeled "girls." In turn, children respond to this differential treatment, albeit sometimes with resistance, by coming to feel and behave accordingly. As Judith Lorber observes, "In social interaction throughout their lives, individuals learn what is expected, see what is expected, act and react in expected ways, and thus simultaneously construct and maintain the gender order" (1997:43). To be sure, Lorber adds, resistance and rebellion have altered gender norms, but thus far they have not erased gender statuses, and most societies continue to rank genders unequally, giving men more social advantages than women.

Sociologists refer to a society that is marked by this kind of inequality between men and women—a society that grants men more power, prestige, and privilege—as a **patriarchy**. In the United States, although women have made great strides over the past few decades, on average they still earn less than men, exercise less authority in the workplace, and exert less economic and political power (Lorber 2012).

Traditionally, boys have been given more freedom than girls to be competitive, aggressive, and risk-takers. Girls have been given less leeway to behave in these ways and have been more closely supervised by their parents. These patterns are mirrored in the generally greater amount of crime committed by boys than girls. Among adults as well, men have higher crime rates than women, not only for conventional crimes of theft and violence, but also for white-collar crimes. To be sure, there are nuances to these patterns that we will explore later in this book. Women are more likely than men to be prostitutes, for instance. But this pattern, too, is consistent with conventional gender norms, given society's tendency to view women as sex objects and men's greater propensity to seek out impersonal sex. At the same time, men are very much in control of the prostitution business, as male pimps act as agents/protectors who live parasitically off women's earnings and often beat them to keep them in their place. More generally, men are more likely to commit sexual violence against women than women are to commit sexual violence against men (see Chapters 2, 6, and 9).

Of course, the social statuses we have been discussing—gender, race/ethnicity, and class—do not exist independently of each other. Rather, they interpenetrate each other in ways that make assumptions about singular statuses tenuous. Sociologists refer to these overlapping domains in terms of the concept of **intersectionalities** (Grabham et al. 2009). The implications of intersectionalities for criminology are illustrated by research conducted by Darrell Steffensmeier and Emilie Allen (1988), who analyzed gender-, race-, and age-specific arrest rates and found that female rates were consistently lower than male rates within the same subgroup, but that subgroup variations indicative of intersectionalities were apparent as well. For example, for crimes against persons, the rate for black females was higher than the rate for white females; for minor property crimes, the rate for urban females approximated or exceeded the rate for rural males; and for both serious and minor property crimes, the rate for younger females was higher than the rate for older males. Other research also finds that gender patterns of crime vary by class and racial status. In a study of urban homicides, for example, Mann (1996) found that over three-fourths of the women arrested for murder were African Americans, and that these women also tended to be unemployed mothers who had not completed high school. Sally Simpson, in her research, too, argued that "race and class combine to produce uniquely situated populations of females" (such as lower-class black women) who "appear to have unique patterns of criminality . . . when compared with their gender and racial counterparts" (1991:115).

Summary

This chapter introduced readers to the interdisciplinary field of criminology, and to sociological criminology in particular. We considered the role of the media and politics in shaping public attitudes and opinions about crime and crime policy, examining the phenomena of crime waves and moral panics (including drug scares) and the politics of federal crime policy over the past few decades. We then introduced a sociological perspective that contextualizes the criminal actions of individuals in terms of broader patterns of social relationships by placing issues of inequality at the center of criminological inquiry and viewing the problem of crime and criminal law in terms of three axes of inequality: class, race/ethnicity, and gender.

2

Counting Crime

In this chapter we offer an overview of our subject matter by exam-
ining quantitative data that attempt to measure the amount and nature of the
crime problem in the United States. Some of these data are gathered by
government agencies, including law enforcement, and some are generated
by criminologists conducting research of their own. As we shall see, the
substantive meaning or interpretation of these data is not readily apparent
simply by taking the numbers at face value. Moreover, in order to evaluate
this information, we need to take into account the ways in which these data
are constructed—that is, we need to consider what is left in and what is left
out of statistical counts of crime.

The *Uniform Crime Reports*

The most widely used data on crime in the United States come from the
official government statistics that have been published annually since 1930
in the Federal Bureau of Investigation's *Uniform Crime Reports (UCR)*.
The *UCR* have their origins in the efforts of J. Edgar Hoover, director of the
Bureau of Investigation (renamed the Federal Bureau of Investigation in
1935), to expand his agency's role in federal law enforcement and the collection of national crime statistics. Hoover received support from the International Association of Chiefs of Police (IACP), whose Committee on Uniform Crime Records published an elaborate guide in 1929 titled "Uniform
Crime Reporting: A Complete Manual for Police." This manual proposed a
standardized crime classification system to be used throughout the country.
The IACP committee developed a schedule or form that all police departments were to voluntarily complete and submit to the federal government
for compilation and publication of statistical information. The US Congress
adopted the committee's recommendations and the FBI began publishing
the *UCR*. Currently, most police departments around the country participate
in the national reporting program (Balkan et al. 1980; Mosher et al. 2002).

The IACP committee's classification scheme was based on a distinction between "offenses which naturally and most inevitably are reported to police agencies and those which are less certain of becoming a matter of record" (cited in Balkan et al. 1980:108). This distinction is reflected in the *UCR* division between **Index crimes**, also known as Part I offenses, and **non-Index crimes**, also known as Part II offenses. In the original formulation, Index offenses included four *crimes against persons,* or violent crimes: homicide, forcible rape, robbery, and aggravated assault; and three *crimes against property:* burglary, larceny-theft, and motor vehicle theft (see Table 2.1). The non-Index offenses include 20 additional (mostly non-violent) categories of violations (see Table 2.4).

Annual data on arrests are published for both Index and non-Index offenses, but data on crimes reported by citizens to the police or those that are otherwise known to or observed directly by the police are published only for Index offenses. Most reported (or known) crimes do not result in an arrest (see Table 2.3), but data on Index offenses are the ones most often cited in media reports and public discussions about how much crime is occurring in society. (Although arson was added to the list of Index property crimes in 1979, published data are only available for arrests.)

The distinction between Index and non-Index crimes implicitly assumes that the former are more serious and thereby more reflective of the real crime problem. This assumption is questionable, however. For example, Table 2.1 shows that about 61 percent of reported Index crimes in 2013 (the latest data available at the time of this writing) were for the nonviolent crime of larceny-theft, which includes shoplifting and bicycle theft,

Table 2.1 Reported *UCR* Index Crimes (2013)

Type of Crime	Number	Percentage[a]
Violent crimes	1,163,146	11.9
Homicide[b]	14,196	0.1
Forcible rape	79,770	0.8
Robbery	345,031	3.5
Aggravated assault	724,149	7.4
Property crimes	8,632,512	88.1
Burglary	1,928,465	19.7
Larceny-theft	6,004,453	61.3
Motor vehicle theft	699,594	7.1
Total Index crimes	9,795,658	100.0

Source: Federal Bureau of Investigation 2013, tab. 1.

Notes: a. It is possible for a single incident of criminality to include more than one crime; for example, a theft could involve both breaking and entering (burglary) and forceful action against an individual (robbery). In such cases, only the most serious of the offenses is recorded for the purpose of the *UCR* statistical record.

b. Homicide = murder and nonnegligent manslaughter.

offenses that most people would agree are relatively less serious. Overall, about 88 percent of Index crimes were property crimes, while about 12 percent were violent crimes. Homicide in particular constituted less than 1 percent. Moreover, the government's preoccupation with drugs is not reflected in the Index crime category, since drug offenses are classified as non-Index offenses. Neither are white-collar crimes listed as Index crimes. To the extent that such crimes (e.g., fraud and embezzlement) are even included as non-Index offenses, they generally consist of those committed by the less affluent rather than by high-status corporate executives.

Table 2.2 presents data on Index crime rates from 1960 to 2013. The crime rate provides a measure of the amount of crime relative to the size of the population, and is calculated by dividing the number of crimes by the size of the population and (according to convention) multiplying this quotient by 100,000. In 2013 the total Index crime rate was 3,099 per 100,000 persons in the United States.

Crime rates are the figures most often used to measure increases or decreases in crime over time. Overall, the most dramatic increases in crime rates over the past five decades took place some time ago, during the 1960s and early 1970s. The reasons for this are complex, but in his analysis of these data Gary LaFree (1998) attributes the rise to a general decline in the legitimacy of social institutions (economic, political, and familial) that occurred during that era, which weakened societal control over individuals and lowered their commitment to the conventional social order. Property crime rates stabilized through the 1980s, although the violent crime rate continued to rise, perhaps because of the increased presence of urban street gangs and the availability of guns among youths (Conklin 2003; Fagan & Wilkinson 1998). In the 1990s, the crime rate began to decline, a trend that

Table 2.2 *UCR* Index Crime Rates (1960–2013)

	Total Index Rate	Violent Rate	Property Rate
1960	1,887	161	1,726
1965	2,449	200	2,249
1970	3,985	364	3,621
1975	5,299	488	4,811
1980	5,950	597	5,353
1985	5,224	558	4,666
1990	5,803	730	5,073
1995	5,276	685	4,591
2000	4,125	507	3,618
2005	3,899	469	3,430
2010	3,346	404	2,942
2013	3,099	368	2,731

Sources: Federal Bureau of Investigation 1976, tab. 2; 1986, tab. 1; 2005, tab. 1; 2010, tab. 1; 2013, tab. 1.

Note: Rate = number of crimes committed per 100,000 population.

has continued to this day. Criminologists have debated the causes of this decline, and we will consider this debate shortly, but first we should review some of the limitations of these data.

Underreporting by Citizens

Evidence from other sources of crime statistics (to be reviewed later) indicates that a large proportion of crime is not reported to the police and hence does not appear in the *UCR*. The reasons for citizen underreporting are numerous. People may believe that the crime was not serious enough to warrant police action or that the police could not or would not do anything about it. They may be uncertain that what they had witnessed or experienced was, in fact, an illegal act, or they may feel that what transpired (even if illegal) was a private matter. Some may be reluctant to inform on the individuals involved in the crime, have something to hide, place a negative value on cooperating with the police, or simply not want to get involved. Some may fear reprisal from the offender or be embarrassed about their own victimization (Sheley 1985).

Criminologists have long known that most of the reported crimes that are known to the police come to their attention because of citizen reports (Reiss 1971). Hence fluctuations in reported crime rates over time may be as much a function of changes in the likelihood of citizen reporting as a function of changes in the level of criminal activity itself. Take, for instance, the reporting of theft. Insurance companies generally require that thefts be reported before claims can be settled, making people with theft insurance more likely to report crimes than those who are uninsured. If, over time, the number of people who are insured increases, then the rate of reported thefts may increase as well.

Historically, one of the most significant areas of unreported crime has involved violence against women, such as rape and domestic battery. Women have remained silent about their victimization for many reasons; for example, they may feel humiliated or embarrassed, fear further violence or retaliation by the offender, or fear hostile questioning or disbelief from the police or other criminal justice officials. Since the 1970s, however, the educational and law reform efforts of the contemporary feminist movement have increased our sensitivity to these issues. The development of crisis centers for rape victims and shelters for battered women, improvements in police training, the addition of female officers, and various legal reforms (such as "rape shield" laws that restrict courtroom questioning of victims' prior sexual conduct, and mandatory arrest policies for domestic batterers) have encouraged women to come forward with complaints. These changes alone could result in higher *UCR* rates of rape and aggravated assault (which may now include more domestic battery cases) independently of actual changes in the occurrence of these crimes (Baumer et al. 2003; Berger et al. 1994; Jensen & Karpos 1993).

The Organizational Production of Crime Data

Crime statistics need to be understood as outcomes of organizational processes that are conditioned by "the interpretations, decisions, and actions of law enforcement personnel" (Kitsuse & Cicourel 1963:137). In one early study, Donald Black (1970) studied police decisionmaking in Boston, Chicago, and the District of Columbia. He found that the preference, attitude, and class status of the complainant (the person who calls the police) had a significant impact on police officers' decisions to record an incident as a crime. Officers were more likely to record a crime when the complainant expressed a preference for formal rather than informal action, was deferential or respectful to the police, and was white-collar rather than blue-collar in status. Black also found that the relational distance between the complainant and the suspect was a factor: the closer the relational distance, such as whether it was a family member or a stranger, the less likely the incident was to be recorded.

Several studies also have found that the relational distance between the complainant and the suspect is especially important in police responses to rape. The closer the relational distance, the more likely the police will label the complaint as "unfounded," as not a real rape (Estrich 1987). Often, the veracity of a woman's complaint is judged according to the interpersonal context of the incident. Complaints by women whose moral character is questioned or whose perceived carelessness is thought to have made them vulnerable to attack are treated more skeptically. Among those least likely to have their complaints treated seriously are juvenile runaways, hitchhikers, and prostitutes; those who are raped in situations involving alcohol and drug use; those who willingly enter the offender's home or apartment; and those considered to be partiers, pleasure seekers, or sexually promiscuous (LaFree 1989; Sanders 1980; Spohn & Tellis 2014). In addition, police officers may distinguish between "good victims" and "bad victims" on the basis of their perception of how well a rape case is likely to stand up in court. As one investigating officer remarked regarding a rape claim: "Generally speaking, I believe something happened. I believe what the lady is saying. . . . But I'm also aware that someone else looking at the incident may see it a little differently" (Beneke 1982:152). Another officer put it this way: "I'm not going to lie to a woman and tell her she's got a case when she hasn't. She'll devote all her time and energy into putting this guy away and it'll be bearing on her mind and then the defense attorney tears her apart and the jury brings back a 'not guilty' verdict. . . . Why give anybody false hopes? . . . I've had enough cases in front of juries so I can just about tell which way it's going to go" (pp. 145–146).

In another study, Barbara Warner (1997) examined the effects of community characteristics on police recording of burglary complaints (911 calls) in 61 neighborhoods in Boston. Warner found that, overall, only 40 percent of the burglary complaints were later verified and recorded by the police as burglaries. The majority of the incidents were downgraded to less serious non-Index offenses or recorded as nonoffenses. The proportion of burglary complaints that were recorded as burglaries ranged across neighborhoods from 14 percent to 58 percent.

Warner found that burglary recording was lower in areas marked by more poverty, and she offered several explanations for this finding. The poor generally receive few public services of all sorts, and police services are no exception. Police may view poor neighborhoods as inhabited by morally unworthy people who get what they deserve. Or police may simply feel that there is no reason to write an official burglary report when so many of the residents are without insurance and the likelihood of recovering the stolen goods is unlikely.

In still another illustrative study, Robert McCleary and colleagues (1982) found that crime rates in one city increased when police administrators removed supervisory sergeants from the radio dispatch bureau, the unit responsible for receiving citizen calls and setting priorities for officers' responses. Requests for police assistance that were dispatched immediately were more likely than requests that were delayed to eventually yield an official crime report. When supervisory sergeants were present, dispatchers were relieved of the responsibility of setting priorities and filtering out less serious calls. But when sergeants were unavailable, dispatchers were more likely to order immediate responses to "play it safe" and "cover their asses." Under these conditions, reported *UCR* crimes increased by about 20 percent.

Additionally, McCleary and colleagues learned about ways in which officers classified offenses that inflated or deflated *UCR* statistics. In one city, uniformed officers were more likely than detectives to classify a broad range of thefts as burglaries. Detectives employed a narrower (and technically accurate) definition of burglary as breaking and entering into a house or enclosed garage. Uniformed officers, on the other hand, recorded breaking through a fence and stealing from a yard as burglaries as well. Differences in such classification decisions increased the number of burglaries in this city by about 150 per month.

Henry Brownstein served more than two years as chief of the Bureau of Statistical Services for New York state's Division of Criminal Justice Services (DCJS), where he "was responsible for the collection, maintenance, and dissemination of official crime and criminal justice data" (1996:19–20). In New York, *UCR* data were voluntarily submitted by over 600 local police departments. *UCR* clerks in different locales had the responsibility of completing forms detailing information about crimes that had been reported in their jurisdiction. These clerks were poorly trained and overworked, and experienced high turnover rates. They had difficulty completing the forms in ways that allowed an understaffed DCJS to clearly differentiate Index from non-Index offenses. It was not always easy, for example, to distinguish murders and nonnegligent (willful) manslaughters, which are Index offenses, from justifiable homicides, accidental deaths, suicides, and negligent manslaughters. Similarly, the line between Index aggravated assaults and non-Index simple assaults was not always clear. Moreover, police departments in different jurisdictions often competed with each other to show that they were "responsible for a greater share of the problem that resources" they hoped would be forthcoming would be used to solve (p. 23). This competition created a problem of duplicate reporting, as departments tried to get credit for the same crimes.

Each month the DCJS received about 800 forms from local police departments. Much discretionary decisionmaking was required to translate these forms into standardized *UCR* categories and to reconcile competing jurisdictional claims. The pressure of FBI deadlines for the submission of *UCR* statistics often meant that this work was hastily performed. Brownstein found that it was not unusual for the DCJS to submit the data for New York state before all the localities in New York City had submitted their forms. Hence the data eventually published in New York state's own *Crime and Justice Annual Report* were at variance from those received by the FBI.

Clearance and Arrest Data

Crimes reported or known to the police are not the only statistical counts of crime included in the *UCR*. Clearance rates and arrest data are other important indicators. The **clearance rate** is essentially the rate of solved crimes. This rate is calculated by dividing the number of reports for each Index crime by the number of arrests for that crime, arriving at a percentage of each crime that is "cleared by arrest." Table 2.3 lists the Index crime clearance rates for 2013. The data show that violent crimes, especially homicide, have higher clearance rates than property crimes. This means, of course, that the chance of the police recovering stolen property is rather slim.

Like official reports, clearance rates are organizationally constructed. While there are times when police departments find lower clearance rates

Table 2.3 Clearance Rates for *UCR* Index Crimes (2013)

Type of Crime	Percentage
Homicide[a]	64
Forcible rape	41
Robbery	29
Aggravated assault	58
Burglary	13
Larceny-theft	22
Motor vehicle theft	14
Arson	21

Source: Federal Bureau of Investigation 2013, tab. 25.
Note: a. Homicide = murder and nonnegligent manslaughter.

advantageous for requesting resources, a department's image is generally enhanced by a higher clearance rate. Hugh Barlow notes that police will "sometimes go to extraordinary lengths to 'clear' crimes" (1996:44). To illustrate his point, Barlow offers the case of Henry Lee Lucas. In 1983, law enforcement identified Lucas as a serial murderer who had confessed to nearly a hundred murders across the country. Barlow writes:

> By 1984 it was reported that he had confessed to 360 murders, and by 1985 the figure stood at an incredible 600 killings in nearly 30 different states. In that same year, however, the *New York Times* reported that Lucas may actually have killed only one person, his mother! As the story unfolded, it became apparent that Lucas had been pressured by eager police into making confessions so that they could clear their books of unsolved murders. The truth will probably never be known, but most of the murders cleared by Lucas's arrest and "confessions" were not committed by him. (p. 44)

In addition to clearance rates, arrest data can be used to examine the proportion of police activity devoted to non-Index offenses. In many respects the emphasis in the *UCR* on Index crimes misrepresents what the police actually do, since more than 80 percent of arrests are for non-Index offenses. Table 2.4 provides the percentage breakdown of the arrests for these crimes in 2013. Taken together, drug and alcohol–related arrests constitute the largest group of offenses, about 30 percent of all arrests (both Index and non-Index). Arrests listed as "all other offenses (except traffic)," a catchall category reflecting a variety of minor state and local laws, constitute nearly 30 percent as well.

Finally, *UCR* arrest data also include information about the age, race/ethnicity, and gender of individuals who are arrested. Unfortunately, arrest data by class are not collected for the nation as a whole, although studies that examine official records from particular localities have consistently found an inverse relationship between class status and arrests, meaning that lower-status people have higher arrest rates than higher-status people (Shaw & McKay 1942; Tracy et al. 1990; Wolfgang et al. 1972). Arrests for race and ethnicity may also be used as a proxy for class status, because of the economic inequality that exists between whites and nonwhites in the United States (see Chapter 1). At the same time, it is important to note that arrest data may not simply reflect a group's actual rate of law violation, as persons who manage to avoid arrest may nevertheless be extensively involved in crime. In other words, there are essentially two ways to interpret these data: they may represent **differential criminal involvement** or **differential likelihood of selection** (Sheley 1985). From this perspective, we can ask whether higher arrest rates are indicative of a group's greater involvement in *these types of offenses* or, as labeling theory suggests, whether they are indicative of members' vulnerability to being apprehended

Table 2.4 Non-Index Offenses as a Percentage of *UCR* Arrests (2013)

Type of Crime	Percentage of Arrests
Other assaults	9.7
Forgery and counterfeiting	0.5
Fraud	1.3
Embezzlement	0.1
Stolen property[a]	0.8
Vandalism	1.8
Weapons[b]	1.2
Prostitution and commercialized vice	0.4
Sex offenses[c]	0.5
Drug abuse violations	13.3
Gambling	0.1
Offenses against family and children	0.9
Driving under the influence	10.3
Liquor laws	3.1
Drunkenness	3.9
Disorderly conduct	4.1
Vagrancy	0.2
Curfew and loitering	0.5
All other offenses (except traffic)	29.0
Suspicion	< 0.1
All non-Index arrests	81.8

Source: Federal Bureau of Investigation 2013, tab. 29.
Notes: a. Stolen property = buying, receiving, and possessing.
b. Weapons = carrying, possessing, etc.
c. Sex offenses = except forcible rape and prostitution.

by police. Of course, it is also possible that both differential involvement and differential selection account for these rates.

National *UCR* data can be used to construct age-specific, race/ethnicity-specific, and gender-specific arrest rates that allow for comparisons between age, race/ethnicity, and gender groups. Such rates are calculated by dividing the number of arrests for individuals in a particular group by the number of persons in that group, and are shown in Table 2.5. The data for age indicate that arrest rates peak in the 15–24-year-old range and decline thereafter. The data for race and ethnicity indicate that the rates are highest for blacks/African Americans, followed by American Indians/Alaskan Natives, Hispanics/Latinos, whites, and Asians/Native Hawaiians/Pacific Islanders. The data for gender indicate that males have higher arrest rates than females.

Explaining the Declining Crime Rate
Having thus far provided an overview and considered the limitations of official crime data, we can now examine the declining crime rate that began in the 1990s. During that decade national attention often focused on New York City, which previously had a reputation as one of the most dan-

Table 2.5 Age-, Race/Ethnicity-, and Gender-Specific Arrest Rates for *UCR* Index Crimes (2013)

	Violent Rate	Property Rate
Age		
10–14	58	271
15–19	279	1,218
20–24	364	1,143
25–29	297	871
30–34	253	727
35–39[a]	173	488
Race/ethnicity		
White	94	350
Black/African American	383	918
Hispanic/Latino	114	375
American Indian/Alaskan Native	165	609
Asian/Native Hawaiian/Pacific Islander	40	112
Gender		
Male	207	517
Female	50	303

Sources: Federal Bureau of Investigation 2013, tabs. 38, 42, 43A; US Census Bureau 2012, tabs. 6–7.

Notes: Rate = number of arrests per 100,000 population of each group.

a. Arrest rates continue to decline with age.

gerous cities in the country. Mayor Rudolph Giuliani, a former federal prosecutor, took the reins of city government in 1994, pledging to make New York safer. Giuliani appointed former New York City transit police chief William Bratton to head the city's police department. Under Bratton's leadership, the New York City Police Department implemented a strategy of aggressive law enforcement against "quality of life" offenses such as jumping subway turnstiles, public drunkenness and underage drinking, truancy, prostitution, panhandling, graffiti-writing, and playing loud music in public (Bratton 1998). This approach was based on the **broken windows** strategy initially developed by criminologists James Wilson and George Kelling (1982)—the idea being that broken windows left unrepaired send a message that no one cares about the community, leaving untended property available for vandals and setting in motion a downward spiral of increasing disorder that emboldens more serious criminals. Thus Bratton hoped that zero tolerance for minor transgressions would have a trickle-down effect on reducing serious crime in the city. He also initiated a computerized system of mapping city "hot spots" to improve police intelligence and deploy officers more effectively. Some NYPD officials, on the other hand, admitted that there was pressure on them to downgrade crimes to reduce rates of serious crime.

In a review of the evidence for the nation as a whole, John Conklin (2003) concluded that police enforcement strategies like those adopted in New York City may have had an impact on declining crime rates, but police alone did not exert an influence independent of other factors (see also Eck & Maguire 2000; Rosenfeld et al. 2007; Zimring 2007). Moreover, Bratton's use of aggressive stop-and-search techniques led to a marked increase in citizen complaints of harassment and brutality by NYPD officers (D. Anderson 1999; Greene 1999).

The age structure of society. Many criminologists attribute the dramatic rise in crime rates during the 1960s and early 1970s, at least in part, to the coming-of-age of post–World War II baby boomers (Cohen & Land 1987; Steffensmeier et al. 1987). Darrell Steffensmeier and colleagues observed, as we saw in Table 2.5, that the types of crime measured by the *UCR* seem to "peak in adolescence or early adulthood [and] then decline fairly steadily" thereafter (1989:806). This pattern, they believe, stems from

> increased sources of criminogenic reinforcement experienced by young people . . . [and] the powerful institutional pressures for conformity that accompany adulthood. Juveniles have not as yet developed either a well-defined sense of self or strong stakes in conformity. . . . They are barred from many legitimate avenues for achieving socially valued goals; their dependent status insulates them from many of the social and legal costs of illegitimate activities; and their stage of cognitive development limits prudence concerning the consequences of their behavior. (pp. 806–807)

As the baby boom generation aged, however, and the size of the youthful population began to decline, property crime rates stabilized (Cohen & Land 1987; Steffensmeier et al. 1987). The violent crime rate, on the other hand, has been more resilient to such demographic shifts, perhaps for reasons we noted earlier (street gangs and gun possession among youths). As for the 1990s, Conklin (2003) estimates that age composition explains from 8 percent (for motor vehicle theft) to 20 percent (for homicide) of the declining crime rate, depending on the particular Index crime that is being assessed.

Economist Steven Levitt (1999), who gained notoriety for his best-selling book *Freakonomics: A Rogue Economist Explores the Hidden Side of Everything* (Levitt & Dubner 2005), also concluded that the changing age structure accounts for only a small proportion of variations in crime rates. More important, as Levitt argued in a provocative empirical study conducted with John Donahue, was the effect of the landmark US Supreme Court *Roe v. Wade* (1973) decision that legalized abortion in the United States (Donahue & Levitt 2001). Legalized abortion, these economists argued, reduced the number of unwanted births to low-income women, thus reducing the number of "at risk" disadvantaged youths who might have been prone to criminality.

The econometric statistical methods used by Donahue and Levitt are complex and have provoked an equally complex empirical literature that questions their analysis. One skeptic, Frank Zimring, noted "the extraordinary difficulty of using trends in crime to test the delayed effects of legal change that happened decades earlier" (2007:85). Zimring also examined data that showed no association between legalized abortion and the percentage of "at risk" births, hence undermining one of the key assumptions of Donahue and Levitt's theory. Another skeptic, Richard Rosenfeld, argued that the economists' theory of abortion, "though not implausible," should have predicted a crime rate decline that began earlier than the 1990s (2004:87).

Additional factors. Most criminologists believe that the declining crime rate can be explained by the confluence of a number of factors, although there is disagreement about which ones are more important for which types of crime. Other hypotheses include stabilization of the crack-cocaine market, implementation of gun control measures, higher rates of incarceration, and the vibrant economy of the 1990s (Blumstein & Wallman 2000). Among these, Conklin (2003) thinks that higher incarceration rates were most important, but Thomas Arvanites and Robert DeFina (2006) found that economic growth had a stronger impact on *UCR* rates of property crime and robbery than incarceration. Additionally, Rick Nevin (2000) found that regulatory environmental policies leading to reductions in lead exposure from motor vehicle exhaust and paint were associated with lower crime rates because, he argues, lead exposure is associated with cognitive problems that put both parents and children at risk of low impulse control and behavioral aggression. Nevin's research, supported by other studies (Dietrich et al. 2001; Wright et al. 2008), is indicative of a connection between policies aimed at regulating the conduct of corporations and the reduction of conventional street crime. Nevertheless, Zimring concludes that the decline in crime is "a classic example of multiple causation, with none of the many contributing causes playing a dominant role" (2007:197).

Other Counts of Crime

Criminologists do not rely exclusively on police-generated *UCR* data to measure the amount of crime that occurs in the United States. **Victimization surveys** and **self-report surveys** are the two major alternative methods of counting crime in this country.

The National Crime Victimization Survey

In the late 1960s, the President's Commission on Law Enforcement and Administration of Justice recommended the implementation of a national survey of crime victimization to supplement the *UCR*. The commission hoped that this effort would provide information on criminal victimizations that remained unreported or unknown to the police. In 1972, the US Department of Justice's Bureau of Justice Statistics (BJS) began conducting the *National Crime Survey,* now called the *National Crime Victimization Survey (NCVS),* to provide annual estimates of victimization. Although the size of the interviewing sample has varied over the years, most recently it includes about 163,000 people from about 92,000 households in the United States (Truman & Langston 2014). During the interview, which occurs in person or by phone, individuals are asked questions about victimizations they experienced over the previous six months. Follow-up interviews are then conducted every six months over a three-year period. The data gathered from these interviews are used to compute estimates of victimization rates for the nation as a whole.

Like Index offenses in the *UCR,* the *NCVS* divides victimizations into two groups: violent crimes and property crimes. The former includes rape/sexual assault, robbery, physical assault, and domestic violence; the latter includes household burglaries, motor vehicle thefts, and other thefts. Table 2.6 lists the percentage of victimizations reported to the police in 2013, and indicates that only about 46 percent of violent victimizations and 36 percent of property victimizations come to the attention of law enforcement authorities.

The *NCVS* suffers from some of the same problems as the *UCR.* There are no questions about drug offenses or white-collar crimes, for example. Homeless individuals are not sampled. Business victimizations have been omitted since the early years of the survey, giving us less information about the fact that "insider" theft from employee pilferage and embezzlement costs businesses more than "outsider" theft from shoplifting, burglary, or robbery; and insider theft accounts for about one-third of all business failures in the United States (Challenger 2004; Reiman 2007). In addition, many respondents forget victimizations, are unaware of the victimizations of family members, or report crimes that occurred before the six-month period. And college-educated respondents, who have more experience with

Table 2.6 Percentage of *NCVS* Victimizations Reported to Police (2013)

Violent crimes	46
Rape/sexual assault	35
Robbery	68
Assault	43
Domestic violence[a]	57
Property crimes	36
Household burglary	57
Motor vehicle theft	76
Theft	29

Source: Truman & Langton 2014, tab. 6.
Note: a. Includes crimes committed by intimate partners and family members.

survey- and test-taking, may report a higher proportion of their victimizations than do less-educated individuals (Sykes & Cullen 1992).

The *NCVS* is administered in a two-stage process. Respondents are first asked several screening questions pertaining to the number of times they have been victimized by each type of offense. If they answer in the affirmative, they are then asked a number of follow-up questions regarding details of the crime and characteristics of the offender. This mode of questioning has been particularly problematic when the information sought concerns rape.

Prior to a survey redesign in 1992, the first stage of the interview asked respondents "whether someone [had] tried to take something from them, rob them, beat them, attack them with a weapon, or steal things from them. *None of these questions ask[ed] whether someone ha[d] tried to rape them.* The question that [was] supposed to elicit rape [read]: 'Did anyone TRY to attack you in some other way?'" (Eigenberg 1990:657). Respondents were thus never specifically asked about rape victimizations. The BJS estimates that the survey redesign alone (which included more direct questioning about rape) more than doubled the reported rate of rape, although that rate declined thereafter (Planty et al. 2013; Rand et al. 1997). Still problematic, however, is the fact that victims of rape and domestic violence may be asked about their experiences while the perpetrator (such as a spouse or partner) is in the room with them.

Last, Table 2.7 presents data on the demographic background of victims of violent crime, which mirrors the *UCR* offender data in many ways. Adolescents and young adults have the highest rate of victimization, which

Table 2.7 Victimization Rates for Violent Crimes by Age, Race/Ethnicity, and Gender (2013)

Age	
12–17	52
18–24	34
25–34	30
35–49	20
50–64	19
65+	5
Race/ethnicity	
Non-Hispanic white	22
Non-Hispanic black	25
Hispanic/Latino	25
American Indian/Alaskan Native	57
Asian/Native Hawaiian/Pacific Islander	7
Biracial/multiracial	90
Gender	
Male	24
Female	23

Source: Truman & Langton 2014, tab. 9.
Note: Rate = number of victimizations per 1,000 persons age 12 or older for each group.

declines with age. Although non-Hispanic blacks and Hispanics/Latinos have only slightly higher rates of victimization than non-Hispanic whites, biracial or multiracial people have the highest rates of any demographic group, followed by American Indians/Alaskan Natives (Asians/Native Hawaiians/Pacific Islanders have the lowest rates). Females and males have comparable rates of victimization, although other data indicate that females are more likely than males to be victimized by sexual violence, and that males are more likely than females to be victimized by nonsexual violence (see Chapters 6 and 8).

Self-Report Surveys

Another source of statistical crime data falls under the rubric of self-report surveys. Here respondents are asked to provide information on offenses they have committed. The first known self-report survey was conducted by Austin Porterfield (1943) with a sample of adolescents and young adults in Fort Worth, Texas. Porterfield was interested in comparing the law-violation rates of youths who had juvenile court records, with the law-violation rates of college students who did not have such records. His survey results revealed comparable rates of crime among these two groups. Porterfield explained his findings in terms consistent with what later became known as labeling theory, suggesting that the higher-class status of college youth had insulated them from arrest.

Self-report surveys, like victimization surveys, tap into a domain of crime that is largely missing from the official record. Unfortunately, there have been few self-report surveys conducted with adults, and some of these have been limited to incarcerated offenders. Most self-report surveys have been conducted with adolescents, often administered in high school settings.

Self-report surveys suffer from memory problems of those who take them, both the forgetting of offenses and the reporting of offenses outside a study's time frame (usually one year prior). Overall, criminologists have found that the surveys contain little distortion due to respondents' intentional deception, but because some evidence suggests that black youths may underreport the extent of their official police records, some researchers suspect that they may also underreport delinquency. Perhaps these youths are more distrustful of how the survey results will be used, or perhaps they dispute the validity of the official charges against them (Hindelang et al. 1981; Mosher et al. 2002; Walker et al. 2007).

These limitations notwithstanding, a large body of adolescent self-report research indicates that delinquent behavior is widespread among youths from *all* social backgrounds. Moreover, the studies that suggest class and race parity in law violation are at variance with *UCR* arrest rates, and these findings have generated a great deal of controversy. They not only raise the specter of discrimination by law enforcement, but also call into question theories of delinquency based on economic and minority-group disadvantage. If delinquency is viewed primarily as a lower-class or racial minority-group problem, as liberals maintain, then the root causes of crime should be sought in the social conditions associated with lower-class and disadvantaged communities. If, on the other hand, there is little relationship between class, race, and delinquency, then the causes can be attributed to factors that affect all social groups, such as declining moral values and low family cohesion (see Chapter 1).

A few decades ago, Michael Hindelang and colleagues (1978) were among the first to argue that the discrepancy between official (*UCR* arrests) and self-report measures of delinquency was "largely illusory," because the two sources of data did not "tap the same domain of behavior." Self-report surveys, they observed, generally ask about a wider range of behaviors than are reported in the *UCR,* and they are skewed toward less serious items that remain largely "outside the domain of behavior that elicits official attention" (pp. 995–996). Thus Hindelang and colleagues argued that there is no relationship between class, race, and *less serious* delinquency, but that the official data do provide a valid measure of *more serious* youthful offenses that are of primary concern to law enforcement authorities.

In another important study, Delbert Elliott and Suzanne Ageton (1980) examined race and class differences for different categories of self-reported offenses based on the *National Youth Survey (NYS),* conducted by the Behavioral Research Institute at the University of Colorado: *predatory crimes against persons* (such as assault and robbery), *predatory crimes against property* (such as burglary and auto theft), *illegal service crimes* (such as prostitution and selling drugs), *public disorder crimes* (such as carrying a weapon, disorderly conduct, and marijuana use), *status offenses* (such as running away and truancy), and *hard-drug use* (such as heroin and cocaine use). Elliott and Ageton found statistically significant race differences for property crimes and class differences for violent crimes (that is, higher rates for black and lower-class youths), but not for the other offense categories. They also found that most of the race and class differences, to the extent they existed, stemmed from a small number of high-frequency or chronic offenders who inflated the overall rates of their respective groups (see also Tracy et al. 1990; Wolfgang et al. 1972). Elliott and Ageton concluded that the differences between their findings and those of earlier self-report studies were "the result of differences in the specific [self-report] measures used" (1980:95).

In analyses of subsequent *NYS* samples, Delbert Elliott and David Huizinga confirmed the results for class variations but not race variations, which suggests that racial influences (to the extent they exist) may best be explained by class influences (Elliott & Huizinga 1983; Huizinga & Elliott 1987). Regardless, the self-report research of Elliott and colleagues points to an important distinction between the **prevalence of offending** and the **incidence of offending**. Prevalence refers to the proportion of a particular group that has engaged in law violation, while incidence refers to the frequency of offending within the subgroup of offenders (Paternoster & Triplett 1988). The theoretical significance of this distinction has been noted by Alfred Blumstein and Elizabeth Grady: "It is reasonable to expect . . . that one set of factors distinguishes between those persons who become involved in crimes the first time and those who do not, and that a different set of factors distinguishes those who persist in crime once involved, from those who discontinue criminality at an early age" (1982:265).

Research by Bradley Wright and colleagues (1999) is noteworthy for adding a new twist to sorting out the relationship between class and delinquency. Using data from New Zealand, they found that low social class promotes delinquency by "increasing individuals' alienation, financial strain, and aggression, and by decreasing [their] educational and occupational aspirations" (p. 176). High social class, on the other hand, promotes delinquency by increasing individuals' inclination toward risk-taking, insulating them from adverse social sanctions, and decreasing their commitment to conventional moral values.

Drug Surveys

Drug surveys are a special type of self-report research. Since 1975, the Monitoring the Future (MTF) project at the University of Michigan's Institute for Social Research has conducted annual surveys of drug use among high school seniors (Johnston et al. 2013). It is not unusual for data released from this and similar reports to become the source of media-generated crime waves or drug scares.

In one illustrative study, James Orcutt and J. Blake Turner (1993) analyzed how *Newsweek* magazine distorted statistical results from the annual MTF survey to make claims about an impending cocaine epidemic. In July 1986, the Institute for Social Research planned to release a study of 1975–1985 drug use trends among high school seniors. But as early as March 17, in a cover story titled "Kids and Cocaine," *Newsweek* scooped the other national media by publishing results from this report, along with an interview with its chief author, Lloyd Johnston, about a "coke plague" (Morganthau 1986:63).

The MTF data indicated that both 30-day prevalence and annual prevalence rates (the proportion of youths using illegal drugs) had risen dramatically between 1976 and 1979, after which drug use *overall* declined until 1985, when the downward trend abated (Johnston et al. 2007). The *Newsweek* story, however, focused on the cocaine data, which did reflect an increase that Johnston characterized as "disturbing" (p. 48). But while the MTF study emphasized the increase in "current use" of cocaine (30-day prevalence), current users constituted less than 7 percent of all high school seniors. Instead, *Newsweek* focused on the 17.3 percent "lifetime" prevalence rate, that is, the proportion of seniors who had used cocaine at any time in their lives—even though the MTF data indicated that lifetime prevalence had in fact remained fairly stable since 1979.

The "Kids and Cocaine" article made the case for a "cocaine [plague] . . . seeping into the nation's schools" by contrasting the 1975 lifetime rate (9 percent) with the higher 1985 rate (17.3 percent), which, as *Newsweek* underscored, amounted to a near doubling of cocaine use (Morganthau 1986:63). It did *not* note, however, that the increase that had occurred prior to 1980 dwarfed the 1980–1985 rise. Including the 1975–1980 data would have shown that the real period of increased cocaine use occurred prior to the emergence of the so-called plague. Then *Newsweek* constructed a glossy, colored graph that accentuated the annual changes in the 1980–1985 period, which pictorially transformed "statistically nonsignificant fluctuations . . . into striking peaks and valleys" and an illusion of increased use overall (Orcutt & Turner 1993:194). By the late 1980s, when MTF data showed a decline in cocaine use among high school seniors, as well as use of other drugs, the cocaine epidemic no longer seemed newsworthy and, ironically, *Newsweek* reported that "in their zeal to shield young people from the plague of drugs, the media and many drug educators have hyped the very real dangers" of cocaine (Martz 1990:74).

Table 2.8 provides MTF data on monthly and annual self-reported drug use by high school seniors from 1993 to 2013. Underage drinking of alcohol, the most widely used substance, declined over this period, as did cigarette smoking. Marijuana use, which increased between 1993 and 2003, remained fairly stable subsequently. Use of other drugs, including cocaine, either declined or remained stable over this 20-year period.

Other self-report surveys are also helpful in shedding light on the racial/ethnic distribution of illegal drug use. Table 2.9 provides data from a

Table 2.8 Self-Reported Use of Selected Drugs by High School Seniors (1993–2013)

	Percentage Using over Past 30 Days			Percentage Using over Past Year		
	1993	2003	2013	1993	2003	2013
Marijuana/hashish	15.5	21.2	22.7	26.0	34.9	36.4
Cocaine	1.3	2.1	0.6	3.3	4.8	2.6
Hallucinogens	2.7	1.8	1.4	7.4	5.9	4.5
Heroin	0.2	0.4	0.3	0.5	0.8	0.6
Amphetamines	3.7	5.0	4.1	8.4	9.9	8.7
Barbiturates	1.3	2.9	2.2	3.4	6.0	4.8
Alcohol	48.6	47.5	39.2	72.7	70.1	62.0
Cigarettes	29.9	24.4	16.3	n/a	n/a	n/a
Steroids	0.7	1.3	1.0	1.2	2.1	1.5

Source: Monitoring the Future 2013, tabs. 2–3.
Note: n/a = data not available.

Table 2.9 Self-Reported Use of Illegal Drugs by Race/Ethnicity, Ages 12 and Older (2012)

	Percent Using over Past Month	Percent Using over Past Year	Percent Using over Lifetime
White	9.2	15.9	51.6
Black/African American	11.3	18.7	46.5
Hispanic/Latino	8.3	15.7	40.8
American Indian/ Alaskan Native	12.7	24.7	64.3
Asian	3.7	7.5	22.8
Native Hawaiian/ Pacific Islander	7.8	18.6	n/a

Source: Substance Abuse and Mental Health Services Administration 2012, tab. 1.19B.
Note: n/a = data not available.

national survey of individuals ages 12 and older conducted by the Substance Abuse and Mental Health Services Administration (2012). These data indicate that although the proportion of blacks who had used drugs over the past month and past year was somewhat higher than the proportion of whites, a higher proportion of whites had used drugs during their lifetime. Additionally, a lower proportion of Hispanics/Latinos, Asians, and Native Hawaiians/Pacific Islanders had used drugs than both whites and blacks over the past month. American Indians/Alaskan Natives are the only group that stands out as having a noticeably higher proportion of users. Nevertheless, these data call into question the "war on drugs" that has resulted in the disproportionate arrest and incarceration of people of color (see Chapter 1).

Counting White-Collar Crime

A major limitation of the three sources of crime data we have discussed thus far—the *UCR,* the *NCVS,* and self-report surveys—is their lack of attention to white-collar crime. In this regard, the work of Edwin Sutherland (1949) and Marshall Clinard and Peter Yeager (1980) on corporate crime remain seminal pieces of research.

Sutherland compiled data on law violations of the 70 largest US corporations, which had an average "life span" up to that time of about 45 years. It is noteworthy that Dryden Press, the publisher of Sutherland's book, forced him to omit the actual names of the corporations for fear of lawsuits. It was not until 1983, three decades after Sutherland's death, that an uncut edition that included the names of the companies was published.

As noted earlier (see Chapter 1), Sutherland did not limit his research to violations of criminal law but included violations of civil and regulatory law as well. Sutherland believed it was appropriate to include the full range of offenses because, in his view, corporate law violations were *potentially* punishable by criminal law, contained the essential elements of criminal intent, and caused harm that was equivalent to or exceeded that caused by conventional crimes.

During the period examined by his research, Sutherland uncovered 980 legal decisions against these corporations. While only 16 percent of these were for violations of criminal law, about 60 percent of the corporations had at least one criminal conviction, and among these the average was four apiece. Overall, each of the 70 corporations had at least one decision against it. Two companies had as many as 50 decisions (Armour, Swift), one had 40 (General Motors), and two had 39 (Montgomery Ward, Sears Roebuck). Over 90 percent of the corporations had four or more violations, perhaps qualifying them for prosecution as habitual or repeat offenders. The largest proportion of violations was for restraint of trade, such as price-fixing and monopolistic practices (31 percent), followed by infringement on patents, copyrights, and trademarks (23 percent), unfair labor practices (16 percent), and misrepresentation in advertising (10 percent). Other violations included commercial and political bribery, tax fraud, manipulation of the stock exchange, short weights and measures, misrepresentation of financial statements, and fraudulent bankruptcies. Importantly, Sutherland found that about half of the companies had engaged in law violations at their origin or in their early years of operation, making crime an essential part of their initial period of capital accumulation.

Years later, Clinard and Yeager collected data on legal actions initiated against the 477 largest US manufacturing corporations during 1975 and 1976. Clinard and Yeager found that about 60 percent of the companies had at least one legal action against them, 50 percent had two or more, and 18 percent had five or more. Over 75 percent of the cases involved what Clinard and Yeager classified as manufacturing violations (consumer health and safety), labor violations (worker health and safety, wage and hour violations, employment discrimination), and environmental violations (pollution). The largest corporations were the chief offenders, with just 8 percent of the companies accounting for over half of all violations. The most frequent offenders were in the motor vehicle, oil refinery, and pharmaceutical industries. Less than 3 percent of the imposed legal sanctions were for criminal offenses, however, and less than 1 percent involved nonmonetary criminal penalties against an officer of the corporation.

The task of collecting such data is daunting, and no criminologist has been able to surpass the scope of Sutherland's or Clinard and Yeager's work. Perhaps if there were a *UCR* or *NCVS* for corporate law violations, we would hear more media reports about corporate crime waves or annual fluctuations in this serious form of criminality.

Summary

This chapter offered an overview of the crime problem through a critical review of several sources of quantitative data that attempt to measure the amount and nature of crime in the United States. We began with the *Uniform Crime Reports,* the data that are compiled from local police departments that can be used to examine fluctuations in crime rates over time and the social distribution of arrests by age, race/ethnicity, and gender. In particular, we examined the issue of the declining crime rate that began in the 1990s. We then turned to other sources of crime data represented by victimization surveys and self-report surveys (including drug surveys) and compared these data to those of the *UCR.* Last, we addressed the problem of accounting for white-collar crime.

3

Individualistic Explanations of Crime

Explaining why people commit crime is a central concern of crim-
inology. It is no doubt a complex task, especially in light of the diverse
forms of crime that exist in any society. Clearly no single explanation can
account for all instances of murder, let alone for crime in its infinite varieties: robbery, sexual assault, drug use, corporate fraud, political corruption, and so forth.

The attempt to explain crime is sometimes characterized as a search for
the causes of crime, where the analyst or researcher tries to locate some
prior trait or event that determines or sets in motion criminal behavior.
Causal explanations rely on both theoretical formulations and empirical
research. Although **theory** is sometimes perceived as a complex maze of
obscure jargon that is irrelevant to the real world, we all use theory—a set
of interconnected concepts or ideas that condense and organize knowledge—to help explain our lives and the world around us. If, for example,
you believe that criminals commit crime because they do not face any credible punishment for their actions, you are invoking a particular theory about
criminal motivation and the societal reaction (or lack thereof) to it. Moreover, theory has practical implications, because proposals to address the
crime problem explicitly or implicitly assume a particular explanation or set
of underlying causes. If the theory associated with a crime control or
reform program is inaccurate, then the program is likely to fail.

In criminology, and the social sciences more generally, theory and
research are intertwined. In other words, theory guides empirical research,
which in turn confirms or disconfirms theory. Unfortunately, it sometimes
seems as if criminology is mired in competing theories and endless empirical tests that produce only mixed or inconsistent results. Nevertheless,
sound and carefully tested theory offers a better guide to social policy than
a hit-or-miss or purely ideological approach.

Much theoretical explanation in criminology is sociological, but some is not. In this chapter we review and critically assess **individualistic explanations** of crime—that is, theories that locate the central causes within the individual rather than within society or the social environment. Our discussion will be organized around three broad areas: *biological, psychological,* and *rational-choice* approaches. Biological and psychological explanations assume that criminals are particular "kinds of persons" who possess some flawed or defective trait or who think about themselves and the world in ways that make the "normal prohibitions against crime relatively ineffective" (Herrnstein 1995:40). Such explanations are especially appealing to those with a conservative political ideology, for they minimize social influences and imply that we do not need to change society to deal with the problem of crime. Rational-choice theory does not assume individual pathology, but it too is limited in its implications for social reform, other than recommending ways to increase the deterrent capability of the criminal justice system.

Biological Explanations

We begin our discussion of individualistic explanations with a consideration of early biological approaches. We then turn to contemporary biosocial criminology.

Early Biological Criminology

Biological thinking about crime, which has evolved considerably over the years, has its historical roots in an ideological perversion of Charles Darwin's (1809–1882) theory of evolution known as **social Darwinism**. Darwin postulated that life had evolved through a process of natural selection or "survival of the fittest" among diverse species, including humans. In the nineteenth century, Herbert Spencer applied this notion to the social realm, asserting that some people had natural qualities that made them more fit, more adaptable members of society, while others lacked such redeeming traits. As such, Spencer's social Darwinism justified social inequality by attributing it to differences in people's natural ability to compete for scarce resources, with the most talented individuals ending up in positions of wealth, power, and responsibility (Hofstader 1959).

It was in this context that Cesare Lombroso, a nineteenth-century Italian physician, emerged as the purported founder of scientific criminology and the biological approach to crime. Lombroso postulated that many criminals were born **atavists**, throwbacks to an earlier stage of human evolution. He believed that these criminals were less highly evolved than law-abiding citizens and that they could be recognized by distinctive physical traits that he considered common among "savages and apes" and the "coloured races"—hairy bodies, curly hair, receding foreheads, long arms, and large skulls, nostrils, jaws, and ears (Lombroso 1876). According to Lombroso, these individuals were unintelligent, excessively idle, insensitive to pain, and lovers of orgies who had an "irresistible craving for evil for its own sake" (cited in Beirne & Messerschmidt 1995:350). Lombroso also believed that women were less evolved than men, and that they were inherently childlike, jealous, and vengeful. He thought that the natural passivity of women made them less inclined toward crime, but that when they did deviate they made for exceptionally wicked criminals (Lombroso & Ferrero 1897).

Upon hearing this, it would be reasonable to wonder how Lombroso could have become a central figure in criminology. Lombroso was a man of his time, when such race and gender prejudice was not uncommon. (Variants of such views continue to persist even today.) But it was Lombroso's attempt to prove his theory with the methods of science that brought him his fame. He measured and recorded in great detail the physical attributes of living and deceased Italian prisoners, compared these findings with data from nonprisoners, and claimed his hypothesis proven.

Nevertheless, Lombroso's research was methodologically flawed. The prisoner and nonprisoner samples were not pure types. The former may have included people who were innocent of the crimes they had been convicted of, and the latter likely included offenders who had not been caught and convicted. Moreover, the alleged physical differences found by Lombroso were rather trivial. And even if the alleged differences were noticeable, the fact that the prisoners were disproportionately Sicilian made the research problematic. For although Sicilians may have tended to have some of the physical traits Lombroso attributed to criminals, their low status in Italian society would have increased their chances of imprisonment (Barkan 2012).

The earliest scientific refutation of Lombroso's work was published by Charles Goring (1913) in the early twentieth century. Goring compared the physical attributes of some 3,000 English prisoners with those of a large control group and found no differences along the lines postulated by Lombroso. He did claim, however, that the criminals in his sample were shorter in height and lighter in weight than noncriminals, leaving the door open for a hereditary or "born criminal" explanation. While Goring cautioned against equating physical difference with abnormality, and he acknowledged possible environmental influences, he was a social Darwinist at heart: "This physical inferiority . . . originating in and fostered by selection, may tend with time to become an inbred characteristic of the criminal classes, just as, with the passage of generations, the upper classes of the noncriminal community have become differentiated in physique from those lower on the social scale" (p. 200).

Contemporary criminologist Nicole Rafter (1992) notes that in the United States **criminal anthropology**, as she calls it, predated Lombroso and continued to have adherents into the twentieth century. Criminal anthropology refers to the practice of studying the criminal "as a physically anomalous human type" (p. 525). William Sheldon (1949), for instance, advanced a theory that body type was associated with personality and behavioral traits. He compared a group of official delinquent and nondelinquent boys according to three body types: the thin and introverted *ectomorph,* the rotund and easygoing *endomorph,* and the muscular and aggressive *mesomorph,* the latter of whom, as one might suspect, was the criminal type in Sheldon's scheme.

Although these studies, like Lombroso's, have been critiqued on methodological grounds, perhaps the strongest criticisms have concerned policy issues. Social Darwinists in the United States had called for "eugenic" solutions to crime and other social problems since the 1870s. **Eugenics**, which means "well born" or "good genes," was a philosophy favoring social intervention to regulate the genetic composition of the population through methods such as compulsory sterilization and restrictions on the marriage and immigration of undesirable groups (i.e., those deemed to be biologically inferior). Involuntary sterilization of people with cognitive disabilities who were institutionalized in hospitals and prisons was common in some states, a practice that was upheld by the US Supreme Court decision of *Buck v. Bell* in 1927. Some 65,000 people were sterilized in a practice that was all too common through the mid–twentieth century, and in some cases even later (Berger 2013).

To be sure, many criminal anthropologists (including Lombroso) were not favorably inclined toward eugenics, but many others (including Goring) were. Some eugenicists even advocated death for the purpose of genetic engineering. In 1900, W. Duncan McKim proposed "a gentle, painless death . . . for the very weak and the very vicious who fall into the hands of the State. . . . [Execution by] carbonic acid gas . . . [is] the simplest, the kindest, and most humane means for preventing reproduction among those whom we deem unworthy of this high privilege" (cited in Rafter 1992:540–541).

The most well-known extermination program of this type was undertaken by Adolf Hitler's Nazi regime during World War II. The physicians in the Nazi program actually learned much from their US counterparts and used the US example to facilitate "a favorable reception for compulsory . . . sterilization in Germany" (Rubenstein & Roth 1987:142). Even prior to Hitler's rise to power, a prominent German medical director wrote to the Ministry of Interior: "What we racial hygienists promote is not at all new or unheard of. In a cultured nation of the first order, in the United States of America, that which we strive toward was introduced and tested long ago" (cited in Rubenstein & Roth 1987:141).

Contemporary Biosocial Criminology
Late in his career, Lombroso retreated from a strictly biological position, acknowledging that crime was the product of a number of factors, some

biological, some not. Similarly, most contemporary biological-oriented criminologists accept the proposition that there is an interaction between biology and the social environment. As such, **biosocial theory** focuses on the purported biological conditions that *predispose* some individuals toward crime. This predisposition interacts with and is activated or triggered by particular environmental conditions that do not produce the same response in individuals with different biological traits. At the same time, according to this view, a person's biology will not produce a definitive or determinant outcome, nor will it prevent one from exerting any conscious control over their actions. Rather, biology operates in conjunction with other influences, each of which increases or decreases the probability or likelihood of criminal behavior. The question is not one of nature *versus* nurture, but of nature *and* nurture (Rafter 2008; Walsh 2012).

Genetics and crime. There is a long tradition of criminological research aimed at documenting the genetic transmission of crime that goes back to Richard Dugdale's *The Jukes: A Study in Crime, Pauperism, Disease, and Heredity* (1877) and Henry Goddard's *The Kallikak Family: A Study in the Heredity of Feeblemindedness* (1912). Dugdale and Goddard traced the criminal histories of family members across successive generations and claimed to have found a disproportionate amount of criminality. Although these particular studies do not stand up to scientific scrutiny, the role of genetic inheritance continues to be a viable issue in criminology. Contemporary research on this subject, which includes studies of twins and adopted children, has produced some intriguing findings.

Several studies of twins have found greater similarity in behavior (whether criminal or noncriminal) among identical or monozygotic twins (one ovum that divided after fertilization by one sperm) than among fraternal or dizygotic twins (two ova fertilized by two separate sperm). These findings suggest a genetic influence on criminality, since identical twins have the same biological makeup while fraternal twins do not. However, critics of these studies have long noted that identical twins are more likely than fraternal twins to be treated similarly by others, and thus their common behavior patterns could just as easily be due to environmental factors (Burt & Simons 2014). Additionally, it is difficult to disentangle genetic characteristics from early childhood and family influences, as family experiences that are common to parents and children include diet, exposure to toxins, neighborhood conditions, and television viewing habits (Fishbein 1990; Moffitt & Caspi 2006; Walters & White 1989).

Some adoption studies have also found greater similarity in criminal behavior between adoptees and their biological parents than would be expected by chance, especially for chronic or repeat offenders. When the biological parent is both criminal and alcoholic, the adoptee's behavior tends to be disproportionately violent. But since adoption agencies often match the class and racial background of adopted and natural parents, it is unclear whether the adoptee's behavior is attributable to genetics rather than environment. In addition, the age at which an individual was adopted needs to be considered, for increased criminality among adoptees has been associated with amount of time spent with biological parents or in orphanages. After reviewing recent genetic research, Anthony Walsh concludes that while "the majority of delinquents have little if any genetic vulnerability to criminal behavior," there may be a small group of "chronic offenders who begin offending prior to puberty and who continue to do so across the life course" who may be influenced by genetic factors (2012:132–133).

Both twin and adoption studies sometimes beg the question of what precisely is being inherited that purportedly causes crime. Clearly no one today seriously believes there is a "bad seed" or crime gene that is inherited. Rather, what biosocial criminologists propose is that there may be genetic predispositions for alcoholism, mental disorders, or temperamental traits such as impulsivity, extroversion, hyperemotionality, and anger that make one more vulnerable to environmental strains that trigger crime (Fishbein 1990; Rowe 1986). One of the most compelling lines of research involves studies that link low levels of the neurotransmitter **serotonin** to low levels of self-control. Low-serotonin individuals appear to respond more slowly to external stimuli and are less inhibited in their aggressive or impulsive behaviors (Crockett et al. 2010).

It is important to remember that whatever the biological disorder, it is often difficult to parse the genetic versus environmental influences. Take the case of a mother's use of alcohol or drugs, which, along with poor prenatal nutrition, can put a child at risk for low IQ, learning disabilities, memory loss, depression, and behavioral aggression. Such effects are caused by parental behavior, not genetics; but insofar as a pregnant woman's ability to eat a balanced diet, receive health care, or obtain access to an alcohol or drug treatment program is inversely related to social class, these are not merely "lifestyle" choices. Diane Fishbein (1990) adds that unhealthy prenatal and ineffective postnatal child-rearing practices are so intertwined that it is difficult to distinguish the effect of one from that of the other. Callie Burt and Ronald Simons go so far as to question the entire premise of most heritability research, noting that genes are not self-activating codes "that can be understood apart from environmental inputs but are only one part of an interactive developmental biopsychosocial system" (2014:225).

Intelligence and crime. One particularly controversial area of biosocial research purports to find a link between a genetic predisposition to low intelligence and crime. This research typically revolves around the measure of IQ (intelligence quotient). Historically, the IQ measure is associated with the work of Alfred Binet, who in 1904 was commissioned by the French Ministry of Public Education to develop a test to measure children's cognitive (linguistic and mathematical) abilities at various age levels. Ironically, in light of subsequent applications, Binet did not think that a person's score on an IQ test was genetic or impervious to accumulated experience. When the IQ test was introduced in the United States, however, a contrary attitude prevailed, even though tests administered to army recruits during World War I indicated that about half scored below the cognitive level expected of a 13-year-old (Katz & Chambliss 1995).

A number of studies have found that low IQ is, in fact correlated with higher rates of official and self-reported juvenile delinquency (e.g., Felson & Staff 2006; Hirschi & Hindelang 1977), though obviously not to those crimes that require higher intelligence, such as computer and financial crimes. How should we interpret the apparent association between low IQ and delinquency? Is intelligence genetic, environmental, or a combination of the two? How much are we limited by our genes? How much does an enriching environment matter? Who would deny the significance of social influences such as parents and teachers who encourage children to read and enjoy learning? Regardless, criminologists often argue that since IQ is associated with the cognitive abilities that lead to academic success, youths with low IQs may be more likely to feel alienated from or dissatisfied with school, which in turn may weaken their stake in conformity and increase their attraction to delinquency.

Perhaps the greatest point of contention regarding the IQ test has been its alleged class and race bias. In their well-publicized book *The Bell Curve,* Richard Herrnstein and Charles Murray (1994) compiled data indicating that African Americans, on average, scored lower on IQ tests than European Americans, while Asian Americans scored the highest. (The bell curve refers to the shape of the distribution of IQ scores in a population from low to middle to high.) Herrnstein and Murray also argued that low IQ or cognitive disadvantage is causally related to a variety of social ills, including out-of-wedlock births, welfare dependency, and crime. Moreover, they claimed that IQ is in large part genetic and that it is *immutable,* impervious to change. Hence government programs such as early childhood education designed to improve the lives of the cognitively disadvantaged are bound to fail.

The Bell Curve has been subjected to numerous criticisms, many of which were previously advanced against earlier works. For example, critics contend that the content of questions on IQ tests advantages individuals who are familiar with the white, middle-class cultural experience. Moreover, the property tax–based system of school funding means that low-income communities will have fewer educational resources for students, who consequently do poorer in school. Schools also use test scores to track students into vertical (high to low) tracks, which in turn become self-fulfilling prophecies of educational attainment, denying some youths access to desirable social roles (Cullen et al. 1997; Felson & Staff 2006).

FURTHER EXPLORATION
Disabilities and Delinquency

Research indicates that youths with cognitive and emotional disabilities are overrepresented among the ranks of youths who are adjudicated as juvenile delinquent and incarcerated in the juvenile justice system in the United States. Studies estimating the prevalence of youths with disabilities in the juvenile justice system vary because these studies employ different criteria for defining disability. In a review of the literature, Kimberly Morris and Richard Morris (2006) found that the percentage of youths in the juvenile justice system who have been diagnosed as having a disability ranges from 28 percent to 58 percent. They also found that the most common category of disabled youths in the juvenile justice system is that of youths with learning disabilities, followed by youths with emotional disorders and then intellectual disabilities. In another review, Christopher Mallett (2013) also notes that disability factors that put youths "at risk" of delinquency are often correlated with other risk factors associated with childhood maltreatment and mental health disorders, and that it is this constellation of factors rather than disability alone that best explains their prevalence in the juvenile justice system.

Morris and Morris (2006) identify three hypotheses that have been advanced to explain the disproportionately high prevalence of youths with disabilities in the juvenile justice system. The **school failure hypothesis** posits that students' impairments lead to school failure, which initiates feelings of rejection, frustration, and low self-esteem that are associated with involvement in delinquency. The **susceptibility hypothesis** posits that it is not school failure per se that leads to delinquency, although school failure is a factor, but rather the neurological and intellectual impairments that lead to poor judgment and hyperactivity-impulsivity. The **differential treatment hypothesis** posits that youths with these disabilities are not more involved in delinquency than other youths, but that school, law enforcement, and other public officials treat them more harshly. Morris and Morris note the inconsistencies in the extant studies and conclude that more research is needed to sort out these factors, as well as the factors that insulate disabled youths from delinquent involvement. They also note the ongoing need for educational and mental health services for those youths with disabilities who are under the jurisdiction and supervision of the juvenile justice system.

In a compelling empirical critique of *The Bell Curve,* Francis Cullen and colleagues (1997) examined data from nearly 500 studies containing over 42,800 offenders. These studies contain measures not only of intelligence and crime but also of respondents' social background (e.g., socioeconomic status, urban versus rural residence, religious participation, living with mother and father). Cullen and colleagues concluded that the association between IQ and crime was at best small, if not insignificant, after taking into account other social influences. Moreover, unlike Herrnstein and Murray's claims about IQ, these social influences are often *amenable to change.*

Cullen and colleagues believe that having "knowledge of an offender's intellectual capacity and aptitude is advantageous in designing" rehabilitative treatment programs. They also advocate a broadened conception of IQ that includes not just the standard linguistic and mathematical criteria but practical intelligence as well—that is, "a person's ability to learn and profit from experience, to monitor effectively one's own and others' feelings and needs, and to solve everyday problems" (pp. 403–404). Nevertheless, they believe that Herrnstein and Murray's thesis and policy conclusions are based more on ideology than on empirical science.

Other biological factors. A complete review of all the biological conditions that have been implicated in criminal behavior would take an entire chapter of its own. In concluding our discussion, therefore, we will mention just a few others. Some research has found that damage to the **prefrontal lobe cortex** of the brain—perhaps caused by an injury, poor nutrition, or substance abuse—is associated with serious juvenile offending. The prefrontal lobe cortex governs functions such as the making of moral judgments and the management of emotions, and damage to it is found in individuals who exhibit disruptive behavior disorders as well as lack of foresight and low impulse control (Cauffman et al. 2005).

Hormones, the "chemical messengers" that help coordinate bodily processes, have also been considered by biosocial criminologists. While some studies have found a correlation between higher testosterone levels and aggressive behavior of males, overall this research tradition has produced inconsistent results, with some studies suggesting that higher testosterone levels may *follow* rather than *precede* aggressive behavior (Walsh 2012).

Research on women offenders has also implicated hormonal factors, which is a line of inquiry that garnered attention in the case of Christine English in the early 1980s. English drove a car over her lover and killed him after they had quarreled over his drinking and infidelity and he had threatened to end their relationship. During the widely reported criminal trial, physician Katharina Dalton testified that English had for years been suffering from a very aggravated premenstrual physical condition—a condition now called **premenstrual syndrome** (PMS)—that made "her irritable, aggressive, impatient, and confused, with loss of self control" (cited in Binder et al. 1988:494). Although English was originally charged with murder, her plea of diminished responsibility resulted in a lesser conviction for manslaughter and a sentence of probation.

In research that brought her notoriety, Dalton (1961) claimed that about half of the 156 women she studied in British prisons had committed their crimes during the eight-day premenstrual/menstrual period. She also claimed that about half of female drivers involved in motor vehicle accidents were in this eight-day phase. PMS research such as this has been vulnerable to the same kinds of criticism as the testosterone studies. Julie Horney (1978), for instance, found that about half of female *passengers* in accidents were also in their eight-day phase. Moreover, most of Dalton's prisoner-subjects had been convicted of nonviolent crimes, particularly theft and prostitution. It is also important to remember that crimes and accidents are stressful events, and stress can bring on early menstruation. So if any weak link does exist between menstruation and behavioral problems, it may be "not because the former causes the latter, but because the latter causes the former" (Tavris 1992:151).

In contrast to PMS research, a more viable line of inquiry links **postpartum** (post-childbirth) influences to women's criminality. Robin Ogle and colleagues (1995), however, believe this connection stems more from environmental factors than from hormonal ones. For example, after childbirth women experience a marked reduction in both sleep and personal space that can cause chronic levels of stress. Often the birth of a child is also accompanied by "severe financial strains due to a host of new expenses and restrictions" on one's ability to earn a living (p. 183). According to Ogle and colleagues, these stresses can induce a state of intense physiological arousal, an autonomic nervous system response that energizes the organism to respond in ways that reduce the arousal. The arousal, which is experienced as a negative condition, may be associated with anger at the stress-inducing stimulus. Women who've had little or no prior history of aggressive behavior do not know how to control this anger and may lash out at the most visible and vulnerable source of their arousal—their child.

Although biosocial criminology acknowledges the interaction between biology and environment, this research tradition has been critiqued for giving causal priority to biology while downplaying social factors. Studies generally rely on relatively small sample sizes and officially labeled offenders, and findings tend to be weak and inconsistent. The focus is on violent criminality and juvenile delinquency to the exclusion of other types of crimes, especially white-collar crime. As David Friedrichs notes, "The pervasiveness of white-collar crime would seem to offer a powerful refutation of the proposition that criminality can be generally explained by biogenic explanations" (2007:201). This research also fails to account for group variations in crime—that is, it fails to explain why crime rates are higher among some groups than others. Thus we are left to assume that entire groups of people must be biologically flawed in some way.

We would be naive to deny that "biological conditions have a profound impact on the adaptive, cognitive, and emotional abilities" of individuals (Fishbein 1990:56). But we must be wary of premature and injudicious applications of biological thinking about crime. At the extreme we have noted the association of biological approaches with eugenics and the historical practice of compulsory sterilization and even extermination. Even when used with the best intentions, to prevent crime by diagnosing and delivering needed services to at-risk children, for example, biological interventions are fraught with ethical problems. Notice that here we are talking about *potential* offenders, children who might someday commit crimes. How will we avoid mistakenly diagnosing children or adversely stigmatizing them with a potentially harmful label or setting in motion a self-fulfilling prophecy? What type of treatment will we employ? Will it be pharmaceutical, psychological, or social? Or will we simply isolate suspect populations?

With convicted offenders as well, imposition of rehabilitative biological treatments is problematic. Fishbein notes that "the appropriate administration of a medication or other treatment may . . . be warranted for some individuals" with an identifiable pathology that played a role in their behavior (1990:54). But she adds that biological variables cannot be manipulated without attention to interacting factors. By the time individuals have entered the legal system, their behavior problems have been so substantially compounded that treating only one facet of their condition will be unlikely to yield the desired therapeutic results.

Psychological Explanations

Like biological approaches, psychological explanations assume that criminals are different than noncriminals. They postulate an assortment of defective mental, emotional, or personality traits that either cause criminal behavior or predispose individuals to the environmental factors that trigger criminal behavior. (Behaviorism, which we will discuss later in this chapter, is an exception.) To a large extent, much of the biological research we have thus far reviewed identifies such traits as intervening between biology and crime, and individual traits such as intelligence are often included as elements of both biological and psychological theories of crime.

Freudian Psychology

One of the earliest psychological formulations was advanced by Austrian physician Sigmund Freud (1856–1939), whose **psychoanalytic theory** was quite influential in early explanations of juvenile delinquency (Friedlander 1947; Healy & Bronner 1936). Freud and his followers believed that the human personality consists of three interdependent yet often conflicting elements: the **id**, **ego**, and **superego**. As Larry Siegel and colleagues explain:

> The id is the unrestrained, primitive, pleasure-seeking component with which each child is born. The ego develops through the reality of living in the world and helps manage and restrain the id's need for immediate gratification. The superego develops through interactions with parents and other significant people and represents the development of conscience and the moral rules that are shared by most adults. . . . All three segments of the personality operate simultaneously. The id dictates needs and desires,

FURTHER EXPLORATION
DNA and the Criminal Justice System

Because of the pervasive influence of television, the American public has been exposed to the use of DNA testing in criminal investigations through shows such as *CSI: Crime Scene Investigation, Forensic Files,* and *Law and Order.* Increasingly, prosecutors are finding that jurors in criminal trials expect them to present a degree of DNA evidence that simply is not available in most cases, and defense attorneys have been exploiting this evidence gap to obtain acquittals for their clients. Apparently, few jurors are fully aware of the limitations and problems associated with this type of evidence (Roane 2005).

DNA, or deoxyribonucleic acid, is found in the cells of the human body and contains an individual's genetic blueprint. Because only identical twins have the same DNA, it can be used to identify crime victims and to establish the statistical likelihood that a suspect was involved in a crime. In criminal investigations, DNA samples are derived from blood, saliva, skin tissue, bone, hair, earwax, sweat, mucus, urine, semen, and vaginal and rectal cells (Turman 2001).

Care must be exercised when gathering and analyzing DNA, to avoid contamination and degradation. Contamination occurs when foreign matter comes into contact with the DNA sample. This can occur if someone sneezes or coughs in the vicinity of the DNA sample or if someone touches some part of his or her body and then touches the areas from which the DNA is extracted. Furthermore, exposure of a DNA sample to heat or humidity accelerates the degradation and makes the sample unstable.

Use of DNA evidence in criminal investigations has increased dramatically in recent years. Nationally there were 343,422 cases processed in 2011, with nearly three-quarters of these cases solved or closed through testing. On the upside, crime laboratories have acquired a greater capacity to process cases—because of technological advances, larger staffs, and use of overtime—but many labs still have backlogs due to increased demand for their services (Nelson et al. 2013). Although DNA testing has been touted for its role in exonerating innocent people accused of crime, in 2014 there were only 22 suspects who were found innocent by DNA evidence (National Registry of Exonerations 2015).

Some civil-liberty concerns about DNA testing have emerged as well. One issue involves other ways collected samples might be used. Because DNA samples can reveal genetic conditions such as sickle cell anemia and schizophrenia, the samples could be used to deny people health insurance or require them to pay higher premiums. Another concern is that the emergence of DNA databases could renew interest in discovering purported "crime genes" that would subject individuals to social control "regardless of whether or not they have violated the law" (Burns & Smith 1999:3). Additionally, several states have reported cases of evidence contamination, falsification of DNA data, inflation of the statistical likelihood of a DNA match, and questionable testimony by forensic experts and laboratory managers (Roane 2005; Tanner 2003).

the superego counteracts the id by fostering feelings of morality and righteousness, and the ego evaluates the reality of a position between the two
extremes. (2003:84)

According to Freudian theory, basic personality formation is completed
in early childhood, and thus early parent-child interaction is of paramount
importance. If parents are neglectful or abusive, or exert too little or too
much discipline, imbalances may develop among the id, ego, and superego,
creating unconscious psychological conflicts within individuals. Later-life
juvenile delinquency and adult criminality may represent a symbolic
expression or acting-out of such conflicts. If parental socialization is weak
or inadequate, for instance, the child's superego will be underdeveloped and
the id will dominate the personality. Later in life this may lead the person to
insist on the immediate gratification of selfish needs, to lack compassion or
sensitivity to others, or to behave impulsively and aggressively. If, on the
other hand, parental discipline is overbearing and punitive, the individual
may become overly rebellious and defiant of authority.

Critics of Freudian psychology contend that it is too speculative. The
postulated personality components are neither observable nor measurable,
requiring one to rely on a psychoanalyst's retrospective "interpretation of a
patient's interpretation of what is occurring in the subconscious" (Sheley
1985:202). Moreover, the influence of early-life events can be significantly
altered by later experiences. Several criminological studies have found, for
example, that earlier involvement in crime is substantially reduced with the
acquisition of adult commitments conducive to law-abiding behavior, particularly marriage and stable employment (see Chapter 4).

Nevertheless, Freud should be credited as being one of the first to draw
attention to the important influence of family socialization. Contemporary
family research suggests that parental affection and support of children,
effective parent-child communication and parental monitoring of peers,
absence of conflict in the home, and positive marital adjustment of parents
mitigate antisocial conduct and increase prosocial behavior among youths
(Cernkovich & Giordano 1987; Dillon et al. 2008; Wright & Cullen 2001).
Criminologists Michael Gottfredson and Travis Hirschi (1990) contend that
effective parenting is the key to individuals' ability to control their impulses
and delay short-term gratifications. Family studies also show that children
who are raised with inconsistent discipline or with overly permissive or
overly harsh discipline, particularly child abuse or neglect, are more likely
to engage in later-life criminality (Patterson & Stouthamer-Loeber 1984;
Widom 1989; Zingraff et al. 1993).

Importantly, the sexual abuse of females by family members and others
is now widely documented (see Chapter 8). Within the home, many girls are
emotionally and physically exploited by fathers and stepfathers (or other relatives or mothers' boyfriends). The psychological trauma associated with

such abuse is often (though not always) extensive, and can include both short- and long-term effects, such as "fear, anxiety, depression, anger and hostility, inappropriate sexual behavior, . . . difficulties in school, truancy, and early marriage" (Chesney-Lind 1989:21–22). Often girls run away from home to avoid further victimization, only to find that life on the streets involves additional exploitation, as some are forced to turn to crime and prostitution in order to survive. Eventually many of these young women are arrested and incarcerated, or they are returned to their homes and forced to remain with the abusers, who continue to exploit them.

Personality and Crime

There are other psychological perspectives that reject Freudian theory (in whole or in part) but that still postulate the existence of developmental personality types or ways of thinking that distinguish criminals from noncriminals. Criminals and delinquents have been variously described as emotionally unstable, mentally disordered, paranoid, schizophrenic, neurotic, egocentric, narcissistic, hedonistic, extroverted, aggressive, impulsive, hostile, defiant, cognitively disabled, insecure, low in self-esteem, lacking foresight, and so forth—the list goes on and on. Among the most extreme of personality types is the **psychopath** or **sociopath**, an individual who is said to lack not only impulse control but also the capacity to experience guilt or a sense of caring, responsibility, or obligation to others. In essence, these individuals lack a conscience (Einstader & Henry 1995).

Sociological critics of personality theory point to the ambiguity of psychological labeling and to the multiple definitions of the personality concept, which "render it so vague that it could mean almost anything" (Sanders 1983:21). Some personality inventories have been faulted for containing similar items in both the personality and the criminality sections of the questionnaire, thereby biasing findings in favor of an association between the two. For example, one section might include an item such as "Sometimes when I was young I stole things" while the other section includes "I have never been in trouble with the law." Sometimes the criminal behavior itself is used as a criterion for the classification of the aberrant personality type. And like the biological research on crime, personality studies tend to rely on relatively small samples and focus on officially labeled criminals and delinquents. Moreover, some studies have found that personality differences *between law violators* are greater than the differences *between offenders and nonoffenders*. The research also finds that the amount of mental disorder among offenders or the amount of crime among the disordered is no more than is found among the general population (Akers & Sellers 2009; Caspi et al. 1994).

To be sure, there are reputable studies that have found personality differences between offenders and nonoffenders, especially for violent individuals (Caspi et al. 1994; Miller & Lynam 2001). But Gottfredson and

Hirschi (1990) argue that the myriad traits identified in this research tradition can best be characterized as a matter of **low self-control**, which is indicative of individuals who have difficulty delaying gratification and tolerating frustration, who are unable to solve problems through verbal rather than physical means, and who are self-centered and indifferent to the needs and feelings of others. They argue that self-control is "for all intents and purposes, *the* individual-level cause of crime" (p. 232). The association between low self-control and criminality is well-documented in the research literature, although not to the exclusion of (or to a greater extent than) other social variables (Baron 2003; Longshore et al. 2004; Pratt & Cullen 2000).

What about the question of white-collar crime? There are a handful of personality studies that address this issue. For the most part, this research indicates that white-collar offenders "fall within the range of normal personality types," but a few studies suggest that these offenders are more likely than nonoffenders to display "a tendency toward risk taking and recklessness, ambitiousness and drive, and egocentricity and a hunger for power" (Friedrichs 2007:202). There is even evidence that the incidence of sociopathy among top corporate executives is four times higher than in the general population, which suggests that business success at the upper echelons of corporate power may be connected to a lack of caring or concern for others (Ronson 2011). As eminent historian R. W. Tawney wrote of the "secret" of capitalism's triumph:

> It concentrates attention upon the right of those who possess or can acquire power to make the fullest use of it for their own self-advancement. By fixing men's minds, not upon the discharge of social obligations, which restricts their energy . . . but upon the exercise of the right to pursue their own self-interest, it offers unlimited scope for the acquisition of riches. . . . It assures men that there are no ends other than their own ends, no law other than their desires, no limit other than that which they think advisable. . . . It relieves communities of the necessity of discriminating . . . between enterprise and avarice, energy and unscrupulous greed, property which is legitimate and property which is theft. (1920:30–31)

Mental Illness and the Insanity Defense

One controversial area involving psychological thinking about crime has been the insanity defense used by some criminal defendants. In the US system of law, the insanity defense is tied to the notion that "illegality alone does not make . . . a crime" (Sykes & Cullen 1992:37). Rather, the illegal act must be accompanied by criminal intent, which in Latin parlance is referred to as *mens rea,* meaning "guilty mind." According to this view, for punishment to be morally justified, the individual must possess criminal intent at the time they committed the crime. (US law does expect that persons will exercise reasonable care to avoid the unintentional harm of others.

If one behaves recklessly—for example, kills someone in a drunk-driving accident—they can be held criminally liable for such conduct.)

The precedent for the insanity defense in the United States derives from English law and the 1843 case of Daniel M'Naghten. M'Naghten was tried for the murder of Edward Drummond, the secretary to Prime Minister Robert Peel. M'Naghten had intended to shoot the prime minister, but killed Drummond by mistake. Apparently M'Naghten suffered from the paranoid delusion that the government was a deadly enemy out to get him. His attorneys claimed he was insane and not legally responsible for his actions. When M'Naghten was found not guilty by reason of insanity, the **M'Naghten Rule** was ushered into the US legal tradition. According to this rule, a defendant can be found not guilty by reason of insanity if it can "be clearly proved that, at the time of the committing of the act, the party accused was laboring under such a defect of reason, from disease of the mind, as not to know the nature and quality of the act he was doing; or if he did know it, that he did not know that he was doing what was wrong" (cited in Sykes & Cullen 1992:48).

In addition to the M'Naghten Rule, another tradition emerged in US law that is known as the doctrine of **irresistible impulse**. Whereas the M'Naghten Rule had recognized only a defect of *reason* as a defense to crime, the irresistible impulse doctrine recognized a defect of *will*. Essentially, the irresistible impulse defense made the cognitive awareness of right and wrong less significant than the ability to control one's actions when an individual was so impaired by mental illness that he or she could not refrain from doing what their reason told them was wrong (Sykes & Cullen 1992).

The American Law Institute, an organization that proposes model penal codes to encourage legal uniformity throughout the United States, also developed a model insanity defense that incorporates elements of both the M'Naghten and irresistible impulse doctrines: "A person is not responsible for criminal conduct if at the time of such conduct as a result of mental disease or defect he lacks *substantial capacity* either to appreciate the criminality of his conduct or to conform to the requirements of law" (cited in Sykes & Cullen 1992:48–49, emphasis added). Importantly, the initial American Law Institute model placed the burden of proof on the prosecution to establish the defendant's sanity; failing that, a defendant could be found insane. This was the model used by the federal government in the notorious case of John Hinckley Jr., who attempted to assassinate President Ronald Reagan in 1981. Reagan, who was hit by a ricocheted bullet, did not receive any lasting injury, but his press secretary, James Brady, was also shot and seriously disabled for life.

At his criminal trial, Hinckley pled not guilty by reason of insanity. He was apparently fascinated with the movie *Taxi Driver* and obsessed with Jodie Foster, the young actress who was featured in the film. Hinckley was trying to impress Foster or at least attract her attention. Sue Titus Reid summarizes the testimony of the defense psychiatrists who took the witness stand on Hinckley's behalf:

> Hinckley was psychotic, was consumed by paradoxical thoughts, was depressed, had hypochondriacal tendencies, hated himself, suffered from schizophrenia spectrum disorder, had an abnormal thought process, thought of himself as a little boy who had done something terrible, and was torn between childish love and dependence on his father and subconscious fantasies about killing him. (1997:128)

The prosecution countered that Hinckley had planned the crime in a cold and calculating manner, and offered its own psychiatric witnesses who testified that Hinckley was legally sane. With the burden of proof on the prosecution, however, the jury ruled in Hinckley's favor.

The insanity defense has always had critics who argue that dangerous criminals will be allowed to avoid prison and set free to commit more crimes. Successful insanity defendants are not set free, however. Like Hinckley, they are remanded to mental hospitals under civil commitment. Release from civil commitment requires the approval of the psychiatric authorities responsible for treating such individuals. Hinckley has not yet (and may never) receive a full discharge, although in December 2003 a federal judge ruled that he could have unsupervised visits with his parents outside the District of Columbia mental hospital where he was committed (Janofsky 2003).

The Hinckley case fueled a public backlash against the insanity defense and spawned the development of legal reforms to curtail its use. One reform adopted by the federal government and a majority of states placed the burden to prove insanity on the defendant. Another reform adopted by some states involved the development of a new legal category: **guilty but mentally ill**. Under the guidelines of this category, defendants may be held criminally responsible for their crimes, but they are first sent to a mental health facility for treatment; afterward they are transferred to a prison to serve the remainder of their sentences (Klofas & Weisheit 1987).

Clearly the public fears that dangerous offenders who use the insanity defense will be deemed fit to reenter society before they are truly cured or rehabilitated. We have all heard of cases where an offender was released from correctional custody only to commit further crimes. But the insanity defense is not the culprit in most of these cases. All told, the insanity defense is attempted by less than 1 percent of felony defendants, only one-quarter of whom are successful, with relatively few of these individuals ever released (Callahan et al. 1991). Be that as it may, the more pressing issue that needs to be addressed is the genuine mental health problems of those individuals who come under the jurisdiction of the criminal justice system. Due to "developments in pharmacology, stricter standards for involuntary commitment, and changes in public expenditures," many individuals who were once held in psychiatric hospitals are now incarcerated in jails and prisons, leading to what some have called the "criminalization of mental illness" (Markowitz 2006:45). Moreover, with about 20 percent of the US population experiencing mental health issues of one kind or another, the availability of psychological treatment becomes an important part of any viable program of crime prevention (Thompson et al. 2003).

Behaviorism

Psychological **behaviorism**, also called "operant conditioning" or "learning-reinforcement" theory, offers another way of understanding individual behavior. Behaviorism, which is associated with the work of B. F. Skinner (1953), differs from Freudian and personality theories in that it focuses on observable behavior rather than on unconscious or personality factors, and it does not assume psychological pathology on the part of the offender. It postulates that "behavior is acquired or conditioned by the effects, outcomes, or *consequences* it has on a person's environment" (Akers 1985:43). Behavior that is reinforced by a reward or positive consequence will persist, while behavior that is unrewarded or punished will be discontinued. Individuals learn to favor particular courses of action, including the criminal variety, depending on the particular mix of rewards and punishments that is attached to their behavior. Rewards and punishments may be *social* or *nonsocial* in nature. The social include favorable or unfavorable reactions from other individuals (e.g., you receive approval or disapproval from parents or friends); the nonsocial include the pleasurable or unpleasurable physical sensations associated with behavior (e.g., you feel euphoric or ill after consuming alcohol or drugs). Learning also takes place through the imitation or modeling of other people's behavior (Akers & Sellers 2009).

Since behaviorist explanations necessarily implicate social relationships, we will defer discussion of the behaviorist approach called "social learning" theory until we consider sociological explanations of crime in Chapter 4. For now it suffices to say that behaviorism postulates that the psychological mechanisms underlying criminal behavior are essentially the same as those underlying law-abiding behavior. Psychologically speaking, most criminals are actually not so different from the rest of us.

Rehabilitative Treatment

Psychological explanations have been influential in establishing the rehabilitative approach to crime prevention and control. These theories suggest therapeutic interventions designed to transform the offender from an individual with an abnormal or maladaptive personality into an individual with a normal personality. Such interventions typically employ professional therapists (e.g., psychiatrists, psychologists, social workers) who attempt to (1) help offenders uncover the childhood root causes of their behavior or gain insight more generally into why they behave as they do, and (2) train

FURTHER EXPLORATION
Jeffrey Dahmer: Murderer Among Us

Between 1987 and 1991, Jeffrey Dahmer committed 16 murders in Milwaukee, Wisconsin. Dahmer targeted gay males, people who often expect harassment from the police and who thus try to avoid contact with them. When stalking his victims, Dahmer chose venues such as shopping malls and gay bathhouses, where anonymity was ensured or where he could blend into the crowd. He would invite his victims to his apartment for a drink or to watch pornographic movies, or he would offer them money to pose for pictures. At his apartment he would immobilize them with the sedative Halcion or hit them with a rubber mallet. Sometimes Dahmer would sexually assault his victims before he killed them, but more often he killed them and then sexually assaulted the corpse. He also cut up his victims, stored body parts in his freezer, and even ate them (Fisher 1997).

Unlike John Hinckley, Dahmer was unsuccessful in his attempt to use the insanity defense. He was convicted, sentenced to life in prison, and later beaten to death by another inmate in 1994. But what some analysts consider to be the real story of the Dahmer case is how he was able "to move about the city . . . with relative impunity, escaping detection" for such a long period of time (Fisher 1997:164). Countless individuals, in both official and unofficial capacities, were in positions to realize what he was doing and take action to stop him.

In 1987, around the time of his second Milwaukee murder, Dahmer was "kicked out of [a] gay bathhouse for drugging another patron to the point [that the victim] . . . had to be taken to a hospital. . . . On another occasion, Dahmer drugged and sexually assaulted two men" at a hotel (Fisher 1997:179). Yet when the police were called to investigate, the victims, fearful of being publicly outed as gay, failed to press charges. The police dropped the matter.

In 1988 after Keison Sinthasomphone, a 13-year-old Laotian boy, managed to escape Dahmer's apartment and alert the police, "Dahmer was arrested for sexual assault and enticing a child for immoral purposes" (Fisher 1997:181). Though he pled guilty to the charges, he served only 10 months in jail. While under probation, Dahmer was required to see several psychiatric professionals, whom he used as a source of Halcion. And social workers who were assigned to do home visits missed the "shrine of bones in his living room because they were afraid—not of him but of visiting the inner-city neighborhood where he lived" (Williams 1999b:10).

Overall, during his murder spree, Dahmer "had at least seven contacts with police, was arrested three times, was put on probation twice, and was jailed once" (Fisher 1997:182). Repeated and urgent calls to the police from women of the mostly black neighborhood where Dahmer lived were seemingly discounted—calls complaining of a stench emanating from his apartment and of his public drunkenness. And with more than a dozen gay men missing in one city alone, no one alerted the community that "a serial killer might be on the loose" (Williams 1999b:10).

In 1991, 14-year-old Konerac Sinthasomphone, brother of Keison, escaped from Dahmer's apartment, drugged and naked. Five African Americans,

continues

continued

aged 11 to 20, came upon him and observed "blood around his buttocks, testicles, and pubic hair" (Fisher 1997:184). One of them called the police as Dahmer appeared at the scene to retrieve Konerac. When the police arrived, Dahmer explained that "Konerac was his roommate, and he was taking him home" (p. 184). The African-American witnesses, emotional and shouting, urged the police to look at Konerac's buttocks, but the officers wouldn't listen and told them to "shut the hell up" and "get lost." Apparently the police preferred to take the word of a murderer, "polite, calm, and white," over a group of exuberant black youths (p. 186).

Dahmer even invited the officers back to his apartment to see photos of Konerac, whom Dahmer said was 19 or 20 years old, posing in black bikini underwear. The officers, who did in fact go to the apartment, later acknowledged detecting an unpleasant odor (which turned out to be a decomposing body). They did nothing, however, leaving Konerac to become Dahmer's twelfth victim. Back at their car, the officers "radioed the police dispatcher and between audible laughs said they had returned 'the intoxicated Asian naked male to his sober boyfriend'" (Fisher 1997:187). One added, amid more laughter, "my partner's gonna get deloused at the station" (p. 187). Even though follow-up calls from worried neighbors continued, the police dismissed the concerns with casual assurances that the 14-year-old was an adult.

Patricia Williams believes that the Dahmer case says a lot about the attitudes of those in power toward those without power. Dahmer's ability to escape suspicion rested on officials' devaluing of gay lives and on a presumption of "adult Asian men as soft, effeminate, exotic, sexualized and perpetually childlike; of blacks as dangerous; and of women, particularly black women, as hysterical and unbelievable" (1999b:10).

individuals to monitor and control their actions more effectively (Einstader & Henry 1995). When applied to at-risk youths, these interventions pose some of the same ethical dilemmas characteristic of biological approaches—issues regarding accurate diagnosis, stigmatizing labels, and unwarranted intrusion into the lives of youths who have not yet committed crimes. On the other hand, failure to intervene to help individuals in need has potential costs as well.

Samuel Yochelson and Stanton Samenow (1976, 1977) are noteworthy for their rejection of "couch therapy" approaches, focusing instead on the criminal's current way of thinking. They are not interested in past environmental influences or the emotional burdens of childhood. Rather, they want to confront the individual's calculating, narcissistic personality. Offenders must acknowledge they are responsible and accountable for their own behavior, and they must reject "errors-in-thinking" by which they rational-

FURTHER EXPLORATION
Media Experiments

One interesting line of behaviorist research involves experiments on the influence of media. In a classic series of experiments with children, Albert Bandura (1973) exposed groups of nursery school youth, in person and through film, to an adult who hit and kicked an inflated Bobo doll. Bandura observed that these children, in comparison to a control group of children who did not witness the Bobo doll episode, played more aggressively for a short period following the exposure. Bandura reasoned that through imitation and modeling, children will duplicate or copy the behavior of others. However, when Bandura introduced a number of additional variables, the experimental results changed. For example, when the adult model was shown being scolded or spanked for striking the doll, the children did not respond in an aggressive manner. This study and other research suggest that the appearance of undesirable consequences will inhibit subsequent aggression in children (Surette 1998).

Experimental research also indicates that some individuals may be more *predisposed* to the influence of media than others. For instance, boys are more affected than girls, and children from families that emphasize nonaggression (e.g., where parents teach children to be kind to others) are less likely to be influenced. According to Ray Surette, "whether or not a particular depiction will cause a particular viewer to act more aggressively is not a straightforward issue. An aggressive effect largely depends on the interaction between each individual viewer, the content of the portrayal, and the setting in which the portrayal is viewed" (1998:125). The following are some of the factors that appear to increase the violence-inducing impact of media: the details of the portrayal and the viewer's real-life circumstances are similar, the aggression is portrayed as justifiable and in a way that does not stir distaste, and aggressive peer models are present during the viewing.

Experiments have also been conducted to measure attitudinal changes among research subjects. In one interesting study, Edward Donnerstein and colleagues (1987) showed male college students a series of R-rated "slasher" films—*Texas Chainsaw Massacre, Maniac, I Spit on Your Grave, Toolbox Murders,* and *Vice Squad*—that included female victims and explicitly violent scenes juxtaposed with erotic scenes. The researchers found that over the course of viewing several films, the students became more desensitized to the violence (they reported seeing fewer violent and offensive scenes) and rated the films as comparatively more entertaining and less degrading to women. In the next stage of the experiment, the students viewed a videotaped reenactment of a rape trial that was based on the transcript of an actual trial. In comparison to a control group of students who had not seen the films, these students expressed less sympathy for the rape victim and perceived her as less worthy and less attractive. They also judged the defendant to be less responsible for the rape and thought that the victim offered less resistance and received less injury. When female college students were included in a similar experiment, they experienced somewhat less desensitization but did have a

continues

continued

negative reaction to the rape victim in the videotaped enactment (Krafka 1985). Other research has found that male viewers enjoyed these types of films more when accompanied by female companions, while female viewers enjoyed them more (and found their male companions more attractive) when the male companion displayed a bravado attitude toward the violence (Zillman et al. 1986).

There is obviously a great deal of difference between the artificial climate of an experiment and the real world, and between behavioral aggression and attitudinal change on the one hand, and criminal violence on the other. It is also possible that persons already predisposed to aggression and violence are the ones most likely to seek out these types of media and thus have the opportunity to be influenced by it (Surette 1998). Even the strongest proponents of the "media violence causes aggression" view acknowledge the reciprocal relationship over time between viewing aggression and acting aggressively (Huesmann & Eron 1986). In other words, viewing violence increases behavioral aggression, but acting aggressively also increases violent viewing.

Moreover, surveys that have attempted to correlate youths' exposure to media violence with aggressive behavior and violent delinquency have yielded inconsistent results. Some longitudinal research has found that viewing media violence during childhood is positively correlated with aggressive behavior in both adolescence and adulthood (Strasburger & Wilson 2002). On the other hand, a study of 281 metropolitan areas found that communities' exposure to television violence (as measured by A. C. Nielsen Company estimates of local audience size for violent programs) was inversely related to *UCR* violent crime rates, perhaps because "high levels of television viewing imply that residents are spending large amounts of time within the relatively safe confines" of their homes (Messner 1986:230). Nonetheless, according to Surette, the issue for most researchers "comes down not to the existence of an effect but to the magnitude of the effect" (1998:128). The same levels of "explained variance" in aggression—that is, "the proportion of the changes in aggression that can be statistically associated with the media"—have been interpreted by some researchers as important and by some researchers as trivial.

ize or blame others for their actions. According to Yochelson and Samenow, only through the development of such "internal deterrents" will the likelihood of future criminality be reduced.

Overall, the rehabilitative record of conventional psychotherapies is weak. Behaviorist interventions that manipulate the distribution of rewards and punishments (e.g., a token economy or point system that grants or denies privileges based on the person's behavior) appear somewhat effective in inducing conformity within correctional settings, but they have negligible impact upon release (Trojanowicz et al. 2001). Successful programs generally require a more comprehensive approach than is typically available. D. A. Andrews and colleagues (1990) believe that the most effective correctional interventions utilize behaviorist and social learning principles and are carefully matched to offenders' particular learning styles and psychological needs. They are also comprehensive in scope, designed to enhance aggression- and stress-management skills as well as academic and vocational skills, change antisocial attitudes and ways of thinking, reduce chemical dependencies, foster familial bonds, modify peer associations and role models, and help offenders access appropriate service agencies (Cullen & Applegate 1997; Pearson et al. 2002).

Rational Choice and Deterrence

Historically predating both biological and psychological approaches, what has come to be known as **classical criminology** emerged in the eighteenth century to counter views that attributed criminal behavior to supernatural forces. In ancient times, for example, it was assumed that people who acted in deviant ways did so because God was testing their faith, punishing them, or using their behavior to warn others. Or else they were seen as sinners who had fallen from God's grace and were tempted or even possessed by the devil or some other evil force (Vold et al. 2002).

By the late nineteenth century to the early twentieth, classical criminology was superseded by other theories of crime—biological, psychological, and sociological (see Chapters 4 and 5). But in the 1960s, classical criminology was revived by economist Gary Becker (1968). Becker argued that economists, who had expertise in cost-benefit analysis as applied to economic affairs, could apply the tools of their trade (i.e., assumptions about rational economic actors, complex statistical techniques) to the crime problem as well. This modern-day version of the classical school is generally referred to as **neoclassical criminology** or **rational-choice theory**.

Classical and Neoclassical Criminology

Classical criminologists of the eighteenth century were part of the European movement known as the **Enlightenment**, or Age of Reason. Enlightenment philosophers believed that humanity need not rely on religious authority to govern its affairs. Instead, rational thought or reason could be used to develop principles of morality and justice. Individuals could agree to enter into a social contract whereby they would surrender some of their individuality and submit themselves to governmental control in exchange for protection of the common good and the maintenance of natural liberties and rights (Vold et al. 2002).

Enlightenment thinkers and classical criminologists like Cesare Beccaria (1738–1794) and Jeremy Bentham (1748–1842) believed in the doctrine of **free will**. In their view, individuals who break the law and violate the social contract *rationally choose* to commit crime because they believe that the pleasures or benefits of such actions outweigh the pains or costs. The role of government is to manipulate this rational calculation of benefits and costs by maintaining a level of punishment that exceeds the potential rewards of crime. In contemporary parlance this is known as the principle of **deterrence**.

The deterrence approach to crime control is often associated with those who believe that the criminal justice system is too lenient and that we should crack down on crime. Ironically, however, the classical criminologists were critics of the excessive punishments of their time: torture and the death penalty. As late as the nineteenth century in England, for instance, the death penalty (or capital punishment) was available for about 200 offenses, most of them property crimes. The classical theorists argued that punishment should be sufficient to offset the benefits of crime, but no more extreme than that. The death penalty, they felt, should not be used as a public spectacle to satisfy the community's desire for revenge or retribution. Rather, punishment should be proportional to the nature of the offense it is designed to deter. As such, the classical criminologists believed that imprisonment should replace torture and the death penalty as the standard mode of punishment (Beirne & Messerschmidt 1995).

Although deterrence remains a core objective of the neoclassical approach, it is not an undifferentiated concept. Even in his day, Beccaria (1764) drew distinctions between the **certainty**, **celerity** (swiftness), and **severity of punishment**. Certainty refers to the likelihood of receiving punishment, celerity to the immediacy of punishment following the offense, and severity to the nature of the punishment itself. According to Beccaria:

> One of the greatest curbs on crime is not the cruelty of punishments, but their infallibility. . . . The certainty of punishment, even if it be moderate, will always make a stronger impression than the fear of another which is more terrible but combined with the hope of impunity. . . . [And] the more promptly and . . . closely punishment follows . . . the commission of a crime, the more just and useful it will be. . . . The criminal is spared the useless and cruel torments of uncertainty. . . . Privation of liberty . . . itself a punishment, should not precede the sentence except when necessity requires. . . . Promptness of punishment is more useful because when the length of time that passes between the punishment and misdeed is less, [it is] so much the stronger and . . . lasting in the human mind. . . . The severity of punishment of itself emboldens men to commit the very wrongs it is supposed to prevent; they are driven to commit additional crimes to avoid the punishment for a single one. The countries and times most notorious for severity of penalties have always been those in which the bloodiest and most inhumane of deeds were committed. (1963:58–59)

Early classical theorists, critics of the punishment practices of their age, appear liberal in their call for moderation. However, use of prison, not reform of society, was their reform agenda. They were primarily concerned with designing a legal system that would discipline those who deviated from the established social order.

Contemporary Deterrence Research

A large body of contemporary deterrence research has examined the impact of punishment on criminal behavior. Much of this research has utilized official crime data for geographical areas like cities, counties, and especially states, and considers both certainty and severity of punishment. (Celerity of punishment is difficult to measure and has been omitted from most studies.) The findings have generally shown that while certainty of punishment (as measured by the proportion of reported crimes that result in arrest, conviction, and incarceration) is more highly associated with lower crime rates than severity of punishment (as measured by the average lengths of sentences), even the effect of certainty is weak (Krohn 2000; Paternoster 1987). In one study, for example, Robert Kane (2006) found a limited (and short-lived) deterrent impact of aggressive policing in different precincts in New York City (as measured by number of arrests per officer and raw arrest counts), although he did find that police efforts to increase the certainty of punishment were more likely to deter economically motivated crimes and crimes that occur in public settings than they were to deter violent crimes.

There are several factors that appear to mitigate the deterrent effect of punishment. Research indicates that individuals' *perceptions* of punishment may be more significant than the actual punishment itself. Perceptual deterrence studies, which typically use self-report data, have generally found that perceived certainty has a greater effect than perceived severity, and that perceived certainty has a greater effect on an individual's decision to *continue* breaking the law than it does on his or her decision to break the law in the first place (Paternoster 1987; Williams & Hawkins 1986). At the same time, research shows that the public's perception of the likelihood of punishment is often at variance with the actual likelihood (Kane 2006; Kleck et al. 2005).

A person's stake in conformity may also affect his or her responsiveness to deterrence. In a study of employee theft, Richard Hollinger and John Clark (1983) found that older employees with more to lose were more deterred by their perceptions of punishment than were their younger coworkers. Similarly, David Matza (1964) observed that as juveniles grew older, many underwent **maturational reform** and desisted from delinquency as they took on the responsibilities of work and family life. Cheryl Carpenter and colleagues (1988) found that by age 16, some juveniles reported being deterred by the fact that they would face greater consequences than they had so far if they continued to offend. These youths recognized that as they grew older they would end up not just in the juvenile justice system but in the more punitive adult criminal justice system.

Other criminologists argue that rational-choice models of deterrence have focused too narrowly on punishment, oversimplified the cognitive or thinking process underlying much criminality, and neglected a number of other factors that affect individuals' decisions to violate the law. Research finds, for instance, that labor market incentives (the relative economic rewards of legal and illegal work) affect decisions to commit crime more than do the risks of punishment (Freeman 1996). In a study of high-risk offenders (adults previously incarcerated, adult drug users, and 17–20-year-old high school dropouts) involved in a federally funded work program, Irving Pilia-van and colleagues found that while "risks of punishment have virtually no impact on criminal behavior . . . persons who perceive greater opportunity to earn money illegally are more likely to violate the law" (1986:114).

Research also suggests that one's internalized or normative evaluation of right and wrong may be more central to the decision to violate the law than are perceptions of punishment, and that informal sanctions or extralegal threats such as shame, embarrassment, and disapproval from family and peers may deter law violation more than does formal punishment (Paternoster 1989; Williams & Hawkins 1986). Harold Grasmick and colleagues (1993) found, for example, that reductions in self-reported drunk driving were more highly associated with increasing levels of shame and embar-

FURTHER EXPLORATION
Deterrence and the Death Penalty

In the 1970s, the US Supreme Court ruled that the Eighth Amendment prohibition against cruel and unusual punishment essentially limited use of the death penalty to the most egregious cases of homicide (see Chapter 12). But although a majority of the US population supports the death penalty in such cases, most criminologists have concluded that "the overwhelming weight of the evidence suggests that the death penalty" does not deter such crimes (Smith 2000:628). Historically, those states that have used the death penalty most often have had the highest rates of homicide. Furthermore, states that have abolished the death penalty have not experienced a rise in homicide, nor have states that reinstated the death penalty experienced a reduction in homicide (Peterson & Bailey 1998; Zimring 2003).

In fact, some criminologists suggest that homicides may even increase as a result of executions, due to what they call a **brutalization effect**. William Bowers and Glenn Pierce argue that executions "devalue life by the example of human sacrifice" and send a message that it is "appropriate to kill those who have gravely offended us" (1980:456). They examined the relationship between monthly executions in New York state between 1906 and 1963 and monthly homicides between 1907 and 1964 and found that, on average, two additional homicides occurred each month following an execution. Similarly, a study of California found that homicides were twice as high during the years (1952–1967) when California was executing an inmate every other month than during the period (1968–1991) when it carried out no executions (Godfrey & Schiraldi 1995). And research that examined the reinstatement of the death penalty in Arizona in 1992 after a 30-year moratorium, and in Oklahoma in 1990 after a 25-year moratorium, found evidence of a brutalization effect as well (Bailey 1998; Thomson 1997).

rassment than with changing perceptions of legal sanctions. They credited the social movement against drunk driving (particularly Mothers Against Drunk Driving) with success in altering moral beliefs and community standards regarding this offense. Similarly, in interviews with corporate officials, Sally Simpson (1992) found that informal factors such as threats to personal reputation and future employment opportunities outweighed formal punishment in decisions to violate the law or engage in unethical business conduct.

In addition, the deterrent effect of punishment may not be substantial because many criminals are not always the rational actors envisioned by classical and neoclassical theory. But this is not the same as saying they are irrational. Rather, it is to say that crimes committed out of emotional or economic desperation or because of chemical dependencies may not involve the kind of cost-benefit calculus that responds to traditional deterrence strategies. To a drug addict, the cost of not stealing the money to pay for one's next fix (inevitable suffering from withdrawal symptoms) probably seems greater than the cost of stealing the money (*possible* arrest, *possible* conviction). Consider also the comments of women who have killed their battering husbands or lovers. Most of those whom Ann Jones (1980) interviewed expressed considerable remorse and sorrow. Some spoke of guilt and depression, "but at the same time, many . . . experienced an exhilarating sense of release. 'Even when I knew I would have to go to prison,' said one woman, 'I felt as if a stone hand had been lifted off my head.' Another said, 'Suddenly I knew that I could take a walk, call my mother, laugh—and it would be all right. For the first time in 11 years, I wasn't afraid'" (p. 320).

In other cases the risk of getting caught may be part of the thrill, or the offender may be rather fatalistic about the prospects of getting caught (Katz 1988). As former Los Angeles gang member Sanyika Shakur recalls: "The total lawlessness [of gang life] was alluring, and . . . the sense of importance, self-worth, and raw power was exciting, stimulating, and intoxicating beyond any other high. . . . Prison loomed in my future like wisdom teeth. . . . [It] was like a stepping stone to manhood" (1993:70, 163). Patrice Gaines, who grew up in a middle-class black family, says that during her youth she was powerfully attracted to the "bad boyz" who daringly defied the law, carried guns, and earned their money through robbery, theft, and drugs:

> Their behavior was an aphrodisiac. When you're a black child who believes she has no control over her life, you create your own definition of freedom. These men exuded freedom. They controlled their lives, working when they wanted to and at what they chose to work at. . . . I wanted the power I thought they possessed, and before long, I reached for it much as . . . [they] did. . . . It was adventure—making up your own rules and knowing how to live the "street life." (1993:5–7)

To be sure, some offenders behave rationally insofar as they try to select targets that minimize the risk of apprehension and maximize the proceeds from crime (Coupe & Blake 2006). Interviews with burglars indicate that they prefer unoccupied single-family homes, homes that have fewer entry barriers (e.g., sophisticated locks, window bars, alarms), homes that appear affluent or that contain "good stuff," and neighborhoods where they fit in or look inconspicuous. And to the extent that thieves fear apprehension, they try to push it from their minds and focus instead on the stash awaiting them (Tunnell 1992; Walsh 1980; Wright & Decker 1994). In his autobiography, Nathan McCall recalls his involvement in armed robbery this way:

> It gave me a rush to know that I'd taken all that money. . . . At the same time, there was this fear that had been nagging me. . . . Cats all around me were getting popped for one thing or another, and being sent to the penitentiary. . . . I figured that sooner or later I'd take a fall, too. Sometimes, when I thought about it, I didn't care. Sometimes I cared a whole lot more than I was willing to admit. . . . I was twenty, half burned out on drugs, depressed, and hopelessly lost. At some point in life . . . I had lost control. (1994:136, 141)

On the night he was arrested for the robbery of a McDonald's restaurant that would send him to prison, McCall remembers: "My intuition . . . was telling me I shouldn't go. . . . Despite the wine I'd guzzled to numb my fear, I was nervous. It just didn't feel right. . . . I wished I could rewind . . . my fucked-up life and reset its course" (pp. 137–138, 140). Some readers of McCall's autobiography will say that his life was simply a product of the choices he made. But others will recognize it is more complicated than that, for many factors impact on the course of one's life as it spins more and more out of control.

Summary

This chapter offered a review and assessment of individual explanations and policies that locate the central causes of criminal behavior within the individual rather than within society or the social environment. We began with biological approaches and considered the evolution of this tradition from now outdated views to contemporary biosocial theory, which focuses on the purported biological conditions that predispose some individuals toward crime. We then examined several psychological approaches, including psychoanalytic theory, personality theory, mental illness and the insanity defense, and behaviorism. Last, we considered rational-choice theory, which assumes that criminals are rational actors who calculate the potential costs and benefits of their criminal and noncriminal options and may be deterred by increasing the certainty and severity of punishment.

4

Microsocial Explanations of Crime

Sociological explanations of crime are as diverse as the individual-istic ones we explored in the previous chapter. We begin our review of these theories by making a distinction between *micro*sociological ("small") and *macro*sociological ("large") levels of analysis.

Macrosociological theories focus on elements of social structure that are characteristic of communities or entire societies. They look at the "big picture," asking why certain groups of people living under particular circumstances commit more crime than other groups living under different conditions. **Microsociological theories**, on the other hand, examine the link between individuals and society by focusing on the process by which "individuals acquire social attributes through interaction with others" (Barlow 1996:468). These explanations acknowledge that people exposed to the same social structure do not necessarily respond in the same way, and that people from dissimilar circumstances do not necessarily respond differently. Microsocial approaches may be understood as **social psychological** insofar as they consider how individuals learn to favor or disfavor criminal courses of action, how they are socialized or controlled through social relationships, and how they interpret or account for the meaning of their actions. In contrast to biological and psychological theories that view criminal offenders as deviant "kinds of persons," microsocial theories emphasize the common ways in which normal people respond to varying social environments.

In this chapter we discuss microsocial theories and in the next chapter we discuss macrosocial approaches. We begin by considering theories that are part of either the symbolic interaction or social learning tradition of sociological analysis, and in some cases both. We then turn to theories that are part of the social control and life-course traditions in criminology.

Symbolic Interaction and Social Learning

Our point of departure for the discussion of symbolic interaction and social learning theories is the seminal work of Edwin Sutherland (1883–1950), whose theory of differential association contains elements of both of these perspectives. Sutherland, who stood heads above his contemporaries when it came to recognizing the problem of white-collar crime (see Chapters 1 and 2), was acutely aware of criminology's restrictive focus on lower-class crime, and he appreciated the need for a general theory that could explain criminal behavior in all strata of society.

Edwin Sutherland and the Theory of Differential Association

Sutherland's **differential association theory** (1947) has been classified as both symbolic interactionist and behaviorist in orientation (Einstader & Henry 1995; Empey & Stafford 1991). **Symbolic interactionism**, whose most influential proponent was George Herbert Mead (1863–1931), is concerned with the symbolic meaning of social action for the individual. The very same experience, Mead noted, could mean different things to different people. Such meanings, and consequently a person's very sense of self or personal identity, are acquired through social interaction with others (Sandstrom et al. 2006). As for the behaviorist strain of Sutherland's work, differential association accepts the proposition that criminal behavior is learned or conditioned through the particular mix of rewards and punishments that are attached to a person's behavior (see Chapter 3).

According to differential association theory, therefore, "criminal behavior is learned in interaction with other persons in a process of communication . . . within intimate personal groups" (cited in Akers & Sellers 2009:86). The learning of crime includes not only "the techniques of committing the crime, which are sometimes very complicated and sometimes very simple," but also "the specific direction of motives, drives, rationalizations, and attitudes" underlying the illegal behavior. A person becomes delinquent or criminal when he or she is exposed to "an excess of definitions favorable to violation of law over definitions unfavorable to violation of law." Since individuals are typically exposed to both crime-inducing and crime-inhibiting associations, what matters is the relative *frequency* (how often you spend time with particular others), *duration* (how much time you spend with them on each occasion), *priority* (how early in life you began associating with them), and *intensity* (how much importance you attach to them) of each.

Perhaps the most obvious example of differential association is the adolescent peer group that provides social approval for participating with others in underage drinking, drug use, gangs, and other forms of crime. Participation in such activities is reinforced through the acquisition of friendship ties, while nonparticipation may lead to exclusion. Even such an egregious crime as gang rape, for some individuals, can be understood in this way. Nathan McCall (1994), for example, recalls how he was initially reluctant to participate in a gang rape as a youth: "I was in no great hurry to have sex in front of a bunch of other dudes. . . . [But] I wasn't about to let it be said that I was scared of pussy." The first time he participated he felt sorry for the 13-year-old girl he and his friends had raped, "knowing she would never be able to live [it] down. . . . But the guilt was short-lived. It was eclipsed in no time by the victory celebration we held after she left" (p. 48).

Consistent with symbolic interactionism, Sutherland was aware that individuals are malleable and subject to change over time in the course of ongoing interactions (Sandstrom et al. 2006). In his book on white-collar crime he presented an account by a young man who underwent a redefinition of self upon entering the labor force after college:

> While I was a student in the school of business I learned the principles of accounting. After I had worked for a time for an accounting firm I found that I had failed to learn many important things. . . . An accounting firm gets its work from business firms and, within limits, must make the reports which those business firms desire. On my first assignment I discovered some irregularities in the books of the firm and these would lead anyone to question the financial policies of that firm. When I showed my report to the manager . . . he said that was not a part of my assignment and I should leave it out. Although I was confident that the business firm was dishonest, I had to conceal this information. Again and again I have been compelled to do the same thing in other assignments. I get so disgusted with things of this sort that I wish I could leave the profession . . . [but] it is the only occupation for which I have training. (Sutherland 1983:239)

Another man described his trouble maintaining employment in retail sales after he graduated from college because he did not like to deceive his customers about price and quality, as his bosses expected him to do. After resigning jobs selling typewriters and then sewing machines, he was in difficult financial straits. As he recalled:

> I occasionally met some of my classmates and they related experiences similar to mine. They said they would starve if they were rigidly honest. . . . My own feelings became less determined than they had been when I . . . got a job in the used-car business. I learned that this business had more tricks for fleecing customers than either of those [businesses] I had previously tried. Cars with cracked cylinders, with half the teeth missing from the fly wheel, with everything wrong, were sold as "guaranteed." When the customer returned and demanded his guarantee, he had to sue to get it and very few went to the trouble. . . . If hot cars would be taken in and sold safely, the boss did not hesitate. . . . I did not quit as I had previously. I sometimes felt disgusted . . . but I [told myself] that I did not have much chance to find a legitimate firm. I knew that the game was rotten but it had to be played. I knew I was dishonest and to that extent felt that I was more honest than my fellows. The thing that struck me . . . was that all these

people were proud of their ability to fleece customers. They boasted of their crookedness and were admired . . . [for] their ability to get away with a crooked deal. . . . Another thing was that these people were unanimous in their denunciation of gangsters, robbers, burglars, and petty thieves. They never regarded themselves as [being part of that group] and were bitterly indignant if accused of dishonesty: it was just good business. (quoted in Sutherland 1983:241–242)

Although this story is anecdotal and from an earlier historical period, the criminological literature is replete with studies that support the general thrust of Sutherland's theory. Self-report delinquency research in particular has confirmed the theory's basic tenets. These studies typically involve broader tests of social learning theory, to which we now turn.

Social Learning Theory

In a large body of theory and research, Akers and Sellers advanced a **social learning theory** of crime that merges principles of differential association theory with those of behaviorist psychology in order to examine processes that "motivate and control criminal behavior" and "promote and undermine conformity" (2009:89). From Sutherland, Akers takes the concepts of *differential association* and *definitions* and adds the behaviorist concepts of *imitation* and *differential reinforcement*. Imitation refers to one's observation and replication of role models' behavior in both actual and simulated environments (e.g., the media). Akers's research indicates that imitation is "more important in the initial acquisition and performance of novel behavior than in the maintenance or cessation of behavioral patterns once established" (p. 93). Differential reinforcement "refers to the *balance* of anticipated or actual rewards and punishments that follow or are consequences of behavior" (pp. 91–92, emphasis added). As noted earlier, rewards and punishments can be both social and nonsocial, and they can range from approval or disapproval of parents and friends to the euphoric or unpleasant physical effects of drugs. Also recall that studies find anticipation of informal sanctions from others to be a more salient deterrent to crime than anticipation of formal sanctions from the law (see Chapter 3).

Akers (1998) acknowledges the macro-level social phenomena that structure environments of social learning, although these are not his primary concern. He is interested in specifying the precise micro-level mechanisms by which learning takes place. On this score, social learning theory has fared rather well in empirical research, especially in studies of juvenile delinquency:

There is abundant evidence to show the significant impact . . . of differential association in primary groups such as family and peers. . . . [Delinquency] may be . . . directly affected by deviant parental models, ineffective and erratic supervision and discipline . . . and the endorsement of values and attitudes favorable to deviance. . . . [I]n general, parental . . . criminality is predictive of . . . children's future [criminality]. . . . The role of the family, [however], is usually as a conventional socializer against delinquency. . . . It provides anticriminal definitions, conforming models, and the reinforcement of conformity through parental discipline. . . . Other than one's own prior . . . behavior, the best single predictor of the onset, continuance, or desistance of . . . delinquency is differential association with conforming or law-violating peers. . . . It is in peer groups that the first availability and opportunity for delinquent acts are typically provided. Virtually every study that includes a peer association variable finds it to be significantly and usually most strongly related to delinquency . . . and other forms of deviant behavior. (Akers & Sellers 2009:99–101)

Moreover, Akers and colleagues (1979) found that differential association and other social learning variables were effective predictors of alcohol and drug use among both male and female adolescents. Similarly, Peggy Giordano (1978) found that peer-group involvement was central to females' acquisition of attitudes favorable to delinquent conduct. She and her colleagues also found females just as likely as males to indicate that they got drugs or alcohol from friends or that they hung out at friends' houses when parents were away: "Females spend as much . . . time in the company of their friends as do males. . . . [Those] who . . . become involved in delinquent acts . . . adopt both a set of attitudes in which they [see] delinquency as appropriate, possible, or desirable . . . and a friendship style in which they . . . encourage each other as a group to act on these orientations" (Giordano et al. 1986:1194).

In terms of practical applications, both social learning theory and differential association theory suggest rehabilitative interventions that utilize group dynamics to reinforce conventional behavior. Such applications are referred to variously as guided group interaction, peer-group counseling, positive peer culture, and **therapeutic communities** (Gottfredson 1987). In juvenile correctional settings, these approaches offer advantages over individual-oriented treatments. Insofar as offenders often manifest their law-violating behavior as part of a group, the group therapy situation is the natural vehicle for personal change or growth:

The [beginning] stages of the group are used to vent hostility and aggression. Initially, the groups' members are self-centered and unable to realistically or meaningfully involve themselves or their peers in the problem-solving process. Later, as the group progresses and the . . . members see that their . . . peers have similar problems and backgrounds, empathy and group identification is facilitated, . . . ultimately produc[ing] insight and new patterns of adaptation. (Trojanowicz et al. 2001:363–364)

These groups are often staffed by ex-offenders and ex-addicts and "show remarkably consistent reductions" in criminal behavior for those who complete the programs (Lipton 1996:12).

FURTHER EXPLORATION
General Strain Theory

Robert Agnew (1992) is noteworthy for developing a micro-level theory of strain that derives from a macro approach we discuss in the next chapter. The latter formulation posits that individuals are structured into a position of "strain" with society because they are frustrated or feel a sense of injustice due to their lack of access to economic and educational opportunities that would enable them to pursue the American dream of financial success and bountiful material consumption. But Agnew argues, in what he calls **general strain theory**, that strain results not simply from the actual or perceived failure to achieve these goals, but more generally from a broader array of stressful or negative life experiences. In accounting for juvenile delinquency, he posits that these sources of strain include the actual or anticipated *removal* of "positively valued stimuli" (such as the death of a parent, end of a romantic relationship, or moving from one's neighborhood), as well as the actual or anticipated *presentation* of "negatively valued stimuli" (such as an abusive parent, an unfair teacher, or hostile peers). Agnew also proposes that the relationship between strain and delinquency is mediated by a youth's *emotional reactions* (such as frustration, depression, or anger) and *coping strategies* (such as talking to others, cathartic physical exercise, or revision of goals) that affect the behavioral outcomes of structurally induced experiences.

More recently, Ronald Simons and Callie Harbin Burt suggest that the elements implicated in general strain theory might also be recast in terms of an expanded view of social learning theory, whereby the lessons communicated and learned through adverse life experiences lead to "a hostile view of people and relationships, a preference for immediate rewards, and a cynical view of conventional norms" (2011:553). Be that as it may, a substantial body of research lends support to general strain theory, while the practical implications suggest the importance of remedial interventions that improve familial, peer, and school relationships and that provide youths with resources that improve their coping strategies, such as the availability of positive adult mentors and anger management and conflict resolution training (Agnew 1995, 2001; Baron 2004).

Techniques of Neutralization

Both social learning and differential association theories make use of the concept of "definitions" when describing the process by which individuals come to define or interpret law-violating behavior as acceptable or unacceptable. In some studies, definitions have been operationalized according to Gresham Sykes and David Matza's concept (1957) of **techniques of neutralization**. Sykes and Matza argued that most law violators have some appreciation or respect for conventional values and must therefore neutralize the hold these values have on them through various self-rationalizations or justifications.

In their research on delinquent youths, Sykes and Matza identified five general techniques of neutralization. *Denial of responsibility* involves the delinquent's assertion that his or her behavior is due to external forces such as "unloving parents, bad companions, or a slum neighborhood" (pp. 667–668).Youths often view themselves as helplessly propelled into unlawful behavior, as "more acted upon than acting." For example, a youth may explain that "the alcohol made me do it" or "the other guy started the fight." *Denial of injury* describes the offender's view that no harm has been caused by his or her actions—for instance, by drinking alcohol, smoking marijuana, or "borrowing" someone's car for a joyride. *Denial of the victim* is used as a way to distinguish people who are deserving targets of crime, such as a black person who's stepped "out of his place," a teacher who's been unfair, or a store owner who's ripped off customers. *Condemnation of the condemners* shifts attention away from the youth and toward the disapproving others, who are viewed as "hypocrites, deviants in disguise, or impelled by personal spite." For example, a youth may resent police officers who are corrupt, teachers who show favoritism, or parents who abuse their children. Finally, *appeal to higher loyalties* involves the imperative to sacrifice the rules of the larger society for the demands of the smaller group, such as the friendship clique or gang.

Critics have faulted Sykes and Matza for failing to establish that techniques of neutralization actually *precede* rather than *follow* delinquent acts, arguing that techniques of neutralization are mechanisms that facilitate the "hardening" of youths already involved in crime (Minor 1984). Others have observed that rationalizations are used not so much to neutralize moral commitments as to minimize risks. For instance, delinquents may rationalize stealing from people they perceive as "careless victims"—that is, as people whose "inefficiency in protecting their possessions makes them 'responsible' in part for their own victimization" (e.g., people who leave their keys in their car, who don't lock up their bicycles, or who leave their houses unlocked) (Carpenter et al. 1988:104).

These criticisms notwithstanding, the techniques-of-neutralization concept sensitizes us to the way in which offenders interpret or account for their actions. Rapists, for example, employ culturally available "rape myths" they have learned from the media and peers (Scully & Marolla 1984). These myths contain neutralization techniques that deny responsibility (e.g., the urge was uncontrollable), deny injury (e.g., she really liked it), and deny the victim (e.g., she was a tease, so she had it coming). As one rapist, a married man, explains: "Sometimes you just get the urge to go out and fuck the living shit out of some broad. . . . It doesn't matter who they are or what they look like. . . . Most women like to get their box battered as much as a man likes to get his balls off. They want to be grabbed and taken hard. It makes them feel like a woman" (Skipper & McWhorter 1981:29; see Chapter 9).

White-collar criminals, as Sutherland observed, rely on comparable rationalizations for their crimes. In a well-documented price-fixing case that came to light in the early 1960s, corporate personnel from General Electric, Westinghouse, and other electrical equipment manufacturers conspired to avoid the competition that would have kept prices down (Geis 1978). The conspirators all testified that this was an ongoing practice before they had been hired by their respective companies and that they were expected to conform. They also denied that they had caused any harm. One GE spokesman rationalized his company's actions this way: "The prices which . . . purchasers . . . have paid during the past years were appropriate to value received and reasonable as compared with the general trends of prices in the economy" (p. 63). And a Westinghouse executive replied, when asked during a Senate subcommittee inquiry about whether he was aware that the meetings he'd had with competitors were illegal: "Illegal? Yes, but not criminal. . . . I assumed that criminal action meant damaging someone, and we did not do that. . . . I thought that we were more or less working on a survival basis in order to try to make enough to keep our plant and our employees" (p. 67). This conspiracy, however, went on for several years and netted the industry millions of dollars in illegal profits.

But white-collar offenders usually don't have to look their victims in the eyes; the victims may remain anonymous to them. The "victim" may not even be an individual, but rather a vast governmental agency, as in the case of Medicare health-care fraud. Moreover, it is generally not a white-collar offender's explicit intention to do harm. As Jeffrey Reiman suggests, in describing a mine disaster:

> What keeps a mine disaster from being [viewed as] a mass murder . . . is that it is not a one-on-one harm. What is important in one-on-one harm is . . . the desire of someone . . . to harm someone . . . else. An attack by a gang on one or more persons or an attack by one individual on several fits the model of one-on-one harm; that is, for each person harmed there is at least one individual who wanted to harm that person. Once he selects his victim, the rapist, the mugger, the murderer all want this person they have selected to suffer. A mine executive, on the other hand, does not want his employees to be harmed. He would truly prefer that there be no accident, no injured or dead miners. What he does want is something legitimate. It is what he has been hired to get: maximum profits at minimum costs. . . . If ten men die because he cut corners on safety, . . . [the] men are dead as an unwanted consequence of his (perhaps overzealous or undercautious) pursuit of a legitimate goal. (2007:72–73)

Last, techniques of neutralization are also apparent in rationalizations by government officials when denials of responsibility or appeals to higher loyalties in the name of "national security" are invoked to justify circumvention of the law. During the early years of the Cold War, for instance, when the former Soviet Union was viewed as the most dangerous adversary of the United States, a secret report prepared for the White House by a group of distinguished citizens headed by former president Herbert Hoover asserted:

> It is now clear that we are facing an implacable enemy whose avowed objective is world domination. . . . There are no rules in such a game. Hitherto accepted norms of human conduct do not apply. . . . If the United States is to survive, long-standing American concepts of fair play must be reconsidered. . . . We must learn to subvert, sabotage, and destroy our enemies by more clever, more sophisticated, more effective methods than those used against us. (cited in Moyers 1988:42).

This rationalization, as we shall see, was used to justify international crimes by the US government that entailed assassinations of foreign leaders, the illegitimate overthrow of foreign governments, and the promulgation of torture around the world (see Chapter 10).

Labeling Theory

Previously we introduced labeling theory's challenge to the legalistic definition of crime (see Chapter 1). Crime, according to labeling theory, is not an objective condition but a process of social definition and the societal reaction to rule-violating behavior. Labeling theory is not concerned with explaining **primary deviation**, the initial impulse for rule violation, but with **secondary deviation**, how labeling transforms the initial behavior into a stable pattern. Drawing on the symbolic interaction tradition, labeling theory is concerned with the process by which individuals develop a sense of personal identity or self through interaction with others. It postulates that labeling of persons as criminal can become a self-fulfilling prophecy that promotes further involvement in crime. The offender internalizes the negative stigma and suffers a decline in self-esteem, while hostile reactions from others reduce opportunities to resume a conventional status (Becker 1963; Schur 1971).

Although results of delinquency research on the effects of labeling on juveniles' self-esteem have been mixed, they do not generally support the proposition that youths experience a decline in self-esteem following arrest or contact with juvenile court. Some studies have found that self-esteem is more likely to decline among youths who are less involved in or committed to delinquency (e.g., first-time, middle-class offenders) than among more involved or committed youths (e.g., high-frequency, lower-class offenders) who already possess a discredited social status, are not highly integrated into mainstream society, and are "less sensitive to and less affected by the judgments of officialdom" (Waegel 1989:113). Labeling may be irrelevant for those already designated as social outsiders, because having delinquent peers and engaging in delinquency may (in the short run) actually increase their self-esteem (Jang & Thornberry 1998; Kaplan et al. 1986).

Issues of self-esteem aside, ethnographic studies of gangs illustrate how excessive official intervention in the lives of youths may make matters worse, as conflict with the police solidifies youths' commitment to the gang (Hagedorn 1988). As one gang member recounts:

> The police . . . would pull me into their car and harass me. I kept telling them that I was not a banger. But they don't believe anything. . . . They asked me questions about . . . friends, guys from the hood who are gang-bangers, and, since I wouldn't tell them what they wanted to hear, they would say things like, "Yes, you are one of those hoodlums from this street. We've been watching you for a long time, and now we got you, and you're going to pay." (quoted in Padilla 1992:85)

According to another youth:

> I was picked up on several occasions . . . because I was Puerto Rican and was walking down the street. I wasn't into gangbanging, but the cops kept asking me questions about my gang and shit. One time . . . [they] picked me up and dropped me off in a white neighborhood . . . [and] took my money so I couldn't catch the bus back to the hood. The white dudes from that neighborhood had a field day with me. . . . I tried protecting myself . . . but I did get the shit smashed out of me. So, what do you do after something like that happens to you? . . . I turned. I became an official member of the [gang]. (pp. 87–88)

The stigmatization associated with official labeling also makes it difficult to find employment after serving punishment for one's crime, and this stigmatization appears to be greater for blacks than for whites. In one study, Devah Pager (2003) found that for both blacks and whites, previously incarcerated job applicants were less likely than non–previously incarcerated applicants to be called back for follow-up job interviews. However, Pager also found that even nonincarcerated black applicants were less likely to be called back for job interviews than previously incarcerated whites (see also Wright 2013). The experience of Nathan McCall (1994), an African American, offers a case in point. After serving three years for armed robbery, he could not land a newspaper job even after receiving a college degree in journalism. As he writes: "Every time I filled out an application and ran across that section about felony convictions, it made me feel sick inside. . . . I knew what they were going to do. . . . A black man with a felony record didn't stand a chance" (p. 234). Through perseverance, however, McCall eventually became a successful journalist, but only after he decided to lie about his criminal record. He hoped that if he got his foot in the door and had a chance to prove himself, people might finally forgive him for his past.

John Braithwaite's observations (1989) about **disintegrative shaming** and **reintegrative shaming** are helpful as we contemplate the obstacles faced by McCall and others like him as they attempted to reintegrate into conventional society. Shaming is social disapproval or condemnation designed to invoke remorse. In disintegrative shaming, the offender continues to be treated as an outsider, is not forgiven for past sins, and thus is more likely to relapse into crime after having difficulty reentering the community. In reintegrative shaming, on the other hand, the offender is shamed, but if remorseful they are forgiven, welcomed back into the fold, and enmeshed in supportive community relationships. Reintegrative shaming has greater cultural support in Japan than in the United States, and this may be one reason why Japan has comparatively lower rates of crime (Vincentnathan 1995).

The fact that labeling may promote criminal identification has led some criminologists to favor a policy of "radical nonintervention" or use of less punitive measures when dealing with some offenders (Schur 1973). Youths who commit minor crimes, for instance, can be diverted from the juvenile justice system into community-based programs that offer various rehabilitative services. Other criminologists who are critical of the overreach of the law have favored a policy of decriminalization—the removal of criminal sanctions—for so-called victimless crimes committed by adults, such as gambling and minor drug use, that for the most part lack the forced victimization of predatory crimes of theft and violence (Meier & Geis 1997). Such nonintervention strategies—especially decriminalization—remain controversial and raise complex issues that we will explore later in the book.

Social Control and the Life Course

The most important micro-level alternative to symbolic interaction and social learning approaches is **social control theory**. This theory had its landmark formulation in a book by Travis Hirschi called *Causes of Delinquency* (1969) and was subsequently extended in work by Robert Sampson and John Laub (1993) on the life course.

Travis Hirschi and Social Control Theory

Hirschi believed that most criminological theories ask the wrong question: Why *do* people engage in criminal behavior? Hirschi thought the more appropriate question to ask is: Why *don't* people engage in criminal behavior? He assumed that human self-interest provided sufficient motivation for crime, and hence what is in need of explanation—the key theoretical issue—is how these impulses are controlled.

According to Hirschi, most micro- and macro-level sociological formulations are essentially "bad things happen to good people" theories—that is, they assume that people are largely benign and naturally prone to conformity unless exposed to disadvantaged opportunities, deviant associations, social stigmatization, and so forth. But these theories, Hirschi argued, fail to address questions like: Why do so many (if not most) economically disadvantaged people *not* commit crime? Why would one be attracted to delinquent peers in the first place?

Following the early work of influential French sociologist Émile Durkheim (1858–1917), Hirschi argued that "the more weakened the groups to which [one] belongs, the less he depends on them, the more he consequently depends only on himself and recognizes no other rules of conduct than what are founded on his private interests" (Durkheim 1952:209). According to Hirschi, conformity arises only if, through the socialization process, a person establishes a bond with the conventional society. When this bond is weak, one is freed from social constraint and is more at risk for delinquency.

Hirschi conceptualized the social bond in terms of four key elements. *Attachment* refers to the ties of mutual affection and respect between children and their parents, teachers, and friends. People with such positive ties (with their parents especially) are reluctant to place those ties in jeopardy by engaging in law-violating behavior. *Commitment* suggests an individual's stake in conformity, as indicated by a youth's willingness to conform to the ideal requisites of childhood (such as getting an education, and postponing smoking, drinking, and sex) and their assessment of anticipated losses associated with nonconformity. *Involvement* refers to participation in conventional activities that minimize idle and unsupervised time (such as chores, homework, organized sports, youth clubs). *Belief* indicates acceptance of the moral validity of laws.

During childhood and adolescence, parents are the key agents of social control, since "the family is the most salient arena for social interaction" at this stage of life (Thornberry 1987:873). In Chapter 3 we noted elements of family life that are associated with the behavior of youths, including (among other things) the degree of parental-child affection and communication. In his self-report survey research, Hirschi (1969) measured attachment to parents by asking youths various questions such as: "Do you share your thoughts and feelings with your parents?" "Do your parents know where you are when you are away from home?" Those who answered affirmatively to questions like these—as well as other measures of the social bond—were less likely to engage in delinquency. Importantly, Hirschi placed emphasis on the *quality* of the relationship between children and parents rather than on the *number* of parents in the home (e.g., single-parent versus two-parent families). All other things being equal, it is desirable to have two parents in the home, but research supports Hirschi's proposition that the quality of family interaction is more important than the number of parents per se (Cernkovich & Giordano 1987; Rankin & Kern 1994; Rebellion 2002).

Although Hirschi's theory has received considerable empirical support through self-report studies, the evidence has appeared most compelling as an explanation of (1) minor rather than serious delinquency, (2) the onset of delinquency rather than the continuation of delinquency, and (3) delinquency in early rather than late adolescence (Agnew 1985; Krohn & Massey 1980; Paternoster & Triplett 1988). Moreover, as Terence Thornberry notes: "Attachment to parents is not . . . an immutable trait, impervious to the effects of other variables. Indeed, associating with delinquent peers, not being committed to school, and engaging in delinquent behavior are so contradictory to parental expectations that they tend to diminish the level of attachment between parents and child" (1987:874).

In his later work with Michael Gottfredson, Hirschi argued that effective familial bonds that promote the development of personal *self-control* in young children are the first line of defense in the fight against crime (Gottfredson & Hirschi 1990; see Chapter 3). However, if the family and then the schools fail in bonding the individual to society, the criminal justice system becomes the last line of defense. Contrary to labeling theory, but consistent with conservative proscriptions for dealing with crime, Hirschi and Gottfredson suggest that law enforcement should be strictly applied to increase the certainty of apprehension, and punishment (not rehabilitative treatment) should be employed, since criminal justice intervention comes too late to effectively reform criminals (Einstader & Henry 1995).

While some social control theorists downplay the significance of class, Terry Williams and William Kornblum ask a question consistent with Hirschi's perspective: How is it that some lower-class youths "manage not only to survive in a community devastated by crime, drug addiction, and violence, but to be recognized as achievers and encouraged to realize their potential as fully as possible"? (1985:16). The answer, for many youths, is family involvement:

> In every low-income community there are young people who work and go to school and fulfill family responsibilities. The largest proportion of these youths is from homes where parents have struggled for years to provide them with as many of the benefits of stability and education as possible, even at great sacrifice to themselves. The influence of family values . . . , the relative security of religious beliefs and practices, fortunate experiences with teachers and school—all of these factors are important in shaping the life chances of young achievers. (p. 17)

At the same time, Williams and Kornblum agree with the African proverb "It takes a village to raise a child." They believe that positive adult mentors who spend time with youths "are among the most precious resources a community can have" (p. 106). Mentors who nurture self-esteem and foster aspirations—whether they are from schools, religious organizations, youth groups, or athletic associations—can make a world of difference in the lives of young people. But Williams and Kornblum follow this observation with advocacy for policies that are consistent with macrosocial approaches we will consider in the next chapter, maintaining that efforts to encourage adult mentoring of disadvantaged youths should be incorporated into government programs that promote "continual opportunities for . . . entry into the economic and social mainstream" (p. 113).

Complicating the Relationship Between Religion and Delinquency

Although the United States is home to one of the most churchgoing populations in the world, contemporary political discourse is filled with lamentations about America's moral decline due to a lack of religious belief and the growth of moral relativism. Religion, many people believe, is one of the key institutions in society that promotes "goodness, morality, concern for the rights and welfare of others, righteousness, and rewards in the hereafter for proper behavior in life" (Binder et al. 1988:465). Within criminology, social control theory suggests an inverse relationship between religion and crime insofar as religion may increase the bond between individuals and society and promote moral beliefs that discourage deviancy.

Most criminological research on religion has focused on juvenile delinquency, and these studies have yielded mixed results. In one of the first major studies that questioned the relationship between religion and delinquency, Travis Hirschi and Rodney Stark (1969) discerned no association between delinquency and church attendance or belief in the supernatural. The researchers explained their findings with the observation that churches are unable to instill neighborly love in their members and that "belief in the possibility of pleasure and pain in another world cannot now, and perhaps never could, compete with the pleasures and pains of everyday life" (pp. 212–213).

Other research suggests that the relationship between religion and delinquency may vary by denomination and geographical context. Several early studies found the lowest rates of delinquency among Jews and persons from fundamentalist or highly ascetic Christian denominations, and that religion appeared to inhibit delinquency more in rural and Southern communities than in urban and non-Southern areas (see Berger 1996:491–494). Research also indicates that the relationship between religion and delinquency is mediated by associations with peers, with youths who have less religious commitment being more vulnerable to the influence of delinquent peers (Burkett & Warren 1987). Stark, however, thinks that the critical issue is not a youth's personal beliefs but the beliefs of most of his or her friends: "In communities where most young people do not attend church, religion will not inhibit the behavior even of those . . . who personally are religious. . . . In communities where most kids are religious, then those who are will be less delinquent than those who aren't" (1984:274–275).

While some criminologists have concluded that the impact of religion is so closely tied to family influences that it has little independent effect

(Cochran et al. 1994; Giordano et al. 2008), Richard Petts (2009) found that religion enhances the effect of parental affection in deterring delinquency and mitigates the increased risk of delinquency among youths in single-parent homes. As such, it seems unwise to dismiss religion as a factor in young people's lives, although the relationship appears strongest for behaviors like alcohol/drug use and teenage sex that are not universally condemned by secular society (Jang & Johnson 2001; Johnson et al. 2000, 2001).

In recent years we have heard more about faith-based efforts to help guide at-risk youths away from gangs, drugs, and violence. Religious leaders now run "safe haven" centers for at-risk youths that combine religious and recreational activities. Some clergy work with police to pull the hardcore kids off the streets—where they can hopefully be reached in a prison ministry—and get the "more winnable" ones into alternative community programs (Leland 1998). Evaluation of faith-based rehabilitation programs for both juveniles and adults, though still in its infancy, is a growing part of contemporary criminological research (O'Conner et al. 2006), although some have raised concerns about the use of tax dollars by religious organizations to proselytize their faith (Goldberg 2007).

Social Bonds Across the Life Course

Robert Sampson and John Laub (1993) have extended social control theory to help explain how the establishment of bonds in adulthood can attenuate and modify previous experiences and patterns of behavior across the **life course**, which may be defined as a developmental pathway or "sequence of culturally defined age-graded roles and social transitions that are enacted over time" (Caspi et al. 1990:15). During childhood and adolescence, the family, school, and peer groups are the most significant sources of informal social control. During young adulthood, higher education, vocational training, work, and marriage are most important. During later adulthood, work, marriage, parenthood, and involvement in community are most important.

Sampson and Laub analyzed longitudinal data collected by Sheldon Glueck and Eleanor Glueck (1950, 1968) on 500 delinquent and 500 nondelinquent males born between 1924 and 1935 who were followed from childhood until they were 32 years of age. They found that childhood and adolescent delinquency were predictive of later-life criminality, but young men who married and found stable employment were more likely to desist from crime than those who did not. Their research supports a theory of "informal social control that recognizes both stability and change in antisocial behavior over the life course" (Sampson & Laub 1990:609).

Sampson and Laub argue that marriage per se does not increase social control, but that close emotional ties and a strong attachment to one's spouse increase the general bond between individuals and society. Marriage also reduces time spent with law-violating peers, as other studies have found as well (Simons et al. 2002; Warr 1998). And while employment per se does not increase social control, it does so when accompanied by job stability, job commitment, and workplace ties. Under these conditions a person develops a social investment in institutions of conformity and becomes embedded in networks of relationships that "create interdependent systems of obligations and restraint that impose significant costs for translating criminal propensities into action" (Laub & Sampson 1993:311). At the same time, Christopher Uggen (2000) found that males in their late twenties and older were more likely than males in their late teens and early twenties to report declines in criminality due to employment.

It is important to understand that the circumstances for personal reform are not entirely of one's own making. Structural features of the labor market, for instance, "have as much to do . . . with employment outcomes . . . as do individual predispositions to work" (Laub & Sampson 1993:318–319). The subjects in Sampson and Laub's study "grew to young adulthood in a period of expanding economic opportunities during the 1950s and 1960s." Some also experienced positive life changes as a result of military experience, which made them eligible for numerous benefits offered by the G.I. Bill.

Sampson and Laub also note that marriage and employment did not have the same impact on everyone in their study because these experiences "only provide the possibility for change to occur" (Laub & Sampson 1993:318). At some point individuals who desist from crime must make a decision to change (E. Anderson 1999; Giordano et al. 2003; Juette & Berger 2008). Importantly, the faith and support that others had given them weighed heavily on their minds. Like many others, McCall (1994) was tempted to return to crime after being released from prison:

> One night . . . I stopped at a convenience store. . . . It was late and there was only one attendant. . . . I thought, I can take this place by myself. . . . I'd been doing that a lot lately. I'd enter stores, case them, and assess my chances of being able to pull off another [robbery]. . . . [That night] I sat there for a long while, struggling inside my head. . . . Then I thought about something . . . that I had . . . that most cats coming out of the joint did not: I had supportive parents. I thought about my mother and stepfather, who had suffered through . . . years of hell with me. . . . I thought about how hard they'd pulled for me since I'd gotten out. They gave me money. I had a place to lay my head. . . . They cared about me. . . . I couldn't let them down. (pp. 236–237)

Life-course research in criminology returns us to the tension between social structure and social action that is a central element of the sociological imagination (see Chapter 1). Individuals are influenced by external constraints but are at times capable of defying the odds. This capacity for per-

FURTHER EXPLORATION
Violently Acquired Spinal Cord Injury

Proportionally, African Americans have a higher rate of disability than other racial/ethnic groups in the United States, an experience that is correlated with greater personal and social risks of living in poverty, including inner-city violence, and with the general health and health-care disparities that exist in the country (Fujiura et al. 1998; Smedley et al. 2003). Moreover, homicide is the leading cause of death among black males ages 15 to 24; and violently acquired spinal cord injury, mainly from gun violence, is the second leading cause of spinal cord injury overall (following motor vehicle accidents) among inner-city residents (Hernandez 2005; Ostrander 2008).

Like people of all racial/ethnic groups with a newly acquired disability, black men face many challenges when learning how to adapt. However, Patrick Devlieger and Gary Albrecht (2000) found that black men were less likely than white men to identify with other people with disabilities or the disability rights movement. Among the men who acquired their spinal cord injuries from gang violence, identification with disability issues was more likely to occur among those who became alienated from unsupportive family and gang friends and who were immersed in a rehabilitation hospital environment that allowed them to adopt an alternative narrative of their lives that moved them beyond gang violence (Devlieger et al. 2007).

For some of these men, the experience of near death was viewed as a "wake-up call," a second chance to turn their lives around (Devlieger et al. 2007; Hernandez 2005). As Melvin Juette remarks, acquiring his disability was "both the worse and best thing that happened to him," because if he had not been shot, he would have "probably ended up in prison or been killed, like so many of [his] former gang associates," friends and enemies alike (Juette & Berger 2008:3). According to another young man: "I got buddies on death row. Buddies that are doing double life and a lot . . . that's dead and quite a few that's on [a] wheelchair. The one[s] in jail will tell you it ain't worth it. The ones in chairs . . . will tell you that it ain't worth it. If I didn't have this disability I [would] probably be dead or in jail doing some real time. It's like a bad thing and a good thing . . . like a blessing in disguise" (Devlieger et al. 2007:1953). Another man put it this way: "Me having this disability now makes me look different at life. I got to be productive. I got to do something that's positive. Anytime of the day I would like to represent not just this chair, but I want to represent everybody that has the disability. Let them know that there is other ways of doing things. Some people say that it took this bullet to wake you up. I tell them, yeah, it's true. I guess that maybe it slowed me down for a reason. Maybe I got a second look on life. I'm not dead. I don't need to go back to that life that I used to live" (p. 1954).

sonal agency or self-efficacy, however, does not emerge spontaneously. It is a capability, like language, that is nurtured through social experience and acquired in varying degrees of proficiency. McCall's ability to eventually steer a successful life course from prison to the *Washington Post* newsroom was in no small part dependent on early family and school experiences that he could fall back on. (Before succumbing to delinquency through peer influences, McCall had been an honor student with a penchant for spelling bees.) He did not create his life completely anew, but continually struggled to overcome social deficits that his involvement in crime had created (e.g., a prison record that limited employment opportunities).

People who desist from crime must overcome considerable adversity in their lives. Life-course research encourages us to reject static models of human behavior in favor of one that recognizes both stability and change in criminal conduct over time.

Summary

This chapter offered a review and assessment of microsociological explanations and policies that focus on how individuals are influenced by their social interactions with others. Under the rubric of symbolic interaction and social learning—the former concerned with the symbolic meaning of criminal action for individuals, and the latter with how individuals learn to favor or disfavor criminal conduct—we considered several approaches: differential association theory, social learning theory, techniques of neutralization, and labeling theory. Under the rubric of social control and the life course, we then considered social control theory, which is concerned with the nature of the social bonds between individuals and society that inhibit or facilitate criminal action, and with how these bonds may be attenuated or modified throughout the course of one's life.

5

Macrosocial Explanations of Crime

Having previously considered microsocial explanations of crime, we now turn to macrosocial approaches. As noted earlier, theories of this bent focus on the "big picture," on why certain groups of people living under particular circumstances commit more crime than other groups living under different conditions. Some of these theories also entail a critique of criminal law and the process of criminalization—that is, why some social harms or analogous social injuries (and the individuals who perpetrate them) are deemed relevant for social control and others are not (see Chapter 1). As such, in this chapter we focus on three general orientations: social disorganization theory, anomie-strain theory, and conflict theory.

Social Disorganization and the Social Ecology of Crime

In the late nineteenth century and early twentieth, influential theorists like Émile Durkheim were concerned with the transition of societies from rural and small-town life to life in the larger urban milieu. Social commentators in the United States characterized the former as consisting of close-knit, extended families and strong communities that were bonded by a spirit of volunteerism and a common religious faith that enabled adults to "keep a firm grip on the process of socializing the young" (Sykes & Cullen 1992:291). But as families immigrated to the United States or moved from rural areas to the cities, they often were isolated from their larger kinship group and enmeshed in a set of fleeting, impersonal neighborhood and workplace relationships. The families of most newcomers and others at the bottom of the class hierarchy were unable to reap the benefits of the new industrial economy and often had to endure the additional stress of overworked parents or prolonged unemployment. Immigrant families in particular, who were unfamiliar with the culture of the new world, had difficulty inculcating in the young the values and skills necessary to successfully compete. Hence the city became filled with criminals and delinquents and a host of unassimilated inhabitants.

To a large extent the contrast between the old and the new way of life was a caricature, a romanticization of the old that reflected a nostalgic view of days gone by. However, commentaries about this state of affairs, as theoretical accounts of crime, were part of an effort to supplant individualistic explanations (concerned with kinds of persons) with sociological explanations (concerned with kinds of places). Liberal social reformers, social workers, sociological academicians, and the like, adopted a paternalistic concern with the plight of city dwellers and hoped to use social science as a guide to the amelioration of social disadvantage (Schwendinger & Schwendinger 1974).

The Contribution of Shaw and McKay

It is in this context that Clifford Shaw and Henry McKay made the most significant contribution to what has been called **social disorganization theory** (Shaw & McKay 1942; Shaw et al. 1929). Shaw and McKay were part of a movement of sociologists at the University of Chicago who pioneered the use of ethnographic field methods to send researchers into the streets to observe and document what was "really happening" in society. They also worked in the tradition of cartographers like European social statistician Adolphe Quetelet (1796–1874), mapping the territorial or ecological distribution of crime and other social conditions. According to Shaw and McKay, the problem of crime was tied to the social ecology of communities that were socially disorganized. Their cartographic research indicated that crime and delinquency were highest in areas marked by concentrated poverty and unemployment, physical dilapidation of buildings, residential overcrowding, absence of homeownership, high residential mobility, influx of immigrant populations of diverse cultures, and lack of "constructive agencies intended to promote well-being and prevent maladjustment" (cited in Sykes & Cullen 1992:292). Importantly, Shaw and McKay did not view economic issues per se as the key to the problem:

> [Rather] children who grow up in these deteriorated and disorganized neighborhoods . . . are not subject to the same constructive and restraining influences that surround those in the more homogenous communities further removed from the industrial and commercial centers. These disorganized neighborhoods fail to provide a consistent set of cultural standards and a wholesome social life for the development of a stable and socially acceptable form of behavior in the child . . . [whose] most vital and intimate social contacts are often limited to the spontaneous and undirected neighborhood play groups and gangs whose activities and standards may vary widely from those of . . . parents and the larger social order. (p. 293)

Moreover, the traditions of these delinquent groups are self-sustaining, transmitted through successive generations. Youths "in these areas have contact not only with other delinquents who are their contemporaries but also with older offenders, who in turn had contact with delinquents preceding them, and so on back to the earliest history of the neighborhood" (Shaw & McKay 1942:168).

The Chicago Area Project. In 1934, Shaw established the Chicago Area Project (CAP), which has been described as "the first systematic challenge to the dominance of psychology and psychiatry in public and private programs for the prevention and treatment of . . . delinquency" (Schlossman et al. 1984:2). The CAP pioneered the practice of community-level approaches to delinquency prevention that used community organizers to help residents exercise more control over their youths and to facilitate cooperative activities among community groups for the solution of common problems. The underlying philosophy of the CAP was that only through the collective mobilization and active participation of the entire community was it possible to impact significantly on the problem of delinquency (Berger 2009b).

The CAP pioneered a number of activities that were later employed in other prevention programs, including the development of recreation and camping programs, youth clubs, and hobby and rap (discussion) groups. The goal of these activities was to provide youths with structured, supervised alternatives to crime; and they also served as springboards for bringing people together, counseling delinquent youths, and providing minimal employment for youth leaders. In addition, the CAP dispatched organizers into the community to provide "curbside counseling" for troubled youths and identify indigenous gang leaders who might be encouraged to commit themselves to the project's goals.

The CAP also interceded in school-related matters by helping to reform curricula, mainstream students who had been incorrectly placed in classes for deficient or incorrigible youths (or conversely, place students who required special treatment into appropriate programs), transfer students to schools with more suitable programs or personnel, and reinstate students who had been expelled for minor delinquencies. Criminal justice interventions involved diverting youths to appropriate community agencies, reforming jails and prisons, and assisting parolees as they returned to community life.

The CAP was not without its problems and critics. It often was difficult to get residents to cooperate and find common ground with other interest groups. Attempts to enlist the help of businesses in expanding employment opportunities for delinquent youths, for example, were not always successful. No effort was made to involve absentee landlords who owned the rental properties, who were only interested in speculative profits, not quality of housing. The project was also forced to rely heavily on the volunteer services of the Polish Catholic Church, which was accused of using the recreational programs to proselytize youths. One of the strongest critics was Saul Alinsky, the CAP's most well-known organizer, who faulted the CAP for its inability to secure needed economic reforms. These, he believed, required more confrontational tactics to force concessions from the political and economic elites of the city. Alinsky was acutely aware of the difficulty of sustaining interest in the project when resources necessary to achieve goals came from sources outside of the residents' control. By the late 1950s the CAP was absorbed by the Illinois Division of Youth Services and transformed into yet another bureaucratic organization that usurped local initiative. Nevertheless, it continues to serve as a prime example of the possibilities of engaging communities in problem-solving prevention efforts that do more than simply respond to crime on a one-to-one, after-the-fact basis (Berger 2009b; Krisberg 2005; Schlossman et al. 1984).

The Decline and Revival of Social Disorganization Theory

To criminologists of a liberal political persuasion, the environmental focus of social disorganization theory was an improvement over individualistic approaches to crime prevention and control. By the 1960s, however, it fell into disfavor among liberals, who began looking to other theories for insight into the crime problem in the United States. Critics of social disorganization theory asked: Were not kinds-of-places theories simply the sociological analogue of kinds-of-persons theories, with entire communities now viewed as pathological, urban areas now seen as inherently criminogenic, and social disorganization now held responsible for breeding personal disorganization? Like most individualistic explanations, the focus was exclusively on lower-class crime (particularly among immigrant groups), and communities were blamed for a problem that was not entirely of their own making. It was as if these communities existed in a vacuum, and capitalist investment decisions leading to uneven economic development did not exist (see Chapter 6). It was as if the poor had power comparable to the wealthy to resist economic and social policies that were not in their interest and that might even increase crime (Balkan et al. 1980).

More recent work in the social disorganization tradition has attempted to respond to these criticisms. Researchers have shown how the **deindustrialization** of the economy—the shift from manufacturing to low-paid service work—and the flight of the middle class (both whites and blacks) from the inner city to the suburbs, have depleted the former of valuable economic and social resources and left behind an even greater concentration of what William Julius Wilson (1987) calls the "truly disadvantaged," or an **urban underclass**. Residential mobility and high population turnover have also weakened informal neighborhood controls and decreased the number of residents who have a long-term stake in the community and who are willing to intercede on each other's behalf to prevent victimization from crime (Bursik & Grasmick 1993). Robert Sampson and colleagues describe this in terms of the phenomenon of **collective efficacy**, or its lack thereof: the social cohesion among neighbors that affects "their willingness to intervene on behalf of the common good" (1997:916).

In support of Shaw and McKay's propositions about the noneconomic correlates of crime, Sampson and W. Byron Groves (1989) found that the effect of economic disadvantage on crime was due to weak local friendship networks, low participation in voluntary organizations, and low supervision of teenage peer groups. They also found that crime was associated with the disproportionate number of (primarily female-headed) single-parent families in these communities, this for the most part a consequence of male joblessness (Sampson 1987; Wilson 1987). Similarly, Leann Tigges and colleagues (1998) found that poor blacks were more likely than nonpoor blacks and nonpoor whites to be socially isolated; that is, they were less likely to live with another adult, less likely to have even one person outside of their household with whom they could discuss important matters, and less likely to be embedded in the types of social networks that provide access to social services and jobs.

Moreover, many poor women raising children alone in socially disorganized neighborhoods lack the parenting skills necessary to effectively discipline their children (Anderson 1999; Williams & Kornblum 1985). Often they have not had adequate parental models and may still be teenagers themselves. Some have succumbed to drugs or become entrapped in abusive relationships. For poor inner-city mothers faced with limited opportunities, insufficient social services, and unsafe housing, life is a constant battle against forces threatening to engulf them. It is a daily struggle to maintain dignity, to keep one's head above the rising tide of hopelessness and despair. As one mother waiting for her son to return safely home from school said: "Mostly, you try to keep them away from the drugs and violence, but it's hard. I tell my oldest boy I don't want him hanging out with the boys who are getting in trouble, and he says, 'Aw, mama, ain't nobody else for me to be with'" (Applebome 1991:1).

Social disorganization theory assumes that frequent interaction among residents helps generate the informal community controls that reduce crime (Bellair 1997). There are conflicting effects of individuals' embeddedness in social relationships, however. Eleanor Miller (1986) found, for example, that females' involvement in **extended domestic networks**—households composed of immediate kin (parents, siblings), extended kin (grandparents, uncles, aunts, cousins), and nonkin (friends, lovers)—was a primary means by which they were recruited into "deviant networks" of street prostitution and hustling. And Mary Pattillo (1998) found that involvement of gang members and drug dealers in networks of law-abiding neighbors and kin sometimes impeded efforts to rid the neighborhood of its criminal elements.

As one resident said, "I didn't wanna give this young man's name [to the police] because his mama is such a sweet lady" (p. 763).

Routine Activities and Crime

In the late 1970s, Lawrence Cohen and Marcus Felson (1979) advanced a **routine activities theory** of crime that moved ecological thinking in a dramatically different direction from traditional social disorganization theory. Cohen and Felson argued that it was possible, theoretically speaking, to bypass explanations of criminal motivation and simply assume there will always be a sufficient number of individuals willing to take advantage of the opportunity to commit crime. What criminologists needed to ascertain were the immediate situational circumstances that enabled such individuals to translate their criminal inclinations into action. The probability of crime increased, they observed, when there was a convergence in physical space and time of three basic elements: *motivated offenders, suitable targets,* and the *absence of capable guardians.*

According to Cohen and Felson, historical changes in the routine patterns of everyday life—such as the dispersion of work and leisure activities away from the home, the increased number of people who have become occupationally and residentially mobile, and the greater participation of women in the work force—have dissolved protective kinship and friendship networks, leaving homes unguarded and individuals vulnerable in the public sphere. In addition, the ever-expanding production of commodities has increased the abundance and variety of goods available to be stolen. Before the advent of the automobile, for example, who could have imagined the crime of motor vehicle theft or car-jacking? Before the mass marketing of athletic clothing and mobile technology, who could have imagined being mugged for a Starter jacket or iPod?

Like social disorganization theory, routine activities theory focuses on the kinds of places that are associated with increased risk of crime. Research indicates that crime is not uniformly distributed across physical space and time. A disproportionate amount occurs along a relatively small number of streets or "hot spots," including areas in or around convenience and large discount department stores, high schools, public housing projects and highrise buildings with easily accessible corridors and poorly monitored areas, drinking establishments, parties, and other places where people hang out in unstructured activities. People whose daily routines or lifestyles take them to these places, especially late at night, are more likely to be victimized by crime. Those who are themselves involved in crime are especially likely to be victimized (Miethe & McCorkle 1998; Sherman et al. 1989).

One criticism of routine activities theory focuses on its inability to adequately account for the victimization of women. Cohen and Felson (1979) argued, for instance, that circumstances that take women outside of the home (such as employment or school) or reduce available guardians (such as being single) increase women's risk of rape and other predatory offenses. But as we previously noted, women (and girls) are often victimized by persons they know, frequently in the privacy of their own homes. While women are vulnerable in both the public and the private spheres of life, the problems of domestic battery, nonstranger rape, intrafamilial sexual abuse, and the like, are not adequately explained by routine activities theory. In fact, Herman and Julia Schwendinger argue that efforts to reduce female dependency on male guardianship may actually decrease sexual violence against women by empowering women "to dictate the basic terms on which men must relate to them" (1983:217). In an analysis of national victimization data from 1980 to 2004, Min Xie and colleagues (2012) found partial support for this hypothesis; that is, *absolute* increases in women's labor force participation, income, and education were associated with decreases in intimate-partner violence. At the same time, they also found evidence of a countervailing "backlash" effect associated with men's resentment of women's gains *relative* to men; that is, reduction in gender inequality, as opposed to women's advancement per se, was associated with more intimate-partner violence.

The issue of domestic violence aside, routine activities theory has also been useful for thinking about the problem of gang rape. Nathan McCall (1994) describes how he and his cohorts would prey on vulnerable adolescent females who were lured under false pretenses to isolated places and then raped by a group of males hiding in wait. Although females attracted to the "bad boy" image may be especially susceptible to this type of manipulation (Gaines 1993; Sikes 1997), these kinds of crimes are not perpetrated only by adolescent street gangs or youths from socially disadvantaged communities. They are a consequence of membership in male peer groups who condone sexual aggression against women. Research suggests, for example, that fraternity gang rapes by white middle-class college students are not uncommon. College campuses bring together in physical space and time the recipe for crime that is predicted by routine activities theory: a group of motivated offenders (male-bonded sexually predatory males) and suitable targets (sorority or female partygoers) who are participating in particular activities (frequent partying or heavy drinking) in the absence of capable guardians (no parental or school supervisors) (Martin & Hummer 1989; Sanday 2007; Schwartz et al. 2001).

Situational crime prevention. In contrast to conventional crime prevention strategies like the CAP that are aimed at changing the behavior of offenders, routine activities theory is directed at modifying the behavior of potential victims. Programs of this nature have been variously called victim prevention, opportunity reduction, target hardening, and **situational crime prevention**. Some of these programs entail measures that can be taken by individuals and businesses, and some involve environmental modification

FURTHER EXPLORATION
Computer Crime

Nowadays, with the advent of computer technology, it is not always necessary for motivated offenders to meet suitable targets in physical space and time in the way hypothesized by routine activities theory, and computer users are often left without capable guardians to protect them. For example, **computer hackers**—individuals who gain access to an individual's or organization's computer system without authorization—can commit their crimes from afar and implant malicious **computer viruses** that cause abundant damage. Viruses are sets of instruction that spread from one system to another and cause a computer to perform unauthorized operations, such as erasing files, changing data, or forcing the system to crash. Hackers have forced businesses to shut down and have caused millions of dollars in damage. They have broken into military computers and stolen sensitive information about weapons systems and battle simulations. Copyright infringement, through the illegal downloading of software, music, and business information, abounds. Computerized power grid systems and electronic voting machines are also susceptible to hacking. Indeed, the country's entire digital infrastructure is increasingly vulnerable to cyber attacks. And this threat comes not just from conventional hackers but from terrorists and agents working for foreign governments (Clarke & Knake 2010; Goldsmith 2010; Rosoff et al. 2007).

Two types of cyberfraud—**identity theft** and **phishing**—have become increasingly common, and some observers are concerned about a growing professional class of **organized online criminals** who operate a cyperspace underground economy that reaps tens of billions of dollars each year. Identity theft involves cybercriminals who access databases that contain information on individuals (e.g., social security numbers, credit reports, ATM and charge accounts) and then use this information for fraud and theft. Corporations that sell private customer information to other companies make the public even more vulnerable to this type of crime (Blitstein 2007; Court 2003; Rosoff et al. 2007).

Phishing refers to cybercriminals who send unsolicited e-mails to Internet users to try to lure unsuspecting "fish" into providing them with passwords and financial data (the "ph" is probably a tribute of sorts to the first generation of "phone freaks" who hacked into telephone company systems of old). The unsolicited e-mails give the appearance of being a legitimate business, typically a business that the fish has used, such as a bank, credit card company, eBay, PayPal, or Amazon.com. The e-mail instructs the recipients to "update" or "validate" their account information in order to keep their accounts active. If the user accepts the bait, a link directs them to a website that imitates the legitimate site, complete with matching logos, colors, and design. If the user submits the information, the data can be used to commit identity theft. These phishing e-mails are sent out in massive quantities (spam), so even if only a small proportion of recipients respond, large amounts of money can be made (Rosoff et al. 2007).

In addition, financial securities fraud has migrated from the "boiler rooms" of the past—where con artists phone volumes of unsuspecting investors—to the Internet. Phony financial advisers and brokers, sometimes using Internet bulletin boards and chat rooms, try to lure the gullible into making fraudulent investments. Some operate "pump and dump" schemes whereby they post fabricated messages about a major development in a small company, hoping to drive up the value of a stock. Then they sell their shares at the peak of the run-up, leaving "other stockholders with near-worthless paper when the stock inevitably plummets" (Rosoff et al. 2007:283).

of entire communities. For example, people can install locks, alarms, window bars, and surveillance cameras in their homes and businesses, and they can erect fences and gates around them. They can put identifying marks on property, hire security guards or private patrols, and acquire large dogs, mace sprays, or guns for protection. They can take courses in karate or other forms of personal defense. Homes, buildings, apartment complexes, and even entire communities can be architecturally designed to ensure that walkways and other public areas are highly visible and well-lighted. Access to particular areas can be reserved for particular legitimate users and prohibited for others. Residents can organize themselves (often with assistance from police) into neighborhood- or community-watch groups and even citizen patrols (Clarke 1992; Newman 1972; Welsh & Farrington 2004).

A potential side effect of situational crime prevention is the problem of **crime displacement**, whereby motivated offenders simply decide to commit their crimes elsewhere or at other times. Research on displacement is mixed, but does suggest that it is not an inevitable consequence of such measures (Weisburd et al. 2006; Welsh & Farrington 1999). Situational crime prevention can be costly, however, providing benefits primarily for those who can afford it, or for those who live in communities already less troubled by crime. Evaluation studies indicate that such prevention strategies have been oversold as a "standalone" approach, and best results have been obtained when these strategies are combined with offender-oriented prevention strategies (Berger 2009b; Rosenbaum 1988).

Crime and the American Dream: Anomie-Strain Theory

In general, ecological theories attribute causal significance to the physical and spatial features of the urban environment. Social disorganization theory in particular views crime as a maladaptive response to urbanization. But the theory's focus on communities overlooks a broader critique of life in the United States, one that locates the source of the crime problem in the organization of society as a whole. This critique was first advanced by Robert Merton (1938) in his seminal article "Social Structure and Anomie."

The Contribution of Robert Merton

Merton drew upon Durkheim's (1897) earlier work on **anomie**, a term the French sociologist used to refer to a state of normlessness whereby individuals were isolated, cut adrift, and lacking in a common bond that brought them into sympathetic relationships with others. Merton also drew upon the theoretical tradition of **functionalism**, derived from Durkheim (1893) as well, which views society as an organism consisting of a number of interdependent parts that contribute to the overall functioning of the whole. In a functionally integrated society, social institutions such as the family, schools, economy, and government help satisfy basic human needs and socialize individuals to adopt their appropriate roles in society. In a dysfunctional society, these institutions break down or are out of balance, straining the relationship between individuals and society and weakening their commitment to the normative legal order (Parsons 1951).

Merton, however, gave Durkheimian theory a peculiarly American twist by arguing that anomie and societal dysfunction were not constituted by normlessness per se but by a disjuncture or lack of integration between *cultural goals* (or values) and *institutionalized means* (or opportunities). Merton believed that the predominant cultural goal of American society was the dream of financial success and bountiful material consumption. People who lacked access to the legitimate means to turn this dream into reality were structured into a relationship of **strain** with society and experienced a sense of frustration, anger, and injustice about their lot in life. In this sense, crime is endemic to a social system that dangles the enticements of materialism before everyone without being able to deliver the goods to all.

Given the pervasive social inequality in the United States, **anomie-strain theory** postulates that the greatest pressures for criminal conduct reside in the lower classes and among disadvantaged racial and ethnic minority groups. Families from these backgrounds often lack the economic and social resources to prepare their children to do well in school, provide them with enriching cultural experiences, bail them out if they get in trouble with the law, finance their college education, and set them up in businesses or professions. Minorities also face the additional problems of discrimination and lack of familiarity with the culture of white middle-class institutional environments. Nevertheless, according to anomie-strain theory, those who turn to crime are not, at heart, different from the rest of us. They share the values we all hold. They are not predisposed to crime; if given the chance, they would prefer to take a more conventional path to success (Williams & Kornblum 1985).

It is important to emphasize the **relative deprivation** component of Merton's insight. It is not poverty per se that is at issue, but *poverty amid affluence* in a society that values particular goals. Hence many studies have found that the level of economic inequality (the distribution of income or wealth) is more strongly related to crime than the level of absolute poverty (the amount of income or wealth) (Blau & Blau 1982; LaFree 1998; Messner 1989; Sampson 1985). Indeed, there are societies around the world that suffer even worse poverty than exists in the United States, but without comparable levels of crime, in part because they have not (yet?) acquired the cultural emphasis on money as the measure of all success, the most important currency of achievement.

In this scheme of things, all else is devalued or set aside. Many of us, for instance, value education mainly as a vehicle for occupational attainment and economic rewards, and we do not hold the acquisition of knowledge or its role in promoting good citizenship in high regard. At the same time, the predominance of the economy as the central element of society makes it difficult for other institutions such as the family to exert positive social controls. Indeed, American society is so "dominated by the schedules, rewards, and penalties of the labor market" that parents are left worrying about finding enough time for their families. Indeed, most people feel fortunate if the "economy has found time for them" (Messner & Rosenfeld 2001:72).

Adaptations to Strain

Merton postulated that individuals adapt to structurally induced anomie or strain in a variety of ways. Figure 5.1 presents his typology of five general modes of adaptation: conformity, ritualism, innovation, retreatism, and rebellion. These adaptations should be conceptualized as behavioral options that emerge out of the particular mix of legitimate and illegitimate opportunities available to individuals differentially situated in the social structure. Often, people develop out-group solutions to common problems, such as through involvement in urban street gangs or organized crime (Cloward & Ohlin 1960; Cohen 1955).

Merton actually had little to say about why some individuals pursue one adaptation or another. That, he acknowledged, would require consideration of individualistic or microsociological criteria (Agnew et al. 2002). He also didn't consider crime to be an automatic consequence of strain. People could pursue noncriminal **conformity** not only through financial success but also by moderating their expectations at particular points in their lives to exact a more realistic fit between goals and means, for instance by delaying short-term gratification to pursue long-term future rewards. **Ritualism**, on the other hand, is a noncriminal adaptation that involves a more permanent scaling down or relinquishment of unattainable success goals and an overemphasis on the institutionalized means in and of themselves (e.g., the bureaucrat who always follows the rules, however irrational they may seem). The ritualist response may entail resigning oneself to working in a dead-end job or to just getting by to make ends meet.

Figure 5.1 Merton's Typology of Modes of Adaptation to Strain

Modes of Adaptation	Cultural Goals	Institutionalized Means
Conformity	+	+
Ritualism	−	+
Innovation	+	−
Retreatism	−	−
Rebellion	±	±

Note: + indicates acceptance; − indicates rejection; ± indicates rejection and substitution.

Innovation in Merton's scheme is arguably the most prevalent criminal adaptation to strain. Innovation occurs when people continue to embrace financial success goals but pursue them through illegitimate means. Such individuals are following the cultural ethos of "winning at all costs" or "anything goes" (Derber 1996). The predominance of property crimes in official statistics is but one indication that innovation is the criminal adaptation of choice. Innovation is also found in the experience of disadvantaged ethnic groups that have used organized crime as a vehicle for upward social mobility and a shortcut to the American dream. As Al Capone once said: "Don't get the idea that I'm one of those goddamn radicals . . . that I'm knocking the American system. . . . Capitalism . . . gives to each and every one of us a great opportunity, if we only seize it with both hands and make the most of it" (quoted in Cockburn 1967:118–119).

Although anomie-strain theory has focused on lower-class criminality, Merton (1968) acknowledged white-collar innovation as well. Take, for example, the nineteenth-century capitalist "robber barons," as they were called, who justified their unethical actions as the legitimate pursuit of property and wealth. As Gus Tyler notes:

> Land grants, covering the acreage of full states, were gained by bribery of colonial legislators and governors. Original accumulations of capital were amassed in tripartite deals among pirates, governors, and brokers. Fur fortunes were piled up alongside the drunk and dead bodies of . . . Indians. Small settlers were driven from their lands or turned into tenants by big ranchers employing rustlers, guns, outlaws—and the law. In the great railroad and shipping wars, enterprising capitalists used extortion, blackmail, violence, bribery, and private armies with muskets and cannons to wreck a competitor and to become the sole boss of a trade. (1967:44–45)

More generally, and up to this very day, corporate innovators respond to pressures of competition, unpredictable economic markets, and government regulatory controls by adapting illegal means to meet the "bottom line," achieve a competitive edge, or quite simply, make as much money as possible (Friedrichs 2007; Passas 1990).

Not all economic crimes, however, are committed for financial success goals. Many are done for the challenge or thrills, out of peer pressure, or to "keep the party going" (Hagan et al. 1998; Jacobs & Wright 1999). Merton recognized that the disjuncture between cultural goals and institutionalized means could produce strain regardless of the nature of the particular goal. Thus David Greenberg (1977) observed that much male delinquency is not a strategy for long-term economic gain but an attempt to satisfy the immediate concerns of adolescence—for example, acquiring a masculine self-image (e.g., through sexual conquests and acts of defiance, including violence) and maintaining an adolescent lifestyle (e.g., purchasing the latest technological devices, fashionable clothes, cigarettes/alcohol/drugs, concert tickets, cars).

Albert Cohen (1955) was one of the first to point out that a major source of strain for youths is not the job market per se but an educational system that was ostensibly designed to prepare them for economic success. Cohen argued that lower-class youths are deprived of the preschool cultural resources available to higher-class youths (e.g., books, educational toys, educated parents) that could help socialize them for school achievement, yet teachers judge them by the same standards as applied to their more

---

FURTHER EXPLORATION
Ethnic Succession in Organized Crime

Since the middle of the nineteenth century, organized crime has provided an illegitimate opportunity structure for disadvantaged immigrant groups seeking a short-term route to the American dream. The Irish were perhaps the first ethnic group to make the successful transition from urban gangs to organized crime, using their muscle to ensure electoral victories for local politicians, who in turn offered criminals protection for their illegal enterprises. By the end of the nineteenth century, Eastern-European Jewish immigrants started to challenge Irish dominance in organized crime, and during the alcohol Prohibition era of the 1920s the Italians began to make their mark (Abadinsky 2007).

Italian-American organized crime benefited from the established traditions of European Mafia groups. In nineteenth-century Sicily, the Mafia (which in Arabic means "place of refuge") constituted a nongovernmental system of organized power that operated through a network of "gangs" or "families." Mafioso served as middlemen or mediators between the Italian elite and the peasantry—delivering votes, arbitrating disputes, and offering protection in exchange for remuneration or immunity to do as they pleased. Such men were respected for their loyalty to family and kin and for the ability to maintain their authority, even if that required the use of violence (Abadinsky 2007).

In the United States, each new wave of immigration brought forth new ethnic groups who imitated as well as fought with those who came before them. Intergroup competition was lessened somewhat by an expanding US economy, which generated more legitimate opportunities for the offspring of earlier arrivals, thus reducing the group's involvement in organized crime. This pattern of entering into and exiting out of organized crime has been dubbed **ethnic succession in organized crime** (Abadinsky 2007).

Despite the Italian-American dominance, which lasted from the Prohibition era to the 1970s, non-Italians made substantial contributions. Meyer Lansky, for example, a man of Polish-Jewish descent, played a major role during Prohibition and in the post-Prohibition development of the heroin trade and the casino-hotel industry. And Chinese groups have operated in US urban communities with significant Chinese populations since the beginning of the twentieth century (Abadinsky 2007).

continues

continued

Some time ago, Frank Hagan observed that the Italian Mafia in the United States, also known as La Cosa Nostra ("this thing of ours"), consisted of a "dwindling empire with . . . remaining strongholds" in just a few areas of the country (1998:400). It had lost control of the heroin market and had become a marginal player in the cocaine trade. The federal government had successfully prosecuted a number of key leaders and had exerted greater supervisory authority over the distribution of Teamsters Union pension funds that the Mafia once controlled and used to finance some of its operations. Members facing prison terms no longer observed the traditional "code of silence," trading concessions from the government (including access to witness-protection programs) for information about the criminal activities of others. Hence the solidarity once considered central to the Mafia's successful reign was crumbling. Currently, other prominent groups involved in organized crime include black, Latino, Asian, and Russian organizations, as well as white outlaw motorcycle gangs (Abadinsky 2007; Reuter 1995).

privileged peers. Hence lower-class youths are more likely to experience the strain of school failure, lose their stake in conformity, and engage in delinquency. Research suggests, however, that school failure is associated with delinquency among youths of all social classes, and that low-achieving, middle-class youths may even be more delinquent than their lower-class counterparts (Agnew 2001; Maguin & Loeber 1996; Wright et al. 1999).

Greenberg (1977) noted that youths' experience of school strain often derives from the rules and regimentation of the school itself, the boredom and perception that education is a waste of time, and the denial of adolescents' autonomy at a point in life when they are trying to establish their independence. Some students view school as a hostile territory and express resentment directly through vandalism of school property and even assaults against teachers. Indeed, much juvenile crime is committed on school grounds and involves crime against other students (including what is nowadays called bullying). Proximity to high schools is also related to higher crime rates in adjacent residential areas (Agnew 2001; Lawrence 1998; Roncek & Faggiani 1985).

In addition to innovation, Merton described two other deviant (often criminal) adaptations to strain: retreatism and rebellion. **Retreatism** involves withdrawing altogether from the pursuit of legitimate success goals, whether through legal or illegal means. Retreatists are individuals who have essentially dropped out of society and adopted escapist lifestyles, sometimes fueled by alcoholism and drug addiction. Retreatists may also be homeless or suffer from mental disorders: "They are in society but not of it. . . . [They] piece out an existence by eating little, sleeping a lot, and abandoning the effort to create patterns of daily life they can respect. . . . Some finally succeed in annihilating the world by killing themselves" (Merton 1964:219). This is how Kenny Hall remembers his addiction to drugs:

> There was no participation in this thing that we call life. . . . I woke up, I got my drugs, and I went to sleep. . . . I was sleeping in basements. . . . I was sleeping on rooftops. . . . I didn't want to be seen during the daylight hours . . . [so] I would catch the [subway] . . . and . . . just ride it all day long. . . . I felt that ashamed about myself. . . . I would come out at night when the sun went down. . . . I would walk on the side of the building in the shadows where no one could see me. . . . I would do what I had to do to satisfy my addiction. . . . When the sun would come up, I would go back underground again. (Moyers 1991)

Similarly, Margaret, a drug addict and prostitute, observes: "I think using drugs is like committing suicide. Only you doing it slower. . . . Instead of taking a gun and blowing your brains out. . . . It might take you a lotta years, but eventually it's gonna kill you. If it don't kill you, it's gonna lame you or something" (Pettiway 1997:38, 50).

The last of Merton's adaptive types is **rebellion**, the rejection of legitimate goals and means and the substitution of new ones. Cohen, for instance, characterized the delinquent adaptation as largely "nonutilitarian, malicious, and negativistic" (1955:25). Delinquent boys "not only reject the dominant values system, but do so with a vengeance. They 'stand it on its head' . . . exalt its opposition . . . engage in malicious, spiteful, 'ornery' behavior of all sorts to demonstrate not only to others, but to themselves . . . their contempt for the game they have rejected" (1966:66).

In his book *Monster,* Sanyika Shakur (1993) describes the nonutilitarian nature of gang violence in the inner city, where groups fight over symbolic possession of "turf" that none of the combatants own. As he says of his years with the Eight Tray (83rd Street) Crips: "I don't own a brick on 83rd. . . . I don't own a brick in this country. . . . You ain't fighting for nothing" ("Eight Tray Gangster" 1993). Later in life, however, Shakur strove for a different kind of rebellion. "Little did I know," he writes, "that I had been resisting all my life. By not being a good black American I was resisting. But my resistance was retarded because it had no political objective" (Shakur 1993:330). In prison, Shakur was exposed to the political ideology of the revolutionary New Afrikan Independence Movement, which has as one of its objectives the securing of separate land (even separate states) for African-American people. "My personal belief is that separation is the solution. . . . This country's . . . experiment of multiculturalism has failed. Perhaps it was never designed to work" (p. 332).

Shakur came to this conclusion in prison after being exposed to the ideas of Malcolm X, a man who had undergone a transformation in prison from street hustler to political activist with the Nation of Islam. Shakur was impressed with Malcolm's fiery rhetoric: "Out of frustration and hopeless-ness our young people have reached the point of no return. We no longer endorse patience and turning the other cheek. We assert the right of self-defense by whatever means necessary, and reserve the right of maximum retaliation against our racist oppressors, no matter what the odds against us are" (quoted in Shakur 1993:214). Quite clearly, Shakur's goals are contro-versial and unrealistic. More than a few African Americans might sympa-thize with the spirit of his sentiments, however.

A Decade of Liberal Reform

One of the most dynamic eras in the annals of crime prevention history was the 1960s, when federal programs predicated on anomie-strain theory pro-vided the rationale for liberal policies aimed at improving the economic and educational opportunities of low-income and minority youths. Along with the Chicago Area Project, they remain the prototypes for contemporary offender-oriented prevention efforts. The programs of the 1960s, which were part of President Lyndon Johnson's War on Poverty, had two basic thrusts: (1) opportunity programs that were administered by social service professionals, and (2) comprehensive community action projects that mobi-lized residents to engage in local collective action (Berger 2009b).

Opportunity programs. The Economic Opportunity Act of 1964 authorized involvement of the US Department of Labor in delinquency prevention through the Neighborhood Youth Corps and the Job Corps. The Neighbor-hood Youth Corps included both summer and year-round training and work programs for youths, some of whom were enrolled in school and some of whom were not. The Job Corps placed low-income urban youths in residen-tial centers for job training and had both an urban and a rural component. The urban centers trained youths in skilled trades such as auto mechanics and carpentry. The rural centers often emphasized forest-conservation skills but provided training for many other jobs as well (Quadagno & Fobes 1995).

In addition, the Department of Health, Education, and Welfare (HEW) and the Department of Housing and Urban Development (HUD) established a broad range of prevention initiatives. HEW's Upward Bound program tried to facilitate educational achievement by increasing the motivation and skills of disadvantaged youths. HUD's Model Cities program provided inner-city youths with college prep courses, college scholarships, and job placements, as well as direct social services such as counseling, drug abuse treatment, assistance to unwed mothers, and recreation and teen clubs.

Although the aim of these programs was to provide equal opportunity for individuals to compete in the US economy, they did not always fulfill their promise. At times they merely offered job training without a concomi-tant guarantee of employment upon completion of the program. African-American trainees even experienced discrimination from some of the skilled trade unions (Quadagno & Fobes 1995). Evaluation studies measuring the effects of these efforts on the long-term labor status of youths and on rates of delinquency were mixed and often unimpressive (Currie 1985; McGahey 1986). Rather than reaching hard-core delinquent or at-risk youths, the programs tended to help those who were more motivated and upwardly mobile to begin with. They were important in strengthening the black middle class, but left behind an intransigent underclass that remains living in urban squalor. Moreover, the success of some only increased the sense of relative deprivation and strain among those who remained behind (LaFree & Drass 1996; Wilson 1987).

Comprehensive community action projects. These projects began in 1961 under the auspices of John Kennedy's President's Committee on Juvenile Delinquency and Youth Crime and continued under the Office of Economic Opportunity. These were large-scale, multidimensional programs established under federal control but rooted in local communities. In many respects, these programs were direct descendants of the earlier Chicago Area Project. But in the 1960s, New York City's Mobilization for Youth project was the model for such efforts (Berger 2009b).

Mobilization for Youth aimed to achieve the following objectives: (1) create job opportunities through work subsidies, vocational training, and career guidance; (2) improve educational opportunities through teacher training, development of relevant curricula and teaching methods, increased contacts between parents and schools, and preschool programs; (3) provide services to youths and families, including recreational opportunities, rap (discussion) groups, child care, and counseling; and (4) establish neighborhood councils and mobilize low-income residents for social action to redress grievances in areas such as housing, health care, and employment discrimination.

Inspired by Mobilization for Youth, the federal government offered funding and planning assistance to other communities to set up their own comprehensive community action projects, which expanded to more than a thousand by the mid-1960s. However, the social action component of these projects led to withdrawal of political support. In the Mobilization for Youth project, for instance, residents were encouraged to participate in strikes, protests, and confrontations with public officials. The intended goal was to make political leaders aware that the community was an organized interest group that demanded their attention.

Mobilization for Youth was thus a classic case of "biting the hand that feeds you," and it was not long before it was derailed by accusations that it had communist sympathies and had misused government funds. Community organizers favoring social action strategies were purged and funds were curtailed. The remaining comprehensive community action projects were transformed into predominately counseling and treatment programs, or programs stressing vocational, educational, or legal assistance.

It is doubtful there was ever full political support for the dramatic social changes attempted in the name of anomie-strain theory. When put into practice, these programs probably exceeded what Merton himself might have imagined. Nevertheless, many advocates of social change continue to believe that the programs of the 1960s contained the essential ingredients of effective crime prevention that are needed to this very day.

Conflict Theory

In Chapter 1, we contrasted the consensus and conflict perspectives on crime. The former assumes that there is general agreement in society about which behaviors should be legal and which should be illegal. The latter, which is part of a broader theoretical tradition called **conflict theory**, assumes that definitions of crime and the enforcement of criminal laws often lack societal consensus and are subject to the assertion of economic and political power and the struggles of competing groups in society. Issues of social inequality and the ways in which law-violating behavior emerges from social conflict are part of this framework as well. Additionally, some of the approaches that are part of the domain of conflict theory are also embedded in the tradition of critical criminology, as also discussed earlier. Critical criminology, essentially an offshoot of conflict theory, rejects a legalistic definition of crime in favor of one that defines it as a violation of human rights or as analogous social injury, and it is concerned with how structures of inequality impact the criminalization process in ways that advance the interests of societal elites at the expense of those who are disadvantaged. In the following sections on conflict theory, we discuss three variations of this viewpoint: group conflict, feminist criminology, and peacemaking criminology.

Group Conflict

We begin our discussion of group conflict with a consideration of class conflict. We then turn to issues related to racial conflict and culture conflict.

Class conflict. Class conflict theory in criminology has its roots in the work of nineteenth-century German social theorists Karl Marx (1818–1883) and Frederich Engels (1820–1895), who advanced a critique of capitalism and the class conflict they thought was endemic to this system. According to Marx and Engels, **capitalism** is an economic system based on private rather than public ownership of the determinative means of production (factories, technology, raw materials), one that pits *owners* (and their managers), who wish to lower labor and production costs, against *workers*, who wish to improve wages and working conditions. **Class conflict** between capitalists and workers is the term they used to characterize the ways in which each side attempts to defend and advance their competing interests.

Richard Quinney (1977) is the twentieth-century criminologist most known for advancing this framework as a general theory of crime in capitalist society. According to Quinney, crime occurs in all classes of society, but criminal law is unevenly enforced and most often directed against subordinate groups. Corporations commit crimes of **economic domination** that include financial crimes such as price-fixing and corporate fraud, and physically harmful crimes related to defective consumer products, dangerous working conditions, and environmental pollution. Workers, in turn, commit **crimes of accommodation and resistance** that include stealing from employers, sabotaging the production process (such as not tightening bolts on the assembly line), participating in illegal strikes, and joining dissident political groups. In addition, governments commit **crimes of repression** that include police brutality, illegal domestic surveillance, and agent provocateuring, the latter of which involves deployment of undercover officers who infiltrate nonviolent protest groups and agitate for the adoption of violent measures that are used to justify legal crackdowns against them (Marx 1981), as well as the overthrow of foreign governments and assassination of foreign leaders who oppose capitalist interests (see Chapters 9 and 10).

One of the central characteristics of a capitalist economic system is the creation of a **surplus population** of potential laborers who are more or less permanently unemployed. This population provides a large pool of workers whom employers can hire when needed (such as when workers strike or are unwilling to do menial work) and who keep wages down by increasing competition for jobs. Individuals in this group are the most vulnerable to involvement in **street crime**—predatory theft, violence, drug use and trafficking, and gang criminality, which are the primary concern of the criminal justice system (see Chapter 6). Although the surplus population is a volatile and potentially rebellious group, street crime for the most part only exacerbates the plight of the disadvantaged, as it is primarily committed not against the affluent but against the most vulnerable people in society (Balkan et al. 1980; Quinney 1977). At the same time, class conflict theory posits that the criminal justice system is used in times of high unemployment to absorb and control the surplus supply of laborers, a proposition that is supported by research that finds that prison admissions in the United States increase during times of higher unemployment and growth of the urban underclass (Chiricos & Delone 1992; Hochstetler & Shover 1997; Michalowski & Carlson 1999).

Nevertheless, the emphasis of class conflict theorists on the criminogenic qualities of capitalism should not be misconstrued as an assertion that *only* capitalism causes crime. While corporate crime does not exist in communist countries, for instance, government corruption and illegal markets in monetary currencies and other commodities are common. There does appear to be less street crime in these societies than in capitalist societies like the United States, but this is more likely due to greater government repression than to success at satisfying economic needs. Nevertheless, as Ronald Akers and Christine Sellers (2009:251) ask, "If there is something inherently criminogenic" about capitalism, why do different capitalist nations have dissimilar rates of crime? Clearly, sweeping generalizations about capitalism fail to account for such variations.

Racial conflict. Another type of social conflict occurs when racial minority groups struggle to overcome their oppression. In the United States, for example, the struggle for civil rights for African Americans has been marked by both nonviolent and violent forms of rebellion.

Civil disobedience, the deliberate yet nonviolent public refusal to obey a law that one thinks is unjust, was an important tactic used by the civil rights movement to overcome legalized segregation in the South. As noted in Chapter 1, Rosa Parks is noteworthy in this regard for refusing to move to the back of the bus, as she was required by law to do. More broadly, during the 1950s and 1960s, Southern blacks were arrested countless times for "sitting-in at lunch counters, libraries, and movie theatres, . . . for 'kneeling-in' at segregated churches . . . [and] for peacefully marching after being unfairly denied parade permits" (Barkan 2012:363). As Martin Luther King Jr. wrote in his famous "Letter from a Birmingham Jail" in 1963:

> One has not only a legal but a moral responsibility to obey just laws. Conversely, one has a moral responsibility to disobey unjust laws. . . . Any law that uplifts the human personality is just. Any law that degrades human personality is unjust. All segregation statutes are unjust because segregation distorts the soul and damages the personality. . . . [But] in no sense do I advocate evading . . . the law. . . . One who breaks an unjust law must do so openly, lovingly, and with a willingness to accept the penalty. . . . [That person] is in reality expressing the highest respect for law. (King 1994:463)

King's noble stance, however, did not stop the FBI from investigating him for subversive activities. According to a 1976 report of the Senate Select Committee on Intelligence, headed by Senator Frank Church, King was targeted by an "intensive [FBI] campaign . . . to 'neutralize' him as an effective civil rights leader" from late 1963 to his death in 1968:

> The FBI gathered information about Dr. King's activities through an extensive surveillance program in order to obtain information about the "private activities of Dr. King and his advisors" to use to "completely discredit" them. . . . The FBI mailed Dr. King a tape recording made from microphones hidden in his hotel rooms which one agent testified was an attempt to destroy Dr. King's marriage. The tape recording was accompanied by a note which Dr. King and his advisors interpreted as threatening to release the tape unless Dr. King committed suicide. (cited in Church Committee 1978:161–162)

The letter read, in part: "King, there is only one thing left for you to do. . . . You are done. There is no way out. . . . You better take it before your filthy, abnormal fraudulent self is bared to the nation" (cited in Garrow 1981:126). The Church Committee noted that the FBI's surveillance program against King was not only "vastly excessive in breadth" but also illegal (1978:162). The FBI is permitted by law to investigate persons suspected of crimes, but it is not allowed to investigate persons for the purpose of discrediting them as political leaders.

Social protests of this nature can also spill over into violence, as in the case of urban race riots, and African Americans have at times rioted in response to real or perceived brutality by the police. In 1992, for example, riots occurred in Los Angeles and other parts of the country after the acquittal of the police officers accused of beating Rodney King, an African American who had been stopped for speeding (see Chapter 11). According to Steven Barkan, such incidents represent "small-scale political revolts stemming from blacks' anger over their poverty and others aspects of racial oppression by white society" (2012:360).

Arguably the most well-known period of urban race rioting in the United States occurred in the 1960s. During that era, some 500 riots involving an estimated 350,000 participants caused massive property damage and

---

FURTHER EXPLORATION
The Occupy Protest Movement

From September 2011 to February 2012, the Occupy protest movement garnered the attention of the national media. Although Occupy was (and is) an international movement, the protests in the United States began in New York City's Wall Street district and spread to scores of cities around the country. On September 17, 2011, about a thousand people gathered in downtown Manhattan and marched up and down Wall Street, the geographical and symbolic center of international finance capitalism. The protest, which popularized the distinction between "the 99 percent" and "the 1 percent," evolved to include people who camped out in public places all around the country, most notably in New York City's Zucotti Park, which is located just two blocks from Wall Street (Boghosian 2013).

Police arrested nonviolent protesters and used pepper spray against those who would not disperse, heightening media coverage. Undercover officers who infiltrated the movement also acted as agent provocateurs who agitated the protesters to become more violent, hence justifying further police crackdowns. Although the Occupy movement has generally abandoned its tactic of occupying public places, it continues as a broad collection of groups, international in scope, that are working to ameliorate the exacerbating economic inequality associated with contemporary global capitalism (Boghosian 2013).

the deaths of nearly 250 people, most of whom were shot by police and National Guard troops. These riots were most common in cities with depressed economic conditions, and they were viewed by a large number of African Americans as a positive event that brought national and international attention to their plight (Cohen 1967; Downes 1968; Myers 1997). In this regard, some evidence suggests that the riots were an impetus for increased aid to the black community in the form of more federal welfare funding and the passage of equal employment opportunity legislation (Betz 1974; Piven & Cloward 1971). However, the riots also provoked a backlash among whites and brought forth more punitive responses from police in the form of increased arrests and use of deadly force (Barkan & Snowden 2001).

Culture conflict. Still another variant of conflict theory focuses on **culture conflict**, which has its roots in work by Thorsten Sellin (1938), who defined this type of conflict as occurring "when persons acting according to the norms and violations of their own group violate those of another group that have been enacted into law" (Akers & Sellers 2009:229). During the Prohibition era (1919–1933), for example, people who drank alcohol were in violation of the Eighteenth Amendment to the US Constitution. The **prohibition movement**, also known as the temperance movement, was composed mainly of pious, middle-class rural and small-town Protestants who believed that drinking was sinful. They were especially concerned about the cultural practices of working-class Catholic immigrants and other urban dwellers whose presence in the United States appeared to threaten the Protestant way of life (Gusfield 1963). Today, many people believe that the government's prohibitionist drug policies, especially laws against marijuana use, constitute an unfair and unnecessary overreach of the law, and that drug abuse should be treated as a medical rather than a criminal problem (see Chapter 7). Abortion law is another area where culture conflict emerges. Some people believe that abortion is murder, while others consider it a private matter that should be subject to a woman's right to make decisions about what is done to her own body.

Culture conflict also occurs in cases where foreign immigrants "violate the laws of a new country simply by behaving according to the customs of the old" (Akers & Sellers 2009:229). One case in Wisconsin involving an Ethiopian immigrant who was convicted for possession of khat illustrates this point. Khat is a plant that is routinely chewed in East Africa and the Arabian Peninsula as a stimulant. During the trial, the attorney for the defendant argued (unsuccessfully): "Every culture has their stimulant. This is their stimulant. There's been no evidence that [khat] has any adverse effect on anybody" (quoted in Trevelen 2006:A1). Omar Jamal, the executive director of the Somali Justice Advocacy Center in neighboring Minnesota, complained that prosecutions like this are "an excuse to get us, because [they think] we're all terrorists" (p. A5).

Feminist Criminology

The branch of conflict theory known as **feminist criminology** has been advanced by criminologists who are dissatisfied with the neglect of gender in much theorizing about crime (conflict theory included). **Feminism** is a social movement concerned with understanding and alleviating the oppressive conditions that women (and girls) experience as a group. According to Meda Chesney-Lind, gender is as important as class and race as a system of stratification, and a feminist approach to crime requires explanations "that are sensitive to its patriarchal context" (1989:19; see Chapter 1).

According to feminist criminologists, traditional criminology had marginalized women's experiences and ignored, neglected, or misrepresented female offenders and victims. Albert Cohen, for instance, well known for his research on male gang delinquency, once dismissed females in this way: "For the adolescent girl as well as for the adult woman, relationships with the opposite sex and those personal qualities which affect the ability to establish such relationships are central in importance. . . . Dating, popularity with boys, pulchritude, and 'charm,' clothes, and dancing are preoccupations so central and so obvious that it would be useless pedantry to attempt to document them" (1955:142, 147). Similarly, in his influential book *Causes of Delinquency,* Travis Hirschi relegated girls to a footnote that said: "In the analysis that follows, the 'non-Negro' becomes 'white,' and girls disappear" (1969:35). And in his treatment of rape, Menachim Amir blamed the female rape victim for being "the one who is acting out, initiating the interaction between her and the offender, and by her behavior . . . generates the potentiality for criminal behavior of the offender or triggers this potentiality, if it existed before" (1971:259).

Beginning in the mid-1970s, however, criminologists began to take women's and girls' offending and victimization more seriously. In her book *Sisters in Crime: The Rise of the New Female Offender,* Freda Adler asserted, "The phenomenon of female criminality is but one wave in . . . the rising tide of female assertiveness—a wave which has not yet crested and may even be seeking its level uncomfortably close to the high-water mark set by males" (1975:1). According to Adler, medical and technological advances and the women's rights movement had freed women from unwanted pregnancies, lightened the burden of housework, and encouraged them to pursue formerly male-dominated endeavors in both the legitimate spheres of education and work as well as the world of crime.

Other research at the time, however, indicated that most of the increases in female criminality had occurred in the area of nonviolent property offenses (larceny-theft, forgery, fraud, embezzlement) and that these changes could be explained by rising divorce rates, increased number of female heads of households, a downturn in the economy, and increased opportunities for theft afforded by self-service retail outlets, consumer credit, and government welfare (Steffensmeier 1978; Steffensmeier & Cobb 1981). Moreover, as discussed in Chapter 2, rates of female criminality have by no means reached the "high-water mark" set by males, leading feminist criminologists to ask why traditional criminology has focused on male offenders without highlighting the gender dynamics underlying males' greater inclination to criminality or females' disinclination to criminality and consequent prosocial behavior (Daly & Chesney-Lind 1988; Messerschmidt 1993; Morash & Chesney-Lind 1991). At the same time, research by Peggy Giordano and Stephen Cernkovich led them to conclude that contemporary females now face a multidimensional and often contradictory set of behavioral scripts about what is "likely, possible, unlikely and impossible" for them to do, and that they are capable of simultaneously identifying with and enacting both traditional and nontraditional gender norms and expectations (1979:469).

Whereas traditional criminology has tended to distinguish "them" (the law breakers) from "us" (the law-abiding), feminist criminology highlights what are often "blurred boundaries" between victimization and criminalization, such as when girls flee abusive households and their street survival strategies result in their arrest and incarceration (Daly & Chesney-Lind 1988; see Chapter 3). Walter DeKeseredy and Martin Schwartz (1996) illuminate such interconnections when they note that the problem of male violence *against women* is related to the problem of male violence *against men*. Given the evidence that indicates that "children who grow up watching their mother being abused are more likely than other children to become delinquents and adult criminals both inside *and* outside the home," they suggest that "one way to reduce street crime against *men* is to reduce violence in the home against *women*" (pp. 478–480).

More broadly with regard to the problem of sexual victimization, the emergence of the anti-rape and anti-battery women's movements of the 1970s has led to greater awareness and legal reforms to protect women and girls (Rose 1977; Tierney 1982). These patterns of male violence against women (and girls) are now understood not simply as a product of individual pathology but as "an extension or exaggeration of conventional sexual relations" and power differentials between women and men, as neither "an aberration nor a particularly unusual occurrence" (Jackson 1978:27, 29). Even pornography, at least in its violent modality, is now viewed as a social problem. As Laura Lederer explained, "We noted the inconsistency in allowing (or even encouraging) women and young girls to be set up as sexual objects and willing victims in all forms of mass media, while at the same time protesting victimization of females in real life. We began to make the connections between media violence to women and real-life violence" (1980:16–17; see Chapter 8).

Peacemaking Criminology

Although the notion of conflict theory may imply a clash or confrontation of interests, one variant of this perspective, often associated with critical criminology, is known as **peacemaking criminology**. This perspective, initially advanced by Hal Pepinsky and Richard Quinney (1991), makes a distinction between war-making and peacemaking approaches to crime. Whereas war-making entails the belief that threats to our personal and collective security can be traced to identifiably evil people who must be suppressed "by killing them, separating them from the social fabric in which they live, or intimidating them into remaining in their proper place and conforming to the social roles their betters prescribe for them," peacemaking involves attempts to weave and reweave ourselves "with others in a social fabric of mutual love, respect, and concern" (Pepinsky 1999:56, 59).

FURTHER EXPLORATION
The Legitimization of Gay and Lesbian Sex

Feminist criminologists have been at the forefront of the gay and lesbian rights movement and efforts to advance understanding and acceptance of sexual diversity. Historically the laws that criminalized sodomy in every state in the United States were not "stand-alone statutes . . . [but] part of a much larger package of law that prohibited all forms of nonprocreative and nonmarital sex" (John D'Emilio, quoted in Graff 2003:A22). Sodomy was considered immoral, regardless of the sex of one's partner, because it allowed people to enjoy sex without the possibility of producing a child.

In 1969 a historic uprising occurred when police officers in New York City's Greenwich Village raided the Stonewall Inn gay bar. Although police raids were common and patrons "were expected to endure humiliation, slurs, and brutality in silence," one hot summer night the accumulated anger and frustration bubbled over and patrons of the bar as well as the throng of supporters who gathered "fought back against the police so valiantly that the cops were forced to retreat" (Feinberg 1996:7). The uprising, which came to be known as the **Stonewall Rebellion**, continued for four nights and now marks the birth of the contemporary gay and lesbian movement in the United States.

In the past few decades, two cases involving prosecution for sodomy have resulted in landmark US Supreme Court decisions. In the 1986 case of *Bowers v. Hardwick,* an Atlanta police officer came to the home of Michael Harwick with a warrant to arrest him for failing to appear in court to face a charge of carrying an open bottle of beer outside a bar. The officer was let into the house by one of Hardwick's roommates and found Hardwick having consensual sex with a male friend in his bedroom. Both Hardwick and his friend were arrested for violating the state sodomy law. The US Supreme Court, in a five-to-four decision, upheld Georgia's statute, ruling there was no constitutional right to privacy for homosexual conduct.

Twelve years later, in 1998, a Texas county sheriff's office received a false tip about an armed man in a Houston apartment. When the investigating officer arrived on the scene, he drew his gun and pushed open the unlocked

continues

continued

apartment door, only to find John Lawrence and Tyrone Garner locked in an embrace. Arrested for "deviate sexual intercourse," Lawrence and Garner were handcuffed and hauled off to jail in their underwear. The two were released the next day and fined for violating Texas's "Homosexual Conduct Law" (Graff 2003).

In the 2003 case of *Lawrence v. Texas,* however, the US Supreme Court struck down the Texas ban on same-sex sodomy, thereby correcting, in David Cole's words, "the wrong the Court committed in *Bowers v. Hardwick* . . . when it narrowly upheld a sodomy statute with the tortured reasoning that since gays and lesbians have been repressed and vilified from time immemorial, it cannot be unconstitutional to continue to do so" (2003:5). Justice Anthony Kennedy, writing the majority opinion, asserted that the law criminalizing consensual gay sex "demeans the lives of homosexual persons . . . [who] are entitled to respect for their private lives" (cited in Bull 2003:35).

Although **homophobia**—the fear and disdain of anyone who is not heterosexual—continues to persist, even just a few years ago no one could have anticipated how rapidly the acceptance of sexual minorities, including the acceptance of **transgendered** people—those who traverse or blur conventional gender boundaries—would have proceeded. By now the military's policy of "don't ask, don't tell," which kept gay, lesbian, and transgendered people in the closet, has been abolished, and even the legitimization of nonheterosexual marriage is on a trajectory that is unlikely to be reversed.

Peacemaking criminology participates in a grand tradition of social prophecy consistent with Judeo-Christian teachings and other social philosophies, including ideas of Mahatma Gandhi and Martin Luther King Jr. (Quinney 1999). In the prophetic tradition, human beings are seen as estranged from their fundamental state of goodness. Imagining the possibility of a better world is considered the first step toward its realization. According to Quinney, such an imagining requires recognition of the "interconnection between the inner peace of the individual and the outer peace of the world. The two develop and occur together. The struggle is to create a humane existence, and such an existence comes only as we act peacefully towards ourselves and one another" (2000:21). Beyond this, we must acknowledge that while "few are guilty . . . all are responsible. If we admit that the individual is in some measure conditioned or affected by the spirit of society, an individual's crime discloses society's corruption" and requires us all to take responsibility to think and act in ways that will make the world a better place in which to live (Heschel 1962:16).

As such, peacemaking criminology encourages us to view crime as a social relationship of **power**, which may be defined as the ability to impose one's will on another (or others) despite attempted resistance (Gerth & Mills 1946). According to John Hagan, "To perpetuate a crime . . . is to impose one's power on others, while to be punished for . . . crime is to be subject to the power of others" (1989:1). Thus, crime may be understood as an act of power that inflicts suffering and denies the humanity of another, and the most fundamental cause of crime may be seen as *any* social process that equates differences among people with evaluations of worth and that allows people the "delusion that they are unconnected to those with whom they interrelate" (Henry & Milovanovic 1994:124). From this point of view, the search for the causes of crime somehow misses the point. Crime is not something apart from ordinary social life but is an integral part of society, for the ability to subject one to the power of another is much of what passes for family life, the practice of business, and the exercise of government authority (Beirne & Messerschmidt 1995).

According to peacemaking criminologists, the elimination of crime will require the elimination of suffering more generally. They believe that the strategy of waging war on crime through punitive policies is fundamentally flawed, for to participate in this strategy is to participate in the very power dynamics that are constitutive of crime itself. They ask that we search for another way, the way of peace, which entails strategies of negotiation and conflict resolution, redemption and reconciliation, and nonviolent resistance to social injustice. Ultimately, peacemaking criminologists argue, it will be necessary to establish a *just social order* before we can establish *law and order* (Pepinsky & Quinney 1991).

Summary

This chapter offered a review of macrosociological explanations and policies that focus on the community- and nationwide conditions that influence criminal action in the United States. Under the rubric of social disorganization and the social ecology of crime, we considered two approaches. First, we examined work in the tradition of social disorganization theory, which is concerned with the ways in which the ecological confluence of urbanization and adverse socioeconomic conditions have led to the development of socially disorganized neighborhoods where law-abiding adults have lost control over youths, and delinquent groups and gangs have developed autonomous traditions that are transmitted from one generation to the next over time. Second, in a dramatically different approach to ecological thinking about crime, routine activities theory bypasses a concern with these causes and focuses instead on the immediate situational circumstances—the availability of suitable targets and the absence of capable guardians—that enable criminally motivated individuals to translate their criminal inclinations into action.

Next, under the rubric of crime and the American dream, we considered anomie-strain theory, which focuses on the social disjuncture or lack of integration between the cultural goal of financial success and the lack of institutionalized means or opportunities for individuals to achieve this goal. We also examined varying modes of individual adaptation to this social condition, including criminal innovation, retreatism, and rebellion. Last, we explored conflict theory, considering several perspectives—group conflict (including class, racial, and culture conflict), feminist criminology, and peacemaking criminology—that view crime and criminal law as subject to the assertion of economic and political power and the struggles of competing groups in society.

Part 2 _____
Patterns of Criminality and Victimization

6

Street Crime

Street crime is the term we use to refer to the constellation of crimes that are committed by offenders in the lower strata of society—predatory theft, violence, drug use and trafficking, and gang criminality, which are the primary concern of the criminal justice system in the United States. As we have noted previously, capitalist countries like the United States are marked by considerable class and racial/ethnic inequality. In this system a numerical minority of the population reaps a disproportionate amount of economic gain and consequent social privilege and political power, which some believe is deserved and others think is not. As we have seen, much macrosocial theory in one way or another focuses on the criminogenic impact of inequality. In this chapter we explore this relationship further by examining how transformations in the economy and urban landscape have affected the nature of street crime in the United States. We also look at the particular problem of racial inequality and explore in depth varying patterns of street crime activity.

The Economic Context
Alvin Gouldner observed that the social order cannot "be understood without making the concerns of economics focal and problematic, . . . without clarifying and focusing on the problem of scarcity" (1970:95). In this section we discuss the relationship between capitalist development and urbanization, illuminate the complexity of the relationship between unemployment and crime, and consider the problem of homelessness in the United States.

Capitalist Development and Urbanization
It is a truism that capitalist development and urbanization go hand-in-hand, and over the course of the twentieth century changing patterns of economic production dramatically changed the urban landscape of the United States.

In earlier years, manufacturing plants were built in and around downtown factory districts that were adjacent to working-class neighborhoods. This pattern of urban land use promoted labor solidarity and union organizing. Over time, however, the larger corporations began moving their manufacturing plants to outlying suburbs, where taxes were lower, land was cheaper, and the quality of life was more pristine, precipitating a depletion of the economic base of the central or inner cities and undermining the social solidarity of working-class areas (Gordon 1978; Robinson 1993).

The transformation of the urban scene was also influenced by the large-scale migration of (largely rural) African Americans from the South to the North and the West Coast. After the Civil War, Southern blacks had remained a source of cheap farm labor for white plantation owners. But such economic exploitation, along with adverse crop conditions, an abundant labor supply, and the mechanization of agriculture (to say nothing of white racial violence against blacks), encouraged African Americans to look elsewhere in their search for the American dream. During World War I, Northern employers actively encouraged black migration to meet the demands of the war economy and to ease the labor shortage, which had been worsened by the curtailment of European immigrant labor. At other times, however, African Americans constituted a surplus labor supply that was used by employers to suppress white workers' wages and replace white workers who went on strike. Black migration tapered off during the depression era of the 1930s but accelerated during World War II and continued through the 1960s. While about half of African Americans still live in the South, they are one of the most urbanized segments of the US population and are especially concentrated in large metropolitan areas (Palen 2005; Robinson 1993).

Over the years, capitalists also sought a more favorable business climate by shifting economic production away from the core cities of the northeastern and north-central regions of the United States to the southern and western states, where labor unions were weaker and wage scales were lower. At the same time, the federal government's subsidization of highway construction and home loans favored suburban growth, which was motivated as well by middle- and working-class "white flight" from neighborhoods populated by racial minorities. Financial lending institutions engaged in **redlining**—the discriminatory practice of denying loans to home buyers/ owners and small businesses in minority communities—and rarely invested in the inner city, contributing further to the depreciation of neighborhoods and property values. Don Wallace and Drew Humphries (1993) attribute rising urban crime rates, in part, to these trends. In their research they found that "central city hardship"—an index of several measures of socioeconomic disadvantage of central cities relative to their outlying suburban areas—was positively related to higher rates of crime. Other studies as well found the degree of suburbanization in a metropolitan area associated with higher rates of inner-city crime (Farley 1987; Shihadeh & Ousey 1996). To be sure, crime exists in the suburbs as well as in urban areas, and among suburban communities crime rates vary with class composition and with opportunities to commit crime (such as the presence of large shopping centers and malls). And while suburban poverty has increased over the years, street crime remains more acute in the depleted urban core (Palen 2005; Press 2007).

According to Steven Margolin and Judith Schor (1990), the 1950s and 1960s were the golden age of postwar capitalism, when economic growth—and the G.I. Bill—created unprecedented prosperity for many white people in the United States. This was an era in which capitalists and organized labor reached a grand bargain, as unions were able to negotiate higher wages and benefits that spread gains in economic productivity and contributed to the growth of the middle class. By the 1970s, however, technological advancements had led to more automated efficiencies in the work process and a decline in manufacturing jobs. Although computerization has since created new opportunities for skilled workers, these jobs require more formal education than previous entry-level manufacturing jobs, leaving others trying to eke out an existence in the economy through low-paid service work in "big box" stores like Walmart, fast food restaurants, and the like. Capitalists seeking low-wage workers have shipped jobs overseas, labor union membership has fallen dramatically, and formerly privileged white workers find themselves resentful because they must now compete with racial/ethnic minorities and women for the jobs that remain (Bluestone & Harrison 1982; Hamm 1993; Reich 2007).

Additionally, the flight of whites and now middle-class blacks as well has depleted the urban core of valuable economic resources and left behind an intransigent urban underclass, a matter we will take up in more detail later in this chapter. Suffice it to say now that these structural or macrolevel changes in the economy have impacted life in communities across the country, denying poor minorities especially the very jobs that had historically encouraged urban migration in the first place. Even **gentrification**—the redevelopment of declining areas to attract more affluent residents—only serves to deprive the poor of affordable housing. Under these conditions, street crime has become part of the repertoire of economic activity, along with government subsidies (including welfare and food stamps) and temporary or part-time low-paid work, of all too many people in the United States (Carlson & Michalowski 1997; Hagedorn 1988; Venkatesh 2008).

Complicating the Relationship Between Unemployment and Crime

Several criminological theories—from macro-level social theories to the micro-level theory of rational choice—converge in the expectation that unemployment increases the level of crime by affecting people's assessment of criminal versus noncriminal options. Yet in a review of the literature published in 1987, Theodore Chiricos reported on an apparent "consensus of doubt" among criminologists regarding the connection between unemployment and crime. Some studies had found a positive relationship, some a negative relationship, and some no relationship between unemployment and crime. Conservative critics of liberal prevention policies used these findings to dismiss programs that attempted to increase job opportunities for the disadvantaged (Wilson & Herrnstein 1985).

In a review of more than 60 quantitative studies, Chiricos (1987) tried to explain the inconsistent findings. He noted that property crimes (especially burglary and larceny) in these studies were more likely than violent crimes to be positively associated with unemployment. A positive relationship between unemployment and crime was more likely in studies that examined varying rates of unemployment and crime within a single city (intracity data) than in those that compared multiple cities or metropolitan areas (intercity/metropolitan data) or that used longitudinal national data. Chiricos reasoned that intracity data may be more sensitive to the social context or "milieu effects" of unemployment in a particular area; in other words, high unemployment in "a particular neighborhood or section of a city or county . . . creates a climate of hopelessness or anomie with [criminogenic] consequences even for those not directly unemployed (e.g., teenagers or others not in the labor force)" (p. 95). More recently, Daniel Mears and Avinash Bhati (2006) argued that "resource deprivation" in a particular area of a city has a spillover effect on crime in adjacent or spatially proximate areas. In a study of 343 "neighborhood clusters" in Chicago, they found that resource deprivation—as measured by an index that includes the unemployment rate, median household income, and the percentage of the population living below the poverty level—was positively associated with homicide rates in neighboring communities. These findings support Herman and Julia Schwendinger's (1993) contention that investments in economic-oriented prevention programs would help not only the participants who are directly involved, but other residents as well.

An additional problem with research on the relationship between unemployment and crime is that the official government measure of unemployment includes only those individuals who are considered temporarily unemployed and who continue to look for work. It therefore excludes those who are more or less permanently unemployed. Thus the 1970s was a period of economic hardship marked by rising **structural unemployment** in what class conflict theorists call the "surplus population" (see Chapter 5), wherein unemployment becomes a long-term rather than transitory state, and wherein those living at the margins of the economy increasingly lose faith in the possibility of advancement. According to Susan Carlson and Raymond Michalowski: "During periods of structural unemployment, a larger proportion of those who will lose jobs will be unable to reenter the labor force, or will do so at wages and under working conditions considerably less attractive than in the jobs they lost. Similarly, a larger share of young people hoping to enter the workforce for the first time will meet with failure or will find only dead-end 'hamburger' jobs" (1997:217). They therefore argue that the relationship between the official rate of unemployment and crime may be weak, because the official unemployment rate has become decoupled from the plight of the structurally unemployed, who are the most likely to engage in crime.

Still another issue that complicates the relationship between unemployment and crime is the possible countervailing effect of unemployment, which may increase the incentive or motivation for crime but also decrease the opportunity for crime. The latter is an expectation of routine activities theory, because when unemployment rises, there are fewer economic goods (suitable targets) available to be stolen and more unemployed people at home (capable guardians) to protect their property (see Chapter 5). Studies attempting to evaluate this countervailing effect, like the research on the relationship between unemployment and crime as a whole, have been inconsistent (Arvanites & DeFina 2006; Kleck & Chiricos 2002). On the other hand, research that examines the effects of both unemployment and deterrence variables (i.e., the certainty and severity of punishment) finds that unemployment has as much (or more) impact than punishment on lowering the crime rate (Chiricos 1987). In addition, studies show that prison inmates are more likely than the general population to be unemployed prior to incarceration, that unemployment prior to incarceration is a strong predictor of recidivism following release, and that ex-convicts who find employment have lower recidivism rates (Conklin 2003). Research also finds that black ex-inmates who gain employment earn less money and experience less wage growth during the course of their postincarceration employment histories than do their white counterparts (Lyons & Pettit 2011).

Terence Thornberry and R. L. Christenson (1984) were among the first to point out that the relationship between unemployment and crime may be reciprocal or mutually reinforcing. In a longitudinal study of nearly a thousand males born in Philadelphia in 1945, they found that unemployment was an immediate or short-term stimulus to increased criminal activity, but that crime over the long term also increased the likelihood of unemployment. John Hagan (1993) adds that involvement in early-life delinquency may actually precede unemployment in people's lives. Involvement in crime, especially for poor urban youths, embeds individuals in networks of criminal associations (including gangs) and at the same time distances them from networks of "job contacts that initiate and sustain legitimate occupational careers" (p. 469). This makes it increasingly difficult for youths to outgrow their youthful ties, and eliminates possibilities for employment even before they become apparent. Unemployment, in turn, becomes a significant problem for accomplishing the transition to adulthood, making it more likely that earlier involvement in criminality will be sustained. Hagan's own self-report survey research and several ethnographies of the urban poor support this hypothesis (Anderson 1999; Moore 1991; Padilla 1992; Sullivan 1989). Other criminologists suggest that it is not just employment but also the *quality* of work that affects an individual's incentive to engage in crime; that is, commitment to the conventional social order is also influenced by the degree to which work provides people with dignity, appreciation from others, and a sense of meaningful participation in community life (Currie 1985; Uggen 1999).

Homelessness and Crime

Prior to the structural economic changes we have been describing, the homeless population in the United States consisted primarily of unemployed, alcoholic men who were over 50 years of age. The homeless were less visible than they are today, living mainly in skid-row areas of large cities or hobo villages alongside railroad tracks (Wagner 2012). Currently, the homeless are more diverse and more visible on the streets and other public areas like beaches, parks, and train and bus stations. Some even rent storage lockers to live in because that is all they can afford, even though it is illegal to use these facilities for this purpose (Rickert 2008). In his study of a low-income housing project in Chicago, Sudhir Venkatesh (2008) learned about **squatters**—people who took refuge in the stairwells or abandoned rooms of high-rise apartment complexes, and who were expected to pay gang members, who patrolled and controlled the buildings, for "permission" to live there.

The decline in affordable low-income housing has been a major factor in the rise of homelessness. Beginning in the 1980s, during the presidential administration of Ronald Reagan, cities began experiencing dramatic reductions in single-room occupancy hotels, rooming houses, and the like, as federal housing subsidies for low-income people were dramatically cut (Palen 2005). Some 610,000 people in the United States are homeless on any given day, 36 percent of whom do not have access to sheltered facilities. Many actually have part-time or full-time jobs but are unable to afford rent, and many more live on the brink of destitution. About 62 percent of the homeless population is male and 38 percent is female, with 36 percent constituted by families and 22 percent being under the age of 18. About 42 percent is non-Hispanic white and 37 percent is black, while the remainder is divided among other ethnic/racial groups. Nearly 10 percent of the homeless population is made of veterans and 26 percent is suffering from serious mental illness (Substance Abuse and Mental Health Services Administration 2011; US Department of Housing and Urban Development 2013).

The problem of homelessness is arguably a national disgrace, even more so because the homeless, like the poor more generally, suffer more health problems than the general population and die at an earlier age (Substance Abuse and Mental Health Services Administration 2011). They also experience higher rates of criminal victimization, with the nonwhite homeless having higher rates of victimization than the white homeless (Coston 1992; Fitzpatrick et al. 1993). At the same time, the homeless also commit crimes themselves, stealing and prostituting to survive and often to support drug or alcohol addictions. One study of the Southern California beach community of Santa Monica found that the homeless were responsible for about half of the serious felonies in the city (Melekian 1990). A study of homeless shelters in New York City also found that nearly a quarter of the occupants had been incarcerated within the past two years (Metraux & Culhane 2006).

Since the homeless commit crimes against other homeless people, even shelters are riddled with theft, drugs, and violence. Homeless youths in particular are preyed upon by their adult counterparts, who quite literally attempt to take the clothes off their backs. One boy describes his experience in a shelter this way: "I was just a kid. . . . They were pushing me around. . . . They asked me to take my clothes off, they wanted to steal my clothes . . . four against me" (Hagan & McCarthy 1997:45). Another boy recalls: "I fell asleep . . . and . . . in the middle of the night . . . I wake up and there's two guys at my bed. . . . One guy's trying to yank my boots off, and the other guy's undoing my pants. . . . Another night . . . I saw a guy get his face cut open, because he refused to give another a cigarette. They . . . cut . . . with the knife . . . and that's when I said . . . 'I'm out of here'" (pp. 45–46).

In a study of homeless youths in Toronto and Vancouver, Canada, Bill McCarthy and colleagues (2002) found that some homeless youths form fictive "street families" that provide mutual support and protection that minimizes their victimization from predatory violence. One youth described a street family as "basically a group of friends . . . you can count on . . . to help you" (p. 848). Another youth said that a street family consisted of "people loving and caring for you . . . being there for you. It feels better . . . than just being . . . alone when you don't know what to do" (p. 845). And another remarked: "The difference between a street sister or brother and an average person is . . . you know they are solid, that they're not going to rat, they are not going to steal from you. . . . Being solid is if somebody walks up to a group of us and picks on one person . . . your street brother or sister is going to stand up for that person" (p. 850).

Racial Inequality in Urban Context

A particular manifestation of the economic context we have been discussing involves the question of race. We begin here by noting that much of the involvement of racial minorities in street crime can be explained from a class perspective. Clifford Shaw and Henry McKay (1942) found, for instance, that the ecological association between crime and adverse economic conditions in the city of Chicago persisted over the first three decades of the twentieth century, regardless of the race or ethnic group residing in the area (see Chapter 5). In a follow-up study, Robert Bursik and Jim Webb (1982) documented a similar pattern in Chicago through the 1940s. During this time, crime rates remained fairly stable, but since the 1950s racial/ethnic turnover has been accompanied by greater destabilization of these areas and increased crime.

William Julius Wilson (1987), whose work we introduced in Chapter 5, attributes the destabilization in Chicago and other urban areas to the general decline in entry-level manufacturing jobs as well as the movement of these jobs from the cities to the suburbs and overseas. These trends have deprived African-American residents of the job opportunities enjoyed by earlier arrivals. Wilson argues that the structural correlates of crime and economic disadvantage—including poverty, joblessness, and family instability—are not race-specific; crime rates can be expected to vary with such community conditions irrespective of racial composition (Krivo & Peterson 1996; Sampson & Wilson 1995). But what Wilson wants us to understand is how these conditions have come to be concentrated in certain black communities.

The Urban Underclass

Wilson's work (1987) addresses a profound paradox that developed over the last few decades of the twentieth century: conditions for some minorities, especially African Americans, deteriorated at a time when civil rights and antidiscrimination laws were expanding. According to Wilson, the civil rights movement opened up opportunities for educated and middle-class blacks to advance, but left behind the less educated and those with few job skills. Furthermore, as Gary LaFree and Kriss Drass (1996) noted, while expanded educational opportunities may have improved the prospects for graduates, they may have lowered the prospects for nongraduates, because an increasingly educated work force may produce an educational inflation effect whereby "jobs are increasingly filled by those with more advanced credentials" and less educated workers are replaced with more educated ones (p. 617).

Wilson's thesis is consistent with research on the relationship between income inequality and crime, which finds that crime rates among blacks (over time and between geographical areas) are more highly associated with intraracial (within-group) inequality than with interracial (between-group) inequality (Harer & Steffensmeier 1992; LaFree & Drass 1996). In other words, it is inequality among blacks rather than inequality between blacks and whites that is associated with the most variation in crime rates. Similarly, Ramiro Martinez (1996) found that intra-Latino inequality, not Anglo-Latino inequality, was most highly related to rates of Latino homicide.

Expectations of racial/ethnic minority involvement in crime are consistent with anomie-strain theory, which postulates that the absence of economic opportunities produces the greatest pressure for crime among disadvantaged groups. And the importance of within-group measures of inequality makes sense in light of strain theory's proposition about relative deprivation. Also, **reference-group theory** predicts that members of a group will be more likely to look internally rather than externally for standards of comparison. "People assess how well, or badly, they are faring economically not by comparing themselves with the population as a whole, but with particular reference groups with whom they share some status attribute" (Harer & Steffensmeier 1992:1036). As one black resident of a dilapidated housing project said: "I'm not African American. . . . I'm a nigger. . . . *Niggers* are the ones who live in this building. . . . *African Americans* live in the suburbs. African Americans wear ties to work. Niggers can't find no work" (Venkatesh 2008:16).

Furthermore, according to Wilson (1987), as both whites and middle-class blacks migrated to the suburbs, the inner city was deprived not only of financial resources but also of social resources: positive role models who reinforce conventional values; provide networks of informal social control; and offer support for schools, churches, and recreation and other community organizations. Remaining are fewer "old heads" who are respected for their wisdom about avoiding crime and staying out of trouble. Left to fill the void is a growing informal economy of off-the-books enterprises (such as unlicensed cabs, house cleaning, and home and car repair), welfare dependency, and street crime (Anderson 1999; Pattillo 1998; Robinson 1993; Venkatesh 2008).

While Wilson (1991) generally aligns himself with the liberal side of the political spectrum, he has criticized liberals for failing to acknowledge the "social dislocations" that have become part of the urban underclass. Male unemployment and imprisonment have reduced the number of reliable marriage partners, and female-headed households and out-of-wedlock births have risen. The increase in single-parent families has occurred in the larger society as well, but it is more pronounced among the poor (Brooks-Gunn et al. 1993; Krivo & Peterson 1996; Sampson & Wilson 1995). Although it is no surprise that a single mother in poverty has difficulty providing her children with the economic, social, and cultural resources they need to succeed, it is important to not misconstrue Wilson's position as a "decline in family values" argument. Rather, Wilson views these social dislocations not as a cause but as a *consequence* of structural changes in the economy that, in his view, have been exacerbated by the "blaming the poor" rhetoric of some conservative politicians and the failure (or absence) of government policies vis-à-vis the inner city.

FURTHER EXPLORATION
Immigration and Crime

In April 2007, an emotionally disturbed college student, Korean-born Cho Seung-Hui, went on a shooting rampage at Virginia Tech university, killing 32 people (Thomas 2007). The following June, former senator Fred Thompson, a 2008 Republican presidential candidate, told an audience at the Prescott Bush Awards Dinner in Stamford, Connecticut, that the problem of *illegal* immigration meant that "we are now living in a nation that is beset by people who are suicidal maniacs and want to kill countless men, women, and children" (quoted in NewsMax 2007). It seemed as if Thompson was alluding to the Virginia Tech incident, even though Cho's family had *legally* immigrated into the United States when he was eight years old. To be sure, illegal immigration is a serious issue, but there is little doubt that many politicians have exploited this concern to muster votes. While they clamor for increased law enforcement aimed at curtailing illegal immigration, few call for more law enforcement against the employers who illegally hire undocumented workers. Moreover, the irony of linking immigration to other forms of crime is that there is little evidence that immigration increases crime. In fact, there is evidence that immigrants actually commit less crime than similarly situated natives.

Social disorganization, anomie-strain, and culture conflict theories all predict a positive association between immigration and crime because new immigrants tend "to settle in urban neighborhoods characterized by poverty, substandard housing, poor schools, and high crime rates" (Lee et al. 2001:561). However, a large body of quantitative research using both intercity and intracity data—most often examining Latino immigration, but not exclusively so—indicates that, all other things being equal, communities with

continues

Wilson (1987) also argues that there are **concentration effects** to these socioeconomic conditions that create and sustain a condition of social isolation. Patterns of residential segregation associated with expanded suburban housing markets and the construction of government-funded housing projects have geographically concentrated the minority poor (Krivo & Peterson 1996; Massey & Denton 1993; Sampson 2013). Freeways have divided and isolated core sectors of heavily populated cities, further separating residents from centers of employment. Minority workers also experience employer discrimination and lack familiarity with the cultural norms of the white-dominated workplace. Deficits in workplace experience accumulate over the life course and the resultant social disadvantages are passed on to the next generation (Anderson 1999; Sharkey 2013; Tienda & Stier 1996). Moreover, punitive incarceration policies further destabilize minority communities by weakening family and community ties that might otherwise foster informal

continued

a higher proportion of immigrants have less street crime (Hagan & Palloni 1999; Lee et al. 2001; Martinez et al. 2010; Sampson et al. 2005).

Skeptics of the **more immigrants, less crime hypothesis** that is supported by these studies point out that immigrants who come into the country illegally may be less likely to report crimes by other immigrants (as well as crimes by nonimmigrants) because they fear deportation if they come forward to the police (Skogan 2006). They also suggest that a reason immigrants may commit less crime is that they are deterred by this fear. Although most studies do not distinguish between legal and illegal immigrants, there is little evidence that the two groups vary in their rates of crime (Hagan & Palloni 1998). On the other hand, proponents of the "more immigrants, less crime hypothesis" cite the traditional family values, higher rates of marriage, and extended family supports that construct ethnic enclaves of stability within these communities (Hagan & Phillips 2008; Sampson et al. 2005). They also note that immigrants with low-paying jobs may be more motivated to work longer hours and may have more hope about the future than similarly situated natives (Lee et al. 2001). At the same time, some research indicates that as subsequent generations of immigrants become acculturated to US society, their rates of crime increase (Martinez & Valenzuela 2006; Sampson et al. 2005). Moreover, the growing presence of immigrant gangs and organized crime networks in some urban centers cautions against an overly sanguine view of the relationship between immigration and crime (Hayden 2004). Ellis Cose concludes that we need to start asking "some broader questions about assimilation, about how to ensure that people, once outsiders, don't forever remain marginalized" within our nation (2007–2008:74).

social controls among youths, hence exacerbating the intergenerational transmission of disadvantage (Foster & Hagen 2007; Roettger & Swisher 2011; Rose & Clear 1998).

Persistent residential segregation by race also means that the black middle class is exposed to more criminogenic influences than the white middle class (Logan & Stults 1999). Black middle-class neighborhoods are more likely than white middle-class neighborhoods "to be nestled between areas that are less economically stable and have higher crime rates" (Pattillo 1998:751). As Robert Sampson and Wilson note: "In not one city over 100,000 in the US do blacks live in ecological equality with whites. . . . The 'worst' urban contexts in which whites reside are considerably better than the average context of black communities" (1995:42). It bears repeating, however, that Wilson's insightful analysis of racial inequality is not meant to suggest that the problems of the urban poor are the fault of the people who live in the inner city or that residents prefer to live under such conditions. Rather, Wilson urges us to recognize that crime prevention efforts that do not address the intersection of race and class are inevitably bound to fail.

Beyond the Subculture of Violence

An alternative approach to explaining minority involvement in crime focuses specifically on the problem of violence. According to Marvin Wolfgang and Franco Ferracuti's (1967) **subculture of violence theory**, a subculture exists among lower-class minority groups, one that contains elements of mainstream, white middle-class culture but is more supportive of the use of physical force in everyday social interactions. This acceptance of force increases the probability of violent confrontations in response to jostles, insults, threats, or displays of weapons. Avoidance of violence by group members is more difficult, because it may lead to rejection by one's peers and loss of self-esteem.

Quantitative research testing this proposition has typically analyzed the relationship between the proportion of a given population that is nonwhite (measured by the percentage that is black or Latino) and rates of homicide. These studies provide no direct measure of subcultural values, however, and much research finds that the connection between nonwhites and homicide can be accounted for by socioeconomic factors, including concentrated neighborhood disadvantage (Feldmeyer 2010; Griffiths 2013; Parker 1989; Sampson 1985).

Research has also tested the proposition that this subculture of violence is more pronounced in some regions of the United States than others. Studies have found that the South (followed by the West) has the highest rate of homicide (Huff-Corzine et al. 1986; Nelsen et al. 1994). Interestingly, homicide rates among *Southern whites* are especially high. In addition, survey evidence indicates that in some defensive or retaliatory situations (such as responding to someone breaking into one's house, to someone seen beating a woman, and to someone seen beating a child after the child has accidentally damaged another's car), whites are more willing than blacks to use violence (Cao et al. 1997; Ellison 1991; Shoemaker & Williams 1987). As discussed in Chapter 1 regarding stand-your-ground laws, this inclination can be fatal. Lynn Curtis (1975) adds that individuals throughout all sectors of society are influenced by multiple value systems. Mainstream cultural media, for example, often glamorize violence; and physical prowess, aggression, and sexual conquest, as means to assert dominance over others, are all part of the "subterranean values" of conventional culture (Matza & Sykes 1961). In any case, the United States is a rather violent nation. It has the highest homicide rate among industrial democracies, and even if homicides committed by African Americans were excluded, the US rate would still be a statistical outlier (Zimring & Hawkins 1997).

Sampson and Wilson approach the issue of crime and cultural values differently than do Wolfgang and Ferracuti. In Sampson and Wilson's view, cultural influences exist but "vary systematically with structural features of the urban environment. . . . Community contexts . . . shape . . . [the] cognitive landscapes or ecologically constructed norms . . . regarding appropriate standards and expectations of conduct. That is, in structurally disorganized slum communities . . . a system of values emerges in which crime, disorder, and drug use are less than fervently condemned and hence expected as part of everyday life" (1995:41, 50). It is true that there are voices in these communities that denounce these practices, but these voices are being heard less often than in the past.

In his ethnographic research in Philadelphia, Elijah Anderson (1999) describes an oppositional street culture, or **code of the street**, that characterizes the inner-city, African-American community. Even the most conscientious and concerned parents, he notes, feel that it is important to encourage their children to be "streetwise," to learn how to handle themselves on the street. The heart of the street code is "respect," being treated with proper deference. Even a fleeting or awkward glance, or eye contact that lingers too long, can be taken as a sign of disrespect, or "dissing." Anderson argues that this code is a cultural adaptation to residents' lack of faith in the ability of the criminal justice system to offer them protection without discrimination. Under these circumstances, residents take on the responsibility of self-protection (Kubrin & Weitzer 2003; Venkatesh 2008). Children witnessing disputes in the street see that "might makes right": "In almost every case the victor is the person who physically won the altercation, and this person often enjoys the esteem and respect of onlookers" (Anderson 1994:86). Under these conditions, humility or "turning the other cheek" is no virtue and can in fact be dangerous. Failure to respond to intimidation or dissing from another only encourages further victimization.

Ruth Horowitz (1987) found a similar code of personal honor in a Chicano community in Chicago. Here "honor revolves around a man's ability to command deference in interpersonal relations . . . [and avoid] any aspersions on his masculinity" (p. 440). Gang youths and nongang youths differ in that the former "seek out and initiate challenges to another's honor as one way of publicly asserting . . . and enhancing their reputation," whereas the latter only defend their honor upon provocation (p. 441). In the culture of the gang, considerable value is placed on acquiring a reputation (or "rep") for oneself and the gang, and younger gang members "want to match or outdo the reputation of their predecessors" (Moore 1991:60). These youths take pride in being *loco* (crazy) or *muy loco* (very crazy) and in describing themselves as violent.

William Harvey (1986) suggests that the minority experience of powerlessness, alienation, frustration, and anger has coalesced in what he describes as a **subculture of exasperation**. Unable to vent their hostility toward whites or those in power, minorities channel their aggression in exhibitions of toughness against those they interact with on a daily basis. As Nathan McCall, an African American, once thought, "I can't do much to keep whites from dissin' me, but I damn sure can keep black folks from doing it" (1994:55). Charles Silberman (1978) adds that the depletion of positive role models in the black community has made it difficult for youths to learn how to control their rage. Moreover, contemporary popular media such as gangsta rap reinforce and romanticize the value placed on rebellion and opposition to mainstream culture (Kitwana 2002; Kubrin 2005).

Alvin Poussaint (1983) sees elements of self-hatred in intraracial crime, which is the leading cause of death among black youths (Messerschmidt 1997). According to Poussaint, some black people are still psychologically scarred, still bear a legacy of internalizing the negative image imposed on them by their white oppressors. Offenders and victims often share a low self-image and low threshold for frustration. Recall how Sanyika Shakur said he "had little respect for life when practically all my life I had seen people assaulted, maimed, and blown away . . . and no one seemed to care" (1993:102; see Chapter 1). McCall (1994) points out how this attitude pervaded his relationships with black women, which were marked by violence and sexual exploitation. Exploiting a black woman "was another way for a guy to show the other fellas how cold and hard he was. It wasn't until I became an adult that . . . I realized that we thought we loved sisters but we actually hated them. We hated them because they were black and . . . on some level much deeper than we realized, we hated . . . ourselves" (p. 50).

Finally, Wilson (1991) sees another consequence of the "cognitive landscape" of the urban poor: individuals' perception of their self-efficacy and ability to exercise personal agency to improve their lives over the long term are undermined (see Chapter 1). "People may seriously doubt that they can do or accomplish what is expected, or they may feel confident of their abilities but nonetheless give up trying because they believe that their efforts will ultimately be futile due to an environment that is unresponsive, discriminatory, or punitive. . . . Such beliefs affect the level of challenge that is pursued, the amount of effort expended in a given venture, and the degree of perseverance when confronting difficulties" (p. 11).

Nevertheless, minority children growing up poor do not face completely homogeneous life chances. In his research, Anderson (1999) found that residents distinguished between what they described as **decent families** and **street families,** two orientations that often exist simultaneously within the same extended family network. The so-called decent families are composed mainly of the working poor and "tend to be better off financially than their street-oriented neighbors" (Anderson 1994:83). Parents in these families socialize their children to accept mainstream values of hard work, self-reliance, respect for authority, and self-improvement through education. They tend toward strict child-rearing practices and encourage their children

FURTHER EXPLORATION
Rural and Suburban School Shooters

In Pearl, Mississippi, in October 1997, 16-year-old Luke Woodham went to his high school and opened fire on his classmates, killing two and wounding seven others. Between December of that year and May 1998, the news media reported on five other similar incidents that occurred in such unlikely places as West Paducah, Kentucky; Jonesboro, Arkansas; Edinboro, Pennsylvania; Fayetteville, Tennessee; and Springfield, Oregon. All told, these other shootings resulted in the deaths of nine students and two teachers and the wounding of 32 others (Berger 2009a).

These incidents were by no means the first or the last crimes of this nature that have occurred in rural and suburban communities in the United States (Frantz et al. 2014). But arguably the paradigmatic case is the one that occurred at Columbine High School in Littleton, Colorado, in April 1999, when Eric Harris and Dylan Klebold went on a shooting rampage, killing 12 students and a teacher and then taking their own lives (Larkin 2007). It was the largest mass murder to occur in the country between the time Timothy McVeigh bombed the Alfred Murrah Federal Building in Oklahoma City in 1996 and the attacks on the World Trade Center and Pentagon on September 11, 2001 (see Chapter 10).

Although inner-city schools experience more violence than schools in rural and suburban areas, it is the latter violence that attracts the bulk of media attention. With each new incident, similar claims of disbelief emerge from school officials and residents: "How could it happen *here*?" "This isn't the inner city." "We're not that kind of people." The consistency of these remarks has prompted Patricia Williams to wonder why black youths are so readily feared while white youths like Harris and Klebold seem "so shrouded in presumptions of innocence . . . [even] after professing their love for Hitler, declaring their hatred for . . . [minorities] on a public website, . . . downloading instructions for making bombs, accumulating ingredients, assembling them under the protectively indifferent gaze . . . [of] parents and neighbors, stockpiling guns and ammunition . . . [and] procuring hand grenades and flak jackets" (1999a:9). Like the probation officers who were supervising Harris and Klebold after the youths had burglarized a car, who described them as intelligent boys with lots of promise, classmates and teachers continued to insist that the two killers were really "good boys" at heart.

Most of the youths who have committed these crimes have been white adolescent males with easy access to firearms and a tendency to perceive violence as a transcending experience—that is, as an experience that made them feel omnipotent. Often the youths had previously been harassed, bullied, and branded as social outcasts by other students; and in their eyes, they were seeking revenge. As Luke Woodham explained, "Murder is not weak and slow-witted, murder is gutsy and daring. . . . I killed because people like me are mistreated every day" (Cowley 1998:25). Harris and Klebold had plotted their crime over a period of eight months, and Klebold had written on a website: "That's the only way to solve arguments with all you fuckheads. I just kill! . . . I don't care if I live or die in the shoot out, all I want to do is kill and injure as many pricks as I can" (Larkin 2007:159–160).

to "walk a straight moral line" and to be on guard against trouble that might come their way. Parents from street families, on the other hand, lack effective parenting skills and socialize their children to accept the code of the street. Their lives are often disorganized and complicated by problems with drug or alcohol use and other self-destructive behaviors. Children are left to fend for themselves and "come up hard" on the street.

According to Anderson, the large majority of inner-city families "try to approximate the decent-family model" (1994:83). But children from these families interact daily with children from the street and "have a chance to go either way" (p. 86). They realize they must choose a direction, and the choice they make will depend largely on how fully they have been socialized by their parents. On the other hand, children from street families rarely absorb the values of decent families. When they do, the positive influence almost always comes from nonfamily settings—such as church, youth groups, or school—where they have the opportunity to become involved with caring adult mentors (Williams & Kornblum 1985).

The Illegal Economy

As noted earlier, the informal economy of urban underclass communities consists of off-the-books enterprises, government subsidies, and crime, the last of which is marked by what criminologists call **systemic violence**. Systemic violence refers to the social context in which those involved in illegal enterprises have no recourse in the civil courts to resolve disputes, and hence violence is used as a mechanism to enforce informal contractual agreements and discipline members in criminal organizations (Reuter 2009).

In this section we discuss four dimensions of the illegal economy— teenage thievery, street robbery, the drug trade, and street prostitution— associated with the consequences of class and racial inequality we have thus far reviewed; and in the following section we consider urban gangs. In doing so, we also address gender variations in these types of street crimes.

Teenage Thievery

In his ethnography of Brooklyn, New York, Mercer Sullivan (1989) studied three urban neighborhoods: Projectville was a largely black community, Hamilton Park was predominately white, and La Barriada was a mixture of Hispanics and whites. Projectville had the highest rate of poverty (52 percent), followed by La Barriada (43 percent), and Hamilton Park (12 percent). Projectville also had the highest overall crime rate, and Hamilton Park the lowest, while La Barriada had the highest rate of violent crime.

Sullivan found that male youths in all three neighborhoods progressed through a series of life stages that influenced their involvement in and commitment to crime. During the early to middle teen years, youths from the same neighborhood began hanging out together in loosely knit groups and participating in turf fights with youths from surrounding areas. They also stole items like radios, bicycles, and clothes, primarily for use rather than for sale on the open market; and when they did sell stolen property, they had no idea of its actual market value. Importantly, these early-life forays into crime prepared them for more serious later-life criminality. Engaging in theft helped them revise their conception of "property rights" as no longer fixed but as "something over which [they] could exert control" (Robinson 1993:317). And from fighting, they learned how to acquire and use weapons in violent crimes.

By the middle teenage years, the youths had acquired more experience in crime. They were now physically stronger and had a greater desire to consume commodities.

> [They also] learned more about the value of stolen items and about the networks for converting them to cash; they were better able to weigh the risks and benefits between types of crime, as well as between crime and legitimate employment. The motivation for crime now became economic, a means of support rather than an occasional excursion to vary the day-to-day boredom of just hanging out . . . and as a youth took on crime as his main source of income, he dropped out of street fighting. (Robinson 1993:317)

Along the way, opportunities for legitimate employment, when available, reduced the incentive to engage in crime. The Hamilton Park white youths in particular had somewhat greater access to networks of legitimate employment and were thus the most likely to opt out of crime. Overall, Sullivan (1989) found that by their late teens, most youths chose to desist from crime because escalating criminality increased their risk of apprehension. The housing projects where the Projectville black youths lived, for example, afforded limited opportunities for profitable theft. When these youths began committing robberies and purse snatchings outside of their own neighborhoods, they increased their exposure and hence their chances of getting caught. But some who became disillusioned with violent theft became attracted to drug sales instead.

Street Robbery

Robbery is generally considered a quintessential male crime because it entails an exercise of masculine domination over others. Earlier we described the culture of respect and personal honor that lies at the heart of the "code of the street" and how males often respond vehemently to "dissing" in order to avoid any insult to their masculinity. Similarly, men who commit robbery are attempting to project a particular image of masculinity to other men. As Jack Katz observes, robbery is not only a means of acquiring money or property but also a means of gaining "an angle of moral superiority over the intended victim" (1988:169). Jody Miller adds that "men accomplish street robberies in a strikingly uniform" way that uses "physical violence and/or a gun placed on or at close proximity to the victim in a confrontational manner" (1998:47). One robber explained that when you "have the gun to his head, [he] can't do nothing but respect that" (p. 48). Another said, "I don't even have to say nothing half the time. When they see that pistol, they know what time it is" (p. 48). While men sometimes rob women, these are deviations from the norm: "Male robbers . . . clearly view the act of robbery as a masculine accomplishment in which men compete with other men for money and status" (p. 50). Masculinity is not accomplished by robbing women, because women are not viewed as "real players" on the streets (p. 50). Additionally, the conspicuous display of the fruits of this labor—such as fashionable clothes and jewelry, and plenty of drugs and alcohol—heightens an individual's status by projecting an image of someone who not only possesses valued commodities but also possesses "things that may require defending" (Anderson 1994:88).

It is not just men who commit street robbery, however. Women do so as well, although in different ways. In her study, Miller (1998) interviewed 37 active street robbers: 14 women and 23 men, nearly all African-American, from an underclass neighborhood in St. Louis, Missouri. She found that women most commonly robbed other women because they were easier targets than men, and women robbers were far less likely to use guns when robbing women. Although women-on-women robberies were most often committed with female accomplices, they were sometimes committed

---

FURTHER EXPLORATION
Fencing of Stolen Property

Fencing refers to the buying and selling of stolen property. Some thieves may fence their goods themselves, selling to people who are unconcerned about the origin of the merchandise. Some who don't steal themselves may be "amateur" fences who sell goods on a part-time basis, typically operating out of their homes and selling to an informal network of acquaintances, friends, and relatives. And some may be "professionals" who are more-or-less full-time businesspeople who have the capital to purchase larger amounts of merchandise (and more expensive merchandise) and are able to tap into a larger consumer market. These individuals typically operate legitimate businesses such as pawn shops or repair shops that serve as a cover for their illegal activities. They may also serve as "tipsters" who let thieves know of attractive targets. In the contemporary era, fencing has increasingly moved to the Internet, where people can sell stolen merchandise through sites like eBay and online auctions (Cromwell et al. 1991; Head 2001; Henry 1978; Steffensmeier 1986).

alone. Women rarely had male accomplices when robbing other women. Occasionally, female victims would defy the stereotype and resist the robbery. One woman recalled an incident where she and a female accomplice confronted another woman following a basketball game:

> She was walking to her car. I was, shit . . . let's get her motherfucking purse. . . . So I walked up to her and I pulled out the knife. I said "up that purse." And she looked at me. I said, "shit, do you think I'm playing?" . . . She was like "shit, you ain't getting my purse. Do what you got to do." I was like "shit, you must be thinking I'm playing." So I took the knife, stabbed her a couple of times on the shoulder, stabbed her on the arm and snatched the purse. . . . She just ran, "help, help." (p. 52)

Although women's robbery of men almost always involved guns and often (but not always) male accomplices, Miller found that women sometimes capitalized on their sexuality to catch male victims off-guard. In these cases, they presented themselves as sexually available to their male targets, at times even drinking and partying at first, making sure to consume less alcohol and drugs than the men they were with. Ironically, it was men's assumption that they could take advantage of women that made them vulnerable. One woman robber recounted the time she went with a man to a hotel room:

> He was . . . drunk . . . [and] didn't have on no clothes. . . . He was like, "shit, . . . ain't you gonna get undressed?" I was like "shit, yeah, hold up" and I went in my purse and I pulled out the gun. He was like "damn, what's up with you gal?" I was like, "shit, I want your jewelry and all the money you got." He was like . . . "bitch you crazy. I ain't giving you my shit." I said, "do you think I'm playing nigger? You don't think I'll shoot your motherfucking ass?" He was like . . . "you ain't gonna shoot me." So then I . . . fired the thing but I didn't fire at him. . . . I snatched his shit . . . [and] ran out the door. (p. 56)

Miller found that some women involved in prostitution also robbed their clients. One woman said she preferred to rob white men, because "they be so paranoid they just want to get away. . . . [And] if you are sucking a man's dick and you pull a knife on them, they not gonna too much argue with you" (p. 55). Los Angeles gang girls interviewed by Gina Sikes (1997) had a similar modus operandi, staking out card clubs, racetracks, and casinos looking for men to rob. As one gang girl said: "The one thing you look for when you choose the man . . . is a wedding ring—a big one. You want to know that he got money and you definitely want someone who's married. Married man's not gonna press charges." Another girl described an incident when she invited a man to a motel room, and when the lights went out, her accomplices burst in with guns. "If a man's half-naked with three girls and a gun on him," she said, "he's gonna give it up" (p. 84).

The Drug Trade

In his ethnography of Puerto Rican gangs in Chicago, Felix Padilla (1992) reports about youths who began their involvement in the drug trade as "runners" or "mules," but who soon realized that the distributors made most of the profits. Sullivan (1989), too, found it was fairly easy for Brooklyn youths to obtain drugs on consignment until they acquired enough capital to stake themselves out; but even though a competent drug dealer could earn between $500 and $1,000 a week in the 1980s, the life chances of these youths remained for the most part dismal. As one youth remarked: "I'm a good businessman. . . . I know how to buy and sell. But I've been ripped off, cut, and arrested. Now, I'm on probation and I won't get off so easy next time. But how am I gonna get a job now? . . . I can't go up to somebody and say, 'Listen, I know how to buy and sell. . . . I've been buying and selling for years'" (p. 175). We will explore the gang context of the urban drug trade later in this chapter. Here we consider gender variations that are part of the drug trade.

Men in criminal organizations prefer to "work, associate, and do business with other men" (Steffensmeier 1983:1013). They do not want to take orders from women, but believe that women should take orders from men. Some researchers have noted a change in women's roles in US urban drug markets, however, with women playing a greater role in contemporary crack-cocaine markets than in the heroin markets of an earlier era (Bourgois 1989; Mieczkowski 1994). As Jeffrey Fagan concluded, in his study of New York City, "the size and seemingly frantic activity of the . . . [cocaine economy] has made possible for women new ways to participate in street networks. Their involvement in drug selling at high income levels defies the gendered norms and roles of the past, where drug dealing was an incidental income source often mediated by domestic partnerships" (1994:210).

Lisa Maher and Kathleen Daly note that the crack-cocaine business was once characterized as an "unregulated market of freelancers engaged in individual entrepreneurial activity," but that as soon as the demand for crack was established, freelancing was "superseded by a more structured system of distribution" (1996:471). In their ethnography of New York drug users in the late 1980s and early 1990s, they found evidence that women's subordinate role in the drug trade had persisted. Their research revealed a hierarchical distribution system of drug business owners who employed several crew bosses, lieutenants, or managers who, in turn, were responsible for organizing and delivering supplies, collecting revenues, and hiring, firing, and paying lower-level street dealers and those who acted as enforcers, lookouts, runners, holders, steerers, and touts (persistent solicitors).

Maher and Daly interviewed more than 200 women drug users and found no one who had filled the role of business owner and only one who had worked in a managerial capacity. They also conducted more extensive interviews with a subgroup of 45 women, all of whom were regular users of smokable cocaine or crack, and more than two-thirds of whom had used heroin at one time. More than 90 percent of these women were homeless, and 80 percent were mothers, although few of their children were living with them during the study period. More than 40 percent had tested positive or believed they were positive for HIV.

The women in Maher and Daly's study most commonly performed the role of steerer or tout (42 percent). At times, some would be given jobs as street-level dealers, but this was largely to fill temporary (though recurring) labor shortages caused by police arrest of male dealers. During the study period, however, only 27 percent of the women were involved in selling or distributing drugs. Only three ran "shooting galleries" (places where people gathered to use drugs), and even these galleries were under the control of or operated by a man or group of men.

About a third of the women in the study "copped" drugs for others, typically white men. As one of these women said, "They'd be . . . people very important, white people like lawyer[s], doctors that come and get off, you'd be surprised" (Maher & Daly 1996:480). Male dealers liked this arrangement because it protected them from undercover police officers, and few men were attracted to this role, because it was considered a low-status activity. Male customers from outside the neighborhood were more likely to trust women (particularly white women) than men to purchase drugs for them. This trust was often misplaced, however. "The combination of naive, inexperienced 'white boyz' and experienced 'street smart' women produced opportunities for additional income by, for instance, simply taking the 'cop' money" and returning to the client claiming that she had been "ripped off" (p. 481). Sometimes the women did not steal the money outright, but simply charged more than the cost of the drug. Sometimes they took some of the drug for themselves or adulterated it with cheaper ingredients.

A few of the women sold drug paraphernalia such as crack pipes, stems, or syringes ("works"). Men who sold "sealed" (new) works were more likely to have suppliers, most often contacts at local hospitals. Women were more likely to sell "used works," which they usually procured from diabetic family members or friends. Others would collect used works strewn around the neighborhood and exchange them for new ones through a needle-exchange program. Sometimes men from outside the area, reluctant to carry drug paraphernalia, would give the women a "hit" of crack in exchange for use of their stem. Women who rented their stems in this way savored the accumulated residue, which they periodically scraped out and smoked. Maher and Daly concluded that the drug market is not an "equal opportunity employer" and that prostitution remains the only consistent option open to women surviving on the streets.

Street Prostitution

Sex work is a term advanced by feminist scholars as well as sex workers themselves to refer to a range of illegal and legal acts that include prostitution, erotic dancing, and the making of pornographic photos and films (Zatz 1997). Lillian Robinson suggests that the term *sex work* has made it easier to talk about the women involved in these "occupations" without denigrating them as immoral or sinful, but it is "a far cry from acknowledging that sex work is the only work or the best work a woman can get, to concluding that it is not a form of exploitation" (1996:184). Indeed, the experience of most sex workers is a far cry from that seen in the popular 1990 film *Pretty Woman,* in which Julia Roberts's character is portrayed as a prostitute who falls in love with one of her rich clients and lives "happily ever after."

Women and girls become involved in prostitution for a variety of reasons. Some are escaping unsavory domestic environments and get caught up in a struggle for survival on the streets (see Chapter 3). Some are from backgrounds that afford them few economic opportunities, and some are drawn to the adventure and lure of what they think will be "easy money." A few simply "enjoy sex and have no qualms about enjoying sex as work" (Alexander 1987:16). Some women prostitute occasionally or sporadically, some consistently for short periods of time, and some for many years. Some are cajoled, deceived, and even physically coerced by pimps and other sex traffickers who keep them mired in what amounts to a life of sexual slavery (Barry 1979; Heil 2012; Potterat et al. 1990).

During the time of her research with Richard Curtis, Maher spent a day hanging out with Bay, a 26-year-old African-American woman, as she "hustled" for cash and crack (Maher & Curtis 1992). Bay was having trouble getting sex work, because she was seven months pregnant. As Maher and Curtis note: "Watching her panhandle change whenever she could, con a junkie out of a stolen bedspread for $1 and re-sell it for $2, get free condoms from health workers and sell them to girls on the stroll, and, finally, try for over an hour to pick up a date, we were left with the indelible impression that, in the absence of sex work, it was difficult, if not impossible, for women to 'get paid' in this neighbourhood" (p. 223).

In Leon Pettiway's study (1997) of drug-addicted, inner-city hustlers, he describes the lives of women who prostitute, sell drugs, shoplift, and perform various kinds of theft and fraud. Some of these women had left home to escape abusive and cruel treatment. For others "the seduction of the fast life, inducements from friends, and environments ridden with drugs and crime were in large measure responsible for their entry into the world" of street hustling (pp. xxvii–xxviii). Margaret, who started turning "tricks" for survival, said that prostitution wasn't foreign to her before she got into it:

> I knew my sisters was doing it. . . . Men always was hitting on me and it just came natural. . . . Wasn't nothing that . . . a woman don't already

FURTHER EXPLORATION
Sex Trafficking and Prostitution in Global Context

Sex trafficking refers to the coercion of people into the commercial sex trade against their will. Ninety-eight percent of the victims of sex trafficking are women and girls. It is the fastest-growing business of organized crime and one of the largest criminal enterprises in the world. While prostitution per se should not be equated with sex trafficking, victims of sex trafficking can be found in some residential brothels, escort services, fake massage parlors, strip clubs, and street prostitution (Barry 1979, 1995; Heil 2012; Walker-Rodriguez & Hill 2011).

Women and girls are recruited into sex trafficking in different ways. In poverty-stricken rural areas of underdeveloped countries, some girls are sold into prostitution by their parents or tricked into leaving their families with false promises of employment or marriage. Some are then recruited or coerced into serving specialized markets for soldiers, sailors, businessmen, or immigrant laborers. In times of war, rape survivors, who are often considered disgraced by their families and communities, are especially vulnerable to networks of pimps and criminal organizations, as are refugees and other socially displaced women and girls.

Moreover, fraudulent employment agencies and dance companies now advertise for what appear to be exciting jobs overseas. Vulnerable women who respond to these solicitations often find that when they arrive at their destination, the anticipated jobs are not available and they have to pay the organization back for expenses incurred. The work they are offered to help them get out of "debt" sometimes includes jobs in bars with duties that they soon learn "extend far beyond being a hostess and serving drinks" (Barry 1979:90). Some of the women who answer these ads know they will be engaging in sex work but do not anticipate the slavery-like conditions they eventually find themselves in. Mail-order-bride businesses also engage in a disguised form of sex trafficking, as would-be brides whose husbands-to-be are unsatisfied are at times turned over to prostitution. And in some cases, women and girls are outright kidnapped, beaten, gang-raped, involuntarily addicted to drugs, and forced to have sex with as many as 50 people a day. Lest one think that sex trafficking in the United States consists only of foreign-born victims who are brought into the country, the United States has its own homegrown problem of interstate sex trafficking as well.

Currently, global economic development has also been accompanied by what Kathleen Barry describes as the "industrialization" and "global diffusion of prostitution," as prostitution, pornography, and other sex services are growing commodities in a number of countries (1995:52). **Sex tourism**—the traveling to a foreign country for the expressed purpose of engaging in sexual activity (including sex with children)—has become all too common, even "an official, planned source of national income" (Kirschenbaum 1991:13). In the United States, of course, Las Vegas, Nevada, is known as the premier city of the commercial sex trade. Although prostitution is technically illegal in Las Vegas, it remains a thriving business there, and in some parts of the state prostitution is legal (Brents et al. 2010; Wonders & Michalowski 2001).

know. Except for when you call yourself a professional. Then you have to learn how to suck . . . real good and stuff like that. How to make them hurry up and reach a climax. . . . How to encourage them . . . [with] all that . . . talking. . . . "Fuck me" or . . . "All this big dick." . . . I never did like that. Moaning and groaning and all. . . . I picked up these rules by just being around. . . . I learnt . . . how to put the rubber on without them knowing, how to go in their pocket [for their money] without them feeling. (pp. 10, 16, 40–41)

But prostitution is not really about pleasing customers; it is about acquiring money and drugs. Charlie told Pettiway that there's no sexual attraction when she is tricking; it's "purely business." She lights a cigarette and tells the customer: "When the cigarette is burnt down, your time's up. If you want more time, that's more money. If you want to touch me, that's even more money" (p. 81). Margaret is equally blunt about oral sex: "When I turn tricks . . . I'm gonna give you two or three minutes and if you can't get it in that . . . time, sorry. . . . Before, I was aiming to please . . . 'cause the money was [better]. But now . . . it don't make me no difference whether they come or not. . . . I ain't making love. . . . They be . . . saying, '. . . you gotta play with my [titties]' [but I say] 'I ain't gotta play with your titties. . . . I'm sucking your dick. That's all I gotta do'" (p. 44).

For Tracy, turning tricks in the projects where she lives seems easier and safer than going downtown to shoplift. However, she does not believe one can "earn an honest living and do drugs too" (p. 192). Likewise, Charlie said: "I wish I hadn't prostituted. . . . It's degrading. . . . It's something I don't want to do, but it's something that my addictions make me do" (p. 95). Drug-addicted women who prostitute have a more difficult time than nonaddicted women maintaining their own standards about whom they will or will not service. If a man "don't want to use no rubber," Margaret lamented, "it be hard . . . to walk away [when he's] got ten . . . or five dollars in his pocket. . . . You want that money so bad" (p. 18).

Although prostitution is sometimes portrayed as a victimless crime, prostitutes are often victimized themselves. Research indicates that a large majority have been physically and sexually assaulted by customers and forced into sexual acts not agreed to. A large majority also report being beaten regularly by their pimps, who "discipline" them for not bringing home enough money, not obeying them, trying to leave, or challenging their authority. Unfortunately, prostitutes who are abused, whether by pimps, customers, or even police, find it virtually impossible to get help, because they typically lack the resources to do so and are vulnerable to arrest (Barry 1995; Heil 2012; Miller et al. 1993).

Bernard Cohen (1980) distinguishes between a **pimp** and a **man**. Both live off the earnings of a prostitute, but a prostitute works *for* a pimp and *with* a man. The "man" is usually a husband or lover who watches over and protects "his woman" and supervises her work. The "pimp" is an agent or companion of several women. He tends to act more as a general manager of the women, since he is not generally on the scene. In her study, Eleanor Miller (1986) found a continuum of managerial types rather than a clear-cut dichotomy between "man" and "pimp," with most falling somewhere in between:

> [W]omen . . . rarely referred to a current manager as "my pimp." He was always . . . "my man." For the female at least, the personal side of the relationship far outweighed the business side in importance. . . . In fact, one of the most common reasons for a "woman" to leave a "man" was when some occurrence made it obvious that the relationship, from his point of view, was entirely for business purposes. On such occasions, women would say, "He wasn't nothin' but a pimp." (p. 39)

Kathleen Barry (1995) describes how pimps looking to recruit a girl or woman target those who appear lonely, naive, or rebellious. If they are fleeing abusive homes or marriages, chances are they have little money and few job skills: "Suddenly he appears, he is friendly, . . . offers to buy her a meal, and . . . gives her a place to spend the night. She hears compliments for the first time in ages, as well as promises that he will buy her new clothes, . . . have her hair done, . . . make [her his] 'foxy lady'" (pp. 204–206). If she seems to be the daring and rebellious type, the pimp may come right out and offer her a proposal. He tells her he is a "businessman" and they could be "partners," that she will be his "woman." He'll give her "some schooling" and her pockets will be "filled with money." If she seems scared or prudish, he'll make "his play for her as a lover," make her feel important, establish a sexual relationship. Then he'll insist that she prove her love for him by prostituting herself. He tells her they need money and "if you love me, you'll do anything for me." If that doesn't work—if she doesn't do what he says—he'll demonstrate his power and reduce her defenses with a beating or sexual assault.

Once a woman has started tricking, pimps often undermine her self-esteem through verbal abuse: "You're nothing but a goddamn whore, . . . you're worthless, . . . you're trash" (Barry 1995:200, 207). Melinda, a former prostitute who eventually got free of her pimp, said that through verbal abuse and beatings her pimp put so much fear in her that she was "afraid to leave him. Yet by that time I was so much in love with him it really didn't matter. . . . When he put his arms around me . . . [and] told me he loved me, I believed everything would work out all right" (p. 200).

Unfortunately, law enforcement does not help women escape from prostitution. Rather, as Miller and colleagues observe, it tends "to strain, if not sever, [the woman's] social connection to her children and the other kin who might be militating against a life of prostitution, and to heighten her feelings of low self-esteem, depression, and hopelessness" (1993:314). Moreover, if she is "dependent on alcohol or other drugs and is not incarcerated for any length of time," which is typically the case, the possible consequences of her arrest, such as losing custody of her children, "may motivate her to retreat even further into alcohol and drug use" and turn tricks to support her habit. Arrest may also strengthen a woman's dependence on her pimp, as he may be the only person available to make arrangements for child care, bail, or legal representation.

Research on prostitutes who become addicted to drugs also has found that the spread of crack-cocaine use has flooded the market with *novice* sex workers who need money for drugs. This trend has been accompanied by a shift in the nature of prostitution from intercourse to fellatio and from indoors to outdoors (cars, alleys, parks, vacant lots), thus deflating the going rate for sexual transactions (Maher & Curtis 1992). One woman described the situation this way: "Women who do crack . . . [will] do anything for five dollars, and it hurts the girls that are out there. . . . [A] guy will come to me and say, 'I'll give you five dollars for a blow job.' . . . Or, 'Do you accept food stamps?' or 'Can I pay you later?'" (Pettiway 1997:90). Some women even exchange sex directly for drugs. As one woman reported, "I've exchanged sex for drugs. . . . This guy that I know, he's a dealer and he wanted some head. So he gave me an eight-ball [3.5 grams of coke] . . . and I gave him a blow job. Other times, guys done gave me like four bags, three bags, and I done gave them a blow job. . . . That's what I mainly do is give blow jobs. . . . I don't really fuck a lot" (Pettiway 1997:16).

The heightened competition for "dates" (customers) has intensified hostility among prostitutes and increased the social isolation they experience. Candy, who had worked the streets for 17 years, said: "These girls out here are just for the drug and theirself—no friendship, everyone's out to cut everyone's throat. . . . [Before] we were friends and we'd help one another out. . . . We'd stick together . . . do a favour, call somebody up, go get a bag of dope. . . . These people don't know how to be ho's" (Maher & Curtis 1992:233–234). As cash and drugs become harder to get, sometimes the "ho's" even rob each other as well as their dates. And when they "be thirsty (needing drugs) . . . they ain't got no time to judge" the character of a date and increasingly end up with "rougher and nastier" men who rob or beat them (pp. 240, 243).

Urban Gangs

Malcolm Klein defines a **gang** as consisting of youths who consider themselves to be a distinct group (usually with an agreed-upon gang name), who are perceived as a distinct group by others in the community, and who have been involved in a sufficient number of crimes so as "to call forth a consistent negative response from neighborhood residents and/or law enforcement agencies" (1971:13). The third element of Klein's definition—a consistent negative response from the community—would exclude as gangs many groups of delinquent youths who manage to avoid negative societal labeling because of their relatively privileged social status. In his classic study "The Saints and Roughnecks," for example, William Chambliss (1973) found that the lower-class Roughnecks were more likely to elicit a negative community reaction than were the middle-class Saints, even though the Saints were extensively involved in illegal activities (see Chapter 1).

Most adolescent delinquency, regardless of class context, occurs in groups (Miller 1980), and C. Ronald Huff thinks that "gangs represent an extreme manifestation of that age-typical emphasis on being together and belonging to something" (1993:6). In William Sanders's opinion (1994), however, it is the violence that distinguishes gangs from other law-violating teenage groups.

Gangs in Historical and Contemporary Context

Frederick Thrasher's (1927) classic study of Chicago youth gangs of an earlier era offers a useful point of departure for a consideration of contemporary urban gangs. Gang members in the 1920s were largely the children of economically disadvantaged, white European immigrants—primarily Irish, Italians, and Poles, but also Germans, Jews, Slavs, and Swedes. Most gang members started out in thievery, which they engaged in as much for sport as for economic gain. Gangs that formed more or less spontaneously as ordinary groups of kids who hung out on the streets were consolidated through rivalry and strife. As Jerome Skolnick observes: "Thrasher traced the rise of gangs to . . . the disintegration of family life, schools, and religion, . . . [the lack of] wholesome alternatives, . . . [and] the corruption and indifference of local politicians. The employment opportunities available to these [youths] usually involved monotonous jobs with low wages that could scarcely compete with the rewards of the gang or with the fun of bonding and stealing" (1992:111).

In many respects, contemporary gangs have not changed in fundamental ways. Youths still join gangs for fun and recreation, to enhance their ability to make money, for physical protection, and for a sense of belonging to a community or alternative family (Sanchez Jankowski 1991). In some Chicano barrios of Los Angeles, for instance, "children, parents, and even grandparents have belonged to the same gang [for decades]. Although the adults fear and disapprove of the violence of today's gangs, they take pride in the tradition of gang membership" and expect the younger generation to preserve and uphold the neighborhood gang name (Skolnick 1992:114). More generally, gangs are often tolerated in their communities because gang youths are not social outsiders among residents; they are sons and daughters, grandchildren, nieces and nephews, the neighbors' kids. The majority of their time is not spent in law-violating activities, and their behavior is appropriate in most social situations (Horowitz 1987; Juette &

Berger 2008). Nevertheless, research indicates that the onset of gang membership is a turning point in the lives of delinquent youths, leading them down a path of escalating and sustained criminality (Krohn et al. 2011; Melde & Esbensen 2011).

Nowadays gangs include older youths who have fewer opportunities to mature out of their situation compared to Thrasher's day (Skolnick 1992). Hence some graduate to organized crime. Observers of the gang scene report that as early as the late 1960s and early 1970s, gangs in some large urban areas, most notably in Chicago and New York, were beginning to be transformed "from territorially oriented younger members to commercially oriented older (19 plus) members," while some black and Latino groups began muscling in on the territories previously controlled by Italian-American organizations (Robinson 1993:312). Needless to say, this transition of control has not always been peaceful.

Ironically, since the 1970s, incarceration of gang members has facilitated gang organization by bringing together a captive population of similarly situated offenders who can be easily recruited into larger, more powerful organizations (Hayden 2004; Irwin 1980; Jacobs 1977). Jeff Fort, for example, a leader of Chicago's Black P (Peace) Stones Nation, formed the Muslim-identified El Rukn (The Foundation) while he was imprisoned in the late 1970s. According to Cyril Robinson's account:

> Soon after his release, [Fort] met with representatives of the Italian syndicate having vice interests in El Rukn territory. Reputedly, the Italian group ordered Fort to keep hands off. After burning down the mob restaurant where the warnings were given, Fort, in turn, ordered the syndicate out of El Rukn territory. . . . By 1981, the El Rukns were investing their drug profits in real estate and other legitimate businesses and were employing pharmacists, doctors, accountants, and lawyers. Satellite clubs or alliances were [also] formed in other parts of the country. (1993:313)

Sanders (1994) studied gangs in San Diego, California, through the 1980s and found that African-American gangs were more likely to sell (but less likely to use) drugs compared to their Chicano counterparts. He did not find San Diego gangs to be particularly well-organized, as gang cohesiveness was rooted more in neighborhood solidarity and loyalty than in a formally structured organization. On the other hand, Martin Sanchez Jankowski (1991)—who studied 37 gangs in Boston, Los Angeles, and New York—argues that most gangs that are in a mature stage of development have identifiable leadership positions and established codes of conduct. Moreover, Jankowski and others have concluded that by the late 1980s, gang organizations of a variety of racial and ethnic backgrounds had become more entrepreneurial in nature, shifting away from turf-fighting and toward more systematic involvement in drug distribution (Padilla 1992; Venkatesh 1997, 2008).

Research also suggests that Asian-American gangs are among the most highly entrepreneurial gangs in the country. Chinese gangs in particular, which can be found primarily in Boston, Los Angeles, New York, and San Francisco (as well as Toronto and Vancouver), have a well-defined hierarchical structure, are well-connected with adult crime groups and fraternal organizations, and have invested in legitimate businesses (Shelden et al. 2004).

In interviews conducted by Skolnick and colleagues (1993), black gang members from Los Angeles reported that perceived economic benefit had become the primary reason for joining gangs. Skolnick and colleagues attributed this change, in part, to the expanded cocaine importation that had dramatically decreased the wholesale cost of the drug. Prospective gang members were now evaluated in terms of their ability to sell drugs. The gang provided members with access to and control of drug markets within the gang's territory, shared information about the drug market (such as sellers, prices, and out-of-town markets), protection from competitors and the police, as well as cash, loans, and "fronting" of drugs, weapons, clothes, and cars.

While black gangs in Los Angeles first appeared in the 1950s, the two infamous supergangs or gang "nations"—the Crips and the Bloods—did not emerge until the late 1960s (Williams 2007). These gangs are said to be "deep," consisting of a large number of sets or factions. In the early 1990s, Léon Bing (1991) reported the existence of 56 Crip sets and 43 Blood sets, while Skolnick and colleagues (1993) found that Crip or Blood crack-cocaine operations could be found in 22 states and at least 28 cities in regions all over the country. Gang members indicated that in the mid-1980s they began traveling extensively to expand their drug business. This expansion was motivated, in part, by pressure from police crackdowns in Los Angeles, saturation of the Los Angeles drug market, and higher prices that could be charged in out-of-town markets. At the same time, other knowledgeable observers believed that large-scale drug operations were still generally being conducted by "individuals and small groups acting on their own rather than for the gang" as a whole (Reiner 1992:72).

In his San Diego study, Sanders (1994) found that black gangs (including Crip and Blood sets) extended their activities over a broad territory, while Chicano gangs were more confined to the barrio and lacked allegiances outside their community. On the other hand, Joan Moore and colleagues characterized Los Angeles Chicano gangs as having a "widespread pattern of nonresident gang membership" and documented several ways in which such nonresident membership developed (Moore et al. 1983:182). Sometimes gang membership was extended to relatives who lived outside the neighborhood. At times, families of gang members moved, but youths maintained affiliation with their original gang. Gangs also formed fighting alliances with gangs in other areas, or factions split apart and affiliated with other groups. Nonresident youths sometimes sought to join a gang because of its activities or reputation. Occasionally the borders of a barrio were unclear, leaving some members living in disputed areas, or freeway construction altered the community ecology, dividing a previously contiguous neighborhood.

In the Chicago area, both black and Latino gangs have grouped around the larger People and Folks gang nations or organizations (Shelden et al. 2004). These Chicago gangs can be traced to the late 1950s and early 1960s, and like the Crips and Bloods, they claim membership in multiple cities. John Hagedorn (1988) documented the emergence of People and Folks sets in Milwaukee, Wisconsin, around 1980, but argued that gangs in Milwaukee developed primarily in response to local conditions. Only four of the original nineteen Milwaukee gangs that he studied were started by former gang youths from Chicago, although an additional four gangs did have former Chicago gang youths as founding members who brought drug and gun connections to the new gang and acted "as cultural carriers of the folkways, mythologies, and other trappings of more sophisticated urban gangs" (Maxson 2006:111).

Nowadays youths claiming gang membership have also appeared in smaller cities, towns, and even rural areas (Skolnick et al. 1993; Takata & Zevitz 1990). In a study of rural/small-town gang origins in southeastern Wisconsin, Linda Stoneall (1997) offered several hypotheses for this development. Whereas Hagedorn (1988) traced the rise of gangs in Milwaukee (a city of about 650,000) to the deindustrialization and persistent racial segregation of that city, Stoneall argued that economic development in smaller communities increased the size and diversity of the population in ways that facilitated gang activity. As families of gang members moved, often to escape the problems of larger cities, youths brought their gang experience and connections with them. Some gang members from larger cities were reaching out to new areas to expand their drug markets, and some were dispersed into new communities through foster-home placements.

At the same time, as Stoneall observed, much of the apparent gang activity in small communities is simply due to cultural diffusion and youth fads, as entertainment media expose nongang youths to urban gang culture, and local peer groups emulate gang names, symbols, and styles. Consequently, teenagers who refer to themselves by the same gang name may not actually be in the same gang, or they may not be in a gang at all. Rather, they may simply be a group of delinquent peers who are "wannabes" merely "playing" at being a gang.

While criminologists continue to debate the distinction between gangs and other law-violating youth groups, it is clear that in some communities gangs have become "a recognized, albeit contradictory, community institution, performing a range of 'positive functions' while simultaneously engaging in behavior that has disrupted community social life" (Venkatesh

FURTHER EXPLORATION
Law-Violating Youth Groups in Suburbia

In their study of law-violating youth groups in the suburbs of Southern California, Wayne Wooden and Randy Blazak (2001) describe two groups: **renegade kids** and **suburban outlaws**. Renegade kids are those who are alienated and bored with the tranquil mediocrity of contemporary suburbia. For these youths, crime is a form of rebellious risk-taking. They find excitement in testing the limits, in challenging authority and getting away with it. Most of what they do is generally harmless to others, but some engage in self-destructive behaviors such as cutting or burning themselves or even suicide. But some renegade kids progress to more serious forms of thievery, property destruction, and violence against others. When they do, they become what Wooden and Blazak call suburban outlaws.

Punkers are a main focus of Wooden and Blazak's portrayal of renegade kids. Punkers are known for their defiant appearance, with their black attire, spiked hair, and pierced rings in their ears, noses, lips, and tongues. Punkers describe themselves as simply interested in rejecting conformity and "doing their own thing," and some claim that their punk identity actually helped them move beyond previous involvement with drugs and alcohol. On the other hand, merchants in shopping malls where punkers congregate think they are prone to shoplifting and are a nuisance to customers.

Still another group of renegade kids in Wooden and Blazak's study is a group of delinquent athletes (jocks) called the *Spur Posse*. Members of this group are known for their sexual exploits, competing with each other to see who can "score" with the most girls. The boys boast of their conquests but consider the girls "sluts," and often they take turns having sex with the same ones. Some are even arrested for rape, sexual assault, and burglary.

Taggers, one of the suburban outlaw groups, include youths who mimic the graffiti-writing "crews" that were first observed among lower-class urban youths (Williams & Kornblum 1985). Tagging offers participants an exciting adrenaline rush, and some of the more extended "pieces" are quite artistic. Nevertheless, the marking of school grounds and property as well as "overhead freeway signs, walls, . . . buses and trains, . . . traffic signs, bridges, and street poles" is perceived by most members of the community as vandalism, pure and simple, as sheer destruction of property (Wooden & Blazak 2001:120).

Wooden and Blazak attribute suburban tagging, in part, to the cultural diffusion of inner-city street culture, whereby enjoying gangsta rap and hip-hop music becomes "for these white 'home boys,' their form of replicating inner-city, black ghetto 'chic'" (2001:122). They also think that suburban tagging is a response to the movement of inner-city gangs into suburbia. Rather than merely mimicking black urban youths, suburban tagger crews form "to compete or oppose them. In effect, the taggers have reversed the direction of gang diffusion from the inner-city outward, as taggers frequently move from "suburban areas along freeways back toward the inner-city,"

continues

continued

leaving their pieces "to indicate their presence and influence along the way" (pp. 122–123). Most taggers want no trouble with inner-city gangs, however. As one youth explained, "We are afraid of gangs. . . . All we want is to be able to write on walls" (p. 124).

Unlike taggers, *skinhead* suburban outlaws tend to embrace violence and attack minority groups, including racial/ethnic groups, immigrants, Jews, and gays. Skinheads are recognizable by their shaved or close-cropped hair, green flight jackets, suspenders, heavy jeans rolled up over industrial boots, and "white power" and Nazi regalia, although not all skinheads look this way. Sometimes these skinheads align themselves with the adult neo-Nazi move- ment and are critical of, if not hostile to, the US government, which they believe promotes the interests of nonwhites over whites (see Chapter 10). But not all skinheads are racist, or if they are, they try to avoid racial violence. These youths are more survivalist in nature, being concerned with their future survival in the event of a nuclear catastrophe or natural disaster. There are even antiracist skinhead groups with racially mixed membership that have formed in reaction to the racist groups.

Stoner gangs, known for their extensive drug and alcohol abuse, are among the most violent suburban outlaws in Wooden and Blazak's study, committing armed robberies, burglaries, and motor vehicle thefts. These youths are also most likely to have been physically (and sexually) abused, rather than merely neglected, by their parents. They share an interest in heavy metal music and attire (e.g., metal-spiked wrist cuffs, collars and belts, and sacrilegious or anti-Christian items), with some engaging in cultlike satanic rituals, including animal sacrifices, which some do to provoke or upset their parents.

1997:107). In his ethnography of the Saints, a pseudonym for an African- American gang in Chicago, Sudhir Venkatesh (1997) found that gang members channeled some of their drug profits to the resident population in order to ingratiate themselves into the social fabric of the housing project in which they were based. The gang distributed groceries and clothing, lent residents money (both interest-free and at exorbitant rates), paid the bail bond for jailed residents, replaced playground equipment, encouraged younger gang members to attend school, and offered protection from other gangs and criminal predators. The residents, in turn, provided the Saints cover, withholding information from the police and refusing "to allow police to enter their apartments without search warrants" (p. 95). As one resident, a prominent leader on a tenant council, remarked:

> [We] stopped cooperating with police a long time ago, 'cause [they] harass us so much and . . . don't do a damn thing anyway. At least the gangs is giving us something, so [a] lot of us prefers to help them 'cause we can

always go to them and tell them to stop the shooting. Police don't do anything for us and they can't stop no shooting anyway. . . . [The Saints] is the
one providing security around here. . . . We all niggers anyway when it
come down to it. (p. 95)

Some residents admitted that the Saints "make our lives miserable, but
if we piss them off, police ain't gonna come 'round here and help us out.
And, shit, I gotta tell you, that most of the time it's nice, 'cause they make
sure I don't get robbed up in here, they walk through the buildings like . . .
police never did that!" (p. 103). Another put it this way: "We have to listen
to [the Saints], 'cause when the police leave, [the Saints] are the ones
who'll let you know if shootings gonna start up again, you know, they'll
tell you if it's safe to go outside at night, or if you can go up north . . . or
if you should just stay in the building" (p. 103). In the words of one Saint,
"We [want] to be part of the community, help our community, 'cause we're
here to stay" (p. 108).

Girls in Gangs

In her research on girls in gangs, Anne Campbell (1987, 1991) interviewed
lower-class minority youths in New York City. One cannot read these young
women's accounts without questioning the adequacy of conventional gender
explanations that emphasize the difference between females and males. The
conventional assumption that males are more violent than females does not
necessarily hold among these youths. As one girl explained: "Round here
you have to know how to fight. I'm glad I got a reputation. That way nobody
will start with me. . . . They're going to come out losing. Like all of us. . . .
We're crazy. Nobody wants to fight us. . . . They say, 'No, man. That girl
might stab me or cut my face'" (1987:462–463).

Meda Chesney-Lind and Randall Shelden (2004) suggest that the moderate increase in female violence that has occurred over the past few
decades may be attributed, in part, to greater involvement of girls in gang-
related offenses, even though females generally remain less involved in
gangs than males (see Chapter 1). Overall, self-reported delinquency of
female gang members is lower than for male gang members, but higher
than for nongang males (Esbensen & Winfree 1998; Miller & Brunson
2000). In a study of gang membership among eighth-grade students in 11
cities, Dana Peterson and colleagues (2001) found that 10 percent of gang
members were involved in all-male gangs and 37 percent of gang members
were involved in majority-male gangs, while only 3 percent of gang members were involved in all-female gangs and 2 percent in majority-female
gangs ("majority-male" and "majority-female" gangs were defined as those
having at least two-thirds of the members as male or female, respectively).
Nearly half of gang members were involved in gender-balanced gangs.
Peterson and colleagues also found that gender patterns of gang offending

varied according to the gender composition of the gangs, with boys in majority-male gangs having the highest rates of delinquency, and girls in all-female and majority-female gangs having the lowest rates.

James Messerschmidt (1997) views the gang milieu as an environment in which girls experiment with and reconfigure the boundaries of femininity. Conventional femininity is the culturally dominant ideal that is organized around "the display of sociability rather than technical competence, fragility in mating scenes, compliance with men's desire for titillation and ego-stroking . . . [and] acceptance of marriage and child care" (Connell 1987:187). According to Messerschmidt, when gang girls act tough and are violent, they are not being unfeminine but are enacting an alternative or oppositional femininity. As such, Peggy Giordano and Stephen Cernkovich (1979) observe that gang girls are capable of identifying with and participating in aspects of both traditional and nontraditional gender roles. Elements of traditionalism still permeate the gang milieu. Girls, for instance, are most often involved in gangs as girlfriends of male gang members or as "little sister" subgroups or female auxiliaries that take their name from the male gang, as with the Latin Queens, named after the Latin Kings (Shelden et al. 2004). One New York City gang girl told Campbell (1991) that when the boys were not around, they could do what they wanted. When the guys were there, however, they were "not allowed" to do as they pleased (p. 244). Similarly, a Los Angeles Chicana told John Quicker: "If it wasn't for [the boys] we wouldn't be around 'cause the guys started [the gang]. . . . The girls never start the gang; the guys do. And the girls that like them or back them up started it with their permission" (1983:101).

In her study of Chicano gangs in Los Angeles, Joan Moore found that boys often treated girls as possessions, "like a piece of ass." As one boy remarked, "It's just there . . . when you want a *chapete* (fuck). . . . The guys treat them like shit. . . . Just to have a partner for the time. . . . And then when they want something you know, get it—wham bam. . . . We used to . . . throw a *linea* (lining up to have sex with a girl), you know what I mean" (1991:54–55). Similarly, in her study of African-American gangs in Fort Wayne, Indiana, Deborah Burris-Kitchen found that girls had difficulty getting the respect they felt they deserved. As one young woman said: "Guys around here don't respect women much. I think it is because of all the rap music bashin' women. I listen to some of this music calling women bitches and ho's and it upsets me. I think the guys around here think sex is all we're good for" (1995:104).

Other females noted a double standard: "Most women get respect if they sellin' drugs, but not if they using. It's ok for guys to use, but not us" (Burris-Kitchen 1995:104). And although gang boys expressed pride over girls' willingness to fight, they were sometimes uncomfortable with or ambivalent about female aggression. As one of Quicker's respondents explained: "I've asked my boyfriend and they all come up with the same answer. 'I don't think a girl should be in . . . the fights.' . . . They say it's right for a guy, but it's not right for girls. . . . That's what they all say, yet they are happy to have their own girls. They're proud. They say our girls do this, our girls are bad. . . . [So] I don't know what they're talking about" (1983:12).

Gang girls—largely lower-class, minority youths—have few opportunities to make it in mainstream society. They come from families where they often have experienced physical and sexual abuse, from families that are frequently "held together by their mothers, who are subsisting on welfare. Most have dropped out of school and have no marketable skills" (Joe & Chesney-Lind 1995:413). The gang represents an alternative family, a social support system that buffers the dismal future that awaits them. But gang girls also recognize that they must negotiate a gender-stratified street environment dominated by males. As one said: "Females who are soft won't make it. . . . Someone think you weak, they goin' take from ya'. Even if you female you got to be willing to shoot" (Burris-Kitchen 1995:93). Campbell notes that gang girls know what it is like to be victimized:

> They know that, to survive, force must be met with more than unspoken anger or frustrated tears. Less physically strong and more sexually vulnerable than boys, they find that the best line of defense is not attack but the threat of attack. The key to this is the development of a reputation for violence, which will ward off opponents. There is nothing so effective as being in a street gang to keep the message blaring out: "Don't mess with me—I'm a crazy woman." (1993:133)

Girls who are unwilling or unable to fight are thus viewed disparagingly. As one girl said: "Tramps. All they think about is screwing. . . . They don't fight. They don't go to rumbles with their guys. . . . They're a bunch of punks" (Campbell 1987:463). Another girl remarked: "You can belong as long as you can back up your shit and don't rat on your homegirls or back away [from a fight. You have to be] able to hold up the hood" (Harris 1988:109).

Although not equal in power, auxiliary female gangs are not mere appendages of male gangs. Girls in gangs have their own leaders and make most of their routine decisions without the boys (Bowker & Klein 1983; Giordano 1978). They take pride in their claims of autonomy and reject "any suggestion that they could be duped or conned by males" (Campbell 1987:460). In a study of San Francisco gangs, David Lauderback and colleagues (1992) found that African-American females were less likely than Latinas to be affiliated with male groups. One black gang, the Potrero Hill Posse, started out as a mixed-gender group, with girls selling drugs for their boyfriends. Eventually, however, the females disaffiliated themselves from the males and formed a gang of their own, requiring members to be adept at either selling drugs (crack cocaine) or shoplifting.

Moore (1991) found that female gangs were not as closely bound to the barrio as were male gangs, and that girls often partied with boys from other gangs. Boys, however, were more likely to date girls who were not in gangs, expressing preference for those they perceived as more likely to fulfill traditional gender roles in the future. As one boy said: "You know that they are going to be good. You know they going to take care of business and . . . be a good housewife" (p. 75). Some girls clearly rejected the traditionalism of male constructions of gender. "Not *me*," said one of Moore's informants, "they didn't treat me like that. They think we're possessions, but we're not. No way, I pick my own boyfriends. . . . You don't tell *me* who to be with" (p. 55).

Some gang girls displayed a defiant view toward conventional expectations of female sexuality while at the same time allowing themselves to be treated as sex objects. For example, some Vice Queens, a black gang in Chicago, unabashedly placed themselves at the boys' disposal, encouraging them to fondle and have sex with them. Although the boys viewed the girls as sex objects, the girls gained status among their female peers by "being able to keep four or five boys 'on the string' without any boys knowing of the others, but at the same time, avoiding sexual relationships with too many boys at one time" (Fishman 1988:21). However, Peggy Orenstein suggests that such girls have simply learned to derive whatever pleasure they can from their subordinate and exploitative position vis-à-vis boys and have "recast mistreatment as excitement" (1994:209).

In her interviews with Latinas in San Antonio, Texas, Sikes (1997) learned that "trains" (sex with a number of gang males in succession) were an option to "jump ins" (physical beatings by gang members) in gang initiation rituals (trains were not an option for male initiates). The girls did not view the trains as rape but considered them "the coward's way in—after all, gang logic goes, all the girl does is lie down and spread her legs" (p. 110). Sikes found that most girls chose the "jump in" option.

Nevertheless, Campbell (1987) observes that serial monogamy, not promiscuity, is the norm for most gang girls, and those who have sex outside of a steady relationship are often condemned. Gang girls may even avoid associating with "'loose' girls whose reputation might contaminate them by association" (p. 452). But once they are involved in a relationship, boys often attempt to exert control over their girlfriends' public appearance and behavior, not allowing them to wear shorts or low-cut blouses, to get "high," or to flirt with other guys. Boys, on the other hand, reserve their prerogative to have other relationships. Masculinity norms make it difficult for boys to turn down an opportunity for sex; in their eyes this would be tantamount to an admission of homosexuality. Girls also accept this view of masculinity and blame other girls for "putting it in his face." In this way, romantic disputes between girls and boys are settled between girls. Nevertheless, the girls' main objective is not so much to "hold on to their man" as to gain the respect of other girls (Campbell 1991; Sikes 1997).

Occasionally, gang girls fight to defend territorial turf and gain recognition for their group. However, much of their fighting occurs in response to competition over boyfriends, assessments of beauty (who is "the cutest"), and negative gossip regarding one's reputation or that of a family member—their mother especially. Fighting among girls is generally less lethal than among boys, since it usually involves fists or knives rather than guns, but gun use among girls does occur (Anderson 1994; Campbell 1993; Harris 1988).

Gang girls who fight or are willing to use violence are not rejecting femininity but are constructing an alternative femininity that combines traditional and nontraditional gender traits. Although participation in a street fight involves physical aggression against rival gang members, it is also defined as an act of *caring* for one's gang and the "hood." Thus, what is generally "considered atypical feminine behavior outside this situation is, in fact, *normalized* within the social context of interneighborhood conflict; girl-gang violence in this situation is . . . permitted and . . . encouraged . . . by *both* boys and girls as appropriate feminine behavior" (Messerschmidt 1997:82). At the same time, girls also perform many conventional feminine roles in the gang, such as child care, cooking, and preparing food and drink for parties. Additionally, gang girls are rather fussy about their physical appearance—their hair, makeup, and clothing (with importance placed on wearing the right brand name)—and are disparaging of their peers who look drab or slovenly. Outside of the gang milieu they are unambiguously feminine. Campbell says that gang girls' concern "with their appearance [and] their pride in their ability to attract men . . . left me in no doubt that they enjoyed being women. They didn't want to be like men and, indeed, would have been outraged at such a suggestion" (1993:113).

Be that as it may, gang girls are often uninformed or misinformed about birth control, and rarely do they or their partners use it. Instead, they view pregnancy as an occupational hazard of sorts. Many of them get pregnant within a year after becoming sexually active, which may begin at or even before puberty. Becoming a mother does not require leaving the gang, and it offers them an alternative source of status. Motherhood is valued, provided that the mother accepts responsibility for her child's welfare. But the ability to care for children often depends on parental or grandparental support and on the (diminishing) availability of government welfare. Abortion is generally condemned for the first pregnancy but is increasingly accepted after that. Wholehearted support for abortion, which might jeopardize their reputations as mothers, is uncommon (Campbell 1987; Moore & Hagedorn 1996; Williams & Kornblum 1985).

In their research in Milwaukee, Joan Moore and John Hagedorn (1996) found that Latina girls had higher hopes of getting married than their African-American counterparts. Forty-three percent of Latina gang members and 75 percent of African Americans agreed with the statement, "I'd rather raise my kids by myself," and 29 percent of the Latinas and none of the African Americans agreed, "All a woman needs to straighten out her life is to find a good man" (pp. 216–217). At the same time, male gang members rarely marry the mothers of their children or contribute financially to their support, although they do take pride in their ability to father children, considering it a public demonstration of masculinity. As one Potrero Hill gang member explained, speaking of her child's father: "They just get you pregnant and . . . go on about their business with somebody else" (Lauderback et al. 1992:69). Moore and Hagedorn (1996) note that Latinas are subject to more traditional gender expectations than are black women, who for generations have been forced to assume independent economic and familial roles. Yet Philippe Bourgois, in his study of a Puerto Rican neighborhood in New York, notes that one of the problems facing inner-city communities today is the increasing number of mothers who are following "the paths of fathers in seeking independent lives in the underground economy or in substance abuse . . . [leaving no one] to cushion the fragmentation of the family unit" (1995:276).

Summary

This chapter opened Part 2 of the book, on patterns of criminality and victimization, by focusing on street crime, the constellation of criminal actions that are committed by offenders in the lower strata of society. We first examined the economic context of street crime, including issues related to capitalist development and urbanization, unemployment, and homelessness, and then turned to related discussions of racial inequality, the urban underclass, and the subculture of violence. The remainder of the chapter focused on the illegal economy and different types of street crime, including teenage thievery, street robbery, the drug trade, street prostitution, and urban gangs.

7

Illegal Drugs

Around the turn of the twentieth century, more than a hundred years ago, there were few laws on the books that prohibited the use of drugs in the United States. Cough elixirs with morphine (an opium derivative) were sold over the counter or ordered by mail from Sears Roebuck. Marijuana was used for migraine headaches, asthma, and other maladies, and was sold in both fluid-extract and cigarette form. Physicians used cocaine as a local anesthetic and a treatment for fatigue and morphine addiction, and it was once the official remedy of the Hay Fever Association. Bordeaux wines, Coca-Cola soft drinks, liquors, cigarettes, tablets, ointments, and sprays contained cocaine. Physicians often prescribed opium to white, middle-aged women from the middle or upper class, the typical users of the time, to alleviate gynecological and nervous disorders, and opium-based products were used to "relieve pain, colds, fevers, athlete's foot, alcoholism, diarrhea, hiccups, and other ailments" (Parsons 2014:27). And because opium was thought to enhance an individual's physical and mental performance, some employers gave it to workers to increase their productivity (Brecher 1972; Musto 1999).

The complex constellation of factors that influenced drug prohibition in the United States included such diverse issues as international treaties, the professionalization of medical practice, law enforcement's interest in expanding its jurisdictional domain, and the financial interests of the pharmaceutical industry (Fang 2014; Levine 2012; Musto 1999; Parsons 2014). In this chapter we expand upon our previous discussions of drug use and trafficking (see Chapters 2 and 6) by focusing on the well-documented connection between drug prohibition and racial and ethnic discrimination in the United States. We then examine upper- and middle-level (primarily white) drug use and drug dealing in the United States, and conclude with a critique of the "war on drugs" and a consideration of alternatives to this dubious policy.

Drug Prohibition and Racial/Ethnic Discrimination

The Early Decades
Opium, the first drug to be legally prohibited in the United States, was used primarily by the Chinese in the nineteenth century. Although the first large wave of Chinese immigrants was composed predominantly of more affluent Chinese, they were succeeded by laborers who worked in the mining industry and built the railroads in the West. By 1875, racism and xenophobia toward the Chinese and fear that lower-paid Chinese workers would displace white workers led to ordinances prohibiting opium dens and opium smoking in San Francisco, California. Similar ordinances were passed the next year in neighboring Nevada. A major impetus for such laws was the belief that opium smoking enhanced workers' productivity, thereby placing nonsmoking whites at a disadvantage in the labor market. Federal legislation attempting to control Chinese drug use was also enacted. In 1887 the US government outlawed the importation of opium *by the Chinese,* even though it remained legal for other groups to import the drug for smoking until 1909. Fear of Chinese immigrants and racial hostility culminated two years later in the passage of the Chinese Exclusion Act, which prohibited immigration of additional Chinese into the country (Helmer 1975; Musto 1999; Parsons 2014).

Cocaine was included with opiates in the Harrison Act of 1914, which regulated the possession and use of narcotics. Cocaine use, which was associated with African Americans, inspired racial fears in whites. Although poverty-stricken blacks used cocaine for relief from bronchial disease and tuberculosis, they did not use it to a greater extent than whites. In fact, it is likely that African Americans experienced lower rates of addiction, because they were less likely to receive medical care and doctors' prescriptions for drugs (Helmer 1975; Kennedy 2003). Nevertheless, the media of those times promoted the myth of blacks' proclivity to drug-induced criminality. In 1903, for example, an article in the *New York Tribune* claimed that "many of the horrible crimes committed in the Southern States by the colored people can be traced directly to the cocaine habit," and in 1914 the *Literary Digest* asserted that "most of the attacks upon white women of the South are a direct result of a cocaine-crazed Negro brain" (cited in Regoli & Hewitt 1997:379–380). Fear of cocaine and its ability to create superhuman strength among African Americans was also, according to David Musto (1999), the chief reason Southern police switched from .32-caliber to .38-caliber pistols. Although relatively few people were incarcerated for drug violations as a result of the Harrison Act compared to subsequent antidrug legislation, the act was disproportionately applied to African Americans. By the end of the 1920s, African Americans, who composed just 9 percent of the population, constituted 23 percent of all incarcerated drug offenders (Kennedy 2003).

Marijuana, a drug originally associated with Mexican immigrants in the Southwest, did not come under the control of the Federal Bureau of Narcotics (FBN) until the late 1930s, although many jurisdictions had statutes outlawing its use by the mid-1920s. The Great Depression, which adversely affected employment opportunities, exacerbated white Americans' fear of Mexican workers, who, like the Chinese, worked for lower wages. Employers in agriculture and other industries supported the anti-Mexican campaign because Mexicans had been successfully organizing unions and strikes. Also fueling the concern about marijuana was the generally accepted notion that violence and sexual promiscuity accompanied its use (see Chapter 1). The FBN, headed by Harry Anslinger, began an aggressive campaign to have marijuana added to the list of controlled substances under its jurisdiction. Finally, in 1937 the Marijuana Tax Act was passed, giving the FBN greatly expanded powers. By 1938, the first full year after the legislation went into effect, one out of every four federal drug convictions involved a violation of this act. Violations of marijuana laws also expedited the deportation of Mexican workers to their home country (Helmer 1975; Musto 1999; Parsons 2014).

The Contemporary War on Drugs
Concern about cocaine use by African Americans resurfaced in the 1980s when media attention focused on crack cocaine (Chiricos 1996; Parsons 2014). Crack, a less expensive form of cocaine consumed primarily by low-income offenders, was frequently portrayed as an instantly addicting substance that incited violence among users. In the midst of a "moral panic," Congress passed the Anti–Drug Abuse Acts of 1986 and 1988, which specified mandatory prison terms for federal drug offenders (the length of time depending on the amount of the drug) and made penalties for possession of crack cocaine a hundred times greater than for possession of comparable amounts of powder cocaine. For instance, a first-time offender convicted in federal court for possession of five grams of crack (about the weight of two pennies and providing 15 to 25 "hits") received a mandatory minimum sentence of five years in prison. The street value of five grams of crack was about $400 at the time. In contrast, an offender would have needed to possess 500 grams of powder cocaine, valued at about $10,000, to receive the same sentence (Wallace 1993).

This federal policy, along with those applied at the state level, disproportionately impacted African Americans. Between 1980 and the early 1990s, for example, the overall proportion of drug-possession arrests of African Americans of all ages increased from 21 percent to about 35 percent, and the proportion of drug-possession arrests of black youths among all juveniles increased from 13 percent to about 40 percent (Mauer 1999). In 1980 the drug arrest rate for white youths was actually higher than for nonwhite youths, but as a result of the subsequent intensified policy of drug prohibition, this situation was reversed (Blumstein 1993; Tollet & Close 1991). Insofar as drug offenses have constituted the largest factor contributing to the rising prison population in the United States, the country's drug policy must be viewed as discriminatory in effect, if not also in intent (Bush-Baskette 1998; Tonry 1995). During the Obama administration, however, the Fair Sentencing Act of 2010 reduced the penalty disparity between possession of crack cocaine and possession of powder cocaine from a 100-to-1 weight ratio to an 18-to-1 ratio (Cratty 2011).

Irrespective of the media's focus on crack cocaine, it is law enforcement's focus on marijuana users that has been the major impetus of drug policy since the 1990s, as well as a major source of differential treatment of African Americans. In recent years, the more than 700,000 marijuana arrests that are made annually account for more than half of all drug arrests (Hart 2013); and although research indicates that whites use marijuana about as often as do blacks (see Chapter 2), the marijuana-possession arrest rate of blacks, who constitute just 13 percent of the US population overall, is six times the rate of whites (Levine 2013). Additionally, most people who are arrested for marijuana possession have only "a small amount hidden in their clothing, vehicle or personal effects," and the police find it during the stop-and-search patrols in the low-income neighborhoods that are the priority of law enforcement (Levine 2013:19). Police who patrol more affluent neighborhoods, on the other hand, do not typically search the vehicles or persons being stopped, so the drug transgressions of this more advantaged class of users, who are primarily white, are less likely to be discovered. Since whites are more likely to benefit from what Harry Levine calls "a de facto legalization of marijuana possession," it makes it difficult for them "to believe that so many people are being arrested for possessing small amounts" of the drug that their more advantaged status allows them to enjoy (2013:20). In this way as well, African Americans accumulate a prior criminal record that adversely impacts the rest of their lives (see Chapter 11).

Upper- and Middle-Level Drug Use and Dealing

Despite this history of drug enforcement, self-report studies indicate that nonwhites do not use more drugs than whites (see Chapter 2). In this section, therefore, we examine upper- and middle-level (primarily white) drug use and drug dealing in the United States.

Upper-Level Drug Dealers

Patricia Adler's (1993) ethnography of 65 upper-level drug dealers and smugglers in the beach communities of Southern California between 1974 and 1980 is arguably the classic sociological study of upper-level drug dealing. The individuals in Adler's study, who were predominately white and

FURTHER EXPLORATION
Methamphetamine

Methamphetamine, also known as "meth," is a drug that is part of a broader class of stimulants called amphetamines. Amphetamines, which were not introduced into the United States until the 1930s, were widely and legally available without a doctor's prescription until a series of federal laws enacted between the 1950s and 1970s curtailed their legal use. These laws ultimately created two separate markets for stimulants—an illegal market and a pre-scription market—such as for drugs like Ritalin and Adderall, used mainly for attention-deficit disorder (ADD), attention-deficit/hyperactivity disorder (ADHD), and narcolepsy, although the prescription market may also be a source of drugs for the illegal one (Parsons 2014). In their study of prescription drug use among college students, A. Rafik Mohamed and Erik Fritsvold found that "those who legally possessed prescription [stimulants] for therapeutic purposes tended to either use their prescriptions in ways that were inconsistent with the ailment or . . . distribute them to their friends and associates, either gratis or for small profits" (2010:72).

Amphetamines like Benzedrine have long been used by individuals not otherwise involved in criminal activities—truck drivers, athletes, students studying all night for exams, and "others seeking to maximize their occupational and work output" (Parsons 2014:59). In the late 1960s, however, the term "speed freak" entered into popular vernacular to refer to individuals who used meth recreationally and addictively, including those who injected it intravenously. By the early 1970s, clandestine "meth labs" emerged, with white outlaw motorcycle gangs accounting for a large proportion of meth production and distribution. "Biker meth," also called "crank," was not usually pure enough to be smoked, but "crystal meth," which derives its name from its crystallized appearance and is also called "ice," is highly smokable (Parsons 2014).

Although crack cocaine dominated media coverage of the drug problem in the 1980s, meth began garnering attention in the 1990s. According to Nicholas Parsons (2014), part of the shift in media interest was generated by the emergence of Mexican criminal organizations in the manufacture and distribution of meth, which turned meth from a white drug issue into a "brown" one, even though the majority of meth *users* were white. Parsons argues that it is because of this racial/ethnic shift that meth became a higher priority for law enforcement and of greater concern for the public.

from middle-class backgrounds, were primarily men, although about 10 percent were women. They dealt in both marijuana and cocaine, with the marijuana smuggled into the United States from Mexico, and the cocaine from South America, primarily from Bolivia and Peru but also from Chile, Colombia, and Ecuador. Adler found that there were far fewer smugglers than dealers, and that awaiting "the outcome of each successful smuggling run was a community of dealers ready to begin the process of distributing the drugs on a wholesale level" (p. 49).

In her study, Adler identified two types of upper-level dealing related to these operations: **straight dealing** and **middling dealing**. Straight dealing involved "purchasing drugs in one quantity and dividing them into smaller units to sell" (1993:49). Middling dealing entailed selling the "purchased drugs intact, without separating them into smaller units" (p. 52). Adler also learned about a third type of dealing based on locally grown marijuana production. The customers of these transactions, which she referred to as **low-volume buyers**, were typically in demand beyond the supply and gave "sellers a position of authority within the transaction" (p. 72).

The smugglers and dealers in Adler's study lived a hedonistic lifestyle that was a major element of what attracted them to the drug trafficking business. As she writes:

> Abandoning the dictates of propriety and the workaday world, they lived spontaneously and intensely . . . [and] rejected society's normative constraints which mandated a lifestyle of deferred gratification, careful planning, and sensible spending. Instead, they embraced the pursuit of self-indulgence. Whether it was the unlimited availability of their favorite

FURTHER EXPLORATION
Money Laundering

Money laundering refers to the process by which illegal "dirty" money is made "clean" and recycled into the legal economy. Under US law, money laundering entails a financial transaction that a person knows to involve illegal proceeds, as well as attempts to conceal or disguise information about these proceeds or failing to comply with transaction reporting requirements (Abadinsky 2007). The upper-level dealers in Adler's study (1993), for example, were aware of the need to account for their income with the Internal Revenue Service. They were therefore careful about overly conspicuous spending and preferred to spend their money on "consumables that left little evidence" (p. 111). They also created businesses such as restaurants, retail stores, and self-employed services that gave them a cover as legitimate businesspeople.

In other instances, upper-level drug dealers employ a variety of other financial schemes to cleanse their money. Some schemes entail use of "dozens of persons (called **smurfs**) to convert cash into money orders and cashier's checks that do not specify payees or that are made out to fictitious persons" and involve less than $10,000 to avoid financial reporting requirements (Abadinsky 2007:327). More sophisticated schemes require the depositing of money abroad into countries such as the Bahamas, Panama, Switzerland, and the Cayman Islands, among others, that allow bank accounts to be numbered without identifying depositors by name. Nowadays the sheer volume and speed of computerized financial transactions make it very difficult to trace or document their illegal nature.

drugs, the illusion of the seemingly bottomless supply of money, the sense of power and . . . freedom they attained, their easy access to sexual satisfaction, or merely the excitement associated with the continual dangers they faced, the dealing crowd was strongly driven by the pleasures they derived from their way of life. . . . Dealers and smugglers plunged themselves fully into satisfying their immediate desires, whether these involved consuming lavish, expensive dinners, drugging themselves to saturation, [or] traveling hundreds of miles to buy a particular item that caught their eye. (1993:83–84)

Adler also found that exiting the drug trade and giving up this lifestyle was typically a gradual process that occurred with aging: "Their initial feelings of exhilaration began to dull as they became increasingly jaded by their own exorbitant drug consumption . . . [and] sensitized to the extreme risks they faced. Cases of friends and associates who were arrested, imprisoned, or killed . . . began to mount . . . [and they] gradually realized that the potential legal consequences they faced were less remote than they had earlier imagined" (p. 131).

College Drug Dealers

In another revealing study of drug dealers, Mohamed and Fritsvold spent six years researching what they call "the silent majority of US drug dealers" who hawk their wares to college students around the country (2010:2). They describe these individuals as "an off-the-radar collection of middle- and upper-class" dealers whose activities "are largely unknown beyond the limits of their social networks [and] whose often flagrant illegal activities are generally carried out without the hindrances of police scrutiny and . . . the stigma of being labeled a criminal" (p. 2). Their research, which began in 2001, was based on some 50 interviews with dealers in Southern California between the ages of 18 and 24 in a geographical area that included the Los Angeles, San Diego, Santa Barbara, San Bernardino, and Riverside metropolitan areas. All but three of the dealers were men and all but three were white (three others were of mixed race/ethnicity).

Mohamed and Fritsvold describe this drug network as "loosely subdivided into several primary strains of fluid, informally organized distribution channels serving one common user base"—college students (2010:5). Marijuana, the most widely used illegal drug, was the main product, but some dealers also "sold modest quantities of cocaine, and others dabbled in party drugs like ecstasy" (p. 12). Like their customer base, the dealers were relatively affluent current or former college students who were actively pursuing traditional educational and occupational pathways to success. All but one of them "were habitual marijuana users in high school; all had a functional understanding of how marijuana markets operated; and many . . . had a strong enough bond with their hometown supply sources to segue this relationship into personal proprietorship" (pp. 21–22). Most of their customers, in turn, had entered college with previous experience using marijuana, and many could be described as "veteran" users who were fairly familiar with "the nuances of marijuana purchasing rituals" (p. 20). While a large number used marijuana exclusively, some experimented with other illegal drugs as well.

Mohamed and Fritsvold make an important distinction between **open drug markets** and **closed drug markets**. In open markets, like those that occur on the streets of inner cities (see Chapter 6), "dealers sell to any potential customers, only screening out those who they suspect of being police or posing some other threat to their operation" (2010:12). In closed markets, like the college market Mohamed and Fritsvold studied, dealers "sell only to customers they personally know or customers who can be vouched for by other customers" (p. 12). Unlike the quick pace of drug-for-money exchanges in open-air street markets, college markets are relatively slow-paced and transactions can take as much as an hour to complete. In large part this is because dealers and customers are often friends or at least acquaintances. The dealers and customers "typically attended the same university, in many cases had known each other since freshman years, were apt to have a class or two together, and were very likely to travel in the same social circles" (p. 25). Dealers generally permitted their customers "to sample the product before committing to a purchase," and after the purchase they would hang out with their customers for a while.

Mohamed and Fritsvold identify several (and often overlapping) motivations for the involvement of these relatively affluent individuals in drug distribution. One is their interest in underwriting the cost of their personal drug use, which is rather extensive. As one dealer named LaCoste said, "I really just do it to smoke, that's the only reason I sell pot" (2010:42). And as Cecilia said, "Not having to buy [pot] . . . is what motivated me. . . . And . . . then you have your four or five friends that you are always sort of servicing, and . . . before you know it you are getting larger and larger sums to service more and more" (p. 44). A related motivating factor is the desire to underwrite other incidental and entertainment expenses that are part of the drug-dealing and drug-using lifestyle. The most successful dealers in the network, for instance, "blew a substantial amount of their profits on partying with friends, supporting the drug use of friends and other hangers-on, high-tech media equipment, 'pimped out' accessories for their cars, and other whimsical expenditures" (p. 5). Many also enjoyed emulating what they perceived as the flamboyant "gangsta" lifestyle.

An inclination for entrepreneurship is another motivating factor, as these relatively affluent dealers "were disproportionately current or former business majors and some already owned and operated their own legitimate small businesses. . . . Early dabbling in the college drug market very quickly revealed ubiquitous demands and minimal market risks; a return on their investment was a virtual lock, and the perceptible risks of adverse social or criminal justice consequences were negligible" (Mohamed & Fritsvold 2010:48). Although LaCoste was confronted by residence-life officials about their suspicions that he was dealing drugs, formal intervention by the university police or administrators was never forthcoming. According to Mohamed and Fritsvold, one reason for universities' reluctance to pursue drug cases is their fear of bad publicity that would discourage recruitment of new students, as well as their fear of alienating affluent parents (like LaCoste's parents) who might otherwise be sources of financial contributions to the university.

The pursuit of status among peers is still another motivating factor. As LaCoste explained: "You can give pot to whoever you want, do whatever you want, buy a ton of shit! . . . If you said, where'd you get pot, where can I get pot? I'm sure my name would be mentioned at least 50 percent of the time. . . . I was like, 'does anybody need weed? . . . Who needs weed? . . . [C]ome and get it!'" (Mohamed & Fritsvold 2010:51). Cecilia added: "Many of my friends expressed . . . a sense of gratitude because they got to stop going to this weird sketchy place where they felt kind of anxious and not really safe and . . . protected" (p. 45). And because they sold drugs to people they knew, these dealers did not consider themselves "drug dealers" at all. As Beefy said: "I don't really like the label [drug dealer]. . . . Call me a supplier, or just a middleman or whatever" (p. 99). And Cecilia explained:

> You are dealing with people who . . . were all in college and who were all your friends. And it depends on what kind of things we are talking about dealing. . . . [I]f we are talking strictly about pot . . . yeah I think sort of a culture goes along with [it] . . . like a decriminalization . . . mantra . . . so it makes it hard to feel like you are a criminal. . . . It is like when you are sixteen and you are drinking alcohol at a high-school party. You know that . . . is not . . . quote-unquote legal, but it certainly doesn't stop you. (pp. 102–103)

According to Mohamed and Fritsvold, the "financial motivation for drug dealing was more about indulgence than necessity" (2010:61). While these drug dealers were "not under the immediate supervision of parents," most were still dependent on them "for tuition, room, board, and other expenses" (p. 59). Their involvement in drug dealing was a way to show others that they were not coddled or spoiled kids, and it gave them a status identity that was distinct from the identity of their parents. Although the vast majority of them stopped selling drugs by the time they graduated from college, a few continued their involvement rather than entering the legitimate work force.

Implications of College Students' Use of Medical Marijuana
In 2012, voters in the state of Colorado passed a ballot measure that approved the legal sale and consumption of **cannabis**, the flowering plant from which

FURTHER EXPLORATION
Pharmacists' Illicit Use of Prescription Drugs

In a study of retail pharmacists sampled from members of the American Pharmaceutical Association, Dean Dabney (2001) found that about 40 percent had used potentially addictive prescription drugs illegally at some time during their professional careers. About 20 percent reported five or more instances and about 6 percent identified themselves as drug abusers at some time. In his research with Richard Hollinger, Dabney also identified two general types of users among these pharmacists: **recreational users** and **therapeutic self-medicators**. Recreational users first began experimenting with alcohol, marijuana, cocaine, and psychedelics during their high school and early college years (Dabney & Hollinger 2002). For these individuals, illicit use of prescription drugs began shortly after they entered pharmacy school, where "they exploited their newly found access to prescription drugs" that were available in training labs and pharmacy internships (p. 191). The majority of recreational users also admitted that one of the main reasons they chose pharmacy as a profession was the opportunity to expand their drug use. Once in pharmacy school, these users rationalized their use as a way to learn about the effects of different drugs. Many managed to convince themselves that their illicit drug use was "actually beneficial to future patients" (p. 192). Once they graduated from pharmacy school, entrance into pharmacy practice expanded their access further as "they quickly realized they had free [rein] over the pharmacy stock" (p. 194). But as their "physical tolerance and psychological dependence progressed," they found themselves in a painful existence of addiction that was harmful to both their professional and personal lives (p. 195).

The therapeutic self-medicators, on the other hand, had little or no experience with illicit drug use before they entered pharmacy school. What little illegal drug involvement they had was with occasional marijuana use. These users claimed they did not begin using prescription drugs illicitly for recreational purposes; rather, they used them to relieve their own medical maladies related to insomnia, a physical injury that occurred as a result of a car accident, sports injury, or similar mishap, or some chronic condition such as arthritis, migraine headaches, back pain, or leg cramps. Over time, however, they inevitably developed "a tolerance for the drugs and . . . had to take larger quantities to achieve the same level of relief" (Dabney & Hollinger 2002:198). For the most part, these users were able to forestall a downward spiral for a longer period of time compared to their recreational-using counterparts, but ultimately these therapeutic self-medicators realized "they were now chemically dependent on one or more of the drugs that they so confidently had been 'prescribing' for themselves" (p. 200).

marijuana, hashish, and hash oil are derived. The law went into effect in January 2014. We will discuss the issue of cannabis legalization later in this chapter. Here we consider the sociological implications for college-age drug users of legalized *medical* marijuana, which preceded full legalization in Colorado through a ballot measure passed more than a decade earlier, in 2000.

In 2009, while studying the college "party scene" at the University of Colorado, Boulder, Patrick O'Brien (2013) discovered an increasing number of students who were obtaining licenses to purchase medical marijuana legally. Although medical marijuana had been legal in Colorado since 2001, in 2009 the Colorado Board of Health abandoned a limit on the number of patients for whom a "primary caregiver" could legally prescribe marijuana. Additionally, the US Department of Justice under the Obama administration announced it would no longer expend federal resources to arrest and prosecute those who operated legally under state medical marijuana laws. Consequently, the number of people receiving licenses to purchase marijuana and the number of licensed dispensaries to meet this demand expanded significantly.

Like the students in Mohamed and Fritsvold's study, the students in O'Brien's study were largely familiar with the norms and processes of illegally distributing and purchasing marijuana, and were willing to allocate the time and money to schedule a physician's visit and pay the state fees that were required to receive a license to gain entrance to a legal medical marijuana dispensary. And as the students began visiting the dispensaries, they realized the significance of a legal medicalized system that offered regulated transactions and insulation from the police, and they underwent a novel learning process about being able to consume marijuana legally. Previously, students had lacked control over their unregulated marijuana-purchasing experience, as the dealers controlled every aspect of the transaction, including the time, location, price, and amount of the purchase. As Madeline explained: "In the illicit market you are at the hands of the dealer, they decide the time and the place and you really don't have any say unless it's your friend or something. You might have to wait for your dealer to go pick it up, wait for them to weigh it all out, and . . . wait for them to come and meet you or wait until they get home, and it's like four hours before you get any marijuana" (O'Brien 2013:428).

Additionally, one of the norms of illegal marijuana transactions is that buyers are encouraged to "smoke out" the dealer as a token of appreciation or to experience and discuss the "high" of the product. As Ethan noted of his appreciation for the new system:

> It's hard to think back to those primitive days when I was buying illegally . . . where you go in to some place you might not want to be . . . and you basically buy whatever pot they have to smoke. I never really liked having to smoke with the guy I buy it from either, you know smoke out your connect for good measure or because they were nice enough to sell you some weed. It's not always a bad thing, but if I'm buying at 1 PM in the afternoon and I have shit to do, I don't want to feel obligated to get high just because I want to have some marijuana at home. (p. 429)

And Jared added: "It's just more efficient. I just go to my dispensary, and I've shopped around so I know the best prices and what dispensary has what I'm looking for. You get your pot in a nice bag, you're in and out in 10 minutes and you . . . don't have to worry about buying crap or having to stock up on bulk. The dispensary will be there" (p. 429).

Other students touted the safety of marijuana dispensaries. As Sarah observed:

> I have had some shady experiences buying weed, and that is never the case with the dispensary. I feel safe in a dispensary. I'm in a public place. . . . [W]hen I was back in New York I had to buy weed from this guy in his forties. He lives on this really sketchy street and I was the only one allowed to go inside. He had the weed in shopping bags and it was awkward. A bunch of his friends were just staring at me. Sometimes it just sucks having to go over to some dude's house to get it. (p. 429)

FURTHER EXPLORATION
College Women's Use of Drugs for Weight Control

Katherine Sirles Vecitis (2012) studied drug use for weight control among white college-age women who were attending a major university. She calls this type of use **instrumental drug use**, because it is done for a particular reason—appetite suppression—in a manner similar to steroid users who use drugs to enhance their athletic performance.

The women in Vecitis's study used two general types of stimulants— legal prescription drugs and illegal street drugs—and were divided into groups who experienced four different temporal trajectories of instrumental drug use for weight control. The largest group reported a history of disordered eating and nonnormative weight loss prior to using prescription drugs for weight loss, while the second largest group reported a history of eating/weight problems prior to using illegal drugs for recreational or medicinal reasons such as ADD or ADHD. A third group used prescription drugs recreationally or medicinally prior to using prescription drugs for weight control, and a fourth group used illegal drugs recreationally and later transformed that use for weight loss.

The women employed a variety of strategies to obtain their drugs. Some obtained prescription stimulants using their own name, including those who claimed they had ADD or ADHD. Some obtained these drugs from their hometown doctor, while others went to the university health center. One woman said: "It's easier to get it at [the student health center] than maybe anywhere else. . . . You're supposed to take all these tests to see if you have

continues

continued

it [ADD or ADHD] but you can say that you had it when you were a kid and
. . . took Ritalin or whatever. . . . So they might not make you go through all
that. And even if you do, you can just fake not being able to pay attention"
(p. 146).

Some women visited multiple physicians in order to maintain their drug
supply. Others went to street dealers or got pills from roommates, friends, or
family. Some used multiple methods in order to stockpile stimulants.
Although appetite suppression was their primary goal, they also liked the side
effects. As one woman said: "Adderall made me want to socialize more,
made me more talkative. I was always in better moods, I had way more
energy and time just seemed to go by fast" (p. 148). Women who used illegal
drugs, including amphetamines and cocaine, also reported "increased energy,
alertness, talkativeness . . . and an overall sense of well-being" (p. 148).
Although these women tended to have easy access to illegal drugs, their suppliers were not as reliable. Additionally, those who used cocaine generally
"snorted" it and found that the effect peaked after 30 minutes and declined
rapidly thereafter. Pharmaceuticals, on the other hand, lasted at least a few
hours. Consequently, women who used cocaine to curb their appetite had to
use it more frequently throughout the day. In addition, insomnia was more
common among users of illegal drugs than among users of pharmaceutical
drugs. As one woman said of the side effects of cocaine: "I'd go days when I
couldn't get any sleep at all which was awful. I had these horrible ugly bags
under my eyes. I was really skinny. . . . I'd force myself to lie in bed and shut
my eyes. My body felt tired but I just couldn't sleep. . . . It gets you all tight
and completely wound up" (p. 150).

In this way, use of marijuana is normalized and consumers do not have
to feel deviant. The dispensaries resemble high-end coffee shops or deli-
catessens. Patrons are greeted and identified in comfortable waiting rooms
adorned with couches, fish tanks, literature, flat-screen televisions, Internet
workstations, and espresso bars, which fosters a sense of well-being.
According to Mark: "It's a huge weight off my shoulders. . . . For my whole
life I was doing something illegal . . . [but] something my friends and I
never thought was that bad. Now the cops can't bother me. I have the right
to smoke some weed" (p. 433). Mark also thought it was remarkable that
when he went into a dispensary, he saw "old ladies, college kids, business
people. . . . [I]t really shows everyone [that] there is a large community of
like-minded" people (p. 437).

Consumers also liked the fact that there were many varieties of marijuana from which they could choose. As Madeline remarked: "Dispensaries have options I'd never seen. I used to buy from this guy with one

kind. With the dispensaries, if you don't like some strain, you've got like 10 others to try out" (p. 434). And Emily observed: "The selection is enormous; you've got candy, brownies, ice cream, olive oil, something for all tastes. . . . I don't like to smoke, really. It hits me really quick and I cough and stuff. The edibles are more gradual and I don't get as paranoid if I just eat a little bit" (p. 435).

The legalization of medical marijuana also moves employment opportunities out of the illegal market and into the legal economy. According to Ethan: "I just think of the jobs this industry provides and that everyone has a chance to get hired. I have a friend who is a major caretaker and he owns a warehouse where he grows and harvests everything. Me, my girlfriend, and about six friends work for him, $20 an hour, just clipping plants, taking care of the grow, and doing what he needs. I've learned a lot. Tons of jobs have popped up, jobs you won't get arrested doing" (p. 430). Also, the availability of knowledgeable "budtenders" in the dispensaries is an advantage to consumers. As Josh said: "It's nice for me to go into a place where people are knowledgeable about the . . . products, strains, effects, strength and all that stuff. I used to just have some idiot who sold me weed. I know how to get high, but you can ask questions and learn new information. . . . With honest information you can make good decisions about how you use marijuana" (p. 435).

Alternatives to the War on Drugs

In their book *The Search for Rational Drug Control* (1992), criminologists Franklin Zimring and Gordon Hawkins argue that for all too long the drug war in the United States has focused not on the *adverse consequences* of drug use but on *drug use itself*. Little distinction has been made between experimental use, casual use, regular use, and addictive use. Drug use has been viewed as a moral problem, and the effort to control drugs has been characterized as a battle between the forces of good and the forces of evil.

This approach, a growing number of criminologists believe, has been both ineffective and destructive. It has failed to stop the selling and use of drugs, and has increased theft and violence associated with drugs that are unrelated to the pharmacological properties of the prohibited substances. Insofar as criminalization heightens the risk of selling drugs, it also increases drug prices, making it more difficult for users to obtain funds through legal means to support their habits. Since the drug market is unregulated, entrepreneurs (including organized crime and criminal gangs) use violence rather than advertising or the courts to gain advantage over competitors and to resolve disputes with competitors, employees, and customers (see Chapter 6). Additionally, users lack safeguards to regulate the potency of the drugs they take and the ingredients that are added to them. Criminalization also creates disrespect for the law by making criminals out of users who are not otherwise involved in other crime, and it forces users to associate with more hardened offenders. Last, criminalization of drugs is the primary source of both corruption in law enforcement and the need of the police to rely on aggressive and controversial tactics, such as military-style policing, undercover surveillance, and use of criminal informants (Fuller 1998; Goode 2005; see Chapter 11).

Therefore, many people think that drugs should either be decriminalized or legalized. **Decriminalization** would reduce the penalties for possession of small quantities of drugs to roughly the equivalent of a traffic offense, while simultaneously maintaining stiff penalties for possession of larger quantities as well as for growing, manufacturing, and selling drugs. **Legalization**, on the other hand, would set up a government-regulated system that is comparable to the one used for alcohol (McBride et al. 2009).

Zimring and Hawkins, however, dispute the notion that drugs represent "a unitary social problem" that compels a choice between criminalization or decriminalization/legalization (1992:110). Instead, they contend, the legal status of each drug should be determined on a case-by-case basis. The harm caused by a drug law should not be worse than the harm caused by the drug itself. In an approach that has been described as a **harm reduction**, they argue that drug policy should focus not on eradicating use per se but on the prevention of drug-related predatory crime, serious injury and death from drug overdoses, drug-related HIV/AIDS and hepatitis cases, driving under the influence, harm to newborns, and drug use by children and adolescents. In this way, harm reduction redefines drug abuse as a public health problem rather than a criminal problem (McBride et al. 2009; Vigilant 2005).

Although Zimring and Hawkins (1992) think that most of the current crop of illegal drugs are too dangerous to be legalized, they maintain that the "war on drugs" approach should be abandoned. The federal government alone spends about $18 billion a year on drug control, less than 30 percent of which is allocated for prevention and treatment (Lock et al. 2002). Drug treatment programs have been especially hurt by the war on drugs, as spending on these interventions has been cut in half since the early 1980s. This policy should be reversed in light of research that shows a substantial drop in criminality following drug treatment (Harrison 2001). Moreover, drug policy for minors "demands a definition of the drug problem . . . that includes tobacco and alcohol," two drugs that cause more harm than the illegal substances (Zimring & Hawkins 1992:135). And since society assumes that minors lack the maturity of judgment to use tobacco or alcohol responsibly, they should not be penalized as harshly as adults for violating drug laws.

Other criminologists who oppose legalization of most illegal drugs nonetheless believe that arrest of users and even petty dealers should be a last resort, and that these offenders should be offered nonpenal alternatives such as rehabilitative treatment and community service, with arrest used if necessary to get them into these programs (Goode 2005). These criminologists also favor the use of needle-exchange programs for intravenous drug users and addicts to prevent the spread of disease, as well as the expansion of **methadone maintenance** programs for heroin addicts. Methadone is a synthetic narcotic that can be administered to addicts with the aim of regulating and gradually reducing their drug use, lowering their involvement in other crimes, and enabling them to hold steady jobs. Although the results of methadone maintenance programs have been mixed, they remain among the most cost-effective forms of treatment available for heroin addiction, often leaving the addict "much better off than on heroin—with respect to his well-being and ours" (Kaplan 1983:222; Vigilant 2005).

Drug Policy in Comparative Perspective

One way to evaluate the war on drugs in the United States is to compare it to policies that have been enacted in other countries that have similar economic and political systems. Several Western European countries, for example, have had more success with drug policies that are less restrictive and punitive than those used in the United States. During the 1920s, when FBN director Harry Anslinger was harassing the American Medical Association for its permissive approach to drug use, the British Royal College of Physicians remained steadfast in its belief that drug addiction was a medical, not a criminal, problem. At that time, "the Englishman with a habit could go to his family physician, get a prescription for heroin—or morphine, or cocaine, or whatever—and pick it up at the corner pharmacy" (Gray 1998:155). In the 1960s, however, the addiction rate in Great Britain doubled, although the total number of addicts in the entire country (1,400) was still just 7 percent of the number in the city of Manhattan, New York, alone (and although the total population of Great Britain was more than 25 times greater than the population of Manhattan). The increase provided the impetus for a change in British drug policy. Addicts were no longer allowed to obtain drugs from a general medical practitioner, and methadone maintenance programs were introduced. This shift in policy was followed by escalating heroin prices and increased violence in the drug trade.

In 1976, the Netherlands adopted a policy of nonenforcement of drug-law violations involving 30 grams or less of cannabis in order "to erect a wall between the so-called soft drugs . . . and hard drugs like heroin and cocaine" (Gray 1998:166). "Youth clubs" and "coffee shops" were permitted to sell cannabis, and during the first seven years of this new policy, it "had little if any effect on levels of [cannabis] use" (MacCoun & Reuter 1997:50). Although cannabis use did increase between 1984 and 1992 in the Netherlands, similar increases were reported in the United States between 1992 and 1996. Even with the more lenient policy in the Netherlands, the rate of cannabis use is no higher there than in the United States, and there is little evidence that cannabis has been a "gateway" to use of harder drugs (Cohen & Sas 1996; MacCoun & Reuter 1997).

Nevertheless, in 1995, under pressure from other European countries, the Dutch Parliament passed legislation reducing by half the number of shops where cannabis could be sold and limiting purchases to five grams, though the legislation did not restrict the number of shops a consumer could visit (*US News & World Report* 1996a). The parliament also authorized the courts to require hard-drug addicts with a history of (nondrug) criminal behavior to undergo two years of compulsory rehabilitation. Otherwise, "people holding small amounts of heroin or cocaine for personal use are ignored," as are lower-level street dealers (Gray 1998:168). The Dutch police do aggressively pursue major drug distributors, however.

Other countries have also dealt with heroin addiction differently than has the United States. In 1994, Switzerland began the first large-scale controlled experiment in heroin maintenance, a three-year program under the supervision of the World Health Organization and the Swiss Academy of Medical Sciences that provided heroin to about a thousand regular users. Evaluation of the program indicated that crime among the addicted subjects declined by 60 percent, that half of the formerly unemployed users found work, and that a third who had been on welfare became self-supporting. Homelessness among these users was eliminated, and improvements in their health were noted. About 8 percent of the users gave up heroin altogether (*The Economist* 1998; Killias et al. 2000).

In Switzerland, hard-core heroin addicts (those who have used heroin for more than two years and have been unsuccessful in previous attempts to stop) are provided drugs, medical advice, and assistance locating employment and housing. Needle-exchange programs and self-injection rooms are also available. In the city of Bern, the nation's capital, this approach has stabilized the rate of HIV transmission, virtually eliminated drug-related deaths, increased the number of addicts who are steadily employed, and reduced the amount of nondrug crime (*The Economist* 1998; Killias et al. 2000).

Italy, whose drug policy has vacillated over the years, has provided criminologists with a "natural experiment" on the effects of drug prohibition. Italy's first antidrug law, the Drug Act of 1923, included no criminal penalties for drug use or possession and provided a maximum sentence of only six months' incarceration for trafficking. And though the maximum sentence for trafficking was increased to three years in 1930, no additional penalties for use or possession were implemented unless the offender was "in a state of serious psychic disorder" (MacCoun & Reuter 2001:231). The Drug Act of 1954 was the first law in Italy to define drug use as a serious crime, increasing sanctions for both use and trafficking to up to eight years in prison. According to Robert MacCoun and Peter Reuter (2001), the 1954 law was passed to enable Italy to comply with various international treaties, not to address an upswing in the drug problem. Nonetheless, the law did not prevent the escalation of soft-drug use in the late 1960s or heroin use in the early 1970s.

In 1975, Italy further reformed its drug laws, lengthening the penalty for trafficking in hard drugs in response to a rise in opiate use and an increase in organized-crime involvement in heroin trafficking. At the same time, the reforms shortened the maximum sentence for trafficking in cannabis, decriminalized drug use, and expanded social, psychiatric, and medical services for addicts. Then, in 1990, following a decade of burgeoning drug deaths and the spread of AIDS among intravenous drug users, Italy once again expanded sanctions for drug trafficking and reestablished criminal penalties for possession of drug quantities that exceeded an "average daily dose." Three years later, however, a successful referendum led to the striking of the phrase "personal use of psychoactive drugs is forbidden," effectively eliminating the criminalization of drug use in the country (Mac-Coun & Reuter 2001). MacCoun and Reuter evaluated the impact of this vacillating drug policy on drug use and drug-induced deaths and concluded that the law had little effect. They suggest that changing cultural trends in drug use and international patterns of drug trafficking influenced Italy's drug problem more than the laws that were in place at any particular point in time.

In 2001, Portugal instituted a comprehensive policy of decriminalization of personal drug use—including cannabis, heroin, and cocaine—that treats possession of up to a 10-day supply as a civil-ordinance violation rather than as a criminal offense, although individuals in possession of larger quantities may face criminal charges for manufacturing or distribution. Individuals who are treated civilly are referred by the police to a Commission for the Dissuasion of Drug Addiction. These commissions are regional panels that consist of up to three professionals, such as medical practitioners, social service workers, and lawyers, who informally "discuss with the offender the motivations . . . [and] circumstances surrounding their offense and are able to provide a range of sanctions" (Hughes & Stevens 2010:1002). Ultimately, the role of these commissions is to impose noncriminal sanctions like fines and community service on nondependent users and to divert dependent users into treatment and education programs. Following the implementation of this policy, illegal drug use among teens declined, new HIV infections among intravenous users plunged, and the number of people in treatment for drug dependence doubled. According to Caitlin Hughes and Alex Stevens, the evidence from the Portuguese case indicates that "combining the removal of criminal penalties with the use of alternative therapeutic responses to dependent drug users . . . can reduce the burden of drug law enforcement on the criminal justice system, while also reducing problematic drug use" (2010:1018).

Last, in an important international development in 2011, the Global Commission on Drug Policy, which included representatives from 15 countries—including former US secretary of state George Schultz, who served under President Ronald Reagan; former UN Secretary-General Kofi Annan, and the former presidents of Brazil, Colombia, Mexico, and Switzerland—concluded that the "global war on drugs has failed, with devastating consequences for individuals and societies around the world" (2011:2). The commission called for replacing "drug policies and strategies driven by ideology and political convenience with fiscally responsible policies and strategies grounded in science, health, security, and human rights" (p. 3).

The Special Case of Marijuana

Many critics of the historical and contemporary record of drug policy in the United States and around the globe believe that marijuana is the illegal drug that is most suitable for decriminalization if not legalization. As far back as 1972, for instance, a bipartisan commission appointed by President Richard Nixon published a 1,184-page report called *Marihuana: A Signal of Misunderstanding,* which called for the nationwide decriminalization of "possession of marijuana for personal use" and "casual distribution of small amounts" (cited in Lee 2013a:23). The commission also called for more research to study the potential medical benefits of cannabis. The psychoactive ingredient in cannabis that causes the "high" sought by recreational users is tetrahydrocannabinol, or THC. In addition to marijuana, high-concentration extracts such as hash and hash oil also contain THC; and other chemical compounds in cannabis called **cannabinoids**, which include THC but also more than a hundred other unique chemicals, have been found to have a number of beneficial medical properties, which is why the notion of using marijuana for medical purposes has gained popularity in recent years. The most commonly known nonpsychoactive medical benefits include decreasing nausea and increasing the appetite of cancer and AIDS patients, but recent research also suggests a number of other potential benefits, including antioxidant properties that suppress the formation of tumors; painkilling effects comparable to acupuncture; and utility in the treatment of epilepsy, stroke, diabetes, cardiovascular disease, Parkinson's disease, Alzheimer's disease, and colitis (Lee 2013a, 2013b).

Back in 1972, Nixon dismissed the recommendations of the *Marihuana* report without even reading it, but this kind of political myopia did not stop the growth of a pro-marijuana social movement. Even before the report, in 1970, the National Organization for the Reform of Marijuana Laws (NORML) had formed as a single-issue consumer advocacy group for people who use America's (and the world's) most popular illegal drug. Although NORML was often viewed as a liberal organization, in 1972 William F. Buckley Jr., the most prominent conservative intellectual in the United States at the time, came out in favor of legalization; and his protégé Richard Cowan, who later served as NORML's executive director, wrote an article in the *National Review* arguing that the criminalization of marijuana consumption made a mockery of conservative principles: "The hysterical myths about marijuana . . . have led [too many] conservatives to condone massive programs of social engineering, interference in the affairs of individuals, [and] monstrous bureaucratic waste" (cited in Lee 2013a:23).

Later, in 1998, an influential report published in *The Lancet,* Great Britain's leading medical journal, expressed an emerging consensus in the medical community that people who smoke marijuana daily for many years risk developing psychological dependency, subtle impairments of memory, bronchitis, and cancers of the lung, throat, and mouth. These are certainly good reasons to avoid using the drug. Importantly, however, *The Lancet* also noted that marijuana poses "less of a threat to health than alcohol or tobacco" and that "moderate indulgence . . . has little ill effect" (cited in Schlosser 1999:47).

As a result of these trends—the cultural acceptance of marijuana use by large segments of the US population, the bipartisan pro-marijuana social movement, and the evolving medical and criminological policy research— nearly 60 percent of the American public now thinks that marijuana use

FURTHER EXPLORATION
Drug Abuse Resistance Education

The Drug Abuse Resistance Education program, better known as DARE, began in Los Angeles during the 1983–1984 academic year as a school-based drug prevention curriculum taught by uniformed police officers that focuses on "enhancing students' self-esteem, decision-making, coping, assertiveness and communications skills" and teaching positive alternatives to drug and alcohol use (Wysong & Wright 1995:285). The curriculum, which was initially designed for fifth- and sixth-graders, consists of 17 weekly sessions of about 45 to 60 minutes each and has been used with youths in lower and higher grades as well. In addition to classroom instruction, several other programmatic elements have been added to DARE over the years, "including the use of selected high school students as DARE 'Role Models' in the elementary grades, informal officer/student contacts, teacher orientation, parental education and community presentations" (p. 285).

DARE has been adopted in nearly 80 percent of US school districts and in more than 50 other countries as well (Hanson 2014). Although it has been touted as a "long-term solution" to the problem of drug use, a consistent body of research long ago established its lack of efficacy (Ennett et al. 1994; Lynam et al. 1999; Wysong & Wright 1995). In an analysis of some 40 research articles that were published between 1991 and 2002, for instance, Steven West and Keri O'Neal (2004) concluded that the program was ineffective in preventing or reducing adolescent drug use. Nevertheless, proponents dismiss these scientific findings and continue to promote the utility of DARE, citing support from parents who seem to like the program. As one DARE advocate said: "I don't have any numbers for you. Our strongest numbers are the numbers that don't show up" (Hanson 2014:2).

should be legal (Riggs 2013). This is a sea change in the prohibitionist attitudes of recent decades. By 2014, therefore, 16 states had decriminalized personal use of marijuana, 13 states had legalized it for medicinal purposes, and 2 states—Colorado and Washington—had legalized it for both recreational and medical use (Lee 2013b; National Organization for the Reform of Marijuana Laws 2014).

At the same time, however, powerful interests resist these trends. These interests include law enforcement bureaucracies that benefit from marijuana prohibition, nonprofit antidrug organizations that receive government and corporate funding, and pharmaceutical companies that view the medical uses of marijuana as a threat to their profits (Fang 2014). Although nearly two-thirds of police officers believe that marijuana laws should be reformed—36 percent think that marijuana should be legalized, regulated, and taxed; 14 percent support relaxed penalties; 11 percent support legalized medical marijuana; and 4 percent support decriminalization—strong financial incentives "have kept nearly every law enforcement professional association opposed to reform" (p. 16). Starting with the Reagan administration in the 1980s, police departments have been encouraged to augment their revenue by seizing and selling property associated with drug arrests, which amounted to about $1 billion between 2002 and 2012 alone. As retired Los Angeles Police Department (LAPD) deputy chief Stephen Downing observes, "In many states, the city government expects police to make seizures, and they expect these seizures to supplement their budgets" (p. 16). Similarly, Florida Polk County sheriff Grady Judd says that seizures from marijuana grow-houses have enabled his department to "meet eligible equipment or other non-recurring needs that could not be met by local funding" (p. 17). And longtime lobbyist John Lovell, who has made a career of channeling federal "drug war" money to California police departments, cites marijuana criminalization as valuable for obtaining funds for overtime pay and hiring of more officers.

In a revealing exposé, Lee Fang also documented the ways in which antidrug nonprofit organizations like the Community Anti-Drug Coalition of America, the Partnership for Drug-Free Kids, and Project SAM (Smart Approaches to Marijuana) receive "a significant portion of their budget from opioid manufacturers and other pharmaceutical companies" (2014:13). These nonprofits take a hard line against medical marijuana and recreational marijuana decriminalization/legalization at the same time that they either endorse or fail to resist pharmaceutical corporations' efforts to expand their market for highly addictive prescription opioid pain medications such as OxyCotin and Vicodin, which are naturally derived from opium poppy or are produced synthetically and "are the most dangerous drugs abused in America, with more than 16,000 deaths annually linked to opioid addiction and overdose," and which account for more deaths than heroin and cocaine combined (p. 13). This coalition, as has become clearly obvious to all but the most naive observers, functions to preserve the revenue that antidrug nonprofits receive from both the government and pharmaceutical corporations while also minimizing the competition to prescription drug profits that medicalization or legalization of marijuana entails.

Summary

This chapter on illegal drugs opened with a historical overview of the connection between drug prohibition and racial/ethnic discrimination in the United States. We then examined upper- and middle-level (primarily white) drug use and drug dealing in the United States, and concluded with a critique of the "war on drugs" and a discussion of alternatives to this dubious policy. We offered insights that can be gained from a comparative analysis of policies enacted in other countries, which indicate that a less punitive approach may be more desirable. We also considered the special case of marijuana, which is arguably the drug that is most suitable for decriminalization if not legalization.

8

Sexual Violence

In this chapter we examine one of the most disconcerting conse-quences of gender inequality in society: sexual violence against women and children. We focus on three broad dimensions of this problem—rape and sexual assault, sexual abuse of children, and battering of women—but begin by situating the problem in the context of what Liz Kelly (1987) calls the **continuum of sexual violence**. According to Kelly, a wide range of sexual violations—from obscene phone calls and flashing to the more extreme forms of rape, battery, and even eroticized murder—have a common functional character, in that their aim is to intimidate, control, and instill fear in women. Deborah Cameron and Elizabeth Frazer add that too many men seem to "feel entitled to . . . unrestricted sexual access to women, even—sometimes especially—against women's will," and that sexual violations "collectively function as a threat to women's autonomy" by limiting their freedom of action and undermining their self-confidence (1987:164). As Susan Brownmiller famously wrote in her groundbreaking book *Against Our Will: Men, Women, and Rape:* "A world without rapists would be a world in which women moved freely without fear of men. That *some* men rape provides sufficient threat to keep all women in a state of intimidation, forever conscious of the knowledge that the biological tool . . . may turn [into a] weapon with a swiftness borne of harmful intent" (1975:209). Furthermore, since men's sexuality is often presumed to be naturally aggressive, women's fear of sexual violence seems inevitable. And to make matters worse, society then places responsibility on *women* to monitor their behavior so they won't be violated. If they are, they may be blamed for their victimization or find that their suffering is "trivialized, questioned, or ignored" (Cameron & Frazer 1987:164).

Suzanne Berne (1991) describes an experience that is all too familiar to many women (and girls) that illustrates the functional similarity of acts that are elements of the sexual violence continuum. She was walking in her neighborhood one winter afternoon when someone called out to her.

She turned to see a man with his pants open, exposing himself. She describes her reaction:

> I [wasn't] afraid, not exactly. But I [was] alone. Sometimes for a woman, this amounts to the same thing. . . . It could have been much worse. I wasn't raped, after all, as someone pointed out later. Only slightly violated. All I got was a small reminder that the world isn't as pleasant and safe as it sometimes appears to be. . . . [That man] is now part of my life; he is my reminder. He lives on that street every time I walk by. . . . He "flashed" me. . . . It [was] a flash, a sudden exposure—of weakness, of aloneness. A woman remembers these moments because the exposure is hers. Ask any woman, and she will tell you exactly where she was . . . when it happened to her. Because it has happened to her. (pp. 10–11)

Berne notes that a particularly insidious aspect of these sorts of intrusions—the "indecent exposure, . . . the construction worker's whistle, the obscene caller's mumbled requests"—is that the man's pleasure depends on the woman's witness (p. 11). He needs her reaction for his thrill. "What happened to me," she writes, does not generally "happen to men. Men are not forced into this sort of collusion." As Carole Sheffield observes, these acts "serve to remind women and girls that they are at risk and vulnerable to male aggression just because they are female" (1989:483–484).

Rape and Sexual Assault

In this section we consider research on the prevalence of rape and sexual assault, and the socially constructed sexual scripts and rape myths that contribute to the problem. We also look at efforts to reform the legal system to make it more responsive to and supportive of women, the role of pornography in creating a cultural climate that sustains and fosters crimes against women, and research on personal resistance strategies that women might use to protect themselves.

The Prevalence of Rape and Sexual Assault

A useful starting point for a discussion of the prevalence of rape and sexual assault entails an attempt to clarify the distinction between the two. According to the definitions used in the *National Crime Victimization Survey,* **rape** refers to

> the unlawful penetration of a person against the will of the victim, with use or threatened use of force, or attempting such an act. Rape includes psychological coercion and physical force, and forced sexual intercourse means vaginal, anal, or oral penetration by the offender. Rape also includes incidents where penetration is from a foreign object (e.g., a bottle), victimization against male and female victims, and both heterosexual

and homosexual rape. Attempted rape includes verbal threat of rape. (cited in Planty et al. 2013:2)

Sexual assault, on the other hand, refers to "a wide range of victimizations, separate from rape or attempted rape. These crimes include attacks or attempted attacks generally involving unwanted sexual contact between a victim and offender. Sexual assault may or may not involve force and includes grabbing or fondling . . . [and] verbal threats" (p. 2).

As such, the *NCVS* distinction is subtle, even unascertainable, especially because the difference between attempted rape and sexual assault appears to involve the question of the offender's intent to commit unwanted penetration. Additionally, since the 1970s, many states in the United States have abandoned use of the term *rape* as a legal category and instead use *sexual assault* or *sexual battery* to designate a continuum of acts (marked by varying degrees of criminal culpability) that include what is conventionally called "rape" and "attempted rape" but also other acts of nonconsensual sexual contact that fall short of penetration or attempted penetration (Berger et al. 1988; Spohn & Horney 1992).

In terms of measuring the prevalence of sexual violence, therefore, the distinction between rape and sexual assault may be a matter of semantics. Thus, a recent *NCVS* study collapses the two, reporting that rape and sexual assault victimizations (combined) of females age 12 and older declined from 5.0 per thousand females in 1995 to 1.8 per thousand females in the 2005–2010 period (Planty et al. 2013). The *NCVS* also reports that between 2005–2010 only about 10 rapes/sexual assaults involved offenders who used a weapon, and about 80 percent involved offenders who were previously known to the female victim: 42 percent were well-known or casual acquaintances, 28 percent were intimate partners (current or former spouses or boyfriends), and just under 10 percent were other relatives. According to other national victimization research, nearly 18 percent of all women will experience rape or attempted rape at some time in their lives, as compared to 3 percent of all men (Rape, Abuse & Incest National Network 2009).

The decline in rape/sexual assault between 1995 and 2005–2010 may reflect, in part, the general decline in crime rates discussed previously in Chapter 2. But the nature of underreporting in the *NCVS* is a factor, too, in getting a handle on the actual prevalence of sexual violence. Recall that the *NCVS* is a general interview survey of victimization, and questions about sexual violence are embedded in the overall survey instrument. Additionally, it is possible for the interview to be conducted in the presence of an abusive intimate partner or relative, which might lead to underreporting of women's victimizations.

In one study designed to avoid the pitfalls of the *NCVS* methodology, Melanie Randall and Lori Haskell (1995) interviewed a random sample of

420 women living in Toronto, Canada. The interviews, which typically took about two hours to complete, were conducted face-to-face in private settings of the respondents' own choosing—mostly their own homes. The inquiries about violence were part of a larger discussion of women's safety. The findings, the researchers concluded, document "the devastating 'normalcy' and pervasive presence of sexual violence in women's lives" (pp. 26–27).

Nearly all of the women (98 percent) in the Randall-Haskell study reported experiencing some form of sexual violation at some time in their lives—"sexually threatening, intrusive, or assaultive . . . experiences [that] ranged from being followed or chased on the street to receiving an obscene phone call, to being sexually harassed at work, to being sexually assaulted and/or raped in childhood or adulthood, to being physically and/or sexually assaulted in an intimate relationship" (1995:14). Over 40 percent of the women reported at least one experience of incestuous and/or nonfamilial sexual abuse before age 16, two-thirds reported at least one instance of sexual assault (from unwanted sexual touching of breasts or genitals to forced sexual intercourse) after age 16, and 40 percent reported completed rape after age 16.

Randall and Haskell argue that it is not "an exaggeration to say that part of the experience of being female . . . typically involves directly expe-

---

FURTHER EXPLORATION
Stalking

Generally speaking, **stalking** refers to "the willful, repeated, and malicious following, harassing, or threatening of another person" (Melton 2000:248). Although stalking is not a new phenomenon, it was not conceptualized as a social problem until 1989, when an obsessed fan shot and killed Rebecca Shaeffer, a television actress he repeatedly had tried to contact. Prior to this event, what came to be termed "stalking" was referred to as "obsession," "sexual harassment," or "psychological rape," and it was portrayed as uncomfortable and annoying rather than as dangerous and violent. The Shaeffer murder, however, became linked to other events, such as the repeated following of Jodie Foster by John Hinckley (see Chapter 3) and the following and stabbing of actress Theresa Saldana, generating a public concern about "celebrity stalking." This concern played a major role in the passage of an anti-stalking law in California in 1990. Other states quickly followed suit, and the National Institute of Justice developed a model anti-stalking code for the states to use when drafting statutes (Emerson et al. 1998; Lowney & Best 1995).

When advocates of battered women made connections between stalking and the harassment and violence women often experience when they attempt

continues

continued

to leave abusive partners, "the link between domestic violence and stalking was quickly recognized" (Melton 2000:248). Stalking became identified as a more serious social problem and was reframed from a *celebrity* issue to a *women's* issue (Lowney & Best 1995).

Research indicates that those who are stalked are most often "the current or former spouses or intimate partners of their stalkers" (Melton 2000:248). In these circumstances, stalking arises "out of efforts to maintain or to recreate a close relationship that has been terminated or that one party sought to terminate" (Emerson et al. 1998:295). Here the parties are or have been "intimately linked" (often they are "exes") or are acquaintances who have been dating. In other circumstances, stalking involves "one-sided attempts to create close, usually romantic relationships" where none existed before. Included here would be (1) *unacquainted stalking,* where the person pursued is a stranger initially encountered in a semipublic or public place; (2) *pseudoacquainted* stalking, where the victim is a celebrity or public figure whom the pursuer has come to feel connected or emotionally attached to; and (3) *semiacquainted* stalking, where the victim is pursued by someone with whom he or she had contact in the past or by someone he or she has minimal present contact (e.g., a coworker in a large firm).

Robert Emerson and colleagues term all of the above circumstances *relational stalking,* since they all "entail unilateral pursuit linked to some admiring or romantic interest in, or implied or specific assertions of rights to, a continuing, close or intimate relationship with another" (1998:295–296). Relational stalking can be distinguished from *revenge stalking,* where there are "no romantic or relational claims" but where the stalker seems to believe that he or she has been maltreated and is "focused on intimidating the victim and perhaps on extracting . . . payback." Psychiatrists, plastic surgeons, judges, and instructors are particularly likely to be targeted by revenge stalkers.

Although all 50 states and the District of Columbia have passed antistalking laws, the legal definitions of stalking differ considerably from place to place. Most statutes require that stalking not be an isolated event, while some specify a minimum number of acts (usually two) that must take place. Some statutes specify particular acts such as surveillance, laying-in-waiting, vandalism, nonconsensual communication, and telephone harassment. Some also consider threats against the victims' immediate family as stalking (Tjaden & Thoennes 1998).

Using a definition of stalking that closely resembles the National Institute of Justice's model code, the *National Violence Against Women Survey* defined stalking as "a course of conduct directed at a specific person that involves repeated [i.e., on two or more occasions] visual or physical proximity, nonconsensual communication, or verbal, written or implied threats, or a combination thereof, that would cause a reasonable person [a high level of] fear." The survey found that 8 percent of women and 2 percent of men in the United States had been stalked at some time in their life, the majority by people the victim already knew. The survey also found "a strong link between stalking and other forms of violence [assault and rape] in intimate relationships" (Tjaden & Thoennes 1998:2–3).

riencing some form of sexual intrusion or violence and/or living with the . . . threat of it" (1995:9). In her research too, Kelly (1987) found that many women experienced sexual interaction not as an "either/or" phenomena— that is, not as *either* consensual *or* forced—but on a continuum moving from choice to pressure to coercion to force. Similarly, Jennifer Dunn's interviews with college sorority women led her to conclude that forcible interaction might best be characterized "as falling along an interpretive continuum ranging from perceptions of violation as relatively nonviolent and unobtrusive to more explicitly threatening and dangerous definitions. . . . What connects meaning conferral along this continuum is the *undesired* character of the interaction from the perspective of the unwilling actor" (1999:441–442). These findings help explain the results of an in-depth survey of more than 6,100 college students in the United States conducted by Mary Koss (1988). Koss found that "only 27 percent of the women whose experience met legal definitions of rape actually labeled themselves as rape victims," and 88 percent of the men who reported perpetrating actions that met legal definitions of rape insisted that what they had done was "not rape" (pp. 16, 19).

One advantage of Randall and Haskell's (1995) methodology, besides its in-depth interview approach, is that it reveals a variety of violations along the sexual violence continuum. It also recognizes that women's pervasive experience of sexual violence cannot really be illuminated by focusing on particular incidents that are independent of one another. We will explore the problem of child sexual abuse later in this chapter, but it suffices here to note that the Randall-Haskell study documented the patterns of victimization and revictimization that all too many girls and women experience as ongoing dimensions of their lives, finding that over 25 percent of the respondents reported sexual abuse or assault in *both* childhood and adulthood, and about 10 percent reported not only childhood sexual abuse *and* adult sexual assault *but also* physical assault in their intimate relationships (see also Schneider 2014).

Sexual Scripts and Rape Myths

Most people tend to view rape as the deviant act of a sick individual. Feminists, on the other hand, have advanced an alternative perspective that views rape as "an extension or exaggeration of conventional sexual relations" and power differentials between women and men, as neither "an aberration nor a particularly unusual occurrence" (Jackson 1978:27, 29). According to this view, rape is not a biological inevitability but a form of socially conditioned sexual aggression that stems from traditional gender socialization and sexual learning (Berger et al. 1986).

James Messerschmidt observes that while sexuality has become "a domain of extensive exploration and pleasure for women . . . it remains simultaneously a site where gendered oppression may occur" (1993:76).

Stevi Jackson (1978) argues that traditional **sexual scripts** have been a major source of the problem. In our society, sexual interactions have traditionally been scripted for an active, aggressive male, the one who seduces, and a passive female, the one who is seduced. The male's role has been to initiate and direct the sexual encounter, the female's role to acquiesce or refuse. She has been socialized to be modest and cautious, to assess the man's desire for a meaningful relationship. Since the man knows that the woman may not want to jeopardize his respect by seeming too eager, however, he often ignores her resistance, presuming it is not indicative of her true feelings and desires. Besides, he may consider failure "to establish dominance over the woman, to make her please him," as a threat to his masculinity (p. 31).

Women are raped in all kinds of situations and by all types of assailants—in their homes and on the street, by strangers and by non-strangers. But with sexual scripts like these, it is easier to understand why **acquaintance rape**—rape involving an assailant the victim knows or is familiar with—is far more common than stranger rape. It is also easier to see how misunderstanding and conflict can occur in potential sexual interactions as each party attempts to negotiate their respective definitions of the situation.

Recall that symbolic interactionism is the sociological perspective that is concerned with the meaning of social action to individuals (see Chapter 4). Symbolic interactionists point out that the very same experience can mean different things to different people. Thus, in sexual interactions men may be surprised when women interpret their advances as overly aggressive, inappropriate, even exploitative, "as foreplay to rape rather than as affection" (Weis & Borges 1973:89). Absence of consent can only be communicated clearly when the woman resists "beyond what is normally expected of women who want intercourse but wish to maintain a 'moral' appearance"—or who at least want to avoid being labeled a "slut" (p. 92). But how can the woman know the amount of resistance that would normally be expected? Might that not vary from man to man or peer group to peer group? And what if she's sexually inexperienced?

All this becomes even trickier to negotiate today as young women reject the traditional double standard and claim their right to sexual desire, and as "Girls Gone Wild" or the latest female celebrity icons mainstream the "hot babe" image. Moreover, in some sense these traditional sexual scripts seem rather quaint when "hooking up" rather than engaging in romantic/emotional relationships becomes more normative. In her exposé of high school and university students in the Washington, DC, area, Laura Sessions Stepp (2007) interviewed a number of young women who assumed that having sex, drinking, and taking drugs were part of the expected, everyday experience of growing up. Young women considered hooking up to be a more affirmative characterization of what used to be called "one-night stands" or "sleeping around," and they felt empowered by being able to "play guys" just like guys have always "played girls." But Stepp also found that these encounters sometimes led to acquaintance rape, what the women called the "gray area" between sex and rape, where a female gets drunk with a guy, goes back to a dorm room or apartment with him, and finds that it is he, not she, who is really in control and that she has no choice but to acquiesce to his forceful advances.

These scenarios are complicated by the culturally available **rape myths** that contain techniques of neutralization or rationalizations that justify rape (see Chapter 4). There is the common presumption, for instance, that a man has urgent sexual needs that prevent him from controlling his behavior and leave him "totally at the mercy of his desires . . . [once his] sexual response has been set in motion" (Jackson 1978:31). This myth places responsibility for limiting sexual activity on the woman. It allows the man to rationalize ignoring her protests, to deny responsibility for forging ahead. She must be careful not to get him too aroused for she may be unable "to control the powerful forces she has unleashed" (p. 31). One convicted rapist likened a man's body to "a coke bottle—shake it up, put your thumb over the opening and feel the tension" (Scully & Marolla 1984:535).

Other rape myths—such as the myth that women secretly want to be raped and eventually relax and enjoy it—allow a man to deny that he has injured the woman: "I didn't hurt her. I just gave her a good screw." There are even rape myths—such as the myth that women are tempting seduc-tresses who invite sexual encounters—that allow men to deny that the woman is a victim at all. Here the man acknowledges that he did rape, but justifies his actions on the grounds that the woman deserved what she got. Sexually assertive women who deviate from traditional scripts are espe-cially likely to be viewed as responsible for provoking the man to rape. Sometimes it's not even what a man considers to be a woman's provocation that leads him to define her as a legitimate victim. Sometimes it's her per-ceived aloofness. Thus, women are placed in a double bind: they are either touchable or untouchable, either looking for sex or thinking they are too good for it. Either way, according to this scenario, they are candidates for rape (Medea & Thompson 1974).

Jackson (1978) observes that rapists do not invent these myths that diminish their responsibility or present their behavior as normal or accept-able. Rather, they adopt them from the larger culture, from the same scripts that structure the sexual interactions of the average couple on a date. Under these circumstances, how can a woman get the man to take her resistance seriously—to recognize that "no" means "no," not "maybe" or "in a little while"? She has been socialized to be nurturing and self-sacrificing, to pro-tect others' feelings, to bolster the male ego, to please and be pleasing. She is supposed to control the pace of the proceedings and to do so gently. Mild protestations may be effective with some, but probably not with a determined man with a shaken "coke bottle." Moreover, it is not only men who have been socialized to ignore and deny the validity of women's feelings, for women have also been taught to question their own feelings and perceptions. Thus, once a woman has allowed an intimate encounter to advance beyond a preliminary stage, not only may the man assume she has committed to going "all the way," but the woman, too, may believe she has relinquished her right to withdraw consent (Foa 1977).

As the man persists, the woman may be too confused and embarrassed to know what to do next. Because her efforts to assert herself have been ineffective, she may simply stop resisting. Acquiescence may indeed seem preferable to the risk of bodily injury or the "humiliation of a lost fight" (MacKinnon 1983:650). Perhaps she resigns herself to what is going to happen, tells herself it will be over soon, tries to put her mind elsewhere. Perhaps she attempts to convince herself he's not really using her, that he's just swept away by her charm. Perhaps she tries to redefine his aggression as romantic or as "hot sex," for eroticizing male dominance would surely seem better than feeling forced or violated. In the end, the man may misread her acquiescence as consent and assume that his seduction techniques were effective after all. Perhaps "his conviction that women will consent if only he tries hard enough" will be reinforced, and it will be even more difficult for the next woman who tries to tell him no (Jackson 1978:32).

Feminist legal scholar Catharine MacKinnon (1983) takes this line or argument further by suggesting that the entire notion of "consent" becomes problematic when male initiative and dominance comprise the normative pattern of sexual interaction and when men are socialized not to be too concerned about what women want. As we have seen, under these conditions it is difficult for women to assess how much resistance is necessary to convince men that they have not granted consent or that they have withdrawn it. A woman may consider it rape, or she may be confused by the fact that she stopped resisting and then *not* define the encounter as such, even though she experienced it as unwanted and nonconsensual. Recall Koss's (1988) findings that only a minority of women whose experiences met legal definitions of rape actually considered themselves to be rape victims, and that a majority of men who reported perpetrating actions that met legal definitions of rape did not think they had committed a crime.

Research also indicates that there are racial/ethnic differences in women's definitions of rape. For example, Linda Williams and Karen Holmes (1981) found that white women, in comparison to black women and Latinas, had a broader definition of what constitutes rape. White women were more likely to define rape as sexual intercourse without a woman's consent (rather than as sexual intercourse that was physically forced) and less likely to consider a woman's behavior or reputation, or her relationship with the offender, as relevant to whether a "real rape" had occurred. Monica Williams, an African American and director of a Los Angeles rape crisis program, suggests why black women may have a narrower view of rape: "I think our image has always been [that black women are] strong and persevering and . . . can take it all, and it doesn't make a difference. . . . I started to notice that [among] most of the women who were assaulted, that it wasn't a priority for them, that they couldn't see that they were hurting. . . . Usually their first concern was their children, or their home or their husband, or how'm I going to make ends meet" (quoted in Matthews 1989:525–526).

The legacy of racism also impacts black women's response to rape. According to Angela Davis, "this country's history of ubiquitous racism in law enforcement," including its use of "the myth of the black rapist" to justify lynchings of black men, has made many black women reluctant to come forward, because they fear it "might well lead to further repressive assaults on their families and communities" (1990:43–44). Marcia Ann Gillespie adds that African-American women have "for the good of the race . . . routinely been expected to put our men first, no matter what. . . . When a woman steps forward and dares to . . . speak about and hold black men accountable for . . . rape, . . . [she] risks becoming a pariah." But Gillespie urges black women to "redefine what is good for the race" by insisting that women's lives matter, too (1993:80–81).

Rape-Law Reform

The common rape scenario that we have been describing is often written off as a "he said, she said" situation. But in a culture where sex has traditionally been scripted for an active male and a passive female, and where it is expected that men may have to be pushy to get what they want, it can be hard to tell the difference between sex and sexual assault. Thus, when a man believes a woman has fabricated charges of rape "after the fact," it may be that her declaration of nonconsent contradicts his experience of the interaction. Moreover, since the law defines the criminality of the act in terms of the *accused's* criminal intent, it becomes difficult to define the act legally as a crime if the man believed that the woman's resistance was not all that genuine (MacKinnon 1983).

According to MacKinnon, the way the law distinguishes between sex and sexual assault is "by adjudicating the level of acceptable force starting just above the level set by what is seen as normal male sexual behavior . . . [not] at the victim's . . . point of violation" (1983:649). Thus, argues MacKinnon, the law adopts the man's perspective:

> [While] many women are raped by men who know the meaning of their acts to women and proceed anyway, . . . women are also violated . . . by men who have no idea of the meaning of their acts to women. To them, it is sex. Therefore, to the law it is sex. . . . The distance between most sexual violations . . . and the legally perfect rape, measures the imposition

of someone else's definition upon women's experiences. Rape, from women's point of view, is not prohibited, it is regulated. (pp. 651–653)

Feminists like MacKinnon have worked to reform the legal system to make it more responsive to and supportive of women. In the past, rape law contained special corroboration rules (not required for other violent crimes) that mandated that prosecutors produce evidence to verify a victim's testimony, because it was assumed that women would deliberately lie about rape in order "to explain premarital intercourse, infidelity, pregnancy, or disease, or to retaliate against an ex-lover or some other man" (Spohn & Horney 1992:24). Prosecutors were also required to demonstrate that a woman had tried to resist her assailant to a degree beyond what was expected of other victims of violent crime. Judges gave jurors special cautionary instructions to warn them that rape was a charge that was easily made but difficult for the defendant to disprove, even if he was innocent. Evidence of a woman's prior sexual history was admissible to impeach her testimony or to show that she had consented to intercourse, because it was assumed that "chastity was a character trait" and that women with premarital or extramarital sexual experiences were more likely to have agreed to sexual relations with the accused (p. 25). And spouses were granted immunity from prosecution on the assumption that when a woman married, she implicitly and irrevocably consented to the sexual advances of her husband (Berger et al. 1988).

Since the mid-1970s, however, states around the country have reformed their laws to eliminate or modify some or all of these practices. One reform redefined the crime of rape as sexual assault, sexual battery, and the like, in order to emphasize the idea that rape is a violent crime and not a crime of uncontrollable sexual passion. Such semantic changes were intended to divert attention from questions about consent, for assault is, "by definition, something to which the victim does not consent" (Bienen 1980:192). Redefining rape as sexual assault also broadened the definition of the crime beyond vaginal-penile intercourse to include oral and anal penetration, sexual penetration with objects, and in some statutes, touching of intimate body parts. Other reforms redefined the crime in gender-neutral terms to protect victims from female offenders and to protect male victims, and some removed or modified the spousal exemption (Berger et al. 1988; Spohn & Horney 1992).

Another set of reforms attempted to eliminate evidentiary rules that made it more difficult to convict offenders. Special corroboration and proof-of-resistance requirements, as well as cautionary jury instructions, were abolished. Reform statutes also introduced **rape shield laws** that limit admissibility of evidence regarding the complainant's prior sexual history. Less restrictive rape shield laws allow admission of evidence of prior sexual conduct after judicial determination of its relevance; more restrictive laws create a general prohibition of such information but allow specific exceptions—for instance, evidence of previous sexual contact between the complainant and defendant. The more restrictive statutes have been criticized for not sufficiently accommodating the defendant's right to present relevant evidence, the less restrictive for providing inadequate protection of the complainant's right to privacy (Berger et al. 1988; Spohn & Horney 1992).

Studies of the impact of rape-law reform indicate that many criminal justice officials continue to operate on the basis of traditional assumptions about rape and fail to consistently comply with the statutes. Decisions regarding rape/sexual assault are still subject to much discretion, and the reforms do not necessarily affect the informal operations of the criminal justice system. Evidentiary reforms involving the victim's prior sexual history, for example, have been aimed at trial procedures, although most cases are handled informally through pretrial plea bargaining (if they go that far). At trial, requirements for closed hearings to determine relevancy of the complainant's prior sexual history are often not held, and this information is often admitted as evidence. Indices of closeness (e.g., dating, cohabiting, marriage) or of prior social interaction (e.g., the woman was acquainted with the accused or had agreed to interact socially with him) are still used by defendants to persuade judges and juries that they believed the woman had consented (Berger et al. 1994; Spohn & Horney 1992; Spohn & Tellis 2014).

The Question of Pornography

In the mid-1970s, many feminists concluded that the problem of violence against women and children required a more direct confrontation with the cultural images that promote a climate that sustains and fosters such crimes, and this critique focused particularly on the issue of pornography (Berger et al. 1991; Lederer 1980; see Chapter 5). Broaching this topic requires recognition that the kinds of sexual imagery people have in mind when they use the term "pornography" vary considerably. We find it useful, therefore, to distinguish between **erotica** and **pornography**. According to Gloria Steinem, erotica involves images or depictions of "mutually pleasurable sexual expression" between consenting subjects "who have enough power to be there by positive choice" (1980:37). Pornography, on the other hand, treats the body as an object to be controlled or dominated. According to Diana Russell, it is "material that combines sex and/or the exposure of genitals with abuse or degradation in a manner that appears to endorse, condone, or encourage" the abuse or degradation. Sexual behavior that is abusive "ranges from derogatory, demeaning, contemptuous, or damaging to brutal, cruel, exploitative, painful, or violent," while sexual behavior that is degrading "is humiliating, insulting, [or] disrespectful" (1993:2–3).

Some researchers argue that pornography is a symptom and not a cause of attitudes that promote sexual violence (Baron & Straus 1989; Schwartz & DeKeseredy 1997). Of course, pornography does not cause violence "in the way a virus causes disease, gravity causes objects to fall or a bell caused Pavlov's famous dogs to salivate" (Cameron & Frazer 1993:371). Individuals who engage in sexual violence are neither "impelled by instinct ... [nor] responding unthinkingly or involuntarily" to pornographic stimuli. Rather, they interpret and "impose meaning on the stimuli" and then act in accordance with this meaning (pp. 368, 370).

Nevertheless, those who are critical of pornography think it plays an important role in shaping some forms of sexual desire and not others. MacKinnon (1986), for instance, believes that pornography is implicated in the "cycle of abuse" of women and children. As she writes, "as long as pornography exists as it does now, women and children will be used and abused to make it, as they are now. And it will be used to abuse them, as it is now" (p. 47). Although people often assume that women in pornographic photos and films are willing participants who make good money, this is, as with women who prostitute or who are victims of sex trafficking, not always the case (see Chapter 6). Many women and children are pressured or coerced by boyfriends, husbands, fathers, or pimps to pose or perform for pornography. They are told to smile, to act like they like what is happening. Even without explicit force, "the compulsion of poverty, of drugs, of the street, of foreclosed alternatives, of fear of retribution for noncooperation can be enforcement enough" (p. 42). And since a child is not considered legally capable of consenting to sex, each and every instance of pornography involving children is "a document of the sexual abuse of the child who was required for its production" (Kelly 1993:116).

To be sure, there are many women (and men) who perform for pornography and who read or watch it without being coerced to do so. Indeed, a number of feminists have accused their antipornography counterparts of overemphasizing the extent to which women are victimized by pornography. They insist that women can be autonomous agents of their own sexuality and can negotiate the risks and dangers of this power-laden terrain for their own purposes (Snitow et al. 1983; Vance 1984). Antipornography feminists respond to this critique by saying they do not deny women's right to be sexually assertive actors, that they do not suggest that pornography turns all men into rapists, and that they do not condemn anyone who enjoys it. But they do assert that although some people like pornography or willingly get involved with it, this does not mean it is without harm (MacKinnon 1986; Russell 1993). In doing so, they point to a body of research from a wide range of sources—including media experiments, survey research, and clinical evidence—that provide legitimate grounds for concern.

Much of the research on pornography involves experimental studies of the effect of sexually violent or aggressive pornography (not erotica) on men in laboratory settings, and these studies have found differences among men in the way they respond to experimental exposure. The research on sexual arousal to pornography, attitudes about women, and laboratory aggression (e.g., administering an electronic shock) indicates that men who are already *predisposed* to sexual aggression—those who report they would be likely to rape if they thought they would not be caught or punished, those who are more sexually aroused by depictions of rape than by depictions of consensual sex, or those who harbor relatively high levels of anger toward women—are influenced by experimental exposure to a greater degree than are men who are not so predisposed. Furthermore, most experimental male subjects are less aroused by rape scenes when female victims are portrayed as abhorring sexual assault than when female victims are portrayed as becoming involuntarily aroused. In general, experimental exposure to the latter type of pornography increases men's aggression against women in laboratory settings, their belief in rape myths that justify sexual violence, their rape fantasies, their insensitivity to rape victims and the trauma of rape, and their self-reported possibility of committing rape (Allen et al. 1995; Donnerstein et al. 1987; Malamuth & Donnerstein 1984).

These findings are not particularly surprising in light of the fact that it is common in sexually violent pornography to depict women as initially resistant if not terrified of rape but becoming "sexually aroused to the point of cooperation" and physically gratified despite their embarrassment or shame (Scully & Marolla 1985:253). Moreover, experimental research has found that even the viewing of nonviolent pornography is associated with less sympathetic attitudes toward rape victims and greater trivialization of rape as a serious crime. Thus, Neil Malamuth, a leading researcher in the field, concluded that the experimental evidence strongly supports the view that at least some types of pornography contribute "to a cultural climate that is more accepting of aggression against women" (1985:405).

Although some analysts discount laboratory experiments because of their artificiality (Durham 1986), survey research also documents the negative experiences that women have had with pornography. In several studies, for example, from 10 to 25 percent of women responded yes to the question: "Have you ever been upset by anyone trying to get you to do what they had seen in pornographic pictures, movies, or books?" (Harmon & Check 1989; Russell 1982; Senn 1993; Stock 1995). Summarizing the results of survey research on men, Robert Jensen notes that pornography can: "(a) be an important factor in shaping a male-dominant view of sexuality, (b) contribute to a user's difficulty in separating sexual fantasy and reality, (c) be used to initiate victims and break down their resistance to sexual activity, and (d) provide a training manual for abusers" (1995:33). By no means does Jensen think that all men who use pornography engage in abusive behavior. But he does conclude that the research suggests that "for some sex abusers, pornography is an integral part of their abuse" (p. 35).

Clinical evidence provided by professional therapists and law enforcement authorities who work with victims or with self-reported and convicted sex offenders also implicates pornography. Cheryl Champion estimates, for instance, that about 40 percent of clinical sex offender cases involve perpetrators who use pornography, typically in a very compulsive and obsessive manner, "for masturbation, fantasy contemplation, and actual acting out of their scenarios" (1986:24). Ray Wyre, who has worked with a wide range of sex offenders over the course of his career as a therapist, notes that sex offenders often use pornography "to justify and legitimate what they do" (1992:236). According to Wyre, pornography can create and reinforce rape and child abuse fantasies that "push men further along [a] continuum of sexual mistreatment of women and children," from inappropriate sexual gestures and conduct to horrendous crimes (p. 246).

It is not just pornography, however, but also mainstream media that trivialize or eroticize violence against women and children. The "Battered Chic" advertisements first introduced in the 1980s, for example, feature models wearing torn or tattered clothing and looking roughed up and bruised. Fashion layouts exhibit women models with frightened expressions, looking over their shoulders at shadowy figures or running from danger. And these are not ads for locks or security devices. They are ads for glamour enhancers like lipstick and hair color. One pantyhose ad presents a woman buried in the sand from the waist *up,* her rear end exposed and legs provocatively displayed in silky hose and high heels while an ominous crustacean inches its way toward her incapacitated body. A jeans ad depicts what appears to be before-and-after shots of rape—a young woman slung over a man's shoulder being carried off to a garage, then hanging out of a car, disheveled, her blouse open. With images like these permeating the culture, it's no wonder that violence can seem sexy to all too many people (Lori 2011; Searles n.d.).

Pornography and sexually charged advertisements and media in general are also implicated in the sexual exploitation of children. As Ellen Bass observes, we are continually bombarded with cultural images that blur "the distinction between woman and girl-child" and that desensitize us to, or even encourage, the sexual use of girls (1983:38). Young girls are often made up to look years older with cosmetics, provocative outfits, and sophisticated hairdos, while adult women are posed seductively sporting pigtails and skimpy girlish clothes, sucking lollipops or holding teddy bears. These images, says Bass, "confuse adult women with children . . . [and] vulnerability with sexual invitation" (p. 42).

Personal Resistance Strategies
In addition to the law reforms discussed earlier, the feminist antiviolence movement has spawned a number of service and prevention efforts for victims, including rape crisis centers, hotlines, improved public lighting,

nighttime-safety transit systems, and rape avoidance and self-defense training. Among these innovations, self-defense training has been particularly controversial, because it has challenged the conventional advice that has been given to women about what to do in the case of a sexual assault, which encourages them not to resist if attacked but to submit to rape in order to avoid further harm (Hazelwood & Harpold 1986). At most, this advice recommends pleading or reasoning with the assailant. Feminists, on the other hand, have generally encouraged women to fight back (Bart & O'Brien 1985; Delacoste & Newman 1981; Searles & Berger 1987).

Many studies now indicate that immediate active resistance (e.g., yelling, fighting, running away), and especially the use of multiple resistance strategies, reduces the likelihood that an attempted rape will be completed. Pleading and arguing seem to be less effective unless used in combination with other verbal strategies such as yelling and calling for help (Bart & O'Brien 1985; Searles & Berger 1987). The research is less clear, however, regarding the question of whether resistance increases the likelihood of additional injury, meaning injury beyond the rape itself. Joan McDermott (1979) found that resisters incurred greater additional injury than nonresisters, although most of these injuries were of a relatively unserious nature, such as bruises, cuts, and scratches. Moreover, women who resisted were much less likely to incur a completed rape. Other studies indicate that the connection between resistance and additional injury may be related to the type of resistance employed. William Sanders (1980) found that those who "struggled" (such as those who attempted to push the attacker away) were more likely than those who fought (such as those who hit, bit, or kicked the attacker) or those who ran away to incur additional serious injury. Gary Kleck and Susan Sayles (1990) found that weaponless forceful resistance was associated with increased injury, but that this resistance was more likely to follow rather than precede the injury. They note that some advice-givers counsel nonresistance because a small proportion of "rapists are indeed incited to further violence by victim resistance." However, they conclude:

> The flaw in this reasoning is that it depends on an unstated, but false, premise that nonresistance does not entail any risks of its own. . . . Advice to not resist depends on the belief that the nonresisting rape victim trades off an increased likelihood of rape completion for a reduced likelihood of injury. Such a trade-off makes sense only if one assumes the additional injury is in some sense a more serious harm . . . than the completion of the rape itself. (p. 160)

It is arguably unwise to give blanket advice to women about what they *should* do if attacked, as if all attack situations are the same, or to criticize what a woman *did* or *did not* do in a stressful and frightening situation. Nevertheless, teaching women and girls psychological and physical self-defense skills, and nurturing in them a strong sense of self-worth, both broadens the range of options they will have and increases the likelihood they will possess the self-confidence and presence of mind to evaluate their options and act in a way that is in their best interests. Regrettably, as Patricia Rozee and colleagues observe, remedies to sexual violence "aimed primarily at behavioral change among women place an unwarranted responsibility on individual women for their own safety. To live a life free of the fear of sexual assault ought to be a right afforded to us by the society in which we live" (1991:351).

FURTHER EXPLORATION
Sexual Violence in the US Military

Sexual misconduct in the military is another element of the rape problem that has been in the news in recent years. The first public reports of this problem occurred during a Tailhook Association convention in Las Vegas, Nevada, in 1991. The Tailhook Association is a nonprofit organization that supports the interests of sea-based aviation such as aircraft carriers. Eighty-three women and seven men who attended the convention reported that they were sexually assaulted or harassed by their fellow attendees (Spahr Nelson 2002). A subsequent Defense Department study in 1995 found that nearly half of women and a third of men in the military reported experiencing "unwanted sexual attention" from military personnel; and 4 percent of women in the air force and coast guard, 6 percent in the navy, 8 percent in the army, and 9 percent in the marines reported being victims of rape or attempted rape in the previous year alone. A 2003 Defense Department study also found that nearly a third of female veterans seeking health assistance from the Department of Veterans Affairs indicated they had experienced rape or attempted rape while serving in the armed forces; and an *Associated Press* investigation uncovered more than 80 military recruiters who had been disciplined in 2005 for sexual misconduct (including rape) with potential recruits (Herbert 2008; Mendoza 2006). Additionally, US military personnel and private mercenaries hired by the Defense Department during the Iraq War raped Iraqi women and children and even circulated pornographic photographs of their crimes (Cienfuegos 2004; CNN 2006b).

   A more recent Defense Department study estimated that about 26,000 sex crimes were committed by US military personnel in 2012 alone, but that only 13 percent of these incidents were reported. Victims allege that they are discouraged by their commanders from filing formal complaints, and that when they do, their complaints are often ignored or mishandled and nothing is done to sanction the perpetrators. There is even one case where an officer who was eventually suspended for repeatedly groping female colleagues was in charge of supervising army prosecutions of sexual assault cases. Even when wrongdoing is implicitly acknowledged, complainants are expected to continue to serve alongside their unprosecuted offenders. Victims favor the creation of an independent reporting/prosecution agency outside the chain of command that is more interested in remedying the problem than in avoiding bad publicity for the military (Goodman 2013; Heppler 2014; Thompson 2011).

Sexual Abuse of Children

According to Bass (1983), whenever a child is used sexually by an adult, whether or not there is physical force or even the threat of it, coercion is involved. "There can be no equality of power, understanding, or freedom in sex between adults and children. Children are dependent upon adults: first for their survival; then for affection, attention, and an understanding of what the world in which they live is all about" (pp. 26–27). Because a child is not legally capable of giving informed consent to sex, sexual interaction with a child is by definition abuse, an illegal act everywhere in the United States.

Child sexual abuse is distressingly common. Studies provide varying estimates of its prevalence, however, due to divergent research samples and definitions of abuse. Underreporting is also a serious problem. David Knudsen reviewed numerous studies and estimated that "at least 30 percent of girls and 20 percent of boys experience some form of sexual abuse" (1992:112). As we have seen, Randall and Haskell (1995) found even higher percentages of abuse among the women they interviewed, and over a quarter of the women who reported abuse said they were abused before age eight. One study using a national sample found that 98 percent of girls and 83 percent of boys who are abused are victimized by men (Finkelhor et al. 1990).

Child sexual abuse varies widely, from fleeting encounters to intense incestuous relations. Overall, according to Andrea Nelson and Pamela Oliver (1998), girls are more likely than boys to be abused by family members, and they tend to experience their first abuse at a younger age compared to abused boys. The duration of abuse also tends to be longer for girls than for boys. Although girls and boys appear equally likely to experience sibling incest, girls are much more likely to experience incestuous abuse by parents. Nelson and Oliver describe incestuous abuse of boys as relatively rare yet traumatic and usually occurring at the hands of men. Boys' abuse contacts are most common with adult acquaintances who are not relatives. Nevertheless, some clinicians consider mother-son incest to be very underreported rather than very rare (Lawson 1993).

The Abuse of Girls

Although both girls and boys may be victimized by sexual abuse, the most common form involves the abuse of a girl by an older male. Bass describes how the experience can shape a girl's view of herself and her world:

> When a man sexually uses a child, he is giving that child a strong message about her world: He is telling her that she is important because of her sexuality, that [sex is what] men want ... from girls, ... that relationships are insufficient without sex. He is telling her that she can use her sexuality as a way to get the attention and affection she genuinely needs, that sex is a

tool. When he tells her not to tell, she learns there is something about sex that is shameful and bad; and that she, because she is a part of it, is shameful and bad. . . . She learns that the world is . . . not to be trusted, that even those entrusted with her care will betray her; that she will betray herself. (1983:27)

The sense of betrayal is especially intense when the abuser is a family member. In the most commonly reported type of incest, father-daughter incest, including incest between stepfathers and stepdaughters, "the father, in effect, forces the daughter to pay with her body for affection and care that should be freely given" (Herman 1981:4). This gross misuse of power shatters the protective bond that should exist between parent and child.

According to Judith Herman, a child who has to live with the abuser is a child who is trapped in a harmful environment, who must somehow "find a way to preserve a sense of trust in people who are untrustworthy, safety in a situation that is unsafe, [and] control in a situation that is terrifyingly unpredictable" (1992:96). This is a formidable task for anyone, let alone a child with an undeveloped system of psychological defenses. Adaptation to this kind of untenable climate requires constant alertness. Abused children tend to become minutely attuned to the abusers' state of mind, often developing "extraordinary abilities to scan for warning signs of attack" (p. 100). When they perceive a threat, they almost reflexively try to protect themselves by avoiding the abuser—becoming as inconspicuous as possible, hiding, even running away—or by placating the abuser with demonstrations of obedience, by trying to be "good."

These desperate efforts are never completely successful, however, and the child must live with the knowledge that the most powerful adult in her intimate life is a threat, and that the other adults—especially her mother—who should be protecting her are not. The child experiences this lack of protection as a sign of indifference at best, as complicit betrayal at worst, and the feeling of abandonment may be "resented more keenly than the abuse itself" (Herman 1992:100). To avoid utter despair, the abused child desperately seeks to preserve faith in her parents and a sense of attachment to them. She resorts to a variety of psychological defenses as she struggles to construct an account of her fate that will absolve one or both parents of responsibility and blame. Sometimes she "tries to keep the abuse a secret from herself." She uses denial, suppression of thoughts, and dissociative states to wall the abuse off "from conscious awareness and memory," so she can believe that "it did not really happen." Or, she will "minimize, rationalize, and excuse, so that whatever did happen was not really abuse." In either case, when the child cannot alter or escape "the unbearable reality in fact," she resorts to altering it "in her mind." Although these alterations of consciousness are sometimes deliberate, they often become habitual. When the abuse is prolonged as well as early and severe, some children even "form separated personality fragments with their own names, psychological functions, and sequestered memories." These alter egos, sometimes called multiple personalities, enable the child "to cope resourcefully with the abuse while keeping both the abuse and the coping strategies outside of ordinary awareness" (pp. 102–103).

Reality cannot always be avoided by dissociation, however, and at times the child attempts to make sense of the abuse by blaming herself. This not only serves to justify the abuse but also enables the child "to preserve a sense of meaning, hope, and power. If she is bad, then her parents are good. If she is bad, then she can try to be good." If she tries hard enough, maybe her parents will forgive her and start treating her with kind-

---

FURTHER EXPLORATION
Sexual Abuse and the Catholic Church

The abuse of children by members of the Catholic clergy had been known for some time, but the scandal did not generate much media attention until early in the first decade of the twenty-first century. A study conducted by the John Jay College of Criminal Justice in conjunction with the US Roman Catholic church found that over 10,600 abuse claims involving 4 percent of US clergy had been made since 1950. Researchers were able to substantiate about 63 percent of these claims, although about 30 percent could not be investigated because the clergymen had died. Nevertheless, about $1 billion was paid by US churches to settle these abuse claims. In 2003, the Boston Archdiocese alone agreed to pay $85 million to more than 500 people who claimed they were sexually abused by priests, and at least 325 priests were removed from their positions or forced to resign. By the end of the decade, the problem increasingly took on international dimensions, and in 2011–2012 alone, more than 380 priests were defrocked (Heilprin & Winfield 2014; Lavoie 2003; Zoll 2004a, 2004b).

Since most of the allegations made public have involved priests and teenage boys, a leading Vatican official asserted that gay men should not be ordained as priests and that those already ordained should be removed from the clergy. This comment led the president of a national gay Catholic group to retort: "This is nothing more than a vicious, transparent attempt to shift the blame in an effort to deny institutional culpability in the scandal. . . . This [abuse] is about violence against children and abuse of power. It has nothing to do with sexual orientation" (quoted in Freiberg 2002:29). In fact, the Catholic Church has for centuries turned "a blind eye to the sexual exploits of priests regardless of their sexual orientation" (Dahir 2002:32). A. W. Richard Sipe, a psychotherapist and former monk who has studied clergy sexuality for over four decades, concludes that "gay priests respect their vows of celibacy in the same proportion as straight priests" (quoted in Freiberg 2002:29). Moreover, as Sipe observes, sexual orientation is hard to categorize, since many priests are psychosexually immature and have not "really sorted out their sexuality" (p. 30).

ness and concern. Unfortunately, her belief in her innate badness is likely to be reinforced by parental blame, by her own understandable rage or aggressive response to mistreatment, by her "participation in forbidden sexual activity," and by any "enforced complicity in crimes against others"—for example, if she is silent about a sibling who is also being abused (Herman 1992:103–104).

These experiences can have lifelong consequences, because the sense of inner badness can be hard to shed even as an adult. As a woman, the survivor of child sexual abuse will likely have low self-esteem and difficulty fully crediting herself for her achievements, perceiving her "performing self" as inauthentic (Herman 1992). She may hunger for love and nurturance while fearing exploitation and abandonment. Her low self-esteem may undercut her faith in her own judgment and make her vulnerable to abuse by others, and being used sexually at an early age may also be an inducement to prostitution by lessening her resistance to viewing herself as a "saleable commodity" (James & Meyerding 1977:41). In her work with Andrea Dworkin, MacKinnon estimates that 65–75 percent of women in prostitution are survivors of child sexual abuse (Dworkin & MacKinnon 1988); and as Kathleen Barry observes, a prostitute with an abusive past "may place her need for affection above the abuse" of her pimp (1979:102).

The Abuse of Boys

Most studies of sexual contact between adults and children ask respondents about "unwanted" or "abusive" experiences. However, Nelson and Oliver (1998) maintain that adolescents can sometimes be "sexual subjects" for adults, not just sexual objects or victims. Conceptualizing consent/coercion as a continuum rather than as an either/or phenomenon, Nelson and Oliver chose to avoid "abuse language" when they asked more than 900 Wisconsin undergraduates the following screening question: "When you were 15 years [old] or younger, did you experience sexual contact with an adult?" (adults were defined as being 18 or older).

Among the cases where there was at least a four-year gap between the child and the adult, Nelson and Oliver found that 98 percent of girls' contacts were with men and 69 percent of boys' contacts were with women (this percentage of woman-boy contacts is higher than is usually found in studies that use "abuse" language). Adult-girl contacts were more common than adult-boy contacts, and girls' experiences were much more likely than boys' to be repeated and incestuous. Although *both boys and girls* usually defined their contacts with *men* as coercive and harmful, *boys* often defined their contacts with *women* as consensual and not harmful. What was crucial for most respondents was "whether the adult 'asked' or persuaded the child into sexual activity rather than 'taking,' unilaterally initiating sexual activity without trying to gain the child's cooperation" (Nelson & Oliver 1998:568). Generally speaking, women were more likely to "ask," and men were more likely to "take." But even when manipulated and dominated by a woman, boys over age 10 tended to report feeling that "their sense of masculine potency had been enhanced in the encounter" (p. 573). Despite the fact that US laws increasingly define sexual abuse in gender-neutral terms, Nelson and Oliver conclude:

> The constructions of masculine and feminine are so strong as to make it impossible for sexual contact between women and boys to have the same social meaning . . . as contact between men and girls. Dominance in woman-boy contacts is less straightforward than in man-girl contacts. [And] the sexual exploitation of a boy by a woman may not be experienced by the boy or seen by others as status-reducing victimization, but rather as status-enhancing "sex with a woman." (p. 560)

Although it is important to note that most of the woman-boy contacts reported in this study involved *adolescent* males and relatively *young* women (under age 22), some of the males who had defined their woman-boy contacts as not harmful did reveal some confusion and tension as they

---

FURTHER EXPLORATION
Rape of Adult Men

Although rape is most commonly committed by men against women and girls, about 10 percent of rape or attempted rape victims are male (Rape, Abuse & Incest National Network 2009). And just as fear of homophobia silences boys who have been sexually abused, it also silences men who have been raped, regardless of sexual orientation. Knowing that heterosexual victims might not want to be presumed gay or that gay victims might not want to be outed, offenders may try to get victims to ejaculate in order to discourage them from reporting the crime. That tactic is often effective, because although one can have an involuntary sexual response during a coerced encounter, ejaculation often confuses the victim and makes him feel complicit. Responses of others frequently compound the problem. As rape survivor Fred Pelka observes, police often ask, "Did you come?" and friends want to know how the victim could "let something like this happen?" (1995:251).

People generally assume that a male perpetrator who rapes another man must be gay or bisexual. But rape is often a way to exert control, to confirm one's "own power by disempowering others" (Pelka 1995:251). Overcoming another man—rather than a woman or child—and perhaps forcing an undesired sexual response, can make a man, regardless of sexual orientation, feel powerful. Likewise, being victimized, being taken and used, can make a man feel like a traitor to his gender, since he no longer fits our culture's "definition of masculinity, as one empowered, one always in control." Pelka (1995) encourages other male survivors to challenge this specious definition by breaking their silence.

attempted to evaluate whether they had been *less* masculine because they had been subordinate and dominated, or *more* masculine because they had exhibited virility at an early age. Some of the respondents may have been attempting to put the best possible face on incidents that they experienced with some ambivalence if not outright distress.

Mike Lew (1990) argues that woman-boy sexual activity is rarely treated as abusive and that boys who attempt to talk about their pain or confusion often find that their experience is ignored, denied, trivialized, or even romanticized, written off as initiation into manhood or "scoring." Males, after all, are expected to be sexual aggressors, to be "strong enough to protect themselves against unwanted attention from . . . the 'weaker sex'" (p. 58). They may thus try to redefine their experiences so that they better fit the perceptions of others, even to the extent of joking or bragging about them. A society that confuses sexual abuse with sex places the boy "in a powerful double bind. If he enjoyed the experience, then it wasn't abusive. If he didn't, he must be homosexual" (p. 55). And if the perpetrator is male, the boy is often presumed likely to become gay, if not thought likely to be so already. So in addition to dealing with the experience of exploitation, the youth finds himself confronting societal homophobia. If he defines himself as heterosexual (or hasn't yet thought much about sexual orientation), he may wonder, "Does this *mean* I'm gay?" If he defines himself as gay, he may wonder, "Is this *why* I'm gay?" or "Did this happen to me *because* I'm gay?" Girls exploited by women may struggle with these questions as well.

Battering of Women

National victimization research finds that about one in four women has been physically assaulted by an intimate partner at some time in her life, and that about 85 percent of all assaults by intimate partners involve women victims (Rennison 2003; Tjaden & Thoennes 2000). Confronting this violence, undermining it, is an uphill battle in a culture that normalizes, even eroticizes, violence. A photo in *Hustler* magazine titled "Battered Wives" illustrates this eroticization of violence. A man in a chef's hat and apron has just pulled a naked woman out of a large mixing bowl. There he stands, holding the woman by the neck with a pair of tongs, her body dripping with gooey batter. The caption reads: "This photo shows why it's no wonder that wife-beating has become one of society's stickiest problems! But today's liberated women should have expected this kind of response when they decided that men should do more of the domestic chores like cooking. Still, there's absolutely no excuse for doing something this bad. Now he's going to have to beat her just to smooth out all those lumps" (cited in Russell 1993:41).

The eroticization of violence permeates not just pornographic magazines, but also advertising, song lyrics, music videos, movies, comic books, video games, and the like—virtually all forms of entertainment. Even Alex Comfort, a physician no less, tells readers in his best-selling book *The New Joy of Sex: The Gourmet Guide to Lovemaking for the Nineties* that while "normal resentments" often build up between two people who live together, violent sex "tends to discharge them" (1991:98–99).

When sexual aggression is normalized, it is common to write off abuse or even murder as a "crime of passion." In 1989, a New York City Police Department officer, Felix Key, dragged Jean Singleton into the street, riddled her body with bullets, then killed himself as well. Singleton had been attempting to end their relationship because Key was extremely overprotective and jealous. Although the NYPD had previously disciplined Key for holding another woman at gunpoint and threatening her, the department's official spokesperson refrained from using the word "murder," instead describing "the killings as 'a lover's quarrel between the two of them'" (Jones 1994:125). And the front-page headline of the *New York Post* read: "Tragedy of a Love Sick Cop"—language that practically invites us to sympathize with the murderer.

The Experience of Battering

According to Ann Jones, the fusion of violence with love and sex gives an aggressive man "an excuse for assault: 'I did it because I love you so much'" (1994:121–122). And it gives a victimized woman an explanation that can snare her in understanding, compassion, and forgiveness for her assailant, often keeping her stuck in the relationship, hoping against hope to work things out. Although Lisa Bianco had divorced her battering husband, Al Matheney, this did not stop Matheney from breaking into her house to beat and rape her. Matheney explained to Bianco that he was doing it because he loved her. Bianco wanted him prosecuted because, as she said, "If I don't do something, it's just going to happen again" (p. 43). Matheney was convicted of assault, although the rape charge was dropped after a probation consultant told the court that the two "very possibly could have been having a wonderful social affair with sex involved" (p. 119). At the sentencing hearing, Matheney's attorney explained to the judge: "Mr. Matheney . . . could never let go of this woman. . . . Just to call it love would be wrong. Although I'm sure that's what Al perceives it as. I perceive it as an obsession. A love obsession." Two years later, after Matheney was released on furlough, he clubbed Bianco 20 times with a stolen shotgun, smashing her head brutally while busting the gun into three pieces. When asked why he did it, he said it was because he "still loved her."

If even murder can be characterized simply as "love gone wrong," portraying an assault as sexually motivated opens the door to dismissing it as "rough sex" that somehow got out of hand (Jones 1994). If the victim can't be discredited on the witness stand, can't be convincingly portrayed as "that kind of woman," perhaps the jury can be made to feel sorry for the poor sex-obsessed fellow. As Andrea Dworkin observes:

> On the same day the [Los Angeles] police who beat Rodney King were acquitted in . . . [1992], a white husband who had raped, beaten, and tortured his wife, also white, was acquitted for marital rape in South Carolina. He had kept her tied to a bed for hours, her mouth gagged with adhesive tape. He videotaped a half hour of her ordeal, during which he cut her breasts with a knife. The [jurors] . . . saw the videotape. Asked why they acquitted, they said he needed help. . . . There were no riots afterward. (1997:49)

Abuse is disguised not only by the "language of love" but also by the label "domestic violence," a euphemism that keeps us dispassionately distant from the horrific spectacle of human suffering (Jones 1994). Advocates for battered women seeking funding for their services originally used this term to avoid offending men who controlled the distribution of funds. So effective was the label at hiding the reality of woman battering that when congressional legislation titled the Domestic Violence Act was proposed in 1978 to fund services for battered women, it was mistaken by many to be legislation aimed at combating political terrorism.

We prefer the term **battering**, which David Adams defines as "controlling behavior that serves to create and maintain an imbalance of power" between the batterer and the person being battered (1988:191–192). Adams argues that a violent act is "any act that causes the victim to do something she does not want to do, prevents her from doing something she wants to do, or causes her to be afraid." He believes that violence does not have to be narrowly defined as "physical contact with the victim," since the intimidation generated through such things as "punching walls, verbal threats, and psychological abuse" can have the same effect. Psychological abuse—that is, "behavior that directly undermines the self-determination or self-esteem" of the victim—is especially powerful when paired with physical violence, because "covert controls" are reminders of the potential for additional violence. Swearing, shouting, sulking, or spewing accusations are particularly frightening and effective when "'reinforced' by periodic or even occasional violence."

Jones adds that "battering is not a series of isolated blow-ups. It is a *process of deliberate intimidation intended to coerce the victim to do the will of the victimizer.* . . . The batterer is not just losing his temper, not just suffering from stress, not just manifesting 'insecurity' or a spontaneous reaction 'provoked' by something the victim did" (1994:88–89). Rather, these are excuses for violence that are effective at convincing the woman to give him another chance. He's not really a bad man, she tells herself. He didn't mean it. He wasn't himself. But of course he *was* himself. He wasn't out of control. He was exercising control.

Although battering husbands are often traditionalists who believe in male superiority and men's right to head the family (Pagelow 1984), Linda Gordon's historical research on four decades of family violence in Boston found that batterers were "not ideologues defending the dominance of their sex. . . . [They were men who] were using violence to increase their control over particular women, defending real material benefits" (1988:286–287). The "sense of entitlement" these men had "was so strong it was experienced as a need." Then, as now, disappointment of their expectations—a hot meal, a cold beer, a tidy house, an ironed shirt, well-behaved kids, sex *now*—meant punishment, lessons the little lady had better learn *once and for all.*

But even the apologies the batterer may make when he thinks his punishment "got out of hand" or "went too far" are designed to control. He pleads:

> I'm sorry. I didn't mean to hit you so hard. You just get me so mad. I'm sorry. I didn't mean those things I said—it was just the booze talking. You know I love you. I'm sorry. I just had such a bad day. I didn't mean to hurt you. Why did you make me do that? Don't you know I'm trying to control my temper. I'm sorry. I just can't take it when you dress like that and men look you up and down. You're my woman after all. Who do they think they are? Who do you think you are? I'm sorry. You know I love you. Why can't you just do what I say? I'm sorry. I'll try not to get so angry. You know I can't live without you. (Searles n.d.)

Although the apologies are often intermingled with blame or denial, the professed remorse and promise of reform can be seductive indeed. Dubbed by psychologists as the **honeymoon phase**, these periods of supposed repentance can lull women into letting their guard down (Walker 1979). Although women often mistake these periods for love, they "are not respites from battering, as they appear, but part of the coercive process, pressuring women to forgive and forget, to minimize and deny, to *submit,* and thus to appear complicitous" (Jones 1994:93).

Many women who are in abusive relationships, however, do not consider themselves to be "battered women." The notion of a battered woman conjures up images of helpless victims beaten down by more or less constant physical assaults. Women who have endured abuse appreciate the incredible vigilance, courage, and self-discipline it takes to survive day after day, and they often see themselves as strong women who somehow manage to cope. Living in an atmosphere of persistent threat, with violence both capricious and inevitable, a woman hems herself in. She "may give up bits and pieces of herself: her preferences, her opinions, her voice, her friends, her job, her freedom of movement, her sexual autonomy. She may learn to lie, or at least to keep the truth to herself. She may learn to say that sex was good when it wasn't, or that she's sorry when she's not. Unable ever to give the 'right' answer, she may retreat into silence" (Jones 1994:94). Her apparent passivity is often mistaken for submission, even masochism, but she doesn't give in. She lies low—at first while she attempts to make some sense of what is happening, then while she tries one thing after another to get him to change. Finally, when she realizes nothing she does to appease him will stop the abuse, she contemplates leaving, checks out her options, and perhaps—with tremendous determination and at enormous risk—squirrels away a dollar here, a dollar there, for her "ticket to freedom."

A women's gradual decision to leave an abusive relationship is significantly affected by her economic resources and access to social support networks and services. When she finally does try to leave, she will likely face an escalation of the violence, sometimes with lethal consequences. The batterer often thinks, "If I can't have her, no one will." In fact, Dworkin notes that "more battered women are killed after they leave than before" (1997:43). So if guilt, shame, love, pity, poverty, tattered self-esteem, sense of duty, family pressure, religious obligation, the specter of homelessness, the questions that ring in her ears—What will the *kids* do without a dad? What will *he* do without me?—don't keep her stuck, fear often will (Choice & Lamke 1997; Goetting 1999; Stanko 1997).

In 1989, Nicole Brown Simpson asked the police to arrest her husband, Hall of Fame football star and Hollywood celebrity O.J. Simpson. It was the ninth time the police had been called, but the first time he was arrested. Dworkin (1997) wonders how many beatings women have to endure before the violence is taken seriously. Nicole's divorce was finalized in 1992. But although she had escaped her marriage, she had not escaped the task of negotiating her safety, as O.J. continued to intimidate, threaten, stalk, and assault her. What O.J. called his "desire for reconciliation" was for Nicole pure hell. This is commonly part of the torment of "escape" for a battered woman: freedom is near, but the abuser won't let her have it.

A few months before Nicole was murdered—along with her friend Ronald Goldman, who happened onto the scene of the crime—she told her mother: "I'm scared. . . . I go to the gas station, he's there. I go to the Payless Shoe Store, . . . he's there. I'm driving, and he's behind me" (quoted in Dworkin 1997:45). Nicole told her sister Denise, among others, that she expected O.J. to kill her and get away with it. Much of the evidence of her fear and despair, however, was called "hearsay" and excluded from her ex-husband's criminal trial. Nicole did what many abused women do: she tried to leave a trail. She kept a diary in which she carefully recorded descriptions of numerous physical assaults. And five days before that fateful June 1994 night, when Nicole and Goldman were brutally and repeatedly stabbed—Nicole's throat was slashed so deeply that she was almost decapitated—she phoned a shelter for battered women, terrified that O.J. was going to kill her. The jury was never informed of this call nor allowed to hear excerpts from her diary. Why? Because Nicole could not be cross-examined! All told, most of the evidence of stalking and beating—from 1977 to May 1994—was excluded from the trial. O.J. was subsequently found not guilty of criminal homicide but was later found civilly liable for the "wrongful deaths" of the two victims at a civil trial, where the burden of proof for the plaintiffs was less onerous than for the prosecutor in the criminal case.

So what else could Nicole have done? Killed O.J.? If she had, she likely would have gone to prison. Self-defense law generally only protects battered women who kill if their assailant is brandishing a weapon. If a woman takes the weapon into her own hands to kill the assailant when he is not armed, she will likely go to prison and be separated from her children (Jones 1994; Schneider 2014). Even though Nicole had managed to divorce her abuser, she was still murdered. But what about the women who cannot escape?

Angela Browne (1987) compared two groups of women who had been involved in abusive intimate relationships: one group consisted of women who had killed their partners, and the other consisted of women who had not. She found that the women who killed their partners had been assaulted more often and had sustained more frequent and more severe injuries. They had also been forced to endure more rape and other forced sexual activities. And the men they killed were more likely to have abused alcohol or drugs and have threatened to kill them, compared to the men who were not killed. Russell Dobash and colleagues (1992) add that whereas females are more likely to kill their male partners after long periods of *enduring* abuse, males are more likely to kill their female partners after long periods of *inflicting* abuse.

These findings are mirrored in Rachel Zimmer Schneider's study (2014) of battered women who killed—and were convicted—for their self-defensive actions. One woman was literally held prisoner in her own home. Her "husband would nail the windows shut and take the cords to all the phones in the house when he would leave. He would lock the door with a key and the only way to open it from the inside was with a key" (p. 29). To be sure, most women are not subjected to this extreme type of surveillance, but a lot of them have to keep tabs on where they go, how long they are away from the house, and how many minutes it takes to drive to the store and back. Some women in Schneider's study described having broken bones, bruises, and black eyes; being raped and forced to have sex with other people; and being purposefully isolated from any support networks. One woman reported having a hot curling iron inserted into her vagina. Another had Drano poured down her throat as her husband told her, "You gonna die bitch" (p. 28). Under circumstances like these, killing her abuser may be a woman's only option. She may fear that her own death is imminent if she fails to take preemptive action—it's either "kill or be killed."

She may do it to protect her children, who may also be being abused (Browne 1987).

About a year after Nicole and Goldman were killed, a housekeeper at the home of another football celebrity dialed 911 in Missouri City, Texas. Felicia Moon fled in a car in fear of her life, and her husband, Warren Moon, took off in hot pursuit. According to Anita Hill's account, when Felicia returned to the house, she explained to the police that Warren "had strangled her to the point where she 'saw black'" (1997:172). Felicia allowed "the police to take pictures of her scratches and . . . bruises," but said that she "did not want to press charges . . . at that time" (p. 172). Moon was arrested nevertheless. At trial, Felicia testified that she had initiated "the violence by throwing a candleholder" and that the housekeeper had mistaken Warren's efforts "to calm her for aggression" (p. 174). The photographed scratches, she explained, could have been from her own fingernails. Moon was found not guilty.

As a black woman married to a famous black man, Felicia was confronted with a special dilemma, a dilemma that influenced her decision to

---

FURTHER EXPLORATION
Partner Abuse in Gay and Lesbian Relationships

It is not just partners in heterosexual relationships who experience the problem of battering. Research indicates that the rate of violence in gay and lesbian relationships is comparable to the rate in heterosexual ones. And as in heterosexual relationships, once violence occurs, it tends to recur and to escalate in severity over time (Island & Letellier 1991; Renzetti 1992).

In addition to the physical, emotional, and sexual abuse we have described as part and parcel of heterosexual battery, Barbara Hart (1996) calls attention to another form of coercion that is available to gay and lesbian batterers: **homophobic control**. Homophobic control of partners is possible because our society is homophobic and because gays and lesbians sometimes internalize the antigay prejudice they grow up with. Examples of homophobic control include threatening to tell the victim's family, friends, or employer that he or she is gay or lesbian; informing the partner that he or she "has no options because the homophobic world will not help" them; insisting that they deserve to be abused because of their sexual orientation; and telling a lesbian partner that no one will believe she has been battered because lesbians are not violent (p. 189). Turning to relatives for support is often difficult or impossible if the victim is uncomfortable coming out to them or if the victim's relationships are already strained or severed due to conflicts over their sexual orientation. Victims may not feel welcome at shelters or services designed for heterosexual women, and they may not reside in an area where

continues

---

continued

the relatively few programs created specifically for gays or lesbians exist. They may also live in a community where there are few gays and lesbians who are "out," and may therefore feel that their abusive partner is their only source of support or only possible lover. And if a gay man's battering partner has AIDS, he may feel incredibly guilty leaving him; if *he* is the one with AIDS, he may be highly dependent on his abuser for physical assistance and financial support (Bornstein et al. 2006; Letellier 1996; Renzetti 1996).

Pam Elliott (1996) conceptualizes gay and lesbian partner abuse as a power issue. Some people, she believes, will abuse their partners if "given the opportunity to get away with [it] . . . because they hunger for control over some part of their lives" (pp. 3–4). Just as "some heterosexual men abuse their partners because they can get away with it in our sexist society, . . . some lesbians and gay men abuse their partners because they can get away with it in our homophobic society."

Unfortunately, the power dynamic in gay and lesbian partner abuse is not always recognized. When survivors of abuse seek help, counselors, shelter volunteers, and police officers may wrongly assume that since both persons are the same sex, the situation is one of *mutual* battering. According to Connie Burk, the executive director of the Seattle-based Advocates for Abused and Battered Lesbians, when officers have trouble determining who the abuser is, it is not uncommon for the abused partner to be arrested if "they're bigger or more butch" (quoted in Friess 1999:294). And it is not just ignorance or homophobic attitudes that impede justice. In some states, laws against battering do not even cover same-sex intimate cohabitants (Wallace 1999). Given these additional hurdles, it is not surprising that gays and lesbians are generally less likely than heterosexuals to report partner abuse to the police.

---

cast herself as the aggressor. Felicia had to save her husband's reputation "not only for himself but for the entire African American community" (Hill 1997:178). Warren Moon was a positive role model for African Americans, and Felicia "ultimately decided that the loss of her reputation would be less damaging to her standing in the community than would be her disloyalty to a black male hero." Black men have had a long history of suffering from white people's injustice, and her acknowledgment of intraracial battery would only serve to isolate Felicia. As Joyce King, a black woman who directs a shelter for battered women in Boston, said: "Those of us who want to have a dialogue about [battery] are frozen out. When I try to talk to black women about the problem, they tell me that we have to be careful what we say and how we say it . . . because of how black men are treated in society. . . . Race is more important than gender" (Hill 1997:183). Thus, after the trial in which Warren was acquitted, one juror commented that Felicia's "injuries were typical of those found in any marriage," a sad commentary on Felicia's sacrifice and the public's ease at trivializing abuse (p. 186).

Mandatory Arrest Policies

Traditionally, police have been reluctant to make arrests in cases of domestic violence involving battered women, viewing such incidents as private matters and as diversions from "real" police work (Miller 1993; Sherman & Berk 1984). Feminist critique of this hands-off approach led criminologists to experiment with different methods of intervention. In a landmark "field experiment" conducted in the early 1980s, Lawrence Sherman and Richard Berk (1984) randomly assigned police officers in Minneapolis to three experimental groups. In one, the officers merely advised the parties and attempted to mediate the dispute; in another, they ordered the offender out of the house for a period of about eight hours; and in a third, they made an arrest. To monitor occurrence of further violence, victims were contacted every two weeks for six months and official records were examined. The findings indicated that the arrest option resulted in significantly less violence during the follow-up period.

Encouraged by these findings, police departments around the country began to adopt mandatory arrest policies, and the National Institute of Justice funded several replication experiments in other cities (Mignon & Holmes 1995; Miller 1993). But since each experimental study was conducted a little differently, the results were inconsistent. In all the cities studied, arrest appeared to deter batterers in the short run, for at least 30 days (Jones 1994). In some cases, arrest appeared to deter batterers for a six-month period, as it had in Minneapolis, but in other instances arrest either had no impact or was associated with *increased* battering over the course of the study period (Berk et al. 1992; Dunford et al. 1990; Pate & Hamilton 1992; Sherman & Smith 1992). In a (nonexperimental) statistical analysis of victimization data, Lisa Dugan and colleagues (2003) found that victims in states with mandatory arrest laws were no more likely than victims in states without these laws to report incidents to the police, and third-party witnesses were less likely to report incidents when mandatory arrest policies were in place. Dugan (2003) also found that cities with mandatory arrest laws had higher rates of spousal homicides against wives.

Several years after his Minneapolis study, Sherman (1992) warned that mandatory arrest policies could backfire by making some offenders even more angry and hostile toward their accusers, and he recommended that these policies be repealed. Other researchers disagreed, however, believing that an association between arrest and increased battering did not warrant a conclusion that arrest backfires and causes increased violence. According to Ann Jones, there is "a big difference between *failing to stop* violence and *causing* violence to escalate" (1994:159). J. David Hirschel and Ira

Hutchinson add that even if arrest is not effective in deterring violence, it is "a more conscionable choice than nonarrest," since nonarrest legitimates abuse and leaves victims to fend for themselves (1992:73).

A number of explanations have been offered for the inconsistent research findings. In some studies there was considerable subject attrition, with less than half of the victims remaining in the interview sample by the end of the study period (Miller 1993; Sherman & Smith 1992). In other instances, police officers did not implement the mandatory arrest policy, believing that the women were not really in dangerous situations, or if they were, that they had chosen to remain in them (Ferraro 1989). When officers received more training regarding the problem of intimate-partner violence, however, they were more likely to implement the policy (Mignon & Holmes 1995). Another variation in the studies involved the length of time that arrested batterers were held in custody. This ranged from a couple of hours to over a week (Sherman et al. 1991). Moreover, those who were arrested were not necessarily prosecuted and convicted. One study found that those who were prosecuted and subsequently served jail time *and* a period of probation had lower battering rates than those who were prosecuted and subsequently received jail time *or* probation (Thistlethwaite et al. 1998).

Finally, there were sociodemographic variations in the experimental findings. Mandatory arrest was more effective in deterring offenders who had a greater stake in conformity. Studies consistently showed that those who were employed were more likely to be deterred than those who were unemployed (Berk et al. 1992; Pate & Hamilton 1992; Sherman & Smith 1992). Some studies also found that married men, high school graduates, and white men were more likely to be deterred than unmarried men, high school dropouts, and black men (Maxwell et al. 2002; Moore 1997; Sherman 1992).

Sherman (1992) concludes that police confronting the problem of intimate-partner violence should have discretionary options, such as offering to take the victim to a shelter (if there is one nearby), rather than the constraint of mandatory arrest. Dugan's research (2003) suggests that strengthening civil protection and child custody provisions for women, and increasing penalties for men who violate these orders, may have a greater impact on reducing domestic violence than mandatory arrest. On the other hand, Berk and colleagues believe that mandatory arrest studies do not offer any definitive policy implications other than "the general warning that a particular arrest will not necessarily lead to a beneficial outcome," and that the research does "not provide a sound rationale for abandoning" mandatory arrest as a reasonable strategy (1992:706). Other researchers are even more definitive in their support of the mandatory arrest approach, believing that women need more law enforcement protection, not less (Jones 1994;

Stanko 1997). Many women, especially poor inner-city women who cannot afford to leave public housing, or women isolated in rural areas, are "sitting ducks" for further assault if there are no serious consequences for offenders. Research also finds that mandatory arrest is "the single most significant factor impacting the likelihood of arrest" in cases involving lesbian couples (Pattavina et al. 2007:374). Clearly there is an urgent need for a comprehensive program of expanded community services for victims and offenders, including shelters and counseling. These, in conjunction with effective law enforcement, will undoubtedly constitute the best strategy overall (Miller 1993; Sullivan 1997; Websdale 1995).

Batterer Intervention Programs

Elizabeth Stanko, among others, believes that law enforcement is the key to solving the problem of intimate-partner violence, because some abusers will be "deterred by nothing except confinement" (1997:634). Nevertheless, even with laws against battering on the books in every state, getting them applied when a man attacks his wife rather than his employer or neighbor—his fellow man—is a challenge. Police officers, reluctant to look behind the curtain of privacy that has traditionally shielded family matters from public scrutiny, have hesitated to arrest when men continue to claim their ancient privilege to "chastise" their wives; and prosecutors and judges, afraid of breaking up families, have sat on their hands. Often, as Jones points out:

> Each branch of the criminal justice system . . . evades its duty by blaming another branch. Police say there's no point in making arrests when prosecutors won't prosecute, and prosecutors in turn say they can't prosecute when (a) police don't arrest, or (b) judges won't sentence anyway. Judges say that women waste the court's time. Blaming the victim allows everyone . . . to pass the buck; and buckpassing conveniently enables individuals within the system to acknowledge a problem without doing anything about it. They'd like to help, but . . . what can they do? . . . Why doesn't she just leave? (1994:145)

It bears underscoring that it is not the victim but the battering partner who is the problem, and research indicates that "batterers vary in their ability to desist, in their techniques of control, in their patterns of dangerousness, and ultimately, in their lethality" (Ellis & DeKeseredy 1997:597). If paired with legal sanctions, batterer intervention programs (especially if begun early) may be effective in interrupting some abusers' pattern of behavior. Those most likely to respond to intervention programs are **sporadic batterers**, those "who are in the first or initial stages of violence progression and who are neither generally violent nor serious alcohol or drug abusers with a lengthy record of criminal and deviant conduct" (p. 597).

The most widely used intervention curriculum is known as the feminist-oriented **Duluth Model**, which was developed by the nonprofit Minnesota Program Development agency in Duluth, Minnesota, in the early 1980s. The goal of the Duluth Model is to transform batterers

> into nonthreatening listeners who are emphatic, honest, accountable, and egalitarian in their parenting, housework, and familial decision making . . . [and] thus to change men from patriarchal authoritarians bent on controlling women into pro-feminist men. . . . Many programs relying on the Duluth Model also incorporate anger-management and skill-building approaches, focusing on improved communication, assertiveness training, and conflict management. (Schrock & Padavic 2007:626)

Regrettably, evaluations of these programs have not shown them to be particularly successful, and critics think they give women a false sense of security that batterers are being reformed, "thereby encouraging them to stay in dangerous relationships" (Shrock & Padavic 2007:627). In one study, Douglas Schrock and Irene Padavic (2007) found that program facilitators were fairly successful in getting batterers to agree to admit responsibility for their actions, use egalitarian language, and adopt cognitive strategies to control their anger. But the men were resistant to attempts to get them to express emotions and to give up their expectation that "as hardworking men they were entitled to a patriarchal dividend." Moreover, "graduates of the program were as likely as dropouts to continue their violence" (pp. 625–626).

Douglas Adams notes that some facilitators "collude with batterers by not making their violence the primary issue" or by downplaying the central power dimensions of battering (1988:177). He also suggests that intervention programs that focus on reducing the batterer's stress or improving his anger management and coping skills tend to gloss over the fact that a man who is abusive at home is often quite capable of behaving appropriately if he thinks it is in his interests to do so—with police officers, neighbors, his boss and coworkers, and so forth. That the man is "selectively abusive" indicates that he already has "an established set of control skills" (p. 191). When he is at home, however, he is "at work on his own agenda, which is to train 'his' woman to be what he wants her to be, and only what he wants her to be, all the time" (Jones 1994:89).

Adams favors batterer intervention programs that begin with a focus on the protection of the batterer's partner, whereby the man is expected to make "safety plans" in which he commits to "respecting the woman's fears and stated limits about the relationship, fully complying with restraining and vacate orders, eliminating drug or alcohol use if it has accompanied violent behavior, and ceasing any pressure or intimidation tactics intended to change his partner's plans or to deny her contact with others" (1988:192–193). He also recommends battery programs—or a local program for battered women if one exists—that contact the batterer's partner to inform her of legal protection options and emergency shelter, support, and advocacy services.

While such programs are to be encouraged, they are clearly insufficient. It continues to be necessary to encourage criminal justice officials to take the problem of battery more seriously. Improved and expanded services for battered women and their children are also needed, including shelters and child care that welcome all comers regardless of sexual orientation. More generally, social and economic changes that strengthen women's position in society in general and the family in particular would lessen women's vulnerability and bolster their ability to protect themselves and their children from harm.

Summary

This chapter focused on the problem of sexual violence against women and children. After introducing the concept of the continuum of sexual violence, we examined several manifestations of this phenomenon. The first section, on rape and sexual assault, considered research on prevalence of sexual violence, sexual scripts and rape myths, rape-law reform, the role of pornography, and personal resistance strategies. Next, we examined the sexual abuse of children, addressing the abuse of both girls and boys. Last, we looked at the battering of women, highlighting the experience of battering, the policy of mandatory arrest, and batterer intervention programs.

9

Corporate Crime

Nineteenth-century French sociologist and jurist Gabriel Tarde
noted that the impulse toward criminality derived not from the lower
classes but from the higher stratum of society. According to Tarde: "The
masses are . . . tied to the ideas and fancies of their social superiors. . . .
Criminal propensities . . . typically travel downward and outward—from
the powerful to the powerless" (quoted in Beirne & Messerschmidt
1995:367). Previously we introduced the concept of white-collar crime,
which Edwin Sutherland (1949) defined as crime committed by persons of
respectability and high social status in the course of their occupations (see
Chapter 1). This chapter focuses more specifically on the problem of **corporate crime**, which we define as crime committed by corporate executives
or managers on behalf of the corporations for which they work. The principal driving force of this crime is monetary gain for the corporation. Executives and managers, of course, benefit from the advancement of corporate
interests when they are rewarded for the illegal profits they make for the
organization. This can occur through salary increases and bonuses, promotion within the organization, and company stock options that are part of the
compensation received by corporate officials. In this chapter we examine
the micro- and macrosociological context of corporate crime and review
illustrative instances of crimes involving economic harm as well as physical
harm to workers, consumers, and the environment.

The Internal and External Environment

We begin with a consideration of the causes of corporate crime associated
with the internal and external environments of corporations. The former may
be understood as microsociological insofar as it involves factors that link individuals with their local organizational circumstances, while the latter may be
understood as macrosociological insofar as it involves broader economic or
political forces outside of particular corporations that impact their operation.

Corporate Culture and the (Mis)management of Power
In his research with retired middle-level managers from Fortune 500 corporations, Marshall Clinard (1983) found that about a third of these managers, from a sample of more than fifty corporations, disapproved of the ethical standards practiced in their respective industries. When explaining corporate crime, they tended to downplay external factors such as "corporate financial problems, unfair practices of competitors, or the type of industry" and instead attributed wrongdoing to the internal cultural environment of the organization (p. 70). These managers said that in many cases the ethical history or cultural tradition of the corporation was established long ago by the company founder and was passed on to subsequent generations of managers. More than 90 percent of the middle-level managers felt that top managers, their organizational superiors, were responsible for setting the ethical (or unethical) tone of the corporation. More than 70 percent thought that top management was generally aware of *all* the violations that were occurring in their companies, and an additional 22 percent thought that top management knew about *some* of the violations. The middle managers believed that top management's knowledge was especially likely in cases of product-safety design defects; illegal kickbacks and foreign bribery; and antitrust (including price-fixing), labor, environmental, and tax violations. One manager noted, "Corporations with many violations are being run primarily for the top and bottom line in order to make a buck" (p. 57). Another said, "Violations are likely if top management is seeking to advance their personal reputations and be 'hot shots.'"

Other research indicates that top managers are more likely than middle managers to attribute law violations to financial strains facing the company. According to one top-management official, "Business executives . . . have no right to wrap themselves in the mantle of moral philosophers and judges—especially to the detriment of the interests of their shareholders whose money they are using" (quoted in Silk & Vogel 1976:229). Top management, however, tends to indirectly signal or insinuate its expectations to subordinates rather than issue specific directives to break the law, preferring "not to know" everything their organization is doing and arranging patterns of reporting so that they cannot find out—or that if they do find out, they find out only in such a way that their culpability cannot be proved (Friedrichs 2007; Stone 1975).

Take the case of the Ford Pinto, for example. Between 1971 and 1976, Ford Motor Company manufactured Pinto automobiles that suffered substantial fuel-tank leaks during rear-end collisions at low to moderate speeds. These leaks stemmed from a design problem involving the placement of the gas tank only six inches from the rear bumper. This placement was intended to reduce trunk space to make the car smaller, lighter, and cheaper in order to compete with Japanese and German automakers that had cornered the market on small-car sales. Upon impact, however, large quantities of gasoline could spill out of the Pinto if the tube leading from the tank to the gas cap was severed or if the bolts on the differential housing (the bulge in the middle of the rear axle) punctured the tank. "At that point, all that was needed to ignite the fuel and . . . create an inferno was a spark—from steel against steel or from steel against pavement" (Cullen et al. 2006:147).

At one time it was estimated that Pinto fires caused the deaths of at least 500 burn victims who otherwise would not have been seriously injured, to say nothing of the countless others who suffered serious burn injuries (Cullen et al. 2006; Dowie 1977). This death estimate is probably exaggerated, but a report published by the National Highway Traffic Safety Administration (NHTSA) in 1978 did verify 38 Pinto fires involving 27 fatalities (26 due to burns and 1 due to impact injuries) and 24 nonfatal burn injuries (Birsch & Fielder 1994). As these figures are based on police accident reports, which often fail to report fires or distinguish between deaths due to fires and deaths due to impact, some fire deaths were probably not recorded as such. Douglas Birsch and John Fielder concluded, "It is likely that the number of unnecessary deaths exceeded" NHTSA estimates, "but it is impossible to determine accurately how many deaths there were" (1994:10).

Especially controversial was the fact that the design problem was known to Ford managers and engineers before the Pinto was put on the market. Ford had considered alterations that could have prevented the gas leakage, such as lining the gas tank with a rubber bladder or covering the bolts on the housing with a polyethylene shield. But Ford officials did not think these safety measures were worth the cost. A high-ranking Ford Motor Company engineer recalled, "Whenever a problem was raised that meant a delay on the Pinto," Lee Iacocca, the chief executive officer (CEO) at Ford, "would chomp on his cigar, look out the window and say, 'Read the product objectives and get back to work'" (quoted in Dowie 1977:21). Another said, "Safety wasn't a popular subject around Ford in those days. With Lee it was taboo."

Most corporate employees will do what they are told, in part because all organizations tend to "selectively recruit new members who in many respects match those already there" (Vaughan 1982:1389). New managers are led "through an initiation period designed to weaken their ties with external groups, including their own families, and encourage a feeling of dependence on and attachment" to the company (Clinard & Yeager 1980:63). Employees quickly learn not to question standard operating procedures.

Barbara Toffler (2003) describes a two-week training program that all new employees of the prestigious Arthur Andersen accounting firm were required to attend before formally beginning their jobs. The hiring process had already aimed to screen out people who would not fit into the institutional culture; and the training program was designed to mold new employees, "like raw clay," into an "Arthur Andersen man," what Toffler calls an "android" (p. 25). Later, at an ethics workshop Toffler conducted for Arthur Andersen employees, she asked the attendees what they would do if a superior in the company wanted them to do something they thought was wrong. "No one dared to breathe," until one timid man spoke up: "I guess I might ask a question. But if he insisted I do it, yes, I would." Toffler asked him if he would tell anyone else. He replied, "No. It could hurt my career" (p. 193).

Similarly, in the electrical equipment price-fixing conspiracy discussed in Chapter 4, executives testified that price-fixing had been an ongoing practice before they joined their respective companies and that they were expected to conform. In another case involving the marketing of an anticholesterol drug that was known by company officials to have harmful side effects, "no one involved expressed any strong repugnance or even opposition to selling the unsafe drug. Rather they all seemed to drift into the activity without thinking a great deal about it" (Carey 1978:384).

Dennis Gioia, who worked as Ford Motor Company's field recall coordinator in 1973 during the Pinto controversy, remembers that, at the time, he felt "no strong obligation to recall" the vehicle and saw "no strong ethical overtones to the case whatsoever" (1996:54). The crashworthiness of the Pinto was consistent with federal standards for subcompacts and, from the viewpoint of company personnel, within the range of "acceptable risk." Matthew Lee and M. David Ermann suggest that the Pinto tragedy should not be understood as an outcome of management's explicit intention to do harm, but rather as a case of "institutionally embedded unreflective action" (1999:43), what Diane Vaughan (2005) calls the **normalization of deviance**.

Even when managers have ethical reservations about what they are doing, the pressure from superiors to meet production quotas and target dates can be immense. As one of Clinard's informants told him, "You get the pressure so strong from top management that you will make judgmental efforts to make things come out right even if you use unethical practices such as lying about production or marketing progress . . . [or] cutting corners . . . on quality" (1983:142). Another middle-level manager said, "When we didn't meet our growth targets the top brass really came down on us. And everybody knew that if you missed the targets enough, you were out on your ear" (p. 143).

James Messerschmidt (1997) adds that corporate managers often conflate profit-making with masculinity. "Real" managers, like "real" men, take risks and are willing to "go to the limit" to bring the company success and prove themselves worthy combatants in the competitive struggle for corporate profits. **Man(agerial) masculinity** requires one to set aside personal or emotional concerns and make decisions without regard to the effects on people. In this context a cost-benefit approach is the perfect vehicle for corporate decisionmaking. In the midst of the Pinto controversy, Mark Dowie (1977) published a chart from a Ford Motor Company memorandum that contained calculations regarding the costs and benefits of installing a safety valve in all cars and light trucks to prevent carburetor and other fuel leakages during rollover accidents (see Figure 9.1). Ford reasoned that the costs ($137 million) of installing this valve far outweighed the benefits ($49.5 million). Notice that in this estimate the potential benefits ignored by Ford included saving human lives and avoiding injuries!

Figure 9.1 Ford Motor Company Cost-Benefit Memorandum

Cost of Installing Safety Valve
Vehicle sales: 11 million cars, 1.5 million light trucks
Unit cost: $11 per car/truck
Total cost: (11,000,000 × $11) + (1,500,000 × $11) = $137.5 million

Benefit of Installing Safety Valve
Savings: 180 burn deaths, 180 burn injuries, 2,100 burned vehicles
Unit savings: $200,000[a] per death, $67,000 per injury, $700 per vehicle
Total benefit: (180 × $200,000) + (180 × $67,000) + (2,100 × $700) = $49.5 million

Source: Adapted from Dowie 1977.
Note: a. Ford obtained the $200,000 figure from the National Highway Traffic Safety Administration, which had succumbed to pressure from the auto industry to institutionalize cost-benefit analysis in regulatory decisionmaking. The Ford memorandum was intended to persuade regulators to reject adoption of a new safety standard (Lee & Ermann 1999).

Criminogenic Market Structures

Turning now to the external corporate environment, recall that Sutherland (1949) found that nearly half of the 70 largest US corporations had engaged in law violations at their origin or in their early years of operation, making crime an essential part of their initial period of capital accumulation (see Chapter 2). He also found that corporations within the same industry tended to have comparable rates of law violation, with companies in the meat-packing and mail-order businesses leading the way. Similarly, Marshall Clinard and Peter Yeager's study (1980) of the largest manufacturing corporations in the mid-1970s found that the most frequent offenders were concentrated in three areas: the motor vehicle, oil refinery, and pharmaceutical industries. While a majority of corporations had a record of law violation, 40 percent did not, and just 8 percent accounted for over half of the violations in the Clinard-Yeager study. What makes some corporations more prone to law violation than others? Are there conditions within particular industries or economic markets that are more or less conducive to law violation?

William Leonard and Marvin Weber (1970) introduced the term **criminogenic market structure** to identify elements of the external social environment that produce the strain that generates crime. According to Leonard and Weber, criminogenic market structures consist of industries character-ized by (1) a limited number of manufacturers that can easily collaborate to avoid unprofitable competition, and (2) products that retain an inelastic demand, meaning products that remain in demand and continue to be pur-chased even if prices are increased.

The automobile industry, for example, has relatively few domestic manufacturers due to the formidable entry barriers inherent in a market that requires a high volume of sales in order to maintain a profitable business. Currently, there are only two US-owned companies, General Motors and Ford, with Chrysler, formerly one of the "big three" US automakers, now owned by the Italian company Fiat.

Historically, the automobile industry had a proven reputation for emphasizing style over safety (Nader 1965). But Leonard and Weber (1970) focus on a less acknowledged problem: the pressure manufacturers exert that constrains dealers' ability to operate ethically or within the law. The franchise agreements that manufacturers offer dealers typically require dealers to sell a high volume of vehicles at a low per-unit cost. If dealers fail to comply, they may lose their franchise or receive unfavorable treat-ment from the manufacturer—such as slow delivery or insufficient supply of popular models—forcing dealers to recoup profits elsewhere. For instance, dealers enjoy very high profit margins in their service depart-ments, where an industrywide flat rate is generally charged for particular repairs, which enables dealers to charge customers for more time than is actually spent fixing their vehicles. Dealers also have a monopoly on new parts, which allows them to charge exorbitant prices for these products; and they may charge for unnecessary repairs and unnecessary replacement of parts, as well as for repairs that are not made and parts that are not used. Additionally, dealers have high profit margins on the sale of used vehicles, and they may not disclose mechanical problems to customers. Other dealer practices include turning back odometers on used cars—even on "execu-tive" cars that have been used by dealers themselves. Dealers also cut cor-ners by not inspecting vehicles before they are delivered to customers, and they may fail to honor warranties, claiming that repairs that should be cov-ered are not. But again, according to some criminologists, it is the crimino-genic market structure in the automobile industry that pressures dealers to engage in such practices. As Harvey Farberman notes, a small number of "manufacturers who sit at the pinnacle of an economically concentrated industry" have established an economic policy that "causes lower level dependent industry participants to engage in patterns" of unethical and ille-gal activities (1975:456).

James Coleman (2006), on the other hand, finds the evidence regarding the effect of market structures on corporate crime more difficult to evaluate. Much research on corporate crime, he observes, is based on official records and thus suffers from the same limitations as research on conventional crimes by not including large numbers of unreported cases (see Chapter 2). Coleman suggests, for example, that the high rates of law violation in the motor vehicle, oil refinery, and pharmaceutical industries studied by Clinard and Yeager (1980) may be due, in part, to the fact that large "industries whose products cause serious and clearly identifiable harm to the public or the environment tend to be subject to more stringent regulation than those that do not" (Coleman 2006:218).

Coleman (2006) also notes the inconsistent results of quantitative research in the United States on the association between market structure and official rates of antitrust violations by corporations, where some studies have found higher rates of antitrust violations among firms in highly concentrated industries (industries with few firms), some have found higher rates in moderately concentrated industries, and some have found no relationship at all between antitrust violations and degree of industry concentration. On the one hand, Coleman reasons, antitrust practices like price-fixing are easier to implement in markets dominated by a few large firms; on the other hand, more competitive markets are likely to exacerbate the economic strains that encourage crime. Coleman also notes that these studies tend not to consider the effect of international competition.

Inconsistent findings in studies of corporate bribery of government officials also suggest an ambiguous relationship between market structure and crime. Coleman concludes that in noncompetitive industries dominated by a few firms "*political* bribery aimed at influencing government policies and programs" may be more common, but intense competition in less concentrated industries "appears more likely to be associated with *commercial* bribery [of sales or purchasing agents] to promote the sale of a firm's products" (2006:216, emphasis added). In either case, it is clear that one cannot understand the behavior of corporate organizations without examining the broader market structure in which they do business.

Corporate Financial Crime

In this section on the economic harms of corporate crime, we consider antitrust violations, crimes of high finance and banking, and corporate fraud.

Antitrust Violations

In Chapter 1, we briefly considered the landmark Sherman Antitrust Act of 1890, which aimed to curtail the consolidation of corporate economic power that was undermining competition in the economy. This legislation contained both criminal and civil provisions for the regulation of business combinations that resulted in a restraint of trade (including price-fixing) or the monopolization of an industry. Throughout its history, however, the Sherman Antitrust Act has been weakly enforced, as the law has been interpreted as allowing for business combinations that the government deems "reasonable." Consequently, the moral stigma associated with anti-trust violations that led to the initial passage of the act has been diluted, and the law has had relatively little impact on the growth and consolidation of corporations in the United States (Inverarity et al. 1983; McCormick 1977).

For the most part, enforcement of antitrust law has focused on the most egregious cases of **price-fixing**. In price-fixing, the higher cost of a product that is due to collusion between companies is distributed across millions of customers, so that each person pays only a small additional price. More-over, at the time of the purchase, consumers do not realize they are being victimized by crime. They may think they are being ripped off by greedy companies perhaps, but they do not consider themselves crime victims. Yet corporations make millions of dollars in illegal profits each year from price-fixing activities.

The oil and airline industries have been among the two most frequent targets of law enforcement against price-fixing. During a period of oil shortages in the 1970s, for instance, seven major oil corporations drove up oil prices in what plaintiffs in a civil lawsuit described as an unlawful price-fixing conspiracy. In cases that lingered in the courts for 17 years, the companies eventually settled the lawsuits for a combined $150 million, an amount that was far less than the plaintiffs had asked for (Coleman 2006; Rosoff et al. 2007).

Between 1988 and 1992, the eight leading US airlines of that time used a shared electronic-fare database to artificially inflate prices, sending coded signals to each other to announce future rate hikes that each would match. In an out-of-court settlement totaling $458 million, the companies agreed to provide some 10 million customers with coupons as compensation for their malfeasance. However, the coupons could only be used for a portion of each full-fare ticket and expired in three years. Some analysts estimated that individual customers would have had to buy as many as 60 round-trip tickets before receiving full compensation, which of course they never recouped. The major beneficiaries of the lawsuit were other large corporations. IBM alone received $3.3 million in discounts (Rosoff et al. 2007).

Later, in the mid-1990s, the Clinton administration issued the largest criminal fines in history to individual companies for price-fixing. Archer Daniels Midland (ADM), a grain and soybean–processing conglomerate whose products are used in a wide range of goods, led the way with a record-breaking $100 million criminal fine. ADM's price-fixing violation involved the lysine used in animal feed and the citric acid used in food and beverages. According to an FBI wiretap of a meeting between ADM and a foreign competitor, an ADM executive said: "We have a saying here in this company that penetrates the whole company. Our competitors are our friends. Our customers are the enemy" (Rosoff 2007:72).

ADM agreed to the $100 million fine in order to avoid an even more costly penalty (which the government agreed to waive) for antitrust activity involving its corn syrup. As ADM had $2 billion in cash on hand, it was easily able to absorb the fine. In 1998 and 1999, however, three ADM executives were found guilty and sentenced to two to three years in prison. Later, in 2004, the firm negotiated a $400 million settlement of civil lawsuits associated with its illegal actions (Eichenwald 1999; Rosoff et al. 2007).

The ADM record for price-fixing fines did not stand long, however. It fell in 1998 and 1999 with penalties of $110 to $135 million levied against companies in the graphite electrode industry, which provides the source of heat for steel. In 1999, Mylan Laboratories, the second largest maker of generic drugs in the United States, was also fined $135 million. In this case, Mylan conspired to raise the price for ingredients of two drugs by as much as 3,000 percent! Still, Mylan chairman Milan Puskar said, "We continue to believe we acted properly" (Rosoff et al. 2007:73).

Criminal prosecution for price-fixing requires the government "to prove conscious and covert collusion on the part of the firms involved" (Clinard & Yeager 1980:136). However, such covert collusion is not necessary to subvert competition when the economy is dominated by oligopolistic industries comprising only a few firms. Under these conditions, prices are inflated throughout the industry through the practices of **price leadership** and **price signaling**. Price leadership involves actions by which the leading firm in an industry is the first to raise prices, but with the tacit understanding that other companies will soon follow. Similarly, price signaling involves the announcement of price increases or the publishing of price lists in the media or industry publications, which enables companies to share pricing information without explicit (illegal) collusion.

High Finance and Banking

Some analysts believe that capitalism in the United States today has evolved into a **casino economy**. "In contrast to **industrial capitalism**, where profits are dependent on the production and sale of goods and services," profits in the casino economy of "**finance capitalism** increasingly come . . . from speculative ventures designed to bring windfall profits for having placed a clever bet" in an economy where nothing is "produced but capital gains" (Calavita & Pontell 1990:335–336).

The shift from industrial to finance capitalism—from an economy based on the manufacture of goods to an economy based on the circulation of money—has been under way for some time. In 1950, the financial sector of the US economy garnered just 10 percent of domestic corporate profits. Currently, it earns about 30 percent, more than the manufacturing sector, which has been on the decline (Weissmann 2013). But who benefits from this type of system and is it fair?

Insider trading. A particular problem with the US system of finance capitalism is that many investors do not play by the rules. In 1934, the Securities Exchange Act criminalized **insider trading** to try to ensure fairness in the system. Insider trading occurs when "stockholders, directors, officers, or any recipients of information not publicly available . . . take advantage of such limited disclosure for their own benefit" (Rosoff et al. 2007:247). The logic behind the prohibition is that the legitimacy of capitalism depends upon the expectation of a positive association between the economic risk taken by an investor and the potential return. But "the insider trader collects the highest returns with little risk at all, while the ordinary investor, who assumes most of the risk, is exploited like some naive bumpkin lured into a rigged game of chance" (p. 262).

Between 1934 and 1979, the Securities and Exchange Commission (SEC) took just 53 actions against insider trading. Between 1980 and 1987 alone, it took 177 actions (Friedrichs 2007). Indeed, the 1980s was a period in which the crimes of high-flying insider traders like Ivan Boesky and Michael Milken were in the news. These men made millions of dollars based on insider knowledge of pending corporate mergers and other financial transactions. They also raised money from others by promising high rates of return on high-risk investments aimed at acquiring companies, then "downsizing" the companies by firing workers to save costs and selling off company assets. These investment strategies made millions for insiders while devastating the lives of ordinary workers who lost their jobs. It was once the case that capitalists got rich by putting people to work; now all too many get rich by putting people out of work (Stewart 1991).

Boesky and Milken, among others, were eventually prosecuted for their crimes. In 1987, Boesky was fined $100 million and sentenced to three years in prison, although he made about $200 million in illegal trades alone. In 1989, Milken was fined a record-breaking $600 million and sentenced to two years in prison for financial dealings that had earned him more than $1 billion (Friedrichs 2007; Rosoff et al. 2007).

Perhaps because insider trading continues to be profitable, the practice has by no means been curbed. The widely publicized case of homemaking diva and corporate entrepreneur Martha Stewart reminds us of this truism. In 2003, Stewart was charged with receiving privileged information from her stockbroker, Peter Banovic, based on which she sold about 4,000 shares of the drug company ImClone Systems the day before "a negative government report on the ImClone cancer drug Erbitux sent its share price falling" (McClam 2003:D10). Stewart avoided losses of about $50,000 from the deal.

Stewart claimed that she had a "stop-loss" agreement with her broker to sell her stock if the price went below a certain amount. No evidence of this agreement was found, however, and Stewart was charged and convicted—but not for insider trading per se. Rather, she was convicted for obstruction of justice and lying to investigators about the transaction, for which she served five months in prison. At Stewart's trial, Banovic, who was also indicted, testified that he had been told by his boss at Merrill Lynch to pass on the information about ImClone to Stewart. Her personal assistant also reluctantly testified that Stewart had told her that she had known about the situation and had altered a computer log of a message from Banovic. Upon her release from prison, Stewart remained unrepentant, telling Barbara Walters in an interview: "I didn't cheat anybody out of anything" (quoted in Rosoff et al. 2007:270). Of course, as we have noted, the reason that insider trading is illegal is that it allows a privileged few to make money at the expense of others who are not privy to the information.

Insider trading is not the only way naive investors are disadvantaged in the stock market. They are also duped through intentional manipulation of stock values, such as **pump-and-dump schemes**, whereby con artists or corrupt stockbrokers recommend stocks or issue fraudulent information to drive up their value and then sell their own shares before the stock price collapses (Rosoff et al. 2007). Nowadays, in a practice known as **high-frequency trading**, even legitimate financial firms use complex computer algorithms to exploit minuscule short-term fluctuations in stock value. As Nick Baumann observes, we now live in "a world where investing—if that's what you call buying and selling a company's stock within a matter of seconds—often comes down to how fast you can purchase or offload it, not how much the company is actually worth" (2013:1).

The savings and loan scandal. One of the most devastating financial debacles in the history of the United States involved the savings and loan (S&L) scandal of the 1980s. By the time the borrowed money for the entire taxpayer bailout is finally paid back, the estimated cost may exceed $1 trillion. Moreover, it is no small matter that criminal activity was a major factor in 70 to 80 percent of the failed S&Ls and that as much as 25 percent of the losses was due to crime. The story of what happened to this industry should have been a forewarning about the pitfalls of deregulating financial markets, but regrettably the lesson was not learned (Leopold 2009; Rosoff et al. 2007).

What was this scandal all about? The federally insured S&L system was established in the early 1930s as a depression-era measure designed to ensure the availability of home loans, promote the construction of new homes, and protect depositors from the types of financial devastation (massive investment losses and withdrawal of bank funds) that followed the 1929 stock market crash. Federal regulations prohibited S&Ls from making risky investments, essentially confining them "to the issuance of home loans within 50 miles of their home office" (Calavita & Pontell 1990:331). By the 1970s, however, S&Ls could no longer compete with other financial institutions such as mortgage companies (for home loans) and mutual funds and money markets (for savings investments). They were locked into long-term, low-interest loans they had previously made, and were prohibited by law from offering adjustable-rate mortgages or from paying more than 5.5 percent interest on deposits (even during a period of double-digit inflation).

During the 1970s, the S&L industry's net worth declined dramatically, and by 1980, 85 percent of S&Ls were losing money. At that time a complete bailout of the industry utilizing taxpayer dollars might have cost about $15 billion. But instead of cutting losses at this level, President Reagan and the Democrat-controlled US Congress opted for a strategy of deregulation. Federal legislation passed in the early 1980s phased out restrictions on interest rates and opened up new areas of investment for S&Ls, which were now authorized to "make consumer loans up to 30 percent of their total assets; make commercial, corporate or business loans; and invest in nonresidential real estate worth up to 40 percent of their assets" (Calavita & Pontell 1993:530; Jackson 1990).

The new (de)regulations also gave the S&Ls unprecedented access to funds by removing the 5 percent limit on **brokered deposits**—aggregated deposits placed by middlemen that yielded high interest rates for investors and exorbitant commissions for brokers. These funds were used to finance risky speculative investments that had the potential for either high payoffs or financial calamity. In addition, S&Ls were allowed to provide 100 percent financing to borrowers, essentially giving them risk-free loans. And the government dropped the requirement that S&Ls "have at least 400 stockholders with no one owning more than 25 percent of stock," thereby allowing a single entrepreneur to own and operate a federally insured S&L (Calavita & Pontell 1993:530). At the same time, the amount of federal depository insurance was raised from $40,000 to $100,000 per account.

Deregulation was "the cure that killed" (Calavita & Pontell 1993:312). S&Ls lost billions of dollars through legal investments that were previously illegal, and the deregulated climate opened the industry to insider abuse and crime. Kitty Calavita and Henry Pontell (1990) identify three general categories of criminal activities that occurred: unlawful risk-taking, collective embezzlement, and illegal cover-ups.

Unlawful risk-taking involved S&Ls that extended their investment activities beyond the levels allowed by law—for example, by exceeding the 40 percent limit on commercial real estate loans. S&Ls also compounded the risk they undertook by failing to conduct adequate marketability studies to ensure the feasibility of their investments, as they were required by law to do.

Unlike ordinary instances of embezzlement, which typically entail lone, relatively subordinate employees stealing from the company in which they work, **collective embezzlement** involved the misuse and theft of funds by the S&L's top management. During the 1980s, some S&L owners and managers treated their institutions as personal slush funds, throwing elaborate parties and purchasing expensive luxury goods like artwork, antiques, yachts, airplanes, and vacation homes. They also violated the law by giving themselves and their associates excessive "salaries as well as bonuses, dividend payments, and perquisites" beyond what was "reasonable and commensurate with their duties and responsibilities" (Government Accounting Office, cited in Calavita & Pontell 1990:323). In addition, S&L operators engaged in a number of fraudulent loan schemes. For instance, "straw borrowers" outside the S&L were used to obtain loans on behalf of individuals within the S&L, thus circumventing the legal limit on the proportion of an institution's loans that could be made to insiders. Another scheme involved insiders from one S&L authorizing loans to insiders of another S&L in return for similar loans.

Illegal cover-ups entailed the manipulation and misrepresentation of S&Ls' financial books and records to conceal fraudulent practices from government regulators, hence preventing regulators from learning about an S&L's impending financial insolvency and delaying the closure of the institution. Regulators were not always adversaries of S&Ls, however. Some, who were wooed by lucrative "job offers at salaries several times . . . their modest government wages," even collaborated with S&L operators to protect them from scrutiny and criminal prosecution (Calavita & Pontell 1993:535). Overall, more than a thousand individuals were convicted of felony law violations related to the scandal (Holland 2013).

Consequences of further financial deregulation. One of the most pernicious effects on the US economy has been the consolidation of the financial industry that has accompanied deregulation, beginning in 1999 with the repeal of major components of the Glass-Steagall Act, also known as the Banking Act of 1933. Glass-Steagall was a depression-era law designed to create a wall of separation between traditional *commercial banks,* which receive deposits that are insured by the federal government and lend money to borrowers, and *investment banks,* which raise uninsured capital for risky high-stakes investments, trade in stocks and other financial securities, and manage corporate mergers and acquisitions. Glass-Steagall aimed to prevent a conflict of interest endemic to a financial institution that loans money to the same companies in which it invests and also to prevent institutions from funneling deposits from their federally insured commercial sector into their noninsured investment sector (Cohan 2009; Leopold 2009; Prins 2004).

Like the deregulation of the S&L industry, the repeal of Glass-Steagall regulations by the Graham-Leech-Blyly Act of 1999 was a bipartisan effort, only this time it was enabled by a Republican-controlled Congress and Bill Clinton, a Democratic president, and his secretary of treasury and chief financial adviser, Robert Rubin. Rubin had been an executive at the highly influential investment firm Goldman Sachs, and after leaving public office he accepted a top position at Citigroup, one of the largest financial conglomerates in the world, where he would earn more than $100 million during the following decade (Drum 2010).

The repeal of Glass-Steagall allowed for the consolidation of commercial and investment banks, brokerage houses, and insurance companies, creating a new industry of huge financial "supermarkets." It also put taxpayer money at risk, because if these "too big to fail" institutions became insolvent, the government would have little choice but to bail them out or the entire economy could slide into a depression, as we saw in the latter part of 2008. To make matters worse, the Commodities Future Modernization Act of 2000 was also passed, which exempted many of the financial instruments known as **derivatives** from regulatory oversight (Leopold 2009).

Derivatives are the product of a financial industry looking to attract investors seeking high rates of return. The most commonly known financial securities are traditional stocks and bonds. A *stock* represents a share of ownership in a company, while a *bond* represents a loan for which the investor is owed interest. A derivative, on the other hand, is a "financial instrument whose value is derived from something else, called the underlying or referenced stock, bond, or other financial instrument" (Leopold 2009:193).

A **collateralized debt obligation** is one type of derivative. It is a security that bundles a pool of similar loans like home mortgages or car loans into securities that can be sliced and diced and bought and sold at various degrees of risk. A **credit default swap** is a derivative that functions like an insurance policy by shifting "risk from a party that doesn't want the risk to a party that is willing to accept it . . . for a price" (Leopold 2009:192). In other ways, however, a credit default swap is nothing like an insurance policy as is commonly understood, because neither party to the agreement needs to own the item they are insuring. The investment simply involves a bet on the future value of a particular asset. As professor of corporate and securities law Lynn Stout notes: "The most important thing to understand about derivatives is that they are bets. That's not a figure of speech—they are literally bets. You can make a million dollar bet on a $1,000 horse" (Puzzanghera 2010:1).

One problem with the derivatives market is that investments are based on speculative assumptions and are so complicated that investors (and regulators) have difficulty estimating the actual value of the assets. Under these circumstances, it is easy for investors to get greedy and take on too much risk. Another problem is not only that the derivatives market goes unregulated but also that it multiplies the risk of the original asset many times, spreading the consequences of failed investments throughout the entire economy. If the home mortgage market goes bust, for instance, as it did in 2008, it is not only the original lenders and borrowers who are in financial trouble, but also thousands of other nonprincipals who are invested in mortgages that have been securitized (including those who rely on invested pension funds). Moreover, the interlocking nature of financial institutions that are "too big to fail" means that a problem in one large firm portends problems in other firms as well. When the insurance giant American International Group (AIG) faced bankruptcy, for example, its collapse (without a government bailout) would have undermined major investment banks like Goldman Sachs that had a stake in AIG's collapsing derivative contracts (Cohan 2009; Leopold 2009).

In all fairness, the financial calamity that was a consequence of the derivatives market does not constitute criminality per se. However, many American taxpayers have justifiably felt that they have been robbed by a system that privatizes profit but collectivizes risk and that is riddled with conflicts of interest and outright fraud. Take the case of Jack Grubman, an investment adviser for the brokerage firm Salomon Smith Barney, which is part of the Citigroup conglomerate, who at one time was known as one of the country's "star" stock analysts. Grubman's advice to clients touted stocks in which Citigroup had a vested financial interest, most notably fraud-ridden WorldCom and Global Crossing, in an attempt to drive up stock prices. For his transgressions, Grubman was investigated by the Office of the New York State Attorney General, fined $15 million, and barred from further work in the industry. To help soften the blow, Citigroup agreed to forgive a $15 million loan it had made to Grubman and also to pay his legal fees (Guyon 2005; Prins 2004).

No criminal charges were brought against Grubman, but Robert Citron of Orange County, California, did not escape the arms of the criminal law. Citron, the lone Democrat on the Republican-dominated Orange County supervisory board, was at the center of the largest government bankruptcy in US history. Citron was the money manager for Orange County's investment pool, in which he pooled investments from various public and private sources, including the Orange County school district. He invested heavily in the derivatives market, even borrowing $12 billion in public money to maximize profits for a conservative political district "hungry for revenues in an antitax environment" (Will et al. 1998:368).

For a while, Citron was the darling of Orange County, dubbed a "financial guru" for a financial portfolio that outperformed other investments in the state and nation. One of Citron's colleagues on the supervisory board described him as "a person who has gotten us millions of dollars. I don't know how the hell he does it, but it makes us all look good" (Will et al. 1998:368). But when the investments went bust in 1994, the board declared losses of between $1.5 and $2 billion. Citron blamed Merrill Lynch, the prestigious brokerage firm he used, for giving him bad advice. In turn, Merrill Lynch officials claimed they had advised Citron about the risks he was incurring, although they continued to sell him the very derivatives they said they had warned him about. Susan Will and colleagues suggest that

"Orange County acted like a gambling addict, while Merrill Lynch and other brokerage houses behaved like dealers offering a revenue-starved community new chances to win" (1998:375). Moreover, "the Board of Supervisors, county staff and officials, and the public were as unlikely to challenge Citron's magic as the members of the kingdom were ready to tell the emperor that he was not wearing clothes," content as they were to maintain a posture of "concerted ignorance" (p. 379).

Citron pled guilty to multiple criminal counts, "including misappropriation of public funds and making false material statements in connection with the sale of securities," and he received a one-year jail term and a $100,000 fine (Will et al. 1998:377). Matthew Raabe, assistant treasurer for Orange County, was also convicted on charges related to his involvement in concealing Citron's failed investments; his three-year prison sentence was overturned on appeal due to a conflict of interest stemming from the fact that the prosecutor's office had suffered financial losses from the bankruptcy. Merrill Lynch, which denied any culpability, settled lawsuits totaling $430 million (Rosoff et al. 2007).

Corporate Fraud

Criminal **fraud**, of which corporate fraud is a part, is the deliberate misrepresentation of truth or fact in which someone attempts to induce another into taking action that is financially disadvantageous to them. Enron, one time nominally the eighth largest corporation in the United States (Kuttner 2003), is arguably the poster-child company for the multibillion-dollar problem of corporate fraud that came to light in the early 2000s. But, as we shall see, corporate fraud is not just the province of one company—it is systemic.

Enron. Enron was formed in the 1980s through the merger of two gas pipeline companies. By the early 1990s, under the direction of its first CEO, Kenneth Lay, the Houston-based company became the dominant player in the natural gas and electricity industry, with plants and pipelines operating in the United States and abroad. Lay was a substantial contributor to the political campaign coffers of Republican senator Phil Graham, a champion of deregulation (Graham's wife was also awarded with a well-paying position on Enron's board of directors). He was also a major contributor to then-governor George W. Bush's 2000 presidential campaign and was known to have Bush's ear on energy policy. Although Bush tried to distance himself from Lay when the scandal became public, Lay was in fact an old family friend whom Bush affectionately called "Kenny Boy" (McLean & Elkind 2004).

Enron claimed to be making billions of dollars, and Lay and his executive cohorts—including Jeffrey Shilling, Lay's protégé, who took over as CEO in 2000, and Andrew Fastow, the chief financial officer—were raking

FURTHER EXPLORATION
The Bernard Madoff Ponzi Scheme

Charles Ponzi, a young immigrant from Italy, opened the Financial Exchange Company of Boston in 1919, guaranteeing investors a 50 percent rate of return within 45 days. Ostensibly, Ponzi's plan "was to purchase international postage coupons in countries where the exchange rate was low and then re-sell them in countries with higher rates. Within six months, Ponzi had per-suaded 20,000 investors to give him nearly $10 million" (Rosoff et al. 2007:6). The secret of Ponzi's success was to pay "early investors with new investors' money, thereby attracting more and more investors. At its height, his company had a *daily* cash flow of $250,000." A **Ponzi scheme**, as this type of fraud became known, is dependent upon an ever-increasing supply of investors; but at some point the offender's greed outstrips his luck and the "house of cards" inevitably falls. After an exposé in the *Boston Globe* revealed Ponzi's fraud in 1920, he was arrested, convicted, and sentenced to four years in prison (and was later deported).

More recently, in 2008, a modern-day Ponzi scheme hit the news. Amid the multibillion-dollar taxpayer bailout approved by the government to help prop up failing financial institutions, the FBI initiated a fraud investigation of several major financial and insurance firms. One notable case involved Bernard Madoff, former chairman of the Nasdaq Stock Market and founder of Bernard L. Madoff Investment Securities. Since the early 1990s, Madoff had been perpetrating a fraud that bilked investors out of some $18 billion, with fabricated gains totaling $65 billion, the largest Ponzi scheme in the history of the United States (Foley 2009).

Regulatory authorities had been suspicious of Madoff's investments for some time, because the gains Madoff claimed to deliver were unrealistic. But investors did not complain, feeling they were privy to a "sweet deal" that included no investment fees. No one bothered to ask or find out how Madoff racked up his incredible returns or request statements from a reputable accounting firm. Investors who knew him through common membership in the exclusive Palm Beach Country Club thought they had an inside track on making a lot of money (Frank et al. 2009; Gross 2009).

Madoff said that when he first began the fraud, he felt "compelled" to give investors high returns despite the weak stock market at the time. "When I began the Ponzi scheme," he said, "I believed it would end shortly and I would be able to extricate myself and my clients from [it]. However, this proved difficult and ultimately impossible" (Frank et al. 2009:2). David Shapiro, an economics professor and former FBI agent, observed that Mad-off, like other white-collar offenders, was able to divorce himself from the human impact of his actions. "When you're making all this money and you realize nobody's really checking on you, the temptations become too great," Madoff said (p. 2). He pled guilty to multiple charges and was sentenced to 150 years in prison.

in millions for themselves. The problem was that Enron was hiding massive debt. Barbara Toffler (2003) was working at Arthur Andersen, Enron's accounting firm, at the time. Toffler recalls that "Enron's basic strategy had been to buy an asset such as a power plant or water source and then create markets around it. To create these markets required taking on a lot of debt—debt which, if held on Enron's balance sheet, could have crippled the company's expansion plans and its high-flying stock" (p. 211).

To disguise this debt and other business losses, Enron created an inter-locking network of some 3,000 corporate subsidies. Most notable among these were the companies run by Fastow, which he apparently used to "fun-nel millions of company dollars to himself and a few carefully selected associates" (Toffler 2003:211). While some Arthur Andersen auditors were concerned about being embroiled in a fraud, the top executives at the firm feared losing Enron's annual multimillion-dollar business, which had earned Arthur Andersen $52 million in fees in 2000 and was expected to earn the firm increasingly more in the future, and did nothing about the fraud (Rosoff et al. 2007).

At the same time, Enron created artificial energy shortages that inflated prices, most notably in California, where citizens held hostage to corporate greed suffered from energy blackouts. When the bubble finally burst, in the latter part of 2001, Enron investors lost billions, including the pensions and retirement savings of thousands of people. Although top executives at Enron sold their stock before its value collapsed, more than 30 executives (Lay, Skilling, and Fastow among them) were prosecuted on charges that included fraud, insider trading, and money laundering. Lay died before sen-tencing and had his conviction posthumously vacated by a judge. Skilling was sentenced to pay about $50 million into a restitution fund for Enron victims and 24 years in prison, a sentence that was subsequently reduced to about $40 million and 14 years. Fastow was sentenced to 6 years in prison and 2 years on probation (Fowler 2013; Reiman 2007; Rosoff et al. 2007).

It's not just Enron. Unfortunately, Enron was not an isolated example, as the case of Bernard Ebbers of WorldCom suggests. In the early 1980s, with the breakup of the telephone monopoly AT&T, Ebbers saw an opportunity to sell cheap long-distance telephone service. Starting with a $650,000 loan from a local Mississippi bank, Ebbers built his Long Distance Discount Service company into a wildly successful telecom business, which was renamed WorldCom in 1995 and merged with rival MCI in 1997 (Prins 2004; Reiman 2007; Rosoff et al. 2007).

On the surface, WorldCom was another capitalist success story, but like Enron, the corporation was riddled with debt, including debt incurred by Ebbers to pay for his personal extravagances, such as a shipyard of yachts, acres of farm- and timberland, and the largest ranch in Canada. Ebbers also overbuilt the business, as a result of which the company could no longer service the debt, and he overstated the company's earnings to try to attract investors. When the company declared bankruptcy in 2002, the largest in US history, Ebbers negotiated a severance package for himself of $1.5 million a year for life. But two years later he was indicted on criminal charges and received a prison sentence of 25 years (Pulliam et al. 2002).

Once again, accounting firm Arthur Andersen was implicated in the fraud, since WorldCom was one of its clients. Indeed, Arthur Andersen's client list read like a "who's who" of corporate fraudsters with whom they were complicit, including Global Crossing, Qwest Communications, Sunbeam, Waste Management, and Halliburton. It was Enron, however, that was most responsible for Arthur Andersen's downfall (Rosoff et al. 2007). According to Toffler's (2003) account, officials at the accounting firm shredded boxes of Enron documents and deleted numerous e-mails, allegedly at the behest of company executives, which implicated Arthur Andersen in Enron's malfeasance. This was not the first time that Andersen personnel had shredded documents about a client that had been involved in fraud, and in 2002 the accounting firm was convicted of obstruction of justice. Although the verdict was overturned on appeal on the grounds that the judge's instructions to the jury had been unclear on the requisite "consciousness of wrongdoing" that was required for conviction, the formerly prestigious but now tarnished accounting firm, which had once employed thousands of people in the United States and worldwide, became a mere shadow of itself, fending off civil lawsuits as it withered away (Prins 2004; Rosoff et al. 2007).

The crimes of the Rigas family, though the family was not a client of Arthur Andersen, are worth mentioning here. John Rigas headed Adelphia Communications, a company he founded. Before it declared bankruptcy in 2002, Adelphia was one of the largest cable companies in the country. Evidence indicates that the Rigas family used the company as their personal piggybank and improperly took off-the-books loans and other payouts amounting to $2.3 billion. Several Adelphia executives were convicted, including members of the Rigas family, two of whom received prison terms (Prins 2004; Rosoff et al. 2007).

Around the same time, Dennis Kozlowski, CEO of Tyco, a corporate conglomerate whose products include fiber-optic cable, was also convicted and sentenced to a lengthy prison term for actions that were similar to those engaged in by the Rigas family. Kozlowski looted the company, which was mired in fraud, of millions of dollars for his own personal use (Prins 2004; Reiman 2007; Rosoff et al. 2007).

Halliburton is particularly noteworthy because of the notoriety of its former CEO Dick Cheney. Halliburton is an energy services and supply company with scores of subsidiaries that operate in countries around the globe. During the time Cheney was CEO in the latter half of the 1990s, the company engaged in some of the same questionable accounting practices as had Arthur Andersen's other clients. According to Stephen Rosoff and colleagues, Halliburton "may have tip-toed right up to the fraud line but never crossed it" (2007:325). These practices included overstating accounts receivable from customers, understating accounts payable to vendors, overbilling for services, and misleading investors about liabilities faced through litigation (Bussey 2002; Morgenson 2004).

Cheney cashed out company stock worth about $30 million before he resigned to run for vice president and just prior to the plummeting of Halliburton's stock amid allegations that the company had engaged in fraud. Halliburton and its subsidiaries, most notably Kellogg, Brown, and Root, were also accused of overcharging the Pentagon for fuel it had purchased as part of the "no bid" multibillion-dollar contracts it had awarded to Halliburton without competitive bidding from other companies (Bussey 2002; Rosoff et al. 2007).

Additionally, scores of other corporations in what Naomi Klein (2007) calls the **disaster-capitalism complex**, the amalgam of corporations that profit from war and disaster relief, have collectively reaped billions of dollars through unethical and illegal practices such as fraudulent overcharging, the provision of shoddy products and services, outsourcing contracted work for profit, noncompetitive contracts, and open-ended contracts that allow companies to keep coming back to the government for more and more money. Such practices were especially apparent during the Iraq War and in the aftermath of Hurricane Katrina, which devastated the city of New Orleans in 2005 (Fineman 2005; Roche & Silverstein 2004; Scahill 2007). Jeremy Scahill points to three major military contractors alone—Boeing, Lockheed Martin, and Northrop Grumman—that have "engaged in 108 instances of misconduct since 1995 and have paid fines or settlements totaling $3 billion" but were still awarded $77 billion in government business in 2007 (2009:4).

In 2010, the SEC filed civil charges against the Goldman Sachs investment bank, alleging a fraud that bilked investors out of about $1 billion. The civil suit alleged that Goldman Sachs hired a third party, ACA Management, to select pools of risky mortgages that were marketed as good investments, without disclosing to investors that the securities were also crafted with input from another client, Paulson & Co., that took out insurance derivatives betting on the investments to fail; when the investments did in fact fail, Paulson & Co. made billions of dollars. As SEC enforcement director Robert Khuzami said, "Goldman wrongly permitted a client that was betting against the mortgage market to heavily influence which mortgage securities to include in an investment portfolio, while telling other investors that the securities were selected by an independent, objective third party" (quoted in Gordon 2010:B5). Goldman Sachs settled the suit for $550 million (US Securities and Exchange Commission 2010).

In 2013, the JP Morgan investment bank agreed to a $13 billion settlement with the US government related to charges that it had overstated the value of the mortgages it was selling to investors in the run-up to the aforementioned financial crisis of 2008. In agreeing to the settlement, JP Morgan did not admit to a violation of law but conceded that it "had regularly and knowingly sold mortgages to investors that should have never been sold" (Freifeld et al. 2013:1). The following year, Citigroup and Bank of America agreed to pay $7 billion and $17 billion, respectively, to settle federal investigations of their deceptive mortgage practices (Horwitz & Virtanen 2014). To be sure, these are large sums of money, but Dean Starkman (2014) notes that they pale in comparison to the illegal profits made by these corporations, to say nothing of the financial harm they caused to the American people, which amounted to aggregate losses of about $13 trillion. Moreover, it is the banks' current shareholders, who essentially had nothing to do with the wrongdoings, rather than the culpable corporate executives and upper-level managers, who will bear the brunt of these sanctions; and as of the time of this writing, not a single corporate official has been criminally indicted for their misdeeds in provoking the 2008 financial crisis, a calamity from which the country still has not fully recovered.

Corporate Violence

Corporate crime involves not only financial crimes but also physical violence. In this section we consider three general types of corporate violence: crimes against workers, crimes against consumers, and crimes against the environment.

Crimes Against Workers

Corporate violence against workers falls into two general categories: workplace accidents and postponed violence, such as exposure to disease-causing substances. The injurious consequences of the former are immediate, while the latter may not become apparent for years, even decades.

Workplace accidents. When considering the problem of workplace accidents, the term "accident" should be used advisedly, because in many cases these incidents can be avoided. During the 1980s, for example, the state of Texas recorded 1,436 deaths in the construction industry, more than any other state in the nation. In one illustrative case, a crane operator working for Baytown Construction Company of Texas was electrocuted to death when his crane hit an overhead power line. When the company was cited by the Occupational Safety and Health Administration (OSHA) for violating regulations that require cranes to be operated with at least 10 feet of clearance between power lines and any part of the crane, Baytown blamed the accident on employee misconduct. But OSHA argued that Baytown was responsible, because it had not provided its employee with proper training or safety protection (Rosoff et al. 2007).

In another case, an explosion and fire at a chicken-processing plant in North Carolina in 1991 caused the deaths of 25 workers and injured 56 others. According to Judy Aulette and Raymond Michalowski's account, the fire at Imperial Food Products "started because of the unsafe practice of repairing hoses carrying hydraulic fuel while continuing to maintain cooking temperatures with gas flames under large vats of oil. To minimize downtime, Imperial Food Products routinely left its gas-fired chicken fryer on while repairing adjacent hoses carrying flammable hydraulic fluid" (2006:61). During the repair, the hydraulic line separated from its coupling and began discharging fluid at high pressure. When the fluid sprayed onto a nearby cooker, the explosion was immediate.

Aulette and Michalowski note that there was only one fire extinguisher in the plant and no sprinkler system or "automatic cutoffs on the hydraulic or gas lines" (2006:62). On the day of the fire, neither were there any "working telephones to call the fire department. . . . An employee had to drive several blocks to the fire station to inform them" about the fire (p. 62). All but one of the workers who were killed died from smoke inhalation; the others died from burn injuries. Workers at Imperial Food Products claimed that the company deliberately kept exits locked to keep workers from stealing chicken nuggets. "In addition to locked doors, exits were unmarked and . . . [t]here had never been a fire drill in the plant or any fire safety instruction of employees" (p. 61). Aulette and Michalowski conclude that "the single most important factor . . . [in] the 25 deaths was the lack of readily accessible routes to safety" (p. 60).

Moreover, the state of North Carolina was implicated in the incident, because elected officials had refused to use federal OSHA money to help fund state safety inspections, which "had fallen to their lowest level in 16 years" (Aulette & Michalowski 2006:46). One reason for this was that the state would have had to provide matching funds, which a majority of North Carolina legislators did not support. This practice was also consistent with a long-standing policy in the state of encouraging corporate investment by "limiting unionization and blocking the power of regulatory agencies" (p. 47).

Often the companies involved in industrial accidents have a history of OSHA violations, although the penalties issued are too inconsequential to deter them from further misconduct and thus prevent injuries and save lives. The McWane foundry company, based in Birmingham Alabama, has been one of the most egregious corporate violators. Employing about 5,000 workers in a dozen metal-foundry plants around the country, McWane has been cited for several hundred safety violations since 2005, four times more than all of its six major competitors combined; and its workers have been seriously burned, maimed (including severed limbs), and even killed (Barstow & Bergman 2003; Rosoff et al. 2007).

Another dangerous occupation in which workers are vulnerable to death and injury from explosions, fires, and cave-ins is mining. Six years into the administration of President George W. Bush, mining deaths reached a 10-year high at 47 in 2006 (Frank 2007). Critics blamed this increase on the administration's rollbacks of mine safety regulations, the appointment of former mine industry executives and lobbyists to important regulatory positions, the dramatic cutting of agency budgets and enforcement staff, and the reduction in penalties for law violators. They also noted the administration's opposition to proposals that would "require stronger standards on oxygen availability for mine emergencies, mine rescue teams, communications and tracking devices; . . . immediate notification of accidents and rapid emergency response; . . . [and] mandatory minimum penalties for egregious and repeated violations" (Dreier 2006:6; see also Kennedy 2004).

The explosion at the Sago Mine in West Virginia that killed 12 miners in 2006 was particularly noteworthy for drawing public attention to the problem, especially because the operator of the mine, International Coal Group, had been cited 273 times for safety violations since 2004, although none of the fines had "exceeded $460, roughly one-thousandth of 1 percent of the $110 million net profit" earned by the company in 2005 (Urbina & Lehren 2006:1). Congress responded by passing new mine safety legislation that went into effect in 2009, implementing provisions that had been previously resisted by the Bush administration (Huber 2007). Nonetheless, in 2010 an explosion at the Upper Big Branch mine in West Virginia, operated by Performance Coal Company, killed 29 workers, making it the largest mining disaster in a quarter century. Performance Coal, a subsidiary of Massey Energy Company, also had a significant history of safety violations—in less than a year and a half before the blast it had been cited for 600 violations, and for 57 just a month before. Corporate managers had also been keeping two sets of books on safety conditions—an accurate one for itself and a sanitized one for the federal government (Cooper 2010; Huber 2011; *Huffington Post* 2010).

Postponed violence. Unlike workplace accidents, many occupational hazards experienced by workers are not immediately observable. Rather, they involve debilitating diseases that take a long time to develop, which Rosoff and colleagues (2007) refer to as **postponed violence**. These injuries entail diseases where the link between the cause of the malady and its manifest symptoms may be obscure, especially because the diseases have a long gestation period and "strike only a segment of the exposed population, either randomly or patterned by varying individual vulnerabilities," or because the diseases also have other causes (Calhoun & Hiller 1988:163). Occupational exposure to workplace toxins, for instance, may multiply the risk of cancer from other sources such as cigarette smoke and air pollution.

Exposure to asbestos has been one of the most publicized sources of postponed violence and has affected millions of workers in the United States. Asbestos is a fibrous mineral mined from rock that has been used mainly as a fire retardant in products such as textiles, brake linings in automobiles, and especially construction materials. Asbestos fibers can crumble and become airborne. Long-term inhalation of these fibers can cause several debilitating if not fatal lung diseases, particularly mesothelioma, as well as damage to other internal organs.

The Johns-Manville Corporation has been a major manufacturer of asbestos over the years. Internal company documents going back to the 1930s and 1940s indicate that the company had full knowledge of the harmful effects of its product. To protect itself from financial liability, Johns-Manville had a policy of negotiating settlements with sick workers if they agreed to drop all other claims against the company. In addition, a Johns-Manville medical director advised that workers who had contracted illnesses but who had not yet manifested debilitating symptoms should not be informed of their condition. It was not until 1964 that Johns-Manville finally warned workers of the dangers of asbestos exposure, but by 1972 it was still refusing to install a dust-control system to protect them. Company executives had calculated that it was more profitable to pay worker compensation to disabled employees or to the families of the deceased than to install the system (Calhoun & Hiller 1988).

In 1973, the federal government began implementing various policies to ban some asbestos applications and to ensure that asbestos in schools would be replaced if it did not meet safety requirements. Several asbestos manufacturers lost civil lawsuits and were forced to pay millions of dollars in damages to injured or deceased workers or their families. In 1982, Johns-Manville negotiated a bankruptcy settlement with the government and was allowed to reorganize. The settlement called for Johns-Manville to set up a trust fund of nearly $3 billion to settle claims with injured parties in exchange for immunity from further lawsuits (Calhoun & Hiller 1988; Rosoff et al. 2007).

Mining is another industry in which exposure to asbestos occurs, but here pneumoconiosis, or black lung disease, is a concern as well. Black lung disease is caused by long-term exposure to coal dust, which accumulates in the lungs, reducing lung capacity and leading to respiratory disease. During the first decade of the twenty-first century, black lung disease was on the rise, even among younger workers, which health officials attributed to longer working hours and the drive to extract coal from more difficult locations. One study linked the rise to increased exposure to airborne crystalline silica, a rock by-product that causes scarring of lung tissues, which can be fatal (Davidson 2010; Maher 2009).

Postponed violence to workers also occurs in the textile industry, where exposure to cotton dust causes an irreversible lung disease called byssinosis, or brown lung. The industry's history of denying harm and suppressing information parallels that of the asbestos industry. J.P. Stevens, the second largest textile manufacturer in the United States, is one of the most notorious perpetrators of workplace-induced byssinosis, and it has been singled out by the National Labor Relations Board as "the greatest labor-law violator" in the country (Rosoff et al. 2007:180).

The nuclear power industry, too, has been a source of postponed violence. The problems in this industry were first brought to public attention by the 1983 film *Silkwood,* based on a true story. In the early 1970s, Karen Silkwood was employed by the Kerr-McGee Corporation, a company in Oklahoma that manufactured highly radioactive (and carcinogenic) plutonium fuel for nuclear reactors. Kerr-McGee had a history of careless handling of plutonium—for example, storing the material in leaking drums and shipping it in improper containers. Inside the plant, a number of workers, including Silkwood, were exposed. After Silkwood was elected to be a union representative, she decided to go public in an effort to pressure Kerr-McGee to take measures to protect its employees. She contacted a *New York Times* reporter, saying she had obtained internal company documents indicating that Kerr-McGee had falsified records regarding levels of plutonium exposure in its plant. On her way to deliver the documents to the reporter, she was killed in a car accident. Investigative journalist Jack Anderson claimed there was evidence that Silkwood's car was run off the road and that the documents she was carrying had been stolen. But a 1977 congressional investigation concluded that her death was an accident. Nonetheless, the following year a civil jury found Kerr-McGee liable for having exposed Silkwood to plutonium and was ordered to pay $10.5 million in damages to her estate (Rashke 1981; Rosoff et al. 2007).

Despite incidents such as these, work-related injuries and illnesses continue to be underreported in the United States. A recent survey of occupational health practitioners (including company doctors and nurses) by the US Government Accountability Office found that more than half said they had been pressured to downplay injuries or illnesses, and more than a third said that they had been pressured to provide insufficient medical treatment, because a company wanted to reduce workers' compensation costs or feared hurting their chances of winning contracts. More than two-thirds of occupational health practitioners also said that they knew of employees who feared disciplinary action if they reported injuries (Greenhouse 2009).

Crimes Against Consumers

We now turn to a consideration of corporate violence against consumers, with a focus on the motor vehicle, food, pharmaceutical, and tobacco industries.

Motor vehicles. In addition to the aforementioned Pinto fires, Ford Motor Company was responsible for as many as 300 deaths and even more injuries from the mid-1960s to the mid-1980s because of malfunctioning transmissions that slipped from "park" to "reverse" after the driver and passengers had exited the vehicle. Ford knew about this problem for years but had done nothing about it (Center for Auto Safety 2014b).

Ford, of course, is not alone in endangering consumers from motor vehicles allowed on the market after company officials knew they were dangerous. For instance, the "sidesaddle" fuel tanks on General Motors pickups and trucks built between 1973 and 1991, which were vulnerable to fuel leaks in accidents, are estimated to have caused more than 1,800 deaths, making it "the worst auto crash fire defect in the history of the United States" (Center for Auto Safety 2014a:1). And faulty rear-end latches on Chrysler minivans built between 1984 and 1995 allowed passengers (especially children) in moderate-speed rear-end collisions to be thrown out of the vehicle, killing an estimated 37 people (Safetyforum 2003).

At the turn of the century, Ford once again was embroiled in a major product-defect case. This case involved defective tires manufactured by the Bridgestone Corporation, which were commonly used on Ford's bestselling Explorer sports utility vehicle (SUV) as well as its Ranger and F-series pickup trucks. The tires, which were prone to tread separation that caused blowouts at high speeds, are estimated to have caused more than 270 deaths and more than 800 injuries. As with previous cases discussed here, the tragedies are made even more egregious by the fact that both Bridgestone and Ford knew about the problem but failed to do anything about it. Bridgestone's initial response to the revelation of the defect was to blame Ford, since the Explorer was dangerously prone to rollover accidents because of its top-heavy design: "a relatively narrow wheel base in proportion to the height and weight of the vehicle" (Mullins 2006:138). Indeed, prior to production of the Explorer, Ford officials knew that their Bronco SUV also had rollover problems and that the Explorer was potentially even less stable. They also knew about problems with the front suspension that could contribute to poor vehicle handling during a tire blowout or potential rollover, even though Ford had advertised the vehicle as handling like a car. Additionally, Ford had not notified the National Highway Traffic Safety Administration that it had replaced the tires on SUVs sold in other countries. Some 20 million tires were eventually recalled as both companies settled lawsuits in the millions of dollars (Naughton 2000; Rosoff et al. 2007).

In 2010, Toyota was the automobile company that dominated the news, primarily for problems with sticking gas pedals and sudden acceleration of their vehicles, which caused more than 50 deaths. The Japanese automaker, like other companies before it, withheld information about manufacturing defects that would have alerted consumers and ignored court orders to produce documents. The NHTSA levied a $16.4 million fine for Toyota's delaying tactics and forced the company to recall and repair more than 2 million vehicles (Anderson & Robbins 2010; Booth 2010; Von App 2010).

In 2014, GM was under fire for ignition-switch and power-steering problems with its Cobalt, Saturn Ions, and other small vehicles. The ignition-switch problem in particular, which GM knew about since 2001, has been linked to at least 13 deaths. GM received a record-breaking $35 million fine and was forced to recall some 13.6 million vehicles for an inexpensive repair reminiscent of the Pinto debacle (Durbin 2014; Krisher 2014; Lowy & Krisher 2014).

Foods. A century after Upton Sinclair's famous exposé of the meatpacking industry in his book *The Jungle* (1906), millions of Americans still get food poisoning and some 5,000 die each year from diseased meat and poultry products, some as a result of corporate law-violating practices (Moss 2009; Rosoff et al. 2007). In 1998, for example, the press reported that the Department of Agriculture had been "permitting hundreds of meat and poultry plants to operate virtually uninterrupted even while federal inspectors [filed] tens of thousands of citations against them for unsanitary conditions and food contamination" (Jaspin & Montgomery 1998:A7). One Arkansas plant operated by Tyson Foods was cited for 1,753 "critical" violations in 1996 alone, yet it did not lose a single day of production ("critical" is defined by the Department of Agriculture as a condition "certain" to cause contamination, "certain" to reach consumers, and "certain to have a detrimental effect" on consumers).

More recently, concerns about food have focused on tainted ground beef that has been contaminated with the virulent E. coli bacteria. Ground beef is particularly vulnerable to contamination, because it often consists of "an amalgam of various grades of meat from different parts of cows," with the low-grade ingredients "cut from areas of the cow that are more likely to have had contact with feces," which carries E. coli (Moss 2009:1). Moreover, the components of the product often come from different slaughterhouses from different states and even different countries, making it especially difficult to ensure the quality of the meat and identify the source of problems should they occur. Too often, meat producers' attempts to test for product safety are meager, and we do not learn of the problem until people get sick. In one case, a 22-year-old woman suffered kidney failure, seizures, and paralysis from infected meat she ate at a fast food restaurant. In 2009,

FURTHER EXPLORATION
The China Connection

In the latter part of 2006, the media began reporting on the problem of toxic products imported into the United States from China. The initial concern was over dog and cat food, which was causing "painful, mysterious and sometimes gruesome deaths. . . . Previously healthy pets would suddenly vomit blood and bile, produce bloody diarrhea and lose control of bladder and bowel. Some animals displayed unquenchable thirst, while others refused to eat or drink at all. Victims became lethargic and withdrawn, their limbs wobbly, eyes cloudy and stomachs painfully distended. Then seizures set in" (Goldstein 2007:5). It is estimated that between December 2006 and February 2007 alone, after food importers began monitoring the problem, as many as 39,000 pets were sickened or killed. The problem was finally traced to contaminated wheat gluten in the food.

In the ensuing months, we then learned about "antifreeze in toothpaste, banned antibiotics in farmed seafood and lead paint on Thomas the Tank Engine toys—all imported from China and all unwittingly consumed or otherwise used by Americans for months, if not years" (Goldstein 2007:5). Problems with lead in other toys, children's necklaces, and fake Halloween teeth from China soon came to light. We also learned of Chinese-manufactured baby cribs, some of them bestselling models in the United States, causing the deaths of at least three children who suffered falls resulting from faulty rail design (Possley 2007; Simmons 2007).

Questions were raised as to why the US government was not protecting the public from these harmful products, and the deregulation policies of the George W. Bush administration were harshly criticized. It was actually the *Chicago Tribune,* not the Consumer Product Safety Commission (CPSC), for instance, that discovered the problems with the cribs and pressed a reluctant CPSC to issue a recall. Indeed, Nancy Ford, head of the CPSC, had throughout her term of office resisted congressional efforts to increase her agency's staff and responsibility so that it could more effectively monitor problems like this. But as a result of the China controversy, we may now expect greater public pressure to make the CPSC a more effective instrument of public safety (Possley 2007; Tankersley & Possley 2008).

the Department of Agriculture initiated a recall of beef from nearly 3,000 grocers in 41 states. Additionally, between 2009 and 2011, it issued about 20 recalls for fruits and vegetables that contained pathogens such as E. coli and salmonella (Eng 2011).

Even the food we feed to our infant children has been found to be contaminated, with studies conducted in the mid-1990s finding traces of pesticides in more than half of baby foods tested, including pesticides with neurotoxins and known carcinogenic effects (Rosoff et al. 2007). According to the National Academy of Sciences: "Children are more susceptible than adults to most pesticides. . . . [If they] are exposed to compounds that act in the nervous system during periods of vulnerability, they can be left with lifelong deficits. If they're exposed to carcinogens, it can set the stage for cancer later" (cited in Rosoff et al. 2007:121).

Pharmaceuticals. During the 1980s, the Eli Lilly corporation marketed Oraflex, a painkiller intended for arthritis patients. When the company asked the Food and Drug Administration (FDA) to approve the sale of the drug in the United States, it did not inform the FDA of at least 26 deaths that had been linked to Oraflex overseas. The drug was sold in the United States for about six months, but was withdrawn after reports of deaths began circulating in the news. The company and one executive were criminally prosecuted, entered guilty pleas, and were fined (the company was fined $25,000 and the executive $15,000). Some observers estimate that Oraflex caused the deaths of about 50 people overall, as well as serious liver and kidney damage in more than 900 others (Coleman 2006; Rosoff et al. 2007).

Although the FDA requires foods, drugs, medical devices, and cosmetics to be tested to ensure that they are safe before they are sold to the public, these tests "are seriously weakened by the fact that the manufacturer, not the FDA," typically conducts the tests (Coleman 2006:145). In the case of pharmaceuticals in particular, "drug companies often have an enormous financial stake" in the testing process, and they have powerful incentives "to bias the testing procedures or even falsify the data" (p. 145). Moreover, much of the FDA budget relies substantially on "user fees" provided by the drug companies themselves, and some 30 percent of individuals who serve on the numerous advisory boards that are used by the FDA to purportedly provide objective advice on granting FDA approval have direct ties to the companies whose products are being evaluated (Alonzo-Zaldivar 2006; Singer & Baer 2009).

The circumstances surrounding the "blockbuster" drug Vioxx, manufactured by Merck, is a case in point. Vioxx is an anti-inflammatory drug designed to treat arthritis, acute pain conditions, and dysmenorrhea. Merck put the drug on the market in 1999 until it was withdrawn in 2004 due to reported adverse side effects experienced by thousands of users—including heart attacks, strokes, blood clots, and sudden deaths. Merck had spent over $160 million marketing the drug, which was prescribed to millions of people worldwide, and it had earned a profit of about $2.5 billion annually. A subsequent FDA investigation and civil lawsuits brought against Merck revealed that the company had withheld test data from the FDA that showed some of these adverse effects. In 2007 Merck settled the pending lawsuits for $4.85 billion (Berenson 2007; NewsInferno 2007; Singer & Baer 2009).

In another pharmaceutical case that came to light in 2004, Warner-Lambert, a division of Pfizer, agreed to plead guilty to two felony counts and pay $430 million in criminal and civil penalties for fraudulently promoting Neurontin, an FDA-approved epilepsy drug, for unapproved purposes such as bipolar disorder, pain, migraine headaches, and drug and alcohol withdrawal (Tansey 2004). It is estimated that up to 90 percent of the prescriptions that were sold for Neurontin were issued for unapproved uses, helping to boost sales of the drug from $97.5 million in 1995 to nearly $2.7 billion in 2003. Warner-Lambert engaged in such illegal tactics as paying doctors to listen to sales pitches for unapproved uses; treating doctors to trips to Hawaii, Florida, and the 1996 Atlanta Olympics; paying doctors to allow sales representatives to sit in on patient visits; and planting company operatives in audiences at medical education conferences to contradict unfavorable comments about the drug. Five years later, in 2009, Warner-Lambert's parent company Pfizer was also fined, in this case $2.3 billion, in criminal and civil penalties for fraudulently promoting the painkiller Bextra, which had been removed from the market in 2005 because of concerns about increased risk of heart attack and stroke, as a way to relieve symptoms of osteoarthritis and rheumatoid arthritis (Guilloton 2009).

Tobacco. The tobacco industry is another area of business that has been marked by corporate malfeasance. Smoking has been recognized for decades "as the primary preventable cause of death in the United States" (Rosoff et al. 2007:108). Its role in heart disease and lung cancer is incontrovertible. Even research conducted by the tobacco industry itself, dating back to the 1960s, recognized these adverse effects, although this information was not disclosed until it was leaked three decades later. And it was not until the mid-1990s that we learned that the industry had been manipulating the level of nicotine beyond the amount that occurs naturally in tobacco in order to increase the addictive quality of its product. Internal corporate memos indicate that tobacco company officials viewed cigarettes as nothing more than "nicotine-delivery systems" and saw themselves as being "in the business of selling nicotine" (cited in Rosoff et al. 2007:109). Yet they continued to deny that they manipulated nicotine levels and repeatedly suppressed research that demonstrated nicotine's addictive properties (Wiener 2010).

It is now also clear that tobacco corporations, despite their denials, intentionally marketed their products to teenagers. Internal documents from Philip Morris show that in the 1970s the company commissioned a poll to ascertain the smoking habits of youths as young as 14 years of age. Philip Morris wanted to know which competing brands were discouraging the use of its Marlboro cigarettes among the young. An R.J. Reynolds memo indicates that company officials felt "unfairly constrained from directly promoting cigarettes to the youth market," but they believed it was imperative nevertheless to "offer . . . the '21 and under' group . . . an opportunity to use our brands" (cited in Rosoff et al. 2007:112).

Much of our current knowledge of industry suppression of information comes from the Liggett Group, one of the smallest of the main tobacco corporations, which broke ranks with the industry by agreeing to settle claims against it and by releasing what it described as a "treasure trove of incriminating documents" from 30 years of meetings with other tobacco companies (cited in Rosoff et al. 2007:111). Although most individual lawsuits against tobacco companies have been unsuccessful, in 1998 the attorneys general of all 50 US states settled lawsuits totaling some $250 billion to

FURTHER EXPLORATION
Corporate Violence Against Women

Over the years, corporate violence against consumers has had a particular impact on women, especially in areas related to reproductive issues. One of the most noteworthy cases involved the drug thalidomide. In the early 1960s, thousands of pregnant (mostly European) women who had taken thalidomide, which was prescribed for morning sickness and sleeping disorders, had given birth to severely deformed infants. Although thalidomide was first developed in Europe, Richardson-Merrell, a US corporation, purchased the rights to sell it in the United States even though it knew the drug had already been withdrawn from the German market because of suspected birth defects. The FDA did prohibit the sale of thalidomide in the United States, despite heavy lobbying from Richardson-Merrell, but not before the corporation had distributed free pills for doctors to pass out to patients (Dowie & Marshall 1980).

In the early 1970s, the A.H. Robbins Company marketed an intrauterine device (IUD) for birth control called the Dalkon Shield to about 2.2 million women in the United States and another 2.3 million worldwide. Sold without adequate premarket testing, the Dalkon Shield turned out to be both ineffective and harmful. A design defect in the wick used to insert and remove the IUD allowed bacteria to travel up into the uterus, where it caused infection. Thousands of women who used the device were rendered sterile, suffered miscarriages, or gave birth to stillborn or premature babies with congenital birth defects. At least 18 women in the United States alone died from its use before the FDA forced its withdrawal from the US market. But A.H. Robbins continued to sell the Dalkon Shield abroad for at least another nine months. The company even persuaded the US Agency for International Development (USAID) to distribute it in over 40 countries overseas. One USAID official reported that the IUD was still being used in Pakistan, India, and possibly South Africa five years later. In the late 1980s, after paying millions of dollars to settle thousands of lawsuits, A.H. Robbins agreed to a settlement and declared bankruptcy, reorganized, and established a $2.5 billion fund to compensate victims (Mintz 1985; Perry & Dawson 1985).

In 1980, women bore the costs of another harmful product when Procter & Gamble sent 60 million sample packages of its superabsorbent Rely

continues

continued

tampon to consumers in 80 percent of US households. Unfortunately, Rely not only contained cancer-causing synthetics such as polyurethane, but also allowed potentially deadly bacteria to grow and move from the vagina or cervix into the uterus and then the bloodstream, causing a potentially fatal condition known as **toxic shock syndrome**. Symptoms of this disease include high fever, vomiting, sunburn-like skin rash, peeling skin on hands and feet, and damage to internal organs, including the lungs, which fill with fluid until respiratory or cardiac failure ensues. At Procter & Gamble, complaints about such problems were considered routine—the company had been receiving over a hundred complaints per month—and company officials first attributed them to allergies. In just the first year of distribution, however, the Centers for Disease Control documented 55 fatal and over a thousand nonfatal cases of toxic shock syndrome. Procter & Gamble did bow to FDA pressure to pull Rely off the market, and it agreed to pay for a mass advertising campaign to warn women to stop using the product. But the corporation never admitted that the product "was defective or that they had done anything wrong" (Rosoff et al. 2007:134; see also Swasy 1993).

Another significant case that came to light in the 1990s involved silicone-gel implants used for breast enlargement. Although scientists working for Dow Corning, the leading implant manufacturer, had been concerned about implant leaks and ruptures since the 1970s, Dow falsified some of its quality-control tests and continued to sell the product to some 150,000 women annually for three decades. Dow claims that its critics have not proven any adverse effects from the silicone implant. However, thousands of women have filed legal claims against Dow, alleging that silicone released into their bodies caused tremors, extreme fatigue, and connective tissue diseases such as rheumatoid arthritis, scleroderma, and lupus. Plaintiffs also believe that children breastfed by mothers with silicone in their system have suffered similar symptoms. Dow and other breast-implant manufacturers have lost several multimillion-dollar civil lawsuits. In 1995 Dow went into bankruptcy after determining that an agreement it had made the year earlier to pay over $4 billion in liability costs would not cover the claims against itself (Rosoff et al. 2007).

recoup public funds spent treating tobacco-related illnesses. Additionally, in 2006 a federal district judge found the nation's top tobacco companies guilty of criminal fraud and racketeering for deceiving the public about the health impact of smoking (including secondhand smoke), the addictiveness of nicotine, the safety of so-called light cigarettes, and the targeting of youths (CNN 2006a; Wiener 2010).

Crimes Against the Environment

One does not have to work under hazardous conditions or consume dangerous products to be harmed by corporate violence. Toxic industrial by-products such as carbon dioxide emissions, mercury, and countless synthetic chemicals and gasses continue to pollute our air, land, and waters. These industrial by-products poison fish and wildlife and enter the food chain with deleterious consequences that may not be fully recognized for years. Overall, human exposure to environmental toxins may account for a large proportion of cancer cases (Friedrichs 2007; Reiman 2007).

Corporate polluters—who constitute what Daniel Faber (2008) calls the **polluter-industrial complex**—continue to view these costs of production as "externalities" they can pass on to the public, rather than as "internalities" to be deducted from their profits by finding ways to change the way they do business. In a practice known as **corporate dumping**, some of these externalities are transferred to developing countries with weak regulatory structures, countries to which hazardous products and toxic waste that cannot be sold or disposed of in the United States are shipped abroad. In other instances, entire production operations are relocated abroad. These practices can have a **boomerang effect** when, for example, pesticides that are banned in the United States are shipped overseas for use on foreign crops and then reimported in the food we eat (Frank & Lynch 1992).

Toxic communities. One of the most infamous cases of corporate environmental malfeasance in the United States involved the Hooker Chemical Corporation. During the 1940s and early 1950s, Hooker burned and stored millions of pounds of chemical waste that contained carcinogenic substances such as dioxin and benzene in Love Canal, an abandoned waterway near Niagara Falls. The canal was subsequently covered up and turned into a housing development. By the late 1970s, contaminated black sludge began seeping into the basements of homes, and residents reported an unusually high number of miscarriages, stillborn babies, and infants with birth defects. A 1980 study found that over 900 Love Canal children were suffering from "seizures, learning problems, eye and skin irritations, incontinence, and severe abdominal pains" (Griffin 1988:27). Internal Hooker documents indicate that the company had known about the problem as early as 1958 but failed to notify the residents. In 1984, Hooker settled a lawsuit and agreed to pay $20 million to residents who were forced to move from their homes. In 1995, after 16 years of resistance, Occidental Petroleum, the parent company of Hooker, agreed to reimburse the federal government $129 million for cleaning up the site (Friedrichs 2007; Rosoff et al. 2007).

The 1996 film *A Civil Action,* based on a true story, depicted a similar situation in Woburn, Massachusetts, an industrial suburb of Boston. Since the 1930s, residents had noticed the red coloring and nauseating odor of Lake Mishawum, the source of their water supply. By the 1970s, residents became concerned about a growing number of childhood leukemia cases, which they suspected were associated with the discoloration and onerous smell and taste of their drinking water. In 1979 the cancer-causing contaminants were confirmed by scientists from the Environmental Protection

Agency; and in 1981 the Massachusetts Department of Health released a report attributing the high incidence of leukemia as well as kidney cancer to the pollution (Rosoff et al. 2007).

The following year, eight families filed a civil lawsuit against the Cryovac Division of the W.R. Grace Corporation for its negligent practices in disposing of chemical waste. A jury found in favor of the plaintiffs, but the judge "set aside the verdict on the grounds that the jury had not understood the highly technical data upon which the case had been based" and ordered a new trial (Rosoff et al. 2007:256). A few days later, Grace agreed to an $8 million settlement with the plaintiffs, but in a subsequent investigation was indicted in federal court on 12 criminal counts of providing false information to the EPA. The company agreed to plead guilty to one of the charges and pay the maximum fine of only $10,000.

Over the years, other communities in the United States have suffered problems similar to those in Love Canal and Woburn, and in some cases residents have been forced to evacuate their homes because of leaks from hazardous-waste sites or contaminated drinking water. One recent case involves the poor, Latino farmworker town of Kettleman City, California, where residents have reported an unusual number of serious birth defects in children, primarily cleft lips and palates but also Down syndrome, brain damage, heart problems, and other life-threatening maladies. Residents and environmentalists implicate multiple environmental toxins as the cause of these ailments. Scores of diesel trucks roll through the town spewing toxic fumes every day, and the smell of chemical pesticides that are sprayed in the fields fills the air. Waste Management Inc. operates the biggest toxic-waste dumpsite west of Alabama, just three miles away, and in 2009 alone the dumpsite "accepted 356,000 tons of hazardous waste, consisting of tens of thousands of chemical compounds including asbestos, pesticides, caustics, petroleum products, and about 11,000 tons of materials contaminated with PCBs—now banned chemicals linked to cancer and birth defects" (Leslie 2010:50).

As these types of problems disproportionately affect poor and minority residents, environmentalists have raised concerns about what they call **environmental racism**. One study estimated that about a third of the hazardous-waste landfills in the contiguous United States are located in just five Southern states and that 60 percent of the waste contained in these sites is located in three predominately African-American zip code areas (Bullard & Wright 1989–1990). In the state of Louisiana, the concentration of chemical plants near poor black communities between New Orleans and Baton Rouge is referred to as "Cancer Alley" (Faber 2008). More generally, a large body of research documents the extensive racial and ethnic disparities in exposure to hazardous waste throughout the country, with black and Hispanic residents more likely to be exposed than white residents (Cole & Foster 2001; Mohai & Saha 2007; Stretesky & Lynch 1999). Of course, the displacement of environmental hazards onto developing countries is a form of environmental racism as well.

The animal waste from industrial factory farms, especially those producing pork, is also a problem, particularly compared to small family farms, which produce less waste per acre. The smaller operations are capable of using the waste they produce, as manure, to grow crops on their own land. But the larger operations concentrate a huge amount of waste—a "witch's brew" of toxic pesticides, hormones, antibiotics, and disease-causing viruses and microbes—that cannot safely be absorbed by the adjacent land. For this reason, industrial meat producers typically locate their factories in poor and minority communities that are less able to mount opposition to their harmful environmental practices (Kennedy 2004; Seely 2010).

The poor and working-class people of the coal-rich Central Appalachian region of the country, which ranges from Kentucky and Tennessee to West Virginia and Virginia, have also been victims of the unsafe environmental practice of **strip-mining**, whereby mining companies "blow off hundreds of feet from the tops of mountains to reach the thin seams of coal beneath. Colossal machines dump the mountains into adjacent valleys, destroying forests and communities and burying free-flowing mountain streams in the process" (Kennedy 2004:114). Massey Energy, which controls almost a third of the total coal reserves in Central Appalachia, has been involved in civil litigation with residents who claim that their water supply has been poisoned by the oily toxic sludge that seeps into the groundwater (SourceWatch 2014b). In one case in 2000, a storage pit in Kentucky that is owned by Martin County Coal, a subsidiary of Massey Energy, spilled 300 million gallons of "thick black lava-like toxic sludge," the largest coal-related spill in US history, "containing 60 poisonous chemicals that choked and sterilized 100 miles of rivers and creeks and poisoned the drinking water of 17 communities" (Kennedy 2004:121).

More recently, in 2014, 300,000 residents of Charleston, West Virginia, were left without water for several days due to a spill from the Freedom Works coal-processing plant that released thousands of gallons of 4-methylcyclohexane methanol, a chemical used to "wash" coal to remove impurities and pollutants before burning (Barrett 2014). Ironically, tougher air pollution regulations that have fueled the "clean coal" industry are causing more contaminants to be discharged into waterways. In 2013 alone, the EPA "identified 132 cases where coal-fired power plant waste has damaged rivers, streams, and lakes, and 123 where it has tainted underground water sources" (Cappiello & Borenstein 2014:A5). In many such cases, these pollution practices are legal.

Oil drilling. Environmentalists have long been concerned about the burning of fossil fuels such as coal and oil because of the gaseous by-products that become trapped in the atmosphere—the "greenhouse" effect—raising

Earth's temperature and contributing to the problem of **climate change**. These conditions are dramatically disrupting Earth's ecosystems and patterns of human habitation by melting the polar ice caps and causing sea levels to rise (which can result in flooding of coastal communities and the salinization of underground water supplies) and by altering rainfall patterns and moisture levels in soils (which can adversely affect agricultural production). With increased warming, some parts of the world can expect more draughts while other parts can expect intensified rainstorms, flooding, and snow blizzards as a consequence of increased evaporation from the ocean surface (Ball 2015; Faber 2008; Kennedy 2004).

Over the years, oil spills from offshore drilling have been another by-product of energy production. The infamous spill that occurred off the coast of the once pristine city of Santa Barbara, California, was the first time this problem was brought home to the American people. In January 1969, at the site of a drilling operation that was jointly owned by the Union, Mobil, Texaco, and Gulf oil companies, a viscous black mass erupted from the ocean floor, surging to the surface. Three months later, at least 3 million gallons of oil had spread over more than 800 square miles of ocean and more than 40 miles of some of the finest beach area in the country. Oceanographers described the effect on the fish and wildlife as a "dead sea," noting that it would take "years, even decades, before this area of the ocean returns to normal" (Sethi 1982:241).

The oil industry's response to the disaster, which outraged the residents of Santa Barbara, was simply to note that "such risks are inevitable in major operations of this kind and must be borne in view of the economic returns and the country's growing petroleum needs" (Sethi 1982:247). Numerous lawsuits seeking compensation for damages from the oil companies were forthcoming from property owners, fishermen, boat owners, and other individuals; and the companies agreed to pay several million dollars in out-of-court settlements. Ironically, Union Oil, which had steadfastly maintained that the accident "had been unforeseeable and unpreventable, sued its drilling contractor, the Peter Bawden Company, for negligence," charging that it had caused the spill (p. 259).

In 1989, another major oil spill involved the oil tanker *Exxon Valdez*, which lost nearly 11 million gallons of oil when it struck a reef off the coast of Alaska, devastating the wildlife, environment, and economy of the region. Questions about Exxon Corporation's responsibility for the disaster arose as evidence surfaced that the company had known of the ship captain's drinking problem but had failed to take appropriate action. In addition, Exxon had reduced the size of the crew, causing the remaining crew members to work while fatigued. After the spill, the "clean-up response was slow, and it was clear . . . that nobody involved was adequately prepared to handle a disaster of that magnitude" (Cruciotti & Matthews 2006:154). Alyeska Pipeline Service Company, a consortium of seven oil companies that had the responsibility for developing and implementing cleanup plans, was ill-prepared to do so, causing delays that might have mitigated some of the damaging effects. And both the US Coast Guard and the Alaska Department of Environmental Control were lax in meeting their responsibilities to exert regulatory supervision to both prevent and respond to problems. In the end, Exxon was forced to pay about $1 billion in civil settlements, $500 million in punitive civil damages, and $100 million in criminal fines (Friedrichs 2007; Oliphant 2008).

More recently, in April 2010, the state of Louisiana and the entire Gulf of Mexico region were affected by a devastating explosion at the Deepwater Horizon oil-drilling rig, located 40 miles offshore. The blast killed 11 workers and released millions of gallons of crude oil from the site's oil well, located 5,000 feet below the ocean's surface. By mid-July, the spill had exceeded 180 gallons, far surpassing the *Exxon Valdez* disaster. The oil penetrated the beaches and already fragile coastal wetlands of the Gulf and caused irreparable harm to the fish and wildlife in the area (Bergin 2010; Shapley 2010).

The disaster, regrettably, did not come as a surprise to environmentalists, who for many years had been cautioning against the "drill baby drill" mentality advocated by people like former Alaska governor Sarah Palin, who was the Republican candidate for vice president in 2008. As Tyson Slocum pointedly observed at the time of the spill, British Petroleum (BP), the London-based contractor of the Deepwater Horizon rig, had "one of the worst safety records of any oil company, . . . [paying] $485 billion in fines and settlements to the US government for environmental crimes, willful neglect of worker safety rules, and penalties for manipulating energy markets" in just the few years preceding the explosion (2010:2). In a cascading chain of recriminations and denials that were part of a congressional hearing in May 2010, a BP executive claimed that Transocean, the owner of the rig, was responsible. A Transocean executive, in turn, blamed Halliburton, to whom it had subcontracted some of its operations. And a Halliburton executive blamed the other companies, saying it had followed standard industry practices and federal guidelines. The truth of the matter is that everyone was to blame, including the US Department of Interior's Mineral Management Service (Crum 2010; Hebert 2010; Morrison 2010).

Critics of the Mineral Management Service cite the conflict of interest in the agency, whereby it had the function of both regulating oil drilling *and* collecting some $13 billion annually from the leasing of rights to drill in federal waters and lands, which amounts to about 95 percent of the revenue collected by the Department of the Interior as a whole. The Mineral Management Service had given BP a **categorical exclusion** for its Deepwater Horizon rig, which essentially amounted to a waiver of environmental review and a rubber-stamping of BP's operations based on the (dubious) assumption that the project did not pose a significant risk to the environment. Thus BP and its corporate partners were allowed to begin drilling without installing properly functioning safety equipment, including a cement casing around the well that might have plugged a leak in the event of an explosion (Morrison 2010; Power et al. 2010).

Five weeks after the explosion, the press reported on an ongoing Coast Guard hearing that was being conducted in New Orleans. Doug Brown, the chief mechanic aboard the Deepwater Horizon rig, testified about a meeting that had taken place just hours before the blowout in which rig workers and one BP official skirmished over a BP decision "to replace heavy drilling fluid in the well with saltwater" (cited in Kunzelman et al. 2010: A11). The company wanted to remove the heavy fluid so it could use it for another project, but rig workers were concerned that the seawater would provide "less weight to counteract the surging pressure from the ocean depths." According to Brown, the BP official "overruled the drillers, declaring, 'This is how it's going to be.'" Another rig worker submitted a handwritten statement to the Coast Guard, which added: "I overheard upper management . . . saying that BP was taking shortcuts by displacing the well with saltwater instead of mud without sealing the well with cement plugs, [and] this is why it blew out."

In July, Mike Williams, a Transocean engineer who had worked at the Deepwater Horizon rig, testified that the safety system had been in ill repair for months if not years. Williams said that at one point he had been chastised by a superior for activating a gas safety valve that had been placed in bypass mode; the supervisor had told him: "The damn thing has been in bypass for five years. . . . As a matter of fact, the entire fleet runs them in bypass" (quoted in Lin & Boxall 2010:A10). Williams also testified that "the pressure regulator valve, which automatically cuts off natural gas flow when it reaches a certain pressure point, was in bypass mode when a burp of gas shot up from the well into the rig," causing the explosion that set "in motion the worst offshore oil spill in U.S. history."

Additionally, a memo released by the House Committee on Energy and Commerce revealed an internal BP inquiry stating that tests conducted by BP less than an hour before the explosion had detected a buildup of pressure that was an "indicator of a very large abnormality" (cited in Kunzelman et al. 2010:A11). Five hours before the explosion as well, rig workers detected an unexpected loss of fluid from a pipe that indicated a leak in the blowout preventer, a five-story device that is supposed to slam shut in an emergency. After the explosion, when an attempt was made to activate the preventer, there was no hydraulic power to operate the equipment. For its actions, as of the time of this writing, BP has paid out more than $25 billion in legal penalties, lawsuit settlements, and cleanup fees, costing it roughly a mere year's worth of profits, but additional penalties may be forthcoming in the future (Krauss 2013; Kunzelman & McConnaughey 2014).

Hydraulic fracturing and nuclear power. In addition to oil drilling, two other sources of energy production raise concerns: hydraulic fracturing (also known as **fracking**) and nuclear power. Fracking entails a process whereby a highly pressurized toxic mixture of sand and chemicals is released deep into the ground to access hard-to-reach fossil fuels. Evidence is mounting that this method of energy extraction is responsible for contaminating drinking water in homes near fracking sites (Fischetti 2013). Nearby residents have also reported lung problems from breathing contaminated microscopic sand particles in the air around and in their homes (Dirr 2013). Other evidence indicates that fracking-contaminated crops and livestock are finding their way into our food supply (Royte 2012), and that the seismic instability created by breaking up the underground rock has been linked to sinkholes and earthquakes (Behar 2013; Murphy 2013).

Whereas the environmental problems associated with fracking have only become known lately, concern about nuclear power has been around for a long time. In 1979, the cooling system that controlled temperatures in the reactor core at the Three Mile Island nuclear power plant in Pennsylvania malfunctioned and released radioactive coolant into the environment. While the long-term carcinogenic health effects of this accident, which was attributed to mechanical and human error, remain in dispute, it did halt the construction of new nuclear power plants in the United States, lead to the imposition of new safety regulations, and give impetus to the movement protesting nuclear power (Gray & Rosen 2003; Walker 2004).

Building state-of-the-art nuclear power facilities that maximize public safety is very expensive, and according to Christian Parenti (2009), the most pressing issue is what is happening at older facilities that are still in operation. Parenti notes that most of the plants that are currently in operation were "opened in the early 1970s and designed to operate for only 40 years" (p. 26). Yet more than half of these plants have received new licenses to stay open for another 20 years, and they are plagued by deteriorating facilities, lax maintenance, and secrecy.

We do know that about a quarter of US nuclear power plants have had documented leaks of radioactive carcinogenic water that is used to cool the reactors (Parenti 2011). The Oyster Creek plant in New Jersey, for example, was slated to close in 2009 but was granted a 20-year extension by the Nuclear Regulatory Commission in April 2009. One week later, workers at the plant discovered a leak of radioactive water, and in August a more significant leak was discovered, constituting about 7,200 gallons a day that "contained 500 times the acceptable level of radiation for drinking water" (Parenti 2009:26). The leak was caused by the deterioration of old pipes buried in a concrete wall; such pipes become brittle over time and must be routinely replaced with new ones. The pipes in question "had erroneously— or perhaps fraudulently—been listed in [the company's] paperwork as replaced" (p. 26).

An additional problem with the older facilities "is the accumulation of spent fuel rods that sit in pools onsite, next door to the reactors they once fed. Unlike the reactors, spent fuel rod pools are not housed in any sort of hardened or sealed containment structure" (Parenti 2011:9). The uranium in them is highly radioactive, and the fuel rods when exposed to air for a day or two begin to combust, giving off large amounts of cesium-137, an aggressive and long-lasting radioactive element. Once in the environment, this material is absorbed by plants and animals and the people who eat them.

Summary

This chapter on corporate crime began with an examination of the causes of corporate crime that are associated with both the internal environment and the external environment of corporations. The former included a discussion of corporate culture and the (mis)management of corporate power, while the latter included a discussion of criminogenic market structures. The remainder of the chapter focused on different forms of illegal corporate conduct. The section on corporate financial crime addressed antitrust violations and crimes of high finance and banking, including insider trading, the savings and loan scandal, and the consequences of financial deregulation. The section on corporate fraud considered the Enron scandal and similar frauds that occurred in other companies. Last, the section on corporate violence examined crimes against workers, crimes against consumers, and crimes against the environment. The discussion of crimes against workers included workplace accidents and occupationally induced disease; the discussion of crimes against consumers focused on the motor vehicle, food, pharmaceutical, and tobacco industries; and the discussion of crimes against the environment examined communities polluted by toxic waste, oil drilling, hydraulic fracturing, and nuclear power.

10

Political and Government Crime

The criminological category of political and government crime entails a broad array of offenses. For our purposes, we define **political crime** as acts committed by relatively subordinate individuals or groups in pursuit of a political or ideological goal. Often the offenders "believe they are following a higher conscience or morality that supersedes present law and society" (Hagan 1997:2). **Government crime**, on the other hand, involves acts of government officials, sometimes in pursuit of personal financial gain, but sometimes in pursuit of government policies. In this chapter we examine two general categories of political crime—terrorism and hate crimes—and two general categories of government crime—state crimes of foreign policy and corruption of government officials. Whereas political crime involves illegal acts undertaken by relatively subordinate groups or individuals, government crime involves actions of government officials.

Terrorism

Throughout history, politically disenfranchised groups have engaged in nonviolent and violent resistance as a means of political rebellion. In Chapter 5 we considered nonviolent civil disobedience. In this section we consider violence, or more specifically, the problem of terrorism.

Under the leadership of Osama bin Laden, Al-Qaida's attack on the World Trade Center and Pentagon on September 11, 2001, brought the political crime of terrorism to the forefront of the contemporary crime problem. **Terrorism** may be defined as the use or threat of violence intended to accomplish a political goal, whether it is the maintenance of the status quo or radical social change. Terrorists often target innocent people, although they generally do so to affect a government's policies or to overthrow a government altogether. One of the objectives of terrorism is to provoke a government to overreact, to break its own rules about the acceptable use of force and thereby undermine its own credibility. In the process, terrorists hope to polarize society and bring "fence-sitters" over to their side (Gorenberg 2004; Martin 2003; White 2003).

Al-Qaida

Since the 1970s, US citizens overseas have been targets of terrorism resulting from conflicts abroad, but the 1993 bombing of the World Trade Center in New York City demonstrated for the first time that terrorism could happen on America's own soil. The explosion, which left six people dead and more than 1,000 injured, shattered the public's sense of security. The World Trade Center bombing, part of a failed plot to bomb other targets as well, was the act of Islamic extremists working under the leadership of Shaikh Omar Abdul Rahman, a man with a checkered past. Rahman had been expelled from Egypt for being part of a conspiracy in the 1981 assassination of Egyptian president Anwar Sadat, who had entered into a landmark peace accord with Israel. Although Rahman was on the State Department's list of undesirables, he had been given a Central Intelligence Agency (CIA) visa to enter the country. Rahman had been working with the CIA, which had been financing and training Afghan rebels who were resisting the Soviet Union's military occupation of Afghanistan in the 1980s. This was the final decade of the **Cold War**, the diplomatic and "undeclared" military confrontation with the Soviet Union that involved proxy "hot" wars in Vietnam and elsewhere that ended with the dissolution of the Soviet Union (which reverted to Russia) in 1991. Apparently it did not occur to the CIA that Rahman might try to target the United States. Rahman received a life sentence for his role in the bombing conspiracy. The other conspirators were given sentences ranging from 25 years to life (Kinser 2006; White 2003; Wright 2006).

Few Americans at the time had ever heard of Osama bin Laden or Al-Qaida. Bin Laden, an exiled Saudi Arabian millionaire who had gone to Afghanistan to fight against the Soviets, is suspected of financing the 1993 World Trade Center bombing. In addition to the 9/11 attack, he is also believed to be responsible for the 1998 bombings of the US embassies in Kenya and Tanzania (which killed 12 Americans and nearly 300 Africans) and the 2000 bombing of the USS *Cole* during its docking in a Yemen harbor (which killed 17 sailors) (Dreyfuss 2005; Martin 2003; Wright 2006).

Al-Qaida, formed in the chaotic aftermath of the anti-Soviet resistance, recruited "Afghan Arab" veterans who were sheltered by the Taliban, a fundamentalist Islamic military regime that took control of most of the country in the latter half of the 1990s. Although the US government never recognized the Taliban as the legitimate government of Afghanistan, in the years prior to 9/11 the US State Department and some US oil companies were courting and negotiating with Taliban representatives, hoping to ensure their cooperation in the development of oil and gas pipelines in the region (Dreyfuss 2005; Martin 2003; Sperry 2003).

FURTHER EXPLORATION
September 11, 2001

In the year following the 9/11 attack, White House national security adviser and future secretary of state Condoleezza Rice made several public statements in which she claimed that it had been impossible for anyone in the Bush administration to have imagined a threat of terrorists flying planes into buildings on US soil. Later, Rice would have trouble explaining why the contents of a President's Daily Brief titled "Bin Laden Determined to Strike in the US," which had been delivered to the president a month prior to the attack, had not alerted the administration to the threat, because the brief included a reference to the hijacking of planes and "scores of ongoing FBI investigations of Al Qaeda threats, as well as reports of recent efforts by terrorist groups to carry out surveillance of the New York skyline" (Shenon 2008:238).

Be that as it may, it is also true that chief White House terrorist adviser Richard Clarke (2004) had been trying to alert the Bush administration from the moment it took office that Al-Qaida should receive prioritized attention. But the administration was too worried about dictatorial states such as Iraq to heed the warning of Clarke (and others). Both the CIA and the FBI, perhaps for lack of administration support, failed to connect the dots and fully investigate leads regarding Al-Qaida operatives within the United States, including those who were learning how to fly (but not land) planes. In a revealing exposé, Senator Bob Graham (2004) documented a dozen instances where the 9/11 plot could have been discovered and potentially foiled.

Although the Bush administration initially resisted the establishment of an official commission to investigate 9/11, it eventually relented to public pressure, especially from the families of 9/11 victims. The information the bipartisan 9/11 Commission had at its disposal was very controlled, however. The White House appointed Phillip Zelikow, a confidant of Rice and author of a national security strategy paper justifying preventive war, as executive director of the commission. Zelikow saw to it that the commission's work would not jeopardize US ties to Saudi Arabia; hence investigation of Saudi "spies," as Graham (2004) called them, who may have provided financial and logistical support to at least two of the hijackers, was thwarted. The CIA could be blamed for its mistakes, but above all Rice and other high-ranking officials, including President Bush and Vice President Dick Cheney, were to be protected from any culpability. Zelikow also tried to use the 9/11 Commission to air questionable evidence about alleged ties between Iraq and Al-Qaida (Mayer 2009; Shenon 2008).

Gus Martin describes Al-Qaida as a transnational terrorist movement, with members and supporters throughout the Muslim world, and which has as its main goals the linking of disparate "Muslim extremist groups . . . into a loose pan-Islamic revolutionary network" and the removal of "non-Muslim (especially Western) influences from Islamic regions and countries" (2003:234). It has "cells" in many different countries and communicates with members using modern technology. Most Al-Qaida cells "are small and self-sustaining and . . . [only] receive funding when activated for specific missions" (p. 235).

After the 9/11 attack, the George W. Bush administration was successful in putting together an international coalition to topple the Taliban in Afghanistan, but it also began plans to launch a preemptive war against Saddam Hussein in Iraq without international cooperation and in the face of much international opposition (Isikoff & Corn 2006). This war, which some criminologists believe was a violation of international law, was begun in March 2003. It arguably diverted valuable resources from the Afghanistan campaign and enabled bin Laden to reconstitute his base of operations on the Pakistan side of the Afghanistan-Pakistan border, until he was finally killed during the administration of Barack Obama in 2011 (Bergen 2007; Hersh 2004). Although the threat of Al-Qaida remains, the Islamic State of Iraq and Syria (ISIS), also known as the Islamic State of Iraq and the Levant (ISIL), has also emerged as a significant terrorist organization (Levant refers to the Eastern Mediterranean region) (Wood 2014).

Domestic Terrorism
The very real threat posed by Al-Qaida and ISIS has reinforced the stereotype held by many Americans that links persons of Middle Eastern descent to terrorism. Prior to 9/11, however, the greatest terrorist threat facing the United States came not from forces abroad but from those indigenous to the United States. We now turn to a discussion of terrorism as a homegrown product, examining terrorism of both the political "right" and the political "left."

Right-wing terrorism. Other than radical Islamic terrorism, many analysts believe that indigenous white-supremacist groups of the political right pose the most serious domestic terrorist threat to the United States. Few people acknowledged this threat until Timothy McVeigh detonated a rented truck filled with 4,800 pounds of explosives at the Alfred Murrah Federal Building in Oklahoma City on April 19, 1995. The bombing killed 191 men, women, and children, making it "the worst single terrorist incident ever committed" in the United States prior to 9/11 (Hagan 1997:160).

McVeigh and his accomplice, Terry Nichols, were affiliated with the contemporary **militia movement**, which overlaps with and draws members from the broader **patriot movement**, a network of individuals and groups who distrust the US government and who believe that their advocacy of the values of "individualism, an armed citizenry, and minimum interference from government" makes them "the true heirs of the ideals of the framers of the US Constitution" (Martin 2003:313). Bruce Hoffman describes the militias as paramilitary organizations "oriented toward 'survivalism,' outdoor skills, guerrilla training, and outright sedition" (1993:220). They vehemently oppose gun control and promote the stockpiling of arms and supplies in preparation for a final showdown with their enemies.

Being a militia sympathizer or a member of a militia group does not make one a terrorist, however. Many join such groups "out of a sense of powerlessness . . . [and frustration] with the rapid pace of change in the modern world" (White 2003:228). They are people who have never quite "made it," who sense that some vague and shifting "system" has let them down. Joining a militia group can make them feel important; for men, it can give them a place to ground their masculinity (Faludi 1999). Although most militia members were appalled by the Oklahoma City bombing, their paramilitary rhetoric can incite some to violence and spawn extremist sects. Small groups of armed members have broken off into separate cells without centralized leadership, feeling encouraged to act on their own in the interest of the cause: resisting the intrusion of the federal government by whatever means necessary.

The boundaries of the militia movement blur into the domain of organized hate groups. McVeigh, for example, was heavily influenced by *The Turner Diaries,* a right-wing novel written by William Pierce under the pen name Andrew MacDonald (1980). Pierce was the leader of the National Alliance, one of the most organized and well-financed neo-Nazi groups in the United States. The defining characteristic of Nazi ideology is its **anti-Semitism**—the hatred and discriminatory treatment of Jews—but neo-Nazis disdain other groups as well: racial and ethnic minorities, gays and lesbians, feminists, liberals, and people with disabilities. Through flyers, short-wave radio broadcasts, and the Internet, the National Alliance voices its opposition to these groups. In *The Turner Diaries,* a character named Earl Turner joins a violent revolutionary group that overthrows the Jewish-controlled Zionist Occupied Government (ZOG). In the book's narrative, ZOG has "outlawed gun ownership and invested human relations councils with police powers to force" racial integration and interbreeding on members of different racial groups (Hamm 1993:50–51). Turner responds by leading an elite group of combatants called "The Order" in a series of terrorist attacks. The book describes the construction and detonation of bombs and endorses blowing up government buildings, power stations, fuel depots, industrial plants, missile silos, and synagogues, as well as assassinating government officials, liberal media figures, Jews, and other racial/ethnic minorities (Martin 2003; Simi & Futrell 2010).

To be sure, not all militia members are hate-mongers, but many are. Randy Weaver, for instance, was a white separatist and follower of Christian Identity, an anti-Semitic/racist movement derived from a nineteenth-century ideology known as Anglo-Israelism. Christian Identity preaches that white Europeans are the descendants of the lost tribes of Israel and that they have been chosen by God to lead the Aryan nations against the Satanic Jews and their allies. Christian Identity adherents believe in the inevitability of a global race war that only whites will survive. In 1992, Weaver sold an illegal firearm to undercover agents from the Bureau of Alcohol,

Tobacco, and Firearms. He resisted arrest, fled, and holed up with his family in his mountain cabin near Ruby Ridge, Idaho. A federal marshal and Weaver's 14-year-old son were both killed in the shootout that ensued. The next day, before Weaver surrendered, an FBI marksman shot and killed Weaver's pregnant wife (Hagan 1997; Simi & Futrell 2010; White 2003).

Ruby Ridge has become one of the rallying cries of the militant right wing, as has the incident near Waco, Texas, involving David Koresh's Branch Davidian religious sect. In fact, Timothy McVeigh considered the Oklahoma bombing to be retaliation for what happened at Waco, and he planned the bombing to occur two years to the day following the FBI raid of the Branch Davidians' Waco compound (Hagan 1997). The Waco raid stemmed from federal authorities' concern about the huge stockpile of illegal weapons that Koresh was storing in the compound. As agents from the Bureau of Alcohol, Tobacco, and Firearms tried to serve a search warrant, they were met with a hail of gunfire that killed four agents and wounded several others. After a three-month standoff, the FBI stormed the compound, not anticipating that Koresh and his followers would set a suicide-

FURTHER EXPLORATION
Violence Against Abortion Clinics and Doctors

Another movement of the political right, the anti-abortion "pro-life" movement, has also been implicated in terrorism (White 2003). Most of the activism of pro-life advocates, who believe that even legal acts of abortion are murder, has involved civil disobedience, with 40,000 arrests associated with Operation Rescue's campaign of picketing and blocking entrances to abortion clinics in the early 1990s. But the mainstream pro-life movement has also spawned an extremist fringe, and bombings and arsons have become part of the anti-abortion campaign. "Pro-choice" abortion rights advocates and physicians who are willing to conduct abortions have been stalked, harassed, threatened with death, and killed. "Wanted" posters with doctors' names and addresses have even been posted on Internet websites, with names crossed off when doctors are killed (Dodge 1999). In one case, an anti-abortion priest dubbed the murders "justifiable homicide" (quoted in Hagan 1997:103). In another case, a clergyman blamed the violence of anti-abortionists on a new law against blocking clinic access, as these anti-abortionists were now "being forced into" killing (quoted in Gegax & Clemetson 1998:34).

In 2009, George Tiller, one of only a few doctors in the country who performed late-term abortions (for reasons related to the health of pregnant women), was shot to death by an anti-abortion extremist while attending church. On two earlier occasions, his clinic had been bombed and he had been shot and wounded, before the violence directed against him finally took his life (Stumpe & Davey 2009).

fire that would kill more than 70 men, women, and children. Many people blame the FBI for its inability to resolve the incident without the loss of these lives, with the National Rifle Association bemoaning that "not too long ago, it was unthinkable for federal agents wearing Nazi bucket helmets and black storm trooper uniforms to attack law-abiding citizens. Not today" (cited in Russakoff & Kovaleski 1998:114). This is what prompted McVeigh to take his revenge. Although Koresh "had nothing to do with the right-wing movement, he had the right formula: guns, a survivalist compound, and . . . messianic illusions" about saving the world from impending doom (White 2003:225). McVeigh received the death penalty and Nichols a life sentence for their crime.

Active militia and patriot groups were on the decline during the George W. Bush administration, but reached a new high during the Obama administration. The Southern Poverty Law Center (2014), which tracks these groups, found that they increased in number from a low of 137 in 2007 to an unprecedented 1,360 in 2012. According to Michael Waltman, an expert on hate crimes, these groups learned that they could amplify their antigovernment message by using Obama as a rallying point and constructing him "as an alien, not of this country, insufficiently American" (quoted in Gellman 2010:28). Recent violent episodes involving individuals affiliated with these and other hate groups include the killing of a security guard at the US Holocaust Memorial Museum in 2009 and the assassination of Colorado's chief of prisons in 2013. Numerous other violent plots have been thwarted by law enforcement.

Left-wing terrorism. Arguably the high point of left-wing terrorism in the United States was the 1960s and early 1970s, when violent groups emerged from the legal protests and civil disobedience of the anti–Vietnam War and civil rights movements of that era. The Weather Underground Organization, for example, announced in 1969: "Kids know that the lines are drawn; revolution is touching all of our lives. Tens of thousands have learned that protest and marches don't do it. Revolutionary violence is the only way" (cited in Evans 1983:255). The Weather Underground Organization sought to promote chaos through violence in order to catalyze social upheaval and topple the capitalist system. In the early 1970s, the organization took credit for a score of bombings. Although it faded from the scene after that, some former members were involved in incidents as late as the 1980s (Hagan 1997; White 2003).

Since the 1970s, the anti–nuclear power and environmental movements of the political left have used civil disobedience to promote their causes. In 1976, the Clamshell Alliance organized a sit-in of more than 1,400 people at the nuclear construction site in Seabrook, New Hampshire. This demonstration is credited with launching the anti–nuclear power movement in the United States (Dwyer 1983). Over the years, radical environmentalists have chained themselves to trees and logging equipment to prevent the destruction of forests, with some camping out in treetop perches "defying anyone to cut the tree down with them in it" (Gwartney 1998:61). Anti-technology environmentalist Theodore Kaczynski, however, was quite clearly a terrorist. Dubbed "The Unabomber," Kaczynski, who was sentenced to life in prison for his crimes, killed three people and wounded 23 others during nearly two decades of activity that preceded his capture in 1996. In a 35,000-word manifesto that was published (under threat of violence by Kaczynski) in the *Washington Post* and *New York Times* in 1995, Kaczynski wrote:

> The Industrial Revolution and its consequences have been a disaster for the human race. . . . They have destabilized society, have made life unfulfilling, have subjected human beings to indignities, have led to widespread psychological suffering . . . and have inflicted severe damage on the natural world. . . . The positive ideal that we propose is Nature . . . WILD nature: those aspects of the functioning of the Earth and its living things that are independent of human management and free of human interference and control. . . . With regard to revolutionary strategy, the only points on which we absolutely insist are that the single overriding goal must be the elimination of modern technology. (cited in *US News & World Report* 1996b:35)

The environmental philosophy from which Kaczynski derived his worldview is sometimes referred to as **deep ecology**, the belief that human beings are simply "ordinary member[s] of the biological community, no more important than" any other living creature (Eagan 1996:3). **Ecoterrorism**, of which Kaczynski is arguably the most extreme case, is a movement of people who advocate the use of violence and the willful destruction of property in order to "terminate, prevent, or minimize human alteration to any part of the natural environment or its animal species" (Nilson & Burke 2002:1). Some ecoterrorist groups, which are composed primarily of individuals from middle-class backgrounds, formed as offshoots of mainstream environmental groups like Greenpeace, which strongly disapprove of ecoterrorist tactics. The Sea Shepherd Conservation Society, for instance, established by former Greenpeace members, has sunk several whaling ships and rammed about a dozen other vessels over the years.

Earth First!, another ecoterrorist group, was formed for the explicit purpose of sharpening the conflict between the mainstream and radical environmental movements. Although Earth First!ers also engage in acts of civil disobedience, their favorite tactic is to sabotage "logging equipment by inserting spikes into trees to damage saws, or pouring foreign substances into the fuel tanks of logging equipment" (Nilson & Burke 2002:3).

Radicals in the left-wing animal rights movement have also been involved in ecoterrorism (Hagan 1997). Most of these groups engage in peaceful protests against the hunting of deer; the wearing of fur; and the maiming, torturing, and killing of animals in laboratory experiments that test nonessential consumer items such as cosmetics and household cleaning products for human safety. But some activists have vandalized laboratories, freed animals, and thrown red paint (symbolizing blood) on persons wearing fur coats. In 1997, members of the Animal Liberation Front were responsible for the bombing of offices and feed trucks belonging to a Utah fur breeders' agricultural cooperative, causing about $1 million in property damage. The following year, members of the Earth Liberation Front set fire to three buildings and four chairlifts at a Colorado ski resort, damaging property worth about $12 million. The Earth Liberation Front admitted to "starting the fires on behalf of the lynx," which they believed were in danger of losing their natural habitat due to the expansion of the resort (Nilson & Burke 2002:4). In 2003, the Earth Liberation Front also took credit for setting fire to 20 Hummer vehicles worth about $50,000 apiece at a southern California dealership to protest what members perceived as a wasteful extravagance (Madigan 2003). This arson was but one of a series of vandalisms against SUV dealerships that damaged about 50 other vehicles in the area as well. The Earth Liberation Front also claimed responsibility for a fire that destroyed some 1,500 partially built apartments, with damages estimated at $50 million (Martin 2003; Tamaki et al. 2003).

Hate Crimes and Hate Groups

We previously noted the blurred boundaries between right-wing domestic terrorism and organized hate groups. Here we explore further the phenomenon of crimes motivated by hate. **Hate crimes** are political crimes insofar as they involve attempts to preserve or assert the dominance of one group over another. Although history is replete with crimes motivated by hate, since the 1980s hate crimes have been perceived as a distinct form of criminality. Three well-publicized incidents stand out in the emergence of this perception. In 1984, Alan Berg, an outspoken Jewish radio talk show host in Denver, Colorado, was machine-gunned to death by white supremacists who called themselves "The Order" (after *The Turner Diaries* [MacDonald 1980]). Two years later, three black men were chased onto a highway by a mob of whites after the men's car broke down in the Howard Beach area of New York City. One of the black men was killed by the oncoming traffic. Right-wing hate groups saluted the actions of the Howard Beach mob. More than a decade later, in 1998, a middle-age black man, James Byrd, was severely beaten, chained to a truck by his ankles, and dragged to his death by three white men in Jasper, Texas, leaving a trail of blood a mile long. Police found a lighter with white-supremacist symbols at the scene of the crime (Hamm 1993; Van Boven & Gesalman 1998).

Data on Hate Crimes

In 1990, the Hate Crime Statistics Act authorized the federal government to collect hate crime data based on race, ethnicity, religion, and sexual orientation. This legislation was in large part the product of a political alliance that was formed among African-American, Japanese-American, Jewish, gay, and lesbian groups. In 1994, subsequent legislation added crimes based on disability to the list generated under the Hate Crime Statistics Act. Feminists argued that rape and battering against women should be counted as hate crimes, too, but they were unable to convince legislators to include gender-based crimes. Those who opposed this policy thought the addition of gender would make the concept of hate crime too broad, since crimes against women are so pervasive in society. Currently, most states and the District of Columbia report hate crime data to the federal government and have laws covering such crimes. Some laws include special categories of offenses, whiie others simply enhance penalties for existing crimes (Jacobs & Potter 1998; Jenness 1999).

FURTHER EXPLORATION
The Matthew Shepard and Brandon Teena Murders

Russell Henderson and Aaron McKinney, high school dropouts who grew up hard and poor, were reviled for being "losers" in the status-obsessed college town of Laramie, Wyoming. Henderson, who had been battered by his mother's boyfriends, and McKinney, whose mother was known to lock him in the basement, were bullied by everyone they knew. On one fateful night in 1998, Henderson and McKinney finished a pitcher of beer at a local bar and began groping in their pockets to come up with the $5.50 they owed. A petite and graceful young man at the end of the bar offered to help. Matthew Shepard, with his bleached hair, stylish clothes, and shiny patent leather shoes, appeared to Henderson and McKinney to be making a "pass" by offering to pay for their drinks (Minkowitz 1999).

Shepard told Henderson and McKinney that he was gay, and the two boys played along, inviting Shepard to come with them to McKinney's place so they could get to know each other better. But once inside McKinney's truck, McKinney pulled out a gun and smashed its butt into Shepard's head. The boys laughed as they beat their victim again and again with the gun and fists. As Shepard pleaded for his life, they drove him out to a field, tied him to a fence, and left him to die.

Shepard's death galvanized national outrage at hate crimes against gays and lesbians. The 1993 murder of Brandon Teena, memorialized in the 1999 film *Boys Don't Cry,* also raised public consciousness about hate crimes against transgendered people. Brandon Teena, born Teena Brandon, had been living as a man. Two friends of a young woman with whom he was sexually involved forced him to reveal that he had female genitals and then beat and raped him. Several days later they returned to murder him (Wilchins 2003).

At its inception, *hate crime* was an umbrella term developed by a diverse set of political activists to establish a common cause. Although many crimes are motivated by one person's hatred of another, the distinguishing characteristic of a hate crime is the bias or prejudice that an offender holds toward *all* members of another group, with the purpose of the crime being not just to victimize an individual but also to send a message to others. Thus, hate crimes are political insofar as they are intended to marginalize and instill fear among all members of a group, leaving victims and others like them with a pervasive sense of vulnerability. From the offenders' perspective, the victims are interchangeable, because anyone fitting the description can become a suitable target (Martin 1995).

Data collection on hate crimes suffers from the same limitations, such as victim underreporting, as do the *Uniform Crime Reports* (see Chapter 2). Immigrants, for example, may fail to report victimization because they do not speak fluent English or because they come from cultures where victimization brings shame to their families. Undocumented workers who are victimized may face deportation if they go to the police. And gay and lesbian people may refrain from reporting because they fear negative repercussions, such as job loss, rejection by family and friends, and hostile reactions from police and other criminal justice officials. Police may also have trouble determining whether the crime in question was, in fact, a hate crime—that is, whether it was motivated by bias rather than some other factor. The offender and victim may offer different accounts of what transpired, and expressions of bias that did not instigate the crime may emerge during or after the incident (Herek & Berrill 1992; Martin 1995).

With these caveats in mind, Table 10.1 presents data on hate crime incidents by bias motivation for 2012. *Race bias* constituted the most common type of hate crime (48.3 percent), with anti-black bias accounting for 65 percent of the race incidents. *Sexual orientation bias* (19.6 percent) and *religion bias* (19.0 percent) constituted the next largest categories, with anti-Jewish bias accounting for 61 percent of the religious incidents and anti–male homosexual bias accounting for 53 percent of the sexual

Table 10.1 Hate Crime Incidents by Bias Motivation (2012)

	Incidents[a]	Percentage
Race	2,797	48.3
Sexual orientation	1,135	19.6
Religion	1,099	19.0
Ethnicity/national origin	667	11.5
Disability	92	1.6
Total	5,790	100.0

Source: Federal Bureau of Investigation 2012, tab. 1.

Note: a. An incident may include multiple offenses, although only 6 out of 5,796 cases were recorded as such.

orientation incidents. *Ethnicity/national origin bias* constituted 11.5 percent, with anti-Hispanic bias accounting for 58 percent of incidents. And *disability bias* accounted for 1.6 percent of incidents, with the anti–mental disability bias accounting for 80 percent of these.

Among hate crime incidents, crimes against persons constituted 56 percent of the incidents overall, with the most common being simple assault (23 percent of all incidents) and intimidation, meaning threatening words or conduct that instill in the victim a reasonable fear of bodily harm (21 percent of all incidents). The most common nonviolent crime was destruction, damage, or vandalism of property (33 percent of all incidents).

Organized Hate Groups

Only a small proportion of hate crimes are committed by members of organized hate groups, but there are hundreds of these groups that remain active in the United States (Gellman 2010; Levin & McDevitt 1999). The Ku Klux Klan (KKK), whose name derives from the Greek word *kuclos* (meaning "circle"), is perhaps the oldest hate group in the country. Founded by a group of Confederate Army veterans in Tennessee after the Civil War, the KKK was a secret society of men who engaged in public demonstrations and overt intimidation to keep blacks and their white sympathizers (especially Jews) in their place. Known for their white robes and hoods and their cross-burning displays, KKK members whipped, tortured, and killed the people they opposed (Hamm 1993; Martin 2003).

Currently the KKK is but a shadow of its former self, but as we have suggested, it has been supplanted by a virulent mix of contemporary hate groups, including skinheads. The **skinhead movement** originated in Great Britain in the early 1970s among angry, anti-immigrant, working-class youths united by white-power rock music containing violent and racist lyrics. Clark Martell is credited with forming the first skinhead group in the United States. In 1979, this 19-year-old high school dropout received a four-year prison sentence for arson as a result of torching the house of a Latino family in Chicago. In prison he read Adolf Hitler's *Mein Kampf* (My Struggle), and upon his release he joined the Chicago-based American Nazi Party. Martell became interested in white-power rock music and formed his own band. Paraphrasing a passage from *Mein Kampf,* he declared: "Our heads are shaved for battle. Skinheads of America, like the dynamic skinheads in Europe, are working-class Aryan youth. We oppose the capitalist and communist scum that are destroying our Aryan race. The parasitic Jewish race is at the heart of our problem" (quoted in Hamm 1993:39).

Most skinhead groups are organized like other youth gangs, with local names that evolve over time (see Chapter 7). In his research, Mark Hamm (1993) found that not all skinhead youths shave their heads, and most are drawn into the skinhead subculture through peer pressure and a common interest in heavy drinking. These youths are proud of their working-class heritage but are concerned about their prospects of obtaining or maintaining blue-collar employment. The hateful lyrics of white-power rock expose them to the ideology necessary to become "true believers." Jews and racial/ethnic minorities are portrayed in this music "as agents in a conspiracy to threaten the well-being of the average blue-collar worker" (p. 211). This message is conveyed with such powerful emotion that the youths begin linking the musical messages to their concerns about employment, and they become "transformed into adherents of a bizarre form of Nazism." They acquire a sense of participating in something larger than themselves; and once drawn into the subculture, they are exposed to the underground literature and electronic network of adult hate groups (Levin 2002; Simi & Futrell 2010).

The diffusion of hate groups around the country makes detection, infiltration, and control difficult for law enforcement. Another impediment is their advocacy of mainstream conservative issues, which gives them an aura of legitimacy. But even when they do not openly advocate violence, they provide the ideological fervor that provokes some extremists to action. Such individuals become even more dangerous when they believe they are on a mission from God. Christian Identity, a movement noted earlier, is just one of several corrupt permutations of Christian belief that have emerged among the militant right-wingers who use "free-wheeling fundamentalism and violent passages of Christian scripture quoted out of context" to justify their cause (White 2003:228).

State Crimes of Foreign Policy

State crimes are crimes carried out by government officials on behalf of the state or a state agency aimed at maintaining social order or fomenting dissent, as the case may be. In the area of foreign policy, these crimes entail the violation of US law, international law, or the law of the affected nation. US officials have committed these crimes with the objective of keeping foreign markets open to US corporations at all costs (Berger 2011; Friedrichs 2007; Kramer & Michalowski 2005).

Overthrow of Foreign Governments

One type of state crime that has been perpetrated by the United States entails the overthrow of democratically elected foreign governments. The first action of this nature in the post–World War II era took place in Iran in 1953. Here the CIA fomented and funded a successful coup d'état that led to the demise of the democratically elected government headed by Prime Minister Mohammed Mossadegh, who was once dubbed by *Time* magazine as the "Iranian George Washington." Under Mossadegh's leadership, the Iranians had decided to nationalize the oil industry, which was controlled by the British. **Nationalization** refers to the process by which a government assumes domestic control of and/or redistributes ownership of a nation's industries or natural resources, with the purported intent of benefiting the entire nation rather than foreign corporate interests. This process may (but does not always) involve compensation to corporations for the appropriation of their businesses (Kinser 2006).

Mossadegh intended to compensate the Anglo-Iranian Oil Company, a corporation owned principally by the British, which "had held a monopoly on the extraction, refining, and sale of Iranian oil" since 1901 (Kinser 2006:117). At that time, less than 16 percent of the company's profits were paid to Iran, a practice Mossadegh intended to change. Officials in the US administration of President Dwight Eisenhower were concerned that this policy did not bode well for US oil interests in the region. To further that end, the administration decided to employ the CIA. Established by the National Security Act of 1947, the CIA was authorized to gather intelligence about perceived foreign threats to national security and also to engage in covert activities to oppose such threats (Kinser 2006; Moyers 1988).

The method of regime change in Iran, which was called Operation Ajax, employed both propaganda and violence. Journalists, publishers, Islamic clergy, and other opinion leaders were bribed to create a climate of public hostility and distrust toward Mossadegh and his government. Demonstrators were paid to flood the streets of Iran's capitol, Tehran, and converge on parliament to demand Mossadegh's ouster. Gangs of street thugs started riots as the city descended into violence. According to the plan, order would be restored by turning the country back to its ruling monarch, Mohammad Reza Pahlavi, the Shah of Iran, whose influence had been dramatically curtailed under Mossadegh. The Shah's subsequent rule, which lasted for a quarter century, was a brutal dictatorship, until he was overthrown, too, this time by an anti-American Islamic revolution in 1979 (Kinser 2006; Moyers 1988). The consequence of this episode in the history of relations between the United States and Iran was aptly noted by an Iranian diplomat 50 years after the coup: "The 1953 coup and its consequences [were] the starting point for the political alignments in today's Middle East and inner Asia. With hindsight, can anyone say that the Islamic Revolution of 1979 was inevitable? Or did it only become so once the [democratic] aspirations of the Iranian people were temporarily expunged in 1953?" (quoted in Kinser 2006:203).

A year after the Iranian coup, the CIA also engineered the overthrow of Jacob Arbenz Guzmán, the democratically elected president of Guatemala. Guzmán had embarked on an ambitious reform program to redistribute land that was held by a small number of landowners to the impoverished peasantry (less than 3 percent of the landowners controlled more than 70 percent of the land). This action was a direct challenge to the United Fruit Company, a US corporation that owned about one-fifth of Guatemala's arable land, less than 15 percent of which it cultivated. The company persuaded the US government that it could not let Guzmán's reforms stand (Kinser 2006).

In 1959, Fidel Castro took power in Cuba after leading a successful revolution against his dictatorial predecessor, Fulgencio Batista. As Batista had been an ally of the United States, Castro turned to the Soviet Union for military and economic aid and proceeded to nationalize US businesses in Cuba. During the Eisenhower administration, the US government devised a plan to deploy about 1,500 CIA-trained Cuban exiles, with support of US ground troops and planes, to invade the Bay of Pigs and overthrow the Castro government (Kinser 2006; Summers 2000).

After John Kennedy was elected president in 1960, he inherited the anti-Cuban operation. Kennedy reluctantly approved a revised plan that would not involve direct intervention of US troops, expecting the Cuban people to join with the invaders in the revolution. Only supportive air strikes would be forthcoming, provided the invaders could secure a beachhead from which to launch the operation. The invasion took place in April 1961, about four months after Kennedy took office. When Castro's forces launched a successful counteroffensive, the invaders were pinned down at the beach. The CIA and US military thought Kennedy would relent and fully commit US troops and planes. But the president, concerned about a confrontation with the Soviet Union, did not; and the invaders were left defenseless and forced to surrender (Kinser 2006; Summers 2000).

Chile was another Latin American democracy that was dismantled by the US government. In the late 1960s, the CIA and private US corporations funneled millions of dollars into Chile to try to block the election of presidential candidate Salvadore Allende, who had been campaigning on a platform of nationalizing foreign industries, particularly the communication and mining holdings of US corporations. After Allende was elected in 1970, the US government tried to destabilize the Chilean economy by withholding supplies necessary for Chilean industries, pressuring world financial institutions to deny Chile loans, and organizing an international boycott of Chilean products. The CIA supported military leaders who opposed Allende and encouraged them to assassinate General René Schneider, a prominent military figure who opposed military interference in government policies. General Schneider was killed in 1970, and three years later the Allende government was overthrown and Allende was killed too. Thousands of pro-Allende Chileans were arrested, tortured, and murdered or exiled under the dictatorship of General Augusto Pinochet, who came to power after the coup. A similar story has been repeated elsewhere in Latin America and other developing countries: military dictators backed by the US government have ruled through fear, intimidation, and brutality; and government "death squads," some financed or trained by the CIA, have kidnapped, tortured, and murdered those who threaten these US-backed regimes (Kinser 2006; Klein 2007; Summers 2000).

FURTHER EXPLORATION
The Kennedy Assassination

We have noted attempts by the US government to subvert the democratic process in foreign countries. These events are facts of the historical record. But there are other incidents that remain more of a mystery, and attempts to "connect the dots" are often disparagingly dismissed as the ravings of crank "conspiracy theorists" (deHaven-Smith 2010).

Bill Moyers, a respected journalist, is no crank, and he notes that the actions of the US government are made "more chilling" by the assassination of President John Kennedy in Dallas, Texas, in November 1963 (1988:44). No event in US history has been shrouded in more myth and conjecture than this assassination. The Warren Commission, appointed by President Lyndon Johnson and headed by US Supreme Court justice Earl Warren, concluded in 1963 that assassin Lee Harvey Oswald acted alone. Oswald, a former marine who became involved in US intelligence, is believed by some to have been a Soviet defector, by others to have been a double agent. He lived only two days from the time he was arrested until he was shot by Jack Ruby, a night-club owner, while he was being transferred from the city jail to the county jail.

Lamar Waldron and Thom Hartmann (2008) are among those who believe that Oswald, who moved in the shadowy circles of the US government, was a patsy for an assassination plot involving organized crime, a view that finds support in an investigation of the House Select Committee on Assassinations (Blakey & Billing 1981). Waldron and Hartmann muster substantially more evidence than was available to Congress, including interviews with key players and previously classified information that implicate Mafia bosses Santo Trafficante, Johnny Rosselli, and especially Carlos Marcello, the godfather of New Orleans who controlled criminal operations in Louisiana and Texas. These men, among other criminal associates, were furious with the president and his brother Robert Kennedy, both of whom had been investigating organized crime even before coming to the White House, when John was a senator and Robert was a senatorial aid. When President Kennedy appointed his brother as attorney general, the Mafia bosses had reason to feel concerned. In fact, in 1961 Robert Kennedy had succeeded in deporting Marcello, who was born in Tunisia, to Central America. Marcello managed to reenter the United States, but he was under prosecution by the Justice Department at the time of the assassination. Waldron and Hartmann note that Jack Ruby had ties to organized crime as well, citing evidence that he was tasked with eliminating Oswald, so Oswald could not reveal what he knew.

Waldron and Hartmann believe the cover-up may have been related to the government's interest in keeping the hitherto mentioned anti-Cuban operation under wraps, which included the enlistment of organized crime in CIA plots to assassinate Castro. The Mafia had an allied interest in overthrowing Castro, because the Cuban dictator had been closing down their casino gambling operations that had flourished in Havana prior to the Castro revolution.

continues

continued

Having penetrated the US intelligence apparatus, Waldron and Hartmann argue, Mafia bosses were also in a position to know about the Kennedys' secret plan for a second invasion attempt of Cuba in December 1963. Waldron and Hartmann provide evidence of a cover-up in which information was withheld from the Warren Commission in order to conceal this plan, noting that Robert Kennedy, who also was assassinated under suspicious circumstances in 1968, was involved in this cover-up too.

To be sure, the Warren Commission's account that posits Oswald as the lone assassin has its staunch defenders, but much to their chagrin, national polls consistently find that 70 to 80 percent of Americans have doubts about this version of the events (Bugliosi 2007). At a minimum, it is clear that the Warren Commission did not investigate all leads. And so suspicions linger and, as Moyers notes, accusations "persist of a dark, unsolved conspiracy behind [Kennedy's] murder. You can dismiss them, as many of us do, but since we know now what our secret government planned for [others], the possibility remains: once we decide that anything goes, anything can come home to haunt us" (1988:44).

The Vietnam War

Of all the foreign policy events thus far reviewed, US involvement in Vietnam was arguably the most controversial. Vietnam, a French colony since the nineteenth century, had been occupied by the Japanese during World War II. After Japan surrendered in 1945, popular Vietnam leader Ho Chi Minh, an avowed Communist, declared his country's independence (Kinser 2006).

Although the French, with US backing, were determined to resume their control after World War II, Vietnamese guerrilla fighters forced them to capitulate. The French ended their rule over Vietnam in 1954, and by international agreement the country was to be divided between North Vietnam and South Vietnam for two years, after which time an election would be held to choose the leader of a united country. By all accounts, Ho was expected to win the election (Ehrlich & Goldsmith 2009; Kinser 2006).

An independent Vietnam in the midst of the Cold War was not a prospect the US government would easily abide. To counter Ho's leadership in North Vietnam, the US installed Ngo Dinh Diem, a devout Catholic and staunch anti-Communist, as prime minister of South Vietnam. When Ngo and the United States refused to hold the promised 1956 election, tensions between the South and the North mounted. In 1960, the North Vietnamese, known as the Vietcong, launched a guerrilla military campaign aimed at "the elimination of the US imperialists and the Ngo Dinh Diem clique" (quoted in Kinser 2006:154).

FURTHER EXPLORATION
Watergate

Early in the morning of June 17, 1972, five men dressed in business suits entered the headquarters of the Democratic National Committee at the Watergate hotel and office complex in Washington, DC. They were there to check on malfunctioning electronic surveillance equipment they had planted on an earlier trip in order to spy on the Democratic Party. This time they were discovered by the night watchman, who called the police. The burglars, it turned out, were under the employ of President Richard Nixon's reelection campaign, the Committee for the Reelection of the President, dubbed CREEP. They were all former CIA operatives, four of whom were Cuban exiles who had been involved in the anti-Castro campaign.

Nixon assured the American public that the matter was under investigation by the proper authorities and that he knew nothing about what had transpired. He did not anticipate that two years later he would be forced to publicly reveal transcripts of tape-recorded White House conversations and admit that "portions of the tapes . . . are at variance with certain of my previous statements" (quoted in Miller 1974:29).

Even prior to the discovery of the tapes, journalists investigating the burglary—especially Bob Woodward and Carl Bernstein of the *Washington Post*—had made headway in unraveling the case. The press reported that a $25,000 check from Nixon's campaign fund had been deposited in the bank account of one of the Watergate burglars and that the White House had tried to involve the FBI and CIA in a cover-up that linked CREEP officials to the crime. The press also reported that Nixon aides had ordered a burglary of the office of Defense Department analyst Daniel Ellsberg's psychiatrist in an effort to discredit Ellsberg. In 1971, Ellsberg had leaked classified documents known as the Pentagon Papers to the press, revealing how government officials—both Republicans and Democrats—had deceived both Congress and the public about their rationale and plans to escalate the Vietnam War (Bernstein & Woodward 1974; Summers 2000).

The infamous tapes were not discovered until the Senate Select Committee on Presidential Campaign Activities began investigating the case in May 1973 and after White House presidential counsel John Dean had testified about the role he and others (including Nixon) had played in the cover-up. Both the Senate committee and the special prosecutor who was appointed by the Department of Justice asked Nixon to turn over the tapes. The president refused and the dispute moved through the courts. Eventually, in July 1974, the US Supreme Court forced Nixon's hand. The excerpt from the tapes that proved most damaging at the time was a conversation that took place just six days after the Watergate burglary between Nixon and his chief of staff, H. R. "Bob" Haldeman. In this conversation Nixon said: "Now, on the . . . Democratic break-in thing, we're back in the problem area because the FBI is not under control . . . because they've been able to trace the money . . . through the bank sources. . . . [This is going] in some directions we don't want it to go. . . . [T]he only way to solve this . . . is for us to have [deputy CIA director

continues

continued

Vernon] Walters call [acting FBI director L. Patrick] Gray and just say 'Stay to hell out of this, . . . we don't want you to go any further'" (quoted in Miller 1974:26–27). The justification Nixon offered was that to do so would reveal "the whole Bay of Pigs thing."

After transcripts of the tapes were released, the House Judiciary Committee recommended that Nixon be impeached for obstruction of justice, abuse of presidential powers, and illegal withholding of evidence from Congress. When even Republican leaders encouraged Nixon to step down, he reluctantly resigned from office, on August 9, 1974. Vice President Gerald Ford became president, and he pardoned Nixon a month later for all crimes that Nixon *might* have committed and for which Nixon *might* have otherwise been prosecuted (Summers 2000).

Although it was the burglary of the Watergate hotel that initially sparked the scandal, the term **Watergate** is now used to refer to a larger cluster of crimes and abuses of government power, including bribery of the Watergate defendants, other burglaries and illegal wiretappings, tax audits of political foes, dissemination of false and defamatory stories about political rivals, solicitation of campaign contributions in exchange for favors, and appropriation of campaign funds for private use. In the end, a number of White House officials and campaign aides received prison sentences for their crimes, and Nixon was forever tarnished in the eyes of history (Rosoff et al. 2007; Summers 2000).

Ngo was an unpopular leader, even in South Vietnam. As a member of a religious group that represented only 10 percent of the country's population, he lacked a natural following; and his regime was known for cronyism and corruption. He survived two early coup attempts only with the help of CIA money used to bribe dissident leaders, and his increasing reliance on US support only undermined his popularity further (Kinser 2006).

During the Kennedy administration, between 1961 and 1963, US troops under the guise of military "advisers" launched ground and air attacks against the Vietcong. But with the Vietcong establishing control of 20 percent of South Vietnam, the United States faced a decision: Should it draw down the number of troops and withdraw, or should it further escalate its military involvement? The United States, as we now know, chose escalation (Kinser 2006).

Back in Washington, DC, the Kennedy administration decided to replace the unpopular Ngo with a more effective military leader: General Duong Van Minh. Ngo was ousted and killed, but Duong held power for just three months before he, too, was overthrown in another coup, which was followed by a succession of military strongmen who ruled South Vietnam by force while the United States sent in more troops—more than

500,000 by the mid-1960s—in a war that lasted until 1975 and cost the lives of more than 58,000 US troops and more than one million Vietnamese (Douglass 2008; Kinser 2006).

A key event in the escalation of the Vietnam War, which the Vietnamese call the American War, was the passage of the Gulf of Tonkin Resolution in the summer of 1964, which gave President Lyndon Johnson congressional authorization to commence open warfare against North Vietnam. Kennedy, before his assassination in November 1963, had been reluctant to escalate the war. Johnson, on the other hand, was not. He firmly believed in the **domino theory** of Communist aggression; if the Communists were allowed to take over the South, he thought, they would soon push the war to the beaches of Hawaii (Douglass 2008; Kinser 2006).

Prior to the passage of the Gulf of Tonkin Resolution, the US Navy had been deploying destroyers on intelligence-gathering missions off the coast of Vietnam in the Gulf of Tonkin, outside of international waters. These operations were conducted in conjunction with secretive and "undeclared" US and South Vietnamese military strikes against the Vietcong in the area. On August 2, 1964, a Vietcong patrol consisting of three Soviet-built motor torpedo boats confronted the USS *Maddox,* a destroyer that had been part of these operations, in international waters. As the United States dispatched the USS *Turner Joy* destroyer and fighter jets to the area, the captain of the *Maddox* instructed his gun crews to fire three warning shots if the Vietcong came within 10,000 yards of the ship. When the warning shots were fired, the Vietcong launched three torpedoes, which missed their mark, but they did hit the *Maddox* with a round of fire from deck guns. The *Maddox* and fighter jets then turned back the Vietcong, damaging two of the motor torpedo boats and destroying the other (Hickman 2010; Marolda 2010).

Two days later, with the *Maddox* and *Turner Joy* still cruising the area, the *Maddox* picked up a series of radar and sonar signals that suggested another attack. The ship took some evasive maneuvers and fired on the radar targets. When the captain of the *Maddox* reported the incident to the top command, he noted that no actual visual sightings of the Vietcong had been made and that the signals the *Maddox* had received may have been caused by the turbulent weather conditions in the area. In fact, the purported attack was a false alarm; no second attack had taken place. Nonetheless, the propaganda value of the incident was immense, enabling Johnson to garner congressional and public support for passage of the Gulf of Tonkin Resolution and launching a new phase in America's long and costly war (Cohen & Solomon 1994; Hickman 2010; Marolda 2010).

The Iran-Contra Scandal

In the aftermath of Watergate, the US Congress undertook investigations of the CIA and set up mechanisms that allowed for more congressional oversight of the agency. Jimmy Carter, who assumed the presidency in 1977, appointed Admiral Stansfield Turner to direct the agency; and when Turner reduced the number of agents in the covert-operations section from 1,200 to 400, many in the CIA were displeased. They did not consider themselves dispensable. Better to have their old boss, George H. W. Bush—who had served as CIA director during the year prior to Carter's taking office—back at the helm. The election of President Ronald Reagan and Vice President Bush in November 1980 was welcomed by most everyone in the CIA (Chambliss 1988; Mayer 2009).

The most significant cluster of state crimes during the Reagan adminis-tration is known as the **Iran-Contra scandal**. The two elements of this scandal—the Iran component and the Contra component—initially repre-sented two separate foreign policy operations. Iran, as noted earlier, experi-enced an Islamic revolution that replaced the regime that had been installed and supported by the United States back in 1953. In November 1979, anti-American forces seized the US embassy in Tehran, taking hostage more than 50 Americans, who were not released until just after Reagan was inau-gurated on January 1981.

The hostage crisis had been a major problem for the Carter administra-tion. Had Carter been able to pull off an "October surprise" just before the election, he would have had a better chance of winning. Former Carter administration official Gary Sick (1991), among others, believes a deal may have been struck between the Reagan-Bush campaign and representatives of the Iranian government to delay the release of the hostages. There is evi-dence that William Casey, the Reagan-Bush campaign director who later headed the CIA, had met with Iranian arms dealers who had contacts in the Iranian government. Some also allege that the Reagan-Bush campaign had informants within the US military-intelligence community who provided information about US aircraft movements related to the hostage crisis. And some believe that someone associated with the Reagan-Bush camp stole briefing papers from President Carter's reelection campaign before the October presidential debates. While these allegations have not been proven, the history of Watergate and other clandestine actions of the US govern-ment make the allegations entirely plausible to more than a few people knowledgeable about that era (deHaven-Smith 2010; Hagan 1997).

During the early years of the Reagan administration, Iranian forces bombed US (and French) embassies in the Middle East. More than 200 US troops stationed in Beirut, Lebanon, were killed in a suicide bombing. More hostages were taken, including the CIA's station chief in Beirut. The US government's official policy, the public was told, was not to negotiate with terrorists. It was also a violation of the US Arms Export Control Act to sell arms to countries (like Iran) that supported terrorism. But negotiate with Iran the United States did; and selling arms (missiles and missile parts) to Iran it did too, at first through Israel but later directly. In the process, arms-merchant middlemen such as retired US Air Force general Richard Secord and Iranian-born businessman Albert Hakim (now a US citizen) grew rich. Following the arms sales, hostages were not always released, and when they were, more were taken (Brinkley & Engelberg 1988).

This brings us to the Contra part of the Iran-Contra scandal. Like Iran, the Central American country of Nicaragua experienced a revolution in the late 1970s that the US government opposed. Dictator Anastasio Somoza, an ally of the United States, was removed from power, and the Sandinista National Liberation Front took control. The Sandinistas turned to Cuba and the Soviet Union for economic and military aid. The Reagan administration, which believed the Sandinistas were fomenting revolution elsewhere in Latin America, found this unacceptable (Moyers 1988; Kinser 2006).

The Contras, the armed Nicaraguan opponents of the Sandinista regime, did not have popular support in their country. They were essentially a creation of the CIA, which was now directed by Casey. Without the CIA and the money and training it supplied, there would have been no Contras. Although Reagan often compared the Contras to the "founding fathers" of the United States, they included former military officers of the Somoza regime as well as men who condoned terrorism, accepted money from drug traffickers, and even trafficked in drugs themselves (McCoy 2003; Kinser 2006).

In the aftermath of the Vietnam War, the American public did not favor another controversial foreign policy campaign, especially if it threatened to involve US troops. And the CIA-Contra operation did not get good publicity, as the press reported that sea mines had been deployed in Nicaraguan harbors and oil facilities had been burned, and innocent people were being terrorized and killed. Excerpts of a CIA pamphlet on guerrilla warfare that were found in the Contras' possession were reported as well: "It is possible to neutralize carefully selected and planned targets, such as court judges [and] security officials. . . . Professional criminals should be hired to [take] . . . demonstrators to a confrontation with the authorities to bring about uprisings and shootings that will . . . create a martyr" (Alpern 1984:30).

During the early 1980s, the US Congress, which has constitutional power over government appropriations, vacillated in its support of the Contras, approving funds, taking them away, and approving them again. But in a definitive legislative statement, the Boland Amendment, Congress explicitly prohibited any agency of the US government from directly or indirectly supporting any military or paramilitary operations in Nicaragua (Brinkley & Engelberg 1988).

President Reagan signed the Boland Amendment into law in October 1984, creating a perplexing problem for his administration: How could it maintain the Contras when it was now illegal to do so? The task of supporting the Contras was given to the National Security Council, a White House advisory board headed by Robert McFarland. According to McFarland, Reagan instructed him to find a way to keep the Contras together. McFarland assigned a US Marine lieutenant-colonel, Oliver North, the job of working out the details and being the White House liaison to the Contras. North and his associates raised millions of dollars from private groups and individuals in the United States and from foreign allies in the governments of Saudi Arabia, Taiwan, and Brunei. Central American governments such as Costa Rica, El Salvador, Guatemala, and Honduras were also pressured or cajoled (with a promise of military aid) to allow their countries to be used as bases for the Contra resupply operation. At the request of Casey, North worked with Secord and Hakim to create a private (profit-making) organization, which they called "The Enterprise," to coordinate the operation. Senator Daniel Inouye, a decorated World War II veteran, described The Enterprise as "a shadowy government with its own air force, its own navy, its own fundraising mechanism, and the ability to pursue its own ideas of the national interest, free from all checks and balances and free from the law itself" (quoted in Moyers 1988:24). The link between the Iran and Contra initiatives was forged as profits from the Iranian arms sales were diverted through The Enterprise to the Contras. This became, according to North, "an attractive incentive" to continue to sell arms to Iran (quoted in Brinkley & Engelberg 1988:16). Moreover, Casey envisioned The Enterprise as a permanent "off-the-shelf" entity with the standalone capacity to conduct covert operations beyond the purview of Congress.

The secrecy surrounding these operations began to crumble in October 1986, halfway through Reagan's second term, when a Contra resupply plane linked to the CIA was shot down over Nicaragua. The story was covered worldwide, and in November a Lebanese magazine disclosed the arms sales to Iran. Reagan and other White House officials first denied the stories, but soon decided to cut their losses, concede that some improper conduct had occurred, and develop a cover story to protect the president, which cast North in the role of a well-intentioned renegade soldier who had gone too far. But North was not willing to take all of the blame. When he was granted immunity to testify before the (televised) joint House and Senate hearing, which began in May 1987, he became a media sensation—"a defiant hero, an obedient soldier, a blameless scapegoat whose conduct had been dictated or approved by his superiors" (Rosoff et al. 2007:394).

The full story of the Iran-Contra scandal, including Reagan's complicity, was not known until after he left office, and by then any question of impeachment was moot. But several members of The Enterprise and a number of administration officials pled guilty or were convicted of crimes, although the sentences overall were less severe than the ones given to the Watergate offenders (Rosoff et al. 2007).

The Iraq War Controversy
Since August 1990, when Iraqi dictator Saddam Hussein invaded the country of Kuwait, which precipitated the 1991 Persian Gulf War, the country of

Iraq has been a major focus of US foreign policy. But whereas the Persian Gulf War had the support of the international community, the Iraq War, launched in 2003, did not.

Weapons of mass destruction. The prelude to the Iraq War, even before the terrorist attack of September 11, 2001, was the desire of neoconservative policymakers to advance a post–Cold War vision of the US prerogative to engage in unilateral military action to protect vital US interests around the world, including access to Middle Eastern oil. **Neoconservatism** is a political ideology that equates global capitalist markets with "freedom," even when that freedom, as we have seen, needs to be imposed and maintained through military force against a democratically elected population (Klein 2007; Kramer & Michalowski 2005).

In 1992, aides to then–secretary of defense Dick Cheney prepared a neoconservative document titled *Defense Planning Guidance,* which "depicted a world dominated by the United States, which would maintain its superpower status through a combination of positive guidance and over-whelming military might" (Armstrong 2002:78). The first objective of US defense policy, according to the guidelines, should be to prevent the reemergence of a new rival to US dominance. In doing so, it also advocated the use of preemptive military force, or **preventive war**, to achieve this goal (Kramer & Michalowski 2005).

The core ideas of the guidelines were later endorsed in a report titled *Rebuilding America's Defenses: Strategy, Forces, and Resources for a New Century,* which was issued by the neoconservative think tank Project for a New American Century, the members of which included advisers who would later play central roles in the administration of George W. Bush. Early in the Bush administration, months before 9/11, regime change in Iraq and US designs on Iraqi oil were never far from view. The Project for a New American Century recognized, however, that it would be difficult to garner public support for this foreign policy agenda without a "catalyzing event" comparable to Pearl Harbor (quoted in Kramer & Michalowski 2005:459).

That event, as we now know, was 9/11. Within hours after the attack, Secretary of Defense Donald Rumsfeld asked his aides to come up with plans to strike Iraq. To justify these plans, the Bush administration claimed not only that Hussein was implicated in the 9/11 attack, but also that he possessed weapons of mass destruction (WMD)—biological, chemical, and especially nuclear weapons—that posed an imminent threat to the United States. These claims, we later learned, were based on misleading if not fraudulent evidence, with administration officials fully aware of intelligence that contraindicated their assertions. In their view, however, even if there was only a "one percent" chance that Iraq had WMD, preventive war was justified (Clarke 2004; Isikoff & Corn 2006; Suskind 2006).

The media, for the most part, capitulated to the administration's claims. *New York Times* journalist Judith Miller was especially influential for writing articles that cited anti-Hussein Iraq defectors who testified about Hussein's WMD capabilities. Vice President Cheney then cited Miller's articles in his statements to the press as an authoritative source supporting the administration's justification for war. Few people realized at the time that Miller's unwitting reporting and Cheney's deceitful remarks were part of an organized propaganda campaign, or program of **strategic disinformation**—the intentional dissemination of false information for the purpose of achieving political goals (Altheide & Grimes 2005; Judis 2002). Indeed, the Iraqi defectors belonged to a group led by Ahmad Chalabi, the Iraqi National Congress, which was funded by the CIA and Pentagon and used to "sell" the war to the American people. John Rendon, a public relations specialist in the Rendon Group, was hired to organize and disseminate these stories to the press (Bamford 2005; Isikoff & Corn 2006).

Two years into the war, the leak of the "Downing Street Memo," written by Sir Richard Dearlove, head of British foreign intelligence, to Prime Minister Tony Blair in July 2002, revealed that intelligence in the White House had been "fixed around the policy" to invade Iraq and that high-ranking US officials had intentionally ignored CIA warnings that their allegations about Iraqi WMD could not be substantiated by the weight of available evidence (cited in Pincus 2005:A18). (Downing Street is the location of the residence and official offices of the British prime minister.) In other words, there was no genuine effort to find out whether the concerns about Iraq were in fact true—for instance, by giving UN WMD inspectors a chance to make a determination—before US troops were committed to battle (Isikoff & Corn 2006; Suskind 2006).

A month after the invasion and after the Hussein regime was toppled, President Bush decided to celebrate the apparent victory with a photo op, landing on the USS *Abraham Lincoln,* which was stationed 30 miles off the coast of California. Bush exited the plane decked in full flight gear and delivered a speech under a banner that declared "Mission Accomplished," announcing that "major combat operations in Iraq have ended." At the time, Bush and his minions had not anticipated the insurgency that would take the United States into a protracted war, one that cost the lives of more than 4,400 US troops and wounded many thousands of others, to say nothing of other nations' troops, members of the press, and the Iraqis themselves who met similar fates. When all is said and done, and after health care for injured veterans is taken into account, the economic cost of the war may be as much as $3 trillion (Fischer 2014; Stiglitz & Bilmes 2008).

In the fall of 2003, as casualties on all sides mounted, a team of about 1,400 weapons inspectors called the Iraq Survey Group, a joint venture of the CIA and Defense Intelligence Agency, reported that no WMD could be found. The Iraq Survey Group did find evidence that Hussein had reconstituted Iraq's missile program, which would have enabled him to project missiles beyond the 90-mile limit that had been imposed by UN resolutions, but this is an entirely different matter from having a WMD program, constituting an imminent threat to the United States, that required a preventive war to stop. Moreover, the Iraq Survey Group concluded that the Gulf War and subsequent UN inspections had destroyed Iraq's WMD program, that Hussein had not tried to rebuild it, and that ongoing aggressive inspections might have been a suitable alternative to war (Drogin 2003; Kramer & Michalowski 2005; Priest & Pincus 2004).

The mushroom cloud. Arguably the Bush administration's most compelling argument for preventive war was the claim that Hussein had not only WMD, but also nuclear weapons he was capable of launching against the United States. Administration officials, including the president and vice president, repeatedly said the United States could not afford to wait for a "smoking gun" that could come in the form of a "mushroom cloud" (Hersh 2004). Although this claim was not supported by the evidence, it was a powerful one nonetheless. Take the case of Dick Armey, the influential Republican majority leader of the House of Representatives. Armey reports that at first he was skeptical about the rationale for war, until Cheney persuaded him that Hussein would "in the not-too-distant future . . . acquire nuclear weapons" (quoted in Gellman 2008:216). According to Armey, Cheney also told him that Hussein had developed the capability of miniaturizing WMD, including nuclear weapons, that would enable them to be moved by ground personnel. At the time, Armey was cynical about the claim, but when faced with emphatic administration assurances, he lost faith in his own doubts. Later, when he discovered that he had been right to doubt the case for war, he wondered: "Did Dick Cheney . . . purposely tell me things he knew to be untrue? . . . I seriously feel that may be the case. . . . Had I known or believed then what I believe I know now, I would have publicly opposed this resolution right to the bitter end, and I believe I might have stopped it from happening" (quoted in Gellman 2008:221–222).

After the invasion was already under way, particular controversy arose over Bush's January 2003 State of the Union speech, which had preceded the attack, in which he told the world that "the British government has learned that Saddam Hussein recently sought significant quantities of uranium from Africa," suggesting that Iraq had reconstituted its nuclear weapons program. At the time of the speech, however, administration officials knew full well that this claim had been disputed by its own intelligence sources. Indeed, the CIA had previously dispatched former ambassador Joseph Wilson to the country of Niger, the alleged source of the uranium, to investigate this claim. Wilson had concluded, as he later wrote in a scathing *New York Times* opinion piece published in July 2003, that it had not taken him long to determine "that the information was erroneous" and "that it was highly doubtful that any such transaction had ever taken place" (quoted in Kerr 2003:A9). Wilson also noted that Cheney's office was specifically informed of his findings by the CIA and that these findings had been discounted in order to legitimize the administration's efforts to skew intelligence to justify its desire for preventive war. Moreover, it later was revealed that the documents alleging the Niger-uranium connection had come from Italian intelligence sources and had been forged, apparently with the knowledge of high-ranking US administration officials, as part of the organized campaign to garner public support for the war (Giraldi 2005; Isikoff & Corn 2006; Wilson 2005).

If Bush or Cheney had purposely deceived Congress, it would have constituted a crime and an impeachable offense. But the only aspect of the Niger case that resulted in criminal prosecution was related to an article written by conservative political columnist Robert Novak a week after Wilson's *New York Times* piece was published. Novak reported that a White House official had informed him that Valerie Plame, Wilson's wife, was a CIA operative. Novak's outing of Plame, who had worked undercover for three decades and was a specialist in WMD, ended her career and endangered her contacts overseas. While Novak's right to publish the information is arguably protected by the First Amendment, the initial disclosure to the press constitutes a felony punishable of up to 10 years in prison. Wilson thinks the leak of his wife's name was intended to stifle complaints from knowledgeable people inside the government who knew that the administration had misrepresented intelligence about the threat posed by Iraq (Isikoff & Corn 2006; Wilson 2005).

When news of the scandal surfaced, Bush insisted he would do everything in his power to get to the bottom of it. A special prosecutor, Patrick Fitzgerald, was appointed by the Justice Department to investigate the case. The investigation dragged on past the November 2004 presidential election, in which Bush won reelection. Finally, in October 2005, Fitzgerald announced he would seek an indictment against only one individual, I. Lewis "Scooter" Libby, not on charges related to the leak itself, but for obstruction of justice, perjury, and making false statements about the leak. Libby was Cheney's top aide, and Fitzgerald found compelling evidence that other White House officials, including Cheney and Bush's top political adviser, Karl Rove, were directly or indirectly involved. Libby was convicted and sentenced to a prison term of two and a half years, a $250,000 fine, and two years of probation. Bush immediately commuted the prison sentence, leaving Libby to face only the fine and probation. No one else was held responsible for the crime (Corn 2007; Isikoff & Corn 2006).

The Question of Torture
In the spring of 2004, reports of widespread abuse, humiliation, and outright torture of Iraqi prisoners held by US intelligence operatives, military

personnel, and private contractors in the Abu Ghraib prison in Iraq hit the news. Some of the interrogators had taken photos of abused and beaten prisoners, and disseminated these photos on the Internet for the entire world to see, undermining the credibility of the United States. Naked prisoners had been forced to feign homosexual acts and form a pile of naked bodies as smiling interrogators looked on. Prisoners were shown in "stress positions," with electrical wires attached to their bodies and growling dogs standing by. These practices were not unique to Abu Ghraib, however. They also occurred at US facilities in Afghanistan, Guantánamo (Cuba), and other sites. Although the administration blamed these actions on maverick interrogators who had gone too far, and although some lower-level personnel were punished, the practices were systematically sanctioned by high-ranking officials—including Rumsfeld, Cheney, and Bush himself. Moreover, little useful intelligence was gathered from these interrogations, and the large majority of Iraqis and other Muslims who were victimized were completely innocent bystanders to the malaise of the Middle East (Hersh 2004; Mayer 2009; McCoy 2006).

Emergence of the US torture regime. What happened at Abu Ghraib and other US sites did not take place in a historical vacuum, but was an outgrowth of long-standing US policies that began in the aftermath of World War II, in the early years of the Cold War. According to historian Alfred McCoy (2006), at that time and in the years thereafter, the United States exhibited a contradictory stance toward torture. On the one hand, the United States was a leader in the international movement for human rights, opposing torture before the United Nations and other international organizations, and signing treaties, such as the Geneva Conventions, that outlawed torture. On the other hand, the newly formed CIA ignored these humanitarian precepts and instead propagated the practice of torture throughout the world. The rationale for these latter actions was the belief that the United States faced an unscrupulous enemy in the form of Communism and the Soviet Union.

In the 1950s, the CIA commissioned a review of Nazi interrogation techniques, including hypnosis, drugs, electroshock, and psychosurgery, and then began a program of extreme cognitive experimentation on witting and unwitting subjects, with the latter including military personnel and hospital patients who were subjected to experimentation without their consent. Through trial and error and in collaboration with nonagency researchers, the CIA identified what would become the hallmarks of the modern psychological paradigm of **"no touch" torture**, which is aimed, according to one CIA report published in 1963, at "inducing regression of the personality to whatever earlier and weaker level is required for the dissolution of resistance and the inculcation of dependence" (cited in McCoy 2006:51). The report noted that all interrogation techniques, whether physical or psychological, "are essentially ways of speeding up the process of regression" until the assault on the target's identity becomes "mentally intolerable" and they comply with their captor's wishes (p. 51). Research at the time had found that sensory deprivation, for example, which could be achieved through prolonged isolation, was especially effective at inducing the psychological equivalent of acute psychosis in as little as two days.

Self-inflicted pain, a technique learned from the Communists, was another method of "no touch" torture adapted by the CIA. A seminal agency study of Communist interrogation methods in the mid-1950s reported that simply forcing subjects to stand for 18 to 24 hours could cause "excruciating pain," as ankles double in size, blisters erupt oozing "watery serum," heart rates soar, kidneys shut down, and delusions set in—outcomes that the CIA described as "nonviolent" (cited in McCoy 2006: 46). The technique of forcing prisoners into stress positions such as wall-standing was also adopted, whereby subjects are made to stand spread-eagled against a wall, with fingers high above their head against the wall, legs spread apart and feet back, "causing them to stand on their toes with the weight of the body mainly on the fingers" (p. 55). These "self-inflicted" techniques are designed to make a person "feel responsible for their own suffering, thus inducing them to alleviate their agony by capitulating to the power of their interrogators" (p. 52). Other "no touch" torture methods included sleep deprivation; subjection to extremely loud noise and extreme heat and cold; sexual humiliation; and denial of food, liquid, and toileting privileges. **Waterboarding**, in which water is poured down a prisoner's throat to induce a sense of drowning, also became part of the CIA's torture regime. As we shall see, however, a problem with these techniques, besides their moral reprehensibility, is that they may elicit compliant behavior without accurate information, as subjects will tell interrogators whatever they want to hear in order to alleviate their suffering.

Exporting torture. According to McCoy (2006), once a torture regime is unleashed, it becomes difficult to control, as it typically spreads from a limited number of high-valued targets to countless innocent victims. It also tends to move beyond "no touch" techniques to harsher physical methods, as it did during the Vietnam War through the murderous Phoenix program, in which specially trained South Vietnamese counterinsurgency teams, often under the direct supervision of the CIA, tortured and summarily executed Vietcong prisoners. The torture techniques that were used included electroshock to men's testicles and women's vaginas. Overall, an estimated 41,000 Vietcong were killed by this program (Hersh 2004; Mayer 2009; McCoy 2006).

The Phoenix program was a seminal experience for the entire US intelligence community, serving as a model for later counterinsurgency training in Latin America (McCoy 2006). In the mid-1960s, US Army Intelligence launched Project X, which, according to a confidential Pentagon memo, was designed "to develop an exportable foreign intelligence package to provide counterinsurgency techniques learned in Vietnam to Latin American countries" (cited in McCoy 2006:71). A manual that was used at the Army Intelligence School provided training in the use of sodium pentothal, physical beatings, abduction of family members, and execution. For the next quarter century, the US Army propagated these tactics—through direct training and dissemination of manuals—to the militaries of at least 10 Latin American countries.

By the 1980s, international outrage led the United Nations to unanimously approve the Convention Against Torture, which broadly defined torture as "any act by which severe pain or suffering, whether physical or mental, is intentionally inflicted on a person for such purpose as obtaining from him or a third person information or a confession" (cited in McCoy 2006:100). In 1988, President Reagan asked the US Congress to approve the Convention Against Torture and, in his words, "bring an end to the abhorrent practice" (p. 100). At the same time, the Reagan administration proposed 19 reservations that stalled congressional ratification for six years. The main focus of the reservations concerned the issue of psychological torture. The administration thought the definition of "mental pain" in the UN convention was too vague, and drafted a four-part diplomatic exception as a condition of US approval, defining psychological torture as limited to "prolonged mental harm" caused by: "(1) the intentional infliction or threatened infliction of severe physical pain or suffering; (2) the administration . . . of mind-altering substances . . . ; (3) the threat of imminent death; or (4) the threat that another person will imminently be subjected to death . . . or other procedures calculated to disrupt profoundly the sense of personality" (p. 100). In essence, these exceptions were designed to protect the US "no touch" torture paradigm from international sanction.

Nevertheless, in 1992, US Army Intelligence revised its interrogation field manual to more fully comply with the Geneva Conventions and evolving international standards, banning not only physical torture such as beatings and electroshock, but also prolonged stress positions, food deprivation, sleep deprivation, and mock executions. While violation of these guidelines could be prosecuted as crimes under the *Uniform Code of Military Justice,* the manual also stated that torture was not only immoral but also ineffective, yielding "unreliable results [that] may damage subsequent collection efforts, and . . . [inducing] the source to say what he thinks the interrogator wants to hear" (cited in McCoy 2006:102). Moreover, it stated that public disclosure of "torture by US personnel will bring discredit upon the US and its armed forces" and undermine domestic and international support of US foreign policy.

The war on terror. In September 2002, Cofer Black, counterterrorism chief of the CIA, told Congress: "All you need to know . . . is that there was a 'before 9/11' and there was an 'after 9/11.' After 9/11, the gloves came off" (quoted in McCoy 2006:119). Apparently this meant a reversal of even the limited restrictions that had been imposed by the Reagan administration. One mechanism of this change was the development of a legal framework that restricted legal compliance to *state* actors rather than to *nonstate* actors such as Al-Qaida, which were not, in the Bush administration's view, subject to the protections afforded to conventional prisoners of war (McCoy 2006).

In conjunction with the CIA and other intelligence agencies, Secretary of Defense Rumsfeld launched a highly classified program that gave "prior authorization for kidnapping, assassination, and torture" of high-valued targets (McCoy 2006:116). The program included the practice of **extraordinary rendition**, whereby suspects were sent to countries like Egypt and Syria to be tortured by agents of foreign governments. The question remained, however: How much pain and suffering were US personnel allowed to inflict? In an important legal memorandum, Assistant Attorney General Jay Bybee, in collaboration with Vice Presidential Counsel David Addington, answered this question, defining the parameters of permissible actions to include anything other than physical pain that was "equivalent in intensity to the pain accompanying serious physical injury, such as organ failure, impairment of bodily function, or even death" (p. 121).

When the Abu Ghraib prison scandal broke in the spring of 2004, administration officials were forced to condemn the actions of a few "bad apples," while also denying that they had approved the "no touch" techniques, which, at the same time, they denied as constituting torture. By the end of the year, however, several FBI e-mails from Guantánamo that disputed the official denials were made public. One FBI agent had written the FBI director an "urgent report," complaining that prisoners were being subjected to "strangulation, beatings, placement of lit cigarettes into the detainee's ear openings and unauthorized interrogation" (cited in McCoy 2006:158). Another agent reported: "I entered interview rooms to find a detainee chained hand and foot in a fetal position to the floor with no chair, food or water. Most times they had urinated or defecated on themselves and had been left there for 18 to 24 hours" (p. 158). Other agents noted that the torture techniques were producing no intelligence of value while also compromising their own (more effective) rapport-building efforts.

Corruption of Government Officials

Thus far our discussion of government crime has focused on the abuse of state power to achieve foreign policy objectives. In this section we focus on **corruption of government officials** undertaken for their own personal gain. This gain may be both financial and political—that is, it may involve the abuse of public office to accumulate personal wealth, and to acquire, maintain, and exercise political power.

Financial Corruption

Financial corruption occurs at all levels of government: local, state, and federal. This corruption is so common that many people consider it an institutionalized part of government, and it undoubtedly foments a well-deserved cynicism about politics. Here we review a few notable examples.

Examples of local and state corruption. In July 2009, a two-year FBI probe into corruption and money laundering in New Jersey culminated in the arrest of 44 individuals, including three mayors (all Democrats), two state assemblymen (one Democrat, one Republican), and five Syrian-Jewish rabbis. The investigation began when Solomon Dwek, a smooth-talking yet unsuccessful New Jersey real estate developer and prominent member of the Syrian-Jewish community, was arrested for trying to pass a bad check worth $25 million. Dwek turned government informant and gave authorities entry into an extensive network of corruption. Operating under an assumed name, Dwek approached local influence-peddlers and told them he was looking for help getting government approval for various construction projects, such as high-rise buildings. Upon making contacts with public officials who had the appropriate jurisdiction, Dwek offered them $5,000 in cash for an upcoming political campaign or simply as a straight-up bribe, with the promise of more to come. He then handed them the money from the trunk of his car. All too many people accepted his offers, which totaled more than $650,000 to those accused in the criminal complaint (CNN 2009; Halbfinger 2009).

The state of Illinois, whose history of corruption rivals New Jersey's, offers other examples. In the latter part of 2008, Democratic governor Rod Blagojevich became the seventh governor in the history of Illinois to be arrested or indicted for his crimes. His most recent predecessor, Republican George Ryan, was convicted in 2006 on multiple felony counts and sentenced to six years in prison for actions that went back to his tenure as secretary of state during the 1990s. The federal investigation of Ryan, which began in 1994 when a fatal truck accident inadvertently exposed a statewide scheme to trade truck operators' licenses for political contributions, resulted in the conviction of more than 70 former state officials, lobbyists, and truck drivers (Rosoff et al. 2007; Suddath 2008).

The wrongdoing for which Blagojevich is best known, which was part of the federal indictment against him, involved his solicitation of bribes from potential replacements for Barack Obama's position in the US Senate after the 2008 presidential election, a decision that Blagojevich controlled. The indictment also alleged that Blagojevich tried to shake down the owner of the *Chicago Tribune,* who owns the Wrigley Field baseball stadium, by trying to force the newspaper to fire editorial writers who had been critical of Blagojevich in exchange for a tax break for the stadium worth about

$100 million. And the indictment accused him of threatening "to revoke millions in funding for a Chicago children's hospital if its CEO did not pay his campaign a $50,000 tribute" (Scherer 2008:1). Although Blagojevich was acquitted of some charges, a federal jury found him guilty of lying to federal agents and he was sentenced to 14 years in prison (Davey 2011).

Illinois's record of corruption notwithstanding, corruption in the state of Louisiana is second to none. According to research by the *Corporate Crime Reporter* (2007), between 1997 and 2006 Louisiana led the nation in its per capita rate of corruption. Edwin Edwards, for example, an admitted high-stakes gambler who served four gubernatorial terms between 1972 and 1996, was tried twice unsuccessfully before finally being convicted the third time, in 2000, on multiple counts of extortion and racketeering and sentenced to 10 years in prison.

Examples of federal corruption. In the wake of Watergate, corruption by government officials became a higher priority for federal law enforcement. One of the most well-known investigations was the FBI's Operation Abscam, carried out in the late 1970s. Like the previously mentioned New Jersey scandal, Operation Abscam began when a convicted swindler and con artist, Melvin Weinberg, agreed to cooperate with the FBI in an investigation of corrupt New Jersey politicians in exchange for a lighter sentence. Under the direction of the FBI, Weinberg set up a phony investment company called Abdul Enterprises, purportedly owned by a wealthy Arab shaikh who was looking to invest in US businesses. Weinberg introduced prospective targets to FBI agents posing as Middle-Eastern businessmen, offering them lucrative bribes in exchange for "greasing the wheels" on ventures ranging from the receipt of casino licenses to defense contracts and other government business. When all was said and done, Abscam snared six US congressmen (five Democrats and one Republican) and a US senator (Democrat), in addition to several local officials (Rosoff et al. 2007; SourceWatch 2014a).

Following Operation Abscam, during the Republican administration of Ronald Reagan, another FBI investigation focused on US Navy undersecretary Melvyn Paisley, who was responsible for procuring weapons systems for the government worth hundreds of millions of dollars. Paisley sold classified information to defense firms competing for government business, granted contracts to firms that paid him bribes, and awarded a contract to a company that he co-owned. Paisley and a number of other government officials, corporate executives, and defense consultants were convicted of bribery, tax evasion, and fraud. Paisley received a four-year prison term. Around the same time, the Department of Housing and Urban Development became a center of influence-peddling and fraud, as HUD secretary Samuel Pierce and his aides steered lucrative government contracts to Republican

Party benefactors and paid exorbitant consulting fees to Republican political insiders. Although Pierce was not prosecuted, a number of HUD officials were convicted in a scandal that cost taxpayers several billion dollars (Rosoff et al. 2007; Simon 2006).

Cataloging the numerous congresspeople who have been embroiled in corruption scandals would fill a volume of its own, but a few over the past couple of decades are worth mentioning. Among Democrats, Dan Rostenkowski of Illinois, chair of the influential House Ways and Means Committee, stands out for his conviction in 1996 for misappropriating $640,000 of congressional funds for his own personal use during a political career that spanned three decades; he received a prison term of 17 months. In 2002, James Traficant of Ohio was convicted for soliciting bribes, tax evasion, and even extorting money from his own staff by forcing them to return part of their salary to him; he received a prison term of 8 years. In 2005, William Jefferson of Louisiana made the news when FBI agents investigating his involvement in bribery found $90,000 in cash stored in his freezer in his Washington, DC, home; he received a prison term of 13 years, the longest ever imposed on a congressperson for bribery (Courson 2009; Rosoff et al. 2007).

Among Republicans, Randy "Duke" Cunningham of California stands out for receiving $2.4 million in bribes, the most lucrative scheme in the history of congressional bribery, mostly from defense contractors looking for government business and other favors. In addition to cash, Cunningham's benefactors lavished him with a Rolls-Royce, a luxury yacht, museum-quality antiques, Persian rugs, and a mansion in one of the nation's wealthiest communities. In 2005, he was convicted and received a prison term of eight years and four months (Rosoff et al. 2007).

The K Street Project. No account of financial corruption would be complete without mentioning the web of scandal associated with lobbyist Jack Abramoff. Abramoff, a former president of the College Republicans, prided himself as a power broker between his corporate clients and the Republican-controlled Congress that came to power in 1994. Under the leadership of Georgia congressman Newt Gingrich, who served as Speaker of the House from 1994 to 1999, the Republicans advanced their "Contract with America," which was "aimed at restoring the faith and trust of the American people in their government" and which called for a dramatic rollback in the role of the federal government in American society (cited in Continetti 2006:8). Abramoff's chief political ally was Texas congressman Tom DeLay, the Republican majority whip and later majority leader, who was nicknamed "The Hammer" for his reputation for nailing down financial contributions for himself and his political allies. Matthew Continetti describes DeLay as a man "who viewed government as a business—one that maximized the advantages of business so that business would then donate to their political war chests" (2006:16).

Working with antitax activist and Gingrich protégé Grover Norquist—who once said that he wanted to shrink the federal government to a size where it could be drowned in a bathtub—DeLay formed the K Street Project, named after the Washington, DC, business corridor where some of the most powerful corporate lobbyists in the country have their offices. The goal of the K Street Project was nothing less than the wholesale partisan realignment of the lobbying industry with the Republican Party (Continetti 2006; Moyers 2006).

As DeLay and his political allies pressured lobbyists to abandon their ties to the Democratic Party, an orgy of political corruption ensued. But Abramoff was arguably the "poster child" for the scandal. Most noteworthy was Abramoff's role in bilking millions of dollars from the nation's Native American tribes, money he falsely claimed would be spent on lobbying to promote their casino gambling interests. In addition to profiting himself, Abramoff persuaded the tribes to make large campaign contributions to his Republican allies. Then there was the case of the Mariana Islands, a territory of the United States, which was touted by DeLay as a paradise of "free market" capitalism. Garment factory owner Willie Tan courted DeLay and paid Abramoff millions of dollars to lobby on his behalf to seek political support to exempt the Marianas from US immigration and labor laws, enabling Tan to subject his workers to some of the most exploitative conditions in the world, while at the same time labeling his products "Made in America." During this time, Abramoff had access to influential members of the George W. Bush administration, including the president himself (Continetti 2006; Moyers 2006).

While padding their campaign coffers, DeLay and his ilk, such as Congressman Bob Ney of Ohio, were also traveling around the world at taxpayer expense or as guests of corporate lobbyists, flying on corporate jets, staying in luxury hotels, playing golf on high-priced courses, and dining in expensive restaurants. During these junkets, they met with some rather unsavory people, whom Continetti describes as an amalgam of "African dictators. Islamic fanatics. Russians with ties to military intelligence. Israeli guerrillas. Small-time mobsters" (2006:88).

The scandal finally reached the light of day in 2005, and a slew of criminal indictments ensued. Abramoff pled guilty to several counts of fraud and related offenses and received a four-year prison sentence. DeLay was convicted of campaign-law violations but was acquitted after a successful appeal. A score of other lobbyists and Republican Congress members (including Ney) who were part of the Abramoff-DeLay network or who committed similar crimes were convicted and sentenced to pay fines and serve prison terms (Continetti 2006; Moyers 2006; Talking Points Memo 2007).

FURTHER EXPLORATION
The Clinton Presidency

Richard Nixon was never formally impeached, but a quarter century later Bill Clinton was, for matters related to a sexual affair with a young White House intern, Monica Lewinsky. **Whitewater** was perhaps the first Clinton scandal to be given a name. In the late 1970s, Bill and Hillary Clinton became partners with James and Susan McDougal in the 230-acre Whitewater real estate development project, which went bust. The McDougals, who were owners of an Arkansas savings and loan that failed in the 1980s, had engaged in some of the illegal financial schemes available to corrupt S&L operators (see Chapter 9). After Clinton was elected president, the McDougals were convicted of several crimes (Conason & Lyons 2000; Stewart 1996).

If money from the McDougals' illegal transactions had been used to repay Whitewater loans, the Clintons may have benefited indirectly. But according to James Stewart's account, "the Clintons had virtually nothing to do with Whitewater and were simply 'passive' investors" (1996:447). Their only wrongdoings pertaining specifically to Whitewater involved overvaluing assets on financial disclosure forms and overestimating losses on their income tax returns, which amounted to a tax savings of less than $2,000 on overall losses of about $43,000 (Conason & Lyons 2000).

The Clintons managed to dodge the Whitewater bullet, but more troublesome was their pattern of withholding information and making misleading statements. Before coming to Washington, DC, for instance, Hillary had worked for the Rose Law Firm in Arkansas. The McDougals were among her clients. At first, Hillary claimed that her legal work for the McDougals had been minimal, and she denied knowing anything about their crimes. Rose Law Firm records revealed, however, that she had billed the McDougals for over a dozen meetings or conversations. While there is no evidence that she did anything illegal, her lack of forthrightness left a contrary impression (Conason & Lyons 2000; Stewart 1996).

Throughout Clinton's presidency there were numerous occasions when his aides denied press reports or stonewalled official inquiries into their actions. In one case, Webster Hubbell, a former Rose Law Firm lawyer who was appointed by Clinton to be an associate attorney general in the US Department of Justice, was forced to resign in the face of a criminal indictment for income tax evasion and mail fraud related to his practice of overbilling clients at the law firm. Hubbell received a prison sentence of nearly two years, but during an 18-month period following disclosure of his crime he received $500,000 in consulting fees from various Clinton associates. One $100,000 fee was paid by a subsidiary of the Lippo Group, an Indonesia-based conglomerate that was accused of illegally funneling foreign campaign contributions to the Democratic National Committee (Stewart 1996).

The Republican majority in Congress was determined to pursue Clinton's alleged wrongdoings, and it authorized an investigation by the Office of Independent Counsel. Kenneth Starr, a highly partisan Republican attorney,

continues

continued

was appointed to head the inquiry. During his investigation, Starr, who had unlimited taxpayer money at his disposal, spent about $2.45 million alone on private investigators over a four-year period. When the investigation of Whitewater turned up empty, he turned his attention to Clinton's greatest vulnerability, his reputation for sexual infidelity, an opportunity that was afforded by a sexual harassment lawsuit that had been initiated against the president by Paula Jones, an Arkansas public employee, in 1994 (Conason & Lyons 2000).

Jones's allegations stemmed from a state-sponsored conference she helped staff at an Arkansas hotel, which Clinton attended in May 1991 during the presidential campaign. She alleged that Clinton had spotted her in the hotel and wanted to meet her. A state trooper who was a member of the then-governor's security detail brought her up to Clinton's room. Although Jones said nothing about it at the time, she later claimed Clinton had made harassing sexual advances (Conason & Lyons 2000).

After losing a court challenge to postpone the Jones lawsuit until after his presidency, Clinton was required to give a deposition in which he was asked about a consensual sexual relationship he had had with Monica Lewinsky. Under oath, in January 1998, Clinton denied the allegation and then told the public he "did not have sexual relations with that woman." Seven months later, in the face of DNA evidence (traces of Clinton's sperm) found on Lewinsky's dress, Clinton admitted he had not told the full truth about the affair; and questions remained as to whether he had committed perjury in the Jones deposition and in subsequent testimony he had given before a grand jury (Conason & Lyons 2000).

Starr issued a report that made the case for impeachment on grounds of perjury and obstruction of justice. In December 1998, a majority of the House of Representatives passed two articles of impeachment against the president (for perjury and obstruction of justice). But two months later Clinton was acquitted in the Senate, where the vote fell far short of the two-thirds majority needed to remove him from office.

Electoral Corruption

As previously noted, corruption of government officials may involve financial gain as well as the abuse of public office to acquire, maintain, and exercise political power. In this section we consider corruption of the electoral process.

The question of voter fraud. In recent years, significant media attention and calls for electoral reform have been directed at the question of fraud committed by individual voters. All over the country, states have passed restrictive photo voter identification laws, among other reforms, that make it more difficult to vote, such as eliminating same-day registration and narrowing the opportunities for early voting. In the case of photo voter iden-tification reforms, citizens are required to have a driver's license or other state-issued photo identification. If they do not have a driver's license, they may be required to produce a birth certificate in order to obtain state-issued identification. Critics of photo voter identification laws think they discrimi-nate against individuals who do not have a driver's license, a condition that is more pronounced among the poor, elderly, and racial/ethnic minorities. In the past, all that was necessary to confirm one's eligibility was a check or utility bill confirming one's address; now there are more legal hoops to jump through (Caldwell 2011; Mayer 2012; Minnite 2010).

Critics of photo voter identification laws acknowledge inaccuracies in voter registration lists and anecdotal cases in which individuals have cast a vote when they were not qualified to do so. But they find little evidence that intentional voter fraud is widespread or that it has influenced any elec-tion in recent years. Lorraine Minnite (2010), who studied elections in Cal-ifornia, Minnesota, New Hampshire, and Oregon, concluded that voter fraud is largely a myth. As she writes:

> The United States has a fragmented, inefficient, inequitable, complicated, and overly complex electoral process run on election day essentially by an army of volunteers. It is practically designed to produce irregularities in the administration: the number of voters signing the poll book do not exactly match the number of ballots cast because of the unexpected crush of citizens who wanted to vote and the fact that a poll worker's bathroom break was not covered; confused voters go here and there trying to cast their ballots in their precinct, the one they voted in eight years ago, only to find their wandering recorded as double votes; absentee ballots do not reach their rightful destination in time, causing anxious voters to show up at the polls where they are again recorded as voting twice; John Smith Sr. on line number twelve in the poll book signs for John Smith Jr. on thirteen . . . ; voter registration applications go unacknowledged so voters send in duplicates, sometimes adding a middle initial or a new last name. (p. 7)

Minnite notes that most of the alleged incidents of voter fraud reported by the media come to their attention from partisan political operatives, yet for the most part "the multitude of alternative explanations for any one irregularity" is not investigated further (p. 7). Testifying for the plaintiffs in a recent federal court case challenging the photo voter identification law passed in Wisconsin, Minnite informed US district judge Lynn Adelman of her research on elections in that state between 2004 and 2012, in which she could verify only one case of intentional voter fraud (Murphy 2014). After reviewing this and other evidence, Judge Adelman concluded:

> The evidence at trial established that virtually no voter impersonation occurs in Wisconsin. The defendants could not point to a single instance of known voter impersonation occurring in Wisconsin at any time in the

recent past. While there is no way to know how many of the 300,000 people who lack the acceptable photo ID will be deterred from voting because of the law, it is absolutely clear that [it] prevents more legitimate votes from being cast than fraudulent votes. (quoted in Trevelen & Hall 2014:A7)

Similarly, Justin Levitt (2014) found only 31 credible cases anywhere in the country (out of more than 1 billion ballots cast) in which an individual showed up at the polls pretending to be someone else. It is our contention, therefore, that the main problem with the electoral process in the United States lies not with the ill intentions of individual voters but with the corruption in the administration of elections and the counting of votes. The place to start in making this case is with the disputed presidential election of 2000, which Minnite describes as a "watershed event" in recent electoral history (2010:1).

The disputed election of 2000. The 2000 election between then–Texas governor George W. Bush (Republican) and Vice President Al Gore (Democrat) came down to the wire. Both candidates needed to win the state of Florida to give them enough Electoral College votes (270) to win the presidency. Before the Florida vote came in, Gore was leading Bush by a margin of 267 to 246. Florida had 25 electoral votes, and Gore needed only 3 more to reach 270. But in a winner-take-all system, a Bush victory in Florida would give him a 271 to 267 victory.

After the Florida polls closed, the media initially declared Gore the winner, based on information gathered from exit polls. But later that evening the media followed the lead of Fox News Channel, a highly partisan conservative network, and retracted its call for Gore and pronounced Bush the winner. Interestingly, the head of Fox's Election Night Decision Desk, who made the call for Bush, was none other than Bush's cousin John Ellis, a man whose impartiality many would question. Ellis made the call at 2:16 A.M., after speaking to Jeb Bush, George's brother and governor of Florida, announcing to his colleagues: "Jebbie says we got it!" (Moore 2008:36). Within minutes, the other networks followed suit, anointing Bush as the next president. As it turned out, this projection was wrong; the race was in fact too close to call, and two hours later the networks retracted their projections. But David Moore argues that it is "difficult to overestimate the impact of the erroneous network call on the post-election political environment," because it created a public perception that Bush had won and that Gore was a "sore loser" who was attempting to reverse the outcome (2008:37).

Although Gore had won the national popular vote by more than half a million votes, the initial Florida vote count placed Bush ahead by 1,784, just 0.03 percent of the 5.9 million ballots cast in the state. Under Florida law, if the vote margin is less than 0.05 percent, a mandatory recount is required. The initial recount was done inconsistently—some of the counties did not actually recount the ballots but merely rechecked the math from election night tabulations—but it reduced Bush's official margin of victory to 327 votes (Corn 2003).

Meanwhile, reports of problems with Florida ballots surfaced that revealed ways in which the election may have been tipped to Bush under questionable circumstances. There was the case of the so-called butterfly ballot, for instance, which listed candidates Bush and Gore on the left side of the ballot and conservative Reform Party candidate Pat Buchanan on the right side. Many Democratic (especially elderly) voters apparently found the ballot confusing, leading them to vote for Buchanan, or for both Buchanan and Gore, when they intended to vote for Gore. These "Democrats for Buchanan" ballots may have given Gore an estimated 6,000 to 9,000 additional votes. And, as we shall see, there were other sources of lost votes that might have won the election for Gore (Corn 2003; Dershowitz 2001; Palast 2003).

Given these problems, the Gore campaign requested an additional hand recount in four heavily Democratic counties, as it was permitted by law to do. It was at this point that the nation was introduced to the problem of antiquated punchcard ballots, which require voters to push a stylus through a perforated hole to dislodge a chad that might be left "hanging" or merely "dimpled." A punchcard system, which is less accurate than an optical-scan system, was used in about 60 percent of Florida precincts, including the four counties that were the target of the Gore recount request. Poor (particularly minority) residents were more likely to have voted with the antiquated technology and hence to have had their ballots discarded. These lost votes were referred to as "undervotes," in comparison to invalidated "overvotes," which included instances where a voter marked or punched a ballot and also specified the name of the same candidate in the space designated for "write-in" votes (Corn 2003; Dershowitz 2001; Palast 2003).

Kathryn Harris, the Florida secretary of state, was in charge of supervising the election process. Despite the obvious conflict of interest, Harris was also cochair of the Bush campaign in the state, where, as noted, Bush's brother Jeb was governor. As the hand recount was still ongoing, Harris predictably exercised her discretionary authority to bring the counting to an end within seven days of the election, as she was permitted (but not required) by law to do. Predictably as well, the Gore campaign filed a legal appeal to extend the recount deadline, while the Bush campaign appealed to stop it (Moore 2008).

As both sides jockeyed for position in the courts, the Gore team received a favorable decision from the Florida Supreme Court, which ruled that a hand recount of the undervotes for the entire state should be undertaken. This statewide recount was begun, but it was soon stopped when the Florida court was reversed by the US Supreme Court. In a slim five-to-four decision in *Bush v. Gore,* the majority sided with Bush and decreed the election over. Thirty-six days after the initial ballots were cast, Harris certified that Bush had won by 537 votes.

Constitutional-law scholar Alan Dershowitz (2001), among others, has characterized the Supreme Court decision as a case of "supreme injustice." Supreme Court justices are nominated by the president (and confirmed by the Senate) and are nowadays chosen as much for their ideological predilections as their legal expertise. The composition of the 2000 Court clearly favored the Republicans, and many think its decision in *Bush v. Gore* was overtly political.

The basis of the Bush campaign's legal argument was that continuing the hand recount would have violated the Fourteenth Amendment of the US Constitution, which says that a person may not be deprived of "the equal protection of the laws." In what was arguably a partisan interpretation of this clause, the Court ruled that continuing the recount would deprive Bush voters (but not Gore voters) of their right to equal protection. The majority-opinion justices reasoned that since the rules governing the hand recount varied from precinct to precinct—for instance, concerning whether or not both "hanging" chads and "dimpled" chads would be counted—the recount would be unfair to those voters whose ballots had been counted by machines before the recount had begun. But, as Dershowitz (2001:61) asks, would not voters whose ballots were not properly counted by machines "suffer much more serious violations of their equal protection rights"? Given the diversity of ballot designs and voting technologies that existed throughout the state (and indeed the entire country), the logical extension of the Court's ruling would have been to invalidate the entire presidential election. As Win McCormack suggests, the majority-opinion justices "speciously ignored the fact that the Florida ballots, prior to any recount, were *already* counted differently, and that the very purpose of recounting was to correct for this discrepancy" (2001:32).

Moreover, the majority's legal logic is inconsistent with the judges' own prior rulings. Previously, these judges had ruled that claims about equal protection violations "should be able to identify with some degree of specificity the alleged victim" and prove that the contested actions had a clear discriminatory purpose (Dershowitz 2001:77). The majority also had previously ruled that the Court's function is to establish legal precedents, not to declare unique dispositions. Yet in *Bush v. Gore* the majority wrote: "Our consideration is limited to the present circumstances, for the problem of equal protection in election processes generally presents many complexities" (p. 81). In other words, as Dershowitz pointedly notes: "In future election cases, don't try to hold the Court to what it said in this case, because it decided this case not on general principles applicable to all cases, but on a principle that has never before been recognized by any court and that will never again be recognized by this court" (p. 81).

A year after the election, a consortium of eight media organizations completed an unofficial hand recount of the Florida vote. The consortium concluded that if the admissible ballots for the entire state had been recounted, Gore would have won by a slim margin of 40 to 400 votes (CNN 2001; Fessenden & Broder 2001). Additionally, journalists uncovered other controversies that had unfairly tipped the election to Bush and would have given Gore a larger margin of victory. Florida election officials, under the direction of Harris, inappropriately did their best to deny former convicted felons from voting. Most states deny felons serving time in prison or on parole the right to vote, but the large majority of states restore the right to vote upon a prisoner's or parolee's completion of their sentence; Florida is one of the states that does not. In 2000 there were an estimated 50,000 to more than 100,000 former felons who had moved to Florida from other states with their voting rights intact. According to Florida court rulings, these individuals have the right to vote. Nevertheless, the Governor's Office of Executive Clemency mailed these people a notice informing them that they were "required to make application for restoration of civil rights in the state of Florida" (cited in Palast 2003:40). Few of these individuals followed up on this "requirement"—a requirement that had been ruled null and void by the Florida courts (Lantigua 2001; Manza & Uggen 2005).

As Florida election officials tried to purge the voter registration lists of people they deemed ineligible to vote, thousands of eligible voters were mistakenly removed. Take the case of the so-called former felons from Texas. ChoicePoint, a private firm with close Republican ties, was hired by the state of Florida to provide the names of Texas ex-felons who had moved to Florida. As it turned out, none of the approximately 8,000 people who were identified and consequently removed from the voter list had actually been convicted of felonies—they had been convicted of misdemeanors. The state also hired Database Technologies of Atlanta, which has since merged with ChoicePoint, to provide it with lists of ineligible voters who had moved to Florida from other states. But the Database Technologies lists contained an error rate of 15 percent, and because African Americans experience higher rates of incarceration than other groups, the majority of people targeted by these purging efforts were black. Since African Americans vote overwhelmingly for Democratic candidates, these efforts disadvantaged Gore (Lantigua 2001; Palast 2003).

Another problem involved the data criteria that were used to match people who appeared on the Database Technologies/ChoicePoint ex-felon lists with people who appeared on the Florida voter lists. According to a vice president of ChoicePoint, Florida officials instructed the company to provide "more names than were actually verified as being a convicted felon" (quoted in Palast 2003:57). One way this was done was to establish criteria that would identify a match even if only part of a name on the ex-felon list matched a name on the voting list. In one case, Reverend Willie David Whiting, a black pastor living in Florida, was confused with Willie J. Whiting, a former felon from Texas, and hence the pastor was denied the opportunity to vote. Florida resident Johnny Jackson Jr. was matched with Texas ex-felon John Fitzgerald Jackson. David Butler of Florida was matched with Ohio ex-felon David Butler Jr. Randall Higgenbotham of Florida was matched with ex-felon Sean Higgenbotham, also of Florida. There were innumerable mistaken matches like these, as well as many misdemeanor offenders who were falsely identified as felons. On top of all this, black residents of one county complained of racial harassment at a highway-patrol checkpoint on a road leading to their polling place (Lantigua 2001). All told, if these types of problems had not occurred, Gore might have received more than 30,000 additional votes (Palast 2003).

Problems with computerized voting. Although the Florida election was marked by the question of antiquated voter technology, it also raised concerns about computerized voting. In Volusia County, for example, the electronic tabulator erroneously subtracted 16,022 votes from Gore's total just minutes before the media networks called the election for Bush. Although this mistake was discovered and corrected, CBS later admitted that it had been critical in its election night decision. Investigators traced the mistake to a second memory card on the system provided by Global Elections Systems (GES) that had been improperly (and suspiciously) uploaded. According to Talbot Ireland, a master programmer for Global Elections Systems, "There is always the possibility that the 'second memory card' or 'second upload' came from an unauthorized source" (quoted in Kennedy 2008:66).

Although the evidence is largely circumstantial, there are grounds for concern that the integrity of democracy in the United States is threatened by corruption through the use of computer technology, where touch-screen voting machines (without paper records) have produced some rather curious results. In the 2002 senatorial election in Georgia, for instance, preelection polls showed decorated disabled war veteran Max Cleland, the Democratic incumbent, ahead of the Republican challenger, Saxy Chambliss, by 5 percentage points; and in the gubernatorial race, the Democratic incumbent, Roy Barnes, was ahead of Republican challenger Sonny Perdue by 11 points. On election day, however, Chambliss won with 53 percent of the vote, and Purdue won with 51 percent (Kennedy 2008).

The computerized voting in the Georgia election was run by Diebold, one of the major makers of electronic-voting machines in the country, which has known ties to the Republican Party. Prior to the election, the president of Diebold's election unit, Bob Urosevich, arrived in Georgia from Diebold headquarters in Texas to personally distribute a software "patch" that was supposed to correct glitches in the computer program. According to Chris Hood, a consultant who worked for Diebold in Georgia, "Diebold employees altered software in some 5,000 machines in DeKalb and Fulton counties—the state's largest Democratic strongholds" (quoted in Kennedy 2008:64). It is possible, Hood believes, that a hidden program on a memory card could have adjusted the votes to a preferred result. But without a paper record that could verify the results in a recount, there is no way of knowing whether or not the machines in Georgia were rigged. As Avi Rubin, a specialist in electronic-voting security observes: "With electronic machines, you can commit wholesale fraud with a single alteration of software. . . . There are a million little tricks you can build into the software that allow you to do whatever you want" (quoted in *Rolling Stone* 2006:54).

Anecdotal evidence for the 2004 presidential election also indicates several cases where votes intended for Democratic candidate Senator John Kerry were recorded for President Bush, votes for Democratic constituencies were undercounted, or Bush was given extra votes (Kennedy 2008; A. Miller 2005; M. Miller 2005). These are not insignificant matters, especially in the state of Ohio, where the entire national election came down to Bush's victory by an official margin of less than 119,000 votes. Questions about the validity of the outcome in Ohio have been fueled by a report of a Republican fundraising letter sent by Walden O'Dell, CEO of Diebold, prior to the election, indicating that he was "committed to helping Ohio deliver its electoral votes to the president" (quoted in Smyth 2003). Bob Fitrakis offers the following examples, some of which were purportedly corrected and some not, of events that may have affected the outcome in Ohio:

> In various polling stations in Democrat-rich inner city precincts in Youngstown and Columbus, voters who pushed touch screens for Kerry saw Bush's name light up. . . . A voting machine in Mahoning County recorded a negative 25 million votes for Kerry. . . . In Gahanna Ward 1B, at a fundamentalist church, a so-called "electronic transfer glitch" gave Bush 4,258 votes when only 638 people had actually voted. . . . In Miami County, at 1:43 a.m. the morning after Election Day, with the county's central tabulator reporting 100 percent of the vote, 19,000 more votes mysteriously arrived; 13,000 were for Bush at the same percentage as prior to the additional votes. . . . In Cleveland, large, entirely implausible vote totals turned up for obscure third party candidates in traditional Democratic African-American wards. (2008:192–193)

Moreover, James Blackwell, the Republican secretary of state in Ohio, made numerous decisions designed to suppress the African-American vote, such as allocating fewer voting machines per capita in large urban areas than in less populated areas, leading to lines requiring voters to wait as long as four to five hours, and in some places as long as ten hours, with many people growing impatient and leaving without voting. None of these problems occurred in Republican-leaning districts (A. Miller 2005).

Summary

This chapter examined a broad array of illegalities that come under the rubric of political or government crime. Whereas political crime involves acts committed by relatively subordinate individuals or groups in pursuit of a political or ideological goal, government crime involves acts of government officials in pursuit of financial gain or government policy. More specifically, we considered two general categories of political crime— terrorism and hate crimes—and two general categories of government crime—state crimes of foreign policy and corruption of government officials.

Our discussion of terrorism focused on Al-Qaida and on right-wing and left-wing domestic terrorism in the United States. Our discussion of hate crimes reviewed available hate crime data and considered the problem of organized hate groups in the country. Our discussion of state crimes of foreign policy examined the US overthrow of foreign governments around the globe, the Vietnam War, the Iran-Contra scandal, and the more recent Iraq War, including the US government's propagation and use of torture. Last, our discussion of government corruption focused on financial crimes of local, state, and federal officials, including the K Street Project lobbying scandal, as well as issues of electoral corruption, including voter fraud, the controversy surrounding the 2000 presidential election, and problems with computerized voting.

Part 3 _____
The Criminal Justice System

11

The Police and Courts

The criminal justice system in the United States consists of three broad areas: the police, courts, and corrections. This chapter will focus on the police and courts, and the next chapter will focus on corrections. We begin by noting the sometimes complementary and sometimes competing objectives of law enforcement in a democratic society, what Herbert Packer (1964) referred to as the **crime control** and **due process models** of criminal justice. Under the crime control model, the suppression of criminal conduct is the primary goal. Under the due process model, legal barriers are erected that make it more difficult to move the accused through the sequential stages of the criminal justice system, therefore protecting individuals from arbitrary and abusive governmental authority. Although due process protections sometimes work to the advantage of criminals, many people believe it is the price we must pay to preserve our liberties. On the other hand, people think such liberties mean little if their safety from criminals is jeopardized.

The Modern Police Force

The modern police force in the United States is a highly decentralized and fragmented system that consists of thousands of departments around the country, mostly at the local level. Policing is primarily a civilian (nonmilitary) activity that is separated from the legislative and judicial branches of government. There is no national police force with general jurisdiction, although federal agencies like the FBI have jurisdiction over federal crimes as well as interstate criminal conduct.

Policing in Historical Perspective

The US system of policing evolved from the English system imported by the early American colonists. In medieval England going back to the eleventh century, local police functions were carried out through an informal system of unpaid citizen volunteers and political appointees. Early English constables, who were responsible not only for ensuring law and order but also for services such as garbage collection, were assisted by night watchmen who patrolled the city ringing bells and assuring everyone that "all was well." By the nineteenth century, however, this informal system of policing could not keep pace with the growing problems of poverty, crime, and public disorder (such as vagrancy, drunkenness, and urban rioting) that accompanied increasing industrialization and urbanization (Barkan & Bryjak 2011; Shelden et al. 2008).

In colonial America, the **constable-watch system** resembled the informal English model. All males were expected to serve as members of the watch, which carried out both daytime and nighttime patrols. As nineteenth-century US cities began experiencing the same problems as their English counterparts, a more formal police system emerged. Economic elites supported an expanded police apparatus to quell worker rebellions and clashes between immigrant ethnic groups. In the cities of the North, the local police were a major antistrike institution employed on behalf of capitalist owners of industry (Harring 1993). At the earliest indication of a strike, police would patrol the area and try to prevent workers from "assembling and maintaining an effective picket line" (Harring & McMullin 1975:13). In the South, the modern police evolved out of a system of citizen slave patrols that were responsible for preventing slave revolts and retrieving runaway slaves (Shelden et al. 2008).

Although the official capacity and legitimate authority to use force is central to policing, firearms did not become standard equipment until late in the nineteenth century. Moreover, the early police did not command much respect from the public. As Samuel Walker observes: "Juvenile gangs made a sport of throwing rocks at the police or taunting them . . . [and people] who were arrested often fought back. . . . Officers responded by beating hostile citizens into submission . . . and excessive use of force [was] commonplace" (1992:9). In addition, police corruption was endemic to nineteenth-century policing. Failure to enforce laws allowed vices like gambling, prostitution, and public drunkenness to flourish. Pickpockets and other professional thieves were tolerated in return for goods or information. Payoffs to officers on the beat were shared with supervisors, and promotions within the department were bought by bribing superiors. In large cities, the police were also an integral part of urban political machines, and the attainment of positions in the police department was influenced more by political connections and favoritism than law enforcement expertise (Barkan & Bryjak 2011).

Policing was an occupation that primarily attracted working-class men, and most officers were drawn from the very working-class population they were expected to control. This led to a problem of conflicting loyalties that made them unreliable enforcers of capitalist rule during times of labor unrest, although the potential for working-class solidarity was often neutralized by recruitment of officers from different ethnic groups. And since police were paid at least twice the rate of ordinary workers, they were able to move into more comfortable neighborhoods, which fostered class identification with the urban elites. Police uniforms and a military-style organization and discipline also served to distance the police from the public (Barkan & Bryjak 2011; Harring 1993; Shelden et al. 2008).

In the early twentieth century, the nature of policing underwent further reform. August Vollmer, who achieved national recognition while serving as the first police chief of Berkeley, California, sought to professionalize police departments by recruiting officers of higher educational background, implementing standardized entrance exams, improving officer training, and using scientific technology such as fingerprinting and crime laboratories in criminal investigations. Nevertheless, in 1931 the National Commission on Law Observance and Enforcement, headed by former US attorney general George Wickersham, found police forces around the country deficient in these areas. The Wickersham Commission, as it was called, also criticized police departments for their frequent use of the "third degree"—the use of physical coercion to gain information from suspects (Barkan & Bryjak 2011; Shelden et al. 2008).

The Wickersham Commission provided further impetus to police reform, as did the image of the dedicated, morally irreproachable FBI agent that was fostered by longtime FBI director J. Edgar Hoover. By the 1960s, "the professional model of the well-trained, highly disciplined, crime-fighting police force had taken hold across the nation" (Adler et al. 2000:110). In big-city police departments, recruits were required to have a high school diploma and undergo psychological testing and background checks. Officer training was also improved, and the traditional foot patrol was replaced by patrol cars equipped with two-way radios, enabling a more rapid response to calls for assistance and allowing supervisors to remain in touch with those on the beat. But as departments began to implement more aggressive stop-and-search patrols, relations between police and the communities they were supposed to serve became increasingly strained. African Americans in particular felt targeted by the stop-and-search police tactic as well as victimized by police brutality. Confrontations between police and citizens precipitated several race riots in the 1960s (see Chapter 5). Advocates of police reform called for remedial measures, including higher educational requirements and better training for officers, the hiring of minority officers, greater attention to police-community relations, and more government oversight over police misconduct.

Organizational Styles of Policing

The work of police officers is subject to a great deal of discretion. **Police discretion** may be defined as "the latitude or flexibility the officer has in deciding how an incident should be handled" (Fuller 1998:85). Discretion is not entirely an individual matter, however, because it is significantly influenced by a department's **organizational style of policing**—the philosophy and methods that govern its operation. In his classic book *Varieties of Police Behavior,* James Q. Wilson (1968) identified three different organizational styles: the watchman, legalistic, and service styles.

The **watchman style** emphasizes the order-maintenance function of policing—the informal handling of disputes—and measures an officer's success by his or her ability to keep the peace on the beat rather than by the number of arrests made. Minor infractions are often ignored as long as order is maintained, and disorderly citizens are advised to leave the area or go home in order to avoid arrest. Officers are provided with little direct supervisory oversight and are encouraged to exercise their own judgment regarding when to enforce the law. Such leeway can be abused, however, if discretionary decisions are based on bribery or discrimination.

In contrast, the **legalistic style** emphasizes a by-the-book approach, whereby officers are expected to enforce the law against all violators. They are rewarded based on the number of calls they handle and the number of arrests they make, and they are expected to be professional, impersonal, and hard-nosed. According to former Philadelphia and Los Angeles police chief Willie Williams (1996), this approach is often equated with a military style of policing, whereby individuals with a military penchant for following orders are recruited and trained to respond quickly to solve immediate problems. In this model, an officer's ability to envision how policing can be improved or performed differently is neither expected nor encouraged (Skolnick & Fyfe 1993).

Finally, the **service style** is common in communities with little serious crime, wherein officers have time to focus on other community needs, such as accident and drug prevention, youth mentoring, and recreational programming. Like watchman departments, service departments emphasize noncustodial methods of intervention: issuing warnings, mediating disputes, and making referrals to nonpolice agencies. Officers are encouraged to develop positive relationships with the community and to relate to citizens in a personal rather than an aloof manner.

Wilson's observations (1968) serve as a useful point of departure for considering two highly significant trends in policing: the increasing militarization of the police and the growing interest in community relations.

Paramilitary policing. Police departments are increasingly making use of what Peter Kraska and Victor Kappeler (1997) call **paramilitary police units** (PPUs), notable for their use of advanced military equipment and technology such as submachine guns, semiautomatic and automatic shotguns, laser sights, tear gas, battering rams, hydraulic door-jamb spreaders, explosives, and fortified tactical cruisers and military armored personnel vehicles. PPU officers "wear black or urban camouflage 'battle dress' uniforms, lace-up combat boots, full body armor, Kevlar helmets, and sometimes goggles with 'ninja' style hoods" (p. 4).

Police administrators and personnel view PPUs as an elite officer core. Most of these units were first formed in the late 1960s and early 1970s "to respond to civil riots, terrorism, barricaded suspects, and hostage situations" (p. 4). Sometimes known as SWAT (special weapons and tactics) teams, PPUs are involved in a range of high-risk activities that require "a squad of officers trained to be use-force-specialists" who have "an intensified operational focus on either the threatened or the actual use of collective force."

According to Kraska and Kappeler, contemporary PPUs do not merely react to preexisting emergencies but proactively seek out dangerous confrontations and at times even provoke an escalation of violence. One PPU officer, for example, described how SWAT teams are used to saturate crime "hot spots" with officers who have, in his words, "bigger guns." As he said: "We send out two, two-to-four-men cars . . . [and] look for minor violations and do jump-outs, either on people on the street or automobiles. After we jump-out the second car provides periphery cover with an *ostentatious display of weaponry*. We're sending a clear message: if the shootings don't stop, we'll shoot someone" (p. 10).

PPUs are also used to serve search warrants and arrest warrants, especially those requiring "no-knock" entries. Some drug raids even take place without warrants, which is apparently legal "if the police have reason to believe that waiting for a warrant would endanger lives or lead to the destruction of evidence" (p. 8). One former PPU member described a drug raid this way: "We did a crack-raid and got in a massive shoot-out in an apartment building. Shots were fired and we riddled a wall with bullets. An MP5 round will go through walls. When we went into the next apartment where the bullets were penetrating, we found a baby crib full of holes; thank god those people weren't home" (p. 9). Often, however, people are in fact home, and in one recent incident in Atlanta, the police threw a flash grenade into a two-year-old's crib. Also known as a stun grenade, this device is a nonlethal explosive that produces a blinding flash of light and loud noise designed to disorient a person. The toddler in this case was seriously injured. In other incidents, PPUs have been deployed against a private poker game, a gay bar, a bar suspected of serving minors, and several barbershops accused of "barbering without a license" (American Civil Liberties Union 2014).

Nowadays PPUs are used not just in the inner-city or large urban departments but in many smaller communities as well. By the mid-1990s, nearly 80 percent of departments with at least 100 officers serving a jurisdiction of at least 50,000 people had PPUs; and 65 percent of departments serving jurisdictions of between 25,000 and 50,000 had them. PPUs are also being used to test military-style equipment that is later introduced into mainstream policing (Kraska & Cubellis 1997; Kraska & Kappeler 1997); and since 2006 alone, the Pentagon has transferred more than $4 billion in surplus military equipment to local and state police departments, including tanks, mine-resistance vehicles, drones, machine guns, and battering rams designed for use in the wars in Iraq and Afghanistan (Apuzzo 2014; *The Week* 2014).

Kraska and Kappeler (1997) note that the growth of PPUs coincided with the popularization of the "war" metaphor of crime control in the 1980s, particularly the war on drugs, with more than 60 percent of SWAT raids deployed for drug searches, many on the basis of unreliable inform-ants (American Civil Liberties Union 2014). SWAT teams are also used to conduct "saturation patrols," whereby extra officers are deployed in certain neighborhoods. According to one SWAT commander, "We focus on quality of life issues like illegal parking, loud music, bums, troubles" (quoted in Bauer 2014:21).

Nevertheless, police officials continue to tout paramilitary policing as a central tool of crime control. If crime, as we are told, is a war, then police may be envisioned as an army that must gain control and maintain occu-pancy of an area by force. As one police chief explained, "It's going to come to the point that the only people that are going to be able to deal with . . . [the problem of crime] are highly trained tactical teams with proper equipment to go into a neighborhood and clear . . . and hold it" (quoted in Bauer 2014:13).

Community policing. A seemingly contradictory approach to paramilitary policing is known as **community policing**, which has its origins in the late 1960s and early 1970s. Previously we described community policing in rather general terms, to identify law enforcement strategies that put police in closer touch with the community (see Chapter 1). Community policing aims to promote trust between citizens and the police and discourage the "us versus them" mentality that is especially prevalent among officers working in minority neighborhoods, where at times police seem unable to distinguish "between law-abiding residents and criminal suspects of the same color" (Williams 1996:224). Andrew Hacker observes that when most "white people hear the cry, 'the police are coming!' . . . it almost always means, 'help is on the way'" (1992:46). But African Americans experience the police quite differently:

> If you have been the victim of a crime, you cannot presume that the police will actually show up; or, if they do, that they will take much note of your losses or suffering. . . . If you are a teenager simply socializing with some friends, the police may order you to disperse and get off the streets. They may turn on a searchlight, order you against a wall. Then comes the com-mand to spread your legs and empty out your pockets, and stand splayed

there while they call in your identity over the radio. You may be a college student and sing in a church choir, but that will not overcome the police presumption that you have probably done something they can arrest you for. (p. 51)

Willie Williams argues that community policing means "changing the prevailing kick-butt-and-take-no-names policy of too many departments" and assigning officers to work *with* rather than *against* the community (1996:219). In community policing, police officials meet regularly with residents, citizen advisory boards, and other community groups to seek input and to learn what the people want from *their* police. There is less reliance on patrol cars, and greater use of foot patrols to provide opportunities for positive encounters, and officers are assigned to the same neighborhood for longer periods of time to enable relationships to develop with residents. As one community policing officer in Chicago remarked: "Every day you go out there and you see people washing their cars or mowing their lawns or playing with the kids. If they see you and know you, they trust you." Before the use of community policing, one resident said that police "only saw the bad guys, not any of the good guys." Since then, however, he's seen "a big difference" (Eig 1996:64).

Community policing replaces an incident-by-incident response to crime with one that seeks comprehensive solutions to community problems. It incorporates a watchman-style emphasis on the informal handling of disputes and a service-style emphasis on prevention and youth programming. Police are considered responsible not only for handling serious crime but also for quality-of-life issues such as noise complaints, graffiti, vagrancy, trash-filled alleys, and abandoned vehicles and buildings. Police, often the first public officials to encounter these problems, can refer residents to other government agencies for remedial action. Earlier we referred to this as the "broken windows" strategy of policing, an approach that encourages police to focus on the little things that conventional law enforcement often ignores (see Chapter 2).

Effective community policing is contingent on a number of factors, including the adequacy of nonpolice follow-up to police referrals, the extent of community participation, the socioeconomic conditions of the community, and the particular type of community policing that is being deployed (MacDonald 2002). Robert Taylor and colleagues note that "the police *cannot* be all things to all people. . . . [They] cannot be an isolated group . . . trying to address major social problems without the combined commitment and resources of the entire city" (1998:3).

Moreover, officers are often resistant to community policing, viewing it as an abrogation of their role as crime fighters. For the most part, police agencies remain cloistered and inflexible, hiring the same type of people and training them the same way as before community policing became

FURTHER EXPLORATION
The Exclusionary Rule

Earlier we noted that the concern with due process is one of the central features of the criminal justice system in the United States, and during the 1960s several US Supreme Court decisions expanded the protections afforded by the Bill of Rights to the states. In *Miranda v. Arizona* (1966), for instance, the Court ruled that the conviction of Ernesto Miranda should be reversed because he had confessed without being informed of his Fifth Amendment right against self-incrimination and his Sixth Amendment right to an attorney. The decision ushered in the now famous **Miranda warning**, which requires that before police question a suspect, they must inform him or her of their right to remain silent and of their right to an attorney prior to and during questioning (and if they cannot afford an attorney, the right to have one appointed by the court), and that anything they say can and will be used against them in court.

The *Miranda* decision and other Supreme Court rulings brought forth criticism from law-and-order advocates who thought that criminals were being allowed to go free on the basis of legal technicalities. One of the most controversial rulings was the *Mapp v. Ohio* (1961) decision regarding "search and seizure" procedures.

The Fourth Amendment to the US Constitution reads: "The right of the people to be secure in their persons, houses, papers, and effects, against unreasonable searches and seizures, shall not be violated, and no warrants shall issue, but upon probable cause, supported by oath or affirmation, and particularly describing the place to be searched, and the persons or things to be seized." In *Weeks v. United States* (1914), the Court ruled that evidence obtained by police in violation of this amendment could be excluded from court. Hence the **exclusionary rule** came into being. The *Weeks* decision applied only to federal cases, however, and it was not until *Mapp v. Ohio* that the rule applied to the states.

The concern about letting criminals go free notwithstanding, research indicates that few felony arrests are dismissed because of search and seizure violations, and these are primarily in cases involving drugs, not violent crimes. In fact, the exclusionary rule has led some police departments to improve officer training about search and seizure regulations and develop closer working relationships with prosecutors about how to obtain evidence that will stand up in court (Reid 2006; Walker 2011).

continues

fashionable. Police are often reluctant to relinquish their role as experts who possess a monopoly on the skills and knowledge necessary to deal with crime. At times, they view community policing as merely a public relations ploy, as a way to enhance their image rather than as a genuine attempt to respond to community concerns (Boostrom & Henderson 1983; Roussell & Gascón 2014). And even where community policing exists, res-

continued

The exclusionary rule is a constantly evolving doctrine, and the Court has articulated several exceptions to it. For example, a warrantless search is permissible when the seized object is in *plain view;* and under the *public safety* exception a search may be conducted if police believe the public is in jeopardy. Under the *inevitable discovery* doctrine, illegally seized evidence is admissible in court as long as the "police would have found it later by legal methods"; and under the *good faith* exception, such evidence is admissible if the officer who secured the evidence reasonably believed he or she was "acting in accordance with the law" (Reid 2006:439).

Police have also been given considerable latitude to search motor vehicles without a warrant. In a 1996 case, for instance, the Court unanimously upheld a stop-and-search in the District of Columbia in which two plainclothes officers in an unmarked vehicle followed two African-American men who were driving a new Nissan Pathfinder in a "high drug area." Although the DC department prohibits plainclothes officers in unmarked vehicles from enforcing traffic ordinances unless the violation threatens public safety, the officers apparently stopped the Pathfinder for remaining too long at a stop sign. After searching the vehicle, they found drugs. The Court ruled that the seized evidence was admissible even in the absence of probable cause or reasonable suspicion (Cole 1999a).

Police may also conduct a search if the person consents to the search, and officers are not obligated to inform citizens of their right to say no (Cole 1999c). Wendy Kaminer reports that in Maryland, police have stopped African-American motorists and asked them "with varying degrees of belligerency, to 'consent' to thorough searches of their cars. If [the motorists] decline, they are not free to leave; they are forced to wait on the side of the road for the arrival of drug dogs, who sniff and paw through their belongings and sometimes urinate in their cars" (1999:38). In addition, police may conduct sweeps of buses and trains that "exploit the fact that the traveler has nowhere to go," making it difficult to withhold cooperation (Cole 1999c:22). One study of police searches in a midsized US city found that nearly one-third were in violation of exclusionary-rule guidelines (Gould & Mastrofski 2004).

idents may remain unaware or unconvinced that the department has undertaken a serious change in orientation. Jerome Skolnick and David Bayley believe that community policing "should be said to exist only when new programs are implemented that raise the level of public participation in the maintenance of public order" (1988:5). As Jonathan Eig maintains, for community policing to really work, "law-abiding residents must feel that there is a social movement afoot, that it's catching on, and that if they join it they might actually improve their neighborhoods. Criminals, in turn, have got to notice that police become much more effective when they have the eyes and ears of neighbors working for them" (1996:68).

Critics of community policing believe it is naive to think that more police contact with residents will necessarily improve relationships. What it may do is increase opportunities for hostile interactions. When officers are given license to exercise discretion on their beats, they may feel that they have been invited "to use force against people who threaten the tranquility of that neighborhood" (Anderson 1999:51). According to Kraska and Kappeler (1997), community policing and paramilitary police units should be viewed not as alternative but as complementary policing strategies. In fact, a majority of the police commanders they interviewed believed it will become increasingly necessary for paramilitary police units to secure neighborhoods and clear them of their unruly elements before community policing will even have a chance to work.

Police Culture and the Work of Policing

Despite the community policing movement, the occupational culture of most police departments has remained fairly stable. According to Jerome Skolnick and James Fyfe (1993), two principal features of police work—danger and authority—combine to produce a distinctive outlook or **working personality** that guides the values, understandings, and behavior of officers, sometimes leading to admirable valor but sometimes leading to brutality or excessive use of force. As James Ahern notes: "The day the new recruit walks through the doors of the police academy he leaves society behind to enter a profession that does more than give him a job, it defines who he is. For all the years he remains . . . he will be a cop" (1972:3).

Although the job-related death rate for police officers is well below that of several other occupations (such as farming, construction, and mining), police are constantly aware of the potential dangers they face (Bayley & Bittner 1999). Police role-calls regularly conclude with the admonition "stay safe out there." As one officer said: "Most of the time this job is boring. . . . You just sit behind the wheel and go where they tell you. . . . But . . . you never forget that the next call you get or car you stop might be your last. . . . You know there's one hell of a lotta people out there who'd love to [knock] off a cop" (Van Maanen 1995:228–229). While officers are weary of colleagues who are hotheads or **hardchargers**—those who seek out and are overzealous in their willingness to rush into dangerous situations—most agree that police work requires courage and a willingness to take risks, and is not for the fainthearted (Herbert 1998).

Additionally, officers believe that both their safety and the effective performance of their job require that citizens respect their authority. To some extent, every stop, frisk, search, arrest, and handcuffing "involves an imposition of force on an essentially unwilling person, no matter how compliant"—and suspects are not always compliant (Skolnick & Fyfe 1993:94).

Although shootings of officers are rare, police continually deal with "people who are willing to fight, struggle, hit, stab, spit, bite, tear, hurl, hide, and run. . . . All except the rawest rookie can show scars on their bodies from continual encounters with low-level violence" (Bayley & Bittner 1999:229). Hence, police may at times decide to use force preemptively to establish control of a situation before it gets out of hand.

Those who resist police demands for compliance can expect to receive some "payback." As the Los Angeles Police Department dispatcher who radioed for an ambulance following the infamous 1991 police beating of Rodney King said, "They should know better than to run, they are going to pay a price when they do that" (quoted in Herbert 1998:359). King had taken police on a high-speed car chase after refusing to submit to a police stop. He was finally forced to the side of the road and ordered out of his vehicle. Four officers, two wielding metal nightsticks, administered dozens of blows while about ten other officers looked on. In another incident, one involving the injury of an LAPD officer, police intensified their surveillance of the community for several weeks, "looking for any pretense to make arrests . . . [in order] to reestablish a sense of police control over an unruly space" (p. 360).

The nature of police work also encourages officers to be suspicious, to be on guard for behavior that seems out of the ordinary. For instance, a person wearing a coat on a warm day may be hiding a sawed-off shotgun or stolen goods; a dirty car with clean license plates (or vice versa) may indicate a stolen vehicle; or a white person in a black neighborhood may be attempting to buy drugs. Boundaries of neighborhoods are often heavily patrolled to prevent anyone from straying out of place, especially when it is lower-class or minority youths who are crossing over into higher-class or white areas. People who are out of place, police think, must be up to no good (Skolnick & Fyfe 1993; Werthman & Piliavin 1967).

Police suspiciousness often leads to the development of stereotypes that identify certain types of people as **symbolic assailants**—"persons whose gestures, language, or attire" trigger suspicion (Skolnick & Fyfe 1993:97). Unfortunately, sometimes one's status as a racial minority can mark him or her as a symbolic assailant. In 1995, for instance, Earl Graves Jr., an African-American business executive, was exiting a commuter train in Manhattan, New York, when he was grabbed and frisked by two police officers. The officers were looking for a 5-foot 10-inch–tall black male suspect with a mustache. Graves, however, stood 6-foot 4-inches and had no mustache (Stout 1995).

In Los Angeles, Christopher Darden (1996), an African-American prosecutor who gained national notoriety during the O.J. Simpson murder trial (see Chapter 8), learned of the racism in the LAPD when he went to work for the Special Investigation Division of the district attorney's office in 1988.

Like any black person in L.A., I could feel the antagonism between African
Americans and the police, but I didn't think a lot about it until it was my
job to investigate and prosecute the police. . . . Most black men knew what
it was like to be driving lawfully down some street when you caught the
eye of a police officer, who spun around and pulled you over . . . looking
for the pile of rock cocaine and the semiautomatic rifle that every black
man obviously carries wherever he goes. . . . You knew what the real crime
was: suspicion of being black. And there were other stories too: stories of
people beaten, kicked, and knocked around by LAPD officers; stories of a
police officer who planted so much evidence his colleagues called him
Farmer; stories of cops who flat-out lied on the stand to get a conviction.
There were even stories of racist cops, guys who collected Nazi paraphernalia and tossed around various racial epithets like gossip at a barbershop.
(pp. 96–97)

Racial Profiling

The experience described by Darden has by no means disappeared and has
become known as "driving while black," or in Earl Graves's case, "walking
while black" (Meeks 2000; Russell 2003). Also known as **racial profiling**,
this practice entails police-targeting of particular groups for more intrusive
law enforcement because of their race, ethnicity, or national origin. Racial
profiling has its roots in the more general practice of criminal profiling,
whereby police officers use demographic traits of *known* offenders to identify *potential* offenders. Individuals who possess these traits then come
under closer scrutiny because they fit the profile of someone who *might*
commit a crime.

The 1992 case of Robert Wilkins, an African-American attorney from
Maryland, was significant in bringing the problem of racial profiling to the
forefront of public attention. Wilkins was returning home from a family
funeral in Chicago with his aunt, uncle, and cousin, Norman El-Amin. El-
Amin was at the wheel of their rented Cadillac when they were stopped by
a white state trooper for speeding on Interstate 68 in western Maryland.
After El-Amin, with Wilkins's encouragement, refused the officer's request
to search the car for contraband, the trooper called for a drug-sniffing
police dog. Wilkins and his relatives were forced to stand on the side of the
road in the rain while the dog searched for the nonexistent drugs. After no
drugs were found, El-Amin was issued a $105 traffic ticket for speeding
(Cole 1999b; Meeks 2000).

With the assistance of the American Civil Liberties Union (ACLU) of
Maryland, Wilkins and his family sued the state of Maryland and in 1995
received a $95,600 settlement (which included legal costs). As part of the
settlement, the Maryland State Police agreed to conduct a comprehensive
investigation of driver stops on Interstates 68 and 95. The completed study
disclosed that African-American motorists were, in fact, disproportionately
singled out for police stops and searches. Over 70 percent of the drivers
stopped and searched by the Maryland State Police between 1995 and 1997

were black, even though blacks composed just 17 percent of the motorists in the state, and even though they were no more likely than whites to have violated a traffic law or have illegal substances found in their vehicles (American Civil Liberties Union 1995).

In addition to Maryland, early studies documented the prevalence of racial profiling in Florida and New Jersey. In a study of traffic stops on Interstate 95 in Florida, about 70 percent of those stopped were black or Latino, even though nonwhites composed only 5 percent of motorists (Curtis 1992). In a study of stops on the New Jersey Turnpike, black drivers accounted for 35 percent of the stops, even though they composed just 14 percent of all drivers and 15 percent of those who were speeding; and black and Latino drivers accounted for about 80 percent of all vehicles that were searched (Kocieniewski & Hanley 2000). More recently, a study of traffic stops in Kansas City, Missouri, found that while race did not play a role in "safety stops" related to clear violations of traffic laws, it was the primary factor in "investigatory stops" related to inquiries into nontraffic crimes. Black drivers were almost three times more likely than their white counterparts to be singled out for investigatory stops, and five times more likely to have their vehicles searched (Epp & Maynard-Moody 2014).

Nor, as we suggested earlier, is racial profiling confined to drivers. An investigation of "stop-and-frisk" practices in New York City in the late 1990s found that more than half of the pedestrians stopped by the police were black, a rate that was double the proportion of blacks among the city's population. Moreover, nearly two-thirds of the pedestrians stopped by the special Street Crime Unit of the New York Police Department were black. And in precincts where blacks and Latinos each constituted less than a tenth of the population, they were stopped 30 percent and 23 percent of the time, respectively (Spitzer 1999).

The controversial practices of the NYPD were highlighted in a 2013 federal court ruling that declared that the "city's highest officials have turned a blind eye to the evidence that officers are conducting stops in a racially discriminatory manner" (cited in *Huffington Post* 2013). This practice reached an all-time high in 2011, during the final years of the administration of Mayor Michael Bloomberg, who first took office in 2002. Under Bloomberg, police stops of pedestrians increased by about 600 percent, with 684,330 alone in 2011, 87 percent of which were of blacks or Latinos. Although 10 percent of these stops resulted in arrest, the court found that nearly 30 percent occurred without any reasonable suspicion.

Proponents of racial profiling contend the practice is necessary for effective law enforcement, yet research questions the efficacy of this procedure. Of importance here is whether or not the stop leads to the discovery of contraband or a crime, the so-called **hit rate**. According to David Harris: "All the studies . . . [that] allow for the calculation of hit rates . . . show higher hit rates *not for blacks and Latinos, but for whites.* In other words, officers 'hit' less often when they use race or ethnic appearance to decide which persons seem suspicious enough to merit stops and searches than they do when they use suspicious behavior and not race as their way of selecting suspects" (2003:82, emphasis added).

In recent years, profiling of Latinos alleged to be illegal immigrants has become more common, particularly in the border states of the South. According to a 1975 US Supreme Court ruling, upheld in subsequent decisions, a "Mexican appearance" is a legitimate reason to stop someone to verify their citizenship status (Hutchinson 2010). Increasingly, this policy has led to "harassment of both immigrants and US citizens, particularly in Latino communities, further marginalizing already vulnerable populations" (American Civil Liberties Union & Rights Working Group 2009:13). Thus, a 2008 survey of Latinos in Southern states found that nearly half of those interviewed said they had been stopped by police under the pretense of some minor offense or no offense at all (Bauer 2009). In Alabama, for example, Victor Marquez was stopped while he was en route to his hometown in Mexico for "failure to maintain a marked lane." Marquez had in his possession $20,000, which he said he and his brother had legally earned and he was taking back to their family. Although Marquez was not arrested or charged with a crime, the money was seized by the police as "drug money." It should be noted that white immigrants from Canada, Europe, and Russia do not generally face this kind of harassment.

Diversity in Policing

Historically, policing was largely a white man's occupation, and it was not until the civil rights and women's movements of the 1960s that sufficient political pressure was mounted to integrate police departments in the United States. As of 2010, about 25 percent of local police officers are racial and ethnic minorities and 12 percent are women (Reaves 2010).

The integration of police departments has not occurred without significant tension, however. Racial/ethnic minorities and women report being more closely supervised and more frequently sanctioned for their mistakes. Common complaints include greater supervisory scrutiny than given to white male officers, undeserved negative performance evaluations, less support from colleagues, and assignment only to minority neighborhoods (Fletcher 1995; Haarr 1997; Williams 1988). Some research indicates that black male officers are more likely than female officers (white or black) to be viewed as competent professionals by white male police. Black women, however, who constitute about a third of women officers, are viewed more negatively than white women officers by both white and black male police. Black male officers sometimes appear even more hostile than white male officers to black women, in part because they compete with black women for scarce affirmative action slots (Dulaney 1996; Fletcher 1995; Martin 1994).

Many people hoped that the quality of policing, especially community policing in minority neighborhoods, would be improved if racial/ethnic minorities were more represented in the profession. Minority officers are less likely than white officers to be viewed by minority residents as intruders, and may therefore legitimate the presence of police in these communities. They may also serve as role models for minority youths, reminding them that legitimate employment opportunities are available to them; and they may help dispel the societal stereotype of criminals, making it more difficult for white officers to perpetuate this stereotype as a taken-for-granted assumption of police culture (Free 1996; Greene 1994).

Still, there are limits to the impact minorities have on policing, and overall there is little evidence that they actually do policing differently than whites. Black officers and white officers, for instance, are equally likely to fire their weapons, use excessive force, and make arrests. It appears that the organizational style of a department is more important than race in accounting for officers' behavior (Black 1980; Fyfe 1981; Walker et al. 2007).

As for women officers, few occupations have resisted the integration of women more vigorously than policing (Martin & Jurik 1996). Traditionally, policing has been a profession that men could use as a resource for demonstrating masculinity, and women's participation challenges their belief that "real policing" is work that only "real men" do. Veteran male officers have been reluctant to work with women on patrol, have refused to teach them the skills they routinely impart to other men, and have not responded quickly when women need backup. The "locker room" culture of police departments has been filled with crude sexist talk, and supervisors have ignored women's complaints of sexual harassment (Fletcher 1995; Haarr 1997; Texeira 2002).

Most criminologists have concluded that female police officers are as capable as male officers. Although some research has found that women are less proficient than men in the use of firearms and that they make fewer arrests, women also receive fewer citizen complaints and appear more effective in using interpersonal skills to deescalate conflict situations without having to use force or make an arrest (Hale & Wyland 1999; Martin & Jurik 1996).

Women have adapted to the male-dominated environment of policing in different ways. Susan Martin (1980) distinguishes between *police*women and police*women* strategies. *Police*women try to gain acceptance from their male colleagues by acting like them, by adopting an aggressive or hard-nosed style. This approach entails the risk of being rejected as unfeminine or being labeled a "dyke" or "bitch." Police*women,* on the other hand, employ a more traditional feminine style, being reluctant to assert their authority or use force and deferring to male partners when on patrol. This approach encourages male officers to adopt a paternalistic or protective stance that reinforces their view that women are not cut out for police work.

Increasingly, women have struck a balance between traditional femininity and masculinity by projecting an image of themselves as both team players and skilled professionals, and by using humor to develop camaraderie with male colleagues and thwart unwelcome sexual advances and harassment (Martin & Jurik 1996).

One understudied element of diversity in policing involves gay and lesbian officers, who experience similar discriminatory treatment as racial/ethnic minorities and women, and more so, given the homophobic attitudes that are prevalent in society and police culture in particular. Thus, gay and lesbian officers often adopt a "faux heterosexual persona . . . and keep their sexual orientation hidden" (Colvin 2012:66). On the other hand, those who are willing to be open about their sexuality may become assets to their departments, helping to more effectively respond to intimate-partner violence involving sexual minorities, hate crimes and bullying, transgender prostitution, and homelessness of gay, lesbian, and transgender youths.

Police Corruption

When Frank Serpico joined the NYPD in 1959, he had every intention of becoming a dedicated and loyal officer. He soon learned, however, that the formal departmental regulations prohibiting corruption and bribery were in conflict with the informal norms of the NYPD culture. When he refused to accept his part of the "take," he was ostracized by his corrupt colleagues and forced to work alone. He was eventually shot and seriously injured during a drug raid after his fellow officers failed to provide him with timely backup (Maas 1973).

Serpico became the most famous police whistleblower in US history, and his story led to a historic official inquiry into police corruption, the Knapp Commission, headed by Judge Whitman Knapp. The Knapp Commission (1972) revealed extensive, routine payoffs among NYPD plainclothes officers involved in gambling and narcotics enforcement. Corruption among uniformed patrol officers was less lucrative but included payoffs from retail businessmen and construction-site operators in exchange for nonenforcement of city ordinances. Patrol officers also received money from traffic violators and prostitutes hoping to avoid legal sanction, from tow-truck operators who received business tips from officers investigating accidents, and from defendants trying to get their cases fixed. The commission found that higher-ranking officers and police officials were on the take as well.

The Knapp Commission distinguished between two general categories of corrupt officers: **grass-eaters** and **meat-eaters**. The more numerous grass-eaters were less aggressive and accepted the smaller gratuities that happened to come their way. The meat-eaters, on the other hand, aggressively sought out opportunities for corrupt financial gain. Though fewer in number, their biweekly or monthly take yielded thousands of dollars apiece.

In the early 1990s, the Mollen Commission's investigation of corruption in the NYPD, headed by Judge Milton Mollen, also uncovered numerous instances of police offering protection to drug dealers, stealing drugs from dealers, and selling and using drugs. Much of this corruption was collaborative group activity, called "crew corruption" by the commission. The commission also identified a corrupt practice known as **testilying**, whereby officers give false testimony in court to cover up violations of due process law during the collection of evidence. One officer "who was working undercover for the . . . commission said he feared that if he did not lie, the other cops would immediately suspect that he was working [for the commission] . . . because *real cops do lie*" (Dershowitz 1996:57). Similarly, an FBI investigation of New York state troopers between 1984 and 1992 found routine faking of fingerprint evidence, whereby officers took a suspect's fingerprints from a police-station booking card or an object the suspect had touched, and then claimed the fingerprints were found at the crime scene. Such practices were justified by even "honest" officers when they believed the suspects were "really guilty" of a crime (Barker & Carter 1999; Hunt & Manning 1991).

In the late 1990s, the CRASH antigang unit that operated in the Rampart district of Los Angeles, fictionalized in the 2001 film *Training Day,* thrust the LAPD into the news again (CRASH is an acronym for "Community Resources Against Street Hoodlums"). In the name of fighting a so-called war on gangs, these officers routinely planted evidence and perjured themselves to get convictions. They also stole and sold drugs, stole money, and engaged in unjustified beatings and even shootings of suspects. More than 30 officers were implicated in the scandal, with criminal charges filed against some of them. The most well-known case involved Rafael Perez, who pled guilty to eight felony counts and cooperated in the investigation of other officers in exchange for a five-year prison term. More than a hundred convictions stemming from arrests by Rampart officers were overturned and scores of lawsuits were filed (Gupta 2003; Rampart Independent Review Panel 2002).

The types of corrupt practices we have been discussing, though perpetrated by a minority of officers, persist because of the informal **code of silence** that the majority of police observe. Officers are understandably reluctant to inform on one another. As Jerome Skolnick and James Fyfe note: "It is not easy in any group to be identified as the rat, the squealer, the busybody, the one person who cannot be trusted. . . . Any member of any group who considers becoming a whistle-blower must know that however laudable one's motives, doing so will forever change one's own life and status in the group" (1993:111). The most practical path to follow is the one of least resistance: "stay out of trouble" and "don't make waves." Nobody is perfect, and drawing attention to someone else may expose one's own derelictions. Indeed, much of the "silent majority" is itself implicated in the

---

FURTHER EXPLORATION
Police Sexual Misconduct

Although police are a politically conservative lot, they do not necessarily uphold traditional "family" values. Studies indicate, for example, that at least half of married male police officers have had adulterous sexual relationships and about a third of all officers have engaged in sexual activity while on duty (Baker 1985; Barker 1986). Moreover, there are many instances where officers have engaged in **police sexual misconduct**—that is, abuse of their authority to seek sexual gratification.

Based on interviews with police officers and supervisors in five states, Allen Sapp (1986) identified several types of police sexual misconduct. *Sexually motivated but nonsexual* contact, for instance, involves male officers who use their position of power to meet potential sexual partners, such as making unwarranted traffic stops of female motorists or by making unnecessary "callbacks" to female crime victims. *Sexually voyeuristic* contact involves attempts by male officers to view females in various stages of nudity, such as patrolling areas where women are known to leave their drapes or blinds open while disrobing, or by seeking out parked cars in areas known to be frequented by lovers.

Police sexual misconduct also occurs when male officers make unnecessary body searches of female suspects and when they have sex with female offenders (including adolescent runaways, truants, and delinquents) in exchange for nonenforcement of the law. Sometimes male undercover officers have sex with prostitutes before making an arrest. As one officer said, "If the whore claims otherwise, no one believes her anyway since they think she is just trying to get her case tossed out." Finally, there is *citizen-initiated* contact by police groupies who are "sexually attracted to the uniform, weapons, or power of the police officer" (Sapp 1986:91–92).

Peter Kraska and Victor Kappeler (1995) warn against dismissing the problem of police sexual misconduct as one of women trading sexual favors or male officers passively confronting sexual opportunities they cannot resist, for much of this misconduct entails the coercive abuse of power and outright force. In their research, they found that more than half of police sexual misconduct cases involved unnecessary strip searches of female suspects and nearly a third involved rape or sexual assault.

---

kind of petty corruption that is commonplace among police. As former LAPD officer Joseph Wambaugh wrote of one fictional officer in his novel *The Choirboys:* He "had accepted a thousand packs of cigarettes and as many free meals in his time. And though he had bought enough clothing at wholesale prices to dress a dozen movie stars, he had never even considered taking a five dollar bill nor was one ever offered except once when he stopped a Chicago grocer in Los Angeles on vacation" (1975:65).

Moreover, there is always some outraged citizen who is going to file a complaint against a police officer, or some reform-minded administrator who will "come down on you for breaking some rules" (Van Maanen 1995:235). The most important thing is not to lose the support of one's colleagues, for an officer's very life depends on others' willingness to provide immediate and unquestioned backup. As one officer said: "I'll put up with a hell of a lot from guys working this sector. I don't care if they're on the take, mean or just don't do any more than they have to. . . . But if some sonofabitch isn't around on a help-the-officer call or shows up after everybody else in the city has already been there, I don't want him working around me" (p. 233).

Police Brutality and Use of Deadly Force

Some use of physical force is necessary and inevitable in police work. Research indicates that about 17 percent of adult arrests involve such force (beyond application of handcuffs), which is most likely to occur when a suspect is resisting (Garner & Maxwell 1999). The most common injuries incurred by suspects are bruises, abrasions, and lacerations. "Officers are trained to use force progressively along a continuum," and official policy requires them to apply "the least amount of force necessary to accomplish their goals" (Adams 1999:5). On the other hand, **police brutality** occurs when officers intentionally exceed their legal authority to use force.

In a landmark study of brutality in the 1960s, a team of researchers under the direction of Albert Reiss (1968) spent seven weeks observing patrol officers' encounters with citizens (crime victims, witnesses, and suspects) in Boston, Chicago, and Washington, DC. The observers found that just 1 percent of these encounters involved instances of excessive force. (Most likely the percentage would have been higher had the police not known they were being watched.) Excluding encounters with victims and witnesses, about 3 percent of encounters with *suspects* involved excessive force. Although these percentages appear low, they add up to a significant number of cases overall.

More recently, a national study by the US Department of Justice in 2008 found that less than 2 percent of persons who had contact with the police said the police used or threatened force against them, with 84 percent of these people thinking the force or threats were unnecessary. Males were more likely than females, and blacks were more likely than whites or Hispanics, to report force or threats of force (Eith & Durose 2011).

Additionally, a study by the National Police Misconduct Reporting Project found that 1,575 officers in the United States were involved in credible complaints about excessive use of force in 2010. The largest category of these complaints entailed use of fists, throw-downs, baton strikes, or other physical attacks (57 percent), followed by tasers (11 percent), chemical weapons (2 percent), police dogs (2 percent), and police vehicles (less than 1 percent). The remainder included the use of firearms and a combination of force types (Packman 2011).

While the National Police Misconduct Reporting Project found there were 127 fatalities associated with these complaints about force, it is important to distinguish between **elective** and **nonelective shootings**. According to James Fyfe (1982), elective shootings involve situations in which the officer shoots when the suspect poses little or no risk to the officer or others. Nonelective shootings involve situations where "the officer has little real choice but to shoot or to risk death or serious injury to himself or others" (p. 710). Nonelective shootings are more likely than elective shootings to be influenced by factors *external* to the police, such as the type and amount of crime in a community and the characteristics of the criminal population in that area. Elective shootings, on the other hand, are more likely to be influenced by *internal* factors, such as a department's formal policies and informal culture, the tactical training given to officers, and the nonlethal technologies like stun guns that are available to subdue resisting suspects (Fyfe 1988).

Shooting incidents rarely fall clearly into one category or the other, however. As Hugh Barlow (1996) observes, an officer may in hindsight regard an encounter as closer to an elective shooting than he or she actually did at the time of the shooting itself. Moreover, "persons who later hear the 'facts' may interpret a situation differently from either the officer involved or any witness. . . . [This makes it] difficult . . . to construct a picture of an encounter that does justice to both the subjective interpretations of participants and the objective characteristics of the event" (p. 338). Fyfe, who was formerly an NYPD lieutenant, notes that in his experience the more ambiguous shooting situations occurred when officers had been encouraged by supervisors and peers "to take charge of threatening situations quickly with as little assistance (and as little inconvenience to colleagues) as possible" (1988:185). In contrast, ambiguous shootings were less likely when officers were encouraged "to use caution, to take cover, and to search for nonlethal means of resolving potential violence."

In his research, Fyfe (1988) examined data on police shootings from New York City, Philadelphia, and Chicago during the 1970s. In Philadelphia and Chicago, 21 and 25 percent of shooting incidents, respectively, involved citizens who were unarmed and made no threat or attempt to attack the police or another person. In New York, only 8.5 percent of shootings involved unarmed individuals. Fyfe observed that in New York the NYPD operated under a "defense of life only" policy that limited the use of deadly force. In Philadelphia and Chicago, on the other hand, "police were given relatively more freedom to use their guns in elective situations" (p. 186; see also White 2001).

In its *Tennessee v. Garner* decision in 1985, the US Supreme Court restricted the type of police shootings that were constitutionally permissible. The case involved a Memphis police officer who had shot and killed Edward Garner, an unarmed, 15-year-old African-American youth who had been fleeing from the police after breaking into an unoccupied residence. The shooting was consistent with the Memphis department's policy on the shooting of fleeing felons (Fyfe 1988).

Data on Memphis police shootings showed that police officers were much more likely to shoot unarmed black suspects than unarmed white suspects (Fyfe 1988). The Court ruled, however, that Garner's rights had been violated not because of discrimination but because the shooting had violated his Fourth Amendment right against unreasonable seizure. According to the Court, police use of deadly force should be restricted to cases where "the officer has probable cause to believe that the suspect poses a significant threat of death or serious physical injury to the officer or others" (cited in Walker 1996:144). The *Garner* decision invalidated the shooting guidelines of some police departments in 34 states, although most large-city departments had already adopted the more restrictive policy on their own.

The issue of race remains one of the most salient issues concerning police shooting of suspects, as African Americans are disproportionately targeted in these incidents (Fyfe 1988). Since there are more white officers than black officers, they account for the largest number of shootings overall. However, it is black officers who are *disproportionately* more likely to be involved in both on-duty and off-duty shootings of blacks. Fyfe attributes this pattern to the fact that black officers are more likely to work and live in neighborhoods where "their chances of encountering [dangerous] situations leading to shooting, justifiable or otherwise, [are] far greater" (1988:196). Fyfe also notes that in high-crime areas, police officers, regardless of their race, are more likely to shoot preemptively at suspects who turn out to be unarmed. These officers, he observes, have greater reason to fear that any furtive movement by the suspect is life-threatening. Thus, Fyfe says, it is no surprise that internal departmental reviews give the benefit of the doubt to police who shoot suspects in neighborhoods perceived as dangerous.

At the same time, considerable research has found higher rates of police shootings of suspects in cities with greater economic and racial inequality and higher percentages of black residents, regardless of the level of crime (Holmes 2000; Jacobs & O'Brien 1998; Smith & Holmes 2014). Criminologists interpret these findings in terms of **minority threat theory**, which posits that dominant groups or public officials who feel threatened by a large racial underclass will be more likely to tolerate, condone, and exercise force to maintain social order and keep minority residents from "getting out of their place" (Blalock 1967).

Brad Smith and Malcolm Holmes suggest, however, that the "mere presence of a relatively large minority population . . . may not be sufficient to explain the differential employment of excessive force" (2014:86). Rather, the very real danger posed to officers who patrol racially segregated neighborhoods "where frustrated, potentially hostile citizens may challenge not only their authority but sometimes their personal safety" needs to be taken into account (p. 86). Homicides of police officers, for example, are in fact higher in cities with a higher degree of segregation of African-American residents (Kent 2010).

Be that as it may, police officers involved in cases of brutality and use of deadly force are rarely prosecuted (Panwala 2002). For instance, a study in San Diego, California, found that not a single officer was prosecuted for any of the 190 civilian shootings that occurred from 1985 to 1990 (Petrillo 1990); and a study in Los Angeles found that prosecutors declined to prosecute 278 cases of "police officers and sheriff's deputies accused of assaulting civilians with fists, clubs, flashlights, leather-covered steel straps, pistol barrels, scalding water and an electric stun gun" that occurred during the 1980s (Freed 1991:1). In the 1991 Rodney King case, the four LAPD officers who beat him were indicted but found not guilty of unlawful assault, although two were found guilty of violating King's civil rights in a subsequent federal trial and sentenced to 30 months in prison. King also won a $3.8 million civil lawsuit against the city of Los Angeles (Gibbs 1996).

Two notorious cases in New York City in the late 1990s are worth mentioning, too. In 1997, Abner Louima, a Haitian immigrant, was arrested by the NYPD for disorderly conduct. He was taken to the stationhouse, where he was beaten and sodomized by NYPD officers with a toilet plunger, resulting in the tearing of a hole through his lower intestine and the bruising of his bladder. One of the officers involved in the beating was convicted and given a lengthy prison term, but three other officers had their convictions overturned on appeal. Louima was awarded $3 million in civil damages from the city of New York (CNN 2002). In 1999, Amadou Diallo, an unarmed African-immigrant street vendor, was killed by four NYPD officers who fired 41 shots, hitting Diallo 19 times. The officers, who were looking for a rape suspect, said they thought Diallo had a gun. They were indicted but acquitted of all criminal charges. The Diallo family was awarded $3 million in civil damages for the death of their loved one (De La Cruz 1999; Feuer 2004; George 2000).

More recently, in 2014, the accumulated outrage over several police killings of unarmed African Americans sparked protests around the country, most notably following two grand jury decisions not to indict police officers for the shooting death of 18-year-old Michael Brown in Ferguson, Missouri, and the choke-hold death of 43-year-old Eric Garner in New York City. Around this time, too, a police officer in Cleveland, Ohio, shot and killed 12-year-old Tamir Rice, who was playing with a pellet gun (McClain 2014).

In recent years, police have increased their use of alternative technologies such as chemical sprays, stun guns, and impact munitions such as rubber bullets with the hope of mitigating the need to use excessive and deadly force. There is evidence that the introduction of these technologies has had that effect, but research also indicates that the availability of these technologies has made police more likely to use nonlethal force (Hubbs & Klinger 2004; Lumb & Friday 1997).

Prosecuting and Defending the Accused

After a suspect is arrested and taken into custody, the criminal justice process moves from the police to the criminal courts, where prosecutors, defense attorneys, judges, and jurors replace police officers as the leading players in a series of formal and informal deliberations that determine a defendant's fate. The criminal court system in the United States is a complex, multitiered set of institutions that operate under state and federal law. The state system was adopted from the English system by the American colonists, and the federal system was established by the US Congress (Adler et al. 2000). Courts in different jurisdictions function independently, and the precise processes vary from one place to another. Here we will consider the core stages or decision points for the processing of adults that are roughly comparable throughout the United States.

Initial Screening

The prosecutor or district attorney is the primary gatekeeper of the court system and is assigned the task of determining the formal charge (if any) that will be filed against an arrested suspect. The prosecutor usually makes this decision in consultation with the police but can decide independently to release a defendant. In a study of the 75 largest urban counties in the country, Gerard Rainville and Brian Reaves (2003) found that about a fourth of all felony arrests were dismissed at this stage in the process.

Technically, the prosecutor is supposed to file charges only when the case meets the standard of **probable cause**—that is, when there is a reasonable basis to believe that the defendant committed the crime. Many cases fail to meet this standard due to insufficient evidence or unreliable witnesses. Informally, the prosecutor also considers whether the case is serious enough to warrant utilization of scarce criminal justice resources, whether the defendant truly intended to commit the crime, and whether the defendant deserves to be held accountable for his or her actions. In addition, the prosecutor may take into account the defendant's prior offense record, age and health, and social standing in the community (Myers 2000).

Some research indicates that gender and racial/ethnic status influence prosecutors' charging decisions. In a study of Los Angeles, for example, Cassia Spohn and colleagues found that prosecutors' decisions to drop or reduce charges revealed "a pattern of discrimination in favor of female defendants and against black and Hispanic defendants" (1987:183). In a study of a city in the US Midwest, Gary LaFree (1980) found that blacks accused of raping white women were given more serious charges than either blacks accused of raping black women or whites accused of raping white women. Similarly, Michael Radelet (1981) found that Florida defendants who had murdered whites were more likely to be charged with first-degree murder than those who had murdered blacks. In another Florida study, Radelet and Glenn Pierce (1985) examined cases of discrepancy between police and prosecutorial assessments of murders as either **felony** or **nonfelony homicides**. Felony homicides, or homicides that occur in the course of another felony crime (such as robbery), carry heavier penalties than nonfelony homicides. Radelet and Pierce found that a murder was most likely to be upgraded (from the initial police assessment) to a felony homicide, and least likely to be downgraded to a nonfelony homicide, when the defendant was black and the victim was white. In an extensive review of the literature, Marvin Free (2002) concluded that prosecutors were consistently more likely to seek the death penalty in homicides involving white victims than in homicides involving black victims.

In the US system of justice, a defendant is entitled to an **initial appearance** before a judge without unnecessary delay, usually within 24 hours following arrest. In minor cases, such as public drunkenness or loitering, the judge may conduct a **summary trial** and issue a sentence in one condensed hearing. If the defendant cannot afford an attorney, the judge will assign a state-appointed attorney or public defender to the case. Only about a third of federal felony defendants and less than a fifth of state felony defendants are able to hire their own private counsel (DeFrances & Marika 2000; Harlow 2000).

In serious misdemeanor and felony cases, the judge—who typically follows the prosecutor's recommendation—also decides whether to keep the defendant confined in jail for pretrial detention or release him or her on bail, on their own recognizance, or under some nonfinancial condition such as an agreement to submit to drug use monitoring or report regularly to a probation officer. The decision regarding pretrial release is of paramount importance, because defendants who are denied release or are unable to make bail are also more likely to be convicted and receive prison terms (Reaves 1991; Williams 2003). In a study of state felony defendants in the largest 75 counties in the United States between 1990 and 2004, Thomas Cohen and Brian Reaves (2007) found that 30 percent were released by posting bail, 32 percent were released under a nonfinancial condition, and 38 percent were detained until trial.

Most defendants who are granted bail cannot afford it and have to pay a bail bondsperson or agency a 10–20 percent fee to front the entire amount. States that prohibit private bonding services may allow defendants to obtain bail by putting up a percentage or some noncash asset such as a real estate holding. Cohen and Reaves (2007) found that less than half of felony defendants who were required to post bail to secure release were able to do so. Additionally, other research found that nonwhite defendants

FURTHER EXPLORATION
The Juvenile Justice System

In 1899, Illinois became the first state to establish a juvenile justice system that was independent from its adult criminal justice system. Today, every state has separate court procedures and correctional facilities that handle juveniles (most often youths under 17 or 18 years of age). Typically these systems have legal jurisdiction over three categories of youths. **Delinquents** are juveniles who violate criminal laws for which adults could also be charged. **Status offenders** include those who commit acts for which adults could not be charged—for example, running away, truancy, curfew violations, and even vague transgressions such as "incorrigibility," "habitual disobedience," and "immoral behavior." And **dependent children** are those who have been so neglected or abused that they need to become wards of the court.

The juvenile system is based on the premise that young people, due to immaturity, are less responsible and blameworthy for their conduct and should therefore be granted special consideration that might not be given to adults. Thus, the system's official mission has been one of rehabilitation through the delivery of psychological and social services that are supposed to be in the "best interest" of the child. Originally the legal formalities of the adult system were viewed as undesirable. When a youth came before a juvenile-court judge, the focus was not on the juvenile's guilt or innocence but rather on how the judge could make an informed assessment of the youth's life circumstances and formulate a course of treatment tailored to his or her particular needs. Hence testimony of any sort, regardless of its legal relevancy, was deemed germane, and attorneys were viewed as a hindrance to the process (Platt 1974; Ryerson 1978).

The absence of due process, however, led to much abuse. In 1964, for instance, 15-year-old Gerald Gault was arrested in Gila County, Arizona, for allegedly making an obscene phone call. Gault was already on probation for being in the company of another boy who had stolen a wallet. A juvenile-court judge sentenced Gault to a juvenile correctional facility for up to six years, without allowing Gault to be represented by an attorney, to confront and cross-examine his accuser, or to be informed of his privilege against self-incrimination. The maximum penalty for an adult committing a similar offense in Arizona at the time was a fine of $50 or a jail term of not more than two months. Gault and his parents appealed the case all the way to the US Supreme Court, which in 1967 ruled that Gault's right to due process of law had been violated. The Court said that juveniles subject to institutional confinement were entitled to most (though not all) of the due process rights enjoyed by adults, including the right to counsel, the right to confront and cross-examine witnesses, and the privilege against self-incrimination. But in a 1971 case, the Court ruled that juveniles did not have a constitutional right to a trial by jury, arguing that a jury was not necessary for a fair hearing or to fulfill the fact-finding function of the court (Binder et al. 1988).

The juvenile system has also been marred by some of the same discriminatory practices that are present in the adult criminal justice system.

continues

continued

Although the evidence is not entirely consistent, the tendency has been for minority and lower-class youths to be treated more severely than higher-status youths, and for females to be treated more leniently than males for serious crimes but more severely for status offenses. Overall, disparities in treatment between nonwhite/lower-class and white/higher-class offenders and between female and male offenders are more apparent at the early stages of juvenile-court processing than at latter stages (Chesney-Lind & Shelden 2004; Engen et al. 2002; Rodriguez 2007a).

Over the past few decades, disillusionment with the rehabilitative ideal and the specter of serious juvenile offenders led nearly every state to either lower the age at which the adult criminal court assumes jurisdiction for teenage defendants or to use a **waiver** procedure to transfer jurisdiction from the juvenile to the adult system, or sometimes both (Griffin et al. 2011). Overall, national-level studies have found that about two-thirds of transferred juveniles were charged with violent crimes, about two-thirds of those transferred were convicted, and about two-thirds of those convicted received prison or jail terms (Rainville & Smith 2003; Strom et al. 1998). On the other hand, some early studies of individual states found that a majority of transferred juveniles were actually nonviolent offenders who often received lighter penalties than they might have received had they remained in the juvenile system, because in the adult system their crimes were considered "lightweight" (Bishop et al. 1989; Howell 1996; Osbun & Rode 1984). More recently, Megan Kurlychek and Brian Johnson found that juvenile offenders in the state of Maryland were "punished more severely than their adult counterparts," primarily for drug crimes (2010:725). They concluded that "not only are the 'get tough' transfer policies leading to substantially disproportionate punishments for juvenile offenders . . . but also that the brunt of this disparity is manifest among nonviolent offenders for whom these policies were initially not designed to target" (p. 747). Thus, some criminologists are pleased with the fact that nationally the number of judicial waivers has been on the decline (Griffin et al. 2011)

were more likely than white defendants to be assigned higher levels of bail regardless of prior record or type of offense they committed. These differential bail levels were most heavily pronounced for drug offenses (Albonetti et al. 1989; Free 2004; Schlesinger 2005).

Following the initial appearance, a judicial determination regarding probable cause may be made at a **preliminary hearing**. This hearing is not "aimed at determining the defendant's guilt or innocence . . . [but] at establishing . . . whether there is sufficient evidence for any reasonable and prudent person to believe a crime has been committed, and whether the defendant committed it" (Daudistel et al. 1979:178). It gives the prosecutor and defense attorney the opportunity to learn about each other's cases and preserve the testimony of witnesses, who may later change their story. In some jurisdictions a **grand jury** may be used instead of a preliminary hearing. In grand jury proceedings the prosecutor presents evidence to a group of 12 to 23 citizens, who rarely reject the recommendation to indict, because defendants "may not even be allowed to present their version of the facts, much less to confront and cross-examine witnesses" (Myers 2000:450). After the preliminary hearing or grand jury decision, the defendant appears before the court for **arraignment** and is asked to plead guilty, not guilty, or no contest (a no contest plea is comparable to a guilty plea except that it cannot be used as an admission of guilt in a subsequent civil proceeding).

Plea Bargaining

Criminal courts in the United States utilize an **adversary system** of criminal justice that puts prosecutors and defense attorneys in an oppositional relationship, with each side dedicated to presenting its best possible case. The trial court is the arena in which the adversary model operates in its purest form. However, more than 90 percent of convictions around the country are attained through informal negotiations known as **plea bargaining**, making a trial the exception rather than the rule (Devers 2011). In plea bargaining, the defendant agrees to plead guilty, waiving his or her Fifth Amendment right against self-incrimination. In exchange for this cooperation, the prosecutor offers something in return—agreeing to reduce the seriousness of the charge and consequently the penalty or, in cases where multiple charges have been brought against the defendant, agreeing to drop some of the charges or recommend to the judge that the sentences be served concurrently rather than consecutively.

Plea bargaining is a common practice because both prosecutors and defense attorneys tend to assume they benefit from its use. Prosecutors are most likely to plea bargain when they have relatively weak cases that may not be provable "beyond a reasonable doubt" if the case goes to trial. Certainty of conviction through plea bargaining often seems preferable to expending considerable time and resources in pursuit of an uncertain outcome (Myers 2000).

Defendants plea bargain for similar reasons. They risk losing at trial and receiving a harsher sentence, as prosecutors forced to go to trial generally ask for the maximum possible penalty in the event of conviction. Defendants also may want to get the ordeal over with as soon as possible and avoid the publicity and higher attorney fees associated with a trial. Thus, one of the defense attorney's most important functions is to get the best possible deal for his or her client when likelihood of acquittal is slim. And since defense attorneys typically believe that their clients are guilty of some charge, if not the current one, they will often attempt to persuade their clients to cop a plea as a matter of course (Blumberg 1967; McIntyre 1987). They try to persuade their clients that the fee they are paying for legal representation will buy them a better deal, even though they may in fact get the same deal on their own. Defendants who benefit the most from plea bargaining—that is, who actually receive lesser sentences than they would have had they gone to trial—are those who have committed less serious crimes and have a cleaner record of prior offenses (Myers 2000; Smith 1986).

Overloaded court dockets are another reason plea bargaining is common. As one New York City prosecutor observed: "Our office keeps . . . [the] courtrooms busy trying 5 percent of the cases. If even 10 percent . . . end in a trial, the system would break down" (Zimring & Frase 1980:506–507). Thus, in *Santobello v. New York* (1971) the US Supreme Court explicitly acknowledged plea bargaining as essential to the management of overloaded courts, and encouraged its properly administered use. The Court also held that prosecutors are obligated to keep the promises they make once an agreement is reached, so that defendants' pleas are made voluntarily and with full knowledge of the consequences (Reid 2006; Shelden et al. 2008).

To a large extent, plea bargaining takes place in a legal marketplace of "going rates" in which similarly situated people are routinely treated in a comparable fashion. Since both prosecutors and defense attorneys are interested in reducing the uncertainty and maximizing the efficiency of their work, they develop a common outlook regarding the disposition that is appropriate for particular kinds of cases. Judges generally approve plea-bargaining agreements because they, too, have a stake in the smooth operation of the system. It is not even unusual for judges to order a continuance (postponement) on the first day of trial to encourage the attorneys to work out a deal. Some judges may even actively participate by supervising negotiations and making bargaining recommendations themselves (Daudistel et al. 1979; Dawson 1992; Myers 2000).

The Trial

Although few choose to exercise it, the Sixth Amendment gives defendants the right to a "speedy and public trial." Technically speaking, defendants are presumed innocent until proven guilty in a court of law, and prosecutors have the burden to prove their guilt beyond a reasonable doubt. Thus, defendants do not need to prove their innocence; they only need to cast reasonable doubt on their guilt. These formal rules serve to balance the informal presumption of guilt that is implicit in a prosecutor's decision to bring a case to trial in the first place.

In many ways, the trial in an adversary system is less "a rational 'fact-finding' process aimed at discovering the 'truth'" and more a process of **impression management** aimed at constructing a desired account of the alleged criminal event (Daudistel et al. 1979:236). Thus, the prosecution and defense present (or ignore) the facts of a case in ways that support the conclusion they have already reached, such as calling witnesses whose testimony is favorable to their point of view and coaching those witnesses about what to say and not say in response to formal questioning. Each side attempts to undermine or damage the credibility of opposing witnesses, whether or not these witnesses are actually telling the truth. Each side makes objections to evidence or lines of questioning they consider damaging to their case, even if they expect the judge to overrule them. Judges play a key role in arbitrating the debate by ruling on objections and motions made by the attorneys, by deciding what evidence can and cannot be introduced, and by instructing the jury about the law governing the case.

Although few defense attorneys harbor illusions about the factual innocence of their clients, they believe it is their job to keep prosecutors honest—to hold them to their legal obligation to prove guilt beyond a reasonable doubt (McIntyre 1987). As one defense attorney admits: "What I knew actually happened was not important. . . . What did matter was whether a version of the 'facts' could be presented that would . . . [cast] doubt . . . [on my] client's guilt" (Subin 1993:31). But as critics say, it is one thing for a defense attorney to attack the prosecutor's case by pointing out its weaknesses; it is quite another to attack the case by advancing utter falsehoods. One defense attorney recalls how he humiliated a rape victim on the witness stand, making "her seem to be little more than a prostitute" (McIntyre 1987:141). This type of questioning is significantly different "from challenging *inaccurate* testimony," whether or not the client is innocent (Subin 1993:36).

Defense attorneys, on the other hand, believe that prosecutors are also known to behave disreputably. One study by the *Chicago Tribune,* for example, uncovered 381 defendants across the country who had had "their homicide convictions thrown out because prosecutors concealed evidence suggesting innocence or presented evidence they knew to be false" (cited in Armstrong & Possley 1999:A3). Two-thirds of these defendants had been sentenced to death. Similarly, a study by the *Pittsburg Post-Gazette* uncovered numerous instances of federal prosecutors "lying, hiding evidence, distorting the facts, engaging in cover-ups, paying for perjury and setting up innocent people in order to win indictments, guilty pleas and convictions" (*Wisconsin State Journal* 1998:A2). According to both newspapers, prosecutors were rarely punished for their misconduct. As one former prosecutor remarked: "It's a result-oriented process. . . . Whatever works is what's right" (p. A2). Additionally, a study by the Center for Public Integrity found that between 1970 and 2002, appellate judges "dismissed criminal charges, reversed convictions or reduced sentences" in more than 2,000 cases due to prosecutors who "stretched, bent or broke rules" (Sniffen 2003:A3). We will discuss the problem of wrongful convictions later in this chapter.

Trial by jury. The Sixth Amendment provides defendants with the right to "an impartial jury," although the US Supreme Court has ruled that this right need not apply to juveniles who are processed in the juvenile justice system or to adults if their conviction would result in a sentence of less than six months of incarceration. Moreover, according to the Court, the right to a jury requires neither a jury of 12 members (6-person juries are allowed in all but capital punishment cases) nor a unanimous jury verdict in noncapital cases (11–1, 10–2, and 9–3 verdicts have been upheld). Nevertheless, most jurisdictions maintain the tradition of 12-member juries and unanimous verdicts for criminal trials (Neubauer 2001).

Defendants may choose either a bench trial (in which the judge decides guilt or innocence) or a jury trial. One landmark study found that judges and juries reach similar conclusions in about three-quarters of cases, but when there is disagreement, juries are more likely to acquit (Kalven & Zeisel 1971). Judges do not have the authority to reverse a jury's verdict of acquittal, but they can reverse a verdict of guilty.

Potential jurors are randomly selected from various sources, such as telephone directories, voter lists, driver's license registries, and property tax lists. Some of these methods result in underrepresentation of low-income and minority residents, who are less likely to register to vote, have a driver's license, or own real estate. And since these groups are also more residentially mobile and less likely to have permanent addresses, they are less likely to receive jury summonses sent through the mail. Moreover, those with lower incomes are more likely to be excused from jury duty for reasons of economic hardship; and women may be granted exemptions for child care and family responsibilities (Benokraitis 1982; Fukurai et al. 1993; Grossman 1994).

The **voir dire** ("to speak the truth") is the next stage in the jury selection process. Here prospective jurors are questioned by the prosecutor and defense attorney under the supervision of the presiding judge. While the Sixth Amendment requires an impartial jury, prosecutors and defense attorneys both prefer jurors who are predisposed to their side of the case. Sometimes they will even hire jury consultants to help them identify the demographic characteristics and attitudes of people who are more likely to convict or acquit. During the voir dire, each side is allowed a limited number of **peremptory challenges**, enabling them to dismiss some jurors without explanation. Each side is also given an unlimited number of **challenges for cause** if they can demonstrate to the judge's satisfaction that a juror will be prejudicial in some way—for example, if the juror knows the defendant, has been the victim of a crime that is similar to the one the defendant is accused of, or has already formulated an opinion on the case due to exposure to pretrial publicity (Barkan & Bryjak 2011).

Until the mid-1980s, prosecutors in some Southern states disproportionately used their peremptory challenges to exclude African-American jurors (Jost 1995). In 1986, however, the US Supreme Court ruled it was unconstitutional to exclude a prospective juror on the basis of race; and in

1994 it ruled it was unconstitutional to exclude a prospective juror on the basis of gender. On the other hand, in a case previously decided in 1986, the Court ruled that jurors who oppose the death penalty can be excluded from juries in capital punishment cases, a decision that disproportionately affects blacks and women, because they are more likely than whites and men to oppose the death penalty (Bohm 1991; Currie & Pillick 1996; Reid 2006).

Research on the effect of gender and race on jurors' decisions is somewhat mixed. In a review of studies of juror voting and gender, Cameron Currie and Aleta Pillick (1996) found that few gender differences exist; rape cases are the exception, with women more likely than men to convict. In a review of studies of juror voting and race, however, Nancy King (1993) found that blacks were more likely than whites to acquit, although both blacks and whites were more likely to acquit defendants of their own race than defendants of another race.

Jury voting along racial lines is nothing new, although throughout most of US history it was predominantly white jurors who refused to convict whites for committing crimes against blacks. Currently, however, the most striking trend in jury verdicts has not been the number of race-based acquittals but the number of **hung juries**. Hung juries occur when unanimity is required but one or more jurors refuse to vote with the majority. The judge then declares a mistrial, and the prosecution must decide whether to seek a new trial. According to Jeffrey Rosen (1997), hung juries occur most often in cities with large minority populations during trials of black men. In these cases, hung juries usually involve a single holdout—most often a black woman—who refuses to convict over the strenuous objections of fellow jurors, both black and white, for reasons that include mistrust of the police, concern about sending yet another black man to prison, or simply having difficulty "sitting in judgment of someone else" (p. 58). These holdouts see the defendants "as their nephews, their sons, . . . their brothers" (p. 62).

Another issue relevant to jury trials involves the doctrine of **jury nullification**, which has a long history in the United States. Nullification refers to a juror's right to disregard the facts of the case or the judge's instructions in order to vote his or her conscience. This right was used by the American colonists in their disputes with the British government, by Northern juries to nullify fugitive slave laws, and by civil rights and antiwar activists during the political turmoil of the 1960s. US courts have upheld the nullification doctrine, though not a juror's right to be informed of it, reasoning that to be moved by conscience to invoke this right is one thing, but to be informed of this prerogative would encourage its abuse (Barkan & Bryjak 2011; Scheflin 1994).

Nevertheless, nullification in political cases is quite different than in the cases resulting in mistrials in contemporary criminal courts. According

FURTHER EXPLORATION
Race, Public Opinion, and the O.J. Simpson Case

In his final summation to the jury in the criminal trial of O.J. Simpson in 1995, African-American defense attorney Johnnie Cochran beseeched the jurors to acquit Simpson for the double murder of his ex-wife and her friend (see Chapter 8), arguing that he had been framed by the LAPD. Mark Fuhrman, the LAPD detective who had found evidence (a bloodied glove) that linked Simpson to the crime, had a reputation as being a racist cop. Cochran accused Fuhrman of planting evidence and told the jurors, nine of whom were black: "There's something in your background . . . that helps you understand that this is wrong" (quoted in Darden 1996:369). The jurors agreed, returning a unanimous verdict for acquittal. Although two white jurors and one Hispanic juror concurred in the decision, much of the white public viewed the verdict as racially biased (Elias & Schatzman 1996).

To be sure, there was a racial divide over opinions about the case, which are reflective of a divide in views about the criminal justice system that remains to this very day. Early on, national polls indicated that 60 percent of blacks but only 23 percent of whites thought that Simpson had been framed or set up by the police (*Newsweek,* Aug. 1, 1994). Just following the verdict, 66 percent of blacks but only 26 percent of whites believed that Simpson had probably not committed the murders; and 85 percent of blacks but only 32 percent of whites agreed with the verdict of not guilty (*Newsweek,* Oct. 16, 1995).

to Eric Holder, an African American who served as a federal court judge and later as US attorney general during the Obama administration: "There are some folks who have been so seared by racism, who are so affected by what has happened to them because they are black, that, even if you're the most credible, upfront black man or woman in law enforcement, you're never going to be able to reach them" (quoted in Rosen 1997:60). On the other hand, Rosen concludes that most jurors are "able to transcend their racially fraught experiences and . . . cast their votes on the basis of a scrupulous evaluation" of the evidence (1997:55). Overall, about three-quarters of all felony trials result in a conviction (*Sourcebook of Criminal Justice Statistics* 2006).

Wrongful Convictions
Wrongful convictions fall into two general (though sometimes overlapping) categories: cases in which the defendant is *factually* innocent, and cases in which the defendant is *legally* innocent. The former entails conviction of defendants who did not commit the crime in question; the latter entails conviction of defendants through illegal means, regardless of whether they are factually innocent or guilty.

Research on convicted offenders who were subsequently exonerated finds that African Americans are disproportionately represented, making up more than half of death-row exonerations since 1973 (Death Penalty Information Center 2014b). Selective law enforcement, racial profiling, overzealousness in the war on drugs, and ineffective legal counsel (often due to the defendant's inability to hire a skilled attorney) contribute to this disparity. Other factors include police solicitation of false confessions, due process violations of search and seizure regulations, and even the planting of evidence and police perjury in court. Police and prosecutors may also decline to follow exculpatory leads as well as suppress exculpatory evidence. The forensics used in the case may be flawed, and informants and witnesses may be unreliable or intentionally deceitful (Free & Ruesink 2012; Huff et al. 1996).

Public pressure to make an arrest and expedite a conviction may also influence a "rush to judgment" that leads to wrongful convictions. All too often, law enforcement agencies place too much emphasis on closing cases expeditiously and on winning at all costs. Take the Dallas County District Attorney's Office, for instance, known for its high rate of wrongful convictions over the years. At one time it was common for prosecutors in this office to think: "Anyone can convict a guilty man; it takes a real prosecutor to convict an innocent one" (quoted in Huff et al. 1996:43).

Eyewitness error in particular is a significant source of wrongful convictions. Various factors are known to influence a witness's perceptions of the crime and the criminal: the amount of time the witness was exposed to the event, the physical distance between the observer and what was being observed, the amount of lighting around the crime scene, and postcrime influences such as whether the witness was given leading information by the police (Huff et al. 1996). Racial stereotypes may also come into play and affect what witnesses of different racial groups "see"—for example, white witnesses who have little previous contact with black people may think that "all blacks look alike"—especially when police lineups include only one person who resembles the alleged perpetrator. Police may also coach witnesses at lineups and, in cases that rely on informants, may even encourage witnesses to lie and perjure themselves in court. Marvin Free and Mitch Ruesink (2012), in their study of nearly 350 wrongfully convicted black men, found that witness error was a factor in about 43 percent of murder cases and 93 percent of rape and sexual assault cases. In many of these cases, the witness was white, raising questions about the accuracy of cross-racial identification.

Although most research on wrongful convictions has focused on men, about 7 percent of the wrongfully convicted are women (Gross & Shaffer 2012). In their research, Ruesink and Free (2005) found that women were less likely than men to be wrongfully convicted of murder, but more likely than men to be wrongfully convicted of drug and child abuse offenses. They also found that black women were more likely than white women to be wrongfully convicted of drug offenses, but that white women were more likely than black women to be convicted of child abuse. In fact, less than 4 percent of wrongful convictions for child abuse involved black women. Ruesink and Free hypothesize that this discrepancy may be a consequence of greater societal intolerance of abuse of white children than black children.

Sentencing the Convicted

Sentencing of convicted offenders is a separate stage in the criminal justice process. In most jurisdictions the sentencing decision is the responsibility of the trial judge, although in some states the trial jury is allowed to determine or recommend sentences. Usually a separate sentencing hearing is held, during which the prosecution and defense attorney argue for or against a particular sentence. At the hearing, a probation officer also reports on the results of a **presentence investigation** he or she has conducted. This report includes information about the offender's background and prior criminal offenses. The probation officer typically makes a sentencing recommendation, which is generally accepted by the judge. Some states also utilize **victim impact statements**, often incorporating them into the presentence investigation report. These impact statements provide victims the opportunity to describe both the harm they have suffered and their views on the appropriate punishment (Barkan & Bryjak 2011).

Models of Sentencing

Excluding death penalty cases, the most basic sentencing decision involves the distinction between **probation**—a period of formal supervision in the community that is given in lieu of incarceration—and incarceration in a jail or prison facility (see Chapter 12). Overall, about 56 percent of adults under correctional supervision are on probation, as are about 69 percent of convicted felony offenders (Glaze & Herberman 2013; Rosenmerkel et al. 2009). Offenders may also serve part of their sentence incarcerated and then part on **parole**, the latter being the time under formal supervision that follows confinement.

The length of the sentences that offenders serve is decided at a separate **sentencing hearing**. For much of the twentieth century, most jurisdictions in the United States used some form of **indeterminate sentence**. An indeterminate sentence entails no specific time period or only a maximum term (or a range involving both a minimum and a maximum term) that an incarcerated inmate must serve. Inmates are periodically reviewed by a parole board of correctional authorities who evaluate their behavior and readiness for release. The guiding correctional principle is **rehabilitation**—that is, the sentence is deemed completed only when an inmate can demonstrate that he or she is sufficiently reformed, meaning capable of becoming a law-abiding member of society, as judged by correctional officials (Barkan & Bryjak 2011; Shelden et al. 2008).

During the 1970s, critics from both the left and the right side of the political spectrum took issue with indeterminate sentencing. The rehabilitation model, everyone agreed, was not working well, as the correctional system had been unable to deliver effective rehabilitative services, and criminal justice officials had been unable to determine who was truly reformed (Lipton et al. 1975). Liberals argued that indeterminate sentencing fostered discriminatory treatment based on class and racial/ethnic status, and that uncertain release dates constituted a "cruel injustice to prisoners, suspending them in a nether world of uncertainty . . . [and] arbitrary decisions" (Adler et al. 2000:315). Conservatives, in turn, complained about dangerous offenders being released too early, and they called for sentencing reforms that would confine criminals for longer periods of time. They argued that **retribution**, not rehabilitation, should be the guiding philosophy of punishment. Also known as "just deserts," retribution entails sentences that are proportionate to the seriousness of the crime, not to the rehabilitative status of the criminal (Wilson 1975).

A **determinate sentence** refers to a term of punishment that is fixed at the outset and not dependent upon the behavior of offenders under correctional supervision. Over the past few decades, state legislatures have been limiting judicial discretion by establishing systems of proportional punishment based on a retributive philosophy. Even where judges retain discretionary authority, they may be required to sentence the offender to a definite period of time. Many states have instituted a form of determinate sentencing known as the **presumptive sentence**. Under this approach, legislatures establish the penalty offenders are expected to receive for particular crimes, but allow judges to shorten or lengthen these sentences if certain *mitigating* or *aggravating* conditions are present. For example, a judge may shorten the sentence if the offender has shown remorse or offered the prosecution assistance in solving other crimes or apprehending other criminals. Conversely, a judge may lengthen the sentence if the offender has a prior criminal record, used a gun during the crime, or seriously injured the victim. Often legislatures will specify the mitigating and aggravating criteria that judges are permitted to consider (Barkan & Bryjak 2011; Reid 2006).

A **mandatory sentence** is more restrictive than a presumptive sentence, because it allows for no judicial discretion whatsoever. Nearly all state legislatures have established mandatory sentences for some crimes, such as murder, crimes involving guns, and some drug offenses. These provisions generally require the offender to serve a minimum period of incarceration, eliminating the possibility of probation (Barkan & Bryjak 2011; Reid 2006).

In the federal system, the Sentencing Reform Act of 1984 authorized the US Sentencing Commission to develop guidelines for federal crimes that were supposed to be "neutral as to race, sex, national origin, creed, and socioeconomic status" (cited in Heaney 1991:203). The commission established a formula whereby a score is given for a particular offense, and additional points are deleted or added for mitigating and aggravating factors. After an offender's total points are computed, a judge determines the sentence by consulting a table that converts the points to the length of the sentence to be served. Currently, about 20 states have adopted similar schemes, which are often referred to as **evidence-based** or **data-based sentencing**. But these schemes, contrary to the intent of the Sentencing Reform Act, often include measures of socioeconomic status, including employment history, educational background, and personal finances, as well as marital status, neighborhood of residence, and family background (including family members' criminal history), which critics believe amounts to profiling offenders and punishing them for "who they are" and not for "what they did" (Starr 2014).

Since the mid-1990s, the federal government and a majority of states have adopted mandatory **"three strikes"** sentences that require prison terms of 25 years to life for anyone convicted of a third felony (or in some states a second or fourth felony). Although three-strikes sentencing is touted by politicians as a way to protect the public from serious criminals, most three-strikes offenders, on their third offense, are sentenced for a nonviolent crime. A notorious case in point is that of Jerry Dewayne Williams, a 27-year-old California man who was sentenced to 25 years to life for a third offense of *stealing a pizza* from a kid at a pizza parlor (Reid 2006; Shichor & Sechrest 1996).

Critics of the three-strikes policy note that it has clogged already overcrowded courts, since defendants facing harsh sentences have little to lose by demanding a trial. Moreover, the enhanced penalty focuses on the wrong age group of offenders—older offenders whose criminality is already declining, especially as they grow into their thirties, middle age, and elderly years. Hence, most of the three-strikes offenders remain in prison years after they no longer pose a threat to the public (Barkan & Bryjak 2011; Reid 2006).

In California, criticism of the three-strikes mandate mounted when judges refused to issue sentences they thought were unjust. One judge refused to sentence 43-year-old Thomas Kiel Brown to life for stealing a $22 baseball cap from a store in a shopping mall, remarking: "No judge I know wants to let dangerous criminals loose. . . . But I'm sure the taxpayer doesn't want to spend more than $500,000 to put a petty thief in jail for stealing a cap" (cited in Reid 2006:477). Then, in 1996, the California Supreme Court upheld a judge's decision to not impose a life sentence on Jesus Romero, a 34-year-old who was convicted of possessing 13 grams of cocaine (Romero's prior convictions were for burglary and attempted burglary). Traditionally, California law had given judges the power to disregard prior convictions when doing so seemed reasonable. In overturning Romero's conviction, the California Supreme Court ruled that it would be a violation of the state constitution if the three-strikes statute was interpreted as removing that judicial prerogative. Hence, a judge who thinks the mandatory sentence is not "in the furtherance of justice" is not required to impose it.

In 2003, however, the US Supreme Court rejected the claim of two defendants that California's three-strikes provision violated the Eighth Amendment's prohibition against cruel and unusual punishment. Gary Ewing and Leandro Andrade had received sentences of 25 years to life and 50 years, respectively (Mears 2003). Ewing's third offense involved stealing three $399 golf clubs from a Los Angeles country club, and Andrade's involved theft of $153 worth of videotapes from two Kmart stores. In a five-to-four decision, the Supreme Court ruled that the three-strikes law represented a "rational legislative judgment, entitled to deference," and said that the Supreme Court would "not sit as a 'superlegislature' to second-guess these policy choices" (cited in Will 2003:74). At the same time, the Court did note the harsh sentences in federal guidelines for crack cocaine as opposed to powder cocaine and ruled that judges had the discretion to reduce the prescribed penalties (see Chapter 7). Graham Boyd, director of the ACLU's Drug Law Reform Project, described the decision as possibly "the first sentencing decision since the mid-1980s that actually talks about justice" (quoted in Cose 2007:53).

Discrimination in Sentencing

Arguably one of the most persistent controversies in criminal sentencing involves concern about the discriminatory treatment of racial and ethnic minorities, who often receive harsher sentences than their racial-majority counterparts. In assessing this issue, however, Joan Petersilia and Susan Turner (1988) think it is important to distinguish between **disparities** and **discrimination**. Disparities occur when legally relevant factors are applied but "have different results for different groups" (p. 92). Discrimination occurs when decisions are based on social status rather than on legitimate criteria.

A considerable body of research finds that legally appropriate criteria such as offense seriousness and prior record account for the sentencing disparities that exist between nonwhites and whites (Barkan & Bryjak 2011; Myers 2000). On the other hand, offense seriousness and prior record may themselves be consequences of previous decisions made by police and prosecutors, as well as consequences of previous sentencing decisions. Police, for instance, are more likely to patrol lower-class areas (which are disproportionately populated by racial/ethnic minorities) than higher-class areas, hence "discovering" more crime, drug use especially (Chambliss 1994; Sampson 1986; see Chapter 7). Irrespective of whether bias is intended against specific individuals, the more active street life of people who have less access to private space makes them more vulnerable to arrest. Ultimately these processes translate into a greater likelihood of lower-class individuals accumulating a prior record of offending, even if only for minor offenses. This process also results in a series of cumulative disadvantages that accrue as a result of prosecutors' initial screening, pre-trial detention, and plea-bargaining decisions (Kutateladze et al. 2014; Schlesinger 2007; Sutton 2013). Given what we now know about racial profiling as well, there may be little distinction between disparities and discrimination after all.

Furthermore, some evidence indicates that judges place more emphasis on offense seriousness and prior record when dealing with minority offenders (Miethe & Moore 1986; Nelson 1994; Welch et al. 1984). Other research suggests that in murder and rape or sexual assault cases, offenders who victimize whites are given more severe sentences than those who victimize blacks, and that black offenders who victimize whites are given the harshest penalties of all (LaFree 1989; Spohn & Spears 1996; Walsh 1987). Moreover, in death penalty cases, the race of the victim is often even "more significant than the race of the offender, and may not only reflect the devalued status of black victims" but also the greater societal outrage at the victimization of members of the racial-majority group (Myers 2000:460; see Chapter 12).

To be sure, research has uncovered stronger evidence of discrimination against minorities convicted of *less* serious crimes than against minorities convicted of *more* serious crimes (Spohn & Cederblom 1991; Unnever & Hembroff 1988). Cases of serious crime call for more severe penalties for all offenders, regardless of minority status, leaving judges less room to exercise discretion based on legally suspect criteria. Similarly, research has shown greater discrimination in the *probation versus incarceration* decision—referred to as the **in/out decision**—than in the decision regarding sentence length for those incarcerated. Apparently, incarcerated offenders constitute a more homogeneous group of serious offenders who receive comparable treatment (Kramer & Steffensmeier 1993; Nelson 1994).

Additionally, research suggests that discrimination is conditional—that is, dependent on other factors. For example, racial minorities are more likely to be incarcerated in the South and in areas with higher proportions of minority residents and higher unemployment rates (Bridges & Crutchfield 1988; Bridges et al. 1987; Chiricos & Crawford 1995). In these places, as predicted by minority threat theory, minorities may be perceived by criminal justice officials as a more volatile, socially disruptive, and potentially rebellious population compared to the majority population.

The effect of race on sentencing is also contingent on gender and age. In this regard, Darrell Steffensmeier and colleagues (1998) examined the effects of race, gender, and age (controlling for offense severity and prior record) on the in/out and length-of-incarceration decision using data from nearly 139,000 cases in the state of Pennsylvania from 1989 to 1992. They found that males received more severe sentences than females, and 21- to 29-year-olds received harsher penalties than 18- to 20-year-olds and those 30 and older (as well, 18- to 20-year-olds received harsher penalties than those 30 and older). Significantly, blacks received more severe sentences than whites in each of their respective gender/age groups. Moreover, the sentencing inequities were the most pronounced for 21- to 29-year-old black males. The one exception to this pattern was for white males 50 years and older, who received somewhat harsher sentences, perhaps due to the sentencing of older drug offenders involved in large-scale or upper-level drug trafficking, compared to black males in the same age group.

Steffensmeier and colleagues argue that race—specifically in the case of the young black male—has become a perceptual shorthand used by judges to make sentencing decisions that involve a high degree of uncertainty about who is and who is not dangerous. Judges make assessments of offenders' past and future behavior that are consistent with societal stereotypes about various social groups. Judges view young black men, compared to other demographic groups, as more committed to street life, more dangerous, and less amenable to reform. They often assume that women, regardless of race, are less blameworthy, viewing them as playing minor roles in crime, as having more health problems, or as victims of domestic abuse (Bickle & Peterson 1991; Daly 1994; Daly & Bordt 1995). Judges assume that both women and older men of any race are more likely to have stable employment histories and responsibility for the care of dependents. On the other hand, since judges view young black men as lacking the social bonds that might insulate them from future criminality, they find less reason to give them a break. Judges also assume that incarcerating women (who might be pregnant) and older men poses greater child welfare and health-care costs to the correctional and social services systems. And they view young black men as better able than whites to "do time" and avoid being victimized in state prisons that are dominated by blacks (see Chapter 12). At the same time, Steffensmeier and colleagues attribute the relatively lighter sentences given to 18- to 20-year-olds (as compared to 21- to 29-year-olds) to judges' view of juveniles "as more impressionable and promising prospects for reform, and as more likely to experience victimization at the hands of [older] predatory inmates" (1998:779).

In a study of more than 89,000 defendants convicted under federal sentencing guidelines between 1993 and 1996, Steffensmeier and Stephen Demuth (2000) also found that Hispanics received the most severe sentences, followed by blacks and then whites. This disparity was most pronounced in **downward departure cases**—meaning cases for which presumptive sentencing guidelines allow "judges to depart from prescribed sentencing ranges" and give a defendant a reduced sentence (p. 705)—

involving drug sentences. Federal guidelines allow for a sentencing reduction when a defendant cooperates with prosecutors and provides **substantial assistance** that facilitates the prosecution of other offenders, and whites were more likely to be the beneficiaries of prosecutorial discretion in these cases.

Many critics of the criminal justice system have hoped that greater minority representation on the judiciary would minimize discriminatory sentencing practices. Susan Welch and colleagues (1988) found that white judges in "Metro City" (an unidentified city in the US Northeast) issued more severe sentences to black offenders than to white offenders, while black judges issued comparable sentences to both blacks and whites. Similarly, Malcolm Holmes and colleagues (1993) found that white judges in El Paso County, Texas, issued harsher penalties to Hispanic offenders than to white offenders, while Hispanic judges issued comparable penalties to both groups.

On the other hand, Cassia Spohn (1990b) found that both black judges and white judges in Detroit sentenced black offenders more severely than white offenders. She suggests that most judges share common attitudes and that judges of both races perceive black offenders as a greater threat. Since judges are selected from the "establishment center" of the legal profession and are socialized to the informal norms of the system, they tend to issue sentences that fall within the range of typical penalties for particular kinds of offenders (Holmes et al. 1993; Uhlman 1978:893). As one African-American judge observes, "No matter how 'liberal' black judges may believe themselves to be, the law remains essentially a conservative doctrine, and those who practice it conform" (Wright 1973:22–23).

In another Detroit study, Spohn (1990a) also found that in sexual assault cases, black female judges issued longer sentences than did black male judges. However, research has not found consistent differences overall in the sentencing practices of female versus male judges of all races, providing further evidence of homogeneity within the judiciary (Gruhl et al. 1981; Kritzer & Uhlman 1977).

Without a doubt, sentencing is a difficult decision that relies on a complex configuration of factors. Judges often make wise and warranted decisions that are based on legally appropriate criteria and reasonable evaluation of an offender's likelihood of reform. All other things being equal, however, some offenders do appear to be treated more inequitably than others.

Summary

This chapter, the first of two on the criminal justice system, focused on the police and courts. We began with a historical overview of policing in the United States and then examined different organizational styles of policing, including paramilitary and community policing. We also considered the nature of police culture and the work of policing, the problem of racial profiling, diversity in policing, police corruption, and police brutality and use of deadly force. Next, we turned to the prosecutorial, defense, and judicial elements of the criminal justice system, examining the process of initial screening, plea bargaining, and trial of criminal defendants, including trial by jury and the problem of wrongful convictions. Last, we addressed the sentencing stage and considered different models of sentencing and the problem of discrimination in sentencing.

12

Punishment and Corrections

Survey research indicates that a large portion of the American public believes that criminal punishments are insufficiently severe, although this sentiment is stronger among men, whites, political conservatives, and religious fundamentalists (Applegate et al. 2000; Johnson 2008; Pickett et al. 2014). Over the past few decades, however, the United States has not been weak-kneed in its resolve to punish criminals. Sentences for convicted offenders have lengthened, and the number of people under correctional supervision has risen dramatically, increasing from 1,840,400 adults in 1980 to 7,022,400 in 2012, a rise of more than 280 percent (Glaze & Herberman 2013; Pastore & Maguire 1998). The number of adults in jails and prisons exceeds 2.2 million, and the US prison incarceration rate of more than 716 per 100,000 population is the highest in the world, exceeding even the rates for Cuba (510 per 100,000) and Russia (475 per 100,000), not to mention the incarceration rates of other Western democracies like England and Wales (148 per 100,000), Canada (118 per 100,000), France (98 per 100,000), and Germany (79 per 100,000) (see Table 12.1).

The correctional system in the United States is a complex apparatus consisting of city and county jails, state and federal prisons, and community-based programs. Jails house individuals awaiting trial and those convicted of minor offenses who are generally serving not more than a year. State facilities contain more than 90 percent of the US prison population, although more than two-thirds of offenders overall are on probation or parole (see Table 12.2). While probation entails a period of community supervision in lieu of incarceration, parole involves community supervision after release from confinement. Community corrections also include a growing array of alternatives to incarceration that are drawing the attention of criminologists and criminal justice practitioners and policymakers. We begin this chapter with a discussion of the death penalty, followed by a consideration of prisons and then community corrections.

Table 12.1 Rates of Prison Incarceration in Selected Countries (2013)

Australia	130
Brazil	274
Canada	118
China	121
Cuba	510
England and Wales	148
France	98
Germany	79
Iran	284
Japan	51
Kenya	121
Mexico	210
Netherlands	82
Russia	475
Saudi Arabia	162
South Africa	294
United States	716

Source: Walmsley 2013.
Note: Rate = number of incarcerated individuals per 100,000 population of each country.

Table 12.2 Number of Adults Under Correctional Supervision (2012)

	Number	Percentage
Probation	3,942,800	56
Jail	744,500	11
Prison	1,483,900	21
Parole	851,200	12
Total	7,022,400	100

Source: Glaze & Herberman 2013, tab. 2.

The Death Penalty

Throughout most of US history, the death penalty, or capital punishment, was considered "an appropriate and justifiable response to crime" (Smith 2000:621). Survey research indicates that about 60 percent of the American public continues to favor the death penalty for the crime of murder, although this proportion drops to about half if respondents are given the option of choosing life without the possibility of parole (Ergun 2014). In either case, the death penalty remains a controversial issue in American society.

Legal Lethality

In the 1972 case of *Furman v. Georgia,* the US Supreme Court ruled that the death penalty had been implemented arbitrarily and unfairly, and hence violated the Eighth Amendment prohibition against cruel and unusual punishment. The penalty, the Court observed, had been administered disproportionately in the South and against the poor and people of color. Nevertheless, the Court stopped short of declaring capital punishment unconstitutional in principle; the problem, it held, was the manner in which it had been applied (Bowers & Pierce 1980).

Use of the death penalty had already been on the decline since the 1930s, and in the years following *Furman* a temporary moratorium on capital punishment was imposed as cases worked their way through the courts. In decisions in 1976 and 1977, the Supreme Court clarified the conditions under which capital punishment may be imposed. States that wished to use the penalty needed to develop guidelines specifying *aggravating conditions* under which it applied—for example, homicides committed in the course of another felony, homicides resulting in the death of more than one person, homicides against public officials, homicides involving especially brutal or heinous acts, homicides by an offender with a prior record of violence, or homicides for pecuniary gain. Moreover, the Court held that capital punishment could not be mandatory, even if such aggravating circumstances were found. Judges and jurors had to be given the opportunity to consider *mitigating conditions* under which the offender's life could be spared. The Court also said that the penalty could not be imposed for nonlethal rape of an adult, as had been done in the pre-*Furman* era (Bowers & Pierce 1980). In 2008, the Court reaffirmed this decision in ruling that a man convicted of child rape could not be executed (Mears 2008). Additionally, in 2002 the Court ruled that execution of persons with intellectual disabilities was unconstitutional, although it allowed states leeway in developing criteria for determining who was eligible for this exemption. And in 2005 it ruled that executions of persons who committed their crimes while they were under 18 years of age was unconstitutional as well (Death Penalty Information Center 2014c, 2014d).

In 1977, Gary Gilmore of Utah became the first offender to be executed in the post-*Furman* period. The annual number of executions since then rose to a high of 98 in 1999 but declined to 39 in 2013 (Death Penalty Information Center 2014a). Southern states have accounted for about 80 percent of the post-*Furman* executions, with Texas alone accounting for 37 percent. As of 2014, 32 states as well as the US government and military have statutory provisions for the death penalty, with the number of death-row inmates exceeding 3,300. Because of postconviction appeals, the average time between the imposition of a death sentence and the actual execution is more than 10 years. On average, it costs more than $2 million to process a capital punishment case from trial to execution, which in the post-*Furman* era has amounted to more than $2.5 billion nationwide "beyond the costs that would have been incurred if life in prison" had been the most severe penalty (Death Penalty Information Center 2009:17). As Mark

Costanzo observes, "Capital trials are more complex and time-consuming than other criminal trials at every stage in the legal process" (1997:62–63). The postconviction appeal stage is generally the most expensive part of all, and about 20 to 30 percent of appeals result in reversal of the conviction and/or sentence, a rate that is many times higher than for noncapital cases (Bohm 1998). Moreover, Michael Radelet and colleagues (1992) found that 416 death penalty defendants in the twentieth century were wrongfully convicted, 23 of whom were executed; and the Death Penalty Information Center (2014b) found that since 1973, 144 people have been released from death row due to posttrial findings of innocence.

Death penalty cases are appealed on grounds of either due process violations or compelling new evidence of innocence. In one case involving the 1980 death of a 16-year-old white girl in Texas, the investigating police officer had told two janitors—one black and one white—that one of them would "hang" for the crime. The officer then turned to the black man, Clarence Lee Brandley, and said, "Since you're the nigger, you're elected" (Radelet et al. 1992:121). Brandley was indicted by an all-white grand jury and initially tried by an all-white trial jury. The first trial resulted in a hung jury, but a second trial resulted in conviction in 1981. Following the trial, misconduct by the police and prosecutor came to light when hair samples and photographs turned up missing. Although Brandley's first appeal was rejected in 1985, subsequent information from an informant and recanted testimony from a trial witness (the other janitor) shed further light on Brandley's innocence. He was granted a new trial in 1989, and nine months later the charges were dropped. All told, Brandley spent nine years on death row for a crime he did not commit. No law enforcement officials were ever reprimanded for mishandling the case (Parker et al. 2001).

In another case, in the state of Florida, Sonia Jacobs was released from death row after an appellate court concluded in 1990 that the prosecution had suppressed exculpatory evidence and that a prosecution witness (who turned out to be the real killer) had lied. Two years earlier, Jacobs's husband and codefendant, Jesse Tafero, had been executed after being "convicted and sentenced to death on exactly the same evidence" (Radelet & Bedau 1998:231).

Samuel Gross (1996) argues that mistaken convictions may be more common in capital murder cases than in other cases because police and prosecutors are under greater public pressure to apprehend the perpetrator as quickly as possible. This pressure may lead them to make hasty judgments, to use informants of questionable reliability, and to coerce suspects into confessions. The greater publicity given to such cases also provides jurors with information damaging to the defendant that might not be admissible in court. And since defendants in capital cases are most often poor, they do not have the resources to challenge a determined prosecutor successfully. Judges typically assign capital cases to inexperienced or mediocre defense attorneys. One study of Kentucky, for instance, found that a quarter of those on death row were represented by attorneys who were subsequently disbarred, suspended, or incarcerated (Kroll 1991). One trial in Alabama had to be postponed when the defense attorney arrived in court drunk; when the case resumed the next day, the defendant was quickly sentenced to death. In four trials in Georgia the attorneys representing African-American defendants used the term "nigger" to refer to their clients, all of whom were sentenced to death. And in Texas a defense attorney simply told the jury at the sentencing hearing: "You are an extremely intelligent jury. You've got that man's life in your hands. You can take it or not. That's all I have to say" (McCormick 1998:64). His client was executed.

In the *Furman* case, a majority of justices on the US Supreme Court were persuaded that the death penalty had been applied in a discriminatory manner. But 15 years later, in *McCleskey v. Kemp* (1987), a more conservative group of justices had the opportunity to revisit the issue. Warren McCleskey had been sentenced to death in Georgia for the murder of a white police officer. McCleskey appealed his case on the basis of statistical evidence that indicated that black offenders who murdered white victims had a higher probability of receiving a death sentence than defendants in cases with other racial patterns of offender and victim. But a majority of justices were not persuaded that *statistical* evidence of racial disparity constituted a sufficient basis upon which to overturn McCleskey's sentence. The decision virtually "eliminated the federal courts as a forum for the consideration of statistically based claims of racial discrimination in capital sentencing" (Baldus & Woodworth 1998:409). As of 2014, about 40 percent of persons on death row are African-American (Death Penalty Information Center 2014e).

Many people believe that if capital punishment is to be used, lethal injection constitutes the most humane method of inducing death. Most states now use lethal injection as the sole means of execution or allow the condemned person a choice between lethal injection and other methods such as electrocution, gas, hanging, or firing squad. Typically the lethal injection procedure entails strapping the person to a gurney and injecting a nonlethal chemical such as sodium pentothal or thiopental to induce unconsciousness. The person is then administered pancuronium bromide, a muscle relaxant, and finally, potassium chloride, which induces cardiac arrest and permanently stops the heart. Complications can arise, however, if the amount of the initial drug is insufficient, the chemicals are administered out of sequence, or the executioners have difficulty locating a usable vein for the insertion of the catheter (Denno 1998). When Stanley Tooky Williams was executed by lethal injection in California in 2005, it took 35 minutes for him to die. One eye witness described the last 10 minutes of his ordeal as "slow, ugly, and torturous. . . . The midsection of Stan's body did not stay still. It began to contort, caving in to the point of distortion—his stomach appeared to have been sucked dry of all internal organs, as it sunk so low it nearly touched his spine" (Williams 2007:346–347). More recently, in 2014, the botched execution of Clayton Lockett in Oklahoma took nearly two hours between the time the execution team tried to find an accessible vein to the time he died (Crair 2014). Nevertheless, the US Supreme Court has upheld the constitutionality of lethal injection as a legal method of capital punishment (Greenhouse 2008).

Women and the Death Penalty

About 2 percent of prisoners on death row are women (Death Penalty Information Center 2014f). The paucity of women receiving capital punishment reflects both their low representation among those convicted of murder and the fact that their homicides are more likely than men's to be domestic crimes and to lack premeditation (see Chapter 8). Women also tend to be viewed by the courts as less blameworthy for their crimes compared to men, and more deserving of consideration (see Chapter 11), and society is less willing to subject women to severe punishments. As Victor Streib observes: "When the ship is sinking, we put women in lifeboats first. When women enter the armed forces, they are kept away from the firing line. . . . We are uncomfortable with subjecting women to death or even danger" (1998:220).

The widely publicized execution by lethal injection of Karla Faye Tucker in Texas in 1998 brought media attention to the issue of women and the death penalty. Prior to the Tucker case, only one woman had been executed in the post-*Furman* era, and Texas had not executed a woman since 1863. Despite Tucker's conviction for the pickaxe murder of two people in a 1983 robbery, she emerged as an appealing and sympathetic media figure, one who sparked "a worldwide debate over redemption and retribution" (O'Shea 1999:343). A born-again Christian who found God on death row, Tucker counseled fellow prisoners and even married a prison minister. The Rutherford Institute, which usually limits its advocacy to cases of religious freedom and human rights, petitioned President Bill Clinton to prevent the execution. Television evangelist Pat Robertson and even Pope John Paul II spoke on Tucker's behalf. While these supporters emphasized Tucker's religious conversion, they had never before made a plea on behalf of a condemned man who had converted to Christianity. Nevertheless, Tucker acknowledged that there had been people who had appealed their cases before "who were just as committed to Christ as I am" but who were executed anyway. The "people" she referred to were men. "If you believe in the death penalty for one," she said, "you believe in it for everyone" (Pearson 1998:A19).

Tucker's appeal for clemency was denied. When asked about the "gender factor" in the case, a spokesperson for then-governor George W. Bush replied, "The gender of the murderer did not make any difference to the victim" (cited in Gillespie 2000:98–99). Neither did it make a difference to protesters carrying signs outside the prison while Tucker was strapped to the gurney, signs that read "Forget injection. Use a pickaxe" and "Axe and you shall receive."

The fact that Tucker was a white woman is also significant, for society's reluctance to execute women varies by the race of the offender. Nearly 40 percent of women executed from 1930 to 1967, for example, were African Americans (Collins 1997). A study of women on death row in 1993 found African-American and Latina offenders to be "overrepresented in the kinds of murders that . . . are at low risk of resulting in the death penalty" (Farr 1997:273). And of the women who were on death row at the time of Tucker's execution, more than 40 percent were women of color (O'Shea 1999).

The Modern Penitentiary
In this section we consider the historical emergence of the modern penitentiary, including the incarceration boom and other trends of the latter part of the twentieth century.

Prisons in Historical Perspective
In colonial America more than 160 offenses, from murder to disrespecting one's parents, were punishable by death. Corporal punishment, fines, and compensation to the victim or victim's family were the preferred penal responses, however. Wealthy offenders were more likely to be fined, while the poor were flogged. **Flogging** with a blunt instrument or whip was a public spectacle that directly involved the citizenry in the **collective ritual of punishment**—the mobilization of moral sentiments that reinforces social solidarity. Although the practice of flogging waned over the years, it remained in use in the United States through much of the twentieth century and was not declared unconstitutional by a federal court until 1968 (Inciardi 1996; Rothman 1971; Shover & Inverarity 1995).

The collective ritual of the **pillory** was also used for corporal punishment in colonial times. Here the offender's head, hands, and feet were secured by a wooden frame. The violator was kept in public view and repeatedly whipped or pelted with rocks and eggs by passersby. It was not unusual for the offender's ears to be nailed to the pillory as well. Another device, the **brank**, was used to punish gossips, perjurers, liars, blasphemers, drunkards, and wife batterers. The brank, also called the "gossip's helm" or "dame's bridle," consisted of a cage that was secured around the head, with "a spike plate or flat dish of iron that was placed in the mouth over the tongue," causing severe pain if the offender tried to speak (Inciardi 1996:492).

Other colonial punishments included branding and use of dunking stools, duncecaps, and signs (such as "I am a fornicator"). The *scarlet letter*, for instance, "made famous by Nathaniel Hawthorne's novel of the same name, was used for a variety of offenses. The adulterous wife wore an *A*, cut from scarlet cloth and sewn to her upper garments. The blasphemer wore a *B*, the pauper a *P*, the thief a *T*, and the drunkard a *D*" (Inciardi 1996:492).

In the late eighteenth century, the Quakers in Pennsylvania pioneered the use of prisons, an innovation that removed the public from direct participation in the collective ritual of punishment. Previously, jails had been used primarily to hold persons who were awaiting court action or who could not pay their debts. Now a separate wing of Philadelphia's Walnut Street Jail, the "penitentiary house," was used to confine convicted offenders, who were kept in solitary confinement. The Quakers viewed the penitentiary as a humane alternative to the cruelty and degradation of existing methods. Locked in isolation, inmates could "be made to contemplate the evil of their ways . . . [and] immerse themselves in self-reflection and penitence" (Barlow 1996:399; see also Clear et al. 2006).

In the early nineteenth century, New York constructed the Auburn Prison, the first institution to use an architectural design that arranged cells in multiple tiers, with the entire facility surrounded by a fortresslike stone wall. Prisoners were confined in separate cells at night but were allowed to eat and work together in small groups during the day. Solitary confinement was reserved for breaches of prison rules, but all inmates were required to maintain complete silence at all times. Hard work and a regimented life were to be the means to one's salvation. Whereas some earlier forms of punishment attempted to discipline the "body" through physical pain, these new methods sought to discipline the "mind" (Clear et al. 2006; Foucault 1979).

The Auburn approach eventually prevailed as the model for the modern penitentiary. Although this approach was considered more humane than earlier punishments, conditions in these institutions were deplorable. They were overcrowded, dirty and dilapidated, physically harsh, and notorious for failing to reform their captives. Through the first half of the twentieth century, prisons in the United States were colloquially referred to as **Big Houses**. Institutions like Alcatraz in California, Sing Sing in New York, and Stateville in Illinois became legendary as human warehouses. Prison guards ruled the Big Houses through the threat and use of force, and boredom terrorized the prisoners' souls (Irwin 1980; Johnson 2002; Shelden et al. 2008).

Beginning in the 1870s, however, prison reformers often advocated a more rehabilitative penal philosophy. The National Prison Association proclaimed that the reformation of criminals required their moral regeneration, "not the infliction of vindictive suffering" (cited in Clear & Cole 1994:57). In 1876 the Elmira Reformatory in New York, under the leadership of Zebulon Brockway, promoted education as the key to successful rehabilitation. Elmira was designed for 16- to 30-year-old, first-time offenders, who were placed in a school-like atmosphere and required to take courses in a variety of academic, vocational, and moral subjects. This approach was incorporated into the philosophy of juvenile "reform schools" as the juvenile justice system developed.

In the nineteenth century, few women were incarcerated, but those who were incarcerated were treated similarly to men. Initially, separate women's quarters were created in men's institutions. Then, in the early 1870s, the first prison operated for and by women was established, in Indianapolis. Reformers considered the fortresslike atmosphere characteristic of men's prisons to be inappropriate for women's institutions, which they thought should be organized around groups of cottages that housed 20 to 50 women in a homelike atmosphere. And inmates, they believed, should be allowed private rooms rather than cells, be given the opportunity to decorate their quarters, and be taught domestic skills thought suitable to their feminine nature, such as ironing, laundering, and cooking (Belknap 2007; Clear et al. 2006).

After World War I, psychological theories of criminality increasingly influenced modern conceptions of rehabilitation, and by the end of the 1920s "rehabilitation as the primary purpose of incarceration became national policy" (Clear & Cole 1994:65–66; see Chapter 3). Diagnostic classification systems were developed to differentiate those who were likely to benefit from rehabilitation from those who were not, and to guide programs of individualized treatment. By the 1940s, the modern "correctional" institution employing primarily group but also individual counseling along with vocational and educational training became the model penitentiary. Prison discipline was less intrusive, and prisoners were allowed more personal amenities as well as recreational, visitation, and mail privileges. But despite all the well-intentioned rhetoric about rehabilitation, prison officials could not deliver on their promises, as genuine reform was overwhelmed by lack of know-how and administrative and fiscal constraints. At best, inmates were left on their own to undergo personal reform, a difficult task in institutions that were still quite grim and punitive (Johnson 2002).

From the early 1960s to the early 1970s, prisons in the United States experienced political turmoil that reflected the civil rights movement of the larger society. Prisoners frustrated with punitive prison practices protested nonviolently and rioted to pressure for reform. The most well-known riot of that era occurred in New York's Attica prison in 1971. More than 2,000 prisoners took over the facility and held guards as hostages, demanding, among other things, improved diet and medical care, religious freedom (especially for black Muslims), education and rehabilitative programming, legal assistance, procedures for handling complaints, and access to the courts. The governor of New York ordered state troopers to reclaim the institution by force, which resulted in the killing of 10 hostages and 29 inmates (Shelden et al. 2008; Welch 2004).

The Attica and other prison protests and riots drew attention to the need for reform and ushered in a wave of civil rights lawsuits by prisoners. As a result, there is now more judicial scrutiny of prison conditions and of the behavior of correctional personnel. At the same time, however, the 1970s witnessed the abandonment of the rehabilitative mandate of prisons in favor of a retributive philosophy (see Chapter 11). The penitentiary has primarily become a custodial institution wherein prisoners are expected to "do their time" in proportion to the seriousness of their offenses.

The Incarceration Boom

Between 1980 and 2012, the US prison population increased by more than 360 percent, and this even after a period of moderate decline in recent years (Glaze & Herberman 2013; Pastore & Maguire 1998; Petersilia 2011). Criminological research shows, however, that crime rates alone do not account for fluctuations in the size of the prison population over time. Several studies have found that prison admissions increase during times of higher unemployment, as incarceration is used to absorb and control the surplus supply of laborers who constitute a potentially rebellious group (Chiricos & Delone 1992; Hochstetler & Shover 1997). Raymond Michalowski and Susan Carlson attributed rising state and federal prison admissions between 1980 and 1992 to the "growth of an urban underclass with declining access to income-replacing social welfare and public-job provisions that began in the 1970s and accelerated throughout the 1980s" (1999:228).

Political factors also affect prison expansion. David Jacobs and Ronald Helms (1996) analyzed state and federal admissions between 1948 and 1989 and found that admission rates were positively associated with the strength of the Republican Party (as measured by the percentage of people who identified themselves as Republican in any given year), independent of the level of crime. They noted that the Republican Party, in comparison to the Democratic Party, has more consistently advanced a law-and-order agenda (see Chapter 1). Jacobs and Helms also found that admission rates increased in the year following presidential elections. They argued that competition for votes caused incumbents from both parties to enact severe penal policies during campaign years in order to appeal to the public's desire to crack down on crime.

David Greenberg and Valerie West's (2001) analysis of state imprisonment rates between 1971 and 1991 yielded results that support and extend previous research. They found that higher rates of imprisonment were associated with higher unemployment, a larger proportion of the population being black, a conservative political culture, lower spending on welfare, and higher per capita state revenues. And in a study of state imprisonment between 1977 and 1996, Thomas Stucky and colleagues (2005) found that Republican control of state legislatures was more likely to increase incarceration rates when competition for electoral votes was high.

Greenberg and West's (2001) research also highlighted the role of increased drug arrests on rising incarceration rates, as discussed in Chapters 1 and 7. Currently, 16 percent of prisoners in state institutions and 51 percent of prisoners in federal institutions are serving time for drug offenses (see Table 12.3). At the same time, as the proportion of prisoners incarcerated for drug offenses increased, the opportunities to receive drug treatment in prison declined (Lock et al. 2002).

African Americans have been especially impacted by punitive correctional policies. The rate of incarceration for black males is six times higher than the rate for white males, and the rate of incarceration for black females is more than two times higher than the rate for white females (see Table 12.4). The rates of incarceration for Hispanics and other minority groups are also higher than the rates for whites. These policies have had the unfortunate effect of further destabilizing minority communities by weakening family and community ties that might otherwise foster informal social controls among youths, and by exacerbating the intergenerational transmission of social disadvantage (Clear 2007; Foster & Hagan 2007; Rose & Clear 1998).

The incarceration boom has created serious problems of prison overcrowding, with many prisons operating well above capacity (Austin et al. 2001). Moreover, this boom has been extraordinarily expensive, with expenditures on state corrections currently approaching $50 billion a year

Table 12.3 Number of Prisoners by Type of Offense (2012/2013)

	State, 2012	Federal, 2013
Drug offenses	210,200 (16%)	98,200 (51%)
Property offenses	247,100 (19%)	11,500 (6%)
Violent offenses	707,500 (54%)	13,600 (7%)
Other offenses	150,200 (11%)	70,400 (36%)
Total	1,315,000 (100%)	193,700 (100%)

Source: Carson 2014, tabs. 13–16.

Table 12.4 Rates of Incarceration by Race/Ethnicity and Gender (2013)

	White	Black	Hispanic	Other[a]
Male	466	2,805	1,134	963
Female	51	113	66	90

Source: Carson 2014, tab. 8.
Notes: Rate = number of incarcerated individuals per 100,000 population of each group. The data include both state and federal prisoners.
   a. "Other" includes American Indians, Alaskan Natives, Pacific Islanders, and persons identifying as two or more races.

nationally, more than three-quarters of which is spent on prisons (Kyckelhahn 2012; Stephan 2004). Money spent on corrections also diverts resources that might otherwise be devoted to crime prevention and general societal needs, with the growth of outlays for corrections outpacing "budget increases for nearly all other essential government services, including transportation, higher education, and public assistance" (Petersilia 2011:27).

The irony of all this, as Franklin Zimring and Gordon Hawkins (1997) observe, is that expanded prison admissions have the greatest impact on less serious offenses—those offenses at the margin between meriting incarceration and meriting more lenient penal sanctions. In California, for example, the state with the largest prison population, "only 27 percent of the additional prison space added between 1980 and 1990 was used to increase the number of prisoners who had been convicted of violent offenses" (p. 18). Nationwide, the *proportion* of prisoners convicted of violent crimes has declined. Zimring and Hawkins are concerned that such correctional policies, which narrow sentencing disparities between life-threatening and non-life-threatening offenses, diminish the deterrent effect of the law, because offenders have less to lose by crossing the threshold of violence. Thus the incarceration boom, in their view, represents a misguided political response to the public's genuine concern about crime. Prison expansion provides little "bang for the buck" in protecting the public against the crimes that it fears most: crimes of violence.

Privatization of Prisons

Earlier we introduced the notion of what Naomi Klein calls the disaster-capitalism complex, the amalgam of corporations that profit from war and disaster relief (see Chapter 9). Corrections has been an area in which such profiting has occurred, leading to what Eric Schlosser calls the **prison-industrial complex**—"a set of bureaucratic, political, and economic interests that encourage increased spending on imprisonment, regardless of the actual need" (1998:54). Architectural and construction firms, investment bankers, and companies selling everything from security cameras to padded cells view this spending not as a burden on taxpayers but as an opportunity to profit (Shelden et al. 2008).

One of the latest trends in corrections, the **privatization** of prisons, is a development that bears close scrutiny. Private companies, which serve a majority of the states and the federal system, contract with the government to build and manage prisons. About 7 percent of the adult prison population is housed in privately operated facilities (Gaes 2008). Although privatization is touted as a way to save money, research indicates that private prisons are not less costly to administer than public institutions. Moreover, private prisons are more likely to cut corners by reducing labor costs, which constitute 60 to 80 percent of prison operating budgets. Correctional officers who work for private companies receive less training, and lower wages and fringe benefits, and have fewer opportunities for promotion than those who work in public institutions. Additionally, research indicates that recidivism rates of prisoners released from private facilities are greater than those released from public facilities (Abramsky 2004; Pratt & Maahs 1999; Schlosser 1998; Spivak & Sharp 2008).

Private prisons usually charge their customers, the taxpayers, a daily rate for each inmate. Like hotels, the companies have an incentive to keep their beds filled. Hence prisoners in private prisons are more likely than those in public institutions to lose credit for "good time" that would lead to earlier release. Additionally, "bed brokers" earn commissions for arranging to locate and transport prisoners from one state to another, and government officials cut deals with companies that agree to share their profits with them (Bates 1998; Schlosser 1998).

Private facilities have also been marked by lax security, with several incidents involving escaped prisoners. The private shipping of prisoners from one state to another also poses considerable security risks, especially when untrained personnel are making the pickups and deliveries. It is not unusual for prisoners to spend a month on the road as transport vehicles visit dozens of states before arriving at their destination. This practice is even less regulated by the government than the interstate shipping of cattle (Schlosser 1998; Shelden et al. 2008).

There is also less accountability in the running of private prisons than in the running of government prisons. A training video from a correctional facility in Texas, operated by Capital Correctional Resources, revealed mistreatment of prisoners originally from Missouri, with correctional officers cursing, kicking, dragging, and zapping them with electronic stun guns while they were lying on the floor. One of the correctional officers had previously served prison time for beating a prisoner when the officer was employed at a Texas state prison. In a Kentucky correctional facility run by the US Corrections Corporation, the company exploited unpaid prison labor for construction and renovation work not only on the prison, but on several churches, a game-room business, a country club, and a private school as well. Company officials had business or personal interests in all of these projects (Schlosser 1998; Shelden et al. 2008).

In the world of privatization, falling crime rates, shorter prison terms, and community alternatives to prison are bad for business. Hence private companies lobby state governments for policies that expand prison construction. One executive from the Corrections Corporation of America, the nation's largest private prison firm, likened profiting from prison to "selling cars, or real estate, or hamburgers" (Schlosser 1998:76). Another executive remarked, in reference to a plan to build prisons in California "on spec" (without a contract to fulfill them): "If you build it in the right place, the prisoners will come."

Living and Working in Prison

Prisons are typically classified as maximum-, medium-, or minimum-security facilities, according to the amount of physical security that is available both within and on the perimeter of the institution. Prisoners are distributed into these institutions on the basis of the seriousness of their offense record and the perceived danger they pose to society. In all prisons, power is divided between the correctional staff and inmates. The staff maintain some semblance "of order as prisoners go through the formal routine of meals, [head] counts, work, recreation, and correctional programs" (Johnson 2002:127). But "outside the formal schedule, on cell block tiers, in recreation areas, [and] on the yard," the prisoners are afforded a degree of self-rule that governs the institution as much as the official rules.

The Society of Captives

In his classic book *The Society of Captives,* Gresham Sykes (1958) described prison life as a response to five types of deprivation or **pains of imprisonment**. According to Sykes, the most basic deprivation is the loss of liberty itself, which consists both of "confinement to the institution" and "confinement within the institution" (p. 65). Although the pain that this deprivation, like many others, induces is more psychological than physical, it produces an intense boredom and loneliness that is more than most of us could bear. Second, prisoners are deprived of most goods and services enjoyed by citizens in the free society. While the public may at times complain about "country club prisons," most inmates lead a rather severe life, the food to eat and roof over their heads notwithstanding.

Deprivation of heterosexual contact is a third pain of imprisonment, leading some prisoners to become involved in homosexual acts they otherwise might not have engaged in, causing some to question their sexual orientation and gender identity, and exacerbating the problem of male-on-male rape. Fourth, prisoners suffer a loss of autonomy as they are subjected "to a vast body of rules and commands which are designed to control [their] behavior in minute detail," from when to eat to when to take a shower (Sykes 1958:73). The fifth deprivation, the loss of physical security, is perhaps the greatest deprivation of all. Nowadays, threats to one's security occur less at the hands of correctional officers than at the hands of other inmates. In either case, the contemporary prison, at least the maximum-security institution, is a rather violent place and bears no resemblance whatsoever to the therapeutic atmosphere envisioned by prison reformers of an earlier era (Johnson 2002; Marcum & Castle 2014; Ross & Richards 2002).

Prisoners adapt to these pains of imprisonment, both individually and collectively, in a variety of ways. One adaptation entails the development of an **informal prison economy**, whereby prisoners barter for commodities such as extra and better food, clothing and personal grooming products, immersion coils for heating water and food, cigarettes, and illegal drugs and alcohol (including prison "home brew"). Some items may be purchased from the prison canteen or commissary with coupons earned from prison work or drawn on personal accounts. They may also be stolen from other inmates or prison facilities (such as the kitchen, canteen, or hospital), mailed in by relatives and friends, or smuggled into the institution from the outside. There is also an informal economy of services, including sex, protection, and legal assistance. Typically, cigarettes are the medium of exchange. They have "a stable and well-known value, and come in 'denominations' of singles, packs, and cartons" (Clear et al. 2006:277–278). The demand for cigarettes remains high among prisoners, and even those who don't smoke keep cigarettes for bartering purposes. Besides, smoking cigarettes is part of the "tough guy" demeanor that helps minimize the chances of being victimized by others (Ross & Richards 2002).

In addition, the prison experience requires adaptation to a **convict code** that governs relationships among prisoners and between prisoners and correctional staff. This code advises prisoners to "do your own time" and "mind your own business"—to keep their distance from staff and above all not squeal or inform on other prisoners. The code also encourages them to respond in kind to threats or assaults from other prisoners or risk becoming perennial targets for further victimization, including rape. As Jack Abbott, a convict who gained notoriety for his book *In the Belly of the Beast,* wrote: "When you walk across the yard or down the tier to your cell, you stand out like a sore thumb if you do not appear either callously unconcerned or cold and ready to kill. Many times you have to 'prey' on someone, or you will be 'preyed' on yourself" (1981:155; see also Ross & Richards 2002; Shelden et al. 2008).

Convicts with a demonstrated capacity for violence often dominate today's prisons, especially state prisons. Most prisoners, however, try to carve out their own private niches, insulating themselves from the violence. They spend as little time as possible in the mess hall, recreational areas, and prison yard; and they stay away from the informal economy. They stick to a few friends, if they can find them, and log long hours alone in their cells. In a survey of 300 prisoners at a maximum-security institution in Tennessee, Richard McCorkle (1992) found that 40 percent said they avoided public areas and nearly 80 percent said they lived as loners. Vulnerable inmates rarely turn to staff for protection, for the convict code inevitably marks those who "snitch" as objects of derision and abuse. For some, voluntary segregation in protective custody is the only safe alternative. Prisoners opting for protective custody remain "confined to their cells for all but a small part of the day," even though such isolated living is difficult and often damaging to their psychological well-being (Lockwood 1977:206).

Many prisoners find they have more time than ever before to read, which is one of the most constructive things they can do while incarcerated. Some may try to earn their General Educational Development (GED)

FURTHER EXPLORATION
Solitary Confinement

Use of solitary confinement in the United States began in the early nineteenth century, but it was later abandoned as a routine practice when correctional officials found that insanity and suicide among prisoners, and an inability to function in society upon release, became commonplace. More recently, in 1989, the Pelican Bay state prison in California became the first supermax facility built exclusively to house prisoners in solitary confinement. Prisoners at Pelican Bay who are unable to psychologically tolerate such social isolation are transferred to a 128-bed psychiatric ward that operates at full capacity. Sans therapists, "group therapy" in the ward consists of listening to music, watching movies, playing games, composing art, or discussing current events in a small room with a few other prisoners, who are each confined to phone booth–sized cages (Shelden et al. 2008; Sullivan 2006).

As of 2014, about 80,000 prisoners are serving time in some form of solitary confinement in the United States, about 30 percent of these in supermax facilities. Most serve more than 5 years in isolation, but some in excess of 20 years. The vast majority of prisoners who serve solitary confinement will one day be released back into society, but we actually know very little about the long-term psychological and social consequences of this severe form of deprivation. What we do know, however, is that recidivism rates of prisoners who have been retained in solitary confinement are higher than for the general prisoner population, and such prisoners are more likely to commit violent crimes upon release (*Solitary Watch* 2014; Sullivan 2006).

certificates or take college courses that are offered on-site or through distance-learning programs. Some join formal religious, cultural-identity, and self-help groups or clubs that are sponsored by the prison and that offer supervised space for meetings (Johnson 2002; Ross & Richards 2002).

Since the 1990s, we have heard more about so-called **supermax prisons**, which are much more expensive to build and operate than traditional maximum-security institutions. Proponents of this method of incarceration believe these facilities are necessary to control violent and seriously disruptive inmates. Prisoners are segregated and their movement and contact with other prisoners and correctional staff are restricted. They are required to spend 23 hours a day locked in cells that may be as small as 8 by 10 feet, and they are tightly monitored by sophisticated electronic surveillance and a higher ratio of correctional officers to inmates than is typical of ordinary prisons. Prisoners are taken out one at a time for a shower or exercise in a small, private pen or room (Cullen & Sundt 2000; *Solitary Watch* 2014; Sullivan 2006).

Race/ethnicity and prison gangs. Racial and ethnic tensions are a significant feature of prison life. In an environment where the majority of prisoners are nonwhite, the power differentials of the outside society are reversed, making whites more vulnerable to victimization compared to other inmates (Bowker 1980; Jacobs 1977; Johnson 2002). As one veteran, white convict observed: "Most whites fuck up right away when they come into prison, because they try to be friendly. . . . If [a white] says hello or even nods to [the black convicts], then he's already doomed. . . . Half of them will think he is just being polite and treating them with respect, but the other half will know he is weak and afraid, because they know that a white man isn't even going to acknowledge them if he's been in prison before, because whites don't speak to [blacks] in prison. These [blacks] are going to move on that guy as soon as the [correctional officer] disappears" (Earley 1992:419).

According to Robert Johnson, life in prison is strikingly similar to life on the streets in low-income, urban neighborhoods, with many prisoners coming from communities that are "as harsh and depriving as the prisons they wind up in" (2002:111). In many respects, the convict subculture may be viewed not simply as an adaptation to the pains of imprisonment but as a continuation of the urban street subculture that is imported into the prison from the outside (see Chapter 6). Consequently, whites (especially those of higher-class background) have greater difficulty adjusting to an institutional environment that is more incongruous with their prior experiences, and they are more likely than nonwhites to commit suicide (Hunt et al. 1993; Rodgers 1995).

Over the past few decades, prison gangs have become an increasingly prominent feature of prison life. Some observers attribute the growth of these gangs since the 1980s to the incarceration boom and the decline of rehabilitation programs, and they characterize the rise of supermax institutions as a response to this problem (Hunt et al. 1993; Sullivan 2006). Prison gangs attract some of the most violent prisoners and exert considerable control over the informal prison economy. Gangs have also expanded their base of operations to the outside, with activities on the streets being dictated at times from behind bars. As noted earlier, the incarceration experience has even facilitated gang organization by bringing together a captive population of similarly situated offenders who can be recruited into larger, more powerful organizations (see Chapter 6).

Prison gangs, which have been documented in virtually every state in the United States, with some having cross-state affiliations, are organized primarily along racial/ethnic lines (black, Latino, and white). According to Mark Fleisher and Scott Decker (2001), the five most influential prison gangs around the country include one black gang (the Black Guerrilla Family), three Latino gangs (La Nuestra Familia, the Mexican Mafia, and the Texas Syndicate), and one white gang (the Aryan Brotherhood) (see also Shelden et al. 2008).

In a study of California prison gangs, Geoffrey Hunt and colleagues (1993) documented the ways in which a new generation of gang members emerged to fill the power vacuum created in the convict subculture as older members were segregated, dropped out of gangs, or went undercover. In the past, for example, Crips and Bloods were more likely to put aside the intra-gang disputes that divided their members on the streets of Los Angeles. As one convict observed: "When they are 'out there' they may fight amongst themselves. . . . But when they get to prison they are wise enough to know, we gotta join collectively to fend off everyone else" (pp. 406–407). Never-theless, intragang disputes persist in prison, and "old school" gang mem-bers complain that the younger generation does not accord them the respect they once received. From their point of view, the younger generation is "needlessly violent and erratic and not 'TBYAS'—thinking before you act and speak."

Women in prison. Women's prisons are fewer in number than men's and more likely to be multiple-classification institutions, housing prisoners of various security risks in the same facility. Some states have no separate prisons for women and either confine them in a separate wing of a men's institution or transfer them to another state. Since the 1970s, several states and the federal government have operated coed prisons, where female and male inmates sleep in separate units but are allowed varying degrees of contact during the day. Prison reformers hoped that coed prisons would nor-malize the incarceration experience and reduce prison violence; and overall, violence is lower in these facilities. But while sexual contact is prohibited, it occurs nevertheless; and women in coed prisons, some of whom become pregnant, are also more likely than men to be sanctioned (and lose "good time" or privileges) for violating the "no sexual contact" policy (Belknap 2007; Clear et al. 2006).

In many respects, the subculture of women's prisons is similar to that of men's. Women find ways to adapt to the pains of imprisonment and adhere to the convict code. Those who establish reputations for fighting and the ability to defend themselves physically achieve the highest status. At the same time, the gender norms of the larger society permeate the institution. Since women have less need to demonstrate toughness and physical prowess, women's prisons are comparatively less violent than men's. Women provide one another with more interpersonal support and are more likely to form **pseudofamilies** by developing emotional bonds with friends and sexual partners. In the male prison subculture, male-on-male rape is accepted while consensual gay relationships are condemned. The opposite is true in women's prisons, where consensual lesbian rela-tionships are more acceptable and the rape of women by other women is rare, although rape by male correctional officers is all too common. Addi-tionally, racial/ethnic divisions are also less salient among women prison-ers, who often form relationships that cut across those lines. At the same time, some white women are more likely than nonwhite women to gain advantage over others by appealing to correctional officers for preferential treatment and assistance in settling disputes (Belknap 2007; Clear et al. 2006; Marcum & Castle 2014).

As with men, both preincarceration and incarceration factors influence women's feelings about and adaptations to prison. In a study of women in two California prisons, the California Institution for Women and the Valley State Prison, Candace Kruttschnitt and colleagues (2000) found that many women had a history of abuse that made them especially sensitive to mistreatment by correctional officers. As one woman remarked: "I was in an abusive relationship for lots of years and . . . I'm still getting abuse. . . . There's a lot of males, mostly [correctional officers]. . . . They have this attitude where [they] know they have full control over us" (p. 702). At the same time, Kruttschnitt and colleagues found that features of the institutional environment influenced women's responses. At the California Institution for Women, which had a more rehabilitative orientation, women expressed more positive views about other prisoners and correctional staff. At Valley State Prison, which had a more custodial orientation and a strict disciplinary regimen, women were more negative about their experiences. The family-like relationships among prisoners often noted in research on women's prisons were absent. As one woman said: "You don't have a friend here. . . . There's no closeness. . . . I don't have anyone I hang around with" (p. 704).

Although female prisoners are less likely than their male counterparts to be violent, they are more likely to be sanctioned for minor rule infractions. In a study of Texas prisons, for instance, Dorothy McClellan (1994) found that women (but not men) were treated like children and cited for hanging their underwear to dry, talking in waiting lines, displaying too many family photographs, and not eating all the food on their plates. Trafficking or contraband violations included lighting another woman's cigarettes, sharing shampoo in the shower, borrowing someone's comb, and possessing an extra pillowcase or bra.

Women in prison are also more likely than men to be sexually harassed and assaulted by correctional officers. According to a report by Amnesty International (1999), male officers in the United States routinely take advantage of their authority by conducting unnecessary strip and pat searches of women, scrutinizing them in showers, and monitoring them by video. The report also noted that male officers threatened to withhold basic needs and privileges (such as food, showers, or family visitations) if women did not provide sexual favors; and women who were raped were threatened with sanctions if they reported being violated.

In addition to this type of abuse, women prisoners, who are more likely than men to have been single heads of households with dependent children, experience more emotional distress as absent parents. Because only about a quarter of incarcerated mothers have dependent children who are living

FURTHER EXPLORATION
Health Care and Illness in Prison

In the United States, prisoners have a constitutional right to medical care, but the quality of that care leaves much to be desired, especially since the rate of HIV/AIDS and other infectious diseases among prisoners is much higher than among the general population (Centers for Disease Control and Prevention 2014). According to Jeffrey Ross and Stephen Richards (2002), prisoners suffering from chronic or acute illnesses will find the medical staff to be few, overburdened, and restricted by bureaucratic red tape that limits the type of medical services and procedures they are authorized to deliver. A life-threatening illness such as cancer, heart attack, or stroke may "require outside intervention, possibly a lawsuit or a letter or phone call from a powerful politician, to get you transferred to a civilian hospital" in order to receive proper treatment (p. 101).

HIV/AIDS is an especially serious problem in prison. About 14 percent of people living with HIV/AIDS in the United States have spent some time in a correctional facility, although most of these individuals were infected before incarceration. Although the majority of HIV/AIDS cases in prison involve men—since there are more men in prison than women—the rate of HIV/AIDS is proportionately higher for women (Braithwaite & Arriola 2003; Centers for Disease Control and Prevention 2014; Krebs 2006; Maruschak 2008).

Additionally, as the number of aging prisoners has increased due to the lengthy sentences that have been issued over the past few decades (McGovern 2013), many "prisons now have geriatric cellblocks filled with elderly prisoners, many of them in wheelchairs, on respirators, or in beds hooked up to machines or intravenous tubes. . . . Some prison systems allow elderly prisoners [or younger ones with terminal diagnoses] . . . to apply for compassionate release . . . to go home and die in the company of . . . loved ones. . . . [But] few prisoners ever make it out the door before they pass away, as the application process may take many months to officially approve" (Ross & Richards 2002:101).

with fathers—about 90 percent of incarcerated fathers have children living with mothers—children of incarcerated mothers are more likely than children of incarcerated fathers to be placed in foster care and to be separated from siblings. Incarcerated mothers are also more likely to have their parental rights terminated (Belknap 2007; Clark 1995; Glaze & Maruschak 2008).

Issues surrounding pregnancy also pose significant problems for women in prison. A study by the Committee on Health Care for Underserved Women (2011) found that from 1990 to 2009 between 6 and 10 percent of incarcerated women were pregnant, and as many as a quarter were either pregnant or had given birth in the previous year. About three-quarters of the states do not have adequate policies (or any policies at all) for the treatment of these women, including the provision of prenatal nutrition counseling, the provision of appropriate nutrition, or HIV/AIDS testing. Pregnant women may also be "required to stand or participate in repetitive, strenuous, physical lifting" that puts them at risk of giving early birth to premature infants (p. 2). These states also allow the **shackling** of women during pregnancy, labor, and delivery. Shackling includes the use of "any physical restraint or mechanical device on a prisoner's body or limbs" and may include not only handcuffs but also leg and belly chains (p. 3). Shackling interferes with the ability of health-care providers to assess and evaluate the mother and fetus, and makes labor and delivery more difficult. All of these factors contribute to higher rates of mortality among infant children of incarcerated women compared to infant children of women who are not incarcerated (Belknap 2007; Wildeman 2012).

Convict Labor and Prison Industries

Prisoners in the United States "have always worked, and making them work [has been] seen as a way to accomplish numerous correctional objectives" (Clear et al. 2006:363). Convict labor has been viewed as a form of punishment, a means of rehabilitation, an escape from idleness, and a source of profit for the institution or government.

In the nineteenth century, prisons leased prisoners to private companies that used the workers to make products that were sold on the open market. In the South, following the Civil War, this system amounted to nothing less than legalized slavery, as African Americans comprised more than 95 percent of prisoners in Southern states (Free 1996). As one South Carolina official observed, "After the emancipation of the colored people, whose idea of freedom from bondage was freedom from work and license to pillage, we had to establish means for their control" (quoted in Sellin 1976:158). Private companies ran their own forced-labor camps where prisoners were beaten by their overseers and forced to work from daylight to dusk, at times in "noxious mud . . . almost to their waists" (p. 150).

In other instances, prison officials allowed private companies to come into the institution and organize production inside the prison walls; or prisons would simply contract to make the goods for the companies, with the companies providing only the raw materials. Some prisons even operated their own businesses and sold their products on the open market. But in the late nineteenth and early twentieth centuries, both private companies and organized labor began lobbying to limit unfair competition from prison industries that operated with minimal labor costs. In the 1930s and 1940s, the US Congress and states around the country banned interstate commerce in prison-made goods. Laws were also passed that required prisons to sell products only to other state agencies, rather than on the open market, and that limited the number of prisoners who could be employed and the kinds of goods that could be produced (Clear et al. 2006).

In the 1970s, the federal government and the states began to reevaluate these restrictive policies. In 1979, Congress lifted its ban on interstate commerce in prison-made goods, provided that prisons met the conditions of the newly created Prison Industry Enhancement Certification Program, commonly known as PIE. This program, which is administered by the US Department of Justice, allows prison-based joint ventures with private industry if prisoners are paid at local prevailing wage rates and other companies are not adversely affected by the arrangement. Prevailing wage rates, however, allow for the deduction of incarceration costs and any training that is required, as well as deductions for Social Security and Medicare taxes, victim compensation payments, and mandatory savings accounts. And work programs that produce goods for foreign export or for sale in intrastate commerce are not covered by PIE regulations (Bureau of Justice Assistance 2002; Johnson 2002; Sexton 1995).

PIE has certified programs in about a quarter of the states that operate private-sector prison industries for a diverse range of corporate enterprises. Still, only a small proportion of prisoner workers participates in the PIE program, and most of the work they otherwise do entails routine manual jobs that do not provide them with marketable employment skills upon release. Relatively few prisoners are engaged in manufacturing work; others work in farming, forestry, ranching, and road construction and maintenance; and most perform menial tasks that are necessary for the functioning of the prison itself, such as mopping floors, laundering, cooking and cleaning in the kitchen, cutting grass, and shoveling snow. Most do not make the prevailing wage rates allowed by the PIE program. According to Michelle Alexander, the typical prisoner earns "less than $3.00 an hour, sometimes as little as 25 cents. Their accounts are then 'charged' for various expenses related to their incarceration, making it impossible . . . to save money that otherwise would allow them to pay off their debts or help them make a successful transition when released from prison" (2010:152; see also Clear et al. 2006; Ross & Richards 2002).

The Work of Correctional Officers

In many respects, issues pertaining to the work of correctional officers parallel those of police. In Chapter 11 we discussed the difference between military and community styles of policing. In corrections there is a similar distinction between **custodial** and **human service styles** of correctional work.

Custodial-oriented correctional officers place utmost priority on maintaining order within the institution. One officer described the prison in which he worked as "a city within a city and we're the policemen" (Lombardo 1997:197). But just as there are overly aggressive police officers, there are overly aggressive correctional officers who use violence—both their own and that of their convict allies—as "one of the tools of their trade" (Johnson 2002:201). Although these officers are a statistical minority, they are tolerated by their colleagues and even viewed as role models. Many officers equate authority with toughness and dominance and will put on a hard-nosed facade to appease their more aggressive colleagues (Toch & Klofas 1982).

So-called **goon squad** officers are those who epitomize the willingness to use force. They are the "physically powerful officers who 'enjoy a good fight' and . . . are called upon to rush to any area of the prison where it is felt that muscle power will restore the status quo" (Bowker 1980:102). Robert Johnson describes them as "the men who 'get the job done' without recourse to such unmanly considerations as tact or persuasion" (2002:216). Other correctional officers maintain order simply by not interfering with the activities of prisoners who dominate the informal economy and convict subculture, and by not protecting weaker inmates who pose little threat to the officers or the overall functioning of the institution. As one officer said of the illicit drugs and sex in prison, "If I got in the middle of that shit, I would be crazy because I will either get seriously hurt or killed" (Stojkovic 1990:225–226). Still other correctional officers resort to petty abuses to gain leverage over prisoners. As one remarked:

> Guy wants to make a phone call? You can make him wait 10, 20 minutes. Guy wants some writing paper? Tell him you don't have any. Guy wants some matches? You can have a drawer full of matches, "I don't have any matches," you tell him. . . . And there's the ways that you can screw around with his property when he's not around. . . . One inmate . . . gave another officer a hard time. . . . This . . . inmate he loves plants. . . . And he had about . . . two dozen. . . . He woke up the next morning and every one of them plants was dead. . . . Say a guy works with . . . woodworking stuff. Just put [a] scratch in his furniture or something. He know[s] how it got there. . . . But there's nothing he can do about it. . . . There's so many ways you can get these guys. (Kauffman 1988:66)

According to Johnson, correctional officers are for the most part "an alienated and . . . embittered lot" (2002:235), and surveys have found that about two-thirds are dissatisfied with their jobs (Cullen et al. 1989; Toch & Grant 1982). But those with a human service orientation, who find more meaning in their work, are more satisfied than others. For them, being a professional means caring about the prisoners, and they "use their authority to help inmates cope with prison life . . . [and] they do the best they can with the resources at their disposal to make the prison a better place in which to live and work" (Johnson 2002:235). As one correctional officer observed: "I often put myself in the inmate's position. If I was locked up and . . . my only contact with authorities would be the officer walking by, it would be frustrating if I couldn't get him to listen to the problem I have.

There is nothing worse than being in need of something and not being able to supply it yourself and having the man who can supply it ignore you" (Jacobs & Retsky 1981:68).

Service-oriented correctional officers fulfill their roles by trying to help prisoners obtain basic goods and services within the institution. As one officer said: "If an inmate hasn't had a change of underwear in two weeks, you should care enough to get him a change of underwear. If he hasn't had a shower in a week, you should care enough to get him a shower" (Earley 1992:269). Some prisoners also need help dealing with the prison bureaucracy—setting up appointments with counselors, getting access to telephone calls and visitors, checking on the status of their prison bank account or their upcoming parole hearing, or getting their prescribed medication or proper work assignment. Perhaps the most important service function of all is providing for the physical security of inmates. According to one officer: "Security doesn't mean keep them from going over the wall. It means you try to make the guy feel . . . that he's not going to get killed or hurt . . . so an inmate can sit next to another inmate in the mess hall or auditorium and . . . [not] have to worry about something happening" (Lombardo 1988:293).

Criminologists have observed that the most common element in the testimonials of reformed prisoners is the self-respect that was fostered in them by caring correctional officers. "This did not mean that the officers were unusually lenient, lax or permissive; it meant only that they treated the men with a personal interest and without pretension or condescension. . . . They were frank, fair and considerate" (Glaser 1969:92–93). Unfortunately, human service correctional officers—who perhaps constitute the majority of officers—often feel they are violating an unofficial code that calls for a tough-minded custodial stance rather than a concerted effort to help prisoners (Johnson 2002). As one officer said: "I am almost ashamed to say it . . . [but] the key to being a good [correctional officer] is having a caring attitude . . . [which] sounds to most staff here as being weak and not very macho. . . . It sounds like you are giving in to the inmate—or at least, that is how the staff interprets it . . . but it is not the same at all" (Earley 1992:269).

Minority and Women Correctional Officers
Issues pertaining to racial/ethnic minorities and women who work in corrections also parallel issues faced by minorities and women who work in policing. Minorities constitute less than 30 percent of employees working in the adult correctional system, with African Americans occupying about two-thirds of the minority positions; these data combine custody/security staff with other staff positions (*Sourcebook of Criminal Justice Statistics* 2003). About a third of correctional employees are women, who are much more likely to work in women's prisons than in men's prisons. There are also fewer women who work in men's prisons than men who work in women's prisons; and women have fewer opportunities for advancement

into supervisory positions in men's prisons than men have in women's prisons (Belknap 2007; Britton 1997).

Some white male correctional officers, like their police counterparts, have resented the entrance of minorities and women into corrections. As one remarked: "What will they think of next? They've lowered the standards so anybody can get in. First they brought in these minorities; some of them can hardly sign their name. Now we've got these women who can't even protect themselves. How do they expect to run a prison? Next thing you know, they'll be bringing kids in here to control the inmates. We might as well give the inmates the keys to the place and go home" (Zimmer 1986:59). Apparently the prospect of women who are capable of doing correctional work is threatening to some male correctional officers' sense of masculinity. As one female officer observed, "They can't go home and talk about how bad and mean they are and what a tough day they have had [if] some little chickie can do the same thing that he is doing" (Owen 1985:158).

While the evidence is mixed, some research suggests that nonwhite and female correctional officers are more likely than white male officers to favor a rehabilitative or human services approach to corrections (Johnson 2002; Van Voorhis et al. 1991; Whitehead & Lindquist 1989). In particular, female officers tend to have better communication skills and are more effective than male officers at defusing inmate violence. Female correctional officers even command more respect than male officers from male prisoners, and the presence of women in male prisons helps normalize the prison environment (Kissell & Katsampes 1980; Owen 1985; Zimmer 1986). Research also suggests that female correctional officers consider female prisoners to be more difficult to manage than male prisoners, "while for male [officers] the reverse is true, suggesting that each sex has less tolerance for . . . the power plays of its own gender" (Pearson 1997:220; Pollock-Byrne 1990).

Nancy Jurik (1985) found that demographic characteristics of correctional officers had less impact on their attitudes toward prisoners and corrections than the organizational features of the workplace, however. Just as individual police officers conform to the organizational styles of their department, individual correctional officers conform to the expectations of superiors who define the operational goals of their institution—that is, whether these officers view the organizational style as custodial or human services in orientation.

In related research, Dana Britton (1997) found that the "organizational logic" of correctional officer training programs generally emphasizes the physical skills perceived as necessary to deal with prisoner violence. Training classes are filled with "war stories" of violence that often intimidate women and lead them to drop out. But the day-to-day reality of prison work, especially in women's prisons, tends to be quite different. Correctional officers consistently describe their job as more of a mental than a physical challenge. As one female officer said: "They try to prepare you . . . for the physical part. But that's not what gets to you, it's the mental part. Playing the games with the inmates, they're constantly trying to figure out a way to get one over on you" (p. 804).

Sexual harassment is also a particular concern for female correctional officers. One woman observed that "on any given night, 10 or 11 guys will be jacking off—or sometimes they'll be lying there with their fly open like they don't notice. . . . They never do that in front of the men" (Britton 1997:805). Female correctional officers, especially younger ones, are also prey to sexual harassment by their male colleagues. Unfortunately, the occupational environment can offset or undermine the professional outlook and sense of mission women recruits bring to the job, and some end up leaving this line of work (Jurik 1985; Martin & Jurik 1996).

Community Corrections

Although a "get tough" retributive philosophy has dominated criminal justice policy in the United States since the 1970s, the majority of offenders under correctional supervision are serving all or part of their sentences in the community, on probation and parole (see Table 12.2). Nevertheless, community corrections receives only a tenth of the money that is spent on corrections overall. This problem is exacerbated by the fact that the United States is experiencing an unprecedented number of prisoners who are reentering society after serving time behind bars, which is a direct outgrowth of the incarceration boom discussed earlier. More than 90 percent of all prisoners are eventually released, and thus the postincarceration population can be expected to grow in future years as more and more inmates complete their prison terms. In this regard, the social costs of abandoning our commitment to rehabilitation in prisons have concerned many criminologists. Funding for rehabilitation programs in state prisons, where most of the nation's prisoners are held, constitutes a mere 1 to 5 percent of state prison budgets (Levrant et al. 1999; Petersilia 2003a, 2003b; Travis & Petersilia 2001).

If these problems are to be remedied, the relative paucity of resources for community corrections and rehabilitation programs inside and outside prison will need to be addressed. Fortunately, there is an emerging political consensus that we can no longer afford to feed the prison-industrial complex. More and more people are starting to recognize that continuing our spending binge on prison expansion is not a cost-effective remedy to our nation's problems (Petersilia 2011).

Probation: Conventional and Alternative Approaches

Probation, a sentence of community supervision given in lieu of incarceration, is the most widely used correctional disposition. John Augustus, a wealthy nineteenth-century Boston shoemaker, is credited with developing this practice by personally providing bail and assistance to some 1,900 men and women. Augustus so impressed the Boston courts that the state of Massachusetts eventually endorsed the idea, becoming in 1880 the first state to employ probation officers statewide. By the 1950s, every state had developed a probationary system of its own (Barkan & Bryjak 2011; Clear et al. 2006).

Historically, probation has been regarded as a cost-effective alternative to prison, especially for nonviolent offenders, and as a means of reducing prison overcrowding. Although probation allows the offender to avoid the brutalizing experience of incarceration, as a standalone sentence it offers little in the way of rehabilitation. Probation officers' caseloads are notoriously too high, leaving little time for anything other than routine checkups (Barkan & Bryjak 2011; DeMichele 2007).

The conditions of probation require an offender to follow certain rules, and failure to comply may result in the revocation of probation and a subsequent jail or prison term. In addition to staying out of trouble and reporting periodically to a probation officer, probationers may be required to abstain from using alcohol, undergo substance abuse treatment and drug testing, receive counseling, refrain from using firearms, pay restitution to their victims, perform community service, and reside in a supervised community **halfway house**—a transitional residence that serves as a bridge between prison and unsupervised residency in the community.

Research on the effectiveness of probation yields disparate results due to the varying conditions under which probation is implemented, the length of the probationary period being examined, the nature of the client population, and whether rehabilitative treatment is part of the program (Geerken & Hayes 1993; Gray et al. 2001). Also at issue is how the effectiveness of probation is measured—whether it is defined broadly as nonviolation of any condition of probation or more narrowly as avoidance of arrest, reconviction, or imprisonment. Nationwide, about two-thirds of probationers successfully complete their probationary terms or receive an early discharge (Bonczar & Maruschak 2013), although "successful completion" often occurs "even when serious, or numerous, technical violations" had been committed during the probationary period (Gray et al. 2001:539). Nevertheless, research indicates that probationers have equal or lower rates of recidivism than offenders with similar offense histories who had been sent to prison and subsequently released, and this result is achieved at lower cost. Additionally, probationers who receive rehabilitative treatment do better than those who do not (Broome et al. 1996; Clear 2007; Petersilia et al. 1985).

Intensive probation and home confinement. **Intensive supervision probation** and **home confinement** offer two alternatives to conventional probation. Under intensive supervision probation, officers work with significantly smaller caseloads, allowing for more frequent visitations with clients. The nature of such supervision programs varies, however, with the best combining probationary supervision with other rehabilitative services, such as education and vocational training, individual and family counseling, and substance abuse treatment. On the other hand, many intensive supervision programs do little more than provide daily visits between probation officers and clients of 10 minutes or less (Clear et al. 2006; Petersilia 2011).

Evaluations of intensive supervision probation programs have been mixed. Some studies found that the rates of probation violation were higher for offenders in these programs than for offenders serving traditional probationary sentences. The higher rates were most likely due to the fact that more extensive supervision increases the likelihood that violations will be discovered. According to Joan Petersilia (2011), these results occurred because most of the funds for intensive supervision probation programs were spent on surveillance mechanisms like drug testing rather than on enhanced social services. In places where intensive supervision probation was implemented according to its original design—that is, where offenders were entered into drug or alcohol abuse, employment, and other community service programs—the recidivism rates were 10 to 20 percent below the rates for nonparticipating offenders. And as with ordinary probation, these results were obtained at less cost than incarceration (Barton & Butts 1990; Petersilia & Turner 1993; Welch 2004).

Home confinement, or house arrest, requires offenders to serve all or part of their sentences within the confines of their homes. Home confinement participants may also be allowed to leave their homes for certain activities, such as to go to work or school, receive medical care, or attend religious services. Most home confinement programs employ some type of **electronic monitoring**, which ranges from something as simple as a telephone call verifying that the probationer is home, to a device that is worn to identify his or her whereabouts. While research has not consistently demonstrated lower recidivism rates among participants in home confinement and electronic-monitoring programs than among ordinary probationers with similar offense histories, many view confinement and monitoring programs as a positive development, allowing for the supervision of offenders at lower labor costs and enabling offenders to maintain family ties and take advantage of educational and employment opportunities (Barkan & Bryjak 2011; Welch 2004).

Critics of intensive supervision probation and home confinement and electronic-monitoring programs have been concerned that the government will abuse its supervisory authority and extend its high-tech monitoring to the general citizenry (Blomberg et al. 1993). They are also troubled about probation officers who have involved neighbors in the surveillance of offenders, creating a network of informants who end up spying on each other. At the same time, for wealthy offenders, home confinement and electronic monitoring may represent nothing more than being "grounded" in luxurious surroundings. Despite these drawbacks, home confinement and electronic monitoring seem particularly appropriate for offenders with special needs, such as pregnant women, AIDS patients, the elderly and terminally ill, and the cognitively disabled (Lilly et al. 1993).

Shock programs and boot camps. **Shock probation** is a sentencing alternative that entails a probationary term that is granted following a brief period of confinement. It is designed to shock or scare offenders out of criminality by giving them a taste of incarceration. Similarly, **shock incarceration** is a military-style "boot camp" experience, usually lasting three to six months, that consists of intense physical activity (drills, exercise, and work), rigid discipline, and regimented daily routines. In some cases, the US Army and Marines have trained correctional officers to serve as drill sergeants in these programs. The basic premise of shock incarceration is that offenders are in need of discipline and self-control; and it is hoped that the program will serve as a crash course in character-building and personal responsibility that will help offenders change their ways (Adler et al. 2000; Barkan & Bryjak 2011; Welch 2004).

Evaluations of shock incarceration, like evaluations of other correctional strategies, have been mixed. The most successful programs combine the boot-camp experience with other rehabilitative interventions, leaving it unclear whether it is the military regimen per se that is responsible for lower recidivism among participants in successful shock incarceration programs (Bourque et al. 1996; MacKenzie et al. 1995; MacKenzie & Souryal 1995; McCorkle 1995). Moreover, some criminologists are concerned that the intense physical and verbal tactics common to boot camps—such as belligerent drill sergeants barking orders and belittling participants—only reinforce an aggressive model of masculinity that underlies much criminal behavior (see Chapter 5). According to Merry Morash and Lila Rucker, the very notion that such tactics will "'train' people to act in a prosocial manner is fraught with contradiction. The idea rests on the assumption that forceful control is to be valued," while empathy toward others is not (1990:214).

Critics also note that boot camps, many of which are privately run with little or no oversight, can be overly harsh. Some youths have reported that they were "punched, kicked and forced to eat dirt for minor infractions such as failing to stand up straight . . . [and that] they had bruised ribs from an exercise in which they were ordered to lie on their backs while counselors ran across their chests in boots" (Spencer 2001:28). Several youths have even died in boot camps.

The inclusion of women in boot-camp programs raises additional concerns. Many women participants have been previously abused by men. For them, the military-style approach may be counterproductive. As one woman boot-camp offender observed: "They get in your face and make you feel like dirt. . . . They grab you and push you around. . . . I have bruises on my arms. . . . For someone like me that's been physically and mentally abused that's all it reminds me of, being abused" (MacKenzie & Donaldson 1996:35). A 13-year-old female boot-camp offender said that the counselors, who liked to be called "sergeant," repeatedly called her a "whore" and "prostitute" (Spencer 2001). On the other hand, some participants have found the program empowering. As one woman said, boot camp taught her to be more assertive, stand up for herself, and not "take anybody's crap" (MacKenzie & Donaldson 1996:35).

The Problem of Prisoner Reentry

In contrast to probation, parole entails release into the community after an offender has served a portion of his or her sentence in confinement. In some states, community correctional officers are assigned caseloads that include both probationers and parolees, while in other states parole is a specialized function. The conditions of parole are generally similar to those of probation, and parole may be revoked and the offender reincarcerated if he or she violates the rules. Nationally, only about half of parolees successfully complete the terms of their parole or receive an early discharge (Glaze & Bonczar 2011).

The practice of parole allows inmates to receive early release from prison for good behavior. But in the late 1980s, the federal government eliminated parole for all new offenders, and many states followed suit, passing **truth-in-sentencing laws** that require inmates to complete all or most of their prison terms before being released from confinement (Seiter & Kadela 2003). Critics contend that denial of parole increases prison overcrowding and removes prisoners' incentive to cooperate while incarcerated. According to Joan Petersilia, it also means that an increasing number of prisoners will "max out" their sentences while incarcerated and will leave prison without any "obligation to report to a parole officer or abide by any other conditions of release" (2003a:3). In the late 1970s, less than 5 percent of prisoners served their full sentences prior to release; currently about 20 percent "max out." But even prisoners who do not serve their entire terms behind bars will find themselves receiving little help readjusting to society. If they happen to live in a state that provides funds upon release (about a third of states do not), they will be given $25 to $200 gate money, which can be "barely enough to cover the cost of a bus ticket back home" (Alexander 2010:152). Sometimes a list of rental apartments or shelters will be provided, "but the arrangements are generally left up to the offender to determine where to reside and how to pay for basic essentials during the first few months" (Petersilia 2003a:4)

Moreover, few prisoners will find opportunities to "make good" when they return home. At the same time that rehabilitative services for prisoners behind bars and after release have been reduced, the US Congress and state legislatures have passed numerous laws and regulations restricting the kinds of jobs for which prisoners can be hired and "easing the requirements for parental rights to be terminated, restricting their access to welfare benefits and public housing, disqualifying them from a host of job training programs, and limiting their right to vote" (Petersilia 2003a:4). Additionally, released offenders generally return to the same communities that facilitated their criminal involvement in the first place, the same ones that have low prospects of employment, especially for those with a criminal record; and studies show that the state of the local economy is significantly related to the degree of offender recidivism (Delgado 2012; Gunnison & Helfgott 2013; Hannon & DeFina 2010).

While the public has supported such policies as a means of cracking down on crime, the abandonment of transition assistance and rehabilitative programming is shortsighted and exacerbates the problems of communities to which prisoners return. Petersilia and Jeremy Travis advocate an alternative approach, whereby correctional agencies "create a seamless set of systems that span the boundaries of prison and community," including "linkages between in-prison job training and community-based employment and job training and between in-prison healthcare and community-based healthcare" (Travis and Petersilia 2001:308). They think that correctional agencies should also be "expected to link mental health services on both sides of the wall [and] to work with community-based domestic violence services when a prisoner with a history of spousal abuse is released."

In their review of prison reentry programs, Richard Seiter and Karen Kadela (2003) found favorable results from prison **work release** (or furlough) programs that allow inmates to work in the community for a few hours to a few days at a time before they are released. Prisoners who participated in work release, especially those who also received vocational training, had lower recidivism rates than those who did not. Seiter and Kadela also found that supervised community halfway houses helped ease the transition from prison to work.

Drug rehabilitation, according to Seiter and Kadela (2003), is one of the most promising areas of correctional programming. Especially effective are programs based on social learning principles and that utilize guided group interaction or therapeutic community designs that rely on the constructive influence of other recovering offenders (see Chapter 4). Lana Harrison (2001) advocates a phased-in **therapeutic continuum** that includes drug treatment in prison followed by both drug treatment and work release in a halfway house facility. More generally, as discussed in Chapter 3, effective correctional interventions entail those that are carefully matched to offenders' particular learning styles and psychological needs, and are designed to enhance skills in managing aggression and stress as well as academic and vocational skills, change antisocial attitudes and ways of

FURTHER EXPLORATION
Drug Courts

Drug courts were first established in Dade County, Florida, which includes the city of Miami, in 1989, and have been expanding ever since, with more than 2,300 around the country by 2010 (DeVall et al. 2012). They operate on the principle that court-ordered treatment in the community is a viable alternative to both incarceration and voluntary treatment. According to Judge Perry Anderson, who has presided over drug courts in the Boston area: "The typical drug court combines substance-abuse treatment in the community, strict case management with direct judicial involvement, regular drug testing, and graduated incentives and sanctions based on performance in treatment. The ultimate reward is avoidance of a jail sentence or the expunging of criminal charges. The ultimate sanction is imprisonment. . . . Drug courts . . . offer a middle way between the war on drugs and the decriminalization of drugs. They protect public safety by providing strict, intense and coordinated supervision of participants . . . and in turning out a high percentage of graduates who are able to maintain their sobriety and obey the law" (2003:45, 48).

Research on the effectiveness of drug courts in facilitating the recovery process for chemically dependent individuals and reducing criminal recidivism is somewhat mixed, but generally favorable enough to encourage a growing number of jurisdictions to experiment with this alternative to incarceration and search for ways to make it more effective. However, because people with prior criminal records are typically excluded from drug courts— and African Americans are more likely to fall into this category—the increased use of this alternative to incarceration has the potential of exacerbating the racial disparity among those convicted of drug offenses, whether or not these offenders are imprisoned (Chase 2014; DeVall et al. 2012; Gregory et al. 2009; Hepburn & Harvey 2007).

thinking, reduce chemical dependencies, foster familial bonds, modify peer associations and role models, and help provide access to appropriate service agencies.

The Restorative Justice Movement

Another array of community correctional programs has been identified with the term **restorative justice**. According to Howard Zehr and Harry Mika, restorative justice involves a process by which all "parties with a stake in a particular offense come together to resolve collectively how to deal with [its] aftermath . . . and its implications for the future" (1998:54). Restorative justice is best understood in contrast to **adversarial justice**, which pits the accused against the accuser and hence encourages offenders "to deny, justify, or excuse their actions, thereby precluding the acceptance of responsibility" (Siegel et al. 2003:272; see Chapter 11). Restorative justice is based on a *social* rather than a *legalistic* view of crime. Crime is defined as a conflict among offenders, victims, and others affected by the wrongdoing, such as family members, schools, and the community at large. "Fairness is assured, not by uniformity of outcomes, but through provision of necessary support and opportunities to all parties" (Zehr & Mika 1998:53). The goal is to empower people to resolve their own differences rather than rely on the government to do justice for them. Whereas adversarial justice aims to establish blame and administer punishment, restorative justice aims to establish obligations and promote healing.

In the distant past, as Andrew Karmen (2004) observes, victims were more involved in the response to law violation than they are today. In modern societies, the government has

> symbolically displaced the wounded person as the injured party, and the courts [have been] transformed from a forum to settle disputes between specific individuals into an arena for ritualized combat between representatives of the state and the accused. If the prosecution [succeeds], the state [inflicts] pain upon its vanquished opponent in order to teach them not to break the law again . . . and to make [them] negative examples . . . [who] serve as a warning to others. (p. 342)

There is little in the process that benefits the victims of crime, outside of the satisfaction that offenders are being punished for their transgressions.

Karmen traces the rise of restorative justice to the emergence of the **victim rights movement** of the past few decades, which aims to give victims a greater role in the criminal justice process. Requiring the offender to make **restitution** to the victim—or in its place, the community—is one way this can be done. Restitution, which is more common in the juvenile justice system than the adult system, is a sanction that requires the offender to compensate the crime victim or the community at large, or both, through some form of monetary payment or service, such as working at a nursing home or hospital, performing grounds work at a city park, or cleaning up graffiti. Typically, restitution is ordered as a condition of probation and is administered through a probation department (Schneider & Finkelstein 1998).

The purpose of restitution is not simply to punish law violators or compensate victims but to make offenders accountable to the *people they have harmed,* thereby erasing "one of the strongest defenses . . . to wrongdoing, [the] inability to empathize . . . with those who have suffered" (Binder et al. 1988:562). By requiring the sacrifice of time and convenience, the expenditure of effort, and the performance of meaningful tasks, it is hoped that offenders will acknowledge and understand their personal and social responsibilities. As Karmen notes, "By making fiscal atonement or contributing services, they can feel cleared of guilt, morally redeemed, and reaccepted into the fold" (2004:295). As such, restitution is consistent with John Braithwaite's (1989) concept of "reintegrative shaming," whereby offenders receive social disapproval that is designed to invoke remorse, but if they are willing to right their wrongs, they are forgiven and welcomed back into the law-abiding community (see Chapter 4).

Restitution orders do not always stipulate that victims should be fully compensated for their financial losses, and much of court-ordered restitution is never paid (Levrant et al. 1999). Nevertheless, some studies report rates of completed payments and lower recidivism that are equal to or comparable to those for other sanctions (Schneider 1986). The programs work best when care is taken to substantiate victim losses, construct appropriate repayment schedules, monitor offender compliance, and keep accurate accounts of monies earned and disbursed. Effective programs must also help unemployed offenders locate jobs. Left on their own, most participants will not succeed. The jobs must pay well enough to provide for the offenders' own living expenses, with enough left over to make payments to victims. According to Karmen:

> If a job pays wages [that are too] low, then the repayment cannot be completed within a reasonable period of time. If nearly all of the offender's earnings are confiscated and handed over to the victim, then commitment to the job and to repaying the debt is jeopardized. If the job is demeaning, then its therapeutic value as a first step in a new lifestyle built on productive employment is lost. If the job is temporary, only for the duration of the restitution obligation, then the risk of returning to . . . crime is heightened. (2004:300)

Some restitution programs are used in conjunction with **victim-offender mediation**, which brings offenders and victims together to work out a fair arrangement under the guidance of a trained mediator or counselor. Beyond restitution, victim-offender mediation gives victims the opportunity to express their anger, indignation, anxieties, and fears, and to get answers to such lingering questions as "Why did you choose to attack me?" or "How did you gain entrance to my home?" or "How could I have avoided this?" Through this process, victims may be helped to achieve some psychological closure to their experience. Offenders, in turn, are given the opportunity to accept responsibility for what they did, express genuine remorse, and agree to do as much as they can "to try to restore the victim to the condition he or she was in before the crime occurred" (Karmen 2004:347).

Research has found greater success in lowering the recidivism rates of juvenile offenders who participated in victim-offender mediation than the rates of adult offenders who did so (Umbreit 1994). Juveniles have been more likely to complete restitution payments that were negotiated with victims than were "similar offenders ordered to make restitution by juvenile court judges who didn't directly involve victims or use mediation" (Karmen 2004:349). In general, however, offenders are more likely than victims to be satisfied with victim-offender mediation conferences. Many victims report feeling even worse after the conferences, because their hopes of achieving emotional closure were not realized or they felt pressured to forgive the offender when they were not psychologically ready to do so (Braithwaite & Daly 1998; Delgado 2000).

John Braithwaite and Kathleen Daly (1998) advocate the **community conferencing** approach, also known as **neighborhood justice**, based on the principle of reintegrative shaming, as a way to accomplish restorative justice. Community conferencing takes place after a warrant for an arrest is issued but before an actual arrest is made. The full power of the criminal justice system is invoked only as a last resort if a suitable victim-offender agreement cannot be worked out and successfully implemented (Karmen 2004).

In community conferencing, both the victim and the offender are allowed to bring members of their immediate and extended families, as well as additional significant others, into the mediation process. This arrangement provides a supportive atmosphere in which victims are given voice in the shaming process and empowered to negotiate assurances that they will be free from future harm. At the same time, the people who care about the offender help foster and ensure his or her community reintegration by agreeing to be responsible for helping to supervise and enforce the agreements the offender has made. In this way, "particular communities of citizens who care about particular people" try to devise unique solutions to problems in ways that seem fair and appropriate to all (Braithwaite & Daly 1998:158). In a study of a restorative program in Arizona that reflects this approach, Nancy Rodriguez found that juveniles who participated "were less likely to recidivate than juveniles in a comparison group," and that girls and offenders with limited criminal histories had the lowest recidivism rates of all (2007b:355).

Sharon Levrant and colleagues (1999) raise several concerns about the restorative justice movement, however. When programs like victim-offender mediation or community conferencing are implemented in lieu of or before a trial, they may lack the due process safeguards that are available in the adversarial system. Evidence against the offender that would be inadmissible in court may be presented and used later at trial if an agreement between victim and offender cannot be reached. Offenders may be pressured to participate under threat of harsher sanctions, and refusal to do so may be used against them in charging and sentencing decisions.

Restorative justice seems to work best for less serious crimes and interpersonal conflicts that are less likely to result in criminal court action in the first place. There is also scant evidence that citizen volunteers, especially in socially disorganized neighborhoods, have the requisite abilities "to effectively mediate conflict between a potentially emotional victim and a resistant offender" (Levrant et al. 1999:12). And it is white-collar offenders, with their greater monetary resources and professional skills, who are best positioned to negotiate, enforce, and fulfill acceptable agreements (Conners 2003; Delgado 2000). Nevertheless, many criminologists believe that community correctional strategies that combine conventional rehabilitative treatment with restorative justice offer a promising alternative to the view that punishing offenders is "the only and best solution to crime," and programs implemented under the rubric of restorative justice have been growing in the United States (Levrant et al. 1999:23; London 2011).

Summary

This chapter considered the nature of punishment and the correctional system in the United States. We began with an examination of the death penalty and then turned to prisons, discussing the historical emergence of the modern penitentiary as well as the incarceration boom and other trends of the past few decades, including the privatization of prisons. We also examined the living conditions and work experiences of prisoners as well as the work of correctional officers. Last, we considered community corrections, including conventional and alternative approaches to probation, the problem of prisoner reentry, and the restorative justice movement.

References

Abadinsky, H. 2007. *Organized Crime*. Belmont, CA: Wadsworth.

Abbott, J. 1981. *In the Belly of the Beast*. New York: Vintage.

Abramsky, S. 2004. "Incarceration, Inc." *The Nation* (July 19–26):22–25.

Adams, D. 1988. "Treatment Models for Men Who Batter." In K. Yllo & M. Bograd (eds.), *Feminist Perspectives on Wife Abuse*. Newbury Park, CA: Sage.

Adams, K. 1999. "What We Know About Police Use of Force." In *Use of Force by Police*. Washington, DC: US Department of Justice.

Adler, F. 1975. *Sisters in Crime: The Rise of the New Female Offender*. New York: McGraw-Hill.

Adler, F., G. Mueller, & W. Laufer. 2000. *Criminal Justice: An Introduction*. New York: McGraw-Hill.

Adler, P. 1993. *Wheeling and Dealing: An Ethnography of an Upper-Level Drug Dealing and Smuggling Community*. New York: Columbia University Press.

Agnew, R. 1985. "Social Control and Delinquency: A Longitudinal Test." *Criminology* 23:47–61.

———. 1992. "Foundation for a General Strain Theory of Crime and Delinquency." *Criminology* 30:47–87.

———. 1995. "Controlling Delinquency: Recommendations from General Strain Theory." In H. Barlow (ed.), *Crime and Public Policy*. Boulder, CO: Westview.

———. 2001. *Juvenile Delinquency: Causes and Controls*. Los Angeles: Roxbury.

Agnew, R., T. Brezina, J. Wright, & F. Cullen. 2002. "Strain, Personality Traits, and Delinquency: Extending General Strain Theory." *Criminology* 40:43–71.

Ahern, J. 1972. *Police in Trouble*. New York: Hawthorn.

Akers, R. 1985. *Deviant Behavior: A Social Learning Approach*. Belmont, CA: Wadsworth.

———. 1992. "Linking Sociology and Its Specialties: The Case of Criminology." *Social Forces* 71:1–16.

———. 1998. *Social Learning and Social Structure: A General Theory of Crime and Deviance*. Boston: Northeastern University Press.

Akers, R., M. Krohn, L. Lanza-Kaduce, & M. Radosevich. 1979. "Social Learning and Deviant Behavior: A Specific Test of a General Theory." *American Sociological Review* 44:636–655.

Akers, R., & C. Sellers. 2009. *Criminological Theories: Introduction, Evaluation, Application*. New York: Oxford University Press.

Albonetti, C., R. Hauser, J. Hagan, & I. Nagel. 1989. "Criminal Justice Decision Making as a Stratification Process: The Role of Race and Stratification Resources in Pretrial Release." *Journal of Quantitative Criminology* 5:57–82.

Alexander, M. 2010. *The New Jim Crow: Mass Incarceration in an Age of Colorblindness*. New York: New Press.

Alexander, P. 1987. "Prostitution: A Difficult Issue for Feminists." In F. Delacoste & P. Alexander (eds.), *Sex Work*. Pittsburgh: Cleis.

Allen, M., D. D'Alessio, & K. Brezgel. 1995. "A Meta-Analysis Summarizing the Effects of Pornography II." *Human Communication Research* 22:258–283.

Alonzo-Zaldivar, R. 2006. "FDA Pledges Conflict Reforms." *Los Angeles Times* (July 25):A12.

Alpern, D. 1984. "A CIA Bombshell." *Newsweek* (Oct. 29):30.

Altheide, D., & J. Grimes. 2005. "War Programming: The Propaganda Project and the Iraq War." *Sociological Quarterly* 46:617–643.

American Civil Liberties Union. 1995. "ACLU Announces Settlement of Lawsuit over 'Racial Profile' Stops" (Jan. 4). www.archive.aclu.org.

———. 2014. *War Comes Home: The Excessive Militarization of American Police* (June 23). www.aclu.org.

American Civil Liberties Union & Rights Working Group. 2009. *The Persistence of Racial and Ethnic Profiling in the United States.* New York.

Amir, M. 1971. *Patterns in Forcible Rape.* Chicago: University of Chicago Press.

Amnesty International. 1999. "'Not Part of My Sentence': Violations of the Human Rights of Women in Custody" (Mar.). www.amnesty.org.

Anderson, C., & D. Robbins. 2010. "In Toyota Cases, Evasion Becomes Tactic." *Associated Press* (Apr. 11). www.yahoo.com.

Anderson, D. 1995. *Crime and the Politics of Hysteria: How the Willie Horton Story Changed American Justice.* New York: Times Books.

———. 1999. "Policing the Police." *American Prospect* (Jan.–Feb.):49–54.

Anderson, E. 1994. "The Code of the Streets." *Atlantic Monthly* (May):81–94.

———. 1999. *Code of the Street: Decency, Violence, and the Moral Life of the Inner City.* New York: Norton.

Anderson, P. 2003. "Treatment with Teeth." *American Prospect* (Dec.):45–48.

Andrews, D., et al. 1990. "Does Correctional Treatment Work? A Clinically Relevant and Psychologically Informed Meta-Analysis." *Criminology* 28:369–404.

Applebome, P. 1991. "As Urban Blight Worsens, Victims Find Their Isolation Is Deepening." *New York Times* (Jan. 28). www.nytimes.com.

Applegate, B., F. Cullen, B. Fisher, & T. Vander Ven. 2000. "Forgiveness and Fundamentalism: Reconsidering the Relationship Between Correctional Attitudes and Religion." *Criminology* 38:719–754.

Apuzzo, M. 2014. "War Gear Flows to Police Departments." *New York Times* (June 8). www.nytimes.com.

Armstrong, D. 2002. "Dick Cheney's Song of America: Drafting a Plan for Global Dominance." *Harper's Magazine* (Oct.):76–83.

Armstrong, K., & M. Possley. 1999. "Study: Prosecutors Sacrifice Justice to Win." *Wisconsin State Journal* (Jan. 11):A3.

Arvanites, T., & R. DeFina. 2006. "Business Cycles and Crime." *Criminology* 44:139–164.

Attinger, J. 1989. "The Decline of New York." *Time* (Sept. 17):36–40, 44.

Aulette, J., & R. Michalowski. 2006. "The Fire in the Hamlet." In R. Michalowski & R. Kramer (eds.), *State-Corporate Crime: Wrongdoing at the Intersection of Business and Government.* New Brunswick, NJ: Rutgers University Press.

Austin, J., et al. 2001. "The Use of Incarceration in the United States." *Critical Criminology* 10:17–41.

Ayres, I., & J. Donahue. 2003. "Shooting Down the More Guns, Less Crime Hypothesis." *Stanford Law Review* 55:1193–1314.

Bailey, W. 1998. "Deterrence, Brutalization, and the Death Penalty: Another Examination of Oklahoma's Return to Capital Punishment." *Criminology* 36:711–733.

Baker, M. 1985. *Cops: Their Lives in Their Own Words.* New York: Fawcett.

Baldus, D., & G. Woodworth. 1998. "Race Discrimination and the Death Penalty: An Empirical and Legal Overview." In J. Acker, R. Bohm, & C. Lanier (eds.), *America's Experiment with Capital Punishment.* Durham, NC: Carolina Academic.

Balkan, S., R. Berger, & J. Schmidt. 1980. *Crime and Deviance in America: A Critical Approach.* Belmont, CA: Wadsworth.

Ball, J. 2015. "Facing the Truth About Climate Change." *New Republic* (Feb.):24–29.

Bamford, J. 2005. "The Man Who Sold the War." *Rolling Stone* (Nov. 18). www.commondreams.org.

———. 2008. *The Shadow Factory: The Ultra-Secret NSA, from 9/11 to the Eavesdropping on America.* New York: Doubleday.

Bandura, A. 1973. *Aggression: A Social Learning Analysis.* Englewood Cliffs, NJ: Prentice Hall.

———. 1997. *Self-Efficacy: The Exercise of Control.* New York: Freeman.

Barkan, S. 2012. *Criminology: A Sociological Approach.* Boston: Prentice Hall.

Barkan, S., & G. Bryjak. 2011. *Fundamentals of Criminal Justice: A Sociological View.* Burlington, MA: Jones and Bartlett Learning.

Barkan, S., & L. Snowden. 2001. *Collective Violence.* Boston: Allyn and Bacon.

Barker, T. 1986. "An Empirical Study of Police Deviance Other Than Corruption." In T. Barker & D. Carter (eds.), *Police Deviance.* Cincinnati: Pilgrimage.

Barker, T., & D. Carter. 1999. "Fluffing Up the Evidence and Covering Your Ass: Some Conceptual Notes on Police Lying." In L. Gaines & G. Cordner (eds.), *Policing Perspectives.* Los Angeles: Roxbury.

Barlow, H. 1996. *Introduction to Criminology.* New York: HarperCollins.

Baron, L., & M. Straus. 1989. *Four Theories of Rape in American Society: A State-Level Analysis.* New Haven: Yale University Press.

Baron, S. 2003. "Self-Control, Social Consequences, and Criminal Behavior: Street Youth and the General Theory of Crime." *Crime & Delinquency* 40:403–425.

———. 2004. "General Strain, Street Youth, and Crime: A Test of Agnew's Revised Theory." *Criminology* 42:457–483.

Barrett, P. 2014. "Meeting Freedom Industries, the Company Behind the West Virginia Chemical Spill." *Bloomberg Businessweek* (Jan. 13). www.businessweek .com.

Barry, K. 1979. *Female Sexual Slavery.* Englewood Cliffs, NJ: Prentice Hall.

———. 1995. *The Prostitution of Sexuality.* New York: New York University Press.

Barstow, D., & L. Bergman. 2003. "At a Texas Foundry, an Indifference to Life." *New York Times* (Jan. 8). www.nytimes.com.

Bart, P., & P. O'Brien. 1985. *Stopping Rape: Successful Survival Strategies.* New York: Pergamon.

Barton, W., & J. Butts. 1990. "Viable Options: Intensive Supervision Programs for Juvenile Delinquents." *Crime & Delinquency* 36:238–256.

Bass, E. 1983. "In the Truth Itself, There Is Healing." In E. Bass & L. Thornton (eds.), *I Never Told Anyone.* New York: Harper and Row.

Bates, E. 1998. "Private Prisons." *The Nation* (Jan. 5):11–18.

Bauer, M. 2009. *Under Siege: Life for Low-Income Latinos in the South.* Montgomery, AL: Southern Poverty Law Center.

Bauer, S. 2014. "The Warrior Cops Suit Up." *Mother Jones* (Nov.–Dec.):18–23.

Baumann, N. 2013. "Too Fast to Fail: Is High-Speed Trading the Next Wall Street Disaster?" *Mother Jones* (Feb.). www.motherjones.com.

Baumer, E., R. Felson, & S. Messner. 2003. "Changes in Police Notification of Rape, 1973–2000." *Criminology* 41:841–872.

Bayley, D., & E. Bittner. 1999. "Learning the Skills of Policing." In L. Gaines & G. Cordner (eds.), *Policing Perspectives.* Los Angeles: Roxbury.

Beccaria, C. 1764/1963. *On Crimes and Punishments.* Indianapolis: Bobbs-Merrill.

Becker, G. 1968. "Crime and Punishment: An Economic Approach." *Journal of Political Economy* 76:493–517.

Becker, H. 1963. *Outsiders: Studies in the Sociology of Deviance.* New York: Free Press.

Beckett, K. 1994. "Setting the Public Agenda: 'Street Crime' and Drug Use in American Politics." *Social Problems* 41:425–447.

Behar, M. 2013. "Whose Fault?" *Mother Jones* (Mar.–Apr.):35–38.

Beirne, P., & J. Messerschmidt. 1995. *Criminology.* Fort Worth: Harcourt, Brace.

Belknap, J. 2007. *The Invisible Woman: Gender, Crime, and Justice.* Belmont, CA: Wadsworth.

Bellair, P. 1997. "Social Interaction and Community Crime: Examining the Importance of Neighbor Networks." *Criminology* 35:677–703.

Beneke, T. 1982. *Men on Rape.* New York: St. Martin's.

Benokraitis, N. 1982. "Racial Exclusion in Juries." *Journal of Applied Behavioral Science* 18:29–47.

Berenson, A. 2007. "Merck Agrees to Settle Vioxx Suit for $4.85 Billion." *New York Times* (Nov. 9). www.nytimes.com.

Bergen, P. 2007. "War of Error: How Osama bin Laden Beat George W. Bush." *New Republic* (Oct. 22):23–27.

Berger, R. (ed.). 1996. *The Sociology of Juvenile Delinquency.* Chicago: Nelson-Hall.

———. 2008. "Agency, Structure, and the Transition to Disability: A Case Study with Implications for Life History Research." *Sociological Quarterly* 49:309–333.

———. 2009a. "Explaining School Shooters: The View from General Strain and Gender Theory." In R. Berger & P. Gregory (eds.), *Juvenile Delinquency and Justice: Sociological Perspectives.* Boulder, CO: Lynne Rienner.

———. 2009b. "Organizing the Community for Delinquency Prevention." In R. Berger & P. Gregory (eds.), *Juvenile Delinquency and Justice: Sociological Perspectives.* Boulder, CO: Lynne Rienner.

———. 2011. *White-Collar Crime: The Abuse of Corporate and Government Power.* Boulder, CO: Lynne Rienner.

———. 2013. *Introducing Disability Studies.* Boulder, CO: Lynne Rienner.

Berger, R., W. Neuman, & P. Searles. 1994. "The Impact of Rape Law Reform: An Aggregate Analysis of Police Reports and Arrests." *Criminal Justice Review* 19:1–23.

Berger, R., P. Searles, & C. Cottle. 1991. *Feminism and Pornography.* Westport: Praeger.

Berger, R., P. Searles, & W. Neuman. 1988. "The Dimensions of Rape Law Reform." *Law & Society Review* 22:329–357.

Berger, R., P. Searles, R. Salem, & B. Pierce. 1986. "Sexual Assault in a College Community." *Sociological Focus* 19:1–26.

Bergin, T. 2010. "Cost of Oil Spill Could Exceed $14 Billion." *Reuters* (May 2). www.reuters.com.

Bergman, J., & J. Reynolds. 2002. "The Guns of Opa-Locka: How US Dealers Arm the World." *The Nation* (Dec. 2):19–22.

Berk, R., A. Campbell, R. Klap, & B. Western. 1992. "The Deterrent Effect of Arrest in Incidents of Domestic Violence: A Bayesian Analysis of Four Field Experiments." *American Sociological Review* 57:698–708.

Berne, S. 1991. "'Excuse Me,' He Said." *New York Times Magazine* (June 30):10–11.

Bernstein, C., & B. Woodward. 1974. *All the President's Men.* New York: Simon and Schuster.

Betz, M. 1974. "Riots and Welfare: Are They Related?" *Social Problems* 21:345–355.

Bickle, G., & R. Peterson. 1991. "The Impact of Gender-Based Family Roles on Criminal Sentencing." *Social Problems* 38:372–394.

Bienen, L. 1980. "Rape III: National Developments in Rape Reform Legislation." *Women's Rights Law Reporter* 6:170–213.

Binder, A., G. Geis, & D. Bruce. 1988. *Juvenile Delinquency: Historical, Cultural, and Legal Perspectives.* New York: Macmillan.

Bing, L. 1991. *Do or Die.* New York: HarperCollins.

Birsch, D., & J. Fielder (eds.). 1994. *The Ford Pinto Case: A Study in Applied Ethics, Business, and Technology.* Albany: State University of New York Press.

Bishop, D., C. Frazier, & J. Henretta. 1989. "Prosecutorial Waiver: Case Study of a Questionable Reform." *Crime & Delinquency* 35:179–201.

Black, D. 1970. "Production of Crime Rates." *American Sociological Review* 35:733–748.

———. 1980. *The Manners and Customs of the Police.* New York: Academic Press.

Black, D., & D. Nagin. 1998. "Do 'Right-to-Carry' Laws Deter Violent Crime?" *Journal of Legal Studies* 27:209–219.

Blakey, G., & R. Billing. 1981. *The Plot to Kill the President: Organized Crime Assassinated JFK.* New York: Times Books.

Blalock, H. 1967. *Toward a Theory of Minority-Group Relations.* New York: Wiley.

Blau, J., & P. Blau. 1982. "The Cost of Inequality: Metropolitan Structure and Violent Crime." *American Sociological Review* 47:114–129.

Blitstein, R. 2007. "Internet Crooks Steal Billions." *Wisconsin State Journal* (Nov. 25):A1, A9.

Blomberg, T., W. Bales, & K. Reed. 1993. "Intermediate Punishment: Redistributing or Extending Social Control?" *Crime, Law, & Social Change* 19:187–201.

Bluestone, B., & B. Harrison. 1982. *The Deindustrialization of America: Plant Closings, Community Abandonment, and the Dismantling of Basic Industry.* New York: Basic.

Blumberg, A. 1967. "The Practice of Law as a Confidence Game." *Law & Society Review* 1:15–39.

Blumstein, A. 1993. "Making Rationality Relevant." *Criminology* 31:1–16.

Blumstein, A., & E. Grady. 1982. "Prevalence and Recidivism in Index Arrests: A Feedback Model." *Law & Society Review* 16:265–290.

Blumstein, A., & J. Wallman (eds.). 2000. *The Crime Drop in America.* New York: Cambridge University Press.

Boghosian, H. 2013. *Spying on Democracy: Government Surveillance, Corporate Power, and Public Resistance.* San Francisco: City Light.

Bohm, R. 1991. "Race and the Death Penalty in the United States." In M. Lynch & E. Patterson (eds.), *Race and Criminal Justice.* Albany, NY: Harrow and Heston.

———. 1998. "The Economic Costs of Capital Punishment: Past, Present, and Future." In J. Acker, R. Bohm, & C. Lanier (eds.), *America's Experiment with Capital Punishment.* Durham, NC: Carolina Academic.

Bonczar, T., & L. Maruschak. 2013. *Probation and Parole in the United States, 2012.* Washington, DC: US Department of Justice.

Bond-Maupin, L. 1998. "'That Wasn't Even Me They Showed': Women as Criminals on *America's Most Wanted.*" *Violence Against Women* 4:30–44.

Boostrom, R., & J. Henderson. 1983. "Community Action and Crime Prevention: Some Unresolved Issues." *Crime & Social Justice* 19:24–30.

Booth, D. 2010. "Toyota Discovers Silence Is Golden." *Vancouver Sun* (May 3). www.vancouversun.com.

Bornstein, D., et al. 2006. "Understanding the Experience of Lesbian, Bisexual, and Trans Survivors of Domestic Violence: A Qualitative Study." *Journal of Homosexuality* 51:159–181.

Bourgois, P. 1989. "In Search of Horatio Alger: Culture and Ideology in the Crack Economy." *Contemporary Drug Problems* 16:619–649.

————. 1995. *In Search of Respect: Selling Crack in El Barrio*. Cambridge: Cambridge University Press.

Bourque, B., M. Han, & S. Hill. 1996. *A National Survey of Aftercare Provisions for Boot Camp Graduates*. Washington, DC: National Institute of Justice.

Bowers, W., & G. Pierce. 1980. "Deterrence or Brutalization: What Is the Effect of Executions?" *Crime & Delinquency* 26:453–484.

Bowker, L. 1980. *Prison Victimization*. New York: Elsevier.

Bowker, L., & M. Klein. 1983. "The Etiology of Female Juvenile Delinquency and Gang Membership: A Test of Psychological and Social Structural Explanations." *Adolescence* 13:739–751.

Braga, A., & G. Pierce. 2005. "Disrupting Illegal Firearms Markets in Boston: The Effects of Operation Ceasefire on the Supply of New Handguns to Criminals." *Criminology & Public Policy* 4:717–748.

Braithwaite, J. 1989. *Crime, Shame, and Reintegration*. New York: Cambridge University Press.

Braithwaite, J., & K. Daly. 1998. "Masculinities, Violence, and Communitarian Control." In S. Miller (ed.), *Crime Control and Women*. Thousand Oaks, CA: Sage.

Braithwaite, R., & K. Arriola. 2003. "Male Prisoners and HIV Prevention: A Call for Action Ignored." *American Journal of Public Health* 93:759–763.

Bratton, W. 1998. *Turnaround: How America's Top Cop Reversed the Crime Epidemic*. New York: Random.

Brecher, E. 1972. *Licit and Illicit Drugs*. Boston: Little, Brown.

Brents, B., C. Jackson, & K. Hausbeck. 2010. *The State of Sex: Tourism, Sex, and Sin in the New American Heartland*. New York: Routledge.

Bridges, G., & R. Crutchfield. 1988. "Law, Social Standing, and Racial Disparities in Imprisonment." *Social Forces* 66:699–724.

Bridges, G., R. Crutchfield, & E. Simpson. 1987. "Crime, Social Structure, and Criminal Punishment: White and Nonwhite Rates of Imprisonment." *Social Problems* 34:345–361.

Brinkley, J., & S. Engelberg (eds.). 1988. *Report of the Congressional Committees Investigating the Iran-Contra Affair*. New York: Random House.

Britton, D. 1997. "Gender Organizational Logic: Policy and Practice in Men's and Women's Prisons." *Gender & Society* 11:796–818.

Brooks-Gunn, J., G. Duncan, P. Klebanor, & N. Sealand. 1993. "Do Neighborhoods Influence Child and Adolescent Development?" *American Journal of Sociology* 99:353–395.

Broome, K., K. Knight, M. Hiller, & D. Simpson. 1996. "Drug Treatment Process Indicators for Probationers and Prediction of Recidivism." *Journal of Substance Abuse Treatment* 13:487–491.

Browne, A. 1987. *When Battered Women Kill*. New York: Macmillan.

Brownmiller, S. 1975. *Against Our Will: Men, Women, and Rape*. New York: Simon and Schuster.

Brownstein, H. 1996. *The Rise and Fall of a Violent Crime Wave: Crack Cocaine and the Social Construction of a Crime Problem*. Guilderland, NY: Harrow and Heston.

Bugliosi, V. 2007. *Reclaiming History: The Assassination of President John F. Kennedy*. New York: Norton.

Bull, C. 2003. "Justice Served." *The Advocate* (Aug. 19):35–38.

Bullard, R., & B. Wright. 1989–1990. "Toxic Waste and the African American Community." *Urban League Review* 13:67–75.

Bureau of Justice Assistance. 2002. *Program Brief: Prison Industry Certification Enhancement Program*. Washington, DC: US Department of Justice.

Burkett, S., & B. Warren. 1987. "Religiosity, Peer Associations, and Adolescent Marijuana Use: A Panel Study of Underlying Causal Structures." *Criminology* 25:109–134.

Burns, R., & J. Smith. 1999. "DNA: Fingerprint of the Future?" *ACJS Today* 18:3–4.

Burris-Kitchen, D. 1995. "Sisters in the Hood." PhD diss., Western Michigan University.

Bursik, R., & H. Grasmick. 1993. *Neighborhoods and Crime: The Dimensions of Effective Community Control.* New York: Lexington.

Bursik, R., & J. Webb. 1982. "Community Change and Patterns of Delinquency." *American Journal of Sociology* 88:24–42.

Burt, C., & R. Simons. 2014. "Pulling Back the Curtain on Heritability Studies." *Criminology* 52:223–262.

Bush-Baskette, S. 1998. "The War on Drugs as a War Against Black Women." In S. Miller (ed.), *Crime Control and Women.* Thousand Oaks, CA: Sage.

Bussey, John. 2002. "Cheney, Halliburton Accused of Fraud." *Wisconsin State Journal* (July 11):A3.

Calavita, K., & H. Pontell. 1990. "Heads I Win, Tails You Lose: Deregulation, Crime, and Crisis in the Savings and Loan Industry." *Crime & Delinquency* 36:309–341.

———. 1993. "Savings and Loan Fraud as Organized Crime: Towards a Conceptual Typology of Corporate Illegality." *Criminology* 31:519–548.

Caldwell, P. 2011. "Who Stole the Election?" *American Prospect* (Nov.):8–11, 13.

Calhoun, C., & H. Hiller. 1988. "Coping with Insidious Injuries: The Case of Johns-Manville Corporation and Asbestos Exposure." *Social Problems* 35:162–181.

Callahan, L., H. Steadman, M. McGreevy, & P. Robbins. 1991. "The Volume and Characteristics of Insanity Defense Pleas: An Eight-State Study." *Bulletin of the American Academy of Psychiatry and the Law* 19:331–338.

Cameron, D., & E. Frazer. 1987. *The Lust to Kill: A Feminist Investigation of Serial Murder.* New York: New York University Press.

———. 1993. "On the Question of Pornography and Sexual Violence: Moving Beyond Cause and Effect." In C. Itzin (ed.), *Pornography: Women, Violence, and Civil Liberties.* New York: Oxford University Press.

Campbell, A. 1987. "Self-Definition by Rejection: The Case of Gang Girls." *Social Problems* 34:451–466.

———. 1991. *The Girls in the Gang.* Cambridge: Blackwell.

———. 1993. *Men, Women, and Aggression.* New York: Basic.

Cantor, D., & K. Land. 1975. "Unemployment and Crime Rates in the Post–World War II United States: A Theoretical and Empirical Analysis." *American Sociological Review* 50:317–323.

Cao, L., A. Adam, & V. Jensen. 1997. "A Test of the Black Subculture of Violence." *Criminology* 35:367–379.

Cappiello, D., & S. Borenstein. 2014. "Spills Not Only Way Coal Pollutes, Data Show." *Wisconsin State Journal* (Jan. 10):A5.

Carey, J. 1978. *Introduction to Criminology.* Englewood Cliffs, NJ: Prentice Hall.

Carlson, S., & R. Michalowski. 1997. "Crime, Unemployment, and Social Structures of Accumulation: An Inquiry into Historical Contingency." *Justice Quarterly* 14:209–239.

Carpenter, C., B. Glassner, B. Johnson, & J. Loughlin. 1988. *Kids, Drugs, and Crime.* Lexington, MA: Lexington Books.

Carson, E. 2014. *Prisoners in 2013.* Washington, DC: US Department of Justice.

Caspi, A., G. Elder, & E. Herbener. 1990. "Childhood Personality and the Prediction of Life-Course Patterns." In L. Robins & M. Rutter (eds.), *Straight and Devious Pathways from Childhood to Adulthood*. New York: Cambridge University Press.

Caspi, A., et al. 1994. "Are Some People Crime-Prone? Replications of the Personality-Crime Relationship Across Countries, Genders, Races, and Methods." *Criminology* 32:163–195.

Cauffman, E., L. Steinberg, & A. Piquero. 2005. "Psychological, Neuropsychological, and Physiological Correlates of Serious Antisocial Behavior in Adolescence: The Role of Self-Control." *Criminology* 43:133–175.

Center for Auto Safety. 2014a. "The C/K Pickup with Unsafe Side Saddle Tanks." www.autosafety.org.

———. 2014b. "Ford Transmissions Failure to Hold in Park." www.autosafety.org.

Centers for Disease Control and Prevention. 2014. "HIV in Correctional Settings." www.cdc.gov.

Cernkovich, S., & P. Giordano. 1987. "Family Relationships and Delinquency." *Criminology* 25:295–321.

Challenger, J. 2004. "Frustrated Employers Looking Closer to Find Good Hires." *California Job Journal* (July 24). www.jobjournal.com.

Chambliss, W. 1973. "The Saints and the Roughnecks." *Society* 11:341–355.

———. 1988. *On the Take: From Petty Crooks to Presidents*. Bloomington: Indiana University Press.

———. 1994. "Policing the Ghetto Underclass: The Politics of Law and Law Enforcement." *Social Problems* 41:177–194.

Chambliss, W., & R. Seidman. 1971. *Law, Order, and Power*. Reading, MA: Addison-Wesley.

Champion, C. 1986. "Clinical Perspectives on the Relationship Between Pornography and Sexual Violence." *Law & Inequality* 4:22–27.

Chase, T. 2014. "Wisconsin Drug Courts Grow, but Racial Disparities Persist." *Cap Times* (Aug. 17). http:host.madison.com.

Chenge, C., & M. Hoekstra. 2013. "Does Strengthening Self-Defense Law Deter or Escalate Violence? Evidence from Expansions to Castle Doctrine." *Journal of Human Resources* 48:821–854.

Chesney-Lind, M. 1989. "Girl's Crime and Woman's Place: Toward a Feminist Model of Female Delinquency." *Crime & Delinquency* 35:5–29.

Chesney-Lind, M., R. Shelden, & K. Joe. 1996. "Girls, Delinquency, and Gang Membership." In C. Huff (ed.), *Gangs in America*. Thousand Oaks, CA: Sage.

Chiricos, T. 1987. "Rates of Crime and Unemployment: An Analysis of Aggregate Research Evidence." *Social Problems* 34:187–212.

———. 1996. "Moral Panic as Ideology: Drugs, Violence, Race, and Punishment in America." In M. Lynch & E. Patterson (eds.), *Justice with Prejudice*. Guilderland, NY: Harrow and Heston.

Chiricos, T., & C. Crawford. 1995. "Race and Imprisonment: A Contextual Assessment of the Evidence." In D. Hawkins (ed.), *Ethnicity, Race, and Crime*. Albany: State University of New York Press.

Chiricos, T., & M. Delone. 1992. "Labor Surplus and Punishment: A Review and Assessment of Theory and Evidence." *Social Problems* 39:421–446.

Choice, P., & L. Lamke. 1997. "A Conceptual Approach to Understanding Abused Women's Stay/Leave Decisions." *Journal of Family Issues* 18:290–314.

Church Committee. 1978. "Report of the Senate Select Committee on Intelligence." In M. Ermann & R. Lundman (eds.), *Corporate and Governmental Deviance*. New York: Oxford University Press.

Cienfuegos, E. 2004. "Rape of Iraqi Girls by US Mercenaries Was Rampant in Baghdad." www.aztlan.net.

Clark, J. 1995. "The Impact of the Prison Environment on Mothers." *Prison Journal* 75:306–329.

Clarke, R. (ed.). 1992. *Situational Crime Prevention: Successful Case Studies.* New York: Harrow and Heston.

Clarke, R. 2004. *Against All Enemies: Inside America's War on Terror.* New York: Free Press.

Clarke, R., & R. Knake. 2010. *Cyber War: The Next Threat to National Security and What to Do About It.* New York: Ecco.

Clear, T. 2007. *Imprisoning Communities: How Mass Incarceration Makes Disadvantaged Neighborhoods Worse.* New York: Oxford University Press.

Clear, T., & G. Cole. 1994. *American Corrections.* Belmont, CA: Wadsworth.

Clear, T., G. Cole, & M. Reisig. 2006. *American Corrections.* Belmont, CA: Wadsworth.

Clinard, M. 1983. *Corporate Ethics and Crime: The Role of Middle Management.* Beverly Hills: Sage.

Clinard, M., & P. Yeager. 1980. *Corporate Crime.* New York: Free Press.

Cloward, R., & L. Ohlin. 1960. *Delinquency and Opportunity: A Theory of Delinquent Gangs.* New York: Free Press.

CNN. 2001. "Florida Recount Study: Bush Still Wins" (Nov. 11). www.cnn.com.

———. 2002. "Court Overturns Three Convictions in N.Y. Police Torture Case" (Feb. 28). www.cnn.com.

———. 2006a. "Judge Finds Tobacco Racketeering" (Aug. 17). www.cnn.com.

———. 2006b. "U.S. Military Names Soldiers Charged in Rape, Murder Probe" (July 10). www.cnn.com.

———. 2009. "Mayors, Rabbis Arrested in Corruption Probe" (July 23). www.cnn.com.

Cochran, J., P. Wood, & B. Arneklev. 1994. "Is the Religiosity-Delinquency Relationship Spurious? A Test of Arousal and Social Control Theories." *Journal of Research in Crime & Delinquency* 31:92–123.

Cockburn, C. 1967. *"I Claud": The Autobiography of Claud Cockburn.* Harmondsworth: Penguin.

Cohan, W. 2009. *House of Cards: A Tale of Hubris and Wretched Excess on Wall Street.* New York: Doubleday.

Cohen, A. 1955. *Delinquent Boys: The Culture of the Gang.* New York: Free Press.

———. 1966. *Deviance and Control.* Englewood Cliffs, NJ: Prentice Hall.

Cohen, B. 1980. *Deviant Street Networks: Prostitution in New York.* Lexington, MA: Lexington Books.

Cohen, J., & N. Solomon. 1994. "30-Year Anniversary: Tonkin Gulf Lie Launched Vietnam War." *Fairness and Accuracy in Reporting* (July 27). www.fair.org.

Cohen, L., & M. Felson. 1979. "Social Change and Crime Rate Trends: A Routine Activity Approach." *American Sociological Review* 44:588–608.

Cohen, L., & K. Land. 1987. "Age Structure and Crime: Symmetry Versus Asymmetry and the Projection of Crime Rates Through the 1990s." *American Sociological Review* 52:170–183.

Cohen, N. 1967. *Los Angeles Riot Study: Summary and Implications for Policy.* Los Angeles: University of California Institute of Government and Public Affairs.

Cohen, P., & A. Sas. 1996. "Cannabis Use: A Stepping Stone to Other Drugs? The Case of Amsterdam." Center for Drug Research, University of Amsterdam. www.mir.drugtext.org.

Cohen, T., & B. Reaves. 2007. *Pretrial Release of Felony Defendants in State Courts*. Washington, DC: US Department of Justice.

Cole, D. 1999a. *No Equal Justice: Race and Class in the American Criminal Justice System*. New York: Free Press.

———. 1999b. "Standing While Black." *The Nation* (Jan. 4):24.

———. 1999c. "When the Reason Is Race." *The Nation* (Mar. 15):22–24.

———. 2003. "Court Watching." *The Nation* (July 21–28):3–5.

Cole, L., & S. Foster. 2001. *From the Ground Up: Environmental Racism and the Rise of the Environmental Justice Movement*. New York: New York University Press.

Coleman, J. 2006. *The Criminal Elite: Understanding White-Collar Crime*. New York: Worth.

Collins, C. 1997. *The Imprisonment of African American Women*. Jefferson, NC: McFarland.

Colvin, R. 2012. *Gay and Lesbian Cops: Diversity and Effective Policing*. Boulder, CO: Lynne Rienner.

Comfort, A. 1991. *The New Joy of Sex: The Gourmet Guide to Lovemaking for the Nineties*. New York: Pocket.

Committee on Health Care for Underserved Women. 2011. "Health Care for Pregnant and Postpartum Incarcerated Women and Adolescent Females." American College of Obstetricians and Gynecologists. www.acog.org.

Conason, J., & G. Lyons. 2000. *The Hunting of the President: The Ten-Year Campaign to Destroy Bill and Hillary Clinton*. New York: Thomas Dunne.

Conklin, J. 2003. *Why Crime Rates Fell*. Boston: Allyn and Bacon.

Connell, R. 1987. *Gender and Power: Society, the Person, and Sexual Politics*. Stanford: Stanford University Press.

Conners, R. 2003. "How 'Restorative' Is Restorative Justice? An Oppression Theory Critique." In M. Free (ed.), *Racial Issues in Criminal Justice*. Westport: Praeger.

Continetti, M. 2006. *The K Street Gang: The Rise and Fall of the Republican Machine*. New York: Doubleday.

Cooper, M. 2010. "Mine Agency's Powers Limited, Often Unused." *Wisconsin State Journal* (Apr. 11):A4.

Corn, D. 2003. *The Lies of George W. Bush: Mastering the Politics of Deception*. New York: Crown.

———. 2007. "Cheney on Trial." *The Nation* (Mar. 26):11–13.

Corporate Crime Reporter. 2007. "Louisiana Most Corrupt State in the Nation, Mississippi Second, Illinois Sixth, New Jersey Ninth" (Oct. 8). www.corporate crimereporter.com.

Cose, E. 2007. "Sanity and Sentencing." *Newsweek* (Dec. 24):53.

———. 2007–2008. "The Rise of a New American Underclass." *Newsweek* (Dec. 31–Jan. 7):74.

Costanzo, M. 1997. *Just Revenge: Costs and Consequences of the Death Penalty*. New York: St. Martin's.

Coston, C. 1992. "The Influence of Race in Urban Homeless Females' Fear of Crime." *Justice Quarterly* 9:721–729.

Coupe, T., & L. Blake. 2006. "Daylight and Darkness Targeting Strategies and the Risks of Being Seen in Residential Burglaries." *Criminology* 44:431–464.

Courson, P. 2009. "Ex-Rep. Jefferson Convicted of Corruption" (Aug. 6). www .cnn.com.

Court, J. 2003. "Identity Thieves." *The Nation* (Nov. 3):8, 22.

Cowley, G. 1998. "Why Children Turn Violent." *Newsweek* (July 22):22–45.

Crair, B. 2014. "Cruel but Not Unusual." *New Republic* (Apr. 30). www.tnr.com.

Cratty, C. 2011. "New Rules Slashing Crack Cocaine Go into Effect" (Nov. 2). www.cnn.com.

Crockett, M., et al. 2010. "Impulsive Choice and Altruistic Punishment Are Correlated and Increase in Tandem with Serotonin Depletion." *Emotion* 10:855–862.

Cromwell, P., J. Olson, & D. Avary. 1991. *Breaking and Entering: An Ethnographic Analysis of Burglary.* Newbury Park, CA: Sage.

Cruciotti, T., & R. Matthews. 2006. "The *Exxon Valdez* Oil Spill." In R. Michalowski & R. Kramer (eds.), *State-Corporate Crime: Wrongdoing at the Intersection of Business and Government.* New Brunswick, NJ: Rutgers University Press.

Crum, R. 2010. "BP Blames Failed Equipment on Rig." *Wisconsin State Journal* (May 3):A12.

Cullen, F., & B. Applegate (eds.). 1997. *Offender Rehabilitation: Effective Treatment Intervention.* Aldershot: Ashgate.

Cullen, F., P. Gendreau, G. Jarjoura, & J. Wright. 1997. "Crime and the Bell Curve: Lessons from Intelligent Criminology." *Crime & Delinquency* 43:387–411.

Cullen, F., B. Link, J. Cullen, & N. Wolfe. 1989. "How Satisfying Is Prison Work? A Comparative Occupational Approach." *Journal of Offender Counseling Services & Rehabilitation* 14:89–108.

Cullen, F., W. Maakestad, & G. Cavender. 2006. *Corporate Crime Under Attack: The Fight to Criminalize Business Violence.* Cincinnati: Anderson.

Cullen, F., & J. Sundt. 2000. "Imprisonment in the United States." In J. Sheley (ed.), *Criminology.* Belmont, CA: Wadsworth.

Cullen, F., J. Wright, & M. Chamblin. 1999. "Social Support and Social Reform: A Progressive Agenda." *Crime & Delinquency* 45:188–207.

Currie, C., & A. Pillick. 1996. "Sex Discrimination in the Selection and Participation of Female Jurors: A Post-*J.E.B.* Analysis." *Judges' Journal* 35:2–6, 38–42.

Currie, E. 1985. *Confronting Crime: An American Challenge.* New York: Pantheon.

Curtis, H. 1992. "Statistics Show Pattern of Discrimination." *Orlando Sentinel* (Aug. 23):A11.

Curtis, L. 1975. *Violence, Race, and Culture.* Lexington, MA: Lexington Books.

Dabney, D. 2001. "Onset of Illegal Use of Mind-Altering or Potentially Addictive Drugs Among Pharmacists." *Journal of the American Pharmaceutical Association* 41:392–400.

Dabney, D., & R. Hollinger. 2002. "Drugged Druggists: The Convergence of Two Criminal Career Trajectories." *Justice Quarterly* 19:181–213.

Dahir, M. 2002. "The Dangerous Lives of Gay Priests." *The Advocate* (July 23):30–35.

Dalton, K. 1961. "Menstruation and Crime." *British Medical Journal* 2:1752–1753.

Daly, K. 1994. *Gender, Crime, and Punishment.* New Haven: Yale University Press.

Daly, K., & R. Bordt. 1995. "Sex Effects and Sentencing: A Review of the Statistical Literature." *Justice Quarterly* 12:143–177.

Daly, K., & M. Chesney-Lind. 1988. "Feminism and Criminology." *Justice Quarterly* 5:497–538.

Darden, C. 1996. *In Contempt.* New York: Regan Books.

Daudistel, H., W. Sanders, & D. Luckenbill. 1979. *Criminal Justice: Situations and Decisions.* New York: Holt, Rinehart, and Winston.

Davey, M. 2011. "Blogojevich Sentenced to 14 Years in Prison." *New York Times* (Dec. 7). www.nytimes.com.

Davidson, S. 2010. "Black Lung on the Rise Among U.S. Coal Miners" (Jan. 11). www.wsws.org.

Davis, A. 1990. *Women, Race, and Class.* New York: Vintage.

Dawley, D. 1992. *A Nation of Lords: The Autobiography of the Vice Lords.* Prospect Heights, IL: Waveland.

Dawson, J. 1992. "Prosecutions in State Courts." *Bureau of Justice Statistics Bulletin* (Mar.):1–9.

De La Cruz, D. 1999. "Police Charged with Murder." *Wisconsin State Journal* (Apr. 1):A2.

Death Penalty Information Center. 2009. *Smart on Crime: Reconsidering the Death Penalty in a Time of Economic Crisis.* Washington, DC.

———. 2014a. "Executions in the United States." www.deathpenaltyinfo.org.

———. 2014b. "Innocence and the Death Penalty." www.deathpenaltyinfo.org.

———. 2014c. "Intellectual Disability and the Death Penalty." www.deathpenalty info.org.

———. 2014d. "Juveniles and the Death Penalty." www.deathpenaltyinfo.org.

———. 2014e. "Race and the Death Penalty." www.deathpenaltyinfo.org.

———. 2014f. "Women and the Death Penalty." www.deathpenaltyinfo.org.

DeFrances, C., & F. Marika. 2000. *Indigent Defense Services in Large Counties, 1999.* Washington, DC: US Department of Justice.

deHaven-Smith, L. 2010. "Beyond Conspiracy Theory: Patterns of High Crime in American Government." *American Behavioral Scientist* 53:795–825.

DeKeseredy, W., & M. Schwartz. 1996. *Contemporary Criminology.* Belmont, CA: Wadsworth.

Delacoste, F., & F. Newman (eds.). 1981. *Fight Back: Feminist Resistance to Male Violence.* Minneapolis: Cleis.

Delgado, M. 2012. *Prisoner Reentry at Work: Adding Business to the Mix.* Boulder, CO: Lynne Rienner.

Delgado, R. 2000. "Goodbye to Hammurabi: Analyzing the Atavistic Appeal of Restorative Justice." *Stanford Law Review* 52:751–775.

DeMichele, M. 2007. *Probation and Parole's Growing Caseloads and Workload Allocation: Strategies for Managerial Decision Making.* American Probation and Parole Association. www.appa-net.org.

Denno, D. 1998. "Execution and the Forgotten Eighth Amendment." In J. Acker, R. Bohm, & C. Lanier (eds.), *America's Experiment with Capital Punishment.* Durham, NC: Carolina Academic.

Derber, C. 1996. *The Wilding of America: How Greed and Violence Are Eroding Our Nation's Character.* New York: St. Martin's.

Dershowitz, A. 1996. *Reasonable Doubts: The O.J. Simpson Case and the Criminal Justice System.* New York: Simon and Schuster.

———. 2001. *Supreme Injustice: How the High Court Hijacked Election 2000.* New York: Oxford University Press.

DeVall, K., P. Gregory, & D. Hartmann. 2012. "The Potential of Social Science Theory for the Evaluation and Improvement of Drug Courts." *Journal of Drug Issues* 42:320–336.

Devers, L. 2011. "Plea and Charge Bargaining: Research Summary." www.bjs.com.

Devlieger, P., & G. Albrecht. 2000. "The Concept and Experience of Disability on Chicago's Near West Side." *Journal of Disability Policy Studies* 11:51–60.

Devlieger, P., G. Albrecht, & M. Hertz. 2007. "The Production of Disability Culture Among Young African-American Men." *Social Science & Medicine* 64:1948–1959.

Diaz, T. 1999. *Making a Killing: The Business of Guns in America.* New York: New Press.

Dietrich, D., et al. 2001. "Early Exposure to Lead and Juvenile Delinquency." *Neurotoxicology & Teratology* 23:511–518.

Dillon, F., H. Patin, M. Robbins, & J. Szapocznik. 2008. "Exploring the Role of Parental Monitoring of Peers on the Relationship Between Family Functioning and Delinquency in the Lives of African American and Hispanic Adolescents." *Crime & Delinquency* 54:65–94.

Dirr, A. 2013. "Frac Sand a Health Concern." *Wisconsin State Journal* (Oct. 6):C1, C4.

Dobash, R., M. Wilson, & M. Daly. 1992. "The Myth of the Symmetrical Nature of Domestic Violence." *Social Problems* 39:71–91.

Dodge, L. 1999. "Abortion Foes Lose Suit over Web Site." *Wisconsin State Journal* (Feb. 2):A1.

Domhoff, G. W. 2013. "Wealth, Income, and Power." www2.ucsc.edu/whorules america/power/wealth.

Donahue, J., & S. Levitt. 2001. "The Impact of Legalized Abortion on Crime." *Quarterly Journal of Economics* 116:379–420.

Donnerstein, E., D. Linz, & S. Penrod. 1987. *The Question of Pornography: Research Findings and Policy Implications.* New York: Free Press.

Douglass, J. 2008. *JFK and the Unspeakable: Why He Died and Why It Matters.* Maryknoll, NY: Orbis.

Dowie, M. 1977. "Pinto Madness." *Mother Jones* (Sept.–Oct.):18–24, 28–32.

Dowie, M., & C. Marshall. 1980. "The Benedictine Cover-Up." *Mother Jones* (Nov.):43–56.

Downes, B. 1968. "The Social Characteristics of Riot Cities: A Comparative Study." *Social Science Quarterly* 49:504–520.

Dreier, P. 2006. "Why Mine Deaths Are Up." *The Nation* (June 12):5–6.

Dreyfuss, R. 2005. *Devil's Game: How the United States Helped Unleash Fundamentalist Islam.* New York: Owl.

Drogin, B. 2003. "Friendly Fire." *New Republic* (Oct. 27):23–27.

Drum, K. 2010. "Capital City." *Mother Jones* (Jan.–Feb.):37–43, 78–79.

Dugan, L. 2003. "Domestic Violence Legislation: Exploring Its Impact on the Likelihood of Domestic Violence, Police Involvement, and Arrest." *Criminology & Public Policy* 2:283–312.

Dugan, L., D. Nagin, & R. Rosenfeld. 2003. "Exposure Reduction or Retaliation? The Effects of Domestic Violence Resources on Intimate Partner Violence." *Law & Society Review* 37:169–198.

Dugdale, R. 1877. *The Jukes: A Study in Crime, Pauperism, Disease, and Heredity.* New York: Putnam.

Dulaney, M. 1996. *Black Police in America.* Bloomington: Indiana University Press.

Dunford, F., D. Huizinga, & D. Elliott. 1990. "Role of Arrest in Domestic Assault: The Omaha Police Experiment." *Criminology* 28:183–206.

Dunn, J. 1999. "What Love Has to Do with It: The Cultural Construction of Emotion and Sorority Women's Responses to Forcible Interaction." *Social Problems* 46:440–459.

Durbin, D. 2014. "GM Recalls 2.4M More Vehicles." *Wisconsin State Journal* (May 21):B8.

Durham, A. 1986. "Pornography, Social Harm, and Legal Control." *Justice Quarterly* 3:95–102.

Durkheim, É. 1893/1964. *The Division of Labor in Society.* New York: Free Press.

———. 1897/1952. *Suicide.* New York: Free Press.

Dworkin, A. 1997. *Life and Death: Unapologetic Writings on the Continuing War Against Women.* New York: Free Press.

Dworkin, A., & C. MacKinnon. 1988. *Pornography and Civil Rights: A New Day for Women's Equality.* Minneapolis: Organizing Against Pornography.

Dwyer, L. 1983. "Structure and Strategy in the Antinuclear Movement." In J. Freeman (ed.), *Social Movements in the Sixties and Seventies*. New York: Longman.

Eagan, S. 1996. "From Spikes to Bombs: The Rise of Eco-Terrorism." *Studies in Conflict & Terrorism* 19:1–18.

Earley, P. 1992. *The Hot House: Life Inside Leavenworth*. New York: Bantam.

Ebert, R. 1986. *Roger Ebert's Movie Home Companion*. Kansas City, MO: Andrews, McMeel, and Parker.

Eck, J., & E. Maguire. 2000. "Have Changes in Policing Reduced Violent Crime? An Assessment of the Evidence." In A. Blumstein & J. Wallman (eds.), *The Crime Drop in America*. New York: Cambridge University Press.

The Economist. 1998. "On Prescription" (Nov. 28):51–52.

Ehrlich, J., & R. Goldsmith. 2009. "The Most Dangerous Man in America: Daniel Ellsberg and the Pentagon Papers." Documentary film.

Eichenwald, Kurt. 1999. "Three Sentenced in Archer Daniels Midland Case." *New York Times* (July 10). www.nytimes.com.

Eig, J. 1996. "Eyes on the Street: Community Policing in Chicago." *American Prospect* (Nov.–Dec.):60–68.

Eigenberg, H. 1990. "The National Crime Survey and Rape: The Case of the Missing Question." *Justice Quarterly* 7:655–671.

"Eight Tray Gangster: The Making of a Crip." 1993. *Discovery Channel* documentary.

Einstader, W., & S. Henry. 1995. *Criminological Theory*. Fort Worth: Harcourt Brace.

Eith, C., & M. Durose. 2011. *Contacts Between Police and the Public, 2008*. Washington, DC: US Department of Justice.

Elias, T., & D. Schatzman. 1996. *The Simpson Trial in Black and White*. Los Angeles: General.

Elliott, D., & S. Ageton. 1980. "Reconciling Race and Class Differences in Self-Reported and Official Estimates of Delinquency." *American Sociological Review* 45:95–110.

Elliott, D., & D. Huizinga. 1983. "Social Class and Delinquent Behavior in a National Youth Panel." *Criminology* 21:149–177.

Elliott, P. 1996. "Shattering Illusions: Same-Sex Domestic Violence." In C. Renzetti & C. Miley (eds.), *Violence in Gay and Lesbian Domestic Relationships*. New York: Harrington Park.

Ellis, D., & W. DeKeseredy. 1997. "Rethinking Estrangement Interventions and Intimate Femicide." *Violence Against Women* 3:590–609.

Ellison, C. 1991. "An Eye for an Eye? A Note on the Southern Subculture of Violence Thesis." *Social Forces* 69:1223–1239.

Emerson, R., K. Ferris, & C. Gardner. 1998. "On Being Stalked." *Social Problems* 45:289–314.

Emirbayer, M., & A. Mische. 1998. "What Is Agency?" *American Journal of Sociology* 4:962–1023.

Empey, L., & M. Stafford. 1991. *American Delinquency*. Belmont, CA: Wadsworth.

Eng, M. 2011. "Produce Safety Tests in Jeopardy." *Wisconsin State Journal* (July 4):A12.

Engen, R., S. Steen, & G. Bridges. 2002. "Racial Disparities in the Punishment of Youth: A Theoretical and Empirical Assessment of the Literature." *Social Problems* 49:194–220.

Ennett, S., N. Tobler, C. Ringwalt, & R. Flewelling. 1994. "How Effective Is Drug Abuse Resistance Education? A Meta-Analysis of Project DARE Outcome Evaluations." *American Journal of Public Health* 84:1394–1401.

Epp, C., & S. Maynard-Moody. 2014. "Driving While Black." *Washington Monthly* (Jan.–Feb.). www.washingtonmonthly.com.

Ergun, D. 2014. "New Low in Preference for the Death Penalty." *ABC News* (June 5). www.abcnews.go.com.

Esbensen, F., & L. Winfree. 1998. "Race and Gender Differences Between Gang and Non-Gang Youth: Results from a Multi-Site Survey." *Justice Quarterly* 15:505–525.

Estrich, S. 1987. *Real Rape.* Cambridge: Harvard University Press.

Evans, E. 1983. "The Use of Terrorism by American Social Movements." In J. Freeman (ed.), *Social Movements of the Sixties and Seventies.* New York: Longman.

Faber, D. 2008. *Capitalizing on Environmental Injustice: The Polluter-Industrial Complex in the Age of Globalization.* Lanham: Rowman and Littlefield.

Fagan, J. 1994. "Women and Drugs Revisited: Female Participation in the Cocaine Economy." *Journal of Drug Issues* 24:179–225.

Fagan, J. (ed.). 2003. "Handguns and Violent Crime." *Criminology & Public Policy* 2:359–417.

Fagan, J., & D. Wilkinson. 1998. "Guns, Youth Violence, and Social Identity in Inner Cities." *Crime & Justice* 24:105–188.

Faludi, S. 1999. "The Betrayal of the American Man." *Newsweek* (Sept. 13):48–50.

Fang, L. 2014. "The Anti-Pot Lobby's Big Bankroll." *The Nation* (July 21):11–17.

Farberman, H. 1975. "A Criminogenic Market Structure: The Automobile Industry." *Sociological Quarterly* 16:438–457.

Farley, J. 1987. "Suburbanization and Central-City Crime Rates: New Evidence and a Reinterpretation." *American Journal of Sociology* 93:688–700.

Farr, K. 1997. "Aggravating and Differentiating Factors in the Cases of White and Minority Women on Death Row." *Crime & Delinquency* 43:260–278.

Federal Bureau of Investigation. 1976, 1986, 2005, 2010, 2013. *Crime in the United States.* www.fbi.gov.

———. 2012. *Uniform Crime Reports Hate Crime Statistics.* www.fbi.gov.

Feinberg, L. 1996. *Transgender Women.* Boston: Beacon.

Feldmeyer, B. 2010. "The Effects of Racial/Ethnic Segregation on Latino and Black Homicide." *Sociological Quarterly* 51:600–623.

Felson, R., & J. Staff. 2006. "Explaining the Academic Performance-Delinquency Relationship." *Criminology* 44:299–319.

Ferraro, K. 1989. "Policing Woman Battering." *Social Problems* 36:61–74.

Fessenden, R., & J. Broder. 2001. "Ballot Study Finds Court Didn't Give Bush Win." *Wisconsin State Journal* (Nov. 12):A1, A8.

Feuer, A. 2004. "New York Settles Lawsuit with Diallo Family for $3 Million." *New York Times* (Jan. 6). www.nytimes.com.

Fineman, H. 2005. "Money, Money, Everywhere." *Newsweek* (Sept. 26):24–31.

Finkelhor, D., G. Hotaling, I. Lewis, & C. Smith. 1990. "Sexual Abuse in a National Survey of Adult Men and Women: Prevalence, Characteristics, and Risk Factors." *Child Abuse & Neglect* 14:19–28.

Fischer, H. 2014. "A Guide to U.S. Military Casualty Statistics: Operation New Dawn, Operation Iraqi Freedom, and Operation Enduring Freedom." Congressional Research Service Report for Congress (Feb. 19). www.crs.gov.

Fischetti, M. 2013. "Groundwater Contamination May End the Gas-Fracking Boom." *Scientific American* (Sept. 12). www.scientificamerican.com.

Fishbein, D. 1990. "Biological Perspectives in Criminology." *Criminology* 28:27–72.

Fisher, J. 1997. *Killer Among Us: Public Reactions to Serial Murder.* Westport: Praeger.

Fishman, L. 1988. "The Vice Queens: An Ethnographic Study of Black Female Gang Behavior." Paper presented at the conference of the American Society of Criminology, Chicago.

Fishman, M. 1978. "Crime Waves as Ideology." *Social Problems* 25:531–543.

Fitrakis, B. 2008. "As Ohio Goes . . ." In M. Miller (ed.), *Loser Take All: Election Fraud and the Subversion of Democracy, 2000–2008*. Brooklyn: Ig.

Fitzpatrick, K., M. La Gory, & F. Ritchey. 1993. "Criminal Victimization Among the Homeless." *Justice Quarterly* 10:353–368.

Fleisher, M., & S. Decker. 2001. "An Overview of the Challenge of Prison Gangs." *Corrections Management Quarterly* 5:1–9.

Fletcher, C. 1995. *Breaking and Entering: Women Cops Talk About Life in the Ultimate Men's Club*. New York: HarperCollins.

Foa, P. 1977. "What's Wrong with Rape?" In M. Vetterling-Braggin, F. Elliston, & J. English (eds.), *Feminism and Philosophy*. Totowa, NJ: Littlefield, Adams.

Foley, Stephen. 2009. "Madoff: The $18bn Hunt for Justice Continues." *The Independent* (Sept. 29). www.independent.co.uk.

Foster, H., & J. Hagan. 2007. "Incarceration and Intergenerational Exclusion." *Social Problems* 54:399–433.

Foucault, M. 1979. *Discipline and Punish: The Birth of the Prison*. New York: Vintage.

Fowler, T. 2013. "Ex-Enron CEO Skilling's Sentence Cut to 14 Years." *Wall Street Journal* (June 21). www.online.wsj.com.

Fox, R., R. Van Sickel, & T. Steiger. 2007. *Tabloid Justice: Criminal Justice in an Age of Media Frenzy*. Boulder, CO: Lynne Rienner.

Frank, N., & M. Lynch. 1992. *Corporate Crime, Corporate Violence: A Primer*. New York: Harrow and Heston.

Frank, R. 2013. "400 Richest Americans Now Worth $2 Trillion." *CNBC* (Sept. 16). www.cnbc.com.

Frank, R., A. Efrati, A. Lucchetti, & C. Bray. 2009. "Madoff Jailed After Epic Scam." *Wall Street Journal* (Mar. 13). www.online.wsj.com.

Frank, T. 2007. "Coal Mine Deaths Spike Upward." *USA Today* (Jan. 1). www.usatoday.com.

Frantz, A., L. Knight, & K. Wang. 2014. "A Closer Look: How Many Newtown-like School Shootings Since Sandy Hook?" (June 19). www.cnn.com.

Free, M. 1996. *African Americans and the Criminal Justice System*. New York: Garland.

———. 2002. "Race and Presentencing Decisions in the United States: A Summary and Critique of the Research." *Criminal Justice Review* 27:203–222.

———. 2004. "Bail and Pretrial Release Decisions: An Assessment of the Racial Threat Perspective." *Journal of Ethnicity in Criminal Justice* 24:23–44.

Free, M., & R. Ruesink. 2012. *Race and Justice: Wrongful Convictions of African American Men*. Boulder, CO: Lynne Rienner.

Freed, D. 1991. "Police Brutality Claims Are Rarely Prosecuted." *Los Angeles Times* (July 7). www.articles.latimes.com.

Freeman, R. 1996. "Why Do So Many Young American Men Commit Crimes and What Might We Do About It?" *Journal of Economic Perspectives* 10:25–42.

Freiberg, P. 2002. "Mass Confusion." *The Advocate* (Apr. 20):28–31.

Freifeld, K., A. Viswanatha, & D. Henry. 2013. "JP Morgan Agrees $13 Billion Settlement with U.S. over Bad Mortgages." *Reuters* (Nov. 19). www.reuters.com.

Friedlander, K. 1947. *The Psychoanalytic Approach to Juvenile Delinquency*. London: Routledge and Kegan Paul.

Friedrichs, D. 2007. *Trusted Criminals: White Collar Crime in Contemporary Society*. Belmont, CA: Wadsworth.

Friess, S. 1999. "Behind Closed Doors: Domestic Violence." In C. Albers (ed.), *Sociology of Families Readings*. Thousand Oaks, CA: Pine Forge.

Fujiura, G., K. Yamaki, & S. Czechowicz. 1998. "Disability Among Ethnic and Racial Minorities in the United States." *Journal of Disability Policy Studies* 9:111–130.

Fukurai, H., E. Butler, & R. Krooth. 1993. *Race and the Jury: Racial Disenfranchisement and the Search for Justice*. New York: Plenum.

Fuller, J. 1998. *Criminal Justice: A Peacemaking Perspective*. Boston: Allyn and Bacon.

Fuller, J. 2014. "Shooting in the Dark." *American Prospect* (Jan.–Feb.):7–11.

Fyfe, J. 1981. "Who Shoots? A Look at Officer Race and Police Shooting." *Journal of Police Science & Administration* 9:367–382.

———. 1982. "Blind Justice: Police Shootings in Memphis." *Journal of Criminal Law & Criminology* 73:707–722.

———. 1988. "Police Use of Deadly Force: Research and Reform." *Justice Quarterly* 5:165–205.

Gaes, G. 2008. "Cost, Performance Studies Look at Prison Privatization." *National Institute of Justice Journal* (Mar.). www.nij.gov.

Gaines, P. 1993. "Tough Boyz and Trouble." In M. Golden (ed.), *Wild Women Don't Wear No Blues*. New York: Anchor.

Garner, J., & C. Maxwell. 1999. "Measuring the Amount of Force Used By and Against the Police in Six Jurisdictions." In *Use of Force by Police: Overview of National and Local Data*. Washington, DC: US Department of Justice.

Garrow, D. 1981. *The FBI and Martin Luther King Jr.* New York: Penguin.

Gecas, V. 1989. "The Social Psychology of Self-Efficacy." *Annual Review of Sociology* 15:291–316.

Geerken, M., & J. Hayes. 1993. "Probation and Parole: Public Risk and the Future of Incarceration Alternatives." *Criminology* 31:549–564.

Gegax, T., & L. Clemetson. 1998. "The Abortion Wars Come Home." *Newsweek* (Nov. 9):34–35.

Geis, G. 1978. "The Heavy Electrical Equipment Antitrust Cases: Price-Fixing Techniques and Rationalizations." In M. Ermann & R. Lundman (eds.), *Corporate and Governmental Deviance*. New York: Oxford University Press.

Gellman, B. 2008. *Angler: The Cheney Vice Presidency*. New York: Penguin.

———. 2010. "Locked and Loaded." *Time* (Oct. 11):24–33.

George, T. 2000. "N.Y. Verdict Stirs Up Emotions." *Wisconsin State Journal* (Feb. 26):A2.

Gerth, H., & C. Mills (eds.). 1946. *From Max Weber: Essays in Sociology*. New York: Oxford University Press.

Gibbs, J. 1996. *Race and Justice: Rodney King and O.J. Simpson in a House Divided*. San Francisco: Jossey-Bass.

Giddens, A. 1984. *The Constitution of Society: Outline of the Theory of Structuration*. Berkeley: University of California Press.

Gillespie, L. 2000. *Dancehall Ladies: Executed Women in the Twentieth Century*. Lanham, MD: University Press of America.

Gillespie, M. 1993. "What's Good for the Race." *Ms.* (Jan.–Feb.):80–81.

Gioia, D. 1996. "Why I Didn't Recognize Pinto Fire Hazards: How Organizational Scripts Channel Managers' Thoughts and Actions." In M. Ermann & R. Lundman (eds.), *Corporate and Governmental Deviance*. New York: Oxford University Press.

Giordano, P. 1978. "Girls, Guys, and Gangs: The Changing Social Context of Female Delinquency." *Journal of Criminal Law & Criminology* 69:126–132.

Giordano, P., & S. Cernkovich. 1979. "On Complicating the Relationship Between Liberation and Delinquency." *Social Problems* 26:467–481.

Giordano, P., S. Cernkovich, & D. Holland. 2003. "Changes in Friendship Relations over the Life Course: Implications for the Desistance from Crime." *Criminology* 41:293–327.

Giordano, P., S. Cernkovich, & M. Pugh. 1986. "Friendships and Delinquency." *American Journal of Sociology* 91:1170–1202.

Giordano, P., M. Longmore, R. Schroeder, & P. Seffrin. 2008. "A Life-Course Perspective on Spirituality and Desistance from Crime." *Criminology* 46:99–131.

Giraldi, P. 2005. "Forging the Case for War." *American Conservative* (Nov. 21). www.amconmag.com.

Glaser, D. 1969. *The Effectiveness of a Prison and Parole System*. Indianapolis: Bobbs-Merrill.

Glassner, B. 1999. *The Culture of Fear: Why Americans Are Afraid of the Wrong Things*. New York: Basic.

Glaze, L., & T. Bonczar. 2011. *Probation and Parole in the United States, 2010*. Washington, DC: US Department of Justice.

Glaze, L., & E. Herberman. 2013. *Correctional Populations in the United States, 2012*. Washington, DC: US Department of Justice.

Glaze, L., & L. Maruschak. 2008. *Parents in Prison and Their Minor Children*. Washington, DC: US Department of Justice.

Global Commission on Drug Policy. 2011. *War on Drugs: Report of the Commission on Drug Policy* (June). www.globalcommissionondrugs.org.

Glueck, S., & E. Glueck. 1950. *Unraveling Juvenile Delinquency*. New York: Commonwealth Fund.

———. 1968. *Delinquents and Nondelinquents in Perspective*. Cambridge: Harvard University Press.

Goddard, H. 1912. *The Kallikak Family: A Study in the Heredity of Feeblemindedness*. New York: Macmillan.

Godfrey, M., & V. Schiraldi. 1995. *How Homicide Rates Have Been Affected by California's Death Penalty*. San Francisco: Center on Juvenile and Criminal Justice.

Goetting, A. 1999. *Getting Out: Life Stories of Women Who Left Abusive Men*. New York: Columbia University Press.

Goldberg, M. 2007. *Kingdom Coming: The Rise of Christian Nationalism*. New York: Norton.

Goldsmith, J. 2010. "The New Vulnerability." *New Republic* (June 24):21–28.

Goldstein, D. 2007. "Poison for Profit." *The Nation* (July 30–Aug. 6):5–6.

Goode, E. 2005. *Drugs in American Society*. New York: McGraw-Hill.

Goodman, A. 2013. "Pentagon Study Finds 26,000 Military Sexual Assaults Last Year, over 70 Sex Crimes per Day" (May 8). www.nationofchange.org.

Gordon, D. 1978. "Capitalist Development and the History of American Cities." In W. Tabb & L. Sawyers (eds.), *Marxism and the Metropolis*. New York: Oxford University Press.

Gordon, D. 1994a. "Drugspeak and the Clinton Administration: A Lost Opportunity for Drug Policy Reform." *Social Justice* 21:30–37.

———. 1994b. *The Return of the Dangerous Classes: Drug Prohibition and Policy Politics*. New York: Norton.

Gordon, L. 1988. *Heroes of Their Own Lives: The Politics and History of Family Violence*. New York: Viking.

Gordon, M. 2010. "Goldman Charged with Fraud." *Wisconsin State Journal* (Apr. 17):B1, B5.

Gorenberg, G. 2004. "The Terror Trap." *American Prospect* (Jan.):13–15.

Goring, C. 1913. *The English Convict*. London: HMSO.

Gottfredson, G. 1987. "Peer Group Interventions to Reduce the Risk of Delinquent Behavior: A Selective Review and a New Evaluation." *Criminology* 25:671–714.

Gottfredson, M., & T. Hirschi. 1990. *A General Theory of Crime*. Stanford: Stanford University Press.

Gould, J., & S. Mastrofski. 2004. "Suspect Searches: Assessing Police Behavior Under the U.S. Constitution." *Criminology and Public Policy* 3:315–361.

Gouldner, A. 1970. *The Coming Crises of Western Sociology*. New York: Avon.

Grabham, E., D. Coop, J. Krishnadas, & D. Herman. 2009. *Intersectionality and Beyond: Law, Power, and the Politics of Location*. New York: Routledge.

Graff, E. 2003. "In the Bedroom." *American Prospect* (Spring):A22–A23.

Graham, B. 2004. *Intelligence Matters: The CIA, the FBI, Saudi Arabia, and the Failure of America's War on Terror*. New York: Random House.

Grasmick, H., R. Bursik, & B. Arneklev. 1993. "Reduction in Drunk Driving as a Response to Increased Threats of Shame, Embarrassment, and Legal Sanctions." *Criminology* 31:41–67.

Gray, M. 1998. *Drug Crazy: How We Got into This Mess and How We Can Get Out*. New York: Random House.

Gray, M., M. Fields, & S. Maxwell. 2001. "Examining Probation Violations: Who, What, and When." *Crime & Delinquency* 47:558–572.

Gray, M., & I. Rosen. 2003. *The Warning: Accident at Three Mile Island*. New York: Norton.

Greenberg, D. 1977. "Delinquency and the Age Structure of Society." *Contemporary Crises* 1:189–223.

Greenberg, D., & V. West. 2001. "State Prison Populations and Their Growth, 1971–1999." *Criminology* 39:615–653.

Greene, H. Taylor. 1994. "Black Perspectives on Police Brutality." In A. Sulton (ed.), *African-American Perspectives on Crime Causation, Criminal Justice, and Crime Prevention*. Englewood, CO: Sulton.

Greene, J. 1999. "Zero Tolerance: A Case Study of Police Policies and Practices in New York City." *Crime & Delinquency* 45:171–187.

Greenhouse, L. 2008. "Justices Uphold Lethal Injection in Kentucky Case." *New York Times* (Apr. 17). www.nytimes.com.

Greenhouse, S. 2009. "Work-Related Injuries Underreported." *New York Times* (Nov. 17). www.nytimes.com.

Gregory, P., K. DeVall, & D. Hartmann. 2009. "Evaluating Juvenile Drug Courts: Shedding Light into the Theoretical Black Box." In R. Berger & P. Gregory (eds.), *Juvenile Delinquency and Justice: Sociological Perspectives*. Boulder, CO: Lynne Rienner.

Griffin, M. 1988. "The Legacy of Love Canal." *Sierra* 73:26–30.

Griffin, P., S. Addie, B. Adams, & K. Firestine. 2011. *Trying Juveniles As Adults: An Analysis of State Transfer Laws and Reporting*. Washington, DC: US Department of Justice.

Griffiths, E. 2013. "Race, Space, and the Spread of Violence Across the City." *Social Problems* 60:491–512.

Gross, D. 2009. "Membership Has Its Penalties." *Newsweek* (Jan. 12):18.

Gross, S. 1996. "The Risks of Death: Why Erroneous Convictions Are Common in Capital Cases." *Buffalo Law Review* 44:469–500.

Gross, S., & M. Shaffer. 2012. *Exonerations in the United States, 1989–2012: Report of the National Registry of Exonerations.* www.law.umich.edu.

Grossman, J. 1994. "Women's Jury Service: Right of Citizenship or Privilege of Difference?" *Stanford Law Review* 46:1115–1160.

Gruhl, J., C. Spohn, & S. Welch. 1981. "Women as Policymakers: The Case of Trial Judges." *American Journal of Political Science* 25:308–322.

Guarino-Ghezzi, S., & J. Treviño (eds.). 2005. *Understanding Crime: A Multidisciplinary Approach.* New York: Routledge.

Guilloton, S. 2009. "Pfizer Fined $2.3 Billion to Settle Medicare and Medicaid Fraud Case" (Sept. 11). www.examiner.com.

Gunnison, E., & J. Helfgott. 2013. *Offender Reentry: Beyond Crime and Punishment.* Boulder, CO: Lynne Rienner.

Gupta, A. 2003. "Over 2,000 Police Killings in the US in Past Decade." www .baltimore.indymedia.org.

Gusfield, J. 1963. *Symbolic Crusade: Status Politics and the American Temperance Movement.* Urbana: University of Illinois Press.

Guyon, Janet. 2005. "Jack Grubman Is Back: Just Ask Him." *Fortune* (May 16). www.money.cnn.com.

Gwartney, D. 1998. "The Moral High Ground." *Newsweek* (Apr. 10):61.

Haarr, R. 1997. "Patterns of Interaction in a Police Patrol Bureau: Race and Gender Barriers to Integration." *Justice Quarterly* 14:53–85.

Hacker, A. 1992. *Two Nations: Black and White, Separate, Hostile, Unequal.* New York: Ballantine.

Hagan, F. 1997. *Political Crime: Ideology and Criminality.* Boston: Allyn and Bacon.

———. 1998. *Introduction to Criminology.* Chicago: Nelson-Hall.

Hagan, J. 1989. *Structural Criminology.* New Brunswick, NJ: Rutgers University Press.

———. 1992. "The Poverty of a Classless Criminology." *Criminology* 30:1–20.

———. 1993. "The Social Embeddedness of Crime and Unemployment." *Criminology* 31:465–491.

———. 2010. *Who Are the Criminals? The Politics of Crime Policy from the Age of Roosevelt to the Age of Reagan.* Princeton: Princeton University Press.

Hagan, J., R. Levi, & R. Dinovitzer. 2008. "The Symbolic Violence of the Crime-Immigration Nexus: Migrant Mythologies in the Americas." *Criminology & Public Policy* 7:95–112.

Hagan, J., & B. McCarthy. 1997. *Mean Streets: Youth Crime and Homelessness.* Cambridge: Cambridge University Press.

Hagan, J., & A. Palloni. 1998. "Immigration and Crime in the United States." In J. Smith & B. Edmonston (eds.), *The Immigration Debate.* Washington, DC: National Academy Press.

———. 1999. "Sociological Criminology and the Mythology of Hispanic Immigration and Crime." *Social Problems* 46:617–632.

Hagan, J., & S. Phillips. 2008. "Border Blunders: The Unanticipated Human and Economic Costs of the U.S. Approach to Immigration Control, 1986–2007." *Criminology & Public Policy* 7:83–94.

Hagan, J., et al. 1998. "Subterranean Sources of Subcultural Delinquency Beyond the American Dream." *Criminology* 36:309–339.

Hagedorn, J. 1988. *People and Folks: Gangs, Crime, and the Underclass in a Rustbelt City.* Chicago: Lake View.

Halbfinger, D. 2009. "44 Charged by U.S. in New Jersey Corruption Sweep." *New York Times* (July 24). www.nytimes.com.

Hale, D., & S. Wyland. 1999. "Dragons and Dinosaurs: The Plight of Patrol Women." In L. Gaines & G. Cordner (eds.), *Policing Perspectives*. Los Angeles: Roxbury.

Hamm, M. 1993. *American Skinheads: The Criminology and Control of Hate Crimes*. Westport: Praeger.

Hannon, L., & R. DeFina. 2010. "The State of the Economy and the Relationship Between Prisoner Reentry and Crime." *Social Problems* 57:611–629.

Hanson, D. 2014. "Drug Abuse Resistance Education: The Effectiveness of DARE." *Alcohol Abuse Prevention*. www.alcoholfacts.org.

Harer, M., & D. Steffensmeier. 1992. "The Differing Effects of Economic Inequality on Black and White Rates of Violence." *Social Forces* 70:1035–1054.

Harlow, C. 2000. *Defense Counsel in Criminal Cases*. Washington, DC: US Department of Justice.

Harmon, P., & J. Check. 1989. *The Role of Pornography in Woman Abuse*. Toronto: La Marsh Research Programme on Violence and Conflict Resolution, York University.

Harring, S. 1993. "Policing a Class Society: The Expansion of the Urban Police in the Late Nineteenth and Early Twentieth Centuries." In D. Greenberg (ed.), *Crime and Capitalism*. Philadelphia: Temple University Press.

Harring, S., & L. McMullin. 1975. "The Buffalo Police, 1872–1900: Labor Unrest, Political Power, and the Creation of the Police Institution." *Crime & Social Justice* 8:5–14.

Harris, D. 2003. "The Reality of Racial Disparity in Criminal Justice: The Significance of Data Collection." *Law & Contemporary Problems* 66:71–98.

Harris, M. 1988. *Cholas: Latino Girls and Gangs*. New York: AMS Press.

Harrison, L. 2001. "The Revolving Prison Door for Drug-Involved Offenders: Challenges and Opportunities." *Crime & Delinquency* 47:462–485.

Hart, B. 1996. Preface to K. Lobel (ed.), *Naming the Violence: Speaking Out Against Lesbian Battering*. Seattle: Seal.

Hart, C. 2013. "Pot Reform's Race Problem." *The Nation* (Nov. 18):17–18.

Hartjen, C. 1974. *Crime and Criminalization*. New York: Praeger.

Harvey, W. 1986. "Homicide Among Young Black Adults: Life in the Subculture of Exasperation." In D. Hawkins (eds.), *Homicide Among Black Americans*. Lanham: University Press of America.

Hayden, T. 2004. *Street Wars: Gangs and the Future of Violence*. New York: New Press.

Hazelwood, R., & J. Harpold. 1986. "Rape: The Dangers of Providing Confrontational Advice." *FBI Law Enforcement Bulletin* (June):1–5.

Head, W. 2001. "Fences and Fencing." In C. Bryant (ed.), *Encyclopedia of Criminology and Deviant Behavior*. New York: Brunner-Routledge.

Healy, W., & A. Bronner. 1936. *New Light on Delinquency and Its Treatment*. New Haven: Yale University Press.

Heaney, G. 1991. "The Reality of Guidelines Sentencing: No End to Disparity." *American Criminal Law Review* 28:161–232.

Hebert, H. 2010. "Execs Get Oil-Spill Grilling." *Wisconsin State Journal* (May 12):A12.

Heil, E. 2012. *Sex Slaves and Serfs: The Dynamics of Human Trafficking in a Small Florida Town*. Boulder, CO: First Forum.

Heilprin, J., & N. Winfield. 2014. "Hundreds Defrocked Under Benedict." *Wisconsin State Journal* (Jan. 18):A1, A6.

Helmer, J. 1975. *Drugs and Minority Oppression*. New York: Seabury.

Henry, S. 1978. *The Hidden Economy*. London: Martin Robertson.

Henry, S., & D. Milovanovic. 1994. "The Constitution of Constitutive Criminology: A Postmodern Approach." In D. Nelken (ed.), *The Futures of Criminology*. London: Sage.

Hepburn, J., & A. Harvey. 2007. "The Effect of the Threat of Legal Sanction on Program Retention and Completion: Is That Why They Stay in Drug Court?" *Crime & Delinquency* 53:255–280.

Heppler, J. 2014. "The Scourge of Sexual Assault in the U.S. Military." *The Lamron* (Mar. 27). www.thelamron.com.

Herbert, B. 2008. "Now's the Time to Confront Misogyny." *Wisconsin State Journal* (Jan. 19):A8.

Herbert, S. 1998. "Police Subculture Reconsidered." *Criminology* 36:343–369.

Herek, G., & K. Berrill (eds.). 1992. *Hate Crimes: Confronting Violence Against Lesbians and Gay Men*. Newbury Park, CA: Sage.

Herman, J. 1981. *Father-Daughter Incest*. Cambridge: Harvard University Press.

———. 1992. *Trauma and Recovery: The Aftermath of Violence, from Domestic Abuse to Political Terror*. New York: Basic.

Hernandez, B. 2005. "A Voice in the Chorus: Perspectives of Young Men of Color on Their Disabilities, Identities, and Peer-Mentors." *Disability & Society* 20:117–133.

Herrnstein, R. 1995. "Criminogenic Traits." In J. Wilson & J. Petersilia (eds.), *Crime*. San Francisco: Institute for Contemporary Studies.

Herrnstein, R., & C. Murray. 1994. *The Bell Curve: Intelligence and Class Structure in American Life*. New York: Free Press.

Hersh, S. 2004. *Chain of Command: The Road from 9/11 to Abu Ghraib*. New York: HarperCollins.

Heschel, A. 1962. *The Prophets*. Vol. 1. New York: Harper and Row.

Hickman, K. 2010. "Vietnam War; Gulf of Tonkin Incident." *Military History*. www.militaryhistory.about.com.

Hill, A. 1997. "Moon's Paradox." In E. Cose (ed.), *The Darden Dilemma*. New York: HarperPerennial.

Hindelang, M., T. Hirschi, & J. Weis. 1978. "Correlates of Delinquency: The Illusion of Discrepancy Between Self-Report and Official Measures." *American Sociological Review* 44:995–1014.

———. 1981. *Measuring Delinquency*. Beverly Hills, CA: Sage.

Hirschel, J., & I. Hutchison. 1992. "Female Spouse Abuse and the Police Response: The Charlotte, North Carolina, Experiment." *Journal of Criminal Law & Criminology* 83:73–119.

Hirschi, T. 1969. *Causes of Delinquency*. Berkeley: University of California Press.

Hirschi, T., & M. Hindelang. 1977. "Intelligence and Delinquency: A Revisionist Critique." *American Sociological Review* 43:571–587.

Hirschi, T., & R. Stark. 1969. "Hellfire and Delinquency." *Social Problems* 17:202–213.

Hochstetler, A., & N. Shover. 1997. "Street Crime, Labor Surplus, and Criminal Punishment, 1980–1990." *Social Problems* 44:358–368.

Hoffman, B. 1993. "Terrorism in the United States: Recent Trends and Future Prospects." In B. Schechterman & M. Slann (eds.), *Violence and Terrorism*. Guilford, CT: Dushkin.

Hofstader, R. 1959. *Social Darwinism in American Social Thought*. Boston: Beacon.

Holland, J. 2013. "Hundreds of Wall Street Execs Went to Prison During Law Fraud-Related Bank Crises" (Sept. 17). www.billmoyers.com.

Hollinger, R., & J. Clark. 1983. *Theft by Employees*. Lexington, MA: Lexington Books.

Holmes, M. 2000. "Minority Threat and Police Brutality: Determinants of Civil Rights Criminal Complaints in U.S. Municipalities." *Criminology* 38:343–367.

Holmes, M., et al. 1993. "Judges' Ethnicity and Minority Sentencing: Evidence Concerning Hispanics." *Social Science Quarterly* 74:496–506.

Horney, J. 1978. "Menstrual Cycles and Criminal Responsibility." *Law & Human Behavior* 2:25–36.

Horowitz, R. 1987. "Community Tolerance of Gang Violence." *Social Problems* 34:437–450.

Horwitz, J., & M. Virtanen. 2014. "Bank of America Agrees to $17B Settlement Plan." *Wisconsin State Journal* (Aug. 21):A12, A14.

Howell, D. 2013. "The Great Laissez-Faire Experiment: American Inequality and Growth from an International Perspective" (Dec. 4). www.americanprogress.org.

Howell, J. 1996. "Juvenile Transfers to the Criminal Justice System: State of the Art." *Law & Policy* 18:17–60.

Hubbs, K., & D. Klinger. 2004. *Impact Munitions Data Base of Use and Effect.* Washington, DC: US Department of Justice.

Huber, T. 2007. "Mining Reforms Not in Effect." *Wisconsin State Journal* (Aug. 8):A3.

———. 2011. "Officials: Mine Faked Safety Logs." *Wisconsin State Journal* (June 30):A9.

Huesmann, R., & L. Eron (eds.). 1986. *Television and the Aggressive Child: A Cross-National Comparison.* Hillsdale, NJ: Lawrence Erlbaum.

Huff, C. 1993. "Gangs in the United States." In A. Goldstein & C. Huff (eds.), *The Gang Intervention Handbook.* Champaign, IL: Research Press.

Huff, C., A. Rattner, & E. Sagarin. 1996. *Convicted but Innocent: Wrongful Conviction and Public Policy.* Thousand Oaks, CA: Sage.

Huff-Corzine, L., J. Corzine, & D. Moore. 1986. "Southern Exposure: Deciphering the South's Influence on Homicide Rates." *Social Forces* 64:906–924.

Huffington Post. 2010. "West Virginia Mine Explosion: Massey Energy Mine Had Scores of Safety Citations." (Apr. 6). www.huffingtonpost.com.

———. 2013. "Stop and Frisk Violated Rights of New Yorkers, Judge Rules" (Mar. 5). www.huffingtonpost.com.

Hughes, C., & A. Stevens. 2010. "What Can We Learn from the Portuguese Decriminalization of Illicit Drugs?" *British Journal of Criminology* 50:999–1022.

Huizinga, D., & D. Elliott 1987. "Juvenile Offenders: Prevalence, Offender Incidence, and Arrest Rates by Race." *Crime & Delinquency* 33:206–233.

Hundley, K., S. Martin, & C. Humburg. 2012. "Florida 'Stand Your Ground' Law Yields Some Shocking Outcomes Depending on How Law Is Applied." *Tampa Bay Times* (June 1). www.tampabaynews.com.

Hunt, G., S. Riegel, T. Morales, & D. Waldorf. 1993. "Changes in Prison Culture: Prison Gangs and the Case of the 'Pepsi Generation.'" *Social Problems* 40:398–409.

Hunt, J., & P. Manning. 1991. "The Social Context of Police Lying." *Symbolic Interaction* 14:51–70.

Hutchinson, E. 2010. "Arizona Dumped Racial Profiling Back on the Nation's Table." *Huffington Post* (May 4). www.huffingtonpost.com.

Inciardi, J. 1996. *Criminal Justice.* Fort Worth: Harcourt.

Inverarity, J., P. Lauderdale, & B. Feld. 1983. *Law and Society: Sociological Perspectives on Criminal Law.* Boston: Little, Brown.

Irwin, J. 1980. *Prisons in Turmoil.* Boston: Little, Brown.

Isikoff, M., & D. Corn. 2006. *Hubris: The Inside Story of Spin, Scandal, and the Selling of the Iraq War.* New York: Crown.

Island, D., & P. Letellier. 1991. *Men Who Beat the Men Who Love Them.* New York: Harrington Park.

Jackson, B. 1990. "The Savings and Loan Crisis." *CNN* documentary.

Jackson, S. 1978. "The Social Context of Rape: Sexual Scripts and Motivation." *Women's Studies International Quarterly* 1:27–38.

Jacobs, B., & R. Wright. 1999. "Stick-up, Street Culture, and Offender Motivation." *Criminology* 37:149–173.

Jacobs, D., & R. Helms. 1996. "Toward a Political Model of Incarceration: A Time-Series Examination of Multiple Explanations for Prison Admission Rates." *American Journal of Sociology* 102:323–357.

Jacobs, D., & R. O'Brien. 1998. "The Determinants of Deadly Force: A Structural Analysis of Police Violence." *American Journal of Sociology* 103:837–862.

Jacobs, J. 1977. *Stateville: The Penitentiary in Mass Society.* Chicago: University of Chicago Press.

Jacobs, J., & K. Potter. 1998. *Hate Crimes: Criminal Law and Identity Politics.* New York: Oxford University Press.

Jacobs, J., & H. Retsky. 1981. "Prison Guard." In R. Ross (ed.), *Prison Guard/Correctional Officers.* Oxford: Butterworth.

James, J., & J. Meyerding. 1977. "Early Sexual Experiences as a Factor in Prostitution." *Archives of Sexual Behavior* 77:31–42.

Jang, S., & B. Johnson. 2001. "Neighborhood Disorder, Individual Religiosity, and Adolescent Use of Illicit Drugs: A Test of Multilevel Hypotheses." *Criminology* 39:109–141.

Jang, S., & T. Thornberry. 1998. "Self-Esteem, Delinquent Peers, and Delinquency: A Test of the Self-Enhancement Thesis." *American Sociological Review* 63: 586–598.

Janofsky, M. 2003. "Man Who Shot Reagan Allowed to Visit Parents Unsupervised." *New York Times* (Dec. 18). www.nytimes.com.

Jaspin, E., & S. Montgomery. 1998. "Review Uncovers Thousands of Unsafe Meat Shipments." *Wisconsin State Journal* (Jan. 18):A7.

Jenkins, P. 1994. *Using Murder: The Social Construction of Serial Homicide.* New York: Aldine de Gruyer.

Jenness, V. 1999. "Managing Differences and Making Legislation: Social Movements and the Racialization, Sexualization, and Gendering of Federal Hate Crime Law in the US, 1985–1998." *Social Problems* 46:548–571.

Jensen, G., & M. Karpos. 1993. "Managing Rape: Exploratory Research on the Behavior of Rape Statistics." *Criminology* 31:363–385.

Jensen, R. 1995. "Pornographic Lives." *Violence Against Women* 1:32–54.

Joe, K., & M. Chesney-Lind. 1995. "Just Every Mother's Angel: An Analysis of Gender and Ethnic Variations in Youth Gang Membership." *Gender & Society* 9:408–430.

Johnson, B., A. Golum, & J. Fagen. 1995. "Careers in Crack, Drug Use, Drug Distribution, and Nondrug Crime." *Crime & Delinquency* 41:275–295.

Johnson, B., S. Jang, D. Larson, & S. Li. 2001. "Does Adolescent Religious Commitment Matter? A Reexamination of the Effects of Religiosity on Delinquency." *Journal of Research in Crime & Delinquency* 38:22–44.

Johnson, B., D. Larson, Spencer Li, & S. Jang. 2000. "Escaping from the Crime of Inner Cities: Church Attendance and Religious Salience Among Disadvantaged Youth." *Justice Quarterly* 17:377–391.

Johnson, D. 2008. "Racial Prejudice, Perceived Injustice, and the Black-White Gap in Punitive Attitudes." *Journal of Criminal Justice* 36:198–206.

Johnson, R. 2002. *Hard Time: Understanding and Reforming the Prison.* Belmont, CA: Wadsworth.

Johnston, D. (ed.). 2014. *Divided: The Perils of Our Growing Inequality.* New York: New Press.

Johnston, L., P. O'Malley, J. Bachman, & J. Schulenberg. 2007. *Monitoring the Future National Survey Results on Drug Use, 1975–2006.* Vol. 1. Bethesda, MD: National Institute on Drug Abuse.

Johnston, L., et al. 2013. *Monitoring the Future: National Results on Drug Use.* Rockville, MD: National Institute on Drug Abuse.

Jones, A. 1980. *Women Who Kill.* New York: Fawcett.

———. 1994. *Next Time She'll Be Dead: Battering and How to Stop It.* Boston: Beacon.

Jost, K. 1995. "The Jury System: The Issues." *CQ Researcher* 5:995–998.

Judis, J. 2002. "Strategic Disinformation." *American Prospect* (Sept.):12–13.

Juette, M., & R. Berger. 2008. *Wheelchair Warrior: Gangs, Disability, and Basketball.* Philadelphia: Temple University Press.

Jurik, N. 1985. "An Officer and a Lady: Organizational Barriers to Women Working As Correctional Officers in Men's Prisons." *Social Problems* 32:375–388.

Kalven, H., & H. Zeisel. 1971. *The American Jury.* Boston: Little, Brown.

Kaminer, W. 1999. "Taking Liberties: The New Assault on Freedom." *American Prospect* (Jan.–Feb.):33–40.

Kane, R. 2006. "On the Limits of Social Control: Structural Deterrence and the Policing of 'Suppressible' Crimes." *Justice Quarterly* 23:186–213.

Kaplan, H., S. Martin, & R. Johnson. 1986. "Self-Rejection and the Explanation of Deviance: Specification of the Structure Among Latent Constructs." *American Journal of Sociology* 92:384–411.

Kaplan, J. 1983. *The Hardest Drug: Heroin and Public Policy.* Chicago: University of Chicago Press.

Kappeler, V., & G. Potter. 2005. *The Mythology of Crime and Criminal Justice.* Long Grove, IL: Waveland.

Karmen, A. 2004. *Crime Victims: An Introduction to Victimology.* Belmont, CA: Wadsworth.

Katz, J. 1980. "The Social Movement Against White-Collar Crime." In E. Bittner & S. Messinger (eds.), *Criminology Review Yearbook.* Beverly Hills, CA: Sage.

———. 1988. *Seductions of Crime: Moral and Sensual Attractions in Doing Evil.* New York: Basic.

Katz, J., & W. Chambliss. 1995. "Biology and Crime." In J. Sheley (ed.), *Criminology.* Belmont, CA: Wadsworth.

Kauffman, K. 1988. *Prison Officers and Their World.* Cambridge: Harvard University Press.

Kelly, L. 1987. "The Continuum of Sexual Violence." In J. Hanmer & M. Maynard (eds.), *Women, Violence, and Social Control.* Atlantic Highlands, NJ: Humanities International.

———. 1993. "Pornography and Child Abuse." In C. Itzin (ed.), *Pornography: Women, Violence, and Civil Liberties.* New York: Oxford University Press.

Kennedy, J. 2003. "Drug Wars in Black and White." *Law & Contemporary Problems* 66:153–181.

Kennedy, R. 2004. *Crimes Against Nature: How George W. Bush and His Corporate Pals Are Plundering the Country and Hijacking Our Democracy.* New York: HarperCollins.

———. 2008. "Diebold and Max Cleland's Loss in Georgia." In M. Miller (ed.), *Loser Take All: Election Fraud and the Subversion of Democracy, 2000–2008.* Brooklyn: Ig.

Kent, S. 2010. "Killings of Police in U.S. Cities Since 1980: An Examination of Environmental and Political Explanations." *Homicide Studies* 14:3–23.

Kerr, J. 2003. "Envoy: Bush Manipulated Findings." *Wisconsin State Journal* (July 7):A9.

Killias, M., M. Aebi, & D. Ribeaud. 2000. "Learning Through Controlled Experiments: Community Service and Heroin Prescription in Switzerland." *Crime & Delinquency* 46:233–251.

King, M. 1963/1994. "Letter from a Birmingham Jail." In J. Bonsignore et al. (eds.), *Before the Law: An Introduction to the Legal Process.* Boston: Houghton Mifflin.

King, N. 1993. "Postconviction Review of Jury Discrimination: Measuring the Effects of Juror Race on Jury Decisions." *Michigan Law Review* 92:63–130.

Kinser, S. 2006. *Overthrow: America's Century of Regime Change, from Hawaii to Iraq.* New York: Times Books.

Kirschenbaum, C. 1991. "A Potential Landmark for Female Human Rights." *Ms.* (Sept.–Oct.):13.

Kissell, P., & P. Katsampes. 1980. "The Impact of Women Corrections Officers on the Functioning of Institutions Housing Male Inmates." *Journal of Offender Counseling Services & Rehabilitation* 4:213–231.

Kitsuse, J., & A. Cicourel. 1963. "A Note on the Uses of Official Statistics." *Social Problems* 11:131–139.

Kitwana, B. 2002. *The Hip Hop Generation: Young Blacks and the Crisis in African-American Culture.* New York: Basic.

Kleck, G., & T. Chiricos. 2002. "Unemployment and Property Crime: A Target-Specific Assessment of Opportunity and Motivation as Mediating Factors." *Criminology* 40:649–679.

Kleck, G., & S. Sayles. 1990. "Rape and Resistance." *Social Problems* 37:149–162.

Kleck, G., B. Sever, S. Li, & M. Gertz. 2005. "The Missing Link in Deterrence Research." *Criminology* 43:623–659.

Klein, M. 1971. *Street Gangs and Street Workers.* Englewood Cliffs, NJ: Prentice Hall.

Klein, N. 2007. *The Shock Doctrine: The Rise of Disaster Capitalism.* New York: Metropolitan.

Klofas, J., & R. Weisheit. 1987. "Guilty but Mentally Ill: Reform of the Insanity Defense in Illinois." *Justice Quarterly* 4:39–50.

Knapp Commission. 1972. *Knapp Commission Report on Police Corruption.* New York: Braziller.

Knudsen, D. 1992. *Child Maltreatment.* Dix Hills, NY: General Hall.

Kocieniewski, D., & R. Hanley. 2000. "Racial Profiling Routine, New Jersey Finds." *New York Times* (Nov. 27). www.nytimes.com.

Koss, M. 1988. "Hidden Rape: Sexual Aggression and Victimization in a National Sample of Students in Higher Education." In A. Burgess (ed.), *Rape and Sexual Assault II.* New York: Garland.

Krafka, C. 1985. "Sexually Explicit, Sexually Violent, and Violent Media: Effects of Multiple Naturalistic Exposures and Debriefing on Female Viewers." PhD diss., University of Wisconsin–Madison.

Kramer, J., & D. Steffensmeier. 1993. "Race and Imprisonment Decisions." *Sociological Quarterly* 34:357–376.

Kramer, R., & R. Michalowski. 1995. "The Iron Fist and the Velvet Tongue: Crime Control Policies in the Clinton Administration." *Social Justice* 22:87–100.

————. 2005. "War, Aggression, and State Crime: A Criminological Analysis of the Invasion and Occupation of Iraq." *British Journal of Criminology* 45:446–469.

Kraska, P., & L. Cubellis. 1997. "Militarizing Mayberry and Beyond: Making Sense of American Paramilitary Policing." *Justice Quarterly* 14:607–629.

Kraska, P., & V. Kappeler. 1995. "To Serve and Pursue: Exploring Police Sexual Violence Against Women." *Justice Quarterly* 12:85–111.

————. 1997. "Militarizing American Police: The Rise and Normalization of Paramilitary Units." *Social Problems* 44:1–18.

Krauss, C. 2013. "Judge Accepts BP's $4 Billion Criminal Settlement over Gulf Oil Spill." *New York Times* (Jan. 29). www.nytimes.com.

Krebs, C. 2006. "Inmate Factors Associated with HIV Transmission in Prison." *Criminology & Public Policy* 5:113–136.

Krisberg, B. 2005. *Juvenile Justice: Redeeming Our Children.* Thousand Oaks, CA: Sage.

Krisher, T. 2014. "Documents Detail Another Long-Delayed Recall by GM." *Wisconsin State Journal* (Apr. 20):A5.

Kritzer, H., & T. Uhlman. 1977. "Sisterhood in the Courtroom: Sex of Judge and Defendant in Criminal Case Disposition." *Social Science Journal* 14:77–88.

Krivo, L., & R. Peterson. 1996. "Extremely Disadvantaged Neighborhoods and Urban Crime." *Social Forces* 75:619–650.

Krohn, M. 2000. "Sources of Criminality: Control and Deterrence Theories." In J. Sheley (ed.), *Criminology.* Belmont, CA: Wadsworth.

Krohn, M., & J. Massey. 1980. "Social Control and Delinquent Behavior: An Examination of the Elements of the Social Bond." *Sociological Quarterly* 21:529–543.

Krohn, M., J. Ward, T. Thornberry, A. Lizotte, & R. Chu. 2011. "The Cascading Effects of Adolescent Gang Involvement Across the Life Course." *Criminology* 49:991–1028.

Kroll, M. 1991. *Chattahoochee Judicial District: Buckle of the Death Belt.* Washington, DC: Death Penalty Information Center.

Kruttschnitt, C., R. Gartner, & A. Miller. 2000. "Doing Her Own Time? Women's Responses to Prison in the Context of the Old and the New Penology." *Criminology* 3:681–717.

Kubrin, C. 2005. "Gangstas, Thugs, and Hustlas: Identity and the Code of the Street in Rap Music." *Social Problems* 52:360–378.

Kubrin, C., & R. Weitzer. 2003. "Retaliatory Homicide: Concentrated Disadvantage and Neighborhood Culture." *Social Problems* 50:157–180.

Kuhnhenn, J. 2013. "Obama Urges Faster Overhaul." *Wisconsin State Journal* (Aug. 20):A1, A9.

Kunzelman, M., M. Baker, & J. Donn. 2010. "Witness: BP Pushed on Well." *Wisconsin State Journal* (May 27):A1, A11.

Kunzelman, M., & J. McConnaughey. 2014. "Ruling Against BP Could Mean $18B in Fines." *Wisconsin State Journal* (Sept. 5):A1, A6.

Kurlychek, M., & B. Johnson. 2010. "Juvenility and Punishment: Sentencing Juveniles in Adult Criminal Court." *Criminology* 48:725–758.

Kutateladze, B., N. Andiloro, B. Johnson, & C. Spohn. 2014. "Cumulative Disadvantage: Examining Racial and Ethnic Disparity in Prosecution and Sentencing." *Criminology* 52:514–551.

Kuttner, R. 2003. "The Great Crash, Part II." *American Prospect* (June): 47–49.

Kyckelhahn, T. 2012. *State Corrections Expenditures, FY 1982–2010.* Washington, DC: US Department of Justice.

LaFree, G. 1980. "The Effect of Sexual Stratification by Race on Official Reactions to Rape." *American Sociological Review* 45:842–854.

———. 1989. *Rape and Criminal Justice: The Social Construction of Sexual Assault.* Belmont, CA: Wadsworth.

———. 1998. *Losing Legitimacy: Street Crime and the Decline of Social Institutions in America.* Boulder, CO: Westview.

LaFree, G., & K. Drass. 1996. "The Effect of Changes in Intraracial Income Inequality and Educational Attainment on Changes in Arrest Rates for African Americans and Whites, 1957 to 1990." *American Sociological Review* 61:614–634.

Lantigua, J. 2001. "How the GOP Gamed the System in Florida." *The Nation* (Apr. 30):11–17.

Larkin, R. 2007. *Comprehending Columbine.* Philadelphia: Temple University Press.

Laub, J., & R. Sampson. 1993. "Turning Points in the Life Course: Why Change Matters to the Study of Crime." *Criminology* 31:301–325.

Lauderback, D., J. Hansen, & D. Waldorf. 1992. "Sisters Are Doin' It for Themselves: A Black Female Gang in San Francisco." *Gang Journal* 1:57–72.

Lavoie, D. 2003. "$85 Million Payout Goes to Sex Abuse Victims." *Wisconsin State Journal* (Sept. 10):A3.

Law Center to Prevent Gun Violence. 2013. "'Stand Your Ground' Policy Summary" (July 18). http://martgunlaws.org.

Lawrence, R. 1998. *School Crime and Juvenile Justice.* New York: Oxford University Press.

Lawson, C. 1993. "Mother-Son Sexual Abuse: Rare or Underreported?" *Child Abuse & Neglect* 17:261–269.

Lederer, L. (ed.). 1980. *Take Back the Night: Women on Pornography.* New York: Morrow.

Lee, M. 2013a. "Let a Thousand Flowers Bloom." *The Nation* (Nov. 18):23–24, 26, 28.

———. 2013b. "Prescription: Cannabis." *The Nation* (Nov. 18):27.

Lee, M., & M. Ermann. 1999. "Pinto 'Madness' as a Flawed Landmark Narrative: An Organizational and Network Analysis." *Social Problems* 46:30–47.

Lee, M., R. Martinez, & R. Rosenfeld. 2001. "Does Immigration Increase Homicide? Negative Evidence from Three Border Cities." *Sociological Quarterly* 42:559–580.

Leland, J. 1998. "Savior of the Streets." *Newsweek* (June 1):20–25.

Leonard, W., & M. Weber. 1970. "Automakers and Dealers: A Study of Criminogenic Market Forces." *Law & Society Review* 4:407–424.

Leopold, L. 2009. *The Looting of America: How Wall Street's Game of Fantasy Finance Destroyed Our Jobs, Pensions, and Prosperity.* White River Junction, VT: Chelsea Green.

Leslie, J. 2010. "What's Killing the Babies of Kettleman City?" *Mother Jones* (July–Aug.): 45–54.

Letellier, P. 1996. "Twin Epidemics: Domestic Violence and HIV Infection Among Gay and Bisexual Men." In C. Renzetti & C. Miley (eds.), *Violence in Gay and Lesbian Domestic Relationships.* New York: Harrington Park.

Levin, B. 2002. "Cyberhate: A Legal and Historical Analysis of Extremists' Use of Computer Networks in America." *American Behavioral Scientist* 45:958–988.

Levin, J., & J. McDevitt. 1999. "Hate Crimes." *Encyclopedia of Violence, Peace, and Conflict.* San Diego: Academic Press.

Levine, H. 2012. "The Secret of Global Drug Prohibition: Its Uses and Crises." In P. Adler, P. Adler, & P. O'Brien (eds.), *Drugs and the American Dream*. West Sussex: Wiley-Blackwell.

———. 2013. "The Scandal of Racist Marijuana Arrests." *The Nation* (Nov. 18):18–22.

Levitt, J. 2014. "A Comprehensive Investigation of Voter Impersonation Finds 31 Credible Incidents out of One Billion Ballots Cast." *Washington Post* (Aug. 6). www.washingtonpost.com.

Levitt, S. 1999. "The Limited Role of Changing Age Structure in Explaining Aggregate Crime Rates." *Criminology* 37:581–597.

Levitt, S., & S. Dubner. 2005. *Freakonomics: A Rogue Economist Explores the Hidden Side of Everything*. New York: Morrow.

Levrant, S., F. Cullen, B. Fulton, & C. Thomas. 1999. "Reconsidering Restorative Justice: The Corruption of Benevolence Revisited?" *Crime & Delinquency* 45:3–27.

Lew, M. 1990. *Victims No Longer: The Classic Guide for Men Recovering from Sexual Child Abuse*. New York: Harper and Row.

Lilly, J., R. Ball, G. Curry, & J. McMullen. 1993. "Electronic Monitoring of the Drunk Driver: A Seven-Year Study of the Home Confinement Alternative." *Crime & Delinquency* 42:491–516.

Lin, R., & B. Boxall. 2010. "Technician: Key Safety Systems Disabled." *Wisconsin State Journal* (July 24):A10.

Lipton, D. 1996. "Prison-Based Therapeutic Communities: Their Success with Drug-Abusing Offenders." *National Institute of Justice Journal* (Feb.):12–30.

Lipton, D., R. Martinson, & J. Wilks. 1975. *The Effectiveness of Correctional Treatment: A Survey of Treatment Evaluation Studies*. New York: Praeger.

Lock, E., J. Timberlake, & T. Arcury. 2002. "Battle Fatigue: Is Public Support Waning for 'War'-Centered Drug Control Strategies?" *Crime & Delinquency* 48:380–398.

Lockwood, D. 1977. "Living in Protection." In H. Toch (ed.), *Living in Prison: The Ecology of Survival*. New York: Free Press.

Logan, J., & B. Stults. 1999. "Racial Differences in Exposure to Crime: The City and Suburbs of Cleveland in 1990." *Criminology* 37:251–276.

Lombardo, L. 1988. "Alleviating Inmate Stress: Contributions from Correctional Officers." In R. Johnson & H. Toch (eds.), *The Pains of Imprisonment*. Prospect Heights, IL: Waveland.

———. 1997. "Guards Imprisoned: Correctional Officers at Work." In J. Marquart & J. Sorenson (eds.), *Correctional Contexts*. Los Angeles: Roxbury.

Lombroso, C. 1876. *L'Uomo Delinquente (The Criminal Man)*. Milan: Hoepli.

Lombroso, C., & W. Ferrero. 1897/1958. *The Female Offender*. New York: Philosophical Library.

London, R. 2011. *Crime, Punishment, and Restorative Justice*. Boulder, CO: First Forum.

Longshore, D., E. Chang, S. Hsieh, & N. Messina. 2004. "Self-Control and Social Bonds: A Combined Control Perspective on Deviance." *Crime & Delinquency* 50:542–564.

Lorber, J. 1997. "'Night to His Day': The Social Construction of Gender." In L. Richardson, V. Taylor, & N. Whittier (eds.), *Feminist Frontiers*. New York: McGraw-Hill.

———. 2012. *Gender Inequality: Feminist Theories and Politics*. New York: Oxford University Press.

Lori. 2011. "Domestic Violence: Still Not Chic, Artistic, or Cutting Edge." *Feministing* (Aug. 31). www.feministing.com.

Lott, J. 1998. *More Guns, Less Crime: Understanding Crime and Gun Control Laws.* Chicago: University of Chicago Press.

Lowney, K., & J. Best. 1995. "Stalking Strangers and Lovers: Changing Media Typifications of a New Crime Problem." In J. Best (ed.), *Images of Issues: Typifying Contemporary Social Problems.* New York: Aldine de Gruyter.

Lowy, J., & T. Krisher. 2014. "GM Fined $35M over Fatal Defect." *Wisconsin State Journal* (May 17):A1, A6.

Lumb, R., & P. Friday. 1997. "Impact of Pepper Spray Availability on Police Office Use-of-Force Decisions." *Policing: An International Journal of Police Strategy and Management* 20:136–148.

Lynam, D., et al. 1999. "Project DARE: No Effects at 10-Year Follow-Up." *Journal of Consulting and Clinical Psychology* 67:590–593.

Lynch, M. 1996. "Class, Race, Gender, and Criminology: Structured Choices and the Life Course." In M. Schwartz & D. Milovanovic (eds.), *Race, Gender, and Class in Criminology.* New York: Garland.

Lyons, C., & B. Pettit. 2011. "Compounded Disadvantage: Race, Incarceration, and Wage Growth." *Social Problems* 58:257–280.

Maas, P. 1973. *Serpico.* New York: Viking.

MacCoun, R., & P. Reuter. 1997. "Interpreting Dutch Cannabis Policy: Reasoning by Analogy in the Legalization Debate." *Science* 278:47–52.

———. 2001. *Drug War Heresies: Learning from Other Vices, Times, and Places.* New York: Cambridge University Press.

MacDonald, A. 1980. *The Turner Diaries.* Arlington, VA: National Alliance.

MacDonald, J. 2002. "The Effectiveness of Community Policing in Reducing Urban Violence." *Crime & Delinquency* 48:592–618.

MacKenzie, D., R. Brame, D. McDowall, & C. Souryal. 1995. "Boot Camp Prisons and Recidivism in Eight States." *Criminology* 33:327–357.

MacKenzie, D., & H. Donaldson. 1996. "Boot Camp for Women Offenders." *Criminal Justice Review* 21:21–43.

MacKenzie, D., & C. Souryal. 1995. "Inmates' Attitude Change During Incarceration: A Comparison of Boot Camp with Traditional Prison." *Justice Quarterly* 112:325–353.

MacKinnon, C. 1983. "Feminism, Marxism, Method, and the State: Toward Feminist Jurisprudence." *Signs* 8:635–658.

———. 1986. "Pornography as Sex Discrimination." *Law & Inequality* 4:38–49.

Madigan, N. 2003. "Burning of Hummers a Message?" *Wisconsin State Journal* (Aug. 31):A3.

Madrick, J. 2011. *Age of Greed: The Triumph of Finance and the Decline of America.* New York: Knopf.

Maguin, E., & R. Loeber. 1996. "Academic Performance and Delinquency." In M. Tonry (ed.), *Crime and Justice.* Chicago: University of Chicago Press.

Maher, K. 2009. "Black Lung on Rise in Mines, Reversing Trend." *Wall Street Journal* (Dec. 15). www.wsj.com.

Maher, L., & R. Curtis. 1992. "Women on the Edge of Crime: Crack Cocaine and the Changing Contexts of Street-Level Sex Work in New York City." *Crime, Law, & Social Change* 18:221–258.

Maher, L., & K. Daly. 1996. "Women in the Street-Level Drug Economy: Continuity or Change?" *Criminology* 34:465–491.

Malamuth, N. 1985. "The Mass Media and Aggression Against Women: Research Findings and Prevention." In A. Burgess (ed.), *Rape and Sexual Assault.* New York: Garland.

Malamuth, N., & E. Donnerstein (eds.). 1984. *Pornography and Sexual Aggression.* New York: Academic.

Mallett, C. 2013. *Linking Disorders to Delinquency: Treating High-Risk Youth in the Juvenile Justice System.* Boulder, CO: First Forum.

Mann, C. 1993. *Unequal Justice: A Question of Color.* Bloomington: Indiana University Press.

———. 1996. *When Women Kill.* Albany: State University of New York Press.

Manza, J., & C. Uggen. 2005. *Locked Out: Felon Disenfranchisement and American Democracy.* New York: Oxford University Press.

Marcum, C., & T. Castle (eds.). 2014. *Sex in Prison: Myths and Realities.* Boulder, CO: Lynne Rienner.

Margolin, S., & J. Schor. 1990. *The End of the Golden Age.* Oxford, UK: Clarendon.

Markowitz, F. 2006. "Psychiatric Hospital Capacity, Homelessness, and Crime and Arrest Rates." *Criminology* 44:45–72.

Marolda, E. 2010. "Tonkin Gulf Crisis, August 1964." *Naval Historical Center.* www.history.navy.mil.

Martin, G. 2003. *Understanding Terrorism: Challenges, Perspectives, and Issues.* Thousand Oaks, CA: Sage.

Martin, P., & R. Hummer. 1989. "Fraternities and Rape on Campus." *Gender & Society* 3:457–473.

Martin, S. 1980. *"Breaking and Entering": Policewomen on Patrol.* Berkeley: University of California Press.

———. 1994. "'Outsider Within' the Station House: The Impact of Race and Gender on Black Women Police." *Social Problems* 41:383–400.

———. 1995. "'A Cross-Burning Is Not Just an Arson': Police Social Construction of Hate Crimes in Baltimore." *Criminology* 33:303–326.

Martin, S., & N. Jurik. 1996. *Doing Justice, Doing Gender: Women in Law and Criminal Justice Occupations.* Thousand Oaks, CA: Sage.

Martinez, R. 1996. "Latinos and Lethal Violence: The Impact of Poverty and Inequality." *Social Problems* 43:131–146.

Martinez, R., J. Stowell, & M. Lee. 2010. "Immigration and Crime in an Era of Transformation: A Longitudinal Analysis of Homicides in San Diego Neighborhoods, 1980–2000." *Criminology* 48:797–829.

Martinez, R., & A. Valenzuela (eds.). 2006. *Immigration and Crime: Race, Ethnicity, and Violence.* New York: New York University Press.

Martz, L. 1990. "A Dirty Drug Secret." *Newsweek* (Feb. 19):74, 77.

Maruschak, L. 2008. *Medical Problems of Prisoners.* Washington, DC: US Department of Justice.

Marx, G. 1981. "Ironies of Social Control: Authorities as Contributors to Deviance Through Escalation, Non-Enforcement, and Covert Facilitation." *Social Problems* 28:221–246.

Masci, D., & P. Marshall. 2003. "Civil Liberties and the War Against Terrorism." In M. Williams (ed.), *The Terrorist Attack on America.* Farmington Hills, MI: Greenhaven Press.

Massey, D., & N. Denton. 1993. *American Apartheid: Segregation and the Making of the Underclass.* Cambridge: Harvard University Press.

Matthews, N. 1989. "Surmounting a Legacy: The Expansion of Racial Diversity in a Local Anti-Rape Movement." *Gender & Society* 3:518–532.

Matza, D. 1964. *Delinquency and Drift.* New York: Wiley.

Matza, D., & G. Sykes. 1961. "Juvenile Delinquency and Subterranean Values." *American Sociological Review* 26:712–719.

Mauer, M. 1999. *Race to Incarcerate.* New York: New Press.

Maxson, C. 2006. "Gang Members on the Move." In A. Egley et al. (eds.), *The Modern Gang Reader*. Los Angeles: Roxbury.

Maxwell, C., J. Garner, & J. Fagan. 2002. "The Preventive Effects of Arrest on Intimate Partner Violence: Research, Policy, and Theory." *Criminology & Public Policy* 2:51–80.

Mayer, J. 2009. *The Dark Side: The Inside Story of How the War on Terror Turned into a War on American Ideals*. New York: Anchor.

———. 2012. "The Voter-Fraud Myth." *New Yorker* (Oct. 29). www.newyorker.com.

McBride, D., et al. 2009. "Reflections on Drug Policy." *Journal of Drug Issues* 39:71–88.

McCall, N. 1994. *Makes Me Wanna Holler: A Young Black Man in America*. New York: Vintage.

McCarthy, B., J. Hagan, & M. Martin. 2002. "In and out of Harm's Way: Violent Victimization and the Social Capital of Street Families." *Criminology* 40:831–865.

McClain, D. 2014. "It's 1963 Again." *The Nation* (Dec. 29):3.

McClam, E. 2003. "Judge Sets Date for Martha Stewart." *Wisconsin State Journal* (June 20):D10.

McCleary, R., B. Nienstedt, & J. Erven. 1982. "*Uniform Crime Reports* as Organizational Outcomes: Three Time Series Experiments." *Social Problems* 29:361–372.

McClellan, D. 1994. "Disparity in the Discipline of Male and Female Inmates in Texas Prisons." *Women & Criminal Justice* 5:71–97.

McCorkle, R. 1992. "Personal Reactions to Violence in Prison." *Criminal Justice & Behavior* 19:160–173.

———. 1995. "Correctional Boot Camps and Change in Attitude: Is All This Shouting Necessary?" *Justice Quarterly* 12:365–375.

McCorkle, R., & T. Miethe. 2002. *Panic: The Social Construction of the Street Gang Problem*. Upper Saddle River, NJ: Prentice Hall.

McCormack, W. 2001. "Deconstructing the Election: Foucault, Derrida, and GOP Strategy." *The Nation* (Mar. 26):25–34.

McCormick, A. 1977. "Rule Enforcement and Moral Indignation: Some Observations on the Effects of Criminal Antitrust Convictions upon Societal Reaction Processes." *Social Problems* 25:30–39.

McCormick, J. 1998. "The Wrongly Convicted." *Newsweek* (Nov. 9):64.

McCoy, A. 2003. *The Politics of Heroin: CIA Complicity in the Global Drug Trade*. Chicago: Lawrence Hill.

———. 2006. *A Question of Torture: CIA Interrogation, from the Cold War to the War on Terror*. New York: Metropolitan.

McDermott, J. 1979. *Rape Victimization in Twenty-Six American Cities*. Washington, DC: US Government Printing Office.

McGahey, R. 1986. "Economic Conditions, Neighborhood Organization, and Urban Crime." In A. Reiss & M. Tonry (eds.), *Communities and Crime*. Chicago: University of Chicago Press.

McGovern, C. 2013. "The Graying of Our Incarceration Nation." *Truthout* (Dec. 27). www.truth-out.org.

McIntyre, L. 1987. *The Public Defender: The Practice of Law in the Shadows of Repute*. Chicago: University of Chicago Press.

McLean, B., & P. Elkind. 2004. *The Smartest Guys in the Room: The Amazing Rise and Scandalous Fall of Enron*. New York: Portfolio.

Mears, B. 2003. "Supreme Court Upholds Long Sentences Under Three-Strikes-You're-Out Law" (Mar. 5). www.cnn.com.

———. 2008. "Child Rapists Can't Be Executed: Supreme Court Rules" (June 25). www.cnn.com.

Mears, D., & A. Bhati. 2006. "No Community Is an Island: The Effects of Resource Deprivation on Urban Violence in Spatially and Socially Proximate Communities." *Criminology* 44:509–547.

Medea, A., & K. Thompson. 1974. *Against Rape*. New York: Farrar, Straus, and Giroux.

Meeks, K. 2000. *Driving While Black: Highways, Shopping Malls, Taxicabs, Sidewalks—How to Fight Back If You Are a Victim of Racial Profiling*. New York: Broadway.

Meier, R., & G. Geis. 1997. *Victimless Crime? Prostitution, Drugs, Homosexuality, Abortion*. Los Angeles: Roxbury.

Melde, C., & F. Esbensen. 2011. "Gang Membership as a Turning Point in the Life Course." *Criminology* 49:513–547.

Melekian, B. 1990. "Police and the Homeless." *FBI Law Enforcement Bulletin* (Nov.):1–7.

Melton, H. 2000. "Stalking: A Review of the Literature and Direction for the Future." *Criminal Justice Review* 25:246–262.

Mendoza, M. 2006. "Military Recruiters in Sex Cases." *Wisconsin State Journal* (Aug. 21):A3.

Merton, R. 1938. "Social Structure and Anomie." *American Sociological Review* 3:672–682.

———. 1964. "Anomie, Anomia, and Social Interaction." In M. Clinard (ed.), *Anomie and Deviant Behavior*. New York: Free Press.

———. 1968. *Social Theory and Social Structure*. New York: Free Press.

Messerschmidt, J. 1993. *Masculinities and Crime: Critique and Reconceptualization of Theory*. Lanham: Rowman and Littlefield.

———. 1997. *Crime as Structured Action: Gender, Race, Class, and Crime in the Making*. Thousand Oaks, CA: Sage.

Messner, S. 1986. "Television Violence and Violent Crime: An Aggregate Analysis." *Social Problems* 33:218–235.

———. 1989. "Economic Discrimination and Homicide Rates: Further Evidence on the Cost of Inequality." *American Sociological Review* 54:597–611.

Messner, S., & R. Rosenfeld. 2001. *Crime and the American Dream*. Belmont, CA: Wadsworth.

Metraux, S., & D. Culhane. 2006. "Recent Incarceration History Among a Sheltered Homeless Population." *Crime & Delinquency* 52:504–517.

Michalowski, R. 1985. *Order, Law, and Crime: An Introduction to Criminology*. New York: Random.

Michalowski, R., & S. Carlson. 1999. "Unemployment, Imprisonment, and Social Structures of Accumulation: Historical Contingency in the Rusche-Kirchheimer Hypothesis." *Criminology* 37:217–248.

Mieczkowski, T. 1994. "The Experiences of Women Who Sell Crack: Some Descriptive Data from the Detroit Crack Ethnography Project." *Journal of Drug Issues* 24:227–248.

Miethe, T., & R. McCorkle. 1998. *Crime Profiles: The Anatomy of Dangerous Persons, Places, and Situations*. Los Angeles: Roxbury.

Miethe, T., & C. Moore. 1986. "Racial Differences in Criminal Processing: The Consequences of Model Selection on Conclusions About Differential Treatment." *Sociological Quarterly* 27:217–237.

Mignon, S., & W. Holmes. 1995. "Police Response to Mandatory Arrest Laws." *Crime & Delinquency* 41:430–442.

Miller, A. (ed.). 2005. *What Went Wrong in Ohio: The Conyers Report on the 2004 Presidential Election*. Chicago: Academy Chicago.

Miller, E. 1986. *Street Woman: The Illegal Work of Underclass Women*. Philadelphia: Temple University Press.

Miller, E., K. Romenesko, & L. Wondolkowski. 1993. "The United States." In N. Davis (ed.), *Prostitution: An International Handbook on Trends, Problems, and Policies*. Westport: Greenwood.

Miller, J. 1998. "Up It Up: Gender and the Accomplishment of Street Robbery." *Criminology* 36:37–65.

Miller, J., & R. Brunson. 2000. "Gender Dynamics in Youth Gangs: A Comparison of Males' and Females' Accounts." *Justice Quarterly* 17:419–448.

Miller, J., & D. Lynam. 2001. "Structural Models of Personality and Their Relation to Antisocial Behavior: A Meta-Analytic Review." *Criminology* 39:765–795.

Miller, M. 1974. *The Breaking of a President*. Vol. 4. City of Industry, CA: Therapy Productions.

Miller, M. 2005. *Fooled Again: How the Right Stole the 2004 Election and Why They'll Steal the Next One Too (Unless We Stop Them)*. New York: Basic.

Miller, S. 1993. "Arrest Policies for Domestic Violence and Their Implications for Battered Women." In R. Muraskin & T. Alleman (eds.), *It's a Crime: Women and Justice*. Englewood Cliffs, NJ: Prentice Hall.

Miller, W. 1973. "Ideology and Criminal Justice Policy: Some Current Issues." *Journal of Criminal Law & Criminology* 64:141–162.

———. 1980. "Gangs, Groups, and Serious Youth Crime." In D. Shichor & D. Kelly (eds.), *Critical Issues in Juvenile Delinquency*. Lexington, MA: Lexington Books.

Mills, C. 1959. *The Sociological Imagination*. New York: Oxford University Press.

Milwaukee Journal. 1994a. "Clinton Vows to Fight Repeal of Crime Bill" (Dec. 21):A3.

———. 1994b. "The Crime Bill" (Aug. 26):A3.

Minkowitz, D. 1999. "Love and Hate in Laramie." *The Nation* (July 12). www.thenation.com.

Minnite, L. 2010. *The Myth of Voter Fraud*. Ithaca: Cornell University Press.

Minor, W. 1984. "Neutralization as a Hardening Process: Considerations in the Modeling of Change." *Social Forces* 62:995–1019.

Mintz, M. 1985. *At Any Cost: Corporate Greed, Women, and the Dalkon Shield*. New York: Pantheon.

Moffitt, T., & A. Caspi. 2006. "Evidence from Behavioral Genetics for Environmental Contributions to Antisocial Conduct." In P. Wikström & R. Sampson (eds.), *The Explanation of Crime*. New York: Cambridge University Press.

Mohai, P., & R. Saha. 2007. "Racial Inequality in the Distribution of Hazardous Waste: A National-Level Reassessment." *Social Problems* 54:343–370.

Mohamed, A., & E. Fritsvold. 2010. *Dorm Room Dealers: Drugs and the Privileges of Race and Class*. Boulder, CO: Lynne Rienner.

Monitoring the Future. 2013. "Data Tables and Figures." www.monitoringthefuture.org.

Moore, A. 1997. "Intimate Violence: Does Socioeconomic Status Matter?" In A. Cardarelli (ed.), *Violence Between Intimate Partners*. Boston: Allyn and Bacon.

Moore, D. 2008. "Because Jeb Said So: What Really Happened on Election Night in Florida." In M. Miller (ed.), *Loser Take All: Election Fraud and the Subversion of Democracy, 2000–2008*. Brooklyn: Ig.

Moore, J. 1991. *Going Down to the Barrio*. Philadelphia: Temple University Press.

Moore, J., & J. Hagedorn. 1996. "What Happens to Girls in the Gang?" In C. Huff (ed.), *Gangs in America*. Thousand Oaks, CA: Sage.

Moore, J., D. Vigil, & R. Garcia. 1983. "Residence and Territoriality in Chicano Gangs." *Social Problems* 31:182–194.

Morash, M., & M. Chesney-Lind. 1991. "A Reformulation and Partial Test of the Power Control Theory of Delinquency." *Justice Quarterly* 8:347–377.

Morash, M., & L. Rucker. 1990. "A Critical Look at the Idea of Boot Camps as a Correctional Reform." *Crime & Delinquency* 36:204–222.

Morganthau, T. 1986. "Kids and Cocaine." *Newsweek* (Mar. 17):58–65.

Morgenson, G. 2004. "Suit Accuses Halliburton of Fraud in Accounting." *New York Times* (Aug. 6). www.nytimes.com.

Morris, K., & R. Morris. 2006. "Disability and Juvenile Delinquency: Issues and Trends." *Disability & Society* 21:613–627.

Morrison, C. 2010. "Gulf Oil Spill: Who's to Blame? BP, Halliburton, and the Feds Are All Implicated." *BNET* (May 3). www.industry.bnet.com.

Mosher, C., T. Miethe, & D. Phillips. 2002. *The Mismeasure of Crime.* Thousand Oaks, CA: Sage.

Moss, M. 2009. "E. Coli Path Shows Flaws in Beef Inspection." *New York Times* (Oct. 4). www.nytimes.com.

Moyers, B. 1988. *The Secret Government: The Constitution in Crisis.* Cabin John, MD: Seven Locks.

———. 1991. "Circle of Recovery." *PBS* documentary.

———. 2006. "Capitol Crimes." *PBS* documentary.

Mullins, C. 2006. "Bridgestone-Firestone, Ford, and the NHTSA." In R. Michalowski & R. Kramer (eds.), *State-Corporate Crime: Wrongdoing at the Intersection of Business and Government.* New Brunswick, NJ: Rutgers University Press.

Murphy, B. 2014. "Does Anyone Really Impersonate Another Voter?" *Isthmus* (May 16):7.

Murphy, T. 2013. "Revenge of the Swamp." *Mother Jones* (Sept.–Oct.):47–50.

Musto, D. 1999. *The American Disease: Origins of Narcotic Control.* New York: Oxford University Press.

Myers, D. 1997. "Racial Rioting in the 1960s: An Event History Analysis of Local Conditions." *American Sociological Review* 62:94–112.

Myers, M. 2000. "The Social World of America's Courts." In J. Sheley (ed.), *Criminology.* Belmont, CA: Wadsworth.

Nader, R. 1965. *Unsafe at Any Speed: The Designed-In Dangers of the American Automobile.* New York: Grossman.

National Organization for the Reform of Marijuana Laws. 2014. "States That Have Decriminalized." www.norml.org.

National Registry of Exonerations. 2015. "Exonerations by Year: DNA and Non-DNA." www.law.umich.edu.

Naughton, K. 2000. "Spinning out of Control." *Newsweek* (Sept. 11):58.

Nelsen, C., J. Corzine, & L. Huff-Corzine. 1994. "The Violent West Reexamined: A Research Note on Regional Homicide Rates." *Criminology* 32:149–161.

Nelson, A., & P. Oliver. 1998. "Gender and the Construction of Consent in Child-Adult Sexual Contact." *Gender & Society* 12:554–577.

Nelson, J. 1994. "A Dollar or a Day: Sentencing Misdemeanants in New York State." *Journal of Criminal Justice* 31:183–201.

Nelson, M., R. Chase, & L. DePalma. 2013. *Making Sense of DNA Backlogs, 2012: Myths vs. Reality.* Washington, DC: National Institute of Justice.

Neubauer, D. 2001. *America's Courts and the Criminal Justice System.* Belmont, CA: Wadsworth.

Nevin, R. 2000. "How Lead Exposure Relates to Temporal Changes in IQ, Violent Crime, and Unwed Pregnancy." *Environmental Research* 83:1–22.

Newman, D. 2000. *Sociology: Exploring the Architecture of Everyday Life*. Thousand Oaks, CA: Pine Forge.

Newman, G. 1993. "Batman and Justice: The True Story." *Humanity & Society* 17:261–274.

Newman, O. 1972. *Defensible Space: Crime Prevention Through Urban Design*. New York: Macmillan.

NewsInferno. 2007. "Vioxx Lawsuit Settlement Could Rank Among the Largest Defective Drug Settlements" (Nov. 12). www.newsinferno.com.

NewsMax. 2007. "Fred Thompson Raps 'Open Border' Immigration." www.news max.com.

Nilson, C., & T. Burke. 2002. "Environmental Extremists and the Eco-Terrorism Movement." *ACJS Today* (Jan.–Feb.):1–6.

Norton, M., & D. Ariely. 2011. "Building a Better America—One Wealth Quintile at a Time." *Perspectives on Psychological Science* 6:9–12.

O'Brien, Patrick K. 2013. "Medical Marijuana and Social Control: Escaping Criminalization and Embracing Medicalization." *Deviant Behavior* 34:423–443.

O'Conner, T., J. Duncan, & F. Quilard. 2006. "Criminology and Religion: The Shape of an Authentic Dialogue." *Criminology & Public Policy* 5:559–570.

Ogle, R., D. Maier-Katkin, & T. Bernard. 1995. "A Theory of Homicidal Behavior Among Women." *Criminology* 33:173–193.

Oliphant, J. 2008. "Court Slices Exxon Valdez Damage Award." *Baltimore Sun* (June 28). www.weblogs.baltimoresun.com.

Orcutt, J., & J. Turner. 1993. "Shocking Numbers and Graphic Accounts: Quantified Images of Drug Problems in Print Media." *Social Problems* 40:190–212.

Orenstein, P. 1994. *School Girls: Young Women, Self-Esteem, and the Confidence Gap*. New York: Doubleday.

Osbun, L., & P. Rode. 1984. "Prosecuting Juveniles As Adults: The Quest for 'Objective' Decisions." *Criminology* 22:187–202.

O'Shea, K. 1999. *Women and the Death Penalty in the United States, 1900–1998*. Westport: Praeger.

Ostrander, R. 2008. "When Identities Collide: Masculinity, Disability, and Race." *Disability & Society* 23:585–597.

Owen, B. 1985. "Race and Gender Relations Among Prison Workers." *Crime & Delinquency* 31:147–159.

Packer, H. 1964. "Two Models of the Criminal Process." *University of Pennsylvania Law Review* 113:1–68.

Packman, D. 2011. *National Police Misconduct Reporting Project*. www.police misconduct.net.

Padilla, F. 1992. *The Gang as an American Enterprise*. New Brunswick, NJ: Rutgers University Press.

Pagelow, M. 1984. *Family Violence*. New York: Praeger.

Pager, D. 2003. "The Mark of a Criminal Record." *American Journal of Sociology* 108:937–975.

Palast, G. 2003. *The Best Democracy Money Can Buy: The Truth About Corporate Cons, Globalization, and High-Finance Fraudsters*. New York: Plume.

Palen, J. 2005. *The Urban World*. New York: McGraw-Hill.

Panwala, A. 2002. "The Failure of Local and Federal Prosecutors to Curb Police Brutality." *Fordham Law Review* 30:639–662.

Parenti, C. 2009. "Zombie Nuke Plants." *The Nation* (Dec. 7):26–31.

———. 2011. "Hiroshima to Fukushima." *The Nation* (Apr. 4):6–9.

Parker, K., M. Dewees, & M. Radelet. 2001. "Racial Bias and the Conviction of the Innocent." In S. Westervelt & J. Humphrey (eds.), *Wrongly Convicted*. New Brunswick, NJ: Rutgers University Press.

Parker, R. 1989. "Poverty, Subculture of Violence, and Type of Homicide." *Social Forces* 67:983–1007.

Parsons, N. 2014. *Meth Mania: A History of Methamphetamine*. Boulder, CO: Lynne Rienner.

Parsons, T. 1951. *The Social System*. New York: Free Press.

Passas, N. 1990. "Anomie and Corporate Deviance." *Contemporary Crises* 14:157–178.

Pastore, A., & K. Maguire. 1998. *Sourcebook of Criminal Justice Statistics*. Washington, DC: US Department of Justice.

Pate, A., & E. Hamilton. 1992. "Formal and Informal Deterrents to Domestic Violence: The Dade County Spouse Assault Experiment." *American Sociological Review* 57:691–697.

Paternoster, R. 1987. "The Deterrent Effect of the Perceived Certainty and Severity of Punishment: A Review of the Evidence and Issues." *Justice Quarterly* 4:173–217.

———. 1989. "Absolute and Restrictive Deterrence in a Panel of Youth: Explaining the Onset, Persistence/Desistance, and Frequency of Delinquent Offending." *Social Problems* 36:289–309.

Paternoster, R., & R. Triplett. 1988. "Disaggregating Self-Reported Delinquency and Its Implications for Theory." *Criminology* 26:591–625.

Pattavina, A., et al. 2007. "Comparison of Police Response to Heterosexual Versus Same-Sex Intimate Partner Violence." *Violence Against Women* 13:374–394.

Patterson, R., & M. Stouthamer-Loeber. 1984. "The Correlation of Family Management Practices and Delinquency." *Child Development* 55:1299–1307.

Pattillo, M. 1998. "Sweet Mothers and Gangbangers: Managing Crime in a Black Middle-Class Neighborhood." *Social Forces* 76:747–774.

Pearson, F., D. Lipton, C. Cleland, & D. Yee. 2002. "The Effects of Behavioral/Cognitive Programs on Recidivism." *Crime & Delinquency* 48:476–496.

Pearson, P. 1997. *When She Was Bad: Violent Women and the Myth of Innocence*. New York: Viking.

———. 1998. "Discrimination on Death Row." *New York Times* (Jan. 13):A19.

Pelka, F. 1995. "Raped: A Male Survivor Breaks His Silence." In P. Searles & R. Berger (eds.), *Rape and Society*. Boulder, CO: Westview.

Pepinsky, H. 1999. "Peacemaking Primer." In B. Arrigio (ed.), *Social Justice/Criminal Justice*. Belmont, CA: Wadsworth.

Pepinsky, H., & R. Quinney (eds.). 1991. *Criminology as Peacemaking*. Bloomington: Indiana University Press.

Perry, S., & J. Dawson. 1985. *Nightmare: Women and the Dalkon Shield*. New York: Macmillan.

Petersilia, J. 2003a. "Prisoner Reentry and Criminological Knowledge." *The Criminologist* (Mar.–Apr.):1–5.

———. 2003b. *When Prisoners Come Home: Parole and Prisoner Reentry*. New York: Oxford University Press.

———. 2011. "Beyond the Prison Bubble." *National Institute of Justice Journal* (Oct.):26–31.

Petersilia, J., & S. Turner. 1988. "Minorities in Prison: Discrimination or Disparity?" *Corrections Today* 50:92–94.

———. 1993. "Evaluating Intensive Supervision Probation/Parole: Results of a Nationwide Experiment." *National Institute of Justice Research in Brief* (May):1–10.

Petersilia, J., S. Turner, J. Kahan, & J. Peterson. 1985. *Granting Felons Probation: Public Risks and Alternatives*. Santa Monica: RAND.

Peterson, D., J. Miller, & F. Esbensen. 2001. "The Impact of Sex Composition on Gangs and Gang Member Delinquency." *Criminology* 39:411–439.

Peterson, R., & W. Bailey. 1998. "Is Capital Punishment an Effective Deterrent to Murder? An Examination of Social Science Research." In J. Acker, R. Bohm, & C. Lanier (eds.), *America's Experiment with Capital Punishment*. Durham: NC: Carolina Academic.

Petrillo, L. 1990. "When a Cop Shoots, Who Takes a Close Look?" *San Diego Union* (Dec. 21):A1, A10.

Pettit, B., & B. Western. 2004. "Mass Imprisonment and the Life Course: Race and Class Inequality in U.S. Incarceration." *American Sociological Review* 69:151–169.

Pettiway, L. 1997. *Workin' It: Women Living Through Drugs and Crime*. Philadelphia: Temple University Press.

Petts, R. 2009. "Family and Religious Characteristics' Influence on Delinquency Trajectories from Adolescence to Young Adulthood." *American Sociological Review* 74:465–483.

Pickett, T., D. Tope, & R. Bellandi. 2014. "'Taking Back Our Country': Tea Party Membership and Support for Punitive Crime Control Policies." *Sociological Inquiry* 84:167–190.

Piliavan, I., R. Gartner, C. Thornton, & R. Matsueda. 1986. "Crime, Deterrence, and Rational Choice." *American Sociological Review* 51:101–119.

Pincus, W. 2005. "British Intelligence Warned of Iraq War." *Washington Post* (May 13). www.washingtonpost.com.

Piven, F., & R. Cloward. 1971. *Regulating the Poor: The Functions of Public Welfare*. New York: Vintage.

Planty, M., et al. 2013. *Female Victims of Sexual Violence, 1994–2010*. Washington, DC: US Department of Justice, Bureau of Justice Statistics.

Platt, A. 1974. "The Triumph of Benevolence: The Origins of the Juvenile Justice System in the United States." In R. Quinney (ed.), *Criminal Justice in America*. Boston: Little, Brown.

Pollak, J., & C. Kubrin. 2007. "Crime in the News: How Crimes, Offenders, and Victims Are Portrayed in the Media." *Journal of Criminal Justice & Popular Culture* 14:49–83.

Pollock-Byrne, J. 1990. *Women, Prison, and Crime*. Pacific Grove, CA: Brooks/Cole.

Porterfield, A. 1943. "Delinquency and Its Outcome in Court and College." *American Journal of Sociology* 49:199–208.

Possley, M. 2007. "3 Children Die Leading to Massive Crib Recall." *Wisconsin State Journal* (Oct. 22):A3.

Potterat, J., D. Woodhouse, J. Muth, & S. Muth. 1990. "Estimating the Prevalence and Career Longevity of Prostitute Women." *Journal of Sex Research* 27:233–243.

Poussaint, A. 1983. "Black-on-Black Homicide: A Psychological-Political Perspective." *Victimology* 8:161–169.

Poveda, T. 1994. "Clinton, Crime, and the Justice Department." *Social Justice* 21:73–84.

Power, S., N. King, & S. Hughes. 2010. "U.S. to Break Up Oil-Rig Regulator." *Wall Street Journal* (May 12). www.online.wsj.com.

Pratt, T., & F. Cullen. 2000. "The Empirical Status of Gottfredson and Hirschi's General Theory of Crime: A Meta-Analysis." *Criminology* 38:931–964.

Pratt, T., & J. Maahs. 1999. "Are Private Prisons More Cost-Effective Than Public Prisons? A Meta-Analysis of Evaluation Research Studies." *Crime & Delinquency* 45:358–371.

President's Commission on Law Enforcement and Administration of Justice. 1967. *The Challenge of Crime in a Free Society.* Washington, DC: US Government Printing Office.

Press, E. 2007. "The New Suburban Poverty." *The Nation* (Apr. 23):18–24.

Priest, D., & W. Pincus. 2004. "U.S. 'Almost All Wrong' on Weapons: Report on Iraq Contradicts Bush Administration Claims." *Washington Post* (Oct. 7):A1.

Prins, N. 2004. *Other People's Money: The Corporate Mugging of America.* New York: New Press.

Pulliam, S., D. Solomon, & C. Mollenkamp. 2002. "Former WorldCom CEO Built an Empire on Mountain of Debt." *Wall Street Journal* (Dec. 31). www.wsj.com.

Puzzanghera, J. 2010. "Senators Grapple with Derivatives Rules in Financial Overhaul." *Los Angeles Times* (May 19). www.latimes.com.

Quadagno, J., & C. Fobes. 1995. "The Welfare State and the Cultural Reproduction of Gender: Making Good Girls and Boys in the Job Corps." *Social Problems* 42:171–190.

Quicker, J. 1983. *Homegirls: Characterizing Chicana Gangs.* San Pedro, CA: International Universities.

Quinney, R. 1970. *The Social Reality of Crime.* Boston: Little, Brown.

———. 1977. *Class, State, and Crime: On the Theory and Practice of Criminal Justice.* New York: David McKay.

———. 1999. "The Prophetic Meaning of Justice." In B. Arrigo (ed.), *Social Justice/Criminal Justice.* Belmont, CA: Wadsworth.

———. 2000. *Bearing Witness to Crime and Social Justice.* Albany: State University of New York Press.

Radelet, M. 1981. "Racial Characteristics and the Imposition of the Death Penalty." *American Sociological Review* 46:918–927.

Radelet, M., & H. Bedau. 1998. "The Execution of the Innocent." In J. Acker, R. Bohm, & C. Lanier (eds.), *America's Experiment with Capital Punishment.* Durham, NC: Carolina Academic.

Radelet, M., H. Bedau, & C. Putnam. 1992. *In Spite of Innocence: Erroneous Convictions in Capital Cases.* Boston: Northeastern University Press.

Radelet, M., & G. Pierce. 1985. "Race and Prosecutorial Discretion in Homicide Cases." *Law & Society Review* 19:587–621.

Rafter, N. 1992. "Criminal Anthropology in the United States." *Criminology* 30:525–545.

———. 2008. *The Criminal Brain: Understanding Biological Theories of Crime.* New York: New York University Press.

Rainville, G., & B. Reaves. 2003. *Felony Defendants in Large Urban Counties, 2000.* Washington, DC: US Department of Justice.

Rainville, G., & S. Smith. 2003. *Juvenile Felony Defendants in Criminal Courts.* Washington, DC: US Department of Justice.

Rampart Independent Review Panel. 2002. "The Los Angeles Police Department Rampart Division Scandal: Exposing Police Misconduct and Responding to It." In M. Ermann & R. Lundman (eds.), *Corporate and Governmental Deviance.* New York: Oxford University Press.

Rand, M., J. Lynch, & D. Cantor. 1997. *Criminal Victimization, 1973–95.* Washington, DC: US Department of Justice.

Randall, M., & L. Haskell. 1995. "Sexual Violence in Women's Lives: Findings from the Women's Safety Project—A Community Survey." *Violence Against Women* 1:6–31.

Rankin, J., & R. Kern. 1994. "Parental Attachments and Delinquency." *Criminology* 32:495–515.

Rape, Abuse, and Incest National Network. 2009. "Who Are the Victims?" www .rainn.org.

Rashke, R. 1981. *The Killing of Karen Silkwood*. New York: Penguin.

Reaves, B. 1991. *Pretrial Release of Felony Defendants, 1988*. Washington, DC: US Department of Justice.

———. 2010. *Local Police Departments, 2007*. Washington, DC: US Department of Justice.

Rebellion, C. 2002. "Reconsidering the Broken Homes/Delinquency Relationship and Exploring Its Mediating Mechanism(s)." *Criminology* 40:103–135.

Reeves, J., & R. Campbell. 1994. *Cracked Coverage: Television News, the Anti-Cocaine Crusade, and the Reagan Legacy*. Durham, NC: Duke University Press.

Regoli, R., & J. Hewitt. 1997. *Delinquency in Society*. New York: McGraw-Hill.

Reich, R. 2007. *Supercapitalism: The Transformation of Business, Democracy, and Everyday Life*. New York: Vintage.

Reid, S. 1997/2006. *Crime and Criminology*. New York: McGraw-Hill.

Reiman, J. 2007. *The Rich Get Richer and the Poor Get Prison: Ideology, Class, and Criminal Justice*. Boston: Allyn and Bacon.

Reinarman, C., & H. Levine. 1989. "The Crack Attack: Politics and Media in America's Latest Drug Scare." In J. Best (ed.), *Images of Issues: Typifying Contemporary Social Problems*. New York: Aldine de Gruyter.

Reiner, I. 1992. *Gangs, Crime, and Violence in Los Angeles*. Arlington, VA: National Youth Gang Information Center.

Reiss, A. 1968. "Police Brutality: Answers to Key Questions." *Transaction* 5:10–19.

———. 1971. *The Police and the Public*. New Haven: Yale University Press.

Rennison, C. 2003. *Intimate Partner Violence, 1993–2001*. Washington, DC: US Department of Justice.

Renzetti, C. 1992. *Violent Betrayal: Partner Abuse in Lesbian Relationships*. Newbury Park, CA: Sage.

———. 1996. "The Poverty of Services for Battered Lesbians." In C. Renzetti & C. Miley (eds.), *Violence in Gay and Lesbian Domestic Partnerships*. New York: Harrington Park.

Ressler, R., & T. Schachtman. 1992. *Whoever Fights Monsters: My Twenty Years Tracking Serial Killers for the FBI*. New York: St. Martin's.

Reuter, P. 1995. "The Decline of the American Mafia." *Public Interest* 120:89–99.

———. 2009. "Systemic Violence in Drug Markets." *Crime, Law, and Social Change* 52:275–284.

Rickert, C. 2008. "Storage Locker Home for Some." *Wisconsin State Journal* (Jan. 5):A1, A7.

Riggs, M. 2013. "Blowing Smoke." *The Nation* (Nov. 13):13–15.

Roane, K. 2005. "The CSI Effect." *US News & World Report* (Apr. 25):48–54.

Roberts, J., & L. Stalans. 2000. *Public Opinion, Crime, and Criminal Justice*. Boulder, CO: Westview.

Robinson, C. 1993. "The Production of Black Violence in Chicago." In D. Greenberg (ed.), *Crime and Capitalism*. Philadelphia: Temple University Press.

Robinson, L. 1996. "Subject/Position." In N. Maglin & D. Perry (eds.), *"Bad Girls"/"Good Girls": Women, Sex, and Power in the Nineties*. New Brunswick, NJ: Rutgers University Press.

Roche, W., & K. Silverstein. 2004. "War Boosters Do Related Business." *Los Angeles Times* (July 14):A7–A9.

Rodgers, L. 1995. "Prison Suicide: Suggestions from Phenomenology." *Deviant Behavior* 6:113–126.

Rodriguez, N. 2007a. "Juvenile Court Context and Detention Decisions: Reconsidering the Role of Race, Ethnicity, and Community Characteristics in Juvenile Court Processes." *Justice Quarterly* 24:629–655.

———. 2007b. "Restorative Justice at Work: Examining the Impact of Restorative Justice Resolutions on Recidivism." *Crime & Delinquency* 53:355–379.

Roettger, M., & R. Swisher. 2011. "Association of Fathers' History of Incarceration with Sons' Delinquency and Arrest Among Black, White, and Hispanic Males in the United States." *Criminology* 49:1109–1147.

Rolling Stone. 2006. "A Call for Investigation: Electronic Voting Machines Pose a Grave Threat to Democracy" (June 15):54.

Roncek, D., & D. Faggiani. 1985. "High Schools and Crime: A Replication." *Sociological Quarterly* 26:491–505.

Ronson, J. 2011. *The Psychopath Test: A Journal Through the Madness Industry.* New York: Riverhead.

Rose, D., & T. Clear. 1998. "Incarceration, Social Capital, and Crime: Implications for Social Disorganization Theory." *Criminology* 36:441–479.

Rose, V. 1977. "Rape as a Social Problem: A By-Product of the Feminist Movement." *Social Problems* 25:75–89.

Rosen, J. 1997. "One Angry Woman." *New Yorker* (Feb. 24):54–63.

Rosenbaum, D. 1988. "Community Crime Prevention: A Review and Synthesis of the Literature." *Justice Quarterly* 5:323–395.

Rosenfeld, R. 2004. "The Case of the Unsolved Crime Decline." *Scientific American* (Feb.):82–89.

Rosenfeld, R., R. Fornango, & A. Rengifo. 2007. "The Impact of Order-Maintenance Policing on New York City Homicide and Robbery Rates: 1988–2001." *Criminology* 45:355–383.

Rosenmerkel, S., M. Durose, & D. Farole. 2009. *Felony Sentences in State Courts, 2006—Statistical Tables.* Washington, DC: US Department of Justice.

Rosoff, S., H. Pontell, & R. Tillman. 2007. *Profit Without Honor: White-Collar Crime and the Looting of America.* Upper Saddle River, NJ: Prentice Hall.

Ross, J., & S. Richards. 2002. *Behind Bars: Surviving Prison.* Indianapolis: Alpha.

Rothman, D. 1971. *The Discovery of the Asylum.* Boston: Little, Brown.

Roussell, A., & L. Gascón. 2014. "Defining 'Policeability': Cooperation, Control, and Resistance in South Los Angeles Community-Policing Meetings." *Social Problems* 61:237–258.

Rowe, D. 1986. "Genetic and Environmental Components of Antisocial Behavior: A Study of 265 Twins." *Criminology* 24:513–532.

Royte. E. 2012. "What the Frack Is In Our Food?" *The Nation* (Dec. 17):11–18.

Rozee, P., P. Bateman, & T. Gilmore. 1991. "The Personal Perspective of Acquaintance Rape Prevention: A Three-Tier Approach." In A. Parrot & L. Bechhofer (eds.), *Acquaintance Rape.* New York: Wiley.

Rubenstein, R., & J. Roth. 1987. *Approaches to Auschwitz: The Holocaust and Its Legacy.* Atlanta: John Knox.

Ruesink, M., & M. Free. 2005. "Wrongful Convictions Among Women: An Exploratory Study of a Neglected Topic." *Women & Criminal Justice* 15:1–23.

Russakoff, D., & S. Kovaleski. 1998. "Two Angry Men." In B. Schechterman & M. Slann (eds.), *Violence and Terrorism.* New York: McGraw-Hill.

Russell, D. 1982. *Rape in Marriage.* New York: Macmillan.

————. 1993. *Against Pornography: Evidence of Harm.* Berkeley: Russell.

Russell, K. 2003. "'Driving While Black': Corollary Phenomena and Collateral Consequences." In M. Free (ed.), *Racial Issues in Criminal Justice.* Westport: Praeger.

Ryerson, E. 1978. *The Best-Laid Plans: America's Juvenile Court Experiment.* New York: Hill and Wang.

Safetyforum. 2003. "Chrysler Minivan Latch Failure Is a Safety Defect That Involves Children." www.safetyforum.com.

Sampson, R. 1985. "Structural Sources of Variation in Race-Age-Specific Rates of Offending Across Major US Cities." *Criminology* 23:647–673.

————. 1986. "Effects of Socioeconomic Context on Official Reaction to Delinquency." *American Sociological Review* 51:876–885.

————. 1987. "Urban Black Violence: The Effect of Male Joblessness and Family Disruption." *American Journal of Sociology* 93:348–382.

————. 2013. "The Place of Context: A Theory and Strategy for Criminology's Hard Problems." *Criminology* 51:1–31.

Sampson, R., & W. Groves. 1989. "Community Structure and Crime: Testing Social-Disorganization Theory." *American Journal of Sociology* 94:774–802.

Sampson, R., & J. Laub. 1990. "Crime and Deviance over the Life Course: The Salience of Adult Social Bonds." *American Sociological Review* 55:609–627.

————. 1993. *Crime in the Making: Pathways and Turning Points Through Life.* Cambridge: Harvard University Press.

Sampson, R., J. Morenoff, & S. Raudenbush. 2005. "Social Anatomy of Racial and Economic Disparities in Violence." *American Journal of Public Health* 95:224–232.

Sampson, R., S. Raudenbush, & F. Earls. 1997. "Neighborhoods and Violence Crime: A Multilevel Study of Collective Efficacy." *Science* 277:918–924.

Sampson, R., & W. Wilson. 1995. "Race, Crime, and Urban Inequality." In J. Hagan & R. Peterson (eds.), *Crime and Inequality.* Stanford: Stanford University Press.

Sanchez Jankowski, M. 1991. *Islands in the Street: Gangs and American Urban Society.* Berkeley: University of California Press.

Sanday, P. 2007. *Fraternity Gang Rape.* New York: New York University Press.

Sanders, W. 1980. *Rape and Woman's Identity.* Beverly Hills: Sage.

————. 1983. *Criminology.* Reading, MA: Addison-Wesley.

————. 1994. *Gangbangs and Drive-Bys: Grounded Culture and Juvenile Gang Violence.* New York: Aldine de Gruyter.

Sandstrom, K., D. Martin, & G. Fine. 2006. *Symbols, Selves, and Social Reality: A Symbolic Interactionist Approach to Social Psychology and Sociology.* Los Angeles: Roxbury.

Sapp, A. 1986. "Sexual Misconduct and Sexual Harassment by Police Officers." In T. Barker & D. Carter (eds.), *Police Deviance.* Cincinnati: Pilgrimage.

Scahill, J. 2007. *Blackwater: The Rise of the World's Most Powerful Military Army.* New York: Nation Books.

————. 2009. "U.S. War Privatization Results in Billions Lost in Fraud, Waste, and Abuse." *Halliburton Watch* (June 10). www.commondreams.com.

Scheflin, A. 1994. "Jury Nullification: The Right to Say No." In J. Bonsignore et al., *Before the Law: An Introduction to the Legal Process.* Boston: Houghton Mifflin.

Scherer, M. 2008. "Governor Gone Wild: The Blagojevich Scandal." *Time* (Dec. 11). www.time.com.

————. 2013. "Edward Snowden: The Dark Prophet." *Time* (Dec. 11):79–99.

Schlesinger, T. 2005. "Racial and Ethnic Disparity in Pretrial Criminal Processing." *Justice Quarterly* 22:170–192.

———. 2007. "The Cumulative Effects of Racial Disparities in Criminal Processing." *Journal of the Institute of Justice and International Studies* 7:268–285.

Schlosser, E. 1998. "The Prison-Industrial Complex." *Atlantic Monthly* (Dec.):51–77.

———. 1999. "The Politics of Pot: A Government in Denial." *Rolling Stone* (Mar. 4):47–52.

Schlossman, S., G. Zellman, & R. Shavelson. 1984. *Delinquency Prevention in South Chicago: A Fifty-Year Assessment of the Chicago Area Project.* Santa Monica: RAND.

Schneider, A. 1986. "Restitution and Recidivism Rates of Juvenile Offenders: Results from Four Experimental Studies." *Criminology* 24:533–552.

Schneider, P., & M. Finkelstein (eds.). 1998. *RESTTA National Directory of Restitution and Community Service Programs.* Bethesda, MD: Pacific Institute for Research and Evaluation.

Schneider, R. 2014. *Battered Women Doing Time: Injustice in the Criminal Justice System.* Boulder, CO: First Forum.

Schrock, D., & I. Padavic. 2007. "Negotiating Hegemonic Masculinity in a Batterer Intervention Program." *Gender & Society* 21:625–649.

Schulenburg, C. 2007. "Dying to Entertain: Violence on Prime Time Broadcast Television, 1998–2006." www.parentstv.org.

Schur, E. 1971. *Labeling Deviant Behavior.* New York: Harper and Row.

———. 1973. *Radical Non-Intervention: Rethinking the Delinquency Problem.* Englewood Cliffs, NJ: Prentice Hall.

Schwartz, M., & W. DeKeseredy. 1997. *Sexual Assault on the College Campus: The Role of Male Peer Support.* Thousand Oaks, CA: Sage.

Schwartz, M., W. DeKeseredy, D. Tait, & S. Alvi. 2001. "Male Peer Support and a Feminist Routine Activities Theory: Understanding Sexual Assault on the College Campus." *Justice Quarterly* 18:623–649.

Schwendinger, H., & J. Schwendinger. 1970. "Defenders of Order or Guardians of Human Rights?" *Issues in Criminology* 5:12–57.

———. 1974. *The Sociologists of the Chair: A Radical Analysis of the Formative Years of North American Sociology (1883–1922).* New York: Basic.

———. 1993. "Giving Crime Prevention Top Priority." *Crime & Delinquency* 39:425–446.

Schwendinger, J., & H. Schwendinger. 1983. *Rape and Inequality.* Beverly Hills: Sage.

Schworm, P. 2013. "Mandatory Drug Term Critics Hail New US Policy." *Boston Globe* (Aug. 13). www.bostonglobe.com.

Scully, D., & J. Marolla. 1984. "Convicted Rapists' Vocabulary of Motives: Excuses and Justification." *Social Problems* 31:530–544.

———. 1985. "'Riding the Bull at Gilley's': Convicted Rapists Describe the Rewards of Rape." *Social Problems* 32:251–263.

Searles, P. n.d. "Observations on Battered Women." Unpublished.

Searles, P., & R. Berger. 1987. "The Feminist Self-Defense Movement: A Case Study." *Gender & Society* 1:61–83.

Seely, R. 2010. "Big Diaries, Little Oversight." *Wisconsin State Journal* (Feb. 28):A1, A9–A10.

Seiter, R., & K. Kadela. 2003. "Prisoner Reentry: What Works, What Does Not, and What Is Promising." *Crime & Delinquency* 49:360–381.

Sellin, T. 1938. *Culture Conflict and Crime*. New York: Social Science Research Council.
———. 1976. *Slavery and the Penal System*. New York: Elsevier.
Senn, C. 1993. "The Research on Women and Pornography: The Many Faces." In D. Russell (ed.), *Making Violence Sexy: Feminist Views on Pornography*. New York: Teachers College.
Sethi, P. 1982. "The Santa Barbara Oil Spill." In M. Ermann & R. Lundman (eds.), *Corporate and Governmental Deviance*. New York: Oxford University Press.
Sexton, G. 1995. *Work in American Prisons: Joint Ventures with the Private Sector*. Washington, DC: US Department of Justice.
Shakur, S. 1993. *Monster: The Autobiography of an L.A. Gang Member*. New York: Penguin.
Shapley, D. 2010. "So How Big Was the B.P. Oil Spill?" *Daily Green* (July 16). www.thedailygreen.com.
Sharkey, P. 2013. *Stuck in Place: Urban Neighborhoods and the End of Progress Toward Racial Equality*. Chicago: University of Chicago Press.
Shaw, C., & H. McKay. 1942. *Juvenile Delinquency and Urban Areas*. Chicago: University of Chicago Press.
Shaw, C., F. Zorbaugh, H. McKay, & L. Cottrell. 1929. *Delinquency Areas*. Chicago: University of Chicago Press.
Sheffield, C. 1989. "The Invisible Intruder: Women's Experiences of Obscene Phone Calls." *Gender & Society* 3:483–488.
Shelden, R., W. Brown, K. Miller, & R. Fritzler. 2008. *Crime and Criminal Justice in American Society*. Long Grove, IL: Waveland.
Shelden, R., S. Tracy, & W. Brown. 2004. *Youth Gangs in American Society*. Belmont, CA: Wadsworth.
Sheldon, W. 1949. *Varieties of Delinquent Youth*. New York: Harper and Row.
Sheley, J. 1985. *America's "Crime Problem."* Belmont, CA: Wadsworth.
Shenon, P. 2008. *The Commission: The Uncensored History of the 9/11 Investigation*. New York: Twelve.
Sherman, L. 1992. *Policing Domestic Violence: Experiments and Dilemmas*. New York: Free Press.
Sherman, L., & R. Berk. 1984. "Specific Deterrent Effects of Arrest for Domestic Assault." *American Sociological Review* 49:261–272.
Sherman, L., P. Gartin, & M. Buerger. 1989. "Hot Spots of Predatory Crime: Routine Activities and the Criminology of Place." *Criminology* 27:27–56.
Sherman, L., & D. Smith. 1992. "Crime, Punishment, and Stake in Conformity: Legal and Informal Control of Domestic Violence." *American Sociological Review* 57:680–690.
Sherman, L., et al. 1991. "From Initial Deterrence to Long-Term Escalation: Short-Custody Arrest for Poverty Ghetto Domestic Violence." *Criminology* 29:821–850.
Shichor, D., & D. Sechrest (eds.). 1996. *Three Strikes and You're Out: Vengeance as Public Policy*. Thousand Oaks, CA: Sage.
Shihadeh, E., & G. Ousey. 1996. "Metropolitan Expansion and Black Social Dislocations: The Link Between Suburbanization and Center-City Crime." *Social Forces* 75:649–666.
Shoemaker, D., & J. Williams. 1987. "The Subculture of Violence and Ethnicity." *Journal of Criminal Justice* 15:461–472.
Shorrock, T. 2003. "Big Bucks in Iraq." *The Nation* (Nov. 10):5–6.
Shover, N., & J. Inverarity. 1995. "Adult Segregative Confinement." In J. Sheley (ed.), *Criminology*. Belmont, CA: Wadsworth.

Sick, G. 1991. *October Surprise: America's Hostages in Iran and the Election of Ronald Reagan.* New York: Times Books.

Siegel, L., B. Welsh, & J. Senna. 2003. *Juvenile Delinquency: Theory, Practice, and Law.* Belmont, CA: Wadsworth.

Sikes, G. 1997. *8 Ball Chicks: A Year in the Violent World of Girl Gangs.* New York: Anchor.

Silberman, C. 1978. *Criminal Violence, Criminal Justice.* New York: Random.

Silk, L., & D. Vogel. 1976. *Ethics and Profits: The Crisis of Confidence in American Business.* New York: Simon and Schuster.

Simi, P., & R. Futrell. 2010. *American Swastika: Inside the White Power Movement's Hidden Spaces of Hate.* Lanham: Rowman and Littlefield.

Simmons, C. 2007. "More Toys, Necklaces with Lead Are Recalled." *Wisconsin State Journal* (Sept. 27):A3.

Simon, David. 2006. *Elite Deviance.* Boston: Allyn and Bacon.

Simons, R., & C. Burt. 2011. "Learning to Be Bad: Adverse Social Conditions, Social Schemas, and Crime." *Criminology* 49:553–597.

Simons, R., et al. 2002. "A Test of Life-Course Explanations for Stability and Change in Antisocial Behavior from Adolescence to Young Adulthood." *Criminology* 40:401–434.

Simpson, S. 1991. "Caste, Class, and Violence Crime: Explaining Differences in Female Offending." *Criminology* 29:115–135.

———. 1992. "Corporate-Crime Deterrence and Corporate-Crime Control Policies: Views from the Inside." In K. Schlegel & D. Weisburd (eds.), *White-Collar Crime Reconsidered.* Boston: Northeastern University Press.

Sinclair, U. 1906. *The Jungle.* New York: New American Library.

Singer, M., & H. Baer (eds.). 2009. *Killer Commodities: Public Health and the Corporate Production of Harm.* Lanham: Rowman and Littlefield.

Skinner, B. 1953. *Science and Human Behavior.* New York: Macmillan.

Skipper, J., & W. McWhorter. 1981. "A Rapist Gets Caught in the Act." In J. Skipper (ed.), *Deviance: Voices from the Margins.* Belmont, CA: Wadsworth.

Skogan, W. 2006. *Police and Community in Chicago: A Tale of Three Cities.* New York: Oxford University Press.

Skolnick, J. 1992. "Gangs in the Post-Industrial Ghetto." *American Prospect* (Winter):109–120.

———. 1996. "Passions of Crime." *American Prospect* (Mar.–Apr.):89–95.

Skolnick, J., & D. Bayley. 1988. "Theme and Variation in Community Policing." *Crime & Justice* 10:1–37.

Skolnick, J., R. Bluthenthal, & T. Correl. 1993. "Gang Organization and Migration." In S. Cummings & D. Monti (eds.), *Gangs: The Origins and Impact of Contemporary Youth Gangs in the United States.* New York: State University of New York Press.

Skolnick, J., & J. Fyfe. 1993. *Above the Law: Police and the Excessive Use of Force.* New York: Free Press.

Slocum, T. 2010. "The Oil Spill . . . BP's $485 Million in Fines." *Public Citizen* (Apr. 29). www.publiccitizenenergy.org.

Smedley, B., A. Stith, & A. Nelson. 2003. *Unequal Treatment: Confronting Racial and Ethnic Disparities in Health Care.* Washington, DC: National Academy Press.

Smith, B., & M. Holmes. 2014. "Police Use of Excessive Force in Minority Communities: A Test of the Minority Threat, Place, and Community Accountability Hypotheses." *Social Problems* 61:83–104.

Smith, D. 1986. "The Plea Bargaining Controversy." *Journal of Criminal Law & Criminology* 77:949–967.

Smith, M. 2000. "Capital Punishment in America." In J. Sheley (ed.), *Criminology*. Belmont, CA: Wadsworth.

Smyth, J. 2003. "Voting Machine Controversy." *Cleveland Plain Dealer* (Aug. 28). www.commondreams.org.

Sniffen, M. 2003. "First Study on Prosecutorial Misconduct Released." *Wisconsin State Journal* (June 26):A3.

Snitow, A., C. Stansell, & S. Thompson (eds.). 1983. *Powers of Desire: The Politics of Sexuality*. New York: Monthly Review.

Solitary Watch. 2014. "Fact Sheet: The High Cost of Solitary Confinement." www.solitarywatch.com.

Sorensen, J., A. Widmayer, & F. Scarpitti. 1994. "Examining the Criminal Justice and Criminological Paradigms: An Analysis of ACJS and ASC Members." *Journal of Criminal Justice Education* 5:149–166.

Sourcebook of Criminal Justice Statistics. 2003. "Employees of Federal, State, and Private Adult Correctional Facilities." www.albany.edu.

———. 2006. "Judicial Processing of Defendants." www.albany.edu.

SourceWatch. 2014a. "Abscam Bribery Scandal." www.sourcewatch.org.

———. 2014b. "Massey Energy." www.sourcewatch.org.

Southern Poverty Law Center. 2014. "Far-Right Extremist Movement Grows Leaner, Meaner: Threat Remains High." *SPLC Report* (Spring):1, 3.

Spahr Nelson, T. 2002. *For Love of Country: Confronting Rape and Sexual Harassment in the U.S. Military*. New York: Haworth.

Spencer, J. 2001. "Tough Love, Teen Death." *Newsweek* (July 16):28.

Sperry, P. 2003. *Crude Politics: How Bush's Oil Cronies Hijacked the War on Terrorism*. Nashville: WND.

Spitzer, E. 1999. *The New York City Police Department's "Stop and Frisk" Practices*. New York Civil Rights Bureau. www.oag.state.ny.us.

Spivak, A., & S. Sharp. 2008. "Inmate Recidivism as a Measure of Private Prison Performance." *Crime & Delinquency* 54:482–508.

Spohn, C. 1990a. "Decision Making in Sexual Assault Cases: Do Black and Female Judges Make a Difference?" *Women & Criminal Justice* 2:83–105.

———. 1990b. "The Sentencing Decisions of Black and White Judges: Expected and Unexpected Similarities." *Law & Society Review* 24:1197–1216.

Spohn, C., & J. Cederblom. 1991. "Race and Disparities in Sentencing: A Test of the Liberation Hypothesis." *Justice Quarterly* 8:305–327.

Spohn, C., J. Gruhl, & S. Welch. 1987. "The Impact of the Ethnicity and Gender of Defendants on the Decision to Reject or Dismiss Felony Charges." *Criminology* 25:175–191.

Spohn, C., & J. Horney. 1992. *Rape Law Reform: A Grassroots Revolution and Its Impact*. New York: Plenum.

Spohn, C., & J. Spears. 1996. "The Effect of Offender and Victim Characteristics on Sexual Assault Case Processing Decisions." *Justice Quarterly* 13:649–679.

Spohn, C., & K. Tellis. 2014. *Policing and Prosecuting Sexual Assault: Inside the Criminal Justice System*. Boulder, CO: Lynne Rienner.

Stanko, E. 1997. "Should I Stay or Should I Go? Some Thoughts on the Variants of Intimate Violence." *Violence Against Women* 3:629–635.

Stark, R. 1984. "Religion and Conformity: Reaffirming a Sociology of Religion." *Sociological Analysis* 45:273–282.

Starkman, D. 2014. "Wrecking an Economy Means Never Having to Say You're Sorry." *New Republic* (Aug. 25):22–23.

Starr, S. 2014. "Sentencing by the Numbers." *New York Times* (Aug. 10). www .nytimes.com.

Steffensmeier, D. 1978. "Crime and the Contemporary Woman: An Analysis of Changing Levels of Female Property Crime, 1960–1975." *Social Forces* 58:1080–1108.

———. 1983. "Organization Properties and Sex-Segregation in the Underworld: Building a Sociological Theory of Sex Differences in Crime." *Social Forces* 61:1010–1032.

———. 1986. *The Fence: In the Shadow of Two Worlds*. Totowa, NJ: Rowman and Littlefield.

Steffensmeier, D., & E. Allen. 1988. "Sex Disparities in Arrests by Residence, Race, and Age: An Assessment of the Gender Convergence/Crime Hypothesis." *Justice Quarterly* 5:53–80.

Steffensmeier, D., E. Allen, M. Harer, & C. Streifel. 1989. "Age and the Distribution of Crime." *American Journal of Sociology* 94:803–831.

Steffensmeier, D., & M. Cobb. 1981. "Sex Differences in Urban Arrest Patterns, 1934–79." *Social Problems* 29:37–50.

Steffensmeier, D., & S. Demuth. 2000. "Ethnicity and Sentencing Outcomes in U.S. Federal Courts: Who Is Punished More Harshly—White, Black, White-Hispanic, or Black-Hispanic Defendants?" *American Sociological Review* 65:705–729.

Steffensmeier, D., C. Streifel, & M. Harer. 1987. "Relative Cohort Size and Youth Crime in the United States, 1953–1984." *American Sociological Review* 52:702–710.

Steffensmeier, D., J. Ulmer, & J. Kramer. 1998. "The Interaction of Race, Gender, and Age in Criminal Sentencing: The Punishment Cost of Being Young, Black, and Male." *Criminology* 36:763–797.

Steinem, G. 1980. "Erotica and Pornography: A Clear and Present Difference." In L. Lederer (ed.), *Take Back the Night: Women on Pornography*. New York: Morrow.

Stephan, S. 2004. *State Prison Expenditures, 2001*. Washington, DC: US Department of Justice.

Stepp, L. 2007. *Unhooked: How Young Women Pursue Sex, Delay Love, and Lose at Both*. New York: Riverhead.

Stewart, J. 1991. *Den of Thieves*. New York: Simon and Schuster.

———. 1996. *Blood Sport: The President and His Adversaries*. New York: Simon and Schuster.

Stiglitz, J., & L. Bilmes. 2008. *The Three Trillion Dollar War on Terrorism*. New York: Norton.

Stock, W. 1995. "The Effects of Pornography on Women." In L. Lederer & R. Delgado (eds.), *The Price We Pay: The Case Against Racist Speech, Hate Propaganda, and Pornography*. New York: Hill and Wang.

Stojkovic, S. 1990. "Accounts of Prison Work: Corrections Officers' Portrayals of Their Work Worlds." In G. Miller & J. Holstein (eds.), *Perspectives on Social Problems*. Vol. 2. Greenwich, CT: JAI.

Stone, C. 1975. *Where the Law Ends: The Social Control of Corporate Behavior*. Prospect Heights, IL: Waveland.

Stoneall, L. 1997. "Rural Gang Origins: A Wisconsin Case Study." *Sociological Imagination* 34:45–58.

Stout, D. 1995. "Black Businessman Ponders Ordeal As a Suspect." *New York Times* (May 9):B1.

Strasburger, V., & B. Wilson. 2002. *Children, Adolescents, and the Media*. Thousand Oaks, CA: Sage.

Streib, V. 1998. "Executing Women, Children, and the Retarded: Second Class Citizens in Capital Punishment." In J. Acker, R. Bohm, & C. Lanier (eds.), *America's Experiment with Capital Punishment*. Durham, NC: Carolina Academic.

Stretesky, P., & M. Lynch. 1999. "Corporate Environmental Violence and Racism." *Crime, Law, & Social Change* 30:163–184.

Strom, K., S. Smith & H. Synder. 1998. *Juvenile Felony Defendants in Criminal Courts*. Washington, DC: US Department of Justice.

Stucky, T., K. Heimer, & J. Lang. 2005. "Partisan Politics, Electoral Competition, and Imprisonment: An Analysis of States over Time." *Criminology* 43:211–247.

Stumpe, J., & M. Davey. 2009. "Abortion Doctor Shot to Death in Kansas Church." *New York Times* (June 1). www.nytimes.com.

Subin, H. 1993. "The Criminal Lawyer's 'Different Mission': Reflections on the 'Right' to Present a False Case." In M. Katsh (ed.), *Taking Sides: Clashing Views on Controversial Legal Issues*. Guilford, CT: Dushkin.

Substance Abuse and Mental Health Services Administration. 2011. "Current Statistics on the Prevalence and Characteristics of People Experiencing Homelessness in the United States." www.homeless.samhsa.gov.

———. 2012. "Results from the 2012 National Survey on Drug Use and Health: Detailed Tables." www.samhsa.gov.

Suddath, C. 2008. "Illinois Corruption." *Time* (Dec. 11). www.time.com.

Sullivan, C. 1997. "Societal Collusion and Culpability in Intimate Male Violence: The Impact of Community Response Toward Women with Abusive Partners." In A. Cardarelli (ed.), *Violence Between Intimate Partners*. Boston: Allyn and Bacon.

Sullivan, L. 2006. "At Pelican Bay Prison: A Life in Solitary Confinement." *National Public Radio* (July 26). www.npr.org.

Sullivan, M. 1989. *Getting Paid: Youth Crime and Work in the Inner City*. Ithaca: Cornell University Press.

Summers, A. 2000. *The Arrogance of Power: The Secret World of Richard Nixon*. New York: Viking.

Sunstein, C. 2007. "The Most Dangerous Mysterious Right." *New Republic* (Nov. 19):42–47.

Surette, R. 1998/2011. *Media, Crime, and Criminal Justice: Images, Reality, and Policies*. Belmont, CA: Wadsworth.

Suskind, R. 2006. *The One Percent Doctrine: Deep Inside America's Pursuit of Its Enemies Since 9/11*. New York: Simon and Schuster.

Sutherland, E. 1947. *Principles of Criminology*. Philadelphia: Lippincott.

———. 1949. *White Collar Crime*. New York: Dryden.

———. 1983. *White Collar Crime: The Uncut Version*. New Haven: Yale University Press.

Sutton, J. 2013. "Structural Bias in the Sentencing of Felony Defendants." *Social Science Research* 42:1207–1221.

Swasy, A. 1993. *Soap Opera: The Inside Story of Procter & Gamble*. New York: Times Books.

Sykes, G. 1958. *The Society of Captives: A Study of a Maximum Security Prison*. Princeton: Princeton University Press.

Sykes, G., & F. Cullen. 1992. *Criminology*. Fort Worth: Harcourt Brace Jovanovich.

Sykes, G., & D. Matza. 1957. "Techniques of Neutralization: A Theory of Delinquency." *American Sociological Review* 22:664–670.

Szasz, A. 1986. "The Process and Significance of Political Scandals: A Comparison of Watergate and the 'Sewergate' Episode at the Environmental Protection Agency." *Social Problems* 33:202–217.

Takata, S., & R. Zevitz. 1990. "Divergent Perceptions of Group Delinquency in a Midwestern Community: Racine's Gang Problem." *Youth & Society* 21:282–305.

Talking Points Memo. 2007. "TPM Grande Ole Docket." www.talkingpoints memo.com.

Tamaki, J., J. Chong, & M. Landsberg. 2003. "Radicals Target SUVs in Series of Southland Attacks." *Los Angeles Times* (Aug. 23). www.latimes.com.

Tankersley, J., & M. Possley. 2008. "Product Watchdog to Get Overhaul." *Wisconsin State Journal* (Jan. 1):A5.

Tanner, R. 2003. "Forensic Scientists Under Scrutiny After Rash of Errors." *Wisconsin State Journal* (July 7):A3.

Tansey, B. 2004. "Huge Penalty in Drug Fraud Case." *San Francisco Chronicle* (May 14). www.sfgate.com.

Tappan, P. 1947. "Who Is the Criminal?" *American Sociological Review* 12:96–102.

Tavris, C. 1992. *The Mismeasure of Woman*. New York: Simon and Schuster.

Tawney, R. W. 1920. *The Acquisitive Society*. New York: Harcourt, Brace.

Taylor, R., E. Fritsch, & T. Caeti. 1998. "Core Challenges Facing Community Policing: The Emperor *Still* Has No Clothes." *ACJS Today* 27:1, 3–5.

Texeira, M. 2002. "'Who Protects and Serves Me?' A Case Study of Sexual Harassment of African American Women in One US Law Enforcement Agency." *Gender & Society* 16:524–545.

Thistlethwaite, A., J. Wooldredge, & D. Gibbs. 1998. "Severity of Dispositions and Domestic Violence Reduction." *Crime & Delinquency* 44:388–398.

Thomas, E. 2007. "Making of a Massacre." *Newsweek* (Apr. 30):22–31.

Thompson, M. 2011. "Service Members Sue Pentagon over Rapes." *Time* (Feb. 28):16.

Thompson, M., M. Reuland, & D. Souweine. 2003. "Criminal Justice/Mental Health Consensus: Improving Responses to People with Mental Illness." *Crime & Delinquency* 49:30–51.

Thomson, E. 1997. "Deterrence Versus Brutalization: The Case of Arizona." *Homicide Studies* 1:110–128.

Thornberry, T. 1987. "Toward an Interactional Theory of Delinquency." *Criminology* 25:863–891.

Thornberry, T., & R. Christenson. 1984. "Unemployment and Criminal Involvement: An Investigation of Reciprocal Causal Structures." *American Sociological Review* 49:398–411.

Thrasher, F. 1927. *The Gang*. Chicago: University of Chicago Press.

Tienda, M., & H. Stier. 1996. "Generating Labor Market Inequality: Employment Opportunities and the Accumulation of Disadvantage." *Social Problems* 43:147–165.

Tierney, K. 1982. "The Battered Women Movement and the Creation of the Wife Beating Problem." *Social Problems* 29:207–220.

Tigges, L., I. Browne, & G. Green. 1998. "Social Isolation of the Urban Poor: Race, Class, and Neighborhood Effects on Social Resources." *Sociological Quarterly* 39:53–77.

Tjaden, P., & N. Thoennes. 1998. *Stalking in America: Findings from the National Violence Against Women Survey*. Washington, DC: US Department of Justice.

———. 2000. *Extent, Nature, and Consequence of Intimate Partner Violence: Findings from the National Violence Against Women Survey*. Washington, DC: US Department of Justice.

Toch, H., & J. Grant. 1982. *Reforming Human Services: Change Through Participation*. Beverly Hills: Sage.

Toch, H., & J. Klofas. 1982. "Alienation and Desire for Job Enhancement Among Corrections Officers." *Federal Probation* 46:35–44.

Toffler, B. 2003. *Final Accounting: Ambition, Greed, and the Fall of Arthur Andersen*. New York: Broadway.

Tollet, T., & B. Close. 1991. "The Overrepresentation of Blacks in Florida's Juvenile Justice System." In M. Lynch & E. Patterson (eds.), *Race and Criminal Justice*. Albany, NY: Harrow and Heston.

Tonry, M. 1995. *Malign Neglect: Race, Crime, and Punishment in America*. New York: Oxford University Press.

Tracy, P., M. Wolfgang, & R. Figlio. 1990. *Delinquency Careers in Two Birth Cohorts*. New York: Plenum.

Travis, J., & J. Petersilia. 2001. "Reentry Reconsidered: A New Look at an Old Question." *Crime & Delinquency* 47:291–313.

Trevelan, E. 2006. "A Culturally Sensitive Drug Case." *Wisconsin State Journal* (Nov. 16):A1, A5.

Trevelan, E., & D. Hall. 2014. "Federal Judge Rejects Law." *Wisconsin State Journal* (Apr. 30):A1, A7.

Trojanowicz, R., M. Morash, & P. Schram. 2001. *Juvenile Delinquency: Concepts and Controls*. Englewood Cliffs, NJ: Prentice Hall.

Truman, J., & L. Langton. 2014. *Criminal Victimization, 2013*. Washington, DC: US Department of Justice, Bureau of Justice Statistics.

Tunnell, K. 1992. *Choosing Crime: The Criminal Calculus of Property Offenders*. Chicago: Nelson-Hall.

Turman, K. 2001. *Understanding DNA Evidence: A Guide for Victim Services Providers*. Washington, DC: US Department of Justice.

Tyler, G. (ed.). 1967. *Organized Crime in America*. Ann Arbor: University of Michigan Press.

Uggen, C. 1999. "Ex-Offenders and the Conformist Alternative: A Job Quality Model of Work and Crime." *Social Problems* 46:127–151.

———. 2000. "Work as a Turning Point in the Life Course of Criminals: A Duration Model of Age, Employment, and Recidivism." *American Sociological Review* 67:529–546.

Uhlman, T. 1978. "Black Elite Decision Making: The Case of Trial Judges." *American Journal of Political Science* 22:884–895.

Umbreit, M. 1994. "Victim Empowerment Through Mediation: The Impact of Victim Offender Mediation in Four Cities." *Perspectives* (Summer):25–28.

Unnever, J., & L. Hembroff. 1988. "The Prediction of Racial/Ethnic Sentencing Disparities: An Expectation States Approach." *Journal of Research in Crime & Delinquency* 25:53–82.

Urbina, J., & A. Lehren. 2006. "U.S. Is Reducing Safety Penalties for Mine Flaws." *New York Times* (Mar. 2). www.nytimes.com.

US Census Bureau. 2012. *Statistical Abstract of the United States*. www.census.gov.

US Department of Housing and Urban Development. 2013. "The 2013 Annual Homeless Assessment Report to Congress." Washington, DC.

US News & World Report. 1996a. "A Marijuana Mecca Rethinks Its Drug Laws" (Apr. 15):15.

———. 1996b. "The Unabomber's Worldview" (Apr. 15):35.

US Securities and Exchange Commission. 2010. "Goldman Sachs to Pay Record $550 Million to Settle SEC Charges Related to Subprime Mortgage CDO" (July 15). www.sec.gov.

Van Boven, S., & A. Gesalman. 1998. "A Fatal Ride in the Night." *Newsweek* (June 22):33.

Van Maanen, J. 1995. "Kinsmen in Repose: Occupational Perspectives of Patrolmen." In V. Kappeler (ed.), *The Police and Society*. Prospect Heights, IL: Waveland.

Van Voorhis, P., F. Cullen, B. Link, & N. Wolfe. 1991. "The Impact of Race and Gender on Correctional Officers' Orientation to the Integrated Environment." *Journal of Research on Crime & Delinquency* 28:472–500.

Vance, C. (ed.). 1984. *Pleasure and Danger: Exploring Female Sexuality*. Boston: Routledge and Kegan Paul.

Vaughan, D. 1982. "Toward Understanding Unlawful Organizational Behavior." *Michigan Law Review* 80:1377–1402.

———. 2005. "The Normalization of Deviance: Signals of Danger, Situated Action, and Risk." In H. Montgomery, R. Lipshitz, & B. Brehmer (eds.), *How Professionals Make Decisions*. Mahwah, NJ: Lawrence Erlbaum.

Vecitis, K. 2012. "Drugs and Eating Disorders: Women's Instrumental Drug Use for Weight Control." In P. Adler, P. Adler, & P. O'Brien (eds.), *Drugs and the American Dream*. West Sussex: Wiley-Blackwell.

Venkatesh, S. 1997. "The Social Organization of Street Gang Activity in an Urban Ghetto." *American Journal of Sociology* 103:82–111.

———. 2008. *Gang Leader for a Day: A Rogue Sociologist Takes to the Streets*. New York: Penguin.

Vigilant, L. 2005. "'I Don't Have Another Run Left with It': Ontological Security in Illness Narratives of Recovering on Methadone Maintenance." *Deviant Behavior* 26:399–416.

Vincentnathan, S. 1995. "Societal Reaction and Secondary Deviance in Culture and Society: The United States and Japan." In F. Adler & W. Laufer (eds.), *The Legacy of Anomie Theory*. New Brunswick, NJ: Transaction.

Vizzard, W. 2000. *Shots in the Dark: The Policy, Politics, and Symbolism of Gun Control*. Lanham: Rowman and Littlefield.

Vold, G., T. Bernard, & J. Snipes. 2002. *Theoretical Criminology*. New York: Oxford University Press.

Von App, Lisa. 2010. "Toyota to Pay Unprecedented $16.4 Million Fine." *Salt Lake City Page One Examiner* (Apr. 22). www.examiner.com.

Waegel, W. 1989. *Delinquency and Juvenile Control*. Englewood Cliffs, NJ: Prentice Hall.

Wagner, D. 2012. *Confronting Homelessness: Poverty, Politics, and the Failure of Social Policy*. Boulder, CO: Lynne Rienner.

Waldron, L., & T. Hartmann. 2008. *Legacy of Secrecy: The Long Shadow of the JFK Assassination*. Berkeley: Counterpoint.

Walker, J. 2004. *Three Mile Island: A Nuclear Crisis in Historical Perspective*. Berkeley: University of California Press.

Walker, L. 1979. *The Battered Woman*. New York: Harper and Row.

Walker, S. 1992. *The Police in America*. New York: McGraw-Hill.

———. 1996/2011. *Sense and Nonsense About Crime: A Policy Guide*. Belmont, CA: Wadsworth.

Walker, S., C. Spohn, & M. Delone. 2007. *The Color of Justice: Race, Ethnicity, and Crime in America*. Belmont, CA: Wadsworth.

Walker-Rodriguez, A., & R. Hill. 2011. "Human Sex Trafficking." *FBI Law Enforcement Bulletin* (Mar.). www.fbi.gov.

Wallace, D., & D. Humphries. 1993. "Urban Crime and Capitalist Accumulation, 1950–1971." In D. Greenberg (ed.), *Crime and Capitalism*. Philadelphia: Temple University Press.

Wallace, H. 1993. "Mandatory Minimums and the Betrayal of Sentencing Reform: A Legislative Dr. Jekyll and Mr. Hyde." *Federal Probation* 57:9–19.

Wallace, H. 1999. *Family Violence: Legal, Medical, and Social Perspectives.* Boston: Allyn and Bacon.

Walmsley, R. 2013. *World Population List.* International Centre for Prisoner Studies. www.prisonstudies.org.

Walsh, A. 1987. "The Sexual Stratification Hypothesis and Sexual Assault in Light of the Changing Conceptions of Race." *Criminology* 25:153–173.

———. 2012. *Criminology: The Essentials.* Thousand Oaks, CA: Sage.

Walsh, D. 1980. *Break-Ins: Burglary from Private Houses.* London: Constable.

Walters, G., & T. White. 1989. "Heredity and Crime: Bad Genes or Bad Research?" *Criminology* 27:455–485.

Wambaugh, J. 1975. *The Choirboys.* New York: Dell.

Warner, B. 1997. "Community Characteristics and the Recording of Crime: Police Recording of Citizens' Complaints of Burglary and Assault." *Justice Quarterly* 14:631–650.

Warr, M. 1998. "Life-Course Transitions and Desistance from Crime." *Criminology* 36:183–216.

Websdale, N. 1995. "An Ethnographic Assessment of the Policing of Domestic Violence in Rural Eastern Kentucky." *Social Justice* 22:102–122.

The Week. 2014. "A Review of the Program to Militarize the Police" (Sept. 5):4.

Weis, K., & S. Borges. 1973. "Victimology and Rape: The Case of the Legitimate Victim." *Issues in Criminology* 8:71–115.

Weisburd, D., et al. 2006. "Does Crime Just Move Around the Corner? A Controlled Study of Spatial Displacement and Diffusion of Crime Control Benefits." *Criminology* 44:549–591.

Weissmann, J. 2013. "How Wall Street Devoured Corporate America." *The Atlantic* (Mar. 5). www.theatlantic.com.

Welch, M. 2004. *Corrections: A Critical Approach.* New York: McGraw-Hill.

Welch, S., M. Combs, & J. Gruhl. 1988. "Do Black Judges Make a Difference?" *American Journal of Political Science* 32:126–136.

Welch, S., J. Gruhl, & C. Spohn. 1984. "Sentencing: The Influence of Alternative Measures of Prior Record." *Criminology* 22:215–277.

Wellford, C., J. Pepper, & C. Petrie (eds.). 2004. *Firearms and Violence: A Critical Review.* Washington, DC: National Academies Press.

Welsh, B., & D. Farrington. 1999. "Value for Money? A Review of the Costs and Benefits of Situational Crime Prevention." *British Journal of Criminology* 39:345–369.

———. 2004. "Surveillance for Crime Prevention in Public Space: Results and Policy Choices in Britain and America." *Criminology & Public Policy* 3:497–526.

Werthman, C., & I. Piliavin. 1967. "Gang Members and the Police." In D. Bordua (ed.), *The Police.* New York: Wiley.

West, S., & K. O'Neal. 2004. "Project D.A.R.E. Outcome Effectiveness Revisited." *American Journal of Public Health* 94:1027–1029.

Wheeler, S., & M. Rothman. 1982. "The Organization as Weapon in White-Collar Crime." *Michigan Law Review* 80:1403–1426.

White, J. 2003. *Terrorism: An Introduction.* Belmont, CA: Wadsworth.

White, M. 2001. "Controlling Police Decisions to Use Deadly Force: Reexamining the Importance of Administrative Policy." *Crime & Delinquency* 47:131–151.

Whitehead, J., & C. Lindquist. 1989. "Determinants of Correctional Officers' Professional Orientation." *Justice Quarterly* 6:69–87.

Widom, C. 1989. "Child Abuse, Neglect, and Violent Criminal Behavior." *Criminology* 27:251–271.

Wiener, Jon. 2010. "Big Tobacco and the Historians." *The Nation* (Mar. 15):11–17.

Wilchins, R. 2003. "The Problem with 'Passing.'" *The Advocate* (May 13):72.
Wildeman, C. 2012. "Imprisonment and Infant Mortality." *Social Problems* 59:228–257.
Will, G. 2003. "Three Strikes and You're In." *Newsweek* (Mar. 17):74.
Will, S., H. Pontell, & R. Cheung. 1998. "Risky Business Revisited: White-Collar Crime and the Orange County Bankruptcy." *Crime & Delinquency* 44:367–387.
Williams, K., & R. Hawkins. 1986. "Perceptual Research on General Deterrence: A Critical Review." *Law & Society Review* 20:211–236.
Williams, L. 1988. "Police Officers Tell of Strains of Living As a 'Black in Blue.'" *New York Times* (Feb. 14):1, 26.
Williams, L., & K. Holmes. 1981. *The Second Assault: Rape and Public Attitudes.* Westport: Greenwood.
Williams, M. 2003. "The Effects of Pretrial Detention on Imprisonment Decisions." *Criminal Justice Review* 28:299–316.
Williams, P. 1999a. "The Auguries of Innocence." *The Nation* (May 24):9.
———. 1999b. "Smart Bombs." *The Nation* (June 7):10.
Williams, S. 2007. *Blue Rage, Black Redemption: A Memoir.* New York: Touchstone.
Williams, T., & W. Kornblum. 1985. *Growing Up Poor.* Lexington, MA: Lexington Books.
Williams, W. 1996. *Taking Back Our Streets: Fighting Crime in America.* New York: Scribner.
Wilson, J. 1968. *Varieties of Police Behavior: The Management of Law and Order in Eight Communities.* Cambridge: Harvard University Press.
———. 1975. *Thinking About Crime.* New York: Basic.
Wilson, J., & R. Herrnstein. 1985. *Crime and Human Nature.* New York: Simon and Schuster.
Wilson, J., & G. Kelling. 1982. "The Police and Neighborhood Safety: Broken Windows." *Atlantic Monthly* (Mar.):29–38.
Wilson, J. 2005. *The Politics of Truth: Inside the Lies That Put the White House on Trial and Betrayed My Wife's CIA Identity.* New York: Carroll and Graf.
Wilson, W. 1987. *The Truly Disadvantaged: The Inner City, the Underclass, and Public Policy.* Chicago: University of Chicago Press.
———. 1991. "Studying Inner-City Social Dislocations: The Challenge of Public Agenda Research." *American Sociological Review* 56:1–14.
Wisconsin State Journal. 1998. "Newspaper: Prosecutors Lie, Cheat with Impunity" (Nov. 11):A3.
Wolfgang, M., & F. Ferracuti. 1967. *The Subculture of Violence.* London: Tavistock.
Wolfgang, M., R. Figlio, & T. Sellin. 1972. *Delinquency in a Birth Cohort.* Chicago: University of Chicago Press.
Wonders, N., & R. Michalowski. 2001. "Bodies, Borders, and Sex Tourism in a Globalized World: A Tale of Two Cities—Amsterdam and Havana." *Social Problems* 48:545–571.
Wood, G. 2014. "The Secrets of ISIS." *New Republic* (Sept. 15):14–17.
Wooden, W., & R. Blazak. 2001. *Renegade Kids, Suburban Outlaws: From Youth Culture to Delinquency.* Belmont, CA: Wadsworth.
Wright, B. 1973. "A Black Broods on Black Judges." *Judicature* 57:22–25.
Wright, B., et al. 1999. "Reconsidering the Relationship Between SES and Delinquency: Causation but Not Correlation." *Criminology* 37:175–194.
Wright, J., & F. Cullen. 2001. "Parental Efficacy and Delinquent Behavior: Do Control and Support Matter?" *Criminology* 39:677–705.
Wright, J., et al. 2008. "Association of Prenatal and Childhood Blood Lead Concentrations with Criminal Arrests in Early Childhood." *PLOS Medicine* 5:732–740.

Wright, K. 2013. "Boxed In: When a Youthful Brush with the Law Means Being Shut Out of the Workforce Forever." *The Nation* (Nov. 25):20–25.

Wright, L. 2006. *The Looming Tower: Al-Qaeda and the Road to 9/11.* New York: Knopf.

Wright, R., & S. Decker. 1994. *Burglars on the Job: Street Life and Residential Break-Ins.* Boston: Northeastern University Press.

Wyre, R. 1992. "Pornography and Sexual Violence: Working with Sexual Offenders." In C. Itzin (ed.), *Pornography: Women, Violence, and Civil Liberties.* New York: Oxford University Press.

Wysong, E., & D. Wright. 1995. "A Decade of DARE: Efficacy, Politics, and Drug Education." *Sociological Focus* 28:283–311.

Xie, M., K. Heimer, & J. Lauritsen. 2012. "Violence Against Women in U.S. Metropolitan Areas: Changes in Women's Status and Risk, 1980–2004." *Criminology* 50:105–143.

Yancy, G., & J. Jones (eds.). 2013. *Pursuing Trayvon Martin: Historical Contexts and Contemporary Manifestations of Racial Dynamics.* Lanham: Lexington.

Yochelson, S., & S. Samenow. 1976, 1977. *The Criminal Personality.* Vols. 1–2. New York: Jason Aronson.

Younge, G. 2014. "Freelance Stop-and-Shoot." *The Nation* (Mar. 10–17):10–11.

Zatz, M. 1987. "Chicano Youth Gangs and Crime: The Creation of a Moral Panic." *Contemporary Crises* 11:129–158.

Zatz, N. 1997. "Sex Work/Sex Act: Law, Labor, and Desire in Constructions of Prostitution." Signs 22:277–308.

Zehr, H., & H. Mika. 1998. "Fundamental Concepts of Restorative Justice." *Contemporary Justice Review* 1:47–55.

Zillman, D., J. Weaver, N. Mundorf, & C. Aust. 1986. "Effects of Opposite-Gender Companion's Affect to Horror on Distress, Delight, and Attraction." *Journal of Personality & Social Psychology* 51:586–594.

Zimmer, L. 1986. *Women Guarding Men.* Chicago: University of Chicago Press.

Zimring, F. 2003. *The Contradictions of American Capital Punishment.* New York: Oxford University Press.

———. 2007. *The Great American Crime Decline.* New York: Oxford University Press.

Zimring, F., & R. Frase. 1980. *The Criminal Justice System.* Boston: Little, Brown.

Zimring, F., & G. Hawkins. 1992. *The Search for Rational Drug Control.* Cambridge: Cambridge University Press.

———. 1997. *Crime Is Not the Problem: Lethal Violence in America.* New York: Oxford University Press.

Zingraff, M., J. Leiter, K. Myers, & M. Johnson. 1993. "Child Maltreatment and Youthful Problem Behavior." *Criminology* 31:173–202.

Zoll, R. 2004a. "4% of Clerics Accused Since 1950." *Wisconsin State Journal* (Feb. 27):A3.

———. 2004b. "Priest-Abuse Claims Exceed Estimates." *Wisconsin State Journal* (Feb. 11):A1, A7.

Index

About the Book

Now fully revised, *Crime, Justice, and Society* **is designed not only to** introduce students to the core issues of criminology, but also to help them think critically about often-sensationalized topics.

Features of the 4th edition include:

- A student-friendly, streamlined organization
- Firsthand perspectives from offenders, victims, and criminal justice professionals
- Expanded coverage of corporate and government crime
- A focus on the dynamics of class, race, and ethnicity
- A chapter on drug-related crime and antidrug laws
- Discussion of topics in the news: marijuana laws, sex trafficking, stand-your-ground policies, and more

This new edition of a now-classic text—both accessible and sophisticated—will be welcomed by students and instructors alike.

Ronald J. Berger is professor emeritus of sociology at the University of Wisconsin–Whitewater (UW-W). **Marvin D. Free, Jr.,** is professor emeritus of sociology at UW-W. **Melissa Deller** is senior lecturer in sociology at UW-W. **Patrick K. O'Brien** is assistant professor of sociology at UW-W.